INDIANA UNIVERSITY

International Development Research Center

Studies in Development

No. 1

WORLD POPULATION – THE VIEW AHEAD

(ed.) Richard N. Farmer, John D. Long, George J. Stolnitz

No. 2

SOCIALIST MANAGEMENT AND PLANNING:

TOPICS IN COMPARATIVE SOCIALIST ECONOMICS

by Nicolas Spulber

No. 3

THE UN AND THE PALESTINIAN REFUGEES:

A STUDY IN NONTERRITORIAL ADMINISTRATION

by Edward H. Buehrig

No. 4

SOVIET AND EAST EUROPEAN FOREIGN TRADE (1946-1969):

STATISTICAL COMPENDIUM AND GUIDE

by Paul Marer

No. 5

RURAL POLITICS AND SOCIAL CHANGE IN THE MIDDLE EAST

(ed.) Richard Antoun and Iliya Harik

Soviet and East European Foreign Trade, 1946-1969

INTERNATIONAL DEVELOPMENT
RESEARCH CENTER

George J. Stolnitz, Director

Studies in Development: No. 4

PAUL MARER

Soviet and East European Foreign Trade, 1946-1969

STATISTICAL COMPENDIUM AND GUIDE

Computer Programs by

GARY J. EUBANKS

INDIANA UNIVERSITY PRESS

Bloomington and London

Published in Canada by Fitzhenry & Whiteside Limited, Don Mills, Ontario

Library of Congress catalog card number: 72-76945

ISBN: 0-253-39604-2

Manufactured in the United States of America

To Erika

Contents

Foreword   xv

Preface   xvii

Part One. Introduction and Summary

Main Perspectives   1

    Background and Objectives   1
    Major Contributions   2
    Statistical Contents   3
    Main Prospective Uses of the Data   4

Standardization of Trade Classifications   5

    Three Classification Systems   5
    Interrelationships of the Three Systems   7

The Major Statistical Series   11

    Origin-Destination of Total Trade: 9 Countries Plus CEMA
      (Series I)   11
    Commodity Composition of Total Trade: 9 Countries Plus
      CEMA (Series II)   12
    Commodity Composition by East European Trade Partner:
      3 Reporting Countries (Series III)   13
    Commodity Composition of Trade with West Europe:
      7 Countries Plus CEMA (Series IV)   14
    Commodity Composition of Trade with CPEs and Non-CPEs:
      2 Countries (Series V)   15

Part Two. Statistical Series

Conventions and Symbols   17

Contents of Part Two   18

  I. Total Import and Export Trade by East European Country
    with Other Individual East European Countries, Other Centrally
    Planned Economies, More Developed Countries, and Less
    Developed Countries (millions of current dollars)   24

 II. Total Import and Export Trade by East European Country
    by One-Digit CTN Categories (CTN), by One-Digit SITC

Categories (SITC), and by BEC Categories (BEC) (millions
of Current dollars)   44

III. Import and Export Trade of U.S.S.R., Czechoslovakia, and
Poland with Individual East European Countries by One-Digit
CTN Categories (CTN) and by BEC Categories (BEC)
(millions of current dollars)   80

IV. Import and Export Trade of Combined West Europe with
Individual European CEMA Countries by One-Digit SITC
Categories (SITC) and by BEC Categories (BEC) (millions
of current dollars)   224

V. Hungary and Poland: Import and Export Trade with
Combined Centrally Planned and Combined Non-Centrally
Planned Economies by CTN Broad Divisions (millions of
current dollars)   272

Part Three. Notes and Documentation

Key to the Citations   277

A. Constructing the Record   278

Origin-Destinations of Total Trade (Series I)   278
Standardization   278
Special Problems   279

Commodity Composition of Total Trade and Trade by
East European Trade Partner (Series II and III)   281
Standardization According to CTN   281
Standardization According to SITC and BEC   284

Commodity Composition of Trade with West Europe
(Series IV)   285

B. Documentation   286

Statistical Series I   286
Statistical Series II   297
Statistical Series III   302
Statistical Series IV   305
Statistical Series V   308

Part Four. Appendices on Subjects of Special Interest

A. Three Commodity Trade Classifications   309
CEMA Trade Nomenclature (CTN)   309
History   309
Classification System   310
Revised and Enlarged 1971 Edition   319

Contents

Standard International Trade Classification (SITC)   322
  History   322
  Classification System and Limitations   322
Broad Economic Categories (BEC)   325
  Classification System   325

B. Reconciliation of Classifications   327
  CTN to BEC   327
    CTN and BEC Classifications Compared   327
    An Original Conversion Key   329
    Special Problems and Evaluation   332
  SITC to BEC   333
  CTN to SITC   336
    The United Nations' Conversion Key   336
    New Conversion Key for U.S.S.R. Total Trade   336

C. Socialist Trade Prices and the Valuation Problem   342
  Concept of Transaction Value   342
  Transaction Values in "National Devisa Units"   342
  Foreign Trade Prices of East European Countries   344
  Conclusions   345

D. Some Main Problems of Statistical Comparability   347
  Introduction   347
  General and Special Reporting Systems   348
    Concepts and United Nations Recommendations   348
    East European Procedures   349
    Estimated Re-Export Trade of East Germany and
      Hungary   349
  Coverage of Merchandise Trade   353
    United Nations Recommendations   353
    East European Procedures   354
  Transport and Related Expenses   357
  Identification of Partner Country   358
    United Nations Recommendations   358
    East European Procedures   358

E. The Case of the Unspecified U.S.S.R. Residuals   360
  Exports to Less Developed Countries   360
  Commodity Composition of Total Trade   360

F. Trade with United States, Canada, Japan, and Australia   369

G. Available East European Foreign Trade Series in Constant
    Prices, 1938-1970   398

H. IDRC Soviet and East European Foreign Trade Data Bank   399

Bibliography   403

Tables

Part One

1   CTN Classification: Numbering and Titles of One-Digit Commodity Categories and Four Broad Divisions   7

2   SITC Classification: Numbering and Titles of One-Digit Commodity Categories and Two Subtotals   8

3   BEC Classification: Numbering and Titles of 7 Large Economic Classes and 19 Basic Categories   9

4   Correspondence of BEC "Larger" Economic Classes with CTN Categories and Broad Divisions   10

Part Two

See list of Statistical Series tables on p. 18.

Part Three

5   Classification of Countries into MDC and LDC Groups by the United Nations and by East European Countries   280

6   Coverage by Country of West Europe as a Group in Trade with East Europe, 1950-1968   286

7   Trade between West Germany and East Germany, 1950-1969   287

8   Bulgaria's Total Trade, Revised and Unrevised, 1955-1956   288

9   East Germany's Trade with Other Centrally Planned Economies, 1953-1959   291

10 Hungary: Revised and Unrevised Series and Corresponding Adjustments, 1952-1956   292

11 Rumania: Alternative Estimates of Trade with Total CPEs and Total Non-CPEs, 1950, 1955   295

12 Percent of "Specified Trade" Converted from CTN to SITC by Each of the Three Conversion Keys, 1946-1969   300

13 Percent of U.S.S.R. Total Trade Converted to BEC by Special Allocation, 1946-1969   301

14 Percent of Bulgaria's Total Trade Converted to BEC by Special Allocation, 1955-1968   302

15 U.S.S.R. Exports to Bulgaria, Czechoslovakia, and East Germany: Percent of Total Exports Converted to BEC by Special Allocation, 1946-1968   304

16   Czechoslovakia's Imports from East European Countries:
        Percent of Total Imports Converted to BEC by Special
        Allocation, 1958-1968   306

17   Czechoslovakia's Exports to East European Countries:
        Percent of Total Exports Converted to BEC by Special
        Allocation, 1958-1968   307

Part Four

A-1   CEMA Trade Nomenclature (CTN), Three Digits
        (effective 1962-1970)   311

A-2   Revisions in the 1971 CTN: New Codes   321

A-3   Revisions in the 1971 CTN: Transferred Codes   322

A-4   Revisions in the 1971 CTN: Changes in Commodity
        Designations   323

A-5   Standard International Trade Classification, Revised
        (SITC), Two Digits   324

A-6   BEC Aggregates by Broad End Use and Basic SNA Classes   326

B-1   Correspondence of BEC Large Economic Classes with
        CTN Commodity Categories and Groups   327

B-2   A Comparison of BEC Large Economic Classes and
        CTN Broad Divisions   328

B-3   Combined Broad Economic Categories (BEC) and
        Corresponding CTN Headings   330

B-4   Conversion of CEMA Trade Nomenclature (CTN) to
        Combined Broad Economic Categories (BEC)   331

B-5   Conversion of Standard International Trade Classification
        (SITC) to Combined Broad Economic Categories (BEC)   334

B-6   Conversion of CEMA Trade Nomenclature (CTN) to
        Standard International Trade Classification (SITC)   337

C-1   Official Exchange Rates of East European Countries,
        1946-1969   346

D-1   East German Imports for Re-Export, and Re-Exports,
        by Region or Country of Provenance or Destination,
        1950-1966   351

D-2   Hungarian Special Trade, General Trade, Imports for
        Re-Export, and Re-Exports, 1951-1968   352

D-3   Coverage of East Europe's Foreign Trade Statistics
      Compared with U.N. 1970 Recommendations   355

E-1   U.S.S.R. Trade with Less Developed Countries: Comparison
      of LDC Group Total with Sum of Trade Reported by
      Component Countries, 1946-1970   361

E-2   U.S.S.R. Imports by CTN Categories: Comparison of
      Percentage Composition Given (G) and Summed (S),
      1946, 1950, 1955, 1958-1969   362

E-3   U.S.S.R. Exports by CTN Categories: Comparison of
      Percentage Composition Given (G) and Summed (S),
      1946, 1950, 1955, 1958-1969   363

E-4   U.S.S.R. Trade: Comparison of Alternative Estimates
      of Percentage Composition by CTN Categories, 1946,
      1950, 1955, 1958-1969   364

E-5   CTN Classification: Titles of "Alternative" Broad
      Divisions and Corresponding One-Digit CTN Categories   365

E-6   U.S.S.R. Trade by CTN Categories: Comparison of
      Percentage Composition Shown in Various Sources   366

E-7   U.S.S.R. Trade: Comparison of Alternative Estimates
      of Percentage Composition by CTN Categories, 1950,
      1955, 1960, 1965, 1967, 1969   367

E-8   U.S.S.R.: Imports and Exports by CTN Categories plus
      Unspecified Trade, 1950, 1955, 1960, 1965, 1967, 1969   368

F-1   United States Trade with U.S.S.R.: Total, 1946-1969,
      by SITC Categories, 1961-1969   370

F-2   United States Trade with Bulgaria: Total, 1946-1969,
      by SITC Categories, 1961-1969   371

F-3   United States Trade with Czechoslovakia: Total,
      1946-1969, by SITC Categories, 1961-1969   372

F-4   United States Trade with East Germany: Total,
      1946-1969, by SITC Categories, 1961-1969   373

F-5   United States Trade with Hungary: Total, 1946-1969,
      by SITC Categories, 1961-1969   374

F-6   United States Trade with Poland: Total, 1946-1969,
      by SITC Categories, 1961-1969   375

F-7   United States Trade with Rumania: Total, 1946-1969,
      by SITC Categories, 1961-1969   376

F-8   United States Trade with Yugoslavia: Total 1946-1969,
        by SITC Categories, 1961-1969   377

F-9   United States Trade with European CEMA: Total,
        1946-1969, by SITC Categories, 1961-1969   378

F-10   Canada's Trade with U.S.S.R.: Total, 1946-1969,
        by SITC Categories, 1961-1969   379

F-11   Canada's Trade with Bulgaria: Total 1946-1969,
        by SITC Categories, 1961-1969   380

F-12   Canada's Trade with Czechoslovakia: Total,
        1946-1969, by SITC Categories, 1961-1969   381

F-13   Canada's Trade with East Germany: Total,
        1946-1969, by SITC Categories, 1961-1969   382

F-14   Canada's Trade with Hungary: Total, 1946-1969,
        by SITC Categories, 1961-1969   383

F-15   Canada's Trade with Poland: Total, 1946-1969,
        by SITC Categories, 1961-1969   384

F-16   Canada's Trade with Rumania: Total 1946-1969,
        by SITC Categories, 1961-1969   385

F-17   Canada's Trade with Yugoslavia: Total 1946-1969,
        by SITC Categories, 1961-1969   386

F-18   Canada's Trade with European CEMA: Total,
        1946-1969, by SITC Categories, 1961-1969   387

F-19   Japan's Trade with U.S.S.R.: Total, 1950-1969,
        by SITC Categories, 1964-1969   388

F-20   Japan's Trade with Bulgaria: Total, 1960,
        1964-1969, by SITC Categories, 1964-1969   389

F-21   Japan's Trade with Czechoslovakia: Total,
        1958-1969, by SITC Categories, 1964-1969   390

F-22   Japan's Trade with East Germany: Total,
        1951-1969, by SITC Categories, 1964-1969   391

F-23   Japan's Trade with Hungary: Total, 1958-1969,
        by SITC Categories, 1964-1969   392

F-24   Japan's Trade with Poland: Total, 1951-1969,
        by SITC Categories, 1964-1969   393

F-25   Japan's Trade with Rumania: Total, 1960-1969,
        by SITC Categories, 1964-1969   394

F-26   Japan's Trade with Yugoslavia: Total,
        1951-1969, by SITC Categories, 1964-1969   395

F-27   Japan's Trade with European CEMA: Total,
       1961-1969, by SITC Categories, 1964-1969   396

F-28   Australia's Trade with Individual East European
       Countries and European CEMA, 1949/50-1969/70   397

G   Available East European Foreign Trade Series in
       Constant Prices, 1938-1970   398

Figures

1   *Data Bank* System Arrangement   400
2   The Data Structure on Computer Tape   401

Foreword

It would be difficult, in introducing this volume, to steer easily between false modesty and immodesty. From an original limited idea, the enterprise has evolved by leaps and not a few serendipitous bounds to its present claimant status as a signal contribution to the field of international trade. Reactions from numerous consultants, representing a broad array of professional interests, give reason to believe that *Compendium* and the considerably more detailed data bank underlying it will represent a major research resource and contribution, not only to the East Europe specialist, but also to the development economist, trade or development policy maker, and economic historian. For it remains a useful syllogism that foreign trade lies at the heart of East Europe's economic performance and prospect for political autonomy, and that these prospects, in turn, could have multiplier impact on the dozens of nations and large majority of the world's population belonging to the less developed, low-income nations.

Even a cursory review of the *Compendium* contents reveals the enormous efforts that Paul Marer and his staff have put into their preparation. The specialist will appreciate, with equal ease, Mr. Marer's courage in making the attempt at all. Literally hundreds of thousands of statistical and analytic decisions, large and small, have been required along the way, with sometimes seemingly ceaseless iterations and reiterations to accommodate additions, revisions, and corrections. And the product continues to evolve, both with the appearance of new series and as opportunities arise for revising old ones.

The *Compendium* plus the simplified data bank associated with it are part of the Center's substantial program in the field of East European planning transitions, development performance, and systemic change during the postwar period. A group of leading East European economists has been commissioned to prepare a series of interrelated national and thematic investigations on these subject areas. Yugoslavia, Hungary, Poland, and Czechoslovakia have been singled out for the study of national experiences, while comparative foreign trade patterns, industrial organization, the management sector, and East European planning theory and controversies exemplify the topics being presented on a region-wide basis.

This is the second volume on socialist-type economies to

xv

appear in the Center's *Studies in Development* series. The earlier study was *Socialist Management and Planning: Topics in Comparative Socialist Economics* by Nicolas Spulber. Others are now in various stages of preparation. Related publications by other scholars, some involving leading economists from East Europe, have also appeared in the Center's *Working Paper, Occasional Paper,* and *Reprint* series.

George J. Stolnitz, Director
International Development Research Center

Preface

Whatever merit is found in this venture is much to the credit of Indiana University's International Development Research Center for providing the resources, an outstanding staff, and that intangible plus, "the environment," without which this work could not have been completed. I am indebted above all to the director of the Center, George J. Stolnitz, who, in addition to his role as project executive, has found time to subject each of the many drafts to searching scrutiny and advice that few authors are fortunate enough to receive. His insights, critical comments, and numerous editorial suggestions have immeasurably improved the collection and presentation of data.

This volume owes a great deal to the expertise of Gary Eubanks, who designed the computer systems of the underlying data bank. The project under his tutelage has become an occasion of creativity. I am immensely grateful for his skill and infinite patience in solving the endless new problems I posed.

My special appreciation goes further to Robert Campbell of Indiana University for his particularly helpful detailed comments on an earlier version of the manuscript. Parts of earlier drafts were read also by Edward Hewett, Heinrich Machowski, and Alec Nove; to the latter I am especially indebted for calling attention to the important and fascinating problem of unspecified residuals in U.S.S.R. exports.

While the idea of the book was still in its formative stages, the Center received helpful advice from Robert Baldwin, Alan Brown, Franklyn Holzman, Michael Kaser, John Michael Montias, Egon Neuberger, Frederic Pryor, Nicholas Spulber, and Leon Smolinski.

It is a pleasure to acknowledge the conscientious help of my able assistant, Nola Miller, in managing the data files, and the support of the Center staff, headed by Evelyn Lowing, and her successor, Norma Snapp. My special appreciation goes to Sherry Dunham and Anne Waaland for efficiently typing the many drafts and tables, and to Susan Kaplan for helping to edit numerous drafts.

Thanks are due the Slavic-language reference librarians in Bloomington and New York and special appreciation to Gertrude Palmer, of the Statistical Library of the United Nations, for frequently retrieving materials in use, to which I could not have had access without her help.

I owe special thanks to my wife for helping with the calculations, but mainly for being so understanding, always.

None of the foregoing is responsible for the errors and inaccuracies that are bound to be discovered in a work of this magnitude and detail. Any notifications by readers to me of inaccuracies or of newly available data would be greatly appreciated.

Paul Marer
Bloomington, Indiana

Soviet and
East European
Foreign Trade,
1946-1969

PART ONE

Introduction and Summary

Main Perspectives

Background and Objectives

This *Compendium* presents comprehensive data on the value of foreign trade of individual East European countries during the period 1946-69. The data are variously arranged in aggregative terms, by country or region of origin and destination, or by structure according to a number of commodity classifications.

Each table is a complete or abridged reproduction of data contained in a more comprehensive computerized system of tables, the *IDRC Soviet and East European Foreign Trade Data Bank,* which is housed at the International Development Research Center of Indiana University. The *Data Bank* represents a collection of figures some three times as large as that presented here, the difference consisting mainly of additional commodity detail.

Nine East European countries are documented individually: the U.S.S.R., Bulgaria, Czechoslovakia, East Germany, Hungary, Poland, Rumania, Yugoslavia, and Albania. The first seven are regular members of the Council for Mutual Economic Assistance (variously identified as CEMA, CMEA, or COMECON). Yugoslavia has observer status in that organization, and Albania was a member until the early 1960s. The only non-European CEMA member is Mongolia, whose trade is not documented here as a reporting country.

Trade flows of the nine countries represent about 11 percent of world trade. In 1970, the region's total exports and imports each amounted to more than $30 billion.

Detailed and comparable time series on much of this trade have been practically inaccessible in the West until now. Moreover, the available data have often been highly aggregated, incomplete in scope, or deficient in details on composition. Our knowledge of East Europe's international commerce has lagged considerably behind the economic and political importance of the region, with comparatively little known about either general patterns or the possibly unique yet significant aspects. As one result among many, projections of trends have not had adequate empirical foundation. Even East-West trade, for which

1

statistics are generally available from Western sources, cannot be
fully assessed in the absence of detailed information on trade within
East Europe, with which it is clearly interconnected.

Study of the trade of East European countries at the International
Development Research Center is part of a larger project on the economic development of East Europe, which has underscored the need for
a systematized, standardized set of trade statistics for the region. The
fact that no such statistical compilation exists has prompted the considerable scale of the present undertaking. The result, incorporating
the effort of several man-years of compilation, processing, and analysis, is a uniquely comprehensive collection of East Europe's trade, especially designed to facilitate detailed intraregional and international
comparisons.

All data except those on East-West trade have been obtained or
derived from primary East European sources. Statistics on East-West
trade have been assembled from Western sources, which are more
comprehensive and standardized than their East European counterparts.

Major Contributions

The most distinctive feature of the *Compendium* is its provision of
multiple sets of standardized data on commodity composition. First,
the data have been standardized according to the nomenclature in which
they were originally compiled by the national statistical offices of the
reporting countries: the CEMA Trade Nomenclature (CTN) or the
Standard International Trade Classification (SITC). Second, CTN data
have been converted when possible into SITC; both CTN and originally
reported SITC data have been transformed by special procedures into
the United Nations' new trade classification, Broad Economic Categories (BEC). The last marks a substantial advance over other trade
classifications in that its aggregates represent more homogeneous
groupings and because they have been rendered much more comparable
with commodity categories in the standardized national income accounts. The *Compendium* is the first publication to present foreign
trade statistics by the BEC classification.

The three classification systems are outlined beginning on page 5
below and compared in detail in Appendix A. Thus statistical information on East Europe's trade, which has long trailed behind that of most
other regions, can now be said to be more up to date in this respect
than that currently available for the rest of the world.

Geographic distributions have also been standardized and disaggregated. Export as well as import trade flows for each of the nine East
European countries are shown with each of the others (except Albania),
as well as with groups of countries covering the rest of the world.

The most detailed geographic documentation throughout the *Compendium* is for intra-East-European trade, mainly because East Europe
is the dominant trade region for all CEMA countries. In addition, such
data have been less readily available in the West than information on
East-West trade, hence were more needed in detail.

The *Compendium* has been organized so that it can serve both as an easy-to-use reference volume and as an extensively documented technical treatise on its subject. Part One, Introduction and Summary, is a concise guide to the basic statistical tables, which are presented in Part Two. Part Three outlines the methodology used in constructing the tables, with detailed notes and documentation concerning the nature, sources, and organization of the data in Part Two.

Part Four consists of appendices on topics of special interest. They include a comprehensive discussion of the three trade classification systems, in Appendix A; a review of how these systems have been reconciled by new conversion procedures, in Appendix B; and a discussion of valuation problems and their bearing on international comparisons, in Appendix C. Appendix D provides a detailed explanation of statistical definitions used by East European countries in compiling their trade series and compares them with statistical standards recommended by the United Nations.

Appendix E deals with an important but little-known problem: the existence of large unspecified residuals in U.S.S.R. trade. The residuals in commodity composition, as well as in trade with less developed countries, suggest that military-strategic items being commercially traded may be partly or entirely excluded from commodity and country breakdowns.

Appendix F presents data on trade between individual East European countries and the United States, Canada, Japan, and Australia.

Appendix G identifies a set of constant-price series, which the author has calculated from official sources for all East European countries except Rumania and Albania. (These data have been published separately as an International Development Research Center's *Working Paper*.* Finally, Appendix H provides information about the system and availability of the Center's computerized *Data Bank*.

Statistical Contents

The data presented in Part Two are organized into 252 one-page tables, which have been photoreduced from computer printouts. The tables are grouped into five sets, each termed a Series, with the following contents:

I. Total Trade by Origin and Destination (Series I) shows, for each East European country and the European CEMA group as a whole, total export trade and import trade with individual East European countries (except Albania) and with three areas covering the rest of the world: other centrally planned economies (OCPEs),** more developed countries (MDCs), and less developed countries (LDCs).

*Paul Marer, "Soviet and East European Foreign Trade Series in Constant Prices," International Development Research Center *Working Paper* (Bloomington, Ind., 1972).

**The term "centrally planned economies" is used throughout to denote European and Asian communist countries, including Yugoslavia. Although "centrally directed economies" may be more apt, the former expression is retained because its abbreviation, "CPEs," is much more familiar.

Subtotals are shown for the trade of each East European country with all centrally planned economies (East Europe plus OCPEs) and all economies not centrally planned (MDCs plus LDCs).

II. Commodity Composition of Total Trade (Series II) shows, for each East European country and the European CEMA group as a whole, export trade and import trade by commodity categories according to as many as possible of three classification systems. CTN series are shown for all East European countries except Yugoslavia. SITC series are shown for the U.S.S.R., as converted from CTN data; and for Hungary and Yugoslavia, as originally reported. BEC series are shown for the U.S.S.R. and Bulgaria, as converted from CTN data; and for Yugoslavia, as converted from SITC.

III. Commodity Composition of Trade by East European Trade Partner (Series III) shows, for the U.S.S.R., Czechoslovakia, and Poland, export trade and import trade with individual East European countries and the European CEMA group as a whole, disaggregated by commodity classifications. These series are shown according to CTN, as originally reported, and BEC, as converted from CTN data.

IV. Commodity Composition of Trade with Total West Europe (Series IV) shows, for each European CEMA country and for the European CEMA group as a whole, export trade and import trade both according to SITC, as compiled from West European sources by the United Nations, and according to BEC, as converted here from SITC data. Appendix F presents comparable recent information on trade with the United States, Canada, Japan, and Australia.*

V. Special Supplement (Series V) shows, for Hungary and Poland, export trade and import trade with combined centrally planned economies and combined non-centrally planned economies, classified by CTN. Comparable time series for other East European countries are not available.

Main Prospective Uses of the Data

The presentation of materials has been designed to facilitate international comparisons, hence all values are shown in current U.S. dollars. Since data from East European sources are originally given in national-currency "devisa" units — special units of account used by

*Commodity composition of East Europe's trade with LDCs has not been compiled. Only fragmentary information on this score is available from either East European or LDC sources, and much of this has already been published in the West. See James R. Carter, *The Net Cost of Soviet Foreign Aid* (New York: Praeger, 1969); Carole A. Sawyer, *Communist Trade with Developing Countries* (New York: Praeger, 1966); Baard R. Stokke, *Soviet and East European Trade and Aid in Africa* (New York: Praeger, 1967); Vassil Vassilev, *Policy in the Soviet Bloc on Aid to Developing Countries* (Paris: Development Centre of the Organization for Economic Co-operation and Development, 1969); and Jozef Wilczynski, *The Economics and Politics of East-West Trade* (New York: Praeger, 1969).

East European countries to record foreign trade statistics — these data have had to be converted to dollars, using official exchange rates in the absence of a preferable alternative. Since East-West trade data were taken from U.N. or OECD (Organization for Economic Cooperation and Development) publications, they had already been converted to dollars from Western currencies, again at official exchange rates.

In using the data, it is important to recall that trade prices of East European countries often diverge systematically from world market prices. Hence dollar values obtained by official exchange rate conversions are not unequivocally comparable with those obtained similarly for Western countries (see Appendix C).

By presenting the study of the trade of each East European country with each of the others and with uniformly defined groups of other countries, the statistics provide a new tool for linking research on centrally planned economies with mainstream research on foreign trade elsewhere. Although the commodity classes or years for which data could be obtained are still not complete for any country, one can point to numerous topics which can now be explored. The following illustrative list by no means exhausts the possibilities.

Balance-of-trade ratios can be calculated, by country or region, to show where trade is balanced bilaterally, for annual or longer periods, or to document traditional or chronic surplus and deficit areas. Rates of growth and stability of trade in individual East European countries or in the region as a whole can be compared both at much more disaggregated levels than heretofore and with respect to a broader international range of other areas.

Differences in the growth rates of trade between individual East European countries, or with West Europe and other parts of the world, can be associated with commodity composition; and such relationships can be compared with those holding for other regions.

The U.S.S.R.'s role as a supplier of raw materials and as a market for the manufactures of individual East European countries can be explored in considerable economic and geographic depth, as can the extent to which East Europe competes with other suppliers on West European markets.

For the first time comparisons can be made between SITC and BEC aggregates, such as primary products and processed goods, for a great number of trading partners and flows.

Standardization of Trade Classifications

Three Classification Systems

All CEMA countries record commodity composition of trade according to CTN. However, since they do not publish this information in full, considerable effort is needed to standardize composition of total trade and trade by East European partner according to this nomenclature if maximum comparability is to be achieved. The rule followed here was that the attempt should be made for all CEMA countries for which an average of about 80 percent of trade was specified according to given or assignable CTN codes. This involved reconstructing the CEMA classification system — its code numbers and accompanying commodity descriptions — from a variety of East European sources (Appendix Table A-1) and examining their correspondence with published foreign trade statistics by commodity. In many cases the data were found to correspond with CTN classifications even though no codes had been assigned in the original sources.

Nearly all Western countries (including Yugoslavia) and international organizations record commodity composition according to SITC. Since this classification was developed from a customs point of view, its groupings are variously defined according to nature of material, final use, or degree of processing. Because the SITC aggregates have limitations for economic analysis, the U.N. Statistical Commission has been prompted to design a new nomenclature, the BEC, published in 1971.*

Whenever commodity detail in the available East European series was adequate, commodity composition of total trade and trade by partner was converted from original CTN or SITC to BEC by special procedures. These procedures have been designed here especially for data not specified in full commodity detail, as discussed in Appendix B. To assist the reader in using the tables in Part Two, the presentation here is limited to a brief description of each classification system.

The CEMA Trade Nomenclature system is a slightly modified version of the U.S.S.R. "Uniform Commodity Nomenclature of Foreign Trade," which was formally adopted by CEMA members in 1962. CTN is a seven-digit numerical code system, which groups commodities by industrial origin or end use. The first digit represents one of the highly aggregated commodity collections called *categories;* the second digit indicates component commodity aggregations called *groups;* the third, *subgroups;* and so on. The nine *categories* may be combined into four *broad divisions,* as shown in Table 1. Codes and titles at the three-digit level are shown in Appendix A.

The original CTN has undergone several revisions since 1962. Until the most recent (1971) edition, however, the revisions affected neither the basic system nor the definitions of *categories* or *broad divisions.* Hence for practical purposes, the present data (to 1969) are based on a fixed system.

The Standard International Trade Classification system, based on a five-digit commodity nomenclature, was originally prepared by the U.N. Secretariat in 1950. A 1960 revision essentially preserved the original structure at three-digit and higher (one- or two-digit) levels

---

*United Nations, Statistical Office, "Classification by Broad Economic Categories," *Statistical Papers,* Series M, no. 53 (New York, 1971).

Table 1

CTN Classification: Numbering and Titles of
One-Digit Commodity Categories and Four Broad Divisions

CTN		Designation
Broad Division	Category	
I	1	Industrial Machinery and Equipment (including Spare Parts)
II		Fuels, Raw Materials (other than for Food), Other Materials
	2	Fuels, Mineral Raw Materials, Metals
	3	Chemicals, Fertilizers, Rubber
	4	Building Materials and Construction Parts
	5	Raw Materials of Vegetable and Animal Origin (not Food)
III		Foodstuffs and Raw Materials for Foodstuffs
	6	Live Animals not for Slaughter
	7	Raw Materials for the Production of Foodstuffs
	8	Foodstuffs
IV	9	Industrial Consumer Goods (other than Food)

Source: *Statisztikai Szemle* (Budapest, June 1964), pp. 652-58.

of aggregation. The first digit identifies ten commodity *categories* (or *sections*), which may be combined into two subtotals, as shown in Table 2. Codes and titles at the two-digit level are shown in Appendix A.

Table 2

SITC Classification: Numbering and Titles of One-Digit
Commodity Categories and Two Subtotals

SITC Category	Designation
	Primary Products
0	Food and Live Animals
1	Beverages and Tobacco
2	Crude Materials, inedible, except Fuels
3	Mineral Fuels, Lubricants, and Related Materials
4	Animal and Vegetable Oils and Fats
	Manufactured Goods (processed)
5	Chemicals
6	Manufactured Goods, classified chiefly by material
7	Machinery and Transport Equipment
8	Miscellaneous Manufactured Articles
9	Commodities and Transactions, not classified according to kind

Source: United Nations, Statistical Office, "Standard International Trade Classification, Revised," *Statistical Papers*, Series M, no. 34 (New York, 1961).

The Broad Economic Categories system, shown in Table 3, has 19 *basic categories,* which can be combined into 7 *large economic classes.* The *basic categories* can also be aggregated according to two additional criteria. One is by *broad end use,* divided into Primary Products and Processed Goods. The other, by SNA *basic classes* (SNA: System of National Accounts), is divided into Capital, Intermediate, and Consumption Goods. The composition of these aggregates is indicated in Table 3.

The twofold advantage of BEC over SITC has been mentioned earlier. The new nomenclature is expected to supplement and possibly supplant SITC. According to the U.N. Statistical Commission, "national classifications of this type will inevitably be attracted toward it and it will eventually tend to serve as a guideline and ultimately as a standard with wide use."* Therefore BEC data are presented here whenever possible.

Interrelationships of the Three Systems

The transformation of CTN to BEC is facilitated by the relatively small number of *basic categories* in the BEC system and by structural similarities in the two nomenclatures. The 7 BEC *large economic classes* correspond very closely to CTN combinations of one-digit *categories* and two-digit *groups* (Appendix B). Furthermore, by combining BEC's 7 *large economic classes* into 4 *"larger" economic classes,* and after some quantitatively insignificant CTN adjustments (see Appendix B for details), one-digit CTN *categories* or *broad divisions* can be accurately regrouped into "larger" economic classes as shown in Table 4.

Conversion of CTN data to the smaller BEC *basic categories* for the purpose of reconstructing BEC aggregates by *broad end use* or SNA *basic classes* is much more difficult because the CTN data are often not given in adequate detail. Even here, however, it was possible to proceed by combining the original 19 BEC *basic categories* into 11 *combined categories* and preparing a CTN/BEC conversion key, which uses the most highly aggregated (lowest number of digits) CTN code that can be assigned accurately to one of these 11 *combined categories.* The key, cross-classified by BEC and CTN headings, is shown in Appendix B. In assigning one-, two-, or three-digit CTN codes to a BEC *combined category,* certain simplifying conventions and adjustments, also detailed in Appendix B, were necessary.

The transformation of SITC to BEC was effected by a similar conversion procedure. Indeed, the original BEC *basic categories* were originally designed by the U.N. to facilitate such matchup. An SITC/BEC conversion key prepared and published by the U.N. assigns more than 600 two- to five-digit individual SITC codes to appropriate BEC *categories.* Unfortunately, the U.N. key could not be applied directly to convert East-West trade in SITC because this particular series is not

*United Nations, Statistical Office, "Classification by Broad Economic Categories," *Statistical Papers,* Series M, no. 53 (New York, 1971), p. vii.

Table 3

BEC Classification: Numbering and Titles of 7 Large Economic
Classes and 19 Basic Categories

1   Food and Beverages

   11 Primary+

      111 for Industry**
      112 for Household Consumption***

   12 Processed++

      121 for Industry**
      122 for Household Consumption***

2   Industrial Supplies (non-Food)**

   21 Primary+
   22 Processed++

3   Fuels and Lubricants

   31 Primary**+
   32 Processed++

      321 Motor spirit
      322 Other**

4   Machinery, Other Capital Equipment (except Transport), and
     Accessories Thereof++

   41 Machinery and Other Capital Equipment (except Transport)*
   42 Parts and accessories**

5   Transport Equipment++

   51 Passenger motor vehicles
   52 Other

      521 Industrial*
      522 Nonindustrial***

   53 Parts and accessories

6   Consumer Goods Not Elsewhere Specified***++

   61 Durable
   62 Semidurable
   63 Nondurable

7   Goods Not Elsewhere Specified

SNA Basic Classes	Broad End Use
* Capital goods	+ Primary
** Intermediate goods	++ Processed
*** Consumption goods	

Source: United Nations, Statistical Office, "Classification by Broad
Economic Categories," *Statistical Papers,* Series M, no. 53 (New York,
1971), p. 1.

Table 4

Correspondence of BEC "Larger" Economic Classes
with CTN Categories and Broad Divisions

		CTN	
BEC Combined Large Economic Classes		Categories	Broad Division
1	Food and Beverages	7-8	III*
2-3	Industrial Supplies (non-Food) including Fuels and Lubricants	2-5	II
4-5	Machinery, Other Capital Equipment (including Transport), Accessories and Parts	1	I
6**	Consumer Goods Not Elsewhere Specified	6, 9	IV

*Includes CTN category 6, Live Animals Not for Slaughter, usually an insignificant component.
　　**Includes BEC category 7, Goods Not Elsewhere Specified.

available in requisite detail. However, item-by-item examination of the U.N. key reveals that a close approximation of BEC *categories* can be obtained in most cases from either two- or three-digit SITC. The transformation procedure described in Appendix B converts two- or three-digit SITC data to the same 11 BEC *combined categories* that were used for CTN/BEC conversions. A corollary advantage is that the resulting BEC series are also comparable with those obtained from CTN.

The biases introduced by combining original BEC *categories* or by making simplifying assumptions in conversions are examined in Appendix B. The discussion there suggests that whenever original data were available in the detail required by the conversion keys, the resulting BEC series do in fact provide a reasonably reliable empirical foundation for analysis and for making international comparisons.

The feasibility of transforming CTN to SITC was also explored, since despite the limitations of SITC, it is still the nomenclature of Western trade statistics. However, to achieve adequate correspondence between CTN and SITC headings (so that accurate one-digit SITC *categories* could be obtained after conversion), a minimum of three-digit CTN would be necessary. Since no CEMA country publishes commodity composition fully in this depth, information at best being available in some mixture of one, two, and three digits, conversion to SITC is impossible or only approximate, depending on the proportion of trade specified in three-digit CTN.

The one country for which a CTN/SITC conversion seemed worth attempting was the U.S.S.R. (total trade only), using a sequentially defined three-part conversion key, detailed in Appendix B. The commodity composition of the U.S.S.R.'s total trade can therefore be compared directly with those of Western countries. However, the fact that the U.S.S.R. specifies less than 100 percent of its trade in CTN circumscribes the usefulness of all series, CTN as well as SITC and BEC.

The Major Statistical Series

Origin-Destination of Total Trade: 9 Countries
Plus CEMA (Series I)

Full coverage for 1946-69, showing trade with East Europe (except Albania) by country and with the rest of the world by groups of countries has been possible for the U.S.S.R., East Germany, Hungary, Poland, and Yugoslavia. Some years are missing before 1950 and 1951-54 or 1956-57 for Bulgaria, Czechoslovakia, and Rumania. For Albania, the full matrix is available only for 1950-64.

Practically all data have been obtained directly or derived indirectly from official statistical publications of reporting countries. Missing entries have been available in secondary sources in a few cases, such as national or international publications issued by an agency other than the reporting country's central statistical office. Secondary sources have been carefully screened to assure that the data were originally based on official sources and were consistent with the rest of the series. For practical purposes all data (in all five series) are based on official statistics.

As a general rule, trade shown for country groups (example: MDCs) or subtotals generated within a table (example: CPEs) represent the simple sums of trade documented for individual countries. Officially given subtotals were used only when not all national components were available. They are identified by code "G" (example: Table I.M.B, Bulgaria's imports from "Total Non-CPEs," 1957-59 and 1961). Entries coded "W" indicate that data were obtained as a balancing estimate. For example, trade with "Total Non-CPEs" might be the difference between total imports and those from "Total CPEs" (example: Table I.M.B, 1952-54). Unrevised series that are known to have been superseded by revised data are included only if revised data were not available; these series are identified by the code "Z" (example: Table I.M.B, 1952-54).

If trade with one or at most a few countries was not available from a reporting country's sources, a missing entry could sometimes be obtained from trade-partner sources to complete an origin or destination row for a particular year. These entries are identified by code "X" (example: Table I.M.C, Czechoslovakia's imports from Yugoslavia, 1946). In a few instances, one- or two-year gaps in trade with country groups were filled by interpolated estimates, coded "Y."

The geographic composition of the country groups outside East Europe has been standardized as fully as possible (exceptions are noted in the documentation). Thus, "Other Centrally Planned Economies"

(OCPEs) includes Cuba uniformly since 1960, regardless of how that country is classified in national publications. Although trade with OCPEs until the early 1960s was dominated by trade with Mainland China, it (along with Albania) is not shown separately as a trade partner, since only a limited number of columns could be presented on a single page.

Presenting both export and import values, in contrast with the standard approach of showing either of these alone, allows for a fuller filling of statistical gaps by the user than would otherwise be possible, and also permits comparing "mirror" series, for example, U.S.S.R. reported exports to Czechoslovakia compared with imports from U.S.S.R. reported by Czechoslovakia.

Careful attention has been given throughout to consistency. The totals of country components or of subtotals by groups of countries have been checked to see that they equal "world" trade as given independently by a reporting country. Discrepancies among sources and other special problems are discussed in the notes to the individual tables, which also give full documentation of sources.

Appendix D takes up topics of special interest for international comparisons. The statistical practice of each East European country is discussed with respect to: (1) system of reporting trade ("general" vs. "special"), (2) commodity coverage of merchandise trade, (3) valuation procedures (c.i.f. vs. f.o.b.), and (4) system of identifying trade-partner country. In the special case of Hungary, whose trade is reported according to both the "general" and the "special" systems, it was possible to estimate re-export trade, which is also presented in Appendix D.

Commodity Composition of Total Trade: 9 Countries
Plus CEMA (Series II)

For each CEMA country plus Albania an attempt has been made to obtain coverage by 9 CTN *categories* and 4 *broad divisions* throughout 1946-69. It was possible to assemble a full matrix by *broad divisions* for 1950 and continuously since 1955 for all but two CEMA countries and for CEMA as a group. The exceptions are East Germany, for which data are not available for 1956-59 and since 1965, and Rumania, which published no commodity detail for 1956-58. For some countries, CTN details are also available prior to 1950 and for 1951-54. For Albania, a full matrix can be presented only for 1950, 1955, and 1960-64. In almost all cases, structure by CTN *categories* is available whenever *broad division* totals are shown. In many cases *broad division* entries were not reported in official publications, but could be obtained by summing *categories*.

For the U.S.S.R. alone, the sum of *categories* is consistently less than the value of total trade independently given in the official statistics (Appendix E). *Category* totals for the U.S.S.R. have been obtained through computer aggregation of very detailed commodity specifications in CTN. For all other countries, the *category* or *broad division* totals as shown in official publications exhaust the given total.

Standardization of CEMA commodity statistics is based on the nomenclature in effect officially since 1962 and unofficially since 1954. As noted earlier, the revisions in the nomenclature between 1954 and 1970 have been minor and apparently have not affected the aggregative groupings shown here through 1969. Effective January 1971, a new edition of CTN has reclassified some commodities among *broad divisions* (Appendix A).

Comprehensive data on composition for the first postwar decade were not published until the mid-1950s. Since in all cases they represent new or revised series, consistency of aggregates over time is probably not a major problem. However, some CEMA countries have made special adaptations of the nomenclature; in one known case, Hungary, the comparability of aggregates would have been affected had we not made appropriate adjustments, as explained in the documentation to Table II.CTN.M.H.

Yugoslavia, which is not a CEMA member, has been compiling commodity composition in SITC since the early 1950s. It is presented here by one-digit commodity *categories*. The commodity compositions of two other countries are also shown in SITC: for Hungary, published officially since 1960, and for the U.S.S.R., converted here since 1946 from CTN data.

Adequate detail to transform original CTN or SITC data into BEC is available for three countries only: the U.S.S.R. since 1946, Bulgaria since 1955, and Yugoslavia since 1952. BEC tabulations on imports and exports of each of the countries are presented in two sets of tables: BEC-1 shows the 11 *combined categories,* and BEC-2 records *broad end use* and SNA *basic classes* aggregates.

Commodity Composition by East European Trade Partner:
3 Reporting Countries (Series III)

No CEMA country publishes comprehensive information on commodity composition of trade with partner countries. The best statistics available yield partner country series by CTN *categories* (each obtained through aggregation of two- and three-digit details), which are consistently less than the reported total trade with that country. Hence, the inclusion of a country in this series had to be determined judgmentally, on the basis of what was deemed to be an adequate feasible approximation. The criterion used was that no less than three-fourths to four-fifths of a CEMA country's trade with all East European partner countries could be specified in value terms, according to given or assignable CTN codes, over a period of at least ten years.*

Data on trade by partner and with CEMA as a group are presented for three countries: the U.S.S.R. 1946-68, Czechoslovakia 1958-68, and

*Yugoslavia, which publishes detailed SITC statistics by partner countries, has not been included since it trades primarily with West Europe.

Poland 1958-68. For each of these countries both import and export trade with each East European country (except Albania) is shown. Hence, out of 28 possible bilateral channels (Albania excluded) between pairs of the eight East European countries, 18 have been recorded. The trade flows of these three countries with each other and with the rest of East Europe represent more than 90 percent of intra-East-European trade (Albania excluded).

Furthermore, in each instance it has been possible to provide the corresponding data by BEC. These are presented in two sets of tables: BEC-1 for the 11 *combined categories* and BEC-2 for the two sets of aggregates: by *broad end use* and SNA *basic classes*.

Commodity Composition of Trade with West Europe:
7 Countries Plus CEMA (Series IV)

This Series presents commodity composition of trade of individual CEMA countries and that of the European CEMA group as a whole with total West Europe by SITC *categories* for 1950-68 (East Germany 1951-68). Each country matrix is complete in that data are shown for all years and each annual sum of *categories* equals total trade, independently given. It has been possible to convert all SITC data in this Series to BEC, shown by *combined categories* as well as by the *broad end use* and SNA *basic classes* aggregates.

CEMA's trade with West Europe approximates its trade with all MDCs, since West Europe predominates within the MDC group. Additional information, involving the commodity composition of trade with the United States, Canada, and Japan, and total trade with Australia, is presented in Appendix F.

All SITC data in Series IV were obtained from U.N. publications. The number of commodity designations has varied over time, increasing from about 20 in 1950 to nearly 200 by 1964. In the tables presented here, only the 10 SITC *categories* and the *primary* versus *manufactures* subtotals are shown. These data were obtained from the *Data Bank*, where special procedures were required because of the variable number of commodity designations available from year to year.

Approximately 50 export and 50 import commodity groups (some representing combined commodity designations) have been included in the *Data Bank* for each CEMA country for most years. Each commodity group was assigned an SITC code (example: 271) or code span (271-276). The number of commodity groups (degree of disaggregation processed) was determined, subject to data availability, by two objectives: to obtain both comparable two-digit SITC series and adequate SITC detail for conversion to BEC, the latter sometimes requiring three-digit information. Gaps in SITC data were overcome whenever possible through the use of estimates, largely based on distributions calculated for other years.

Two special problems warrant attention here. First, since Yugoslavia's trade is classified consistently with East Europe, it has been subtracted everywhere from the West Europe totals given by the U.N. U.N. publications include Yugoslavia with West Europe for all years except 1950-53 and 1964-65. Second, the U.N. has occasionally added a number of smaller countries to West Europe, because either they had started to trade with East Europe or relevant statistics had become available. Such newly included cases are Greece and Iceland since 1952, Portugal and Ireland since 1958, and Spain since 1964. Although no adjustment has been made here for this inconsistency, the distortion is believed to be small. In 1968 the proportion of CEMA trade with all countries added to the West Europe total subsequent to 1950 was only some 5 percent of total East-West trade, and this share was probably smaller in preceding years. There should be no appreciable effect on percentage composition during any year or on its changes over time.

Notes to this Series in Part Three present a detailed discussion of data problems; as noted, Appendix B describes SITC/BEC conversion procedures.

Commodity Composition of Trade with CPEs and Non-CPEs:
2 Countries (Series V)

This set of tables presents for Hungary and Poland commodity composition of trade with combined centrally planned economies ("socialist countries") and combined non-centrally planned economies ("capitalist countries"). Composition is according to CTN *broad divisions;* the periods covered are 1949-69 for Hungary and 1950-69 for Poland.

The conventions and symbols used in presenting the major statistical series in Part Two are shown on p. 17; the key to the citation code for Parts Three and Four, on p. 277.

PART TWO

Statistical Series

Conventions and Symbols

Part Two consists of five series, identified by the Roman numerals I through V. The letter M designates imports, X exports. Individual East European countries and total CEMA are identified by a mnemonic code of letters, as follows:

    U = U.S.S.R.
    B = Bulgaria
    C = Czechoslovakia
    G = East Germany
    H = Hungary
    P = Poland
    R = Rumania
    Y = Yugoslavia
    A = Albania
 CEMA = Regional total, excluding Yugoslavia and Albania.

Within each series, the tables are ordered in this geographic sequence, except where countries with inadequate data are excluded. As noted, the abbreviations CTN, BEC, and SITC indicate commodity nomenclature.

The table titles reflect all these identifying characteristics. For example, Table III.CTN.X.U-R represents commodity composition of U.S.S.R. exports to Rumania according to CEMA Trade Nomenclature (in this case by nine commodity *categories*), in short, it denotes "U.S.S.R. Exports to Rumania by CTN Categories."

A horizontal line in the body of the table indicates a break in the series, as explained in the documentation to the individual tables in Part Three.

17

Contents of Part Two

I.M. Total Imports by East European Country from Other Individual East European Countries, Other Centrally Planned Economies, More Developed Countries, and Less Developed Countries (millions of current dollars)

U	U.S.S.R., 1946-1969 (f.o.b.)	24
B	Bulgaria, 1950, 1952-1969 (f.o.b.)	25
C	Czechoslovakia, 1946-1969 (f.o.b.)	26
G	East Germany, 1946-1969 (f.o.b)	27
H	Hungary, 1946-1969 (c.i.f.)	28
P	Poland, 1946-1969 (f.o.b.)	29
R	Rumania, 1948-1969 (f.o.b.)	30
Y	Yugoslavia, 1946-1969 (c.i.f.)	31
A	Albania, 1946-1967 (f.o.b.)	32
CEMA	European CEMA Group (excluding Albania), 1950, 1952-1969 (f.o.b., except Hungary, c.i.f.)	33

I.X. Total Exports by East European Country to Other Individual East European Countries, Other Centrally Planned Economies, More Developed Countries, and Less Developed Countries (millions of current dollars)

U	U.S.S.R., 1946-1969 (f.o.b.)	34
B	Bulgaria, 1950, 1952-1969 (f.o.b.)	35
C	Czechoslovakia, 1946-1969 (f.o.b.)	36
G	East Germany, 1946-1969 (f.o.b.)	37
H	Hungary, 1946-1969 (f.o.b.)	38
P	Poland, 1946-1969 (f.o.b.)	39
R	Rumania, 1948-1969 (f.o.b.)	40
Y	Yugoslavia, 1946-1969 (f.o.b.)	41
A	Albania, 1946-1967 (f.o.b.)	42
CEMA	European CEMA Group (excluding Albania), 1950, 1952-1969 (f.o.b.)	43

II.CTN.M. Total Imports by One-Digit CTN Categories (millions of current dollars)

U	U.S.S.R., 1946-1969 (f.o.b.)	44
B	Bulgaria, 1950, 1955-1969 (f.o.b.)	45
C	Czechoslovakia, 1948-1969 (f.o.b.)	46
G	East Germany, 1950, 1955, 1960-1965, 1969 (f.o.b.)	47
H	Hungary, 1949-1969 (c.i.f.)	48

P Poland, 1946-1969 (f.o.b.)   49
R Rumania, 1950, 1955, 1959-1969 (f.o.b.)   50
A Albania, 1950, 1955, 1960-1964 (f.o.b.)   51
CEMA European CEMA Group (excluding East Germany and
   Albania), 1950, 1955-1969 (f.o.b., except Hungary, c.i.f.)   52

II.CTN.X. Total Exports by One-Digit CTN Categories (millions of
   current dollars)

U U.S.S.R., 1946-1969 (f.o.b.)   53
B Bulgaria, 1950, 1955-1969 (f.o.b.)   54
C Czechoslovakia, 1948-1969 (f.o.b.)   55
G East Germany, 1950, 1955, 1960-1965, 1967, 1969 (f.o.b.)   56
H Hungary, 1949-1969 (f.o.b.)   57
P Poland, 1946-1969 (f.o.b.)   58
R Rumania, 1950, 1955, 1959-1969 (f.o.b.)   59
A Albania, 1950, 1955, 1960-1964 (f.o.b.)   60
CEMA European CEMA Group (excluding East Germany
   and Albania), 1950, 1955-1969 (f.o.b.)   61

II.SITC.M. Total Imports by One-Digit SITC Categories (millions of
   current dollars)

U U.S.S.R., 1946-1969 (Converted from CTN; f.o.b.)   62
H Hungary, 1960-1969 (Originally Given; c.i.f.)   63
Y Yugoslavia, 1952-1969 (Originally Given; c.i.f.)   64

II.SITC.X. Total Exports by One-Digit SITC Categories (millions of
   current dollars)

U U.S.S.R., 1946-1969 (Converted from CTN; f.o.b.)   65
H Hungary, 1960-1969 (Originally Given; f.o.b.)   66
Y Yugoslavia, 1952-1969 (Originally Given; f.o.b.)   67

II.BEC.M. Total Imports by BEC Categories (Table 1) and Two Sets of
   BEC Aggregates (Table 2) (millions of current dollars)

U U.S.S.R., 1946-1969 (f.o.b.)   68
B Bulgaria, 1955-1968 (f.o.b.)   70
Y Yugoslavia, 1952-1969 (c.i.f.)   72

II.BEC.X. Total Exports by BEC Categories (Table 1) and Two Sets of
   BEC Aggregates (Table 2) (millions of current dollars)

U U.S.S.R., 1946-1969 (f.o.b.)   74
B Bulgaria, 1955-1968 (f.o.b.)   76
Y Yugoslavia, 1952-1969 (f.o.b.)   78

III.CTN.M. Imports of U.S.S.R., Czechoslovakia, and Poland from Individual East European Countries by One-Digit CTN Categories
   (millions of current dollars)

U-B U.S.S.R. from Bulgaria, 1946-1968 (f.o.b.)   80
U-C U.S.S.R. from Czechoslovakia, 1946-1968 (f.o.b.)   81
U-G U.S.S.R. from East Germany, 1946-1968 (f.o.b.)   82
U-H U.S.S.R. from Hungary, 1946-1968 (f.o.b.)   83
U-P U.S.S.R. from Poland, 1946-1968 (f.o.b.)   84
U-R U.S.S.R. from Rumania, 1946-1968 (f.o.b.)   85
U-Y U.S.S.R. from Yugoslavia, 1946-1968 (f.o.b.)   86
U-CEMA U.S.S.R. from European CEMA (excluding
        Albania), 1946-1968 (f.o.b.)   87

C-U Czechoslovakia from U.S.S.R., 1958-1968 (f.o.b.)   88
C-B Czechoslovakia from Bulgaria, 1958-1968 (f.o.b.)   89
C-G Czechoslovakia from East Germany, 1958-1968 (f.o.b.)   90
C-H Czechoslovakia from Hungary, 1958-1968 (f.o.b.)   91
C-P Czechoslovakia from Poland, 1958-1968 (f.o.b.)   92
C-R Czechoslovakia from Rumania, 1958-1968 (f.o.b.)   93
C-Y Czechoslovakia from Yugoslavia, 1958-1966 (f.o.b.)   94
C-CEMA Czechoslovakia from European CEMA
        (excluding Albania), 1958-1968 (f.o.b.)   95

P-U Poland from U.S.S.R., 1958-1968 (f.o.b.)   96
P-B Poland from Bulgaria, 1958-1968 (f.o.b.)   97
P-C Poland from Czechoslovakia, 1958-1968 (f.o.b.)   98
P-G Poland from East Germany, 1958-1968 (f.o.b.)   99
P-H Poland from Hungary, 1958-1968 (f.o.b.)   100
P-R Poland from Rumania, 1958-1968 (f.o.b.)   101
P-Y Poland from Yugoslavia, 1958-1968 (f.o.b.)   102
P-CEMA Poland from European CEMA
        (excluding Albania), 1958-1968 (f.o.b.)   103

III.CTN.X. Exports of U.S.S.R., Czechoslovakia, and Poland to Individ-
    ual East European Countries by One-Digit CTN Categories (mil-
    lions of current dollars)

U-B U.S.S.R. to Bulgaria, 1946-1968 (f.o.b.)   104
U-C U.S.S.R. to Czechoslovakia, 1946-1968 (f.o.b.)   105
U-G U.S.S.R. to East Germany, 1946-1968 (f.o.b.)   106
U-H U.S.S.R. to Hungary, 1946-1968 (f.o.b.)   107
U-P U.S.S.R. to Poland, 1946-1968 (f.o.b.)   108
U-R U.S.S.R. to Rumania, 1946-1968 (f.o.b.)   109
U-Y U.S.S.R. to Yugoslavia, 1946-1968 (f.o.b.)   110
U-CEMA U.S.S.R. to European CEMA (excluding
        Albania), 1946-1968 (f.o.b.)   111

C-U Czechoslovakia to U.S.S.R., 1958-1968 (f.o.b.)   112
C-B Czechoslovakia to Bulgaria, 1958-1968 (f.o.b.)   113
C-G Czechoslovakia to East Germany, 1958-1968 (f.o.b.)   114
C-H Czechoslovakia to Hungary, 1958-1968 (f.o.b.)   115
C-P Czechoslovakia to Poland, 1958-1968 (f.o.b.)   116
C-R Czechoslovakia to Rumania, 1958-1968 (f.o.b.)   117

C-Y   Czechoslovakia to Yugoslavia, 1958-1966 (f.o.b.)   118
C-CEMA   Czechoslovakia to European CEMA
        (excluding Albania), 1958-1968 (f.o.b.)   119

P-U   Poland to U.S.S.R., 1958-1968 (f.o.b.)   120
P-B   Poland to Bulgaria, 1958-1968 (f.o.b.)   121
P-C   Poland to Czechoslovakia, 1958-1968 (f.o.b.)   122
P-G   Poland to East Germany, 1958-1968 (f.o.b.)   123
P-H   Poland to Hungary, 1958-1968 (f.o.b.)   124
P-R   Poland to Rumania, 1958-1968 (f.o.b.)   125
P-Y   Poland to Yugoslavia, 1958-1968 (f.o.b.)   126
P-CEMA   Poland to European CEMA (excluding
        Albania), 1958-1968 (f.o.b.)   127

III.BEC.M. Imports of U.S.S.R., Czechoslovakia, and Poland from Individual East European Countries by BEC Categories (Table 1)
and Two Sets of BEC Aggregates (Table 2) (millions of current
dollars)

U-B   U.S.S.R. from Bulgaria, 1946-1968 (f.o.b.)   128
U-C   U.S.S.R. from Czechoslovakia, 1946-1968 (f.o.b.)   130
U-G   U.S.S.R. from East Germany, 1946-1968 (f.o.b.)   132
U-H   U.S.S.R. from Hungary, 1946-1968 (f.o.b.)   134
U-P   U.S.S.R. from Poland, 1946-1968 (f.o.b.)   136
U-R   U.S.S.R. from Rumania, 1946-1968 (f.o.b.)   138
U-Y   U.S.S.R. from Yugoslavia, 1946-1968 (f.o.b.)   140
U-CEMA   U.S.S.R. from European CEMA (excluding
        Albania), 1946-1968 (f.o.b.)   142

C-U   Czechoslovakia from U.S.S.R., 1958-1968 (f.o.b.)   144
C-B   Czechoslovakia from Bulgaria, 1958-1968 (f.o.b.)   146
C-G   Czechoslovakia from East Germany, 1958-1968 (f.o.b.) 148
C-H   Czechoslovakia from Hungary, 1958-1968 (f.o.b.)   150
C-P   Czechoslovakia from Poland, 1958-1968 (f.o.b.)   152
C-R   Czechoslovakia from Rumania, 1958-1968 (f.o.b.)   154
C-Y   Czechoslovakia from Yugoslavia, 1958-1966 (f.o.b.)   156
C-CEMA   Czechoslovakia from European CEMA
        (excluding Albania), 1958-1968 (f.o.b.)   158

P-U   Poland from U.S.S.R., 1958-1968 (f.o.b.)   160
P-B   Poland from Bulgaria, 1958-1968 (f.o.b.)   162
P-C   Poland from Czechoslovakia, 1958-1968 (f.o.b.)   164
P-G   Poland from East Germany, 1958-1968 (f.o.b.)   166
P-H   Poland from Hungary, 1958-1968 (f.o.b.)   168
P-R   Poland from Rumania, 1958-1968 (f.o.b.)   170
P-Y   Poland from Yugoslavia, 1958-1968 (f.o.b.)   172
P-CEMA   Poland from European CEMA
        (excluding Albania), 1958-1968 (f.o.b.)   174

III.BEC.X. Exports of U.S.S.R., Czechoslovakia, and Poland to Individual East European Countries by BEC Categories (Table 1) and
Two Sets of BEC Aggregates (Table 2) (millions of current dollars)

U-B U.S.S.R. to Bulgaria, 1946-1968 (f.o.b.)   176
U-C U.S.S.R. to Czechoslovakia, 1946-1968 (f.o.b.)   178
U-G U.S.S.R. to East Germany, 1946-1968 (f.o.b.)   180
U-H U.S.S.R. to Hungary, 1946-1968 (f.o.b.)   182
U-P U.S.S.R. to Poland, 1946-1968 (f.o.b.)   184
U-R U.S.S.R. to Rumania, 1946-1968 (f.o.b.)   186
U-Y U.S.S.R. to Yugoslavia, 1946-1968 (f.o.b.)   188
U-CEMA U.S.S.R. to European CEMA
     (excluding Albania), 1946-1968 (f.o.b.)   190

C-U Czechoslovakia to U.S.S.R., 1958-1968 (f.o.b.)   192
C-B Czechoslovakia to Bulgaria, 1958-1968 (f.o.b.)   194
C-G Czechoslovakia to East Germany, 1958-1968 (f.o.b.)   196
C-H Czechoslovakia to Hungary, 1958-1968 (f.o.b.)   198
C-P Czechoslovakia to Poland, 1958-1968 (f.o.b.)   200
C-R Czechoslovakia to Rumania, 1958-1968 (f.o.b.)   202
C-Y Czechoslovakia to Yugoslavia, 1958-1966 (f.o.b.)   204
C-CEMA Czechoslovakia to European CEMA
     (excluding Albania), 1958-1968 (f.o.b.)   206

P-U Poland to U.S.S.R., 1958-1968 (f.o.b.)   208
P-B Poland to Bulgaria, 1958-1968 (f.o.b.)   210
P-C Poland to Czechoslovakia, 1958-1968 (f.o.b.)   212
P-G Poland to East Germany, 1958-1968 (f.o.b.)   214
P-H Poland to Hungary, 1958-1968 (f.o.b.)   216
P-R Poland to Rumania, 1958-1968 (f.o.b.)   218
P-Y Poland to Yugoslavia, 1958-1968 (f.o.b.)   220
P-CEMA Poland to European CEMA (excluding   222
     Albania), 1958-1968 (f.o.b.)

IV.SITC.M. Imports of Combined West Europe from Individual European CEMA Countries by One-Digit SITC Categories (millions of
current dollars)

U U.S.S.R., 1950-1968 (c.i.f.)   224
B Bulgaria, 1950-1968 (c.i.f.)   225
C Czechoslovakia, 1950-1968 (c.i.f.)   226
G East Germany, 1951-1968 (c.i.f.)   227
H Hungary, 1950-1968 (c.i.f.)   228
P Poland, 1950-1968 (c.i.f.)   229
R Rumania, 1950-1968 (c.i.f.)   230
CEMA European CEMA (excluding Albania),
     1950-1968 (c.i.f.)   231

IV.SITC.X.   Exports of Combined West Europe to Individual European
CEMA Countries by One-Digit SITC Categories (millions of current dollars)

U   U.S.S.R., 1950-1968 (f.o.b.)   232
B   Bulgaria, 1950-1968 (f.o.b.)   233
C   Czechoslovakia, 1950-1968 (f.o.b.)   234
G   East Germany, 1951-1968 (f.o.b.)   235
H   Hungary, 1950-1968 (f.o.b.)   236
P   Poland, 1950-1968 (f.o.b.)   237
R   Rumania, 1950-1968 (f.o.b.)   238
CEMA   European CEMA (excluding Albania)
     1950-1968 (f.o.b.)   239

IV.BEC.M.   Imports of Combined West Europe from Individual European CEMA Countries by BEC Categories (Table 1) and Two Sets
of BEC Aggregates (Table 2) (millions of current dollars)

U   U.S.S.R., 1950-1968 (c.i.f.)   240
B   Bulgaria, 1950-1968 (c.i.f.)   242
C   Czechoslovakia, 1950-1968 (c.i.f.)   244
G   East Germany, 1951-1968 (c.i.f.)   246
H   Hungary, 1950-1968 (c.i.f.)   248
P   Poland, 1950-1968 (c.i.f.)   250
R   Rumania, 1950-1968 (c.i.f.)   252
CEMA   European CEMA (excluding Albania),
     1950-1968 (c.i.f.)   254

IV.BEC.X.   Exports of Combined West Europe to Individual European
CEMA Countries by BEC Categories (Table 1) and Two Sets of
BEC Aggregates (Table 2) (millions of current dollars)

U   U.S.S.R., 1950-1968 (f.o.b.)   256
B   Bulgaria, 1950-1968 (f.o.b.)   258
C   Czechoslovakia, 1950-1968 (f.o.b.)   260
G   East Germany, 1951-1968 (f.o.b.)   262
H   Hungary, 1950-1968 (f.o.b.)   264
P   Poland, 1950-1968 (f.o.b.)   266
R   Rumania, 1950-1968 (f.o.b.)   268
CEMA   European CEMA (excluding Albania),
     1950-1968 (f.o.b.)   270

V.CTN.MX.   Hungary and Poland: Import and Export Trade with Combined Centrally Planned (Table 1) and Non-Centrally Planned
Economies (Table 2) by CTN Broad Divisions (millions of current
dollars)

H   Hungary, 1949-1969 (imports c.i.f., exports f.o.b.)   272
P   Poland, 1946-1969 (f.o.b.)   274

TABLE I.M.U
USSR IMPORTS, 1946-69
(MILLIONS OF CURRENT DOLLARS,* F.O.B.)

YEAR	BULGARIA	CZECH.	EAST GERMANY	HUNGARY	POLAND	RUMANIA	YUGOSL.	OTHER CPE'S	TOTAL CPE'S	MDC'S	LDC'S	TOTAL NON-CPE'S	TOTAL IMPORTS
1946	51.7	32.2	50.3	10.6	108.4	22.4	24.8	96.3/W	396.8/G	313.2	58.9	372.1	768.9
1947	38.2	39.0	21.8	17.2	137.1	27.3	29.6	128.9/W	439.1/G	243.2	62.7	305.7	744.8
1948	64.9	135.9	61.8	28.6	173.7	91.6	46.3	151.8/W	754.4/G	288.0	181.6	469.6	1224.0
1949	55.2	205.0	146.3	66.9	186.4	99.6	10.7	247.4/W	1017.5/G	350.1	121.6	471.7	1489.2
1950	66.9	201.6	160.1	83.2	210.0	139.2	—	275.2/W	1136.2/G	227.0	92.7	319.7	1455.9
1951	74.0	253.1	327.9	114.1	264.1	139.2	—	421.8/W	1594.2/G	301.2	95.3	396.6	1990.8
1952	109.0	299.3	365.2	140.6	350.9	196.0	—	500.3/W	1961.3/G	430.9	113.9	544.8	2506.1
1953	124.7	312.3	483.3	172.3	367.3	229.7	—	555.1/W	2244.8/G	444.2	80.0	524.2	2769.0
1954	136.7	318.1	617.7	166.7	338.0	194.7	1.1	666.4/W	2439.3/G	586.2	156.2	742.4	3181.7
1955	121.4	386.6	506.4	146.4	286.7	209.8	17.4	743.5/W	2418.3/G	446.4	195.8	642.2	3060.5
1956	144.7	396.4	626.3	120.8	283.3	235.3	49.7	879.2/W	2735.8/G	600.3	276.6	876.9	3612.6
1957	198.1	385.6	764.3	106.8	255.9	190.0	56.9	868.0/W	2825.5/G	698.2	414.0	1112.2	3937.7
1958	203.1	512.1	815.9	161.9	265.1	233.6	50.9	999.4/W	3242.0/G	657.0	450.6	1107.5	4349.5
1959	260.8	581.9	889.4	206.6	316.6	249.4	53.1	1239.2/W	3797.0/G	788.2	488.0	1276.2	5073.2
1960	298.6	652.4	929.1	248.2	386.7	280.0	53.1	1130.2/W	3978.3/G	1115.5	534.6	1650.1	5628.4
1961	326.1	697.7	875.9	326.8	476.9	340.8	54.6	1048.1/W	4146.7/G	1117.3	563.5	1680.9	5827.6
1962	390.0	824.8	1073.8	388.8	564.2	348.8	46.1	929.1/W	4565.5/G	1305.5	584.3	1889.9	6455.4
1963	444.8	950.5	1303.7	423.1	614.5	410.2	87.0	752.5/W	4986.4/G	1423.7	648.7	2072.3	7058.7
1964	533.3	968.9	1327.7	481.6	717.9	421.1	120.9	775.1/W	5346.4/G	1763.6	626.4	2390.1	7736.5
1965	615.5	1035.4	1284.7	515.3	780.7	441.0	188.7	748.5/W	5609.8/G	1632.8	815.7	2448.4	8058.3
1966	654.1	919.4	1238.0	511.9	733.2	405.4	192.8	609.0/W	5263.8/G	1778.4	870.5	2649.0	7912.8
1967	773.8	982.2	1412.7	597.1	902.4	424.3	232.6	620.4/W	5945.5/G	1815.2	775.9	2591.1	8536.6
1968	891.3	990.0	1605.3	669.0	1031.5	456.4	217.1	506.3/W	6367.0/G	2182.9	860.0	3042.9	9409.9
1969	974.7	1114.7	1629.3	719.1	1124.2	449.4	227.8	456.9/W	6696.0/G	2528.3	1102.3	3630.6	10326.7

* CONVERTED FROM NATIONAL DEVISA UNITS THROUGH OFFICIAL EXCHANGE RATES. NOTE THE LIMITATIONS DISCUSSED IN THE EXPLANATORY TEXT.

G SUBTOTAL GIVEN
W BALANCING ESTIMATE

TABLE I.M.8
BULGARIA'S IMPORTS, 1950, 1952-69
(MILLIONS OF CURRENT DOLLARS, * F.O.B.)

YEAR	USSR	CZECH.	EAST GERMANY	HUNGARY	POLAND	RUMANIA	YUGOSL.	OTHER CPE'S	TOTAL CPE'S	MDC'S	LDC'S	TOTAL NON-CPE'S	TOTAL IMPORTS
1950	66.5	21.1	5.0	6.4	11.1	3.5	-	-	113.7	17.3	1.5	18.7	132.5
1952	90.1/Z	20.0/Z	11.3/Z	5.9/Z	7.8/Z	2.4/Z	-	2.3/Z	139.7/Z	16.7/Y	1.9/Y	18.5/WZ	158.3/Z
1953	97.4/Z	23.5/Z	18.6/Z	9.2/Z	15.6/Z	4.5/Z	-	5.5/Z	174.4/Z	23.0/Y	2.8/Y	25.8/WZ	200.2/Z
1954	90.1/Z	26.9/Z	24.9/Z	8.4/Z	7.5/Z	9.1/Z	-	4.7/Z	171.6/Z	21.2/Y	2.9/Y	24.1/WZ	195.7/Z
1955	118.5	41.6	23.0	13.2	10.5	10.8	.6	5.0	223.3	23.1	3.5	26.6	249.9
1956	103.7	36.2	33.2	8.9	7.0	9.2	2.0	5.7	206.0	36.8	8.3	45.1	251.1
1957	174.9	32.3	32.2	8.4	10.9	5.7	4.1	7.0	275.6	46.7/Y	9.9/Y	56.6/G	332.1
1958	193.1	36.2	39.2	10.2	17.0	4.5	2.2	10.2	312.6	45.0/Y	8.9/Y	53.9/G	366.5
1959	286.4	52.9	51.1	15.3	22.3	6.6	8.1	14.4	457.2	103.2/Y	19.1/Y	122.2/G	579.4
1960	332.3	61.9	70.3	11.5	21.5	9.1	8.4	15.8	530.8	86.8	15.0	101.8	632.6
1961	355.6	55.3	84.4	13.4	22.6	7.4	7.9	18.0	564.6	82.7/Y	18.6/Y	101.4/G	666.0
1962	442.6	60.9	67.7	14.9	24.1	12.7	5.8	21.5	650.2	104.8	29.7	134.5	784.7
1963	500.4	81.4	97.2	17.8	33.8	11.5	8.5	18.4	769.0	138.8	25.5	164.3	933.2
1964	560.9	63.4	90.1	17.2	35.2	6.9	9.6	20.3	803.5	211.4	47.5	258.9	1062.4
1965	588.6	76.5	84.6	19.7	45.8	9.2	20.5	29.4	874.4	262.2	41.1	303.3	1177.7
1966	706.5	77.9	104.0	28.9	42.7	16.2	22.8	28.9	1027.9	407.9	42.4	450.3	1478.3
1967	782.8	98.2	126.2	29.8	47.3	21.0	27.5	31.8	1164.7	345.2	62.0	407.2	1571.9
1968	946.2	82.7	150.5	30.3	64.4	20.0	32.5	40.3	1366.9	328.9	86.5	415.4	1782.3
1969	973.8	79.1	152.6	32.4	81.7	15.7	17.9	40.8	1393.9	259.7	95.7	355.5	1749.3

* CONVERTED FROM NATIONAL DEVISA UNITS THROUGH OFFICIAL EXCHANGE
RATES. NOTE THE LIMITATIONS DISCUSSED IN THE EXPLANATORY TEXT.

G   SUBTOTAL GIVEN
W   BALANCING ESTIMATE
Y   OTHER ESTIMATE
Z   OFFICIAL UNREVISED

TABLE I.M.C
CZECHOSLOVAKIA'S IMPORTS, 1946-69
(MILLIONS OF CURRENT DOLLARS,* F.O.B.)

YEAR	USSR	BULGARIA	EAST GERMANY	HUNGARY	POLAND	RUMANIA	YUGOSL.	OTHER CPE'S	TOTAL CPE'S	MDC'S	LDC'S	TOTAL NON-CPE'S	TOTAL IMPORTS
1946	27.1	7.9	7.5/X	11.8	.6	3.9	14.4/X	-	73.2			133.0/W	206.3
1947													578.8
1948	111.7	11.0	9.6	21.3	40.6	27.4	49.2	.1/W	270.7/G	322.2	88.5	410.7/G	681.4
1949													718.1
1950	192.2	15.0	29.9	34.0	57.9	21.3	-	10.6	360.9	223.2	55.3	278.5	639.4
1951									551.8/G	265.2/Y	79.7/Y	344.9/G	896.7
1952	319.1								621.0/G	187.9/Y	67.1/Y	255.0/G	876.0
1953	343.9	20.3	60.8	73.5	100.3	36.0	-	58.6	693.4	131.0	54.9	185.8	879.2
1954	350.3	21.3	75.3	77.5	80.7	37.6	2.2	56.5	701.4	147.2/Y	84.2/Y	231.4/W	932.9
1955	365.4	24.3	97.9	77.1	76.1	41.7	7.4	64.7	754.6	169.2	128.9	298.1	1052.7
1956	390.0	31.8	118.2	64.9	77.0	28.5	6.7	75.0	792.0	262.9	130.8	393.8	1185.8
1957	535.6	47.4	144.3	73.3	60.0	26.7	5.8	78.9	972.0	287.2	127.6	414.9	1386.9
1958	451.8	41.4	162.1	90.4	71.5	22.4	15.0	102.8	957.4	264.3	135.6	399.9	1357.3
1959	598.0	44.3	175.0	87.0	82.0	42.5	10.7	115.1	1154.5	292.8	155.2	448.0	1602.5
1960	630.5	57.1	198.2	93.9	110.6	64.3	24.7	114.7	1294.0	344.1	177.7	521.7	1815.7
1961	656.0	65.7	230.0	135.8	141.1	54.0	16.8	95.7	1395.3	413.1	215.4	628.5	2023.8
1962	781.5	65.0	228.4	139.5	145.0	60.1	21.3	92.0	1532.6	363.8	173.8	537.5	2070.2
1963	842.7	69.3	232.0	131.1	146.1	52.9	22.6	91.3	1588.7	370.6	201.1	571.7	2160.5
1964	912.9	72.6	254.0	146.8	193.3	74.6	44.3	64.6	1763.2	468.6	197.4	666.0	2429.2
1965	954.8	89.2	287.9	171.4	208.6	94.3	71.8	83.3	1961.4	502.0	209.3	711.3	2672.7
1966	914.7	63.9	318.2	171.8	179.7	92.2	73.8	109.0	1923.3	582.4	230.4	812.8	2736.2
1967	965.4	78.8	320.2	150.8	199.2	86.5	52.9	75.6	1929.3	544.1	206.8	750.9	2680.2
1968	1036.2	90.3	399.6	181.3	247.9	109.3	59.6	95.0	2219.2	654.6	203.5	858.1	3077.3
1969	1105.2	99.0	415.0	191.0	260.2	139.0	63.8	100.4/W	2373.7/G	713.7	207.1	920.8/G	3294.4

G SUBTOTAL GIVEN
W BALANCING ESTIMATE
X MIRROR ESTIMATE
Y OTHER ESTIMATE

* CONVERTED FROM NATIONAL DEVISA UNITS THROUGH OFFICIAL EXCHANGE RATES. NOTE THE LIMITATIONS DISCUSSED IN THE EXPLANATORY TEXT.

TABLE I.M.G
EAST GERMANY'S IMPORTS, 1946-69
(MILLIONS OF CURRENT DOLLARS,* F.O.B.)

YEAR	USSR	BULGARIA	CZECH.	HUNGARY	POLAND	RUMANIA	YUGOSL.	OTHER CPE'S	TOTAL CPE'S	MDC'S	LDC'S	TOTAL NON-CPE'S	TOTAL IMPORTS
1946	–	–	.9	–	9.8	–	–	–	10.7	54.0	–	54.0	64.8
1947	.4	.9	1.8	1.0	14.1	–	2.2	–	20.5	137.9	–	137.9	158.4
1948	55.8	5.8	17.0	2.0	33.4	.5	7.9	–	122.3	144.1	–	144.1	266.4
1949	110.0	6.2	25.0	5.2	63.7	.8	1.0	–	204.5/G**	107.5	1.1	108.7	313.1
1950	194.1	5.0	41.9	24.9	87.1	3.3	–	.1/W	356.4/G	112.7	.5	113.2	469.7
1951	271.8	9.4	45.1	14.1	82.7	7.5	–	13.0/W	443.7/G	155.4	8.5	163.9	607.6
1952	333.3	11.1	49.5	29.1	94.9	14.8	–	47.3/W	580.1/G	182.5	10.2	192.7	772.8
1953	458.4	18.0	58.4	34.3	111.9	14.9	–	54.0/W	749.9/G	227.1	5.6	232.6	982.5
1954	456.5	24.7	76.9	48.0	111.8	21.5	.9	71.1/W	811.5/G	277.0	11.3	288.2	1099.7
1955	422.1	31.0	70.7	62.1	114.6	37.9	1.7	93.3/W	833.5/G	315.0	30.6	345.6	1179.1
1956	557.1	34.4	105.4	39.2	106.9	29.1	3.5	92.4/W	965.9/G	327.9	44.3	372.2	1338.1
1957	736.1	26.6	118.9	47.1	103.0	21.0	6.0	105.2/W	1163.9/G	408.2	62.2	470.4	1634.3
1958	700.2	30.4	141.9	70.6	84.7	30.1	24.0	124.2/W	1206.1/G	415.9	81.1	497.0	1703.1
1959	924.5	45.2	154.7	81.9	104.7	32.8	24.3	138.9/W	1507.0/G	434.3	75.9	510.2	2017.2
1960	958.1	54.7	187.0	93.5	108.8	52.0	44.2	122.4	1620.5	482.9	91.1	574.0	2194.5
1961	1070.7	55.9	218.1	103.8	102.3	50.3	26.9	69.5	1707.3	466.9	76.4	543.4	2250.7
1962	1246.2	76.1	224.6	98.5	108.3	43.5	36.3	75.6	1909.1	415.0	83.4	498.3	2407.5
1963	1172.8	72.7	216.0	95.3	108.5	36.9	37.4	75.9	1815.6	428.4	86.5	515.0	2330.6
1964	1211.1	80.5	249.8	112.3	144.8	63.1	64.5	49.5	1975.7	552.8	105.1	658.0	2633.7
1965	1205.0	93.7	262.7	124.1	140.2	72.7	78.3	69.6	2046.4	638.4	124.8	763.3	2809.7
1966	1384.5	108.3	293.7	151.7	154.6	66.5	67.9	79.6	2306.8	780.4	127.9	908.3	3215.1
1967	1417.7	114.4	318.1	153.3	164.8	70.8	66.5	88.9	2394.3	751.5	133.1	884.5	3278.9
1968	1492.6	122.3	328.8	171.5	224.4	77.2	57.6	83.5	2558.1	703.9	130.9	834.8	3392.9
1969	1744.3	145.2	367.7	208.3	260.8	111.7	43.6	94.1	2975.9	974.8	153.9	1128.8	4104.6

* CONVERTED FROM NATIONAL DEVISA UNITS THROUGH OFFICIAL EXCHANGE RATES. NOTE THE LIMITATIONS DISCUSSED IN THE EXPLANATORY TEXT.

** SUM OF TOTAL CPE'S, 1949   211.9
GIVEN TOTAL OF CPE'S   204.5
(SEE EXPLANATORY TEXT)

G   SUBTOTAL GIVEN
W   BALANCING ESTIMATE

TABLE I.M.H

HUNGARY'S IMPORTS, 1946-69

(MILLIONS OF CURRENT DOLLARS,* C.I.F.)

YEAR	USSR	BULGARIA	CZECH.	EAST GERMANY	POLAND	RUMANIA	YUGOSL.	OTHER CPE'S	TOTAL CPE'S	MDC'S	LDC'S	TOTAL NON-CPE'S	TOTAL IMPORTS
1946	15.5	.1/Y	3.4	-	.4/Y	.3/Y	2.2/Y	-	21.9			9.6/W	31.5
1947	14.5	.7/Y	12.4	.3/X	2.7/Y	2.4/Y	15.6/Y	-	48.6			75.2/W	123.8
1948	29.4	1.3/Y	20.0	.6/X	4.8/Y	4.2/Y	27.4/X	-	87.7			80.5/W	168.3
1949	61.8	4.1	29.7	2.2	15.2	13.4	6.6	.0	133.1	144.6/W	10.5	155.0/G	288.1
1950	77.4	6.4	32.6	8.2	31.1	22.2	-	.9	178.8	122.2/W	14.7	136.9/G	315.7
1951	100.5	5.7	51.6	22.4	36.2	17.5	-	25.7	259.6	107.0/W	27.4	134.4/G	394.0
1952	118.1	5.7	73.0	39.5	33.7	22.3	-	38.9	331.2	112.3/W	16.0	128.3/G	459.5
1953	141.7	9.9	69.8	40.6	28.2	20.5	-	45.0	355.5	117.5/W	14.3	131.9/G	487.4
1954	146.4	12.0	67.2	52.5	25.3	16.5	.7	39.7	360.3	148.1/W	23.2	171.3/G	531.6
1955	99.1	10.2	56.3	49.5	26.6	18.6	2.5	39.5	302.4	212.7/W	39.2	251.9/G	554.2
1956	107.4	12.1	55.2	44.3	23.4	12.9	6.4	36.6	298.4	158.0/W	24.8	182.8/G	481.2
1957	236.7	12.5	78.8	70.3	35.3	17.0	10.5	35.9	497.0	166.7/W	18.7	185.4/G	682.4
1958	194.3	9.3	76.4	71.4	32.0	13.7	15.9	37.5	450.5	151.2/W	29.3	180.4/G	630.9
1959	255.7	10.4	88.1	90.5	40.0	22.8	13.2	49.2	569.8	191.7/W	31.4	223.1/G	792.9
1960	302.9	13.1	111.8	100.9	49.5	41.5	20.4	47.1	687.3	251.7/W	36.7	288.4/G	975.8
1961	356.3	13.7	103.4	104.9	58.0	24.4	19.1	32.8	712.5	272.3/W	40.7	313.0/G	1025.5
1962	416.7	15.3	126.1	117.1	67.0	39.1	11.3	28.1	820.6	260.4/W	67.7	328.1/G	1148.7
1963	432.4	15.0	150.0	132.9	79.8	35.9	12.3	42.0	900.2	318.8/W	86.5	405.3/G	1305.5
1964	497.4	23.9	154.6	133.2	95.2	41.5	23.9	26.2	995.9	402.4/W	96.2	498.6/G	1494.6
1965	553.3	22.1	134.5	131.2	88.3	38.8	27.3	22.7	1018.2	406.7/W	95.4	502.1/G	1520.3
1966	517.3	28.4	133.0	151.6	91.7	33.0	29.6	31.1	1015.7	436.0/W	113.8	549.8/G	1565.5
1967	591.9	39.7	152.1	194.0	111.5	39.4	32.2	22.2	1183.1	487.0/W	105.2	592.2/G	1775.3
1968	648.1	28.8	160.5	196.4	112.7	36.2	29.8	22.3	1234.7	462.6/W	105.3	567.9/G	1802.6
1969	713.2	31.5	140.9	191.8	117.4	38.5	46.9	25.8	1305.9	526.3/W	95.6	621.8/G	1927.7

G   SUBTOTAL GIVEN
W   BALANCING ESTIMATE
X   MIRROR ESTIMATE
Y   OTHER ESTIMATE

* CONVERTED FROM NATIONAL DEVISA UNITS THROUGH OFFICIAL EXCHANGE
  RATES. NOTE THE LIMITATIONS DISCUSSED IN THE EXPLANATORY TEXT.

TABLE I.M.P
POLAND'S IMPORTS, 1946-69
(MILLIONS OF CURRENT DOLLARS,* F.O.B.)

YEAR	USSR	BULGARIA	CZECH.	EAST GERMANY	HUNGARY	RUMANIA	YUGOSL.	OTHER CPE'S	TOTAL CPE'S	MDC'S	LDC'S	TOTAL NON-CPE'S	TOTAL IMPORTS
1946	101.0	-	2.3	7.8	1.3	.5	1.3	-	114.1	29.1/Y	2.6/Y	31.7/G	145.8
1947	80.7	7.3	6.3	7.5	3.8	.5	4.6	-	110.6	192.6/Y	17.0/Y	209.6/G	320.1
1948	120.2	6.0	53.5	29.7	4.0	5.8	26.2/W	-	245.4/G	249.0/Y	22.0/Y	271.0/G	516.4
1949	118.5	8.5	69.5	47.2	11.7	9.0	4.5	.4	269.4	333.6/Y	29.4/Y	363.0/G	632.5
1950	192.4	12.0	87.9	76.9	24.7	11.6	-	2.7	408.3	238.8	21.1	259.8	668.2
1951	241.2	9.8	84.5	135.5	28.0	12.5	-	23.7	535.2	344.8/Y	44.2/Y	389.0/G	924.2
1952	275.0	11.7	92.7	119.2	30.7	17.5	-	35.6	582.6	239.4/Y	41.0/Y	280.4/G	863.0
1953	263.5	9.5	82.2	128.0	31.5	13.2	-	27.9	555.9	179.3/Y	39.0/Y	218.4/G	774.2
1954	336.7	15.7	80.0	136.5	29.2	13.0	-	30.0	641.3	206.7/Y	55.4/Y	262.2/G	903.5
1955	313.6	6.9	79.7	121.8	30.6	11.9	3.8	36.6	604.9	247.1	79.7	326.9	931.8
1956	344.3	10.6	102.9	135.2	23.1	14.1	8.9	38.3	677.4	298.5	46.0	344.4	1021.8
1957	421.9	14.6	77.1	164.9	20.7	15.6	17.8	45.5	778.0	408.6	64.9	473.5	1251.5
1958	334.0	18.7	94.5	155.5	33.8	12.3	22.3	43.2	714.3	445.9	66.6	512.5	1226.8
1959	452.3	22.1	112.9	187.2	36.6	21.1	25.0	65.7	923.0	414.2	82.3	496.6	1419.6
1960	465.3	20.2	127.1	186.4	46.1	20.5	15.3	68.6	949.5	443.8	101.7	545.5	1495.0
1961	489.7	20.8	162.9	202.7	59.0	24.0	39.0	56.0	1054.2	544.3	88.2	632.5	1686.7
1962	577.8	31.2	198.6	234.9	68.2	40.2	39.2	56.0	1246.2	529.4	109.8	639.2	1885.4
1963	647.2	32.9	193.0	253.4	75.9	33.3	34.8	55.6	1326.0	527.8	125.2	653.0	1979.0
1964	642.4	31.9	193.1	235.8	82.6	29.5	40.5	50.3	1306.1	605.8	160.3	766.1	2072.2
1965	728.4	39.8	244.1	271.4	105.7	44.7	63.0	50.4	1547.5	573.8	219.0	792.8	2340.3
1966	791.7	43.8	233.1	280.3	104.1	41.0	56.6	53.2	1603.9	709.2	181.0	890.2	2494.1
1967	921.1	45.0	235.2	292.1	104.0	50.2	47.3	42.0	1736.9	756.6	151.3	907.9	2644.8
1968	1010.7	47.3	228.6	296.2	97.7	57.5	40.0	60.0	1838.0	825.3	189.9	1015.1	2853.1
1969	1200.2	64.1	244.7	320.0	116.6	60.2	52.6	55.1	2113.5	892.0	204.2	1096.2	3209.7

G   SUBTOTAL GIVEN
W   BALANCING ESTIMATE
Y   OTHER ESTIMATE

* CONVERTED FROM NATIONAL DEVISA UNITS THROUGH OFFICIAL EXCHANGE
  RATES. NOTE THE LIMITATIONS DISCUSSED IN THE EXPLANATORY TEXT.

TABLE I.M.R
RUMANIA'S IMPORTS, 1946-69
(MILLIONS OF CURRENT DOLLARS,* F.O.B.)

YEAR	USSR	BULGARIA	CZECH.	EAST GERMANY	HUNGARY	POLAND	YUGOSL.	OTHER CPE'S	TOTAL CPE'S	MDC'S	LDC'S	TOTAL NON-CPE'S	TOTAL IMPORTS
1946													21.7/Y
1947													64.8/Y
1948									76.0/G			50.0/G	126.0/Y
1949									145.0/G			42.0/G	187.0/Y
1950									200.0/G			43.4/G	243.4
1951									215.0/G			53.0/G	268.0/Y
1952									275.0/G			52.0/G	327.0/Y
1953									322.0/G			63.0/G	385.0/Y
1954									251.0/G			87.0/G	338.0/Y
1955									344.0/G			117.9/G	461.9
1956									235.0/G			167.0/G	402.0
1957									318.0/G			174.0/G	492.0
1958	253.8	3.3	39.0	36.1	15.0	12.8	3.6	18.3	381.8	79.9	20.0/W	99.9	481.7
1959	234.7	5.0	49.2	44.8	18.4	17.8	1.7	32.4	403.9	78.9	19.2/W	98.1	502.0
1960	265.9	8.6	63.9	51.9	25.8	23.1	4.9	29.7	473.6	152.5	21.8/W	174.2	647.9
1961	298.8	14.1	76.3	58.6	29.4	32.0	12.4	26.5	548.1	228.3	38.3/W	266.6	814.7
1962	370.5	17.1	88.7	55.6	36.5	35.1	8.4	22.3	634.2	271.0	35.9/W	307.0	941.1
1963	399.3	13.7	101.6	64.3	34.0	41.0	5.5	35.1	694.3	275.6	52.1/W	327.7	1022.0
1964	493.1	13.9	96.5	68.5	42.7	41.1	10.3	28.6	794.6	326.4	47.2/W	373.6	1168.1
1965	406.2	13.1	69.6	62.5	28.1	37.1	12.4	30.7	659.6	330.8	86.7/W	417.5	1077.1
1966	394.1	15.0	69.7	84.4	30.9	43.6	17.1	39.4	694.2	411.2	107.8/W	519.0	1213.2
1967	396.5	25.5	90.2	92.5	34.7	47.0	22.9	40.9	750.2	731.4	64.6/W	795.9	1546.1
1968	427.0	25.6	100.5	90.8	34.6	58.4	28.3	58.8	824.0	701.0	83.9/W	784.9	1609.0
1969	464.8	32.6	108.6	84.3	42.8	68.2	23.8	62.3	887.3	758.6	94.6/W	853.2	1740.5

* CONVERTED FROM NATIONAL DEVISA UNITS THROUGH OFFICIAL EXCHANGE RATES. NOTE THE LIMITATIONS DISCUSSED IN THE EXPLANATORY TEXT.

G SUBTOTAL GIVEN
W BALANCING ESTIMATE
Y OTHER ESTIMATE

TABLE I.M.Y
YUGOSLAVIA'S IMPORTS, 1946-69
(MILLIONS OF CURRENT DOLLARS,* C.I.F.)

YEAR	USSR	BULGARIA	CZECH.	EAST GERMANY	HUNGARY	POLAND	RUMANIA	OTHER CPE'S	TOTAL CPE'S	MDC'S	LDC'S	TOTAL NON-CPE'S	TOTAL IMPORTS
1946	8.1	1.6	6.1	1.0	2.3	2.7	3.0	-	24.7	10.3	.3	10.5	35.2
1947	37.6	5.4	29.9	7.0	8.5	5.5	1.1	-	94.9	60.6	10.5	71.1	166.1
1948	34.1	5.3	53.7	13.1	13.7	23.1	5.4	.7	148.9	137.9	19.6	157.5	306.5
1949	3.9	.1	18.8	3.9	8.9	6.6	.1	.5	42.8	216.8	35.3	252.0	294.8
1950								5.4	5.4	184.7	40.5	225.2	230.7
1951								2.0	2.0	340.4	41.3	381.6	383.7
1952								3.3	3.3	325.5	44.2	369.7	373.0
1953								.2	.2	362.3	32.8	395.1	395.3
1954	1.1	.6	1.1	.2	.9		.1	.6	4.5	284.3	50.5	334.8	339.4
1955	14.4	1.3	7.3	2.2	2.8	4.2	.7	.0	33.0	353.1	54.8	407.9	440.9
1956	70.5	2.2	12.1	3.2	6.4	7.9	2.9	4.1	109.1	316.5	48.5	365.0	474.1
1957	69.0	4.2	19.0	7.6	19.7	19.2	3.7	7.8	150.2	452.9	58.2	511.1	661.3
1958	57.8	5.3	27.4	26.3	35.6	35.9	4.7	2.7	195.7	431.1	58.2	489.3	684.9
1959	57.6	4.7	23.2	28.9	31.6	20.3	3.7	2.8	172.6	446.6	67.9	514.5	687.1
1960	56.9	7.2	26.2	37.4	36.6	37.8	9.0	1.2	212.4	508.0	106.0	614.0	826.3
1961	32.0	9.9	19.8	37.6	32.8	28.6	8.4	2.4	171.5	656.0	82.6	738.7	910.2
1962	59.1	10.4	25.8	36.3	20.9	32.1	3.5	5.7	194.0	595.5	98.1	693.7	887.6
1963	72.9	9.6	43.0	49.2	25.3	33.2	6.7	1.4	241.3	667.2	148.0	815.2	1056.5
1964	100.1	16.7	82.2	72.7	35.2	59.6	10.2	9.3	386.0	752.4	184.6	937.0	1323.2
1965	107.9	22.1	70.6	63.1	30.8	57.1	16.0	7.5	375.2	734.4	178.4	912.8	1288.0
1966	145.7	36.9	93.2	87.9	35.4	72.1	22.5	13.9	507.7	880.4	187.3	1067.7	1575.4
1967	163.8	19.8	94.7	68.9	31.8	41.6	21.7	22.8	465.1	1073.6	168.7	1242.3	1707.3
1968	188.3	22.8	103.1	70.8	34.1	44.6	22.2	8.5	494.4	1145.5	156.9	1302.4	1796.8
1969	168.2	23.0	119.9	77.6	43.8	47.0	25.0	6.9	511.3	1375.8	246.6	1622.5	2133.8

* CONVERTED FROM NATIONAL DEVISA UNITS THROUGH OFFICIAL EXCHANGE RATES. NOTE THE LIMITATIONS DISCUSSED IN THE EXPLANATORY TEXT.

TABLE I.M.A
ALBANIA'S IMPORTS, 1946-67
(MILLIONS OF CURRENT DOLLARS,* F.O.B.)

YEAR	USSR	BULGARIA	CZECH.	EAST GERMANY	HUNGARY	POLAND	RUMANIA	YUGOSL.	OTHER CPE'S	TOTAL CPE'S	MDC'S	LDC'S	TOTAL NON-CPE'S	TOTAL IMPORTS
1946														2.05
1947														30.27
1948														18.18
1949														12.89
1950	8.20	.35	3.70	-	3.73	3.70	2.37	-	-	22.06	-			22.06
1951	23.41	.43	5.08	.86	2.61	2.66	4.18	-	-	39.22	.34	-	.34	39.56
1952	13.71	1.87	4.93	2.83	3.38	2.53	2.42	-	-	31.66	.13	-	.13	31.79
1953	21.22	1.46	6.62	2.58	2.25	2.76	2.66	-	-	39.56	.47	-	.47	40.03
1954	10.71	2.09	4.25	2.50	2.40	2.24	1.40	-	-	25.61	.23	-	.23	25.83
1955	15.66	2.41	6.23	6.14	4.34	2.85	2.64	.20	1.27	41.73	1.07	.03	1.10	42.83
1956	16.70	.82	5.43	5.13	2.07	2.04	1.41	.15	4.09	37.85	.86	.10	.96	38.81
1957	25.99	1.32	6.37	4.25	1.55	3.28	1.69	.40	5.90	50.75	2.06	.50	2.56	53.31
1958	44.70	2.30	10.49	5.68	3.76	4.74	2.72	.53	1.68	76.60	1.79	.22	2.01	78.61
1959														85.29
1960	45.67	2.67	7.84	5.44	2.57	3.42	2.15	.30	6.97	77.03	4.04	.01	4.04	81.08
1961	22.49	1.87	10.32	4.04	3.31	3.98	1.30	.22	19.75	67.27	4.89	.08	4.96	72.23
1962	.03	.47	8.71	2.42	1.66	3.17	.91	.56	43.79	61.72	2.70	.17	2.87	64.59
1963	-	.61	10.11	3.62	2.09	4.52	1.61	.34	43.20	66.10	4.50	.15	4.64	70.74
1964	-	.80	9.44	5.18	2.26	7.38	2.37	1.09	63.54	92.06	5.77	.30	6.07	98.13
1965														107.78
1966														118.90
1967														130.00

* CONVERTED FROM NATIONAL DEVISA UNITS THROUGH OFFICIAL EXCHANGE RATES. NOTE THE LIMITATIONS DISCUSSED IN THE EXPLANATORY TEXT.

TABLE I.M.CEMA

IMPORTS OF THE EUROPEAN CEMA GROUP (EXCLUDING ALBANIA), 1950, 1952-69

(MILLIONS OF CURRENT DOLLARS,* F.O.B., EXCEPT HUNGARY, C.I.F.)

FROM YEAR	USSR	BULGARIA	CZECH.	EAST GERMANY	HUNGARY	POLAND	RUMANIA	YUGOSL.	OTHER CPE'S	TOTAL CPE'S	MDC'S	LDC'S	TOTAL NON-CPE'S	TOTAL IMPORTS
1950	722.6	105.3	385.1	280.1	173.3	397.3	201.1		289.4	2754.2**	941.2	185.7	1170.3**	3924.6
1952	1135.6	137.5	534.6	535.3	206.3	487.3	253.1		624.4	4491.0***	1169.6	250.0	1471.7***	5962.6
1953	1304.9	182.3	546.2	731.4	320.9	623.3	318.8		746.0	5095.8***	1122.1	196.7	1381.8***	6477.6
1954	1380.1	210.4	569.1	906.8	329.8	563.4	292.4	4.9	868.5	5376.4**	1386.5	333.2	1806.7**	7183.1
1955	1318.8	193.9	634.9	798.7	329.5	514.6	330.6	33.4	982.8	5481.1**	1413.4	477.7	2009.0**	7490.1
1956	1502.5	233.5	696.1	957.4	256.8	495.6	329.2	77.2	1127.2	5910.4***	1684.5	530.7	2382.2**	8292.6
1957	2105.2	299.2	692.7	1176.0	256.3	465.1	276.0	101.1	1140.4	6830.1**	2015.7	697.3	2887.0**	9717.1
1958	2127.2	306.2	899.9	1280.2	381.9	483.2	316.6	133.9	1335.7	7264.7	2059.3	791.9	2851.2	10115.9
1959	2751.5	387.8	1039.7	1438.1	445.6	583.2	375.2	136.2	1655.0	8812.4	2303.4	871.0	3174.3	11986.7
1960	2955.0	452.2	1204.1	1536.7	519.0	700.2	467.4	170.9	1528.6	9534.0	2877.3	978.4	3855.7	13389.7
1961	3227.1	506.3	1313.6	1556.5	668.3	832.8	501.0	176.7	1346.6	10128.8	3125.0	1041.2	4166.2	14295.0
1962	3835.3	594.6	1523.8	1777.5	746.3	943.6	544.4	168.3	1224.5	11358.3	3249.9	1084.7	4334.6	15692.9
1963	3994.8	648.3	1692.4	2084.0	777.1	1023.8	580.7	208.2	1070.9	12080.3	3483.7	1225.6	4709.3	16789.6
1964	4317.7	756.2	1726.3	2109.3	883.2	1227.6	636.7	313.9	1014.7	12985.4	4331.1	1280.2	5611.3	18596.7
1965	4436.4	873.4	1822.8	2122.2	964.2	1300.7	700.8	462.0	1034.8	13717.3	4346.7	1592.0	5938.7	19656.1
1966	4708.7	913.5	1726.9	2176.5	999.3	1245.6	654.3	460.6	950.3	13835.7	5105.5	1673.9	6779.4	20615.1
1967	5075.2	1077.0	1876.1	2437.1	1069.8	1472.1	692.3	481.8	921.8	15104.0	5430.0	1498.8	6929.7	22033.7
1968	5560.7	1205.6	1891.1	2738.9	1184.3	1739.4	756.7	465.0	866.3	16408.0	5859.2	1659.9	7519.1	23927.1
1969	6201.6	1347.0	2055.6	2793.0	1310.2	1912.6	814.6	476.2	835.4	17746.2	6653.5	1953.5	8606.9	26353.0

* CONVERTED FROM NATIONAL DEVISA UNITS THROUGH OFFICIAL EXCHANGE RATES. NOTE LIMITATIONS DISCUSSED IN THE EXPLANATORY TEXT.

** SUM OF COMPONENTS LESS THAN SUBTOTAL DUE TO MISSING RUMANIAN SERIES.

*** SUM OF COMPONENTS LESS THAN SUBTOTAL DUE TO MISSING CZECHOSLOVAK AND RUMANIAN SERIES. (USSR COLUMN DOES INCLUDE TRADE WITH CZECHOSLOVAKIA).

TABLE I.X.U
USSR EXPORTS, 1946–69
(MILLIONS OF CURRENT DOLLARS,* F.O.B.)

YEAR	BULGARIA	CZECH.	EAST GERMANY	HUNGARY	POLAND	RUMANIA	YUGOSL.	OTHER CPE'S	TOTAL CPE'S	MDC'S	LDC'S	TOTAL NON-CPE'S	TOTAL EXPORTS
1946	83.9	29.0	41.0	10.2	106.4	30.3	18.4	59.0/W	378.3/G	232.3	43.0	275.3	653.7
1947	62.4	44.3	43.7	16.2	104.4	37.7	37.7	135.7/W	482.1/G	267.1	21.6	288.7	770.8
1948	79.4	141.8	91.4	34.4	132.9	48.2	34.4	205.4/W	768.1/G	466.4	73.6	540.0	1308.1
1949	94.0	206.0	116.1	83.7	136.9	111.3	2.9	346.7/W	1097.5/G	278.6	71.1	349.7	1447.2
1950	100.0	220.4	185.8	126.9	241.4	113.9	—	511.8/W	1500.2/G	262.1	32.3	294.4	1794.6
1951	115.9	290.1	298.7	121.8	310.7	142.9	—	597.8/W	1877.8/G	339.7	73.3	413.0	2290.8
1952	117.9	363.3	432.9	150.3	362.3	226.0	—	677.3/W	2330.1/G	385.2	74.6	459.8	2789.9
1953	109.6	348.8	505.1	157.7	328.9	220.8		840.7/W	2511.4/G	386.2	50.1	436.3	2947.7
1954	108.4	351.6	482.7	153.0	413.4	212.7	2.0	927.8/W	2651.5/G	473.7	97.9	571.5	3223.1
1955	127.4	355.9	478.7	115.3	431.8	267.8	16.4	933.0/W	2726.3/G	558.3	142.0	700.3	3426.6
1956	108.4	373.7	571.3	126.9	357.2	212.0	69.1	914.2/W	2732.9/G	614.3	267.8	882.1	3615.0
1957	172.4	551.3	862.1	249.7	430.9	250.8	73.1	714.1/W	3304.4/G	714.1	362.9	1077.0	4381.4
1958	200.6	446.8	799.8	200.6	376.8	251.3	51.1	809.3/W	3136.2/G	702.4	460.6	1163.0	4299.2
1959	289.9	603.0	1030.1	259.8	486.4	232.4	46.2	1183.8/W	4131.6/G	887.9	430.8	1318.7	5450.3
1960	329.0	630.8	1051.7	311.4	490.8	260.7	55.1	1082.0/W	4211.4/G	1014.8	337.4	1352.2	5563.6
1961	356.2	652.7	1209.1	359.3	530.7	291.8	35.9	885.4/W	4321.1/G	1093.4	583.9	1677.3	5998.4
1962	447.8	770.7	1372.7	411.1	594.1	374.8	72.3	861.8/W	4905.2/G	1137.0	988.3	2125.3	7030.5
1963	495.4	849.0	1313.9	443.4	662.5	399.0	96.3	839.8/W	5099.4/G	1261.1	911.9	2173.0	7272.4
1964	567.4	900.8	1385.2	492.7	660.0	493.1	134.9	772.8/W	5406.8/G	1312.0	964.4	2276.4	7683.3
1965	588.4	925.9	1363.0	545.9	726.7	402.8	145.1	858.5/W	5556.3/G	1495.7	1122.7	2618.3	8174.6
1966	697.1	894.0	1406.8	504.6	803.2	386.3	213.9	967.0/W	5872.8/G	1756.4	1211.8	2968.2	8841.0
1967	762.8	967.4	1416.2	585.5	912.2	394.6	280.3	1057.8/W	6376.8/G	1934.1	1341.1	3275.2	9652.2
1968	949.3	1038.1	1506.4	675.4	1050.1	416.7	289.1	1208.9/W	7134.0/G	2096.8	1403.4	3500.2	10634.2
1969	974.3	1109.7	1739.0	700.0	1199.0	476.4	244.8	1238.9/W	7682.0/G	2284.3	1689.0	3973.3	11655.3

G   SUBTOTAL GIVEN
W   BALANCING ESTIMATE

* CONVERTED FROM NATIONAL DEVISA UNITS THROUGH OFFICIAL EXCHANGE RATES. NOTE THE LIMITATIONS DISCUSSED IN THE EXPLANATORY TEXT.

TABLE I.X.B
BULGARIA'S EXPORTS, 1950, 1952-69
(MILLIONS OF CURRENT DOLLARS,* F.O.B.)

YEAR	USSR	CZECH.	EAST GERMANY	HUNGARY	POLAND	RUMANIA	YUGOSL.	OTHER CPE'S	TOTAL CPE'S	MDC'S	LDC'S	TOTAL NON-CPE'S	TOTAL EXPORTS
1950	63.8	17.2	6.5	5.6	11.8	2.3	-	.4	107.6	8.4	1.1	9.5	117.1
1952	97.7/Z	21.3/Z	11.0/Z	6.1/Z	9.8/Z	2.9/Z	-	3.1/Z	151.9/Z	16.1/Y	2.8/Y	18.9/WZ	170.8/Z
1953	104.5/Z	18.8/Z	20.3/Z	9.8/Z	9.2/Z	2.8/Z	-	8.5/Z	174.0/Z	26.5/Y	5.2/Y	31.7/WZ	205.7/Z
1954	108.3/Z	21.2/Z	29.6/Z	12.1/Z	13.9/Z	6.5/Z	.2/Z	9.5/Z	201.2/Z	25.7/Y	5.6/Y	31.3/WZ	232.5/Z
1955	119.4	25.5	32.5	10.1	7.0	9.3	1.3	6.8	211.9	19.7	4.7	24.4	236.2
1956	147.1	32.1	39.5	13.1	10.9	9.9	2.2	7.5	262.4	30.4	9.2	39.7	302.1
1957	200.8	46.9	25.6	9.7	14.0	7.0	5.7	8.2	317.9	40.2/Y	12.0/Y	52.1/G	370.1
1958	200.4	40.7	29.7	7.9	19.4	3.2	5.6	15.5	322.4	39.3/Y	11.5/Y	50.8/G	373.2
1959	259.4	42.3	46.8	10.6	22.3	4.9	5.7	13.2	405.3	48.0/Y	13.8/Y	61.8/G	467.1
1960	307.3	54.7	56.2	11.6	20.3	8.4	8.0	13.6	480.1	71.4	20.0	91.4	571.5
1961	336.8	65.9	75.6	14.0	22.1	13.8	12.7	12.9	554.0	82.9/Y	25.6/Y	108.5/G	662.6
1962	388.2	63.8	80.3	16.2	32.7	16.7	12.1	26.8	636.9	101.4	34.3	135.6	772.6
1963	445.7	70.1	80.8	16.3	32.8	13.9	8.9	16.4	685.0	107.8	41.3	149.1	834.0
1964	521.3	73.2	82.4	23.3	30.9	13.8	14.4	21.4	780.8	147.9	51.0	198.9	979.7
1965	613.6	91.4	108.4	21.9	39.4	13.8	22.2	23.2	933.8	186.2	55.7	242.0	1175.8
1966	663.6	62.8	107.6	26.4	44.1	14.9	33.5	44.1	997.0	238.6	69.4	308.0	1305.0
1967	772.2	80.3	117.9	36.4	44.4	26.1	21.5	36.3	1135.1	239.9	83.2	323.1	1458.2
1968	893.8	88.5	120.9	28.5	47.5	25.5	28.5	37.1	1270.4	243.7	101.0	344.7	1615.1
1969	979.7	101.5	149.1	30.6	65.0	30.7	25.0	41.1	1422.6	263.8	107.9	371.7	1794.4

G SUBTOTAL GIVEN
W BALANCING ESTIMATE
Y OTHER ESTIMATE
Z OFFICIAL UNREVISED

* CONVERTED FROM NATIONAL DEVISA UNITS THROUGH OFFICIAL EXCHANGE
RATES. NOTE THE LIMITATIONS DISCUSSED IN THE EXPLANATORY TEXT.

TABLE I.X.C
CZECHOSLOVAKIA'S EXPORTS, 1946-69
(MILLIONS OF CURRENT DOLLARS,* F.O.B.)

YEAR	USSR	BULGARIA	EAST GERMANY	HUNGARY	POLAND	RUMANIA	YUGOSL.	OTHER CPE'S	TOTAL CPE'S	MDC'S	LDC'S	TOTAL NON-CPE'S	TOTAL EXPORTS
1946	34.3	6.3	.9/X	7.6	2.8	3.8	6.1/X	-	61.7			224.1/W	285.9
1947													571.4
1948	120.1	15.6	9.9	22.2	52.9	23.8	52.2	1.8	298.5	331.8	122.8	454.6	753.1
1949													806.3
1950	197.9	19.7	41.3	33.5	87.6	37.9	-	9.0	427.0	270.0	82.1	352.1	779.0
1951									521.2/G	239.0/Y	85.2/Y	324.2/G	845.3
1952	291.0								629.2/G	173.5/Y	71.5/Y	245.0/G	874.2
1953	321.3	38.3	61.3	70.4	101.8	110.3		72.6	776.0	147.5	70.0	217.5	993.6
1954	348.6	39.2	81.1	67.2	84.3	42.4	1.1	84.5	748.4	156.1/Y	100.9/Y	257.0/W	1005.4
1955	402.8	43.3	79.7	64.0	102.8	37.5	6.1	73.6	809.9	196.5	169.6	366.1	1176.1
1956	428.5	36.0	140.3	58.9	99.2	35.0	13.5	88.5	899.8	252.9	234.6	487.5	1387.3
1957	398.1	33.8	132.2	76.0	78.2	37.1	18.8	110.3	884.4	273.6	199.9	473.5	1357.9
1958	497.1	36.3	157.5	77.4	94.9	37.8	25.0	141.0	1066.9	256.5	189.9	446.4	1513.3
1959	587.4	53.5	178.1	86.1	114.9	60.6	21.9	148.1	1250.5	292.9	183.8	476.7	1727.2
1960	658.7	61.5	195.6	111.7	128.3	63.6	23.9	151.4	1394.7	321.7	213.2	534.9	1929.6
1961	713.4	57.1	213.6	104.2	164.0	75.7	18.1	96.7	1442.8	362.0	241.7	603.7	2046.4
1962	828.4	64.7	229.0	125.0	201.0	88.1	24.6	69.2	1630.8	334.3	228.5	562.8	2193.6
1963	956.5	80.0	222.1	152.7	195.6	100.7	46.8	104.5	1858.8	376.7	226.3	603.0	2461.7
1964	961.7	63.1	266.0	158.1	192.8	92.9	76.3	90.8	1901.7	424.8	249.5	674.2	2575.9
1965	1022.9	61.8	277.1	132.2	248.8	68.9	69.2	84.7	1965.6	459.1	264.0	723.1	2688.7
1966	920.5	81.5	297.4	132.2	236.5	69.4	95.3	95.4	1928.3	511.0	305.9	816.9	2745.2
1967	977.2	91.7	318.6	152.4	234.9	89.5	96.4	90.7	2051.3	546.7	266.4	813.1	2864.4
1968	1008.0	82.0	328.1	167.4	231.7	99.7	106.7	107.5	2131.0	577.5	297.0	874.5	3005.5
1969	1124.5	80.7	359.8	138.5	248.2	106.8	136.0	98.9/W	2293.4/G	696.4	329.9	1026.3/G	3319.7

G   SUBTOTAL GIVEN
W   BALANCING ESTIMATE
X   MIRROR ESTIMATE
Y   OTHER ESTIMATE

* CONVERTED FROM NATIONAL DEVISA UNITS THROUGH OFFICIAL EXCHANGE RATES. NOTE THE LIMITATIONS DISCUSSED IN THE EXPLANATORY TEXT.

TABLE I.X.G

EAST GERMANY'S EXPORTS, 1946-69

(MILLIONS OF CURRENT DOLLARS,* F.O.B.)

YEAR	USSR	BULGARIA	CZECH.	HUNGARY	POLAND	RUMANIA	YUGOSL.	OTHER CPE'S	TOTAL CPE'S	MDC'S	LDC'S	TOTAL NON-CPE'S	TOTAL EXPORTS
1946	-	-	7.5	-	12.4	-	-	-	19.9	54.1	-	54.1	74.0
1947	.0	.4	6.8	.3	4.5	-	2.2	-	14.3	224.8	-	224.8	239.1
1948	47.9	1.9	15.7	.6	39.9	.8	3.1	-	109.9	136.4	-	136.4	246.2
1949	132.6	6.2	20.5	2.2	46.5	1.2	5.9	-	213.5/G**	115.8	.9	116.7	330.2
1950	153.7	3.2	30.2	8.0	78.8	3.0	-	-.1/W	276.9/G	126.4	2.7	129.1	406.0
1951	329.8	8.3	45.1	22.2	122.6	10.3	-	24.2/W	562.4/G	144.4	5.9	150.3	712.7
1952	306.3	11.4	47.3	35.9	105.4	20.8	-	27.6/W	554.7/G	171.8	12.2	184.0	738.7
1953	433.4	19.9	56.6	42.6	108.5	31.2	-	70.5/W	762.8/G	196.4	8.3	204.7	967.5
1954	586.7	23.9	73.0	46.9	133.9	25.8	.6	113.4/W	1004.1/G	260.6	21.5	282.1	1286.1
1955	522.6	21.2	93.8	46.1	123.8	24.8	1.9	116.6/W	950.8/G	302.1	41.7	343.8	1294.6
1956	569.3	32.4	109.8	47.7	139.0	28.5	3.4	116.3/W	1046.4/G	320.0	48.4	368.4	1414.8
1957	809.7	29.8	140.6	63.2	151.1	33.9	8.7	141.8/W	1378.8/G	381.8	73.3	455.2	1833.9
1958	846.0	36.4	150.6	61.2	143.9	34.6	25.3	172.7/W	1470.8/G	366.2	77.6	443.9	1914.7
1959	941.5	50.7	171.5	86.5	176.4	47.8	29.8	148.8/W	1653.0/G	415.3	73.2	488.5	2141.5
1960	924.7	69.0	192.1	94.2	184.0	48.3	34.2	125.5	1672.1	445.1	90.2	535.3	2207.4
1961	912.0	83.7	229.1	99.4	208.3	58.8	39.4	101.2	1731.9	447.9	101.6	549.5	2281.5
1962	1092.8	63.8	217.2	112.5	233.1	55.2	35.0	60.5	1870.2	417.7	90.1	507.7	2378.0
1963	1276.5	97.8	229.6	121.9	250.0	63.2	49.1	55.3	2143.6	482.1	87.5	569.5	2713.1
1964	1383.6	87.0	251.5	124.3	235.3	63.0	67.1	63.6	2275.3	549.3	107.0	656.3	2931.6
1965	1310.6	97.3	291.9	126.6	269.4	67.2	60.9	72.8	2296.7	634.5	138.5	773.1	3069.8
1966	1276.5	105.3	309.8	141.0	279.7	85.3	85.6	102.9	2386.0	649.5	169.5	819.0	3205.0
1967	1407.8	125.1	316.2	183.5	284.6	89.9	64.9	127.1	2599.1	686.1	170.9	857.0	3456.1
1968	1567.3	151.6	402.2	193.5	291.5	89.5	75.8	132.1	2903.6	725.1	162.6	887.6	3791.2
1969	1657.6	152.5	414.5	185.5	315.2	84.3	74.8	149.3	3033.8	930.5	188.9	1119.4	4153.2

G SUBTOTAL GIVEN
W BALANCING ESTIMATE

* CONVERTED FROM NATIONAL DEVISA UNITS THROUGH OFFICIAL EXCHANGE
  RATES. NOTE THE LIMITATIONS DISCUSSED IN THE EXPLANATORY TEXT.

** SUM OF TOTAL CPE'S, 1949   215.1
   GIVEN TOTAL OF CPE'S   213.5
   (SEE EXPLANATORY TEXT)

TABLE I.X.H
HUNGARY'S EXPORTS, 1946-69
(MILLIONS OF CURRENT DOLLARS,* F.O.B.)

YEAR	USSR	BULGARIA	CZECH.	EAST GERMANY	POLAND	RUMANIA	YUGOSL.	OTHER CPE'S	TOTAL CPE'S	MDC'S	LDC'S	TOTAL NON-CPE'S	TOTAL EXPORTS
1946	16.0	.3/Y	5.7	–	.7/Y	1.0/Y	1.3/Y	–	25.0			10.6/W	35.5
1947	13.4	1.4/Y	12.3		3.0/Y	4.0/Y	5.1/Y	–	40.2			48.5/W	88.7
1948	33.7	3.7/Y	15.6	1.0/X	7.9/Y	10.7/Y	13.7/X	–	87.4			77.2/W	164.6
1949	69.9	5.4	28.4	2.0/X	11.5	15.7	7.9	1.6	145.5	124.8	10.3	135.0/G	280.5
1950	95.0	6.3	34.7	24.2	27.0	25.4	–	4.2	216.7	97.2	14.6	111.8/G	328.5
1951	129.1	5.1	52.3	13.4	32.0	14.6	–	25.2	271.7	103.8	20.2	124.1/G	395.7
1952	148.3	7.2	57.7	30.1	35.8	18.7	–	26.6	324.3	92.7	21.1	113.8/G	438.1
1953	187.2	9.1	70.0	35.9	32.2	25.7	–	34.3	394.4	81.5	22.3	103.8/G	498.2
1954	171.9	8.7	75.4	48.9	29.0	15.1	.9	35.7	385.6	103.9	29.8	133.7/G	519.2
1955	152.9	8.7	79.1	64.9	31.9	19.4	3.6	43.5	404.0	152.3	44.7	197.0/G	601.0
1956	120.8	5.8	62.6	38.5	22.7	12.1	6.8	37.8	307.0	144.4	35.6	179.9/G	486.9
1957	105.9	8.6	75.8	49.6	21.9	12.1	21.6	34.7	330.1	123.2	34.6	157.8/G	487.9
1958	158.8	9.8	92.4	75.3	33.6	15.1	38.5	68.0	491.5	155.5	36.6	192.1/G	683.5
1959	208.6	15.6	87.1	89.9	39.0	18.1	31.4	50.6	540.5	183.2	45.9	229.1/G	769.6
1960	256.5	11.9	93.9	100.7	45.5	25.9	37.3	52.8	624.6	199.2/W	50.2	249.4/G	873.9
1961	331.9	13.7	137.7	110.3	59.6	28.5	32.6	52.6	767.0	204.8/W	57.2	262.0/G	1028.9
1962	391.8	15.0	137.0	104.9	70.8	36.5	22.0	32.5	810.5	214.3/W	74.5	288.8/G	1099.3
1963	427.9	16.7	132.7	106.9	78.5	34.0	25.2	27.2	849.1	274.9/W	81.8	356.7/G	1205.8
1964	490.2	16.6	149.0	121.9	84.4	42.1	36.3	22.1	962.6	303.2/W	86.0	389.2/G	1351.8
1965	525.4	20.3	179.3	135.1	105.1	28.7	29.2	34.8	1057.8	342.6/W	109.1	451.7/G	1509.5
1966	526.8	29.4	171.4	157.5	105.1	30.1	32.1	36.7	1088.9	409.0/W	95.4	504.4/G	1593.3
1967	613.4	31.4	153.2	163.9	101.6	37.2	30.4	35.8	1166.8	425.5/W	108.9	534.3/G	1701.1
1968	683.1	28.9	181.8	174.7	101.3	35.3	34.1	46.3	1285.6	415.1/W	88.4	503.5/G	1789.1
1969	725.6	31.5	197.6	219.4	116.9	42.1	43.6	40.9	1417.6	542.7/W	123.3	666.1/G	2083.7

* CONVERTED FROM NATIONAL DEVISA UNITS THROUGH OFFICIAL EXCHANGE RATES. NOTE THE LIMITATIONS DISCUSSED IN THE EXPLANATORY TEXT.

G SUBTOTAL GIVEN
W BALANCING ESTIMATE
X MIRROR ESTIMATE
Y OTHER ESTIMATE

TABLE I.X.P
POLAND'S EXPORTS, 1946-69
(MILLIONS OF CURRENT DOLLARS,* F.O.B.)

YEAR	USSR	BULGARIA	CZECH.	EAST GERMANY	HUNGARY	RUMANIA	YUGOSL.	OTHER CPE'S	TOTAL CPE'S	MDC'S	LDC'S	TOTAL NON-CPE'S	TOTAL EXPORTS
1946	58.5	.5	4.0	8.5	1.8	1.0	1.3	.2/W	75.7/G	46.8/Y	4.0/Y	50.8/G	126.6
1947	70.5	3.0	14.7	9.8	3.5	.8	6.8	.1/W	109.1/G	126.3/Y	10.9/Y	137.2/G	246.2
1948	110.7	7.8	45.0	39.7	4.3	5.5	21.7	.2/W	234.9/G	273.0/Y	23.4/Y	296.4/G	531.3
1949	120.2	13.8	53.2	64.7	13.5	9.3	4.8	1.3	280.7	311.4/Y	26.7/Y	338.1/G	618.8
1950	154.1	11.6	58.2	88.1	26.9	13.0	—	9.0	360.8	251.9	21.5	273.4	634.2
1951	180.5	7.5	87.5	88.2	31.0	11.0	—	28.6	434.3	294.9/Y	32.5/Y	327.3/G	761.7
1952	247.2	8.0	83.5	102.5	28.0	8.8	—	27.3	505.3	237.9/Y	32.2/Y	270.1/G	775.4
1953	274.5	14.5	95.2	111.2	27.5	9.5	—	36.3	568.8	225.5/Y	36.6/Y	262.1/G	831.0
1954	329.0	7.0	77.2	112.5	24.5	9.8	—	41.7	601.7	224.4/Y	42.7/Y	267.1/G	868.8
1955	280.5	9.6	75.3	125.1	26.4	12.6	3.7	45.3	578.4	280.0	61.4	341.3	919.7
1956	270.2	6.4	76.2	107.5	24.8	19.1	7.2	68.7	580.2	342.4	62.2	404.6	984.7
1957	258.5	11.9	61.1	125.3	32.6	17.0	18.2	53.3	577.9	338.1	58.9	397.0	975.0
1958	265.2	17.1	72.5	106.4	28.6	13.6	34.0	82.9	620.4	340.2	98.7	439.0	1059.4
1959	313.0	17.0	80.6	136.9	37.1	17.6	20.6	59.1	681.9	379.9	83.3	463.2	1145.1
1960	390.2	27.6	113.1	124.7	46.5	23.2	36.7	68.2	830.2	395.5	99.8	495.3	1325.5
1961	485.0	21.6	146.8	109.7	55.1	32.5	26.2	62.2	939.1	451.5	113.0	564.5	1503.6
1962	568.7	24.3	145.8	117.6	63.6	35.1	31.5	47.7	1034.3	489.7	122.2	611.8	1646.1
1963	617.5	34.5	144.7	120.5	79.0	41.2	33.2	52.5	1123.1	512.2	134.8	647.0	1770.0
1964	721.7	35.2	195.9	164.5	89.8	39.7	55.7	48.1	1350.6	577.2	168.6	745.8	2096.4
1965	781.4	44.9	208.4	153.1	85.9	35.8	54.1	45.0	1408.7	639.3	179.9	819.2	2227.9
1966	741.2	44.5	178.3	160.6	91.5	46.2	75.0	62.8	1400.1	692.8	179.2	872.0	2272.1
1967	901.8	51.3	202.7	175.7	113.4	46.5	48.5	71.3	1611.2	724.9	190.4	915.3	2526.6
1968	1042.1	63.4	245.5	229.2	110.3	57.7	51.9	78.3	1878.5	781.3	198.0	979.3	2857.8
1969	1121.4	80.6	270.5	277.9	115.0	66.1	63.3	69.3	2064.0	841.0	236.5	1077.5	3141.5

* CONVERTED FROM NATIONAL DEVISA UNITS THROUGH OFFICIAL EXCHANGE RATES. NOTE THE LIMITATIONS DISCUSSED IN THE EXPLANATORY TEXT.

G SUBTOTAL GIVEN
W BALANCING ESTIMATE
Y OTHER ESTIMATE

TABLE I.X.R
RUMANIA'S EXPORTS, 1946-69
(MILLIONS OF CURRENT DOLLARS,* F.O.B.)

YEAR	USSR	BULGARIA	CZECH.	EAST GERMANY	HUNGARY	POLAND	YUGOSL.	OTHER CPE'S	TOTAL CPE'S	MDC'S	LDC'S	TOTAL NON-CPE'S	TOTAL EXPORTS
1946													22.5/Y
1947													42.0/Y
1948									98.0/G			48.0/G	146.0/Y
1949									132.0/G			44.0/G	176.0/Y
1950									180.0/G			32.4/G	212.4
1951									215.0/G			44.0/G	259.0/Y
1952									263.0/G			35.0/G	298.0/Y
1953									276.0/G			65.0/G	341.0/Y
1954									262.0/G			88.0/G	350.0/Y
1955									303.0/G			118.7/G	421.7
1956									279.0/G			164.0/G	443.0
1957									291.0/G			120.0/G	411.0
1958	235.3	4.7	22.7	30.2	14.1	12.5	5.0	32.5	356.9	86.3	25.2/W	111.4	468.3
1959	250.1	6.6	35.0	35.5	22.8	22.0	4.1	37.8	413.7	82.1	26.7/W	108.7	522.4
1960	281.4	9.2	62.6	53.9	42.0	20.9	7.9	45.3	523.2	152.1	41.7/W	193.8	717.0
1961	351.2	9.1	56.8	53.0	25.0	24.6	9.0	27.6	556.2	192.9	43.3/W	236.2	792.5
1962	343.3	11.7	58.3	46.6	38.3	40.1	4.1	17.1	559.6	193.1	65.2/W	258.4	818.0
1963	412.9	11.8	55.0	41.9	36.7	33.2	8.8	39.2	639.4	219.7	56.0/W	275.6	915.0
1964	421.8	6.9	75.2	71.0	40.9	29.1	10.1	32.8	687.8	233.1	79.2/W	312.2	1000.1
1965	438.4	9.2	95.3	71.7	38.5	45.0	16.4	41.4	755.9	255.2	90.5/W	345.7	1101.5
1966	409.8	17.4	92.3	66.7	32.9	41.3	21.8	53.2	735.4	332.4	118.4/W	450.8	1186.2
1967	432.9	20.7	87.0	69.8	37.9	49.5	21.0	67.3	786.0	443.3	166.0/W	609.3	1395.4
1968	455.7	19.9	112.8	77.1	36.6	58.6	25.2	83.6	869.4	448.2	151.0/W	599.1	1468.6
1969	454.9	20.8	140.8	121.3	39.1	61.4	35.0	97.2	970.4	520.4	142.3/W	662.7	1633.1

* CONVERTED FROM NATIONAL DEVISA UNITS THROUGH OFFICIAL EXCHANGE RATES. NOTE THE LIMITATIONS DISCUSSED IN THE EXPLANATORY TEXT.

G SUBTOTAL GIVEN
W BALANCING ESTIMATE
Y OTHER ESTIMATE

TABLE I.X.Y
YUGOSLAVIA'S EXPORTS, 1946-69
(MILLIONS OF CURRENT DOLLARS,* F.O.B.)

YEAR	USSR	BULGARIA	CZECH.	EAST GERMANY	HUNGARY	POLAND	RUMANIA	OTHER CPE'S	TOTAL CPE'S	MDC'S	LDC'S	TOTAL NON-CPE'S	TOTAL EXPORTS
1946	23.4	.9	14.4	.1	.3	1.4	.6	.1	41.3	12.1	.7	12.8	54.1
1947	28.4	3.0	31.9	4.6	14.2	5.9	1.5	.6	90.1	66.6	7.0	73.6	163.7
1948	45.5	2.9	46.5	5.3	27.4	23.7	2.0	.7	153.9	127.3	15.7	143.1	296.9
1949	9.3	.2	8.7	.7	5.2	3.8	.0	.4	28.3	157.8	12.6	170.4	198.7
1950	-	-	-	-	-	-	-	.2	.2	134.2	20.0	154.2	154.3
1951	-	-	-	-	-	-	-	1.1	1.1	161.8	15.9	177.7	178.8
1952	-	-	-	-	-	-	-	1.3	1.3	227.2	18.0	245.2	246.5
1953	-	-	-	-	-	-	-	.7	.7	149.8	35.4	185.3	186.0
1954	1.5	.0	2.9	.2	.9	-	.1	.7	6.2	185.4	48.8	234.1	240.4
1955	17.9	.5	7.3	2.1	2.8	3.9	.8	.2	35.5	173.8	47.3	221.1	256.6
1956	42.2	1.4	8.2	4.4	6.3	8.9	2.3	4.5	78.3	207.4	37.6	245.1	323.3
1957	48.9	4.1	8.6	10.4	12.0	16.2	4.4	4.5	109.1	238.0	47.9	285.9	395.1
1958	36.4	1.9	19.5	26.4	14.1	22.0	2.4	5.6	128.3	256.4	56.7	313.1	441.4
1959	47.2	8.0	16.4	26.7	13.1	33.9	1.8	2.8	149.7	249.8	77.1	326.9	476.6
1960	52.7	8.5	25.7	46.4	20.4	22.1	6.0	1.9	183.7	295.9	86.4	382.4	566.1
1961	50.9	8.5	16.9	30.2	18.0	40.5	10.7	5.1	180.7	298.5	89.7	388.1	568.8
1962	43.3	6.2	21.3	35.3	11.1	42.3	7.3	1.3	168.1	359.6	162.8	522.4	690.4
1963	85.4	8.9	23.2	37.9	12.3	38.2	5.0	3.6	214.5	430.7	145.1	575.8	790.3
1964	116.1	10.0	44.8	63.2	24.1	39.2	9.8	5.0	312.3	437.7	143.1	580.8	893.2
1965	187.6	20.4	71.0	76.1	26.0	64.2	12.9	7.4	465.5	462.0	164.1	626.0	1091.5
1966	193.7	17.8	67.6	64.4	29.4	56.3	16.7	9.7	455.6	586.7	177.7	764.4	1220.1
1967	219.2	19.9	50.1	63.0	30.1	45.9	22.7	10.4	461.5	640.1	150.1	790.2	1251.7
1968	207.5	29.3	54.8	55.3	28.8	37.0	22.2	9.1	443.0	652.8	167.9	820.7	1263.7
1969	206.4	23.1	62.8	44.0	44.1	46.9	23.7	6.3	457.3	819.4	197.7	1017.2	1474.5

* CONVERTED FROM NATIONAL DEVISA UNITS THROUGH OFFICIAL EXCHANGE
RATES. NOTE THE LIMITATIONS DISCUSSED IN THE EXPLANATORY TEXT.

TABLE I.X.A
ALBANIA'S EXPORTS, 1946-67
(MILLIONS OF CURRENT DOLLARS,* F.O.B.)

YEAR	USSR	BULGARIA	CZECH.	EAST GERMANY	HUNGARY	POLAND	RUMANIA	YUGOSL.	OTHER CPE'S	TOTAL CPE'S	MDC'S	LDC'S	TOTAL NON-CPE'S	TOTAL EXPORTS
1946														1.91
1947														4.75
1948														8.33
1949														5.82
1950	4.06	.17	.61	-	.73	.49	.42	-	-	6.48	-	-		6.48
1951	4.82	.36	1.71	-	1.04	.82	.23	-	-	8.99	.16	-	.16	9.15
1952	7.47	.43	2.06	.51	1.34	.97	.30	-	-	13.08	-	-		13.08
1953	5.29	.53	2.31	1.05	.70	.80	.28	-	-	10.95	.04	-	.04	10.99
1954	5.37	.77	1.66	1.33	1.02	.71	.06	-	-	10.93	.01	-	.01	10.93
1955	5.42	.70	2.20	1.30	1.69	1.25	.03	.05	-	12.63	.37	-	.37	13.00
1956	8.59	.59	3.30	1.92	1.06	1.01	.67	.09	.72	17.96	.96	.09	1.05	19.01
1957	14.97	.52	4.85	2.81	1.55	1.87	.56	.44	.68	28.24	.64	.15	.79	29.03
1958	13.65	1.15	4.89	2.55	1.61	2.55	.51	.94	.81	28.66	.53	.02	.55	29.21
1959														34.01
1960	24.20	1.60	7.79	4.71	3.58	2.73	.65	.40	2.34	48.00	.49	.07	.56	48.56
1961	21.07	1.69	9.65	4.61	2.55	3.98	.37	.27	3.29	47.47	.99	.11	1.10	48.58
1962	-	2.05	10.44	4.85	1.52	4.90	1.16	.44	12.94	38.30	2.22	.39	2.61	40.90
1963	-	2.30	5.90	3.14	2.48	4.05	1.82	.50	24.58	44.76	2.82	.50	3.32	48.08
1964	-	.78	11.42	6.08	1.63	5.81	2.40	1.37	25.97	55.46	4.05	.41	4.46	59.92
1965														68.88
1966														73.34
1967														78.88

* CONVERTED FROM NATIONAL DEVISA UNITS THROUGH OFFICIAL EXCHANGE RATES. NOTE THE LIMITATIONS DISCUSSED IN THE EXPLANATORY TEXT.

TABLE I.X.CEMA
EXPORTS OF THE EUROPEAN CEMA GROUP (EXCLUDING ALBANIA), 1950, 1952-69
(MILLIONS OF CURRENT DOLLARS,* F.O.B.)

YEAR	TO USSR	BULGARIA	CZECH.	EAST GERMANY	HUNGARY	POLAND	RUMANIA	YUGOSL.	OTHER CPE'S	TOTAL CPE'S	MDC'S	LDC'S	TOTAL NON-CPE'S	TOTAL EXPORTS
1950	664.4	140.9	360.6	345.8	200.9	446.6	195.5		534.5	3069.3**	1016.1	154.3	1202.8**	4271.9
1952	1090.5	144.5	573.1	576.5	220.3	513.3	277.1		761.9	4758.4****	1077.2	214.5	1326.7****	6085.1
1953	1321.0	191.5	589.5	733.8	308.0	580.6	400.3		1063.0	5463.6***	1063.7	192.5	1321.2**	6784.7
1954	1544.5	187.2	598.3	754.7	303.7	674.6	312.2	4.7	1212.5	5854.5**	1244.4	298.2	1630.6***	7485.1
1955	1478.2	210.3	629.5	780.9	262.0	697.2	371.3	33.0	1218.8	5984.3**	1508.9	464.1	2091.7**	8075.9
1956	1536.0	189.1	654.3	897.1	271.3	629.0	316.7	102.1	1233.0	6107.7**	1704.5	657.8	2526.2**	8633.9
1957	1773.0	256.5	875.7	1194.9	431.1	696.1	357.9	146.0	1062.4	7084.6**	1871.0	741.6	2732.6**	9817.2
1958	2202.8	304.8	825.6	1198.8	389.8	681.0	355.7	184.5	1321.9	7465.0	1946.5	900.0	2846.5	10311.6
1959	2559.9	433.3	1019.6	1517.1	502.9	861.0	381.5	159.8	1641.4	9076.6	2289.3	857.3	3146.6	12223.2
1960	2818.8	508.2	1147.2	1582.6	617.5	889.8	430.1	203.3	1538.8	9736.3	2599.7	852.6	3452.3	13188.5
1961	3130.3	541.4	1289.0	1771.3	657.1	1009.4	501.2	173.9	1238.7	10312.1	2835.4	1166.3	4001.7	14313.8
1962	3613.2	627.3	1392.9	1952.0	766.8	1171.8	606.3	201.8	1115.5	11447.5	2887.5	1603.0	4490.5	15938.1
1963	4136.9	736.3	1481.0	1886.0	850.0	1252.6	652.1	268.4	1134.8	12398.2	3234.3	1539.4	4773.8	17172.0
1964	4500.4	776.3	1645.5	2091.0	929.1	1232.5	744.5	394.7	1051.6	13365.7	3547.3	1705.8	5253.0	18618.7
1965	4692.3	822.0	1792.1	2108.4	951.0	1434.3	617.1	397.1	1160.5	13974.8	4012.6	1960.4	5973.0	19947.8
1966	4538.3	975.2	1708.5	2196.5	928.6	1509.9	632.2	557.2	1362.0	14408.6	4589.8	2149.5	6739.2	21147.9
1967	5105.2	1082.8	1806.9	2262.1	1109.0	1627.2	683.7	563.1	1486.3	15726.4	5000.5	2326.9	7327.4	23054.0
1968	5650.1	1295.1	2069.1	2436.5	1211.8	1780.7	724.4	611.3	1693.8	17472.6	5287.6	2401.4	7689.0	25161.6
1969	6063.7	1340.4	2234.5	2866.3	1208.7	2005.7	806.4	622.5	1735.6	18883.8	6079.2	2817.8	8897.0	27781.0

* CONVERTED FROM NATIONAL DEVISA UNITS THROUGH OFFICIAL EXCHANGE RATES. NOTE LIMITATIONS DISCUSSED IN THE EXPLANATORY TEXT.

** SUM OF COMPONENTS LESS THAN SUBTOTAL DUE TO MISSING RUMANIAN SERIES.

*** SUM OF COMPONENTS LESS THAN SUBTOTAL DUE TO MISSING CZECHOSLOVAK AND RUMANIAN SERIES. (USSR COLUMN DOES INCLUDE TRADE WITH CZECHOSLOVAKIA).

TABLE II.CTN.M.U
USSR IMPORTS, 1946-69
(MILLIONS OF CURRENT DOLLARS,* F.O.B.)

YEAR	BROAD DIV I 1	2	3	4	5	BROAD DIV II (2-5)	6	7	8	BROAD DIV III (6-8)	BROAD DIV IV 9	NOT SPECIFIED	TOTAL IMPORTS
1946	219.3	166.4	10.7	10.9	142.1	330.1		38.7	64.4	103.1	33.4	82.9	768.9
1947	132.3	159.7	21.9	8.2	137.9	327.7		84.0	84.9	168.9	37.2	78.7	744.8
1948	110.0	233.0	69.0	14.7	342.9	659.5		152.1	89.2	241.3	111.3	101.8	1224.0
1949	214.9	339.7	69.0	25.9	300.0	734.5		125.8	104.9	230.7	154.8	154.3	1489.2
1950	313.0	371.0	84.2	19.9	224.2	699.3		132.4	111.4	243.9	95.8	103.9	1455.9
1951	413.3	501.0	238.1	18.8	233.6	991.4		171.0	148.0	319.0	149.0	118.0	1990.8
1952	540.2	670.3	215.0	28.1	362.4	1275.9		206.4	208.4	414.9	173.9	101.2	2506.1
1953	760.9	776.5	99.8	26.3	357.4	1260.1		176.1	286.7	462.8	181.9	103.3	2769.0
1954	972.7	728.1	92.9	18.3	433.4	1272.8		187.6	425.4	613.0	199.7	123.7	3181.7
1955	925.3	753.1	103.0	19.4	387.1	1262.7	0.2	202.7	410.9	613.8	146.8	112.0	3060.5
1956	895.3	989.9	208.4	32.7	469.0	1700.0	0.2	227.1	359.7	587.0	341.0	89.3	3612.6
1957	940.4	1027.8	206.2	38.9	622.1	1895.0	0.1	199.1	362.8	562.0	447.7	92.7	3937.7
1958	1064.5	1006.2	279.4	48.6	596.1	1930.3	0.3	223.0	409.3	632.7	617.3	104.7	4349.5
1959	1351.9	1079.0	303.6	45.4	631.3	2059.3	0.2	243.3	393.8	637.3	912.1	112.6	5073.2
1960	1675.2	1178.9	337.2	45.1	648.9	2210.1	0.8	211.2	463.0	675.0	961.8	106.3	5628.4
1961	1734.4	1086.1	411.2	53.9	592.0	2143.2	2.2	188.1	627.8	818.1	999.3	132.6	5827.6
1962	2245.1	1143.5	425.9	55.8	584.8	2210.0	1.4	139.2	598.5	739.4	1137.9	123.0	6455.4
1963	2466.0	1048.3	441.1	59.3	687.7	2236.4	1.7	361.0	538.1	900.5	1288.4	167.3	7058.7
1964	2665.0	940.4	425.1	42.3	708.3	2116.2	1.7	675.1	858.7	1535.4	1187.4	232.4	7736.5
1965	2692.3	999.8	499.4	47.3	792.4	2339.0	2.1	619.7	995.7	1617.4	1142.3	267.2	8058.3
1966	2564.9	885.8	507.3	50.8	824.7	2268.5	2.1	655.8	888.5	1546.4	1292.1	240.9	7912.8
1967	2916.9	646.7	521.0	61.8	836.0	2065.4	1.4	318.7	1023.2	1343.3	1664.3	546.7	8536.6
1968	3474.5	745.4	553.0	71.7	798.3	2168.4	2.3	313.1	961.3	1276.8	1842.8	647.5	9409.9
1969	3873.1	886.9	618.5	76.2	904.5	2486.2	0.7	291.1	1033.4	1325.2	1915.6	726.5	10326.7

CTN BROAD DIVISIONS AND CATEGORIES

I. 1. INDUSTRIAL MACHINERY AND EQUIPMENT (INCLUDING SPARE PARTS)

II. FUELS, RAW MATERIALS (OTHER THAN FOOD), OTHER MATERIALS
2. FUELS, MINERAL RAW MATERIALS, METALS
3. CHEMICALS, FERTILIZERS, RUBBER
4. BUILDING MATERIALS AND CONSTRUCTION PARTS
5. RAW MATERIALS OF VEGETABLE AND ANIMAL ORIGIN (NOT FOOD)

III. FOODSTUFFS AND RAW MATERIAL FOR FOODSTUFFS
6. LIVE ANIMALS (NOT FOR SLAUGHTER)
7. RAW MATERIAL FOR THE PRODUCTION OF FOODSTUFFS
8. FOODSTUFFS

IV. 9. INDUSTRIAL CONSUMER GOODS (OTHER THAN FOOD)

TABLE II.CTN.M.B
BULGARIA'S IMPORTS, 1950, 1955-69
(MILLIONS OF CURRENT DOLLARS,* F.O.B.)

YEAR	BROAD DIV I 1	2	3	4	5	BROAD DIV II (2-5)	6	7	8	BROAD DIV III (6-8)	BROAD DIV IV 9	TOTAL IMPORTS
1950	49.3	43.7	14.0	0.8	13.8	72.3	0.1	3.9	0.6	4.6	6.2	132.5
1955	128.5	60.7	16.9	1.0	23.1	101.7	0.5	8.5	2.3	11.4	8.4	249.9
1956	106.1	73.8	21.5	1.5	33.8	130.5	0.3	1.5	2.6	4.4	10.1	251.1
1957	99.6	89.4	31.2	2.5	48.3	171.4	0.3	17.4	4.4	22.2	39.0	332.1
1958	130.9	102.1	30.7	2.8	49.5	185.0	0.4	4.6	3.4	8.5	42.1	366.5
1959	226.1	136.6	52.2	4.0	71.8	264.6	0.5	21.3	8.0	29.8	58.9	579.4
1960	273.4	156.2	43.1	5.7	73.1	278.0	0.7	14.8	17.6	33.1	48.0	632.6
1961	310.8	167.6	43.8	5.0	69.7	286.1	0.3	8.5	17.5	26.4	42.7	666.0
1962	357.4	190.5	47.8	5.3	86.0	329.6	0.5	19.7	23.5	43.8	54.0	784.7
1963	430.3	222.8	60.4	6.7	81.4	371.3	0.4	34.2	32.2	66.8	64.9	933.2
1964	447.3	276.1	69.2	7.4	107.5	460.2	1.4	57.2	39.5	98.0	56.8	1062.4
1965	513.6	313.9	75.8	11.1	119.2	520.1	0.8	36.1	48.0	84.9	59.1	1177.7
1966	696.3	376.1	101.0	11.5	138.3	626.9	0.3	38.3	48.9	87.5	67.5	1478.3
1967	769.8	378.2	124.6	11.9	136.9	651.6	1.4	18.2	58.6	78.2	72.2	1571.9
1968	799.7	430.2	154.7	12.9	162.7	760.5	0.9	37.9	78.4	117.3	104.8	1782.3
1969	712.0	474.7	133.8	12.6	175.3	796.4	0.6	51.4	72.6	124.5	116.4	1749.3

CTN BROAD DIVISIONS AND CATEGORIES

I. 1. INDUSTRIAL MACHINERY AND EQUIPMENT (INCLUDING SPARE PARTS)

II. FUELS, RAW MATERIALS (OTHER THAN FOR FOOD), OTHER MATERIALS
2. FUELS, MINERAL RAW MATERIALS, METALS
3. CHEMICALS, FERTILIZERS, RUBBER
4. BUILDING MATERIALS AND CONSTRUCTION PARTS
5. RAW MATERIALS OF VEGETABLE AND ANIMAL ORIGIN (NOT FOOD)

III. FOODSTUFFS AND RAW MATERIAL FOR FOODSTUFFS
6. LIVE ANIMALS (NOT FOR SLAUGHTER)
7. RAW MATERIAL FOR THE PRODUCTION OF FOODSTUFFS
8. FOODSTUFFS

IV. 9. INDUSTRIAL CONSUMER GOODS (OTHER THAN FOOD)

* CONVERTED FROM NATIONAL DEVISA UNITS THROUGH OFFICIAL EXCHANGE RATES. NOTE THE LIMITATIONS DISCUSSED IN THE EXPLANATORY TEXT.

TABLE II.CTN.M.C
CZECHOSLOVAKIA'S IMPORTS, 1948-69
(MILLIONS OF CURRENT DOLLARS,* F.O.B.)

YEAR	BROAD DIV I 1	2	3	4	5	BROAD DIV II (2-5)	6	7	8	BROAD DIV III (6-8)	BROAD DIV IV 9	TOTAL IMPORTS
1948	49.3	136.8	59.4	3.5	185.0	384.8	1.3	132.8	94.9	228.9	18.5	681.4
1949	52.4					464.2				189.5	12.1	718.1
1950	71.4					390.2				161.0	16.8	639.4
1951	93.6					518.2				267.1	17.8	896.7
1952	105.6					518.0				227.9	24.6	876.0
1953	123.5	239.0	64.2	4.4	169.2	476.8	0.6	162.0	103.1	265.6	13.3	879.2
1954	111.5					492.8				306.3	22.2	932.9
1955	139.6	254.9	89.5	9.3	210.9	564.5	0.3	168.3	136.7	305.3	43.3	1052.7
1956	203.5	303.1	102.6	10.0	237.0	652.7	0.6	177.4	114.3	292.2	37.4	1185.8
1957	260.0	365.4	108.9	12.4	262.4	749.1	0.7	194.2	128.3	323.2	54.6	1386.9
1958	253.5	353.6	111.5	24.7	249.9	739.8	0.4	179.7	137.1	317.2	46.8	1357.3
1959	325.9	405.2	123.6	24.0	292.9	845.8	0.0	215.2	169.7	385.9	45.0	1602.5
1960	393.2	503.5	163.6	15.6	276.1	959.2	1.3	214.6	186.1	402.0	61.3	1815.7
1961	475.9	593.5	178.6	18.8	297.5	1088.4	0.6	189.3	182.9	372.8	86.7	2023.8
1962	542.1	627.4	153.6	16.8	256.3	1054.1	0.4	174.0	209.7	384.2	89.7	2070.2
1963	552.5	616.0	167.2	14.9	279.6	1077.1	0.3	211.5	236.5	448.4	81.8	2160.5
1964	683.1	671.3	183.6	15.7	306.7	1177.3	2.4	254.0	220.3	476.7	92.1	2429.2
1965	799.8	735.8	203.1	33.1	333.1	1305.0	3.3	191.7	233.2	428.2	139.7	2672.7
1966	886.2	656.0	207.7	32.2	345.6	1241.5	2.2	188.9	258.1	449.2	159.3	2736.2
1967	820.3	686.0	213.4	29.7	342.7	1271.8	1.3	192.7	246.0	439.9	148.2	2680.2
1968	963.7	773.8	243.1	43.9	350.6	1411.4	2.9	208.5	273.8	485.2	217.1	3077.3
1959	1050.2	802.6	259.0	61.3	341.6	1464.4	6.9	203.8	296.1	506.8	272.9	3294.4

CTN BROAD DIVISIONS AND CATEGORIES

I. 1. INDUSTRIAL MACHINERY AND EQUIPMENT (INCLUDING SPARE PARTS)

II. FUELS, RAW MATERIALS (OTHER THAN FOR FOOD), OTHER MATERIALS
2. FUELS, MINERAL RAW MATERIALS, METALS
3. CHEMICALS, FERTILIZERS, RUBBER
4. BUILDING MATERIALS AND CONSTRUCTION PARTS
5. RAW MATERIALS OF VEGETABLE AND ANIMAL ORIGIN (NOT FOOD)

III. FOODSTUFFS AND RAW MATERIAL FOR FOODSTUFFS
6. LIVE ANIMALS (NOT FOR SLAUGHTER)
7. RAW MATERIAL FOR THE PRODUCTION OF FOODSTUFFS
8. FOODSTUFFS

IV. 9. INDUSTRIAL CONSUMER GOODS (OTHER THAN FOOD)

TABLE II.CTN.M.G
EAST GERMANY'S IMPORTS, 1950, 1955, 1960-65, 1969
(MILLIONS OF CURRENT DOLLARS,* F.O.B.)

YEAR	BROAD DIV I 1	2	3	4	5	BROAD DIV II (2-5)	6	7	8	BROAD DIV III (6-8)	BROAD DIV IV 9	NOT SPECIFIED	TOTAL IMPORTS
1950	25.8					266.3				155.0	22.5	0.0	469.7
1955	40.1					695.7				374.9	68.4	0.0	1179.1
1960	276.5	937.0				1286.0				515.7	116.3	0.0	2194.5
1961	301.6					1339.1				483.9	126.1	0.0	2250.7
1962	305.7					1389.1				606.7	105.9	0.0	2407.5
1963	314.6					1391.4				533.7	90.9	0.0	2330.6
1964	395.1					1596.0				553.1	89.5	0.0	2633.7
1965	421.5	1241.9				1727.9				576.0	84.3	0.0	2809.7
1969	1346.3	1346.3				N.A.				N.A.	291.4	1120.6	4104.6

CTN BROAD DIVISIONS AND CATEGORIES

I. 1. INDUSTRIAL MACHINERY AND EQUIPMENT (INCLUDING SPARE PARTS)

II. FUELS, RAW MATERIALS (OTHER THAN FOR FOOD), OTHER MATERIALS

2. FUELS, MINERAL RAW MATERIALS, METALS
3. CHEMICALS, FERTILIZERS, RUBBER
4. BUILDING MATERIALS AND CONSTRUCTION PARTS
5. RAW MATERIALS OF VEGETABLE AND ANIMAL ORIGIN (NOT FOOD)

III. FOODSTUFFS AND RAW MATERIAL FOR FOODSTUFFS

6. LIVE ANIMALS (NOT FOR SLAUGHTER)
7. RAW MATERIAL FOR THE PRODUCTION OF FOODSTUFFS
8. FOODSTUFFS

IV. 9. INDUSTRIAL CONSUMER GOODS (OTHER THAN FOOD)

* CONVERTED FROM NATIONAL DEVISA UNITS THROUGH OFFICIAL EXCHANGE RATES. NOTE THE LIMITATIONS DISCUSSED IN THE EXPLANATORY TEXT.

TABLE II.CTN.M.H
HUNGARY'S IMPORTS, 1949-69
(MILLIONS OF CURRENT DOLLARS,* C.I.F.)

YEAR	BROAD DIV I 1	2	3	4	5	BROAD DIV II (2-5)	6	7	8	BROAD DIV III (6-8)	BROAD DIV IV 9	TOTAL IMPORTS
1949	50.1					220.0				10.3	7.7	288.1
1950	65.5					227.7				11.3	11.2	315.7
1951	82.5					275.1				29.0	7.5	394.0
1952	99.2					326.7				25.9	7.7	459.5
1953	91.0					330.1				57.9	8.4	487.4
1954	76.2					362.0				74.4	18.9	531.6
1955	63.0	136.4	41.7	2.1	181.8	374.4	0.2	51.1	39.3	97.8	19.0	554.2
1956	58.6	139.6	40.7	2.7	148.3	340.4	0.1	29.6	29.0	62.3	19.8	481.2
1957	84.0	234.8	60.2	2.9	165.1	463.0	0.2	64.6	26.9	91.7	43.7	682.4
1958	106.2	201.7	61.7	4.8	174.1	442.2	0.2	29.7	23.8	53.7	28.8	630.9
1959	202.1	218.2	76.5	7.1	181.1	482.9	0.2	41.7	29.5	71.4	36.5	792.9
1960	271.2	269.7	90.0	9.2	205.7	574.7	0.2	38.8	41.6	80.6	49.2	975.8
1961	261.9	289.8	91.3	10.7	214.4	606.3	0.3	60.2	47.7	108.1	49.3	1025.5
1962	345.0	304.7	103.9	10.1	220.6	639.2	0.3	59.7	50.7	110.7	53.8	1148.7
1963	394.6	345.4	120.8	16.7	231.4	714.3	0.5	63.3	64.7	128.4	68.3	1305.5
1964	437.3	408.3	154.0	18.4	271.2	851.9	0.4	64.0	63.8	128.2	77.2	1494.6
1965	427.1	417.7	151.9	17.4	279.2	866.2	0.4	68.7	77.5	146.6	80.4	1520.3
1966	445.4	415.8	161.1	19.9	304.6	901.4	0.5	48.0	79.9	128.5	90.2	1565.5
1967	574.0					863.3				204.8	133.2	1775.3
1968	467.7					1003.5				194.1	137.3	1802.6
1969	503.2					1065.2				212.5	146.9	1927.7

CTN BROAD DIVISIONS AND CATEGORIES

I. 1. INDUSTRIAL MACHINERY AND EQUIPMENT (INCLUDING SPARE PARTS)

II. FUELS, RAW MATERIALS (OTHER THAN FOR FOOD), OTHER MATERIALS

2. FUELS, MINERAL RAW MATERIALS, METALS
3. CHEMICALS, FERTILIZERS, RUBBER
4. BUILDING MATERIALS AND CONSTRUCTION PARTS
5. RAW MATERIALS OF VEGETABLE AND ANIMAL ORIGIN (NOT FOOD)

III. FOODSTUFFS AND RAW MATERIAL FOR FOODSTUFFS

6. LIVE ANIMALS (NOT FOR SLAUGHTER)
7. RAW MATERIAL FOR THE PRODUCTION OF FOODSTUFFS
8. FOODSTUFFS

IV. 9. INDUSTRIAL CONSUMER GOODS (OTHER THAN FOOD)

Series II. CTN. M. Poland 49

TABLE II.CTN.M.P
POLAND'S IMPORTS, 1946-69
(MILLIONS OF CURRENT DOLLARS,* F.O.B.)

YEAR	BROAD DIV I 1	2	3	4	5	BROAD DIV II (2-5)	6	7	8	BROAD DIV III (6-8)	BROAD DIV IV 9	TOTAL IMPORTS
1946	20.4					61.2				51.0	13.1	145.8
1947	56.9					191.8				58.2	13.2	320.1
1948	95.4					314.8				80.1	26.0	516.4
1949	154.4					395.5				65.2	17.4	632.5
1950	216.5					354.8				74.7	22.1	668.2
1951	313.0					488.8				82.3	40.0	924.2
1952	315.7					416.9				102.1	28.3	863.0
1953	321.4					380.5				51.8	20.6	774.2
1954	293.6					456.8				122.1	31.0	903.5
1955	288.1					482.0				121.3	40.4	931.8
1956	339.4	200.6	94.2	8.0	194.0	496.8	0.4	98.1	25.5	124.0	61.7	1021.8
1957	297.5	290.3	103.7	8.4	262.3	664.7	0.5	177.2	40.2	217.9	71.4	1251.5
1958	327.6	312.4	91.8	7.4	250.3	661.9	0.4	95.1	39.2	134.7	102.6	1226.8
1959	390.2	342.4	97.7	8.5	240.5	689.1	0.5	145.9	94.1	240.6	99.7	1419.6
1960	405.2	374.8	119.0	7.2	268.8	769.8	0.5	160.5	78.1	239.1	80.9	1495.0
1961	491.2	449.8	111.3	9.1	267.6	837.9	0.6	177.0	79.9	257.5	100.1	1686.7
1962	626.5	486.5	122.8	11.2	262.1	882.7	0.7	169.8	80.5	250.9	125.2	1885.4
1963	674.5	486.6	120.6	12.7	261.2	881.0	0.4	200.4	98.0	298.9	124.7	1979.0
1964	634.4	538.2	140.0	11.8	318.9	1008.9	0.6	216.4	99.8	316.8	112.2	2072.2
1965	766.7	572.6	186.9	15.1	332.4	1107.0	0.6	211.3	97.2	309.1	157.5	2340.3
1966	874.7	606.1	206.6	17.6	347.5	1177.8	0.8	172.7	114.4	287.8	153.7	2494.1
1967	977.7	666.3	213.9	18.4	330.2	1228.8	0.4	183.4	105.4	289.2	149.1	2644.8
1968	1024.3	732.1	224.3	21.7	367.2	1345.3	0.3	183.6	137.5	321.5	162.0	2853.1
1969	1182.7	835.6	252.6	28.0	393.3	1509.6	0.3	194.1	139.3	333.7	183.7	3209.6

CTN BROAD DIVISIONS AND CATEGORIES

I. 1. INDUSTRIAL MACHINERY AND EQUIPMENT (INCLUDING SPARE PARTS)

II. FUELS, RAW MATERIALS (OTHER THAN FOR FOOD), OTHER MATERIALS
2. FUELS, MINERAL RAW MATERIALS, METALS
3. CHEMICALS, FERTILIZERS, RUBBER
4. BUILDING MATERIALS AND CONSTRUCTION PARTS
5. RAW MATERIALS OF VEGETABLE AND ANIMAL ORIGIN (NOT FOOD)

III. FOODSTUFFS AND RAW MATERIAL FOR FOODSTUFFS
6. LIVE ANIMALS (NOT FOR SLAUGHTER)
7. RAW MATERIAL FOR THE PRODUCTION OF FOODSTUFFS
8. FOODSTUFFS

IV. 9. INDUSTRIAL CONSUMER GOODS (OTHER THAN FOOD)

* CONVERTED FROM NATIONAL DEVISA UNITS THROUGH OFFICIAL EXCHANGE RATES. NOTE THE LIMITATIONS DISCUSSED IN THE EXPLANATORY TEXT.

RUMANIA'S IMPORTS, 1950, 1955, 1959-69
TABLE II.CTN.M.R
(MILLIONS OF CURRENT DOLLARS,* F.O.B.)

YEAR	BROAD DIV I 1	2	3	4	5	BROAD DIV II (2-5)	6	7	8	BROAD DIV III (6-8)	BROAD DIV IV 9	TOTAL IMPORTS
1950	90.3	60.2	11.0	2.8	52.2	126.1	0.1	1.3	0.8	2.1	24.9	243.4
1955	172.0	98.4	24.4	2.4	90.0	215.2	0.1	35.9	19.4	55.4	19.3	461.9
1959	162.9	177.4	35.7	5.4	76.2	294.7	0.8	8.4	16.7	25.9	18.6	502.0
1960	210.5	229.5	48.2	6.8	86.7	371.2	1.9	14.3	16.5	32.7	33.5	647.9
1961	329.6	247.0	53.3	9.3	103.0	412.5	1.7	2.9	21.5	26.0	46.6	814.7
1962	408.3	292.9	55.5	9.8	95.3	453.5	0.8	3.4	25.5	29.6	49.7	941.1
1963	427.1	312.1	69.1	9.0	95.6	485.8	0.4	7.2	31.7	39.3	69.9	1022.0
1964	458.2	383.9	69.6	11.5	111.1	576.2	0.4	40.0	25.0	65.3	68.5	1168.1
1965	419.4	349.1	67.9	15.4	119.4	551.8	0.1	7.6	25.9	33.6	72.3	1077.1
1966	497.1	346.2	87.0	17.5	138.5	589.2	0.3	9.3	28.5	38.1	88.8	1213.2
1967	754.7	384.5	100.1	19.9	138.1	642.6	1.1	10.1	31.4	42.6	106.2	1546.1
1968	751.9	438.6	100.9	21.0	139.6	700.0	0.3	12.7	44.2	57.2	99.9	1609.0
1969	770.7	494.1	117.1	34.8	159.1	805.1	1.9	14.8	49.5	66.3	98.5	1740.5

CTN BROAD DIVISIONS AND CATEGORIES

I. 1. INDUSTRIAL MACHINERY AND EQUIPMENT (INCLUDING SPARE PARTS)

II.   FUELS, RAW MATERIALS (OTHER THAN FOR FOOD), OTHER MATERIALS

   2. FUELS, MINERAL RAW MATERIALS, METALS
   3. CHEMICALS, FERTILIZERS, RUBBER
   4. BUILDING MATERIALS AND CONSTRUCTION PARTS
   5. RAW MATERIALS OF VEGETABLE AND ANIMAL ORIGIN (NOT FOOD)

III.   FOODSTUFFS AND RAW MATERIAL FOR FOODSTUFFS

   6. LIVE ANIMALS (NOT FOR SLAUGHTER)
   7. RAW MATERIAL FOR THE PRODUCTION OF FOODSTUFFS
   8. FOODSTUFFS

IV. 9. INDUSTRIAL CONSUMER GOODS (OTHER THAN FOOD)

* CONVERTED FROM NATIONAL DEVISA UNITS THROUGH OFFICIAL EXCHANGE RATES. NOTE THE LIMITATIONS DISCUSSED IN THE EXPLANATORY TEXT.

TABLE II.CTN.M.A
ALBANIA'S IMPORTS, 1950, 1955, 1960-64
(MILLIONS OF CURRENT DOLLARS,* F.O.B.)

YEAR	BROAD DIV I 1	2	3	4	5	BROAD DIV II (2-5)	6	7	8	BROAD DIV III (6-8)	BROAD DIV IV 9	TOTAL IMPORTS
1950	6.80	3.52	1.16	0.22	1.28	6.18	-	0.90	0.74	1.64	7.44	22.06
1955	17.78	5.96	4.20	0.52	3.78	14.46	0.02	3.86	0.48	4.36	6.22	42.83
1960	38.02	10.26	4.90	1.10	4.80	21.06	0.20	13.84	1.90	15.94	6.06	81.08
1961	26.92	9.82	5.44	0.78	5.34	21.38	-	16.34	3.62	19.96	3.98	72.23
1962	17.98	14.40	6.78	0.96	5.16	27.30	-	8.66	5.80	14.46	4.84	64.59
1963	23.24	17.04	6.66	0.90	4.42	29.02	-	10.84	3.12	13.96	4.52	70.74
1964	48.68	14.68	7.00	1.10	4.54	27.32	-	11.32	4.16	15.48	6.64	98.12

CTN BROAD DIVISIONS AND CATEGORIES

I. 1. INDUSTRIAL MACHINERY AND EQUIPMENT (INCLUDING SPARE PARTS)

II. FUELS, RAW MATERIALS (OTHER THAN FOR FOOD), OTHER MATERIALS

    2. FUELS, MINERAL RAW MATERIALS, METALS
    3. CHEMICALS, FERTILIZERS, RUBBER
    4. BUILDING MATERIALS AND CONSTRUCTION PARTS
    5. RAW MATERIALS OF VEGETABLE AND ANIMAL ORIGIN (NOT FOOD)

III. FOODSTUFFS AND RAW MATERIAL FOR FOODSTUFFS

    6. LIVE ANIMALS (NOT FOR SLAUGHTER)
    7. RAW MATERIAL FOR THE PRODUCTION OF FOODSTUFFS
    8. FOODSTUFFS

IV. 9. INDUSTRIAL CONSUMER GOODS (OTHER THAN FOOD)

* CONVERTED FROM NATIONAL DEVISA UNITS THROUGH OFFICIAL EXCHANGE
  RATES. NOTE THE LIMITATIONS DISCUSSED IN THE EXPLANATORY TEXT.

IMPORTS OF THE EUROPEAN CEMA GROUP (EXCLUDING EAST GERMANY AND ALBANIA), 1950, 1955-69
(MILLIONS OF CURRENT DOLLARS,* F.O.B., EXCEPT HUNGARY, C.I.F.)

TABLE II.CTN.M.CEMA

YEAR	BROAD DIV 1	2	3	4	5	BROAD DIV II (2-5)	6	7	8	BROAD DIV III (6-8)	BROAD DIV IV 9	NOT SPECIFIED	TOTAL EXPORTS
1950	806.0	474.9	109.2	23.4	290.3	1870.4**	0.1	137.6	112.8	497.6**	177.1	103.9	3455.0
1955	1716.5	1303.5	275.5	34.2	892.8	3000.4***	1.3	466.6	608.5	1205.0***	277.2	112.0	6311.1
1956	1602.9	1707.0	467.5	54.9	1082.0	3320.4	1.6	533.7	531.0	1069.9	469.9	89.3	6552.5+
1957	1681.5	2007.7	510.3	65.0	1360.2	3943.2	1.9	652.5	562.7	1217.1	656.3	92.7	7590.7+
1958	1882.7	1976.0	575.2	88.3	1319.8	3959.3	1.7	532.2	612.9	1146.8	837.7	104.7	7931.1+
1959	2658.9	2358.7	689.3	94.4	1493.9	4636.4	3.2	675.8	711.8	1390.9	1170.8	112.6	9969.5
1960	3228.8	2713.0	801.1	89.7	1559.3	5163.0	5.4	654.2	802.8	1462.5	1234.7	106.3	11195.2
1961	3603.8	2833.8	889.6	106.8	1544.2	5374.4	5.6	626.0	977.2	1608.8	1324.8	132.6	12044.3
1962	4524.4	3045.6	909.5	108.9	1505.0	5569.0	4.3	565.9	988.5	1558.7	1510.3	123.0	13285.4
1963	4944.9	3031.3	979.1	119.3	1636.8	5766.5	3.4	877.7	1001.2	1882.3	1697.9	167.3	14459.0
1964	5325.3	3218.2	1041.6	107.1	1823.7	6190.6	6.8	1306.6	1307.0	2620.5	1594.2	232.4	15963.0
1965	5618.9	3388.9	1185.1	139.3	1975.7	6689.0	7.4	1134.9	1477.5	2619.8	1651.4	267.2	16846.4
1966	5964.6	3285.9	1270.7	149.6	2099.1	6805.3	6.2	1112.9	1418.4	2537.5	1851.7	240.9	17400.0
1967	6813.5	2761.8	1172.9	141.6	1783.8	6723.4++	5.6	723.0	1464.6	2398.0++	2273.2	546.7	18754.8
1968	7481.9	3120.1	1275.9	171.2	1818.4	7389.1++	6.9	755.8	1495.2	2451.9++	2563.9	647.4	20534.2
1969	8091.8	3493.8	1381.1	213.0	1973.8	8126.8++	10.4	755.1	1591.0	2569.0++	2734.1	726.6	22248.3

CTN BROAD DIVISIONS AND CATEGORIES

I. 1. INDUSTRIAL MACHINERY AND EQUIPMENT (INCLUDING SPARE PARTS)

II. FUELS, RAW MATERIALS (OTHER THAN FOR FOOD), OTHER MATERIALS

2. FUELS, MINERAL RAW MATERIALS, METALS
3. CHEMICALS, FERTILIZERS, RUBBER
4. BUILDING MATERIALS AND CONSTRUCTION PARTS
5. RAW MATERIALS OF VEGETABLE AND ANIMAL ORIGIN (NOT FOOD)

III. FOODSTUFFS AND RAW MATERIAL FOR FOODSTUFFS

6. LIVE ANIMALS (NOT FOR SLAUGHTER)
7. RAW MATERIAL FOR THE PRODUCTION OF FOODSTUFFS
8. FOODSTUFFS

IV. 9. INDUSTRIAL CONSUMER GOODS (OTHER THAN FOOD)

* CONVERTED FROM NATIONAL DEVISA UNITS THROUGH OFFICIAL EXCHANGE RATES. NOTE THE LIMITATIONS DISCUSSED IN THE EXPLANATORY TEXT.

** SUM OF COMPONENTS LESS THAN SUBTOTAL DUE TO MISSING CZECHOSLOVAK, HUNGARIAN AND POLISH SERIES.

+ TOTAL AND COMPONENTS EXCLUDE RUMANIA.

++ SUM OF COMPONENTS LESS THAN SUBTOTAL DUE TO MISSING HUNGARIAN SERIES.

TABLE II.CTN.x.U
USSR EXPORTS, 1946-69
(MILLIONS OF CURRENT DOLLARS,* F.O.B.)

YEAR	BROAD DIV I 1	2	3	4	5	BROAD DIV II (2-5)	6	7	8	BROAD DIV III (6-8)	BROAD DIV IV 9	NOT SPECIFIED	TOTAL EXPORTS
1946	37.8	80.2	31.2	0.4	235.1	347.0		142.4	42.3	184.8	33.1	51.0	653.7
1947	22.2	130.2	61.6	4.1	243.3	439.2		94.0	34.4	128.4	59.7	121.2	770.8
1948	58.9	217.0	74.0	5.4	306.7	603.1		433.8	38.7	472.4	77.9	95.8	1308.1
1949	132.7	299.0	94.0	4.9	307.9	705.8		228.6	98.8	327.3	72.8	208.7	1447.2
1950	212.6	274.6	74.6	3.8	333.4	686.3		235.4	114.6	350.0	67.1	478.7	1794.6
1951	340.3	399.8	83.7	4.0	467.8	955.2		357.2	128.4	485.7	84.2	425.3	2290.8
1952	453.2	505.3	82.2	5.0	455.6	1048.1		471.2	131.8	603.0	67.4	618.1	2789.9
1953	523.6	641.9	79.7	10.0	480.3	1211.9		319.9	206.3	526.2	70.7	615.4	2947.7
1954	532.3	858.7	100.6	17.1	581.1	1557.4		311.0	159.0	470.0	81.6	581.8	3223.1
1955	599.0	900.4	102.6	16.1	598.3	1617.4	0.7	300.4	109.9	411.0	103.4	695.8	3426.6
1956	624.4	1131.0	120.8	14.3	570.1	1836.2	0.6	243.8	148.1	392.4	100.7	661.2	3615.0
1957	652.1	1502.7	137.2	9.6	619.9	2269.3	0.6	580.2	211.8	792.5	141.7	525.8	4381.4
1958	796.4	1564.5	146.1	7.4	622.7	2340.8	3.1	369.2	155.8	528.1	153.0	480.9	4299.2
1959	1177.7	1791.8	160.3	10.7	693.5	2656.3	3.0	520.6	296.7	820.2	154.2	641.9	5450.3
1960	1143.2	2021.0	185.3	14.2	792.0	3012.5	3.3	503.2	218.3	724.9	157.1	525.9	5563.6
1961	964.9	2265.3	220.8	16.0	850.7	3352.7	1.4	508.1	307.0	816.5	172.1	692.1	5998.4
1962	1168.5	2486.1	217.2	18.2	890.2	3611.7	1.3	566.0	359.1	926.4	180.2	1143.5	7030.5
1963	1435.1	2646.2	240.2	22.4	883.7	3792.5	0.0	467.4	466.1	934.5	187.0	923.2	7272.4
1964	1612.8	2999.1	239.6	29.2	990.8	4258.6	0.3	281.7	306.7	588.7	183.2	1040.0	7683.3
1965	1635.8	3101.2	273.9	39.3	1124.0	4538.4	0.3	315.6	360.4	676.3	188.9	1135.2	8174.6
1966	1838.2	3158.1	323.8	47.4	1237.0	4766.3	0.3	283.1	524.1	807.5	199.7	1229.3	8841.0
1967	2036.0	3292.7	374.7	50.3	1233.1	4950.8	0.1	516.7	612.8	1129.5	238.3	1297.5	9652.2
1968	2301.6	3591.6	415.0	62.8	1308.2	5377.6	0.2	460.7	623.3	1084.2	257.8	1613.0	10634.2
1969	2623.2	4020.0	437.7	69.8	1241.0	5768.4		577.8	636.3	1214.1	272.4	1777.2	11655.3

CTN BROAD DIVISIONS AND CATEGORIES

I. 1. INDUSTRIAL MACHINERY AND EQUIPMENT (INCLUDING SPARE PARTS)

II.   FUELS, RAW MATERIALS (OTHER THAN FOR FOOD), OTHER MATERIALS

2. FUELS, MINERAL RAW MATERIALS, METALS
3. CHEMICALS, FERTILIZERS, RUBBER
4. BUILDING MATERIALS AND CONSTRUCTION PARTS
5. RAW MATERIALS OF VEGETABLE AND ANIMAL ORIGIN (NOT FOOD)

III.   FOODSTUFFS AND RAW MATERIAL FOR FOODSTUFFS

6. LIVE ANIMALS (NOT FOR SLAUGHTER)
7. RAW MATERIAL FOR THE PRODUCTION OF FOODSTUFFS
8. FOODSTUFFS

IV. 9. INDUSTRIAL CONSUMER GOODS (OTHER THAN FOOD)

* CONVERTED FROM NATIONAL DEVISA UNITS THROUGH OFFICIAL EXCHANGE
  RATES. NOTE THE LIMITATIONS DISCUSSED IN THE EXPLANATORY TEXT.

TABLE II.CTN.X.B
BULGARIA'S EXPORTS, 1950, 1955-69
(MILLIONS OF CURRENT DOLLARS,* F.O.B.)

YEAR	BROAD DIV I (1)	2	3	4	5	BROAD DIV II (2-5)	6	7	8	BROAD DIV III (6-8)	BROAD DIV IV 9	TOTAL EXPORTS
1950	-	9.8	0.4	2.1	43.8	56.1	0.1	24.0	35.1	59.2	1.8	117.1
1955	6.2	48.9	4.4	3.8	60.3	117.4		23.1	60.0	83.1	29.7	236.2
1956	12.1	63.3	4.4	5.0	64.7	137.4	0.1	22.6	83.2	105.9	46.7	302.1
1957	27.6	64.4	8.0	5.5	70.3	148.2	0.1	19.4	83.4	102.9	91.4	370.1
1958	31.4	56.0	8.8	3.3	71.2	139.3		14.2	110.2	124.4	78.1	373.2
1959	55.9	50.1	11.6	3.3	96.3	161.4		29.3	137.7	167.0	82.8	467.1
1960	77.7	53.4	12.6	3.2	103.8	173.0		41.9	176.5	218.4	102.4	571.5
1961	103.1	67.4	17.1	5.6	97.7	187.7		30.3	229.4	259.7	112.1	662.6
1962	150.3	69.6	18.4	6.8	111.6	206.3	0.1	35.7	245.1	280.9	135.0	772.6
1963	180.3	70.3	19.1	8.3	150.1	247.8		36.9	244.3	281.2	124.7	834.0
1964	238.1	81.2	24.9	12.1	155.5	273.6	0.2	69.6	276.4	346.2	121.8	979.7
1965	291.3	92.9	25.8	19.0	159.6	297.3		72.3	355.0	427.4	159.9	1175.8
1966	332.5	108.3	31.7	13.6	144.2	297.8	0.3	115.8	369.0	484.8	190.0	1305.0
1967	372.1	104.5	39.2	15.6	168.0	327.4	1.0	110.4	432.1	542.9	215.9	1458.2
1968	426.8	123.5	53.2	18.8	166.0	361.5	0.9	82.6	490.3	573.8	252.9	1615.1
1969	492.1	133.2	53.9	19.1	159.7	365.9		84.4	566.8	652.1	284.4	1794.4

CTN BROAD DIVISIONS AND CATEGORIES

I. 1. INDUSTRIAL MACHINERY AND EQUIPMENT (INCLUDING SPARE PARTS)

II. FUELS, RAW MATERIALS (OTHER THAN FOR FOOD), OTHER MATERIALS
2. FUELS, MINERAL RAW MATERIALS, METALS
3. CHEMICALS, FERTILIZERS, RUBBER
4. BUILDING MATERIALS AND CONSTRUCTION PARTS
5. RAW MATERIALS OF VEGETABLE AND ANIMAL ORIGIN (NOT FOOD)

III. FOODSTUFFS AND RAW MATERIAL FOR FOODSTUFFS
6. LIVE ANIMALS (NOT FOR SLAUGHTER)
7. RAW MATERIAL FOR THE PRODUCTION OF FOODSTUFFS
8. FOODSTUFFS

IV. 9. INDUSTRIAL CONSUMER GOODS (OTHER THAN FOOD)

* CONVERTED FROM NATIONAL DEVISA UNITS THROUGH OFFICIAL EXCHANGE RATES. NOTE THE LIMITATIONS DISCUSSED IN THE EXPLANATORY TEXT.

TABLE II.CTN.X.C
CZECHOSLOVAKIA'S EXPORTS, 1948-69
(MILLIONS OF CURRENT DOLLARS,* F.O.B.)

YEAR	BROAD DIV I 1	2	3	4	5	BROAD DIV II (2-5)	6	7	8	BROAD DIV III (6-8)	BROAD DIV IV 9	TOTAL EXPORTS
1948	152.7	172.9	41.8	38.8	74.5	327.9	0.1	13.1	28.3	41.5	231.0	753.1
1949	219.3					297.9				64.0	225.0	806.3
1950	205.8					276.7				99.3	197.1	779.0
1951	237.0					312.7				122.5	173.2	845.3
1952	294.3					353.4				96.7	129.9	874.2
1953	421.0	255.2	27.9	16.7	66.5	366.3	0.1	35.3	49.9	85.3	121.0	993.6
1954	387.3					390.4				82.1	145.6	1005.4
1955	511.2	336.4	33.8	24.7	66.9	461.8	0.4	32.5	39.6	72.5	130.6	1176.1
1956	558.7	369.5	33.3	29.3	80.1	512.3	0.4	57.1	45.6	103.1	213.4	1387.3
1957	554.6	327.1	35.6	26.5	83.6	472.8	0.8	44.3	49.4	94.6	235.9	1357.9
1958	656.3	328.1	36.3	27.4	79.3	471.0	0.8	44.9	61.9	107.6	278.4	1513.3
1959	761.3	331.6	45.1	30.7	95.3	502.7	1.3	45.4	65.6	112.2	351.0	1727.2
1960	870.3	380.7	54.2	28.6	108.1	571.6	1.5	38.6	61.8	102.0	385.7	1929.6
1961	912.2	403.5	58.8	28.3	116.3	606.9	1.8	43.5	82.0	127.2	400.2	2046.4
1962	1044.1	425.2	59.7	29.7	104.5	619.1	2.6	37.2	67.4	107.2	423.2	2193.6
1963	1177.0	456.4	69.0	32.6	112.6	670.7	2.2	48.3	112.8	163.3	450.6	2461.7
1964	1210.7	537.3	89.0	36.1	119.7	782.1	4.3	42.4	92.0	138.6	444.5	2575.9
1965	1303.6	546.8	101.7	40.4	129.2	818.1	4.7	39.0	79.6	123.3	443.6	2688.7
1966	1364.4	519.3	107.2	42.5	137.8	806.9	2.2	40.8	65.3	108.3	465.6	2745.2
1967	1393.4	512.7	122.4	48.6	133.3	817.0	3.5	46.3	78.9	128.6	525.5	2864.4
1968	1482.5	529.6	130.8	54.2	122.8	837.4	3.3	57.5	79.9	140.7	544.9	3005.5
1969	1689.4	616.0	141.7	57.4	128.6	943.7	3.6	64.0	90.7	158.3	528.2	3319.7

CTN BROAD DIVISIONS AND CATEGORIES

I. 1. INDUSTRIAL MACHINERY AND EQUIPMENT (INCLUDING SPARE PARTS)

II. FUELS, RAW MATERIALS (OTHER THAN FOR FOOD), OTHER MATERIALS
2. FUELS, MINERAL RAW MATERIALS, METALS
3. CHEMICALS, FERTILIZERS, RUBBER
4. BUILDING MATERIALS AND CONSTRUCTION PARTS
5. RAW MATERIALS OF VEGETABLE AND ANIMAL ORIGIN (NOT FOOD)

III. FOODSTUFFS AND RAW MATERIAL FOR FOODSTUFFS
6. LIVE ANIMALS (NOT FOR SLAUGHTER)
7. RAW MATERIAL FOR THE PRODUCTION OF FOODSTUFFS
8. FOODSTUFFS

IV. 9. INDUSTRIAL CONSUMER GOODS (OTHER THAN FOOD)

* CONVERTED FROM NATIONAL DEVISA UNITS THROUGH OFFICIAL EXCHANGE RATES. NOTE THE LIMITATIONS DISCUSSED IN THE EXPLANATORY TEXT.

TABLE II.CTN.X.G
EAST GERMANY'S EXPORTS,1950,1955,1960-65,1967,1969
(MILLIONS OF CURRENT DOLLARS,* F.O.B.)

YEAR	BROAD DIV I 1	2	3	4	5	BROAD DIV II (2-5)	6	7	8	BROAD DIV III (6-8)	BROAD DIV IV 9	NOT SPECIFIED	TOTAL EXPORTS
1950	113.7					214.0				27.6	50.7	0.0	406.0
1955	721.1					411.7				23.3	138.5	0.0	1294.6
1960	1059.5	657.8				728.4				88.3	331.1	0.0	2207.4
1961	1092.8					736.9				77.6	374.2	0.0	2281.5
1962	1139.1					756.2				64.3	418.4	0.0	2378.0
1963	1280.6					784.1				86.8	561.6	0.0	2713.1
1964	1389.6					864.8				96.7	580.4	0.0	2931.6
1965	1458.1	773.6				890.3				92.1	629.3	0.0	3069.8
1967	1703.8					929.7				148.6	673.9	0.0	3456.1
1969	2072.4	892.9				N.A.				N.A.	847.3	340.6	4153.2

CTN BROAD DIVISIONS AND CATEGORIES

I. 1. INDUSTRIAL MACHINERY AND EQUIPMENT (INCLUDING SPARE PARTS)

II. FUELS, RAW MATERIALS (OTHER THAN FOR FOOD), OTHER MATERIALS

   2. FUELS, MINERAL RAW MATERIALS, METALS
   3. CHEMICALS, FERTILIZERS, RUBBER
   4. BUILDING MATERIALS AND CONSTRUCTION PARTS
   5. RAW MATERIALS OF VEGETABLE AND ANIMAL ORIGIN (NOT FOOD)

III. FOODSTUFFS AND RAW MATERIAL FOR FOODSTUFFS

   6. LIVE ANIMALS (NOT FOR SLAUGHTER)
   7. RAW MATERIAL FOR THE PRODUCTION OF FOODSTUFFS
   8. FOODSTUFFS

IV. 9. INDUSTRIAL CONSUMER GOODS (OTHER THAN FOOD)

* CONVERTED FROM NATIONAL DEVISA UNITS THROUGH OFFICIAL EXCHANGE RATES. NOTE THE LIMITATIONS DISCUSSED IN THE EXPLANATORY TEXT.

TABLE II.CTN.X.H
HUNGARY'S EXPORTS, 1949-69
(MILLIONS OF CURRENT DOLLARS,* F.O.B.)

YEAR	BROAD DIV I 1	2	3	4	5	BROAD DIV II (2-5)	6	7	8	BROAD DIV III (6-8)	BROAD DIV IV 9	TOTAL EXPORTS
1949	48.7					62.4				121.2	48.2	280.5
1950	73.9					60.7				128.9	65.1	328.5
1951	91.2					76.4				136.4	91.7	395.7
1952	114.3					89.7				145.9	88.2	438.1
1953	176.1					99.4				122.8	100.0	498.2
1954	170.9					105.6				150.2	92.4	519.2
1955	178.4	85.5	11.2	6.9	41.1	143.3	0.5	68.0	118.1	182.6	96.7	601.0
1956	148.8	65.2	8.9	5.1	34.8	113.1	0.8	60.1	92.0	150.2	74.9	486.9
1957	189.7	52.3	10.9	4.1	36.3	103.6	0.8	31.0	95.8	127.7	66.9	487.9
1958	244.8	96.8	19.3	6.0	38.4	160.4	1.4	44.2	110.2	155.9	122.4	683.5
1959	265.8	99.7	28.7	5.1	50.5	184.1	1.1	47.5	126.4	175.0	144.6	769.6
1960	332.4	116.8	23.9	4.7	60.3	205.8	1.1	49.1	129.8	180.1	155.7	373.9
1961	383.0	134.4	31.0	5.9	55.1	230.4	1.5	46.4	155.6	203.5	212.1	1028.9
1962	397.3	164.7	26.1	5.4	49.2	245.4	1.8	44.4	170.8	216.9	239.7	1099.3
1963	410.6	180.2	29.3	7.2	57.0	273.7	1.9	53.4	223.5	278.9	242.5	1205.8
1964	457.8	210.4	43.2	9.4	73.9	336.9	2.5	52.3	230.4	285.2	271.8	1351.8
1965	494.1	218.9	52.2	12.8	76.3	360.2	3.3	77.5	252.7	333.5	321.7	1509.5
1966	498.0	227.7	57.8	12.8	93.7	391.9	4.2	68.5	272.2	344.8	358.6	1593.3
1967	529.1					377.4				393.1	401.4	1701.1
1968	583.6					389.3				380.0	436.2	1789.1
1969	636.1					499.5				478.0	470.2	2083.7

CTN BROAD DIVISIONS AND CATEGORIES

I. 1. INDUSTRIAL MACHINERY AND EQUIPMENT (INCLUDING SPARE PARTS)

II. FUELS, RAW MATERIALS (OTHER THAN FOR FOOD), OTHER MATERIALS

2. FUELS, MINERAL RAW MATERIALS, METALS
3. CHEMICALS, FERTILIZERS, RUBBER
4. BUILDING MATERIALS AND CONSTRUCTION PARTS
5. RAW MATERIALS OF VEGETABLE AND ANIMAL ORIGIN (NOT FOOD)

III. FOODSTUFFS AND RAW MATERIAL FOR FOODSTUFFS

6. LIVE ANIMALS (NOT FOR SLAUGHTER)
7. RAW MATERIAL FOR THE PRODUCTION OF FOODSTUFFS
8. FOODSTUFFS

IV. 9. INDUSTRIAL CONSUMER GOODS (OTHER THAN FOOD)

* CONVERTED FROM NATIONAL DEVISA UNITS THROUGH OFFICIAL EXCHANGE RATES. NOTE THE LIMITATIONS DISCUSSED IN THE EXPLANATORY TEXT.

TABLE II.CTN.X.P
POLAND'S EXPORTS, 1946-69
(MILLIONS OF CURRENT DOLLARS,* F.O.B.)

YEAR	BROAD DIV I 1	2	3	4	5	BROAD DIV II (2-5)	6	7	8	BROAD DIV III (6-8)	BROAD DIV IV 9	TOTAL EXPORTS
1946	0.1	92.6				112.5				2.5	11.6	126.6
1947	2.4	141.9				174.7				31.4	37.7	246.2
1948	3.4	274.6				374.5				85.1	68.3	531.3
1949	14.6	296.0				399.1				127.7	77.4	618.8
1950	49.3	256.5				355.0				152.6	77.3	634.2
1951	51.9	356.4				516.4				126.4	67.4	761.7
1952	79.2	341.3				482.1				144.2	69.9	775.4
1953	102.1	316.1				480.4				169.1	79.4	831.0
1954	96.5	387.1				534.9				156.3	81.2	868.8
1955	120.1	428.2				592.2				140.9	66.5	919.7
1956	154.0	544.4	29.3	9.3	44.8	627.8	0.5	22.3	92.3	115.1	87.8	984.7
1957	195.0	522.7	26.1	5.2	40.7	594.7	0.2	16.0	106.8	123.1	62.2	975.0
1958	284.3	445.5	38.6	9.6	44.8	538.5	0.4	33.8	144.3	178.6	58.0	1059.4
1959	301.5	445.9	48.0	9.1	57.8	560.8	0.7	35.9	172.0	208.6	74.2	1145.1
1960	371.5	453.8	50.6	9.6	67.1	581.0	0.9	44.0	194.4	239.4	133.6	1325.5
1961	421.6	447.4	51.4	14.3	73.9	587.0	1.5	62.0	258.8	322.2	172.7	1503.6
1962	494.0	482.8	57.0	19.5	83.2	642.5	3.0	55.1	258.1	316.2	193.4	1646.1
1963	585.8	491.7	64.1	24.1	92.2	672.2	3.7	37.6	242.8	284.0	227.9	1770.0
1964	700.9	540.3	76.9	24.5	103.1	744.8	7.1	50.9	333.6	391.6	259.1	2096.4
1965	767.3	559.3	84.7	26.0	112.3	782.3	11.4	66.2	326.6	404.1	274.1	2227.9
1966	802.2	540.4	89.2	24.0	125.0	778.6	9.7	71.7	295.2	376.6	314.7	2272.1
1967	911.3	597.7	98.4	25.5	112.3	833.9	15.3	61.2	315.9	392.4	389.0	2526.6
1968	1056.5	680.5	113.9	23.3	127.5	945.2	16.8	64.7	320.3	401.7	454.3	2857.8
1969	1229.7	739.2	133.2	26.1	138.3	1036.8	26.9	51.7	302.2	380.9	494.1	3141.5

CTN BROAD DIVISIONS AND CATEGORIES

I. 1. INDUSTRIAL MACHINERY AND EQUIPMENT (INCLUDING SPARE PARTS)

II. FUELS, RAW MATERIALS (OTHER THAN FOR FOOD), OTHER MATERIALS

2. FUELS, MINERAL RAW MATERIALS, METALS
3. CHEMICALS, FERTILIZERS, RUBBER
4. BUILDING MATERIALS AND CONSTRUCTION PARTS
5. RAW MATERIALS OF VEGETABLE AND ANIMAL ORIGIN (NOT FOOD)

III. FOODSTUFFS AND RAW MATERIAL FOR FOODSTUFFS

6. LIVE ANIMALS (NOT FOR SLAUGHTER)
7. RAW MATERIAL FOR THE PRODUCTION OF FOODSTUFFS
8. FOODSTUFFS

IV. 9. INDUSTRIAL CONSUMER GOODS (OTHER THAN FOOD)

TABLE II.CTN.X.R
RUMANIA'S EXPORTS, 1950, 1955, 1959-69
(MILLIONS OF CURRENT DOLLARS,* F.O.B.)

YEAR	BROAD DIV I 1	2	3	4	5	BROAD DIV II (2-5)	6	7	8	BROAD DIV III (6-8)	BROAD DIV IV 9	TOTAL EXPORTS
1950	8.9	71.7	3.5	9.4	63.1	147.6		23.0	30.1	53.1	2.9	212.4
1955	25.8	187.2	5.5	16.4	85.0	294.1	0.2	52.6	43.7	96.5	5.4	421.7
1959	78.2	238.8	12.0	16.7	85.9	353.4	0.0	22.9	39.6	62.6	28.3	522.4
1960	119.4	265.4	15.7	18.0	108.1	407.2	0.1	64.3	84.7	149.1	41.5	717.0
1961	127.1	274.4	22.1	19.2	120.6	436.4	0.2	87.0	91.9	179.1	49.9	792.5
1962	147.4	269.3	25.6	20.3	121.9	437.1	0.3	71.5	107.8	179.6	53.9	818.0
1963	150.7	283.5	37.0	23.4	136.1	479.9	0.3	106.2	105.2	212.2	72.2	915.0
1964	182.4	278.5	56.9	27.5	147.6	510.4	0.3	93.8	127.4	221.5	85.7	1000.1
1965	203.9	277.9	70.9	37.4	155.8	542.0	0.2	80.9	153.2	234.2	121.4	1101.5
1966	205.8	288.7	68.5	37.7	169.4	564.2	0.3	113.9	166.7	280.9	135.2	1186.2
1967	264.8	285.9	83.8	37.8	179.3	586.8	0.3	177.8	210.7	388.8	155.0	1395.4
1968	313.3	311.6	90.4	38.5	174.1	614.5	0.5	121.1	207.2	328.8	211.9	1468.6
1969	353.7	336.7	115.5	43.4	168.8	664.3	0.5	125.6	232.5	358.6	256.6	1633.1

CTN BROAD DIVISIONS AND CATEGORIES

I.   1. INDUSTRIAL MACHINERY AND EQUIPMENT (INCLUDING SPARE PARTS)

II.   FUELS, RAW MATERIALS (OTHER THAN FOR FOOD), OTHER MATERIALS

     2. FUELS, MINERAL RAW MATERIALS, METALS
     3. CHEMICALS, FERTILIZERS, RUBBER
     4. BUILDING MATERIALS AND CONSTRUCTION PARTS
     5. RAW MATERIALS OF VEGETABLE AND ANIMAL ORIGIN (NOT FOOD)

III.   FOODSTUFFS AND RAW MATERIAL FOR FOODSTUFFS

     6. LIVE ANIMALS (NOT FOR SLAUGHTER)
     7. RAW MATERIAL FOR THE PRODUCTION OF FOODSTUFFS
     8. FOODSTUFFS

IV. 9. INDUSTRIAL CONSUMER GOODS (OTHER THAN FOOD)

* CONVERTED FROM NATIONAL DEVISA UNITS THROUGH OFFICIAL EXCHANGE
  RATES. NOTE THE LIMITATIONS DISCUSSED IN THE EXPLANATORY TEXT.

TABLE II.CTN.X.A
ALBANIA'S EXPORTS, 1950,1955, 1960-64
(MILLIONS OF CURRENT DOLLARS,* F.O.B.)

YEAR	BROAD DIV I 1	2	3	4	5	BROAD DIV II (2-5)	6	7	8	BROAD DIV III (6-8)	BROAD DIV IV 9	TOTAL EXPORTS
1950	-	4.02	-	-	2.10	6.12		-	0.34	0.34	0.02	6.48
1955	0.06	9.18	-	-	3.42	12.60		0.06	0.28	0.34	0.02	13.00
1960	-	27.14	0.14	0.78	9.36	37.42		0.02	9.54	9.56	1.58	48.56
1961	0.26	27.28	0.10	0.84	5.38	33.60		0.02	12.06	12.08	2.64	48.58
1962	-	25.78	0.22	0.14	2.74	28.88		0.02	10.14	10.16	1.88	40.90
1963	-	23.26	0.12	0.12	7.94	31.44		0.02	12.36	12.38	4.26	48.08
1964	-	32.50	0.06	-	10.36	42.98		0.02	13.82	13.84	3.10	59.92

CTN BROAD DIVISIONS AND CATEGORIES

I. 1. INDUSTRIAL MACHINERY AND EQUIPMENT (INCLUDING SPARE PARTS)

II. FUELS, RAW MATERIALS (OTHER THAN FOR FOOD), OTHER MATERIALS

2. FUELS, MINERAL RAW MATERIALS, METALS
3. CHEMICALS, FERTILIZERS, RUBBER
4. BUILDING MATERIALS AND CONSTRUCTION PARTS
5. RAW MATERIALS OF VEGETABLE AND ANIMAL ORIGIN (NOT FOOD)

III. FOODSTUFFS AND RAW MATERIAL FOR FOODSTUFFS

6. LIVE ANIMALS (NOT FOR SLAUGHTER)
7. RAW MATERIAL FOR THE PRODUCTION OF FOODSTUFFS
8. FOODSTUFFS

IV. 9. INDUSTRIAL CONSUMER GOODS (OTHER THAN FOOD)

* CONVERTED FROM NATIONAL DEVISA UNITS THROUGH OFFICIAL EXCHANGE RATES. NOTE THE LIMITATIONS DISCUSSED IN THE EXPLANATORY TEXT.

TABLE II.CTN.X.CEMA
EXPORTS OF THE EUROPEAN CEMA GROUP (EXCLUDING EAST GERMANY AND ALBANIA), 1950, 1955-69
(MILLIONS OF CURRENT DOLLARS,* F.O.B.)

YEAR	BROAD DIV I 1	2	3	4	5	BROAD DIV II (2-5)	6	7	8	BROAD DIV III (6-8)	BROAD DIV IV 9	NOT SPECIFIED	TOTAL EXPORTS
1950	550.4	612.6	78.5	15.2	440.3	1582.4**	0.1	282.4	179.8	843.1**	411.2	478.7	3865.9
1955	1440.6	1986.7	157.4	67.9	851.6	3226.1***	1.8	476.5	371.4	986.6***	432.2	695.8	6781.3
1956	1497.9	2173.4	196.7	63.1	794.6	3226.8	2.4	405.9	461.1	866.6	523.4	661.2	6776.0+
1957	1619.1	2469.3	217.8	50.9	850.8	3588.7	2.5	691.0	547.3	1240.8	598.0	525.8	7572.3+
1958	2013.2	2490.9	249.0	53.7	856.4	3649.9	5.8	506.4	582.4	1094.6	690.0	480.9	7928.6+
1959	2640.5	2957.9	305.7	75.6	1079.4	4418.6	6.1	701.6	837.9	1545.6	835.1	641.9	10081.7
1960	2914.5	3291.1	342.3	78.3	1239.3	4951.1	7.0	741.1	865.6	1613.7	976.0	525.9	10981.2
1961	2911.8	3596.4	401.2	89.2	1314.3	5401.1	6.3	777.3	1124.7	1908.3	1119.1	692.1	12032.3
1962	3401.6	3897.6	404.0	99.9	1360.6	5762.1	9.1	809.9	1208.3	2027.3	1225.5	1143.5	13560.1
1963	3939.6	4128.3	458.8	118.1	1431.7	6136.9	9.1	750.5	1394.6	2154.3	1305.0	923.2	14458.9
1964	4402.6	4646.8	530.5	138.7	1590.5	6906.5	14.8	590.6	1366.4	1971.8	1366.2	1040.0	15687.1
1965	4695.9	4797.1	609.2	174.9	1757.2	7338.3	19.9	651.4	1527.5	2198.9	1509.7	1135.2	16878.0
1966	5041.0	4842.4	678.3	178.0	1906.9	7605.6	16.7	693.8	1692.5	2403.0	1663.8	1229.3	17942.8
1967	5506.6	4793.6	718.5	177.8	1826.1	7893.3++	19.6	912.3	1650.4	2975.4++	1925.1	1297.5	19597.9
1968	6164.4	5236.9	803.4	197.5	1898.5	8525.6++	21.9	786.5	1720.9	2909.3++	2158.0	1613.0	21370.4
1969	7024.2	5845.1	882.0	215.7	1836.3	9278.6++	32.0	903.3	1828.5	3241.9++	2305.9	1777.2	23627.8

CTN BROAD DIVISIONS AND CATEGORIES

I. 1. INDUSTRIAL MACHINERY AND EQUIPMENT (INCLUDING SPARE PARTS)

II. FUELS, RAW MATERIALS (OTHER THAN FOR FOOD), OTHER MATERIALS

2. FUELS, MINERAL RAW MATERIALS, METALS
3. CHEMICALS, FERTILIZERS, RUBBER
4. BUILDING MATERIALS AND CONSTRUCTION PARTS
5. RAW MATERIALS OF VEGETABLE AND ANIMAL ORIGIN (NOT FOOD)

III. FOODSTUFFS AND RAW MATERIAL FOR FOODSTUFFS

6. LIVE ANIMALS (NOT FOR SLAUGHTER)
7. RAW MATERIAL FOR THE PRODUCTION OF FOODSTUFFS
8. FOODSTUFFS

IV. 9. INDUSTRIAL CONSUMER GOODS (OTHER THAN FOOD)

* CONVERTED FROM NATIONAL DEVISA UNITS THROUGH OFFICIAL EXCHANGE RATES. NOTE THE LIMITATIONS DISCUSSED IN THE EXPLANATORY TEXT.

+ TOTAL AND COMPONENTS EXCLUDE RUMANIA.

** SUM OF COMPONENTS LESS THAN SUBTOTAL DUE TO MISSING CZECHOSLOVAK, HUNGARIAN AND POLISH SERIES.

++ SUM OF COMPONENTS LESS THAN SUBTOTAL DUE TO MISSING HUNGARIAN SERIES.

*** SUM OF COMPONENTS LESS THAN SUBTOTAL DUE TO MISSING POLISH SERIES.

TABLE II.SITC.M.U
USSR IMPORTS, 1946-69
(MILLIONS OF CURRENT DOLLARS,* F.O.B.)

YEAR	PRIMARY					TOTAL PRIMARY	MANUFACTURED				TOTAL MANUFACT.	NOT SPECIFIED	TOTAL IMPORTS
	0	1	2	3	4		5	6	7	8			
1946	74.3	46.6	85.1	90.6	22.9	319.4	9.2	112.1	230.9	14.3	366.6	82.9	768.9
1947	117.0	50.6	129.8	91.0	26.6	414.9	5.9	94.2	136.0	15.1	251.2	78.7	744.8
1948	175.8	76.9	331.6	110.6	41.1	735.9	21.2	207.2	120.1	37.8	386.3	101.8	1224.0
1949	143.1	43.0	340.1	162.8	39.2	728.2	36.9	269.8	244.6	55.4	606.7	154.3	1489.2
1950	161.8	32.3	356.1	168.0	30.4	748.7	34.3	206.7	330.1	32.2	603.3	103.9	1455.9
1951	218.7	43.6	573.5	180.7	34.6	1051.0	45.0	267.0	460.3	49.4	821.8	118.0	1990.8
1952	277.2	74.3	675.2	248.1	44.4	1319.3	49.3	392.9	576.3	67.0	1085.5	101.2	2506.1
1953	275.6	67.7	612.2	265.3	94.3	1315.1	42.2	422.1	829.3	56.9	1350.5	101.3	2769.0
1954	398.9	85.4	620.0	256.1	127.4	1487.9	58.7	397.4	1033.9	80.2	1570.2	123.7	3181.7
1955	428.2	61.1	651.1	250.0	83.0	1473.4	55.0	384.6	957.9	77.7	1475.1	112.0	3060.5
1956	420.4	81.2	915.2	256.4	57.9	1731.2	82.4	548.3	947.0	214.3	1792.1	89.3	3612.6
1957	424.8	104.3	1083.7	208.1	47.9	1868.8	84.4	577.2	983.5	331.1	1976.3	92.7	3937.7
1958	485.8	103.2	1056.1	212.3	59.0	1916.4	117.9	614.0	1105.7	490.9	2328.4	104.7	4349.5
1959	472.0	115.0	1044.1	231.3	56.1	1918.5	117.7	810.7	1397.0	706.8	3042.1	112.6	5073.2
1960	546.1	102.4	1027.2	237.3	37.3	1950.4	157.4	936.4	1719.0	758.8	3571.6	106.3	5628.4
1961	708.4	102.0	975.3	217.0	53.0	2055.8	165.4	888.9	1774.3	810.7	3639.3	132.6	5827.6
1962	652.2	106.9	927.4	198.9	29.6	1915.0	229.7	974.9	2279.6	933.2	4417.4	123.0	6455.4
1963	790.4	146.6	931.1	202.0	32.4	2102.5	319.6	901.5	2487.1	1080.7	4788.8	167.3	7058.7
1964	1366.2	228.4	827.7	183.2	49.6	2655.1	385.7	748.3	2679.5	1035.4	4849.0	232.4	7736.5
1965	1369.5	268.1	963.1	198.6	64.9	2864.2	418.8	807.7	2692.3	1008.1	4926.8	267.2	8058.3
1966	1307.9	270.8	968.0	184.4	38.1	2769.2	439.6	757.3	2562.1	1143.8	4902.7	240.9	7912.8
1967	1092.4	300.4	610.3	185.9	21.3	2210.4	544.7	899.3	2905.3	1430.2	5779.5	546.7	8536.6
1968	986.0	341.9	586.5	166.9	27.9	2109.2	626.0	1006.3	3459.1	1566.7	6658.0	642.7	9409.9
1969	964.3	407.4	700.5	174.7	18.3	2265.3	688.7	1189.2	3846.3	1610.7	7334.8	726.5	10326.7

* CONVERTED FROM NATIONAL DEVISA UNITS THROUGH OFFICIAL EXCHANGE RATES. NOTE LIMITATIONS DISCUSSED IN THE EXPLANATORY TEXT.

SITC CATEGORIES

0   FOOD AND LIVE ANIMALS
1   BEVERAGES AND TOBACCO
2   CRUDE MATERIALS, INEDIBLE, EXCEPT FUELS
3   MINERAL FUELS, LUBRICANTS AND RELATED MATERIALS
4   ANIMAL AND VEGETABLE OILS AND FATS
5   CHEMICALS
6   MANUFACTURED GOODS CLASSIFIED CHIEFLY BY MATERIAL
7   MACHINERY AND TRANSPORT EQUIPMENT
8   MISCELLANEOUS MANUFACTURED ARTICLES

TABLE II.SITC.M.H
HUNGARY'S IMPORTS, 1960-69
(MILLIONS OF CURRENT DOLLARS,* C.I.F.)

YEAR	PRIMARY					TOTAL PRIMARY	MANUFACTURED				TOTAL MANUFACT.	9	TOTAL IMPORTS
	0	1	2	3	4		5	6	7	8			
1960	62.9	4.4	220.0	122.1	5.4	414.8	64.9	192.6	259.2	44.3	561.0		975.8
1961	91.9	6.5	238.1	134.3	5.5	476.4	74.1	215.1	218.3	41.6	549.2		1025.5
1962	105.2	5.3	255.0	139.9	6.0	511.4	85.2	232.0	275.1	44.9	637.3		1148.7
1963	119.6	6.0	250.0	167.1	6.9	549.6	103.0	251.3	340.5	61.1	755.9		1305.5
1964	139.7	8.0	269.9	175.2	7.7	600.5	134.9	268.8	421.5	68.8	894.0	+0.0	1494.6
1965	158.6	6.6	278.4	174.7	10.3	628.6	136.7	273.9	412.1	68.1	890.8	.9	1520.3
1966	134.0	16.1	302.8	172.8	13.8	639.5	144.8	278.2	430.3	71.6	924.9	1.1	1565.5
1967	146.3	32.5	310.3	160.6	9.3	659.1	162.3	307.4	561.5	84.1	1115.3	.8	1775.3
1968	147.0	25.6	306.9	167.9	11.4	658.8	186.5	357.2	516.0	82.7	1142.4	1.5	1802.6
1969	155.2	26.9	312.5	185.3	11.9	691.8	197.6	391.7	554.0	90.3	1233.5	2.4	1927.7

* CONVERTED FROM NATIONAL DEVISA UNITS THROUGH
OFFICIAL EXCHANGE RATES. NOTE LIMITATIONS
DISCUSSED IN THE EXPLANATORY TEXT.

SITC CATEGORIES

0 FOOD AND LIVE ANIMALS
1 BEVERAGES AND TOBACCO
2 CRUDE MATERIALS, INEDIBLE, EXCEPT FUELS
3 MINERAL FUELS, LUBRICANTS AND RELATED MATERIALS
4 ANIMAL AND VEGETABLE OILS AND FATS
5 CHEMICALS
6 MANUFACTURED GOODS CLASSIFIED CHIEFLY BY MATERIAL
7 MACHINERY AND TRANSPORT EQUIPMENT
8 MISCELLANEOUS MANUFACTURED ARTICLES
9 COMMODITIES AND TRANSACTIONS NOT CLASSIFIED
  ACCORDING TO KIND PLUS NOT SPECIFIED

TABLE II.SITC.M.Y
YUGOSLAVIA'S IMPORTS, 1952-69
(MILLIONS OF CURRENT DOLLARS,* C.I.F.)

YEAR	PRIMARY					TOTAL PRIMARY	MANUFACTURED				TOTAL MANUFACT.	9	TOTAL IMPORTS
	0	1	2	3	4		5	6	7	8			
1952	81.4	.0	51.8	29.1	4.6	166.9	17.3	66.0	117.1	5.7	206.1	.0	373.0
1953	111.3	.1	50.2	30.7	5.0	197.3	17.3	50.1	125.6	5.0	198.0	.0	395.3
1954	82.4	.1	50.9	30.0	6.3	169.7	20.7	51.5	91.0	6.0	169.2	.5	339.4
1955	121.1	1.3	77.4	36.5	5.2	241.5	29.4	50.8	111.6	6.9	198.7	.7	440.9
1956	150.9	.0	75.2	46.9	5.6	278.7	33.0	57.7	94.4	10.0	195.1	.3	474.1
1957	146.8	1.0	97.1	65.3	12.9	323.2	48.3	103.8	167.9	14.6	334.6	3.4	661.3
1958	130.5	1.1	84.1	41.2	14.4	271.3	66.8	108.2	215.7	20.3	410.9	2.7	684.9
1959	132.6	.1	95.9	45.3	15.7	289.7	75.3	107.7	192.0	20.6	395.6	1.8	687.1
1960	75.5	.1	118.4	45.0	11.5	250.5	71.4	171.7	304.4	27.1	574.7	1.1	826.3
1961	119.7	1.1	129.7	40.3	15.2	306.0	63.6	184.7	324.2	31.3	603.8	.4	910.2
1962	126.7	3.9	132.2	47.9	14.3	325.0	77.9	162.9	293.5	28.0	562.3	.4	887.6
1963	193.9	7.1	159.0	47.0	10.8	417.8	111.1	186.6	306.8	34.0	638.6	.1	1056.5
1964	163.8	2.5	211.9	66.0	16.0	460.2	138.0	275.3	399.8	49.6	862.7	.3	1323.2
1965	189.0	.6	216.5	72.0	13.4	491.4	118.4	279.1	355.4	43.3	796.2	.3	1288.0
1966	231.0	5.9	212.2	82.4	8.8	540.4	150.5	370.0	459.1	55.0	1034.5	.5	1575.4
1967	174.6	7.5	198.8	84.6	30.8	496.2	167.3	430.7	571.8	69.9	1239.7	.4	1707.3 **
1968	124.1	3.7	198.3	98.0	19.2	443.3	188.3	427.2	645.1	92.8	1353.3	.2	1796.8
1969	141.4	6.0	264.3	103.5	7.2	522.4	220.7	544.2	723.6	122.6	1611.2	.2	2133.8

* CONVERTED FROM NATIONAL DEVISA UNITS THROUGH
OFFICIAL EXCHANGE RATES. NOTE LIMITATIONS
THROUGH OFFICIAL EXCHANGE RATES. NOTE LIMITATIONS
DISCUSSED IN THE EXPLANATORY TEXT.

** SUM OF COMPONENTS GREATER THAN GIVEN
TOTAL. ERROR IN ORIGINAL.

SITC CATEGORIES

0 FOOD AND LIVE ANIMALS
1 BEVERAGES AND TOBACCO
2 CRUDE MATERIALS, INEDIBLE, EXCEPT FUELS
3 MINERAL FUELS, LUBRICANTS AND RELATED MATERIALS
4 ANIMAL AND VEGETABLE OILS AND FATS
5 CHEMICALS
6 MANUFACTURED GOODS CLASSIFIED CHIEFLY BY MATERIAL
7 MACHINERY AND TRANSPORT EQUIPMENT
8 MISCELLANEOUS MANUFACTURED ARTICLES
9 COMMODITIES AND TRANSACTIONS NOT CLASSIFIED
   ACCORDING TO KIND PLUS NOT SPECIFIED

TABLE II. SITC. X. U
USSR EXPORTS, 1946-69
(MILLIONS OF CURRENT DOLLARS,* F.O.B.)

YEAR	PRIMARY					TOTAL PRIMARY	MANUFACTURED				TOTAL MANUFACT.	NOT SPECIFIED	TOTAL EXPORTS
	0	1	2	3	4		5	6	7	8			
1946	179.6	28.1	236.6	33.6	0.0	477.8	12.2	54.2	39.9	18.6	124.9	51.0	653.7
1947	117.7	19.4	284.3	54.4	.4	476.3	20.2	97.6	23.7	31.8	173.2	121.2	770.8
1948	454.9	10.6	381.0	62.6	8.7	917.7	21.6	171.9	62.7	38.6	294.7	95.8	1308.1
1949	268.0	19.4	381.8	75.4	41.8	786.4	25.8	261.9	136.6	27.9	452.1	208.7	1447.2
1950	290.1	15.3	398.4	67.7	52.2	823.8	22.9	217.3	216.1	35.9	492.2	478.7	1794.6
1951	428.6	19.0	495.0	116.1	57.4	1116.1	34.9	338.8	340.3	35.3	749.3	425.3	2290.8
1952	546.9	17.2	505.2	137.0	58.7	1265.0	39.3	385.7	446.1	35.7	906.8	618.1	2789.9
1953	414.3	26.3	546.8	197.3	98.9	1283.7	43.8	453.7	517.9	33.3	1048.7	615.4	2947.7
1954	394.7	30.3	659.2	271.8	64.2	1420.2	50.1	608.0	524.7	38.3	1221.1	581.8	3223.1
1955	372.0	32.1	721.1	329.1	18.0	1472.3	56.4	559.3	592.8	50.0	1258.5	695.8	3426.6
1956	322.0	24.8	734.8	428.2	57.6	1567.3	59.1	644.5	628.3	54.4	1386.4	661.2	3615.0
1957	709.1	21.4	838.3	648.3	80.1	2297.3	66.4	769.3	669.9	52.7	1558.3	525.8	4381.4
1958	485.4	25.7	841.9	651.2	44.2	2048.4	72.6	813.9	823.0	60.4	1769.9	480.9	4299.2
1959	731.3	28.2	924.9	798.0	107.0	2589.4	80.2	872.2	1200.5	66.0	2219.0	641.9	5450.3
1960	665.0	20.3	1070.8	902.4	77.9	2736.4	92.1	975.2	1167.1	66.9	2301.3	525.9	5563.6
1961	723.5	22.8	1176.8	1046.1	97.3	3066.5	102.4	1071.1	1001.7	64.6	2239.8	692.1	5998.4
1962	810.7	18.7	1219.7	1155.8	122.0	3326.7	101.0	1175.9	1225.7	57.7	2560.2	1143.5	7030.5
1963	782.7	22.3	1245.2	1299.0	144.9	3494.1	116.4	1187.1	1485.1	66.4	2855.1	923.2	7272.4
1964	470.7	21.4	1385.4	1380.2	92.8	3350.5	123.7	1444.9	1649.0	75.2	3292.7	1040.0	7683.3
1965	536.2	14.2	1508.7	1403.9	130.2	3593.2	136.6	1558.2	1675.9	75.6	3446.2	1135.2	8174.6
1966	601.9	20.1	1617.8	1448.8	197.3	3885.9	151.6	1605.7	1882.2	86.4	3725.9	1229.3	8841.0
1967	839.7	24.1	1650.4	1550.1	260.3	4324.6	188.6	1648.4	2097.4	95.7	4030.1	1297.5	9652.2
1968	786.5	29.9	1779.5	1702.8	249.4	4548.2	208.4	1789.5	2371.6	103.4	4473.1	1613.0	10634.2
1969	900.1	30.8	1738.2	1821.1	248.7	4738.8	218.9	2121.8	2691.1	107.6	5139.3	1777.2	11655.3

* CONVERTED FROM NATIONAL DEVISA UNITS THROUGH
OFFICIAL EXCHANGE RATES. NOTE LIMITATIONS
DISCUSSED IN THE EXPLANATORY TEXT.

SITC CATEGORIES

0 FOOD AND LIVE ANIMALS
1 BEVERAGES AND TOBACCO
2 CRUDE MATERIALS, INEDIBLE, EXCEPT FUELS
3 MINERAL FUELS, LUBRICANTS AND RELATED MATERIALS
4 ANIMAL AND VEGETABLE OILS AND FATS
5 CHEMICALS
6 MANUFACTURED GOODS CLASSIFIED CHIEFLY BY MATERIAL
7 MACHINERY AND TRANSPORT EQUIPMENT
8 MISCELLANEOUS MANUFACTURED ARTICLES

TABLE II.SITC.X.H
HUNGARY'S EXPORTS, 1960-69
(MILLIONS OF CURRENT DOLLARS,* F.O.B.)

YEAR	PRIMARY					TOTAL PRIMARY	MANUFACTURED					TOTAL MANUFACT.	TOTAL EXPORTS
	0	1	2	3	4		5	6	7	8	9		
1960	161.6	16.3	29.7	22.7	8.7	239.0	47.1	145.8	353.2	88.8		634.9	873.9
1961	174.9	18.7	36.1	21.5	8.9	260.1	56.8	173.7	414.2	124.1		768.8	1028.9
1962	183.2	18.2	37.7	24.2	10.0	273.4	69.5	203.4	410.8	142.3		825.9	1099.3
1963	247.7	21.7	39.8	26.0	10.4	345.6	80.3	213.1	415.4	151.4		860.2	1205.8
1964	251.1	31.0	67.1	23.5	12.6	385.3	93.9	256.0	451.9	164.6	+0.0	966.5	1351.8
1965	295.1	38.3	70.1	23.9	10.7	438.1	112.4	272.1	489.7	197.1	.1	1071.2	1509.5
1966	301.3	40.1	83.8	29.5	12.8	467.5	126.3	286.1	495.5	217.7	.2	1125.6	1593.3
1967	330.6	46.8	91.4	28.9	8.8	506.5	138.0	286.6	522.1	247.9	.2	1194.5	1701.1
1968	311.9	51.6	97.7	31.6	9.2	502.0	141.5	273.6	600.5	271.0	.5	1286.6	1789.1
1969	396.1	57.1	122.4	41.3	13.2	630.1	158.7	353.1	654.4	287.2	.2	1453.4	2083.7

* CONVERTED FROM NATIONAL DEVISA UNITS THROUGH
OFFICIAL EXCHANGE RATES. NOTE LIMITATIONS
DISCUSSED IN THE EXPLANATORY TEXT.

SITC CATEGORIES

0 FOOD AND LIVE ANIMALS
1 BEVERAGES AND TOBACCO
2 CRUDE MATERIALS, INEDIBLE, EXCEPT FUELS
3 MINERAL FUELS, LUBRICANTS AND RELATED MATERIALS
4 ANIMAL AND VEGETABLE OILS AND FATS
5 CHEMICALS
6 MANUFACTURED GOODS CLASSIFIED CHIEFLY BY MATERIAL
7 MACHINERY AND TRANSPORT EQUIPMENT
8 MISCELLANEOUS MANUFACTURED ARTICLES
9 COMMODITIES AND TRANSACTIONS NOT CLASSIFIED
ACCORDING TO KIND PLUS NOT SPECIFIED

TABLE II.SITC.X.Y
YUGOSLAVIA'S EXPORTS, 1952-69
(MILLIONS OF CURRENT DOLLARS,* F.O.B.)

YEAR	PRIMARY					TOTAL PRIMARY	MANUFACTURED				TOTAL MANUFACT.	9	TOTAL EXPORTS
	0	1	2	3	4		5	6	7	8			
1952	94.1	9.8	64.6	3.9	.0	172.4	9.8	60.2	.1	1.5	71.7	2.5	246.5
1953	34.2	7.0	70.1	2.3	.0	113.6	9.9	54.7	2.9	2.9	70.4	2.0	186.0
1954	71.4	10.3	71.3	3.1	.1	156.2	10.5	59.5	8.2	4.7	82.9	1.3	240.4
1955	60.2	19.9	75.2	2.5	.1	157.9	14.0	70.6	4.7	7.1	96.5	2.2	256.6
1956	82.9	26.3	76.4	4.3	.0	190.0	14.4	89.2	14.9	11.7	130.3	3.0	323.3
1957	97.4	26.8	82.0	6.6	.1	212.9	19.4	108.0	26.7	21.7	175.8	6.4	395.1
1958	130.4	37.7	74.8	5.8	.0	248.7	14.6	102.0	47.1	24.5	188.1	4.5	441.4
1959	121.7	23.6	75.9	4.9	.1	226.2	15.6	118.5	82.7	28.9	245.8	4.7	476.6
1960	160.6	26.5	88.5	5.2	1.3	282.1	23.0	134.0	84.7	38.3	279.9	4.1	566.1
1961	168.8	22.3	84.6	6.8	.2	282.7	20.3	129.4	93.9	42.0	285.6	.5	568.8
1962	160.5	29.8	95.6	17.5	.7	304.0	21.6	156.4	157.3	50.5	385.8	.6	690.4
1963	204.4	38.9	108.8	15.4	.1	367.7	25.5	169.2	154.0	72.8	421.5	1.1	790.3
1964	211.8	50.0	118.1	12.1	.5	392.5	37.8	204.5	151.9	105.0	499.2	1.4	893.2
1965	231.0	48.9	110.1	10.7	.5	401.3	59.5	247.6	256.7	126.0	689.8	.4	1091.5
1966	248.6	47.4	107.7	20.9	.3	424.9	69.6	282.3	299.4	143.2	794.5	.6	1220.1
1967	285.2	51.0	106.2	22.5	2.3	467.2	74.2	280.7	254.7	173.8	783.3	1.2	1251.7
1968	219.3	41.8	126.7	12.5	2.2	402.5	76.8	323.9	275.5	184.3	860.5	.7	1263.7
1969	245.8	43.0	141.8	14.4	2.7	447.7	91.5	431.7	300.4	202.5	1026.1	.7	1474.5

* CONVERTED FROM NATIONAL DEVISA UNITS THROUGH OFFICIAL EXCHANGE RATES. NOTE LIMITATIONS DISCUSSED IN THE EXPLANATORY TEXT.

SITC CATEGORIES

0 FOOD AND LIVE ANIMALS
1 BEVERAGES AND TOBACCO
2 CRUDE MATERIALS, INEDIBLE, EXCEPT FUELS
3 MINERAL FUELS, LUBRICANTS AND RELATED MATERIALS
4 ANIMAL AND VEGETABLE OILS AND FATS
5 CHEMICALS
6 MANUFACTURED GOODS CLASSIFIED CHIEFLY BY MATERIAL
7 MACHINERY AND TRANSPORT EQUIPMENT
8 MISCELLANEOUS MANUFACTURED ARTICLES
9 COMMODITIES AND TRANSACTIONS NOT CLASSIFIED ACCORDING TO KIND PLUS NOT SPECIFIED

TABLE II.BEC-1.M.U
USSR IMPORTS, 1946-69
(MILLIONS OF CURRENT DOLLARS,* F.O.B.)

YEAR	CLASS 1	111	112	121	122	CLASS 2	21	22	CLASS 3	31	32	CLASS 4+5	CLASS 6	CLASS 7	TOTAL IMPORTS
1946	103.1	32.1	14.9	8.8	47.3	239.6	107.4	132.1	90.6	71.4	19.1	219.3	33.4	82.9	768.9
1947	168.9	72.2	20.0	20.8	55.9	236.7	137.1	99.6	91.0	76.0	15.0	132.3	37.2	78.7	744.8
1948	241.3	122.9	12.9	40.2	65.3	549.0	346.6	202.4	110.6	85.4	25.1	110.0	111.3	101.8	1224.0
1949	230.7	87.2	13.6	59.0	70.9	571.8	287.8	284.0	162.8	105.9	56.9	214.9	154.8	154.3	1489.2
1950	243.9	104.9	15.6	33.1	90.3	531.3	297.1	234.2	168.0	94.8	73.2	313.0	95.8	103.9	1455.9
1951	319.0	138.1	31.0	39.0	110.9	810.8	495.8	315.0	180.7	95.3	85.3	413.3	149.0	118.0	1990.8
1952	414.9	176.1	43.7	47.0	148.1	1027.8	571.5	456.2	248.1	131.4	116.7	540.2	173.9	101.2	2506.1
1953	462.8	145.4	53.9	56.1	207.3	994.8	505.7	489.1	265.3	131.7	133.7	760.9	181.9	103.3	2769.0
1954	613.0	154.2	73.9	64.4	320.4	1016.7	548.4	468.2	256.1	134.7	121.4	972.7	199.7	123.7	3181.7
1955	613.8	176.0	67.7	92.2	277.9	1012.7	545.6	467.1	250.0	128.8	121.2	925.3	146.8	112.0	3060.5
1956	587.0	193.4	80.0	117.8	195.8	1443.5	803.9	639.7	256.4	132.8	123.7	895.3	341.0	89.3	3612.6
1957	562.0	165.0	102.2	79.8	215.0	1686.9	1006.7	680.2	208.1	102.2	105.9	940.4	447.7	92.7	3937.7
1958	632.7	187.0	132.2	98.1	215.3	1718.0	987.6	730.3	212.3	78.9	133.4	1064.5	617.3	104.7	4349.5
1959	637.3	203.9	118.7	122.6	192.2	1828.0	971.7	856.3	231.3	89.0	142.3	1351.9	912.1	112.6	5073.2
1960	675.0	172.7	122.0	98.9	281.4	1972.8	959.2	1013.6	237.3	97.3	140.0	1675.2	961.8	106.3	5628.4
1961	818.1	154.7	127.2	34.6	501.7	1926.2	903.5	1022.7	217.0	92.7	124.3	1734.4	999.3	132.6	5827.6
1962	739.4	112.3	133.4	70.6	423.1	2011.1	870.3	1140.8	198.9	88.6	110.3	2245.1	1137.9	123.0	6455.4
1963	900.5	323.1	170.0	81.4	326.0	2034.4	910.6	1123.8	202.0	90.4	111.6	2466.0	1288.4	167.3	7058.7
1964	1535.4	631.3	194.6	168.8	540.8	1933.0	842.6	1090.4	183.2	79.3	103.9	2665.0	1187.4	232.4	7736.5
1965	1617.4	579.1	199.9	95.3	743.1	2140.4	935.0	1205.5	198.6	106.9	91.7	2692.3	1142.3	267.2	8058.3
1966	1546.4	610.5	196.7	114.7	624.5	2084.1	951.4	1132.7	184.4	112.7	71.8	2564.9	1292.1	240.9	7912.8
1967	1343.3	276.2	235.6	123.2	708.3	1879.5	578.7	1300.8	185.9	119.0	66.9	2916.9	1664.3	546.7	8536.6
1968	1276.8	272.9	230.3	105.7	667.9	2001.5	573.1	1428.5	166.9	107.0	59.9	3474.5	1842.8	647.4	9409.9
1969	1325.2	245.8	256.0	119.6	703.9	2311.5	667.3	1644.2	174.7	112.1	62.6	3873.1	1915.6	726.5	10326.7

* CONVERTED FROM NATIONAL DEVISA UNITS THROUGH
OFFICIAL EXCHANGE RATES. NOTE LIMITATIONS
DISCUSSED IN THE EXPLANATORY TEXT.

BEC CATEGORIES

1 FOOD AND BEVERAGES
   11 PRIMARY
       111 FOR INDUSTRY
       112 FOR HOUSEHOLD CONSUMPTION
   12 PROCESSED
       121 FOR INDUSTRY
       122 FOR HOUSEHOLD CONSUMPTION

2 INDUSTRIAL SUPPLIES (NON-FOOD)

3 FUELS AND LUBRICANTS
   31 PRIMARY
   32 PROCESSED

4 MACHINERY, EXC. TRANSPORT (W/PARTS)

5 TRANSPORT EQUIPMENT

6 CONSUMER GOODS, N.E.S.

TABLE II.BEC-2.M.U
USSR IMPORTS, 1946-69
(MILLIONS OF CURRENT DOLLARS,* F.O.B.)

YEAR	AGGREGATION I. BASIC SNA CLASSES			AGGREGATION II. PRIMARY VS. PROCESSED		NOT SPECIFIED	TOTAL IMPORTS	RATIO SPECIFIED
	CAPITAL GOODS	INTERMEDIATE GOODS	CONSUMER GOODS	PRIMARY	PROCESSED			
1946	219.3	371.0	95.7	225.9	460.1	82.9	768.9	.8922
1947	132.3	420.7	113.1	305.8	360.8	78.7	744.8	.8944
1948	110.0	822.7	189.6	567.8	554.4	101.8	1224.0	.9168
1949	214.9	880.8	239.2	494.4	840.4	154.3	1489.2	.8964
1950	313.0	837.3	201.7	512.3	839.7	103.9	1455.9	.9286
1951	413.3	1168.5	290.9	760.2	1112.5	118.0	1990.8	.9407
1952	549.2	1499.0	365.7	922.8	1482.1	101.2	2506.1	.9596
1953	760.9	1461.7	443.1	836.7	1829.0	103.3	2769.0	.9627
1954	972.7	1491.4	594.0	911.2	2146.9	123.7	3181.7	.9611
1955	925.3	1530.9	492.3	918.0	2030.5	112.0	3060.5	.9634
1956	875.3	2011.2	616.8	1210.1	2313.2	89.3	3612.6	.9753
1957	940.4	2139.8	764.9	1376.1	2469.0	92.7	3937.7	.9765
1958	1064.5	2215.4	964.9	1385.7	2859.1	104.7	4349.5	.9759
1959	1351.9	2385.8	1223.0	1383.3	3577.3	112.6	5073.2	.9778
1960	1675.2	2481.6	1365.2	1351.2	4170.9	106.3	5628.4	.9811
1961	1734.4	2332.4	1628.2	1278.1	4417.0	132.6	5827.6	.9773
1962	2245.1	2392.9	1694.4	1204.7	5127.7	123.0	6455.4	.9809
1963	2466.0	2641.0	1784.4	1494.2	5397.2	167.3	7058.7	.9763
1964	2665.0	2916.3	1922.8	1747.8	5756.3	232.4	7736.5	.9700
1965	2692.3	3013.4	2085.3	1820.8	5970.2	267.2	8058.3	.9668
1966	2564.9	2993.7	2113.3	1871.3	5800.6	240.9	7912.8	.9696
1967	2916.9	2464.9	2608.2	1209.5	6780.4	546.7	8536.6	.9360
1968	3474.5	2547.0	2741.0	1183.3	7579.2	647.4	9409.9	.9312
1969	3873.1	2851.5	2875.5	1281.2	8318.9	726.5	10326.7	.9296

* CONVERTED FROM NATIONAL DEVISA-UNITS THROUGH
OFFICIAL EXCHANGE RATES. NOTE LIMITATIONS
DISCUSSED IN THE EXPLANATORY TEXT.

TABLE II.BEC-1.M.B
BULGARIA'S IMPORTS, 1955-68
(MILLIONS OF CURRENT DOLLARS,* F.O.B.)

YEAR	CLASS 1	111	112	121	122	CLASS 2	21	22	CLASS 3	31	32	CLASS 4+5	CLASS 6	CLASS 7	TOTAL IMPORTS
1955	11.4	8.8	.9	.3	1.4	88.3	19.4	68.9	13.4		13.4	128.5	8.4	.0	249.9
1956	4.4	1.5	1.3	.4	1.3	114.2	30.9	83.2	16.3		16.3	106.1	10.1	.0	251.1
1957	22.2	17.3	1.5	.5	3.0	147.8	47.5	100.3	23.6		23.6	99.6	39.0	.0	332.1
1958	8.5	4.0	1.6	1.0	1.8	160.3	48.3	112.0	24.8		24.8	130.9	42.1	.0	366.5
1959	29.8	19.4	2.0	2.4	6.1	230.4	73.4	157.1	34.2		34.2	226.1	58.9	.0	579.4
1960	33.1	14.1	2.1	1.3	15.5	235.4	71.0	164.4	42.6	.2	42.5	273.4	48.0	.0	632.6
1961	26.4	7.9	2.3	1.0	15.3	233.1	66.4	166.7	53.0	.2	52.8	310.8	42.7	.0	666.0
1962	43.8	17.4	2.6	2.9	20.9	263.9	75.0	188.9	65.6	.3	65.4	357.4	54.0	.0	784.7
1963	66.8	31.5	5.0	3.2	27.2	293.0	73.7	219.3	78.3	8.1	70.2	430.3	64.9	.0	933.2
1964	98.0	52.2	5.4	6.4	34.1	358.5	104.4	254.1	101.6	32.6	69.0	447.3	56.8	.0	1062.4
1965	84.9	31.0	5.6	5.9	42.4	403.2	109.2	294.0	116.9	39.3	77.6	513.6	59.1	.0	1177.7
1966	87.5	33.6	3.8	5.0	45.1	489.5	135.9	353.5	137.4	47.0	90.4	696.3	67.5	.0	1478.3
1967	78.2	14.2	4.0	5.4	54.7	507.2	142.2	365.0	144.4	40.3	104.1	769.8	72.2	.0	1571.9
1968	117.3	29.0	5.1	9.9	73.3	587.5	167.9	419.6	173.0	47.3	125.7	799.7	104.8	.0	1782.3

* CONVERTED FROM NATIONAL DEVISA UNITS THROUGH
  OFFICIAL EXCHANGE RATES. NOTE LIMITATIONS
  DISCUSSED IN THE EXPLANATORY TEXT.

BEC CATEGORIES

1 FOOD AND BEVERAGES
   11   PRIMARY
        111 FOR INDUSTRY
        112 FOR HOUSEHOLD CONSUMPTION
   12   PROCESSED
        121 FOR INDUSTRY
        122 FOR HOUSEHOLD CONSUMPTION

2 INDUSTRIAL SUPPLIES (NON-FOOD)
   21   PRIMARY
   22   PROCESSED

3 FUELS AND LUBRICANTS
   31   PRIMARY
   32   PROCESSED

4 MACHINERY, EXC. TRANSPORT (W/PARTS)

5 TRANSPORT EQUIPMENT

6 CONSUMER GOODS, N.E.S.

7 GOODS N.E.S. AND UNSPECIFIED

TABLE II.BEC-2.M.B
BULGARIA'S IMPORTS, 1955-68
(MILLIONS OF CURRENT DOLLARS,* F.O.B.)

YEAR	AGGREGATION I. BASIC SNA CLASSES			AGGREGATION II. PRIMARY VS. PROCESSED		NOT SPECIFIED	TOTAL IMPORTS	RATIO SPECIFIED
	CAPITAL GOODS	INTERMEDIATE GOODS	CONSUMER GOODS	PRIMARY	PROCESSED			
1955	128.5	110.8	10.7	29.1	220.8	.0	249.9	1.0000
1956	106.1	132.4	12.6	33.7	217.4	.0	251.1	1.0000
1957	99.6	189.1	43.4	66.2	265.9	.0	332.1	1.0000
1958	130.9	190.1	45.6	53.9	312.6	.0	366.5	1.0000
1959	226.1	286.4	66.9	94.8	484.6	.0	579.4	1.0000
1960	273.4	293.5	65.6	87.4	545.1	.0	632.6	1.0000
1961	310.8	295.0	60.3	76.8	589.2	.0	666.0	1.0000
1962	357.4	349.8	77.5	95.2	689.5	.0	784.7	1.0000
1963	430.3	405.9	97.1	118.3	814.9	.0	933.2	1.0000
1964	447.3	518.7	96.3	194.7	867.7	.0	1062.4	1.0000
1965	513.6	556.9	107.2	185.1	992.6	.0	1177.7	1.0000
1966	696.3	665.6	116.4	220.3	1257.9	.0	1478.3	1.0000
1967	769.8	671.2	130.9	200.7	1371.2	.0	1571.9	1.0000
1968	799.7	799.4	183.2	249.3	1533.0	.0	1782.3	1.0000

* CONVERTED FROM NATIONAL DEVISA-UNITS THROUGH
OFFICIAL EXCHANGE RATES. NOTE LIMITATIONS
DISCUSSED IN THE EXPLANATORY TEXT.

TABLE II.BEC-1.M.Y
YUGOSLAVIA'S IMPORTS, 1952-69
(MILLIONS OF CURRENT DOLLARS,* C.I.F.)

YEAR	CLASS 1	111	112	121	122	CLASS 2	21	22	CLASS 3	31	32	CLASS 4+5	CLASS 6	CLASS 7	TOTAL IMPORTS
1952	81.6	67.5	1.7		12.4	137.7	32.8	104.9	29.1	14.5	14.5	117.2	7.4		373.0
1953	114.0	92.5	1.7		19.8	118.4	28.8	89.6	30.7	15.4	15.4	125.6	6.5		395.3
1954	82.9	68.7	3.8		10.4	127.0	32.4	94.6	30.0	15.0	15.0	91.1	7.8	.5	339.4
1955	122.3	86.1	8.9		27.3	160.3	47.6	112.6	36.5	18.2	18.2	111.8	9.4	.7	440.9
1956	155.5	116.7	7.7		31.0	163.9	46.1	117.8	46.9	23.5	23.5	94.6	12.9	.3	474.1
1957	152.9	111.2	10.5		31.1	253.9	63.0	191.0	65.3	32.7	32.7	168.0	17.7	3.4	661.3
1958	131.8	78.3	14.5		38.9	269.4	54.5	214.9	41.2	20.6	20.6	215.7	24.1	2.7	684.9
1959	133.5	99.1	13.0		21.5	289.4	62.5	226.9	45.3	22.6	22.6	192.1	24.9	1.8	687.1
1960	73.2	38.7	12.1		22.5	370.8	84.9	285.8	45.0	22.5	22.5	304.9	31.4	1.1	826.3
1961	119.3	80.0	14.1		25.2	389.9	92.3	297.6	40.3	20.1	20.1	324.5	35.8	.4	910.2
1962	125.3	86.2	13.2		25.9	387.8	97.9	289.9	47.9	23.9	23.9	293.8	32.4	.4	887.6
1963	187.8	143.1	19.6		25.1	475.6	117.0	358.5	47.0	23.5	23.5	307.1	39.0	.1	1056.5
1964	163.4	90.8	20.7	13.4	38.6	638.5	152.5	485.9	66.0	33.9	32.1	400.5	54.5	.3	1323.2
1965	182.6	122.9	24.4	8.2	27.0	629.5	154.3	475.2	72.0	34.7	37.3	355.6	48.0	.3	1288.0
1966	230.8	140.7	31.0	7.1	52.1	741.2	155.9	585.3	82.4	30.6	51.9	459.6	60.9	.5	1575.4
1967	185.8	59.3	34.8	26.5	65.2	815.7	144.9	670.8	84.6	23.9	60.7	572.7	77.1	.4	1707.3**
1968	122.5	40.8	33.3	12.5	35.9	827.9	144.3	683.7	98.0	26.9	71.0	647.0	101.3	.2	1796.8
1969	129.3	54.7	38.1	3.1	33.4	1043.3	190.5	852.8	103.5	27.0	76.5	727.1	130.4	.2	2133.8

* CONVERTED FROM NATIONAL DEVISA UNITS THROUGH OFFICIAL EXCHANGE RATES. NOTE LIMITATIONS DISCUSSED IN THE EXPLANATORY TEXT.

** SUM OF COMPONENTS GREATER THAN GIVEN TOTAL. ERROR IN ORIGINAL SITC.

BEC CATEGORIES AND LARGE ECONOMIC CLASSES

1 FOOD AND BEVERAGES
  11 PRIMARY
    111 FOR INDUSTRY
    112 FOR HOUSEHOLD CONSUMPTION
  12 PROCESSED
    121 FOR INDUSTRY
    122 FOR HOUSEHOLD CONSUMPTION

2 INDUSTRIAL SUPPLIES (NON-FOOD)
  21 PRIMARY
  22 PROCESSED

3 FUELS AND LUBRICANTS
  31 PRIMARY
  32 PROCESSED

4 MACHINERY, EXC. TRANSPORT (W/PARTS)

5 TRANSPORT EQUIPMENT

6 CONSUMER GOODS, N.E.S.

7 GOODS N.E.S. AND NOT SPECIFIED

TABLE II.BEC-2.M.Y
YUGOSLAVIA'S IMPORTS, 1952-69
(MILLIONS OF CURRENT DOLLARS,* C.I.F.)

YEAR	AGGREGATION I. BASIC SNA CLASSES			AGGREGATION II. PRIMARY VS. PROCESSED		NOT SPECIFIED	TOTAL IMPORTS	RATIO SPECIFIED
	CAPITAL GOODS	INTERMEDIATE GOODS	CONSUMER GOODS	PRIMARY	PROCESSED			
1952	117.2	234.3	21.5	116.6	256.5	.0	373.0	1.000
1953	125.6	241.6	28.0	138.3	256.9	.0	395.3	1.000
1954	91.1	225.7	22.0	119.9	219.0	.5	339.4	.998
1955	111.8	282.8	45.6	160.9	279.4	.7	440.9	.998
1956	94.6	327.6	51.7	194.0	279.8	.3	474.1	.999
1957	168.0	430.5	59.3	217.4	440.5	3.4	661.3	.995
1958	215.7	388.9	77.6	167.9	514.3	2.7	684.9	.996
1959	192.1	433.8	59.4	197.3	488.0	1.8	687.1	.997
1960	304.9	454.5	65.9	158.2	667.0	1.1	826.3	.999
1961	324.5	510.2	75.0	206.6	703.2	.4	910.2	1.000
1962	293.8	521.9	71.5	221.3	665.9	.4	887.6	1.000
1963	307.1	665.7	83.7	303.3	753.2	.1	1056.5	1.000
1964	430.5	808.6	113.8	297.9	1025.0	.3	1323.2	1.000
1965	355.6	832.6	99.5	336.4	951.3	.3	1288.0	1.000
1966	459.6	971.4	143.9	358.2	1216.7	.5	1575.4	1.000
1967	572.7	986.1	177.1	262.9	1473.0	.4	1707.3**	1.000
1968	647.0	979.1	170.5	245.3	1551.4	.2	1796.8	1.000
1969	727.1	1204.6	201.9	310.2	1823.4	.2	2133.8	1.000

* CONVERTED FROM NATIONAL DEVISA UNITS THROUGH
  OFFICIAL EXCHANGE RATES. NOTE LIMITATIONS
  DISCUSSED IN THE EXPLANATORY TEXT.

** SUM OF COMPONENTS GREATER THAN GIVEN
   TOTAL. ERROR IN ORIGINAL SITC.

TABLE II.BEC-1.X.U
USSR EXPORTS, 1946-69
(MILLIONS OF CURRENT DOLLARS,* F.O.B.)

YEAR	CLASS 1	111	112	121	122	CLASS 2	21	22	CLASS 3	31	32	CLASS 4+5	CLASS 6	CLASS 7	TOTAL EXPORTS
1946	184.8	142.4	.1	6.0	36.2	313.4	224.4	89.1	33.6	6.4	27.1	37.8	33.1	51.0	653.7
1947	128.4	94.0	.4	7.2	26.8	384.8	247.3	137.5	54.4	15.6	38.9	22.2	59.7	121.2	770.8
1948	472.4	433.8	.6	5.8	32.3	540.6	331.0	209.6	62.6	12.7	49.9	58.9	77.9	95.8	1308.1
1949	327.3	228.4	.2	11.6	87.1	630.3	319.4	311.0	75.4	22.9	52.6	132.7	72.8	208.7	1447.2
1950	350.0	235.3	3.6	12.9	98.2	618.7	341.9	276.8	67.7	19.3	48.3	212.6	67.1	478.7	1794.6
1951	485.7	356.7	.8	11.4	116.8	839.1	431.3	407.8	116.1	34.1	82.0	340.3	84.2	425.3	2290.8
1952	603.0	470.4	.8	10.8	121.0	911.1	457.3	453.8	137.0	45.6	91.4	453.2	67.4	618.1	2789.9
1953	526.2	318.9	2.8	17.6	187.0	1014.5	463.7	550.8	197.3	80.7	116.7	523.6	70.7	615.4	2947.7
1954	470.0	310.0	.4	14.6	145.0	1285.7	560.2	725.5	271.8	104.7	167.1	532.3	81.6	581.8	3223.1
1955	411.0	297.3	.8	17.3	95.6	1288.3	587.0	701.3	329.1	130.6	198.6	599.0	103.4	695.8	3426.6
1956	392.4	240.9	1.1	14.3	136.2	1408.0	611.5	796.5	428.2	184.9	243.3	624.4	100.7	661.2	3615.0
1957	792.5	577.1	7.8	18.4	189.2	1621.0	666.8	954.2	648.3	323.4	324.9	652.1	141.7	525.8	4381.4
1958	528.1	370.3	3.7	23.8	130.3	1689.5	664.9	1024.7	651.2	330.7	320.6	796.4	153.0	480.9	4299.2
1959	820.2	503.4	7.8	41.1	267.8	1858.3	735.1	1123.2	798.0	390.9	407.1	1177.7	154.2	641.9	5450.3
1960	724.9	489.1	13.3	24.4	198.1	2110.1	829.4	1280.2	902.4	455.2	447.2	1143.2	157.1	525.9	5563.6
1961	816.5	496.2	10.1	35.7	274.6	2306.6	901.4	1405.3	1046.1	536.9	509.2	964.9	172.1	692.1	5998.4
1962	926.4	552.4	16.5	37.9	319.6	2456.0	929.5	1526.5	1155.8	635.2	520.6	1168.5	180.2	1143.5	7030.5
1963	934.5	444.8	24.2	47.1	418.5	2493.5	939.3	1554.2	1299.0	722.0	577.0	1435.1	187.0	923.2	7272.4
1964	588.7	265.3	22.8	45.4	255.1	2878.4	1042.9	1835.5	1380.2	854.4	525.8	1612.8	183.2	1040.0	7683.3
1965	676.3	293.2	32.7	50.3	300.1	3134.5	1127.7	2006.8	1403.9	912.9	491.0	1635.8	188.9	1135.2	8174.6
1966	807.5	266.1	37.8	49.9	453.7	3317.5	1214.3	2103.2	1448.8	939.1	509.7	1838.2	199.7	1229.3	8841.0
1967	1129.5	503.8	33.2	50.6	542.0	3400.7	1236.0	2164.8	1550.1	1006.7	543.4	2036.0	238.3	1297.5	9652.2
1968	1084.2	446.7	38.1	70.4	529.1	3674.9	1345.5	2329.3	1702.8	1084.9	617.9	2301.6	257.8	1613.0	10634.2
1969	1214.1	551.7	36.7	88.4	537.3	3947.3	1295.2	2652.1	1821.1	1196.0	625.1	2623.2	272.4	1777.2	11655.3

* CONVERTED FROM NATIONAL DEVISA UNITS THROUGH
OFFICIAL EXCHANGE RATES. NOTE LIMITATIONS
DISCUSSED IN THE EXPLANATORY TEXT.

BEC CATEGORIES

1 FOOD AND BEVERAGES
  11 PRIMARY
    111 FOR INDUSTRY
    112 FOR HOUSEHOLD CONSUMPTION
  12 PROCESSED
    121 FOR INDUSTRY
    122 FOR HOUSEHOLD CONSUMPTION

2 INDUSTRIAL SUPPLIES (NON-FOOD)
  21 PRIMARY

3 FUELS AND LUBRICANTS
  31 PRIMARY
  32 PROCESSED

4 MACHINERY, EXC. TRANSPORT (W/PARTS)

5 TRANSPORT EQUIPMENT

6 CONSUMER GOODS, N.E.S.

TABLE II.BEC-2.X.U
USSR EXPORTS, 1946-69
(MILLIONS OF CURRENT DOLLARS,* F.O.B.)

YEAR	AGGREGATION I. BASIC SNA CLASSES			AGGREGATION II. PRIMARY VS. PROCESSED		NOT SPECIFIED	TOTAL EXPORTS	RATIO SPECIFIED
	CAPITAL GOODS	INTERMEDIATE GOODS	CONSUMER GOODS	PRIMARY	PROCESSED			
1946	37.8	495.4	69.4	373.4	229.3	51.0	653.7	.9220
1947	22.2	540.4	86.9	357.3	292.2	121.2	770.8	.8427
1948	58.9	1042.7	110.8	778.0	434.4	95.8	1308.1	.9268
1949	132.7	945.8	160.1	570.9	667.6	208.7	1447.2	.8558
1950	212.6	934.5	168.9	600.1	715.9	478.7	1794.6	.7333
1951	340.3	1323.3	201.8	822.8	1042.6	425.3	2290.8	.8143
1952	453.2	1529.3	189.2	974.1	1197.7	618.1	2789.9	.7784
1953	523.6	1548.3	260.4	866.0	1466.3	615.4	2947.7	.7912
1954	532.3	1882.0	227.0	975.3	1666.0	581.8	3223.1	.8195
1955	599.0	1932.1	199.8	1015.7	1715.2	695.8	3426.6	.7970
1956	624.4	2091.4	237.9	1038.3	1915.5	661.2	3615.0	.8171
1957	652.1	2864.9	338.7	1575.1	2280.5	525.8	4381.4	.8800
1958	796.4	2734.9	287.0	1369.5	2448.8	480.9	4299.2	.8881
1959	1177.7	3200.9	429.9	1637.3	3171.1	641.9	5450.3	.8822
1960	1143.2	3526.1	368.4	1787.5	3250.3	525.9	5563.6	.9055
1961	964.9	3884.6	456.8	1944.5	3361.7	692.1	5998.4	.8846
1962	1163.5	4202.1	516.3	2133.7	3753.3	1143.5	7030.5	.8373
1963	1435.1	4284.4	629.7	2130.3	4218.9	923.2	7272.4	.8731
1964	1612.8	4569.4	461.1	2185.4	4457.8	1040.0	7683.3	.8646
1965	1635.8	4882.0	521.7	2366.6	4672.8	1135.2	8174.6	.8611
1966	1838.2	5082.3	691.2	2457.3	5154.4	1229.3	8841.0	.8610
1967	2036.0	5505.2	813.5	2779.6	5575.1	1297.5	9652.2	.8656
1968	2301.6	5894.7	824.9	2915.1	6106.1	1613.0	10634.2	.8483
1969	2623.2	6408.5	846.4	3079.5	6798.6	1777.2	11655.3	.8475

* CONVERTED FROM NATIONAL DEVISA-UNITS THROUGH OFFICIAL EXCHANGE RATES. NOTE LIMITATIONS DISCUSSED IN THE EXPLANATORY TEXT.

TABLE II.BEC-1.X.B
BULGARIA'S EXPORTS, 1955-68
(MILLIONS OF CURRENT DOLLARS,* F.O.B.)

YEAR	CLASS 1	111	112	121	122	CLASS 2	21	22	CLASS 3	31	32	CLASS 4+5	CLASS 6	CLASS 7	TOTAL EXPORTS
1955	83.1	13.0	25.2	5.0	39.8	115.0	91.5	23.5	2.3	2.3		6.2	29.7	.0	236.2
1956	105.9	11.5	35.9	5.6	52.8	131.5	98.9	32.6	6.0	5.7	.3	12.1	46.7	.0	302.1
1957	102.9	9.9	35.7	4.8	52.5	141.5	101.5	40.0	6.8	6.7	.1	27.6	91.4	.0	370.1
1958	124.4	10.9	46.7	1.7	65.1	135.7	99.4	36.3	3.6	3.6		31.4	78.1	.0	373.2
1959	167.0	16.2	59.1	6.6	85.2	159.1	122.3	36.9	2.2	2.2		55.9	82.8	.0	467.1
1960	218.4	24.4	61.3	8.7	123.9	170.9	129.4	41.4	2.1	2.1		77.7	102.4	.0	571.5
1961	259.7	17.8	77.5	6.3	158.1	184.5	135.3	49.2	3.2	2.9	.3	103.1	112.1	.0	662.6
1962	280.9	23.8	81.7	8.1	169.4	203.1	144.9	58.2	3.2	2.9	.3	150.3	135.0	.0	772.6
1963	281.2	20.0	83.3	8.5	169.4	245.1	167.5	77.6	2.6	2.1	.5	180.3	124.7	.0	834.0
1964	346.2	45.2	83.9	12.3	204.7	271.6	169.0	102.6	2.0	.8	1.2	238.1	121.8	.0	979.7
1965	427.3	53.8	93.9	9.2	270.3	295.1	163.2	131.9	2.1	.1	2.1	291.3	159.9	.0	1175.8
1966	484.8	97.0	70.1	9.4	308.3	293.5	147.6	145.9	4.3	.3	3.9	332.5	190.0	.0	1305.0
1967	542.9	92.4	82.7	9.9	358.5	323.6	162.6	161.0	3.8	.6	3.2	372.1	215.9	.0	1458.2
1968	573.8	63.8	88.7	9.9	411.5	353.6	160.3	193.3	7.9	4.4	3.5	426.8	252.9	.0	1615.1

* CONVERTED FROM NATIONAL DEVISA UNITS THROUGH
OFFICIAL EXCHANGE RATES. NOTE LIMITATIONS
DISCUSSED IN THE EXPLANATORY TEXT.

BEC CATEGORIES

1 FOOD AND BEVERAGES
  11 PRIMARY
     111 FOR INDUSTRY
     112 FOR HOUSEHOLD CONSUMPTION
  12 PROCESSED
     121 FOR INDUSTRY
     122 FOR HOUSEHOLD CONSUMPTION

2 INDUSTRIAL SUPPLIES (NON-FOOD)
  21 PRIMARY
  22 PROCESSED

3 FUELS AND LUBRICANTS
  31 PRIMARY
  32 PROCESSED

4 MACHINERY, EXC. TRANSPORT (W/PARTS)

5 TRANSPORT EQUIPMENT

6 CONSUMER GOODS, N.E.S.

7 GOODS N.E.S. AND UNSPECIFIED

TABLE II.BEC-2.X.B
BULGARIA'S EXPORTS, 1955-68
(MILLIONS OF CURRENT DOLLARS,* F.O.B.)

YEAR	AGGREGATION I. BASIC SNA CLASSES			AGGREGATION II. PRIMARY VS. PROCESSED		NOT SPECIFIED	TOTAL EXPORTS	RATIO SPECIFIED
	CAPITAL GOODS	INTERMEDIATE GOODS	CONSUMER GOODS	PRIMARY	PROCESSED			
1955	6.2	135.4	94.7	132.0	104.2	.0	236.2	1.0000
1956	12.1	154.7	135.4	152.2	150.0	-.1	302.1	1.0003
1957	27.6	162.9	179.6	153.8	216.3	.0	370.1	1.0000
1958	31.4	151.9	189.9	160.6	212.6	.0	373.2	1.0000
1959	55.9	184.1	227.1	199.7	267.4	.0	467.1	1.0000
1960	77.7	206.2	287.6	217.3	354.1	.0	571.5	1.0000
1961	103.1	211.8	347.7	233.5	429.0	.0	662.6	1.0000
1962	150.3	236.2	386.2	253.3	519.3	.0	772.6	1.0000
1963	180.3	276.2	377.4	272.9	561.1	.0	834.0	1.0000
1964	238.1	331.1	410.4	298.9	680.8	.0	979.7	1.0000
1965	291.3	360.3	524.2	311.1	864.7	.0	1175.8	1.0000
1966	332.5	404.2	568.4	315.0	990.0	.0	1305.0	1.0000
1967	372.1	429.0	657.2	338.3	1119.9	.0	1458.2	1.0000
1968	426.8	435.2	753.1	317.2	1297.9	.0	1615.1	1.0000

* CONVERTED FROM NATIONAL DEVISA-UNITS THROUGH
OFFICIAL EXCHANGE RATES. NOTE LIMITATIONS
DISCUSSED IN THE EXPLANATORY TEXT.

TABLE II.BEC-1.X.Y
YUGOSLAVIA'S EXPORTS, 1952-69
(MILLIONS OF CURRENT DOLLARS,* F.O.B.)

YEAR	CLASS 1	111	112	121	122	CLASS 2	21	22	CLASS 3	31	32	CLASS 4+5	CLASS 6	CLASS 7	TOTAL EXPORTS
1952	91.0	68.9	6.2		16.0	147.4	51.5	95.9	3.9	1.9	1.9	.1	1.6	2.5	246.5
1953	33.2	12.6	7.4		13.2	142.4	49.6	92.8	2.3	1.1	1.1	3.0	2.9	2.0	186.0
1954	69.6	26.6	12.3		30.7	153.3	54.3	99.0	3.1	1.6	1.6	8.4	4.7	1.3	240.4
1955	62.7	13.3	15.2		34.2	177.1	65.6	111.6	2.5	1.2	1.2	4.8	7.2	2.2	256.6
1956	88.7	23.2	17.8		47.8	200.6	71.3	129.3	4.3	2.1	2.1	15.0	11.8	3.0	323.3
1957	104.4	26.3	18.9		59.2	229.0	73.3	155.8	6.6	3.3	3.3	26.9	21.8	6.4	395.1
1958	139.6	55.3	18.7		65.5	219.6	75.7	143.8	5.8	2.9	2.9	47.4	24.4	4.5	441.4
1959	127.1	42.1	14.4		70.6	228.0	66.5	161.5	4.9	2.5	2.5	83.1	28.8	4.7	476.6
1960	168.2	60.9	14.9		92.4	265.4	75.6	189.8	5.2	2.6	2.6	85.1	38.1	4.1	566.1
1961	174.8	57.9	17.5		99.4	250.2	71.3	178.9	6.8	3.4	3.4	94.3	42.3	.5	568.8
1962	168.3	34.3	19.4		114.5	295.3	83.8	211.5	17.5	8.7	8.7	157.8	51.0	.6	690.4
1963	211.5	43.6	23.1		144.9	334.6	99.6	235.0	15.4	7.7	7.7	154.4	73.1	1.1	790.3
1964	223.9	26.4	22.8	.2	174.4	397.5	116.8	280.7	12.1	1.1	11.0	152.7	105.5	1.4	893.2
1965	245.0	28.7	20.5	.2	195.6	450.4	108.2	342.2	10.7	1.0	9.7	258.5	126.1	.4	1091.5
1966	257.7	60.3	19.7	.0	177.7	494.2	105.5	388.7	20.9	.8	20.1	301.2	145.4	.6	1220.1
1967	303.9	98.5	19.1	2.0	184.2	491.8	102.7	389.1	22.5	1.1	21.4	256.5	175.9	1.2	1251.7
1968	234.9	74.9	17.0	1.8	141.3	548.1	110.5	437.6	12.5	.8	11.6	277.5	190.0	.7	1263.7
1969	261.3	73.9	21.4	.1	165.9	685.9	119.2	566.7	14.4	4.9	9.6	303.1	209.0	.7	1474.5

* CONVERTED FROM NATIONAL DEVISA UNITS THROUGH OFFICIAL EXCHANGE RATES. NOTE LIMITATIONS DISCUSSED IN THE EXPLANATORY TEXT.

** SUM OF COMPONENTS GREATER THAN GIVEN TOTAL. ERROR IN ORIGINAL SITC.

BEC CATEGORIES AND LARGE ECONOMIC CLASSES

1 FOOD AND BEVERAGES
  11 PRIMARY
    111 FOR INDUSTRY
    112 FOR HOUSEHOLD CONSUMPTION
  12 PROCESSED
    121 FOR INDUSTRY
    122 FOR HOUSEHOLD CONSUMPTION

2 INDUSTRIAL SUPPLIES (NON-FOOD)
  21 PRIMARY
  22 PROCESSED

3 FUELS AND LUBRICANTS
  31 PRIMARY
  32 PROCESSED

4 MACHINERY, EXC. TRANSPORT (W/PARTS)

5 TRANSPORT EQUIPMENT

6 CONSUMER GOODS, N.E.S.

7 GOODS N.E.S. AND NOT SPECIFIED

TABLE II.BEC-2.X.Y
YUGOSLAVIA'S EXPORTS, 1952-69
(MILLIONS OF CURRENT DOLLARS,* F.O.B.)

YEAR	AGGREGATION I. BASIC SNA CLASSES			AGGREGATION II. PRIMARY VS. PROCESSED		NOT SPECIFIED	TOTAL EXPORTS	RATIO SPECIFIED
	CAPITAL GOODS	INTERMEDIATE GOODS	CONSUMER GOODS	PRIMARY	PROCESSED			
1952	.1	220.2	23.7	128.5	115.5	2.5	246.5	.990
1953	3.0	157.3	23.5	70.8	113.1	2.0	186.0	.989
1954	8.4	183.1	47.6	94.7	144.3	1.3	240.4	.995
1955	4.8	192.9	56.6	95.3	159.0	2.2	256.6	.991
1956	15.0	228.1	77.3	114.4	206.0	3.0	323.3	.991
1957	26.9	261.9	99.9	121.8	266.9	6.4	395.1	.984
1958	47.4	280.7	108.7	152.7	284.1	4.5	441.4	.990
1959	83.1	275.1	113.8	125.4	346.5	4.7	476.6	.990
1960	85.1	331.5	145.4	154.0	408.0	4.1	566.1	.993
1961	94.3	314.8	159.2	150.1	418.2	.5	568.8	.999
1962	157.8	347.1	184.9	146.3	543.5	.6	690.4	.999
1963	154.4	393.6	241.1	174.0	615.2	1.1	790.3	.999
1964	152.7	436.3	302.7	167.2	724.5	1.4	893.2	.998
1965	258.5	490.1	342.1	158.4	932.3	.4	1091.5	1.000
1966	301.2	575.4	342.8	186.3	1033.1	.6	1220.1	.999
1967	256.3	614.9	379.3	221.4	1029.0	1.2	1251.7	.999
1968	277.5	637.3	348.2	203.2	1059.8	.7	1263.7	.999
1969	303.1	774.3	396.3	219.4	1254.4	.7	1474.5	1.000

* CONVERTED FROM NATIONAL DEVISA UNITS THROUGH
  OFFICIAL EXCHANGE RATES. NOTE LIMITATIONS
  DISCUSSED IN THE EXPLANATORY TEXT.

** SUM OF COMPONENTS GREATER THAN GIVEN
   TOTAL. ERROR IN ORIGINAL SITC.

TABLE III.CTN.M.U-B
USSR IMPORTS FROM BULGARIA, 1946-68
(MILLIONS OF CURRENT DOLLARS,* F.O.B.)

YEAR	BROAD DIV I (1)	2	3	4	5	BROAD DIV II (2-5)	6	7	8	BROAD DIV III (6-8)	BROAD DIV IV 9	NOT SPECIFIED	TOTAL IMPORTS
1946	—	1.1			26.3	27.5		3.0	1.9	4.9	0.0	19.3	51.7
1947	—	2.5			34.7	37.1		0.5		0.5	0.0	0.5	38.2
1948	—	4.8			57.4	62.2		1.4		1.4	0.0	1.3	64.9
1949	—	8.2			33.4	41.6		6.8	0.2	7.0	0.0	6.6	55.2
1950	0.7	10.8			24.2	34.9		11.5	2.6	14.1	0.0	17.1	66.9
1951	—	19.0			27.8	46.8		7.0	6.4	13.4	0.4	13.4	74.0
1952	1.9	29.5			36.7	66.2		11.4	9.8	21.2	1.1	18.6	109.0
1953	1.8	37.8			30.0	67.9		9.8	13.3	23.2	2.3	29.5	124.7
1954	3.6	43.4			33.9	77.3		7.1	15.1	22.2	2.3	31.3	136.7
1955	5.6	31.7	0.3	1.2	30.1	63.4		7.5	27.7	35.2	15.6	1.6	121.4
1956	6.2	33.6	0.4	1.8	29.3	65.1		10.0	35.8	45.8	27.2	0.3	144.7
1957	11.4	27.4	3.7	2.1	33.7	66.9		8.8	36.7	45.5	71.1	3.2	198.1
1958	15.5	28.4	5.0	1.9	26.5	61.8		9.3	47.2	56.5	68.5	0.8	203.1
1959	31.5	26.1	5.5	2.1	46.9	80.6		10.8	66.0	76.8	70.2	1.7	260.8
1960	49.1	26.8	6.3	0.8	34.3	68.2		12.8	88.1	100.9	78.7	1.6	298.6
1961	54.7	22.7	6.2	2.1	33.9	65.0		8.7	108.6	117.3	87.2	1.9	326.1
1962	100.4	26.2	7.5	1.7	38.2	73.5		8.8	108.1	116.9	97.3	1.6	390.0
1963	115.9	26.4	6.2	2.1	49.3	84.0		12.6	129.2	141.8	101.6	1.6	444.8
1964	146.9	25.2	5.1	3.2	68.4	102.0		17.0	162.8	179.8	99.1	5.6	533.3
1965	172.9	19.1	5.4	6.1	52.9	83.4		11.4	212.2	223.6	123.2	12.4	615.5
1966	190.6	16.5	7.2	7.1	55.9	86.8		9.4	218.7	228.1	143.5	5.0	654.1
1967	215.6	7.8	7.8	10.0	65.0	90.6		10.3	259.9	270.0	172.3	25.3	773.8
1968	253.7	17.4	7.1	12.3	69.1	105.9		10.3	285.7	296.0	204.0	31.7	891.3

CTN BROAD DIVISIONS AND CATEGORIES

I. 1. INDUSTRIAL MACHINERY AND EQUIPMENT (INCLUDING SPARE PARTS)

II. FUELS, RAW MATERIALS (OTHER THAN FOR FOOD), OTHER MATERIALS
2. FUELS, MINERAL RAW MATERIALS, METALS
3. CHEMICALS, FERTILIZERS, RUBBER
4. BUILDING MATERIALS AND CONSTRUCTION PARTS
5. RAW MATERIALS OF VEGETABLE AND ANIMAL ORIGIN (NOT FOOD)

III. FOODSTUFFS AND RAW MATERIAL FOR FOODSTUFFS
6. LIVE ANIMALS (NOT FOR SLAUGHTER)
7. RAW MATERIAL FOR THE PRODUCTION OF FOODSTUFFS
8. FOODSTUFFS

IV. 9. INDUSTRIAL CONSUMER GOODS (OTHER THAN FOOD)

* CONVERTED FROM NATIONAL DEVISA UNITS THROUGH OFFICIAL EXCHANGE

TABLE III.CTN.M.U-C
USSR IMPORTS FROM CZECHOSLOVAKIA, 1946-68
(MILLIONS OF CURRENT DOLLARS,* F.O.B.)

YEAR	BROAD DIV 1	2	3	4	5	BROAD DIV II (2-5)	6	7	8	BROAD DIV III (6-8)	BROAD DIV IV 9	NOT SPECIFIED	TOTAL IMPORTS
1946	5.3	15.3				15.3			0.8	0.8	1.7	9.1	32.2
1947	8.7	17.8				17.8			10.3	10.3	0.5	1.7	39.0
1948	24.9	41.0				41.0			9.1	9.1	18.1	42.9	135.9
1949	36.7	48.5				48.5			8.8	8.8	34.2	76.8	205.0
1950	59.1	78.1				78.1			13.3	13.3	21.8	29.2	201.6
1951	78.7	101.7				101.7			16.1	16.1	15.2	41.5	253.1
1952	107.1	127.0				127.0			13.0	13.0	16.2	36.1	299.3
1953	112.1	149.6				149.6			14.9	14.9	6.4	29.3	312.3
1954	145.9	117.4				117.4			12.8	12.8	7.0	35.1	318.1
1955	157.2	121.9	1.4	0.0	1.1	124.4		0.0	10.3	10.3	5.6	89.1	386.6
1956	113.8	127.6	1.1	0.1	2.6	131.4		2.0	5.5	6.5	75.5	69.3	396.4
1957	122.5	120.0	1.9	0.5	4.2	126.6		2.8	13.2	15.2	58.2	63.1	385.6
1958	187.0	145.6	3.4	2.3	4.6	155.9		2.8	17.7	20.5	97.1	51.7	512.1
1959	232.6	108.7	6.4	4.8	5.7	125.6		5.2	21.1	26.4	142.2	55.1	581.9
1960	293.2	113.5	7.5	2.8	6.7	130.5		3.4	21.8	25.2	168.3	35.2	652.4
1961	336.1	120.5	9.8	2.2	6.6	139.1		4.6	23.7	28.3	165.5	28.6	697.7
1962	454.0	118.8	11.7	3.6	3.5	137.6		3.8	19.2	23.1	177.9	32.2	824.8
1963	513.5	134.7	14.9	4.0	5.0	158.6		4.3	21.8	26.0	201.8	50.6	950.5
1964	528.1	149.0	27.6	4.2	5.5	186.3		1.7	4.3	6.0	186.4	62.0	968.9
1965	572.6	149.8	29.3	4.2	6.4	189.7		4.0	12.5	16.5	169.8	86.9	1035.4
1966	491.0	118.5	33.7	3.5	6.7	162.4		2.6	6.5	9.1	172.6	84.2	919.4
1967	508.3	116.7	38.1	5.1	6.9	166.8		4.5	6.6	11.1	206.7	89.4	982.2
1968	517.5	119.9	43.0	4.5	6.8	174.2		6.0	6.3	12.3	213.0	72.9	990.0

CTN BROAD DIVISIONS AND CATEGORIES

I. 1. INDUSTRIAL MACHINERY AND EQUIPMENT (INCLUDING SPARE PARTS)

II. FUELS, RAW MATERIALS (OTHER THAN FOOD), OTHER MATERIALS

2. FUELS, MINERAL RAW MATERIALS, METALS
3. CHEMICALS, FERTILIZERS, RUBBER
4. BUILDING MATERIALS AND CONSTRUCTION PARTS
5. RAW MATERIALS OF VEGETABLE AND ANIMAL ORIGIN (NOT FOOD)

III. FOODSTUFFS AND RAW MATERIAL FOR FOODSTUFFS

6. LIVE ANIMALS (NOT FOR SLAUGHTER)
7. RAW MATERIAL FOR THE PRODUCTION OF FOODSTUFFS
8. FOODSTUFFS

IV. 9. INDUSTRIAL CONSUMER GOODS (OTHER THAN FOOD)

* CONVERTED FROM NATIONAL DEVISA UNITS THROUGH OFFICIAL EXCHANGE RATES. NOTE THE LIMITATIONS DISCUSSED IN THE EXPLANATORY TEXT.

TABLE III.CTN.M.U-G
USSR IMPORTS FROM EAST GERMANY, 1946-68
(MILLIONS OF CURRENT DOLLARS,* F.O.B.)

YEAR	BROAD DIV I 1	2	3	4	5	BROAD DIV II (2-5)	6	7	8	BROAD DIV III (6-8)	BROAD DIV IV 9	NOT SPECIFIED	TOTAL IMPORTS
1946	2.3	5.8				5.8					4.6	37.7	50.3
1947	0.4	2.1				2.1					5.3	14.0	21.8
1948	2.5	1.2	0.5			1.6					15.0	42.7	61.8
1949	21.3	4.1	2.1			6.2					12.6	106.2	146.3
1950	60.7	4.9	6.3			11.2					8.6	79.5	160.1
1951	145.9	27.5	11.7			39.2					18.9	123.8	327.9
1952	197.0	27.4	13.0			40.4					17.9	109.9	365.2
1953	353.0	26.4	10.2			36.6					22.0	71.7	483.3
1954	461.9	26.4	13.8			40.2					25.3	90.2	617.7
1955	393.0	37.0	55.3	1.9	6.5	100.6			0.9	0.9	10.2	1.7	506.4
1956	377.6	38.0	56.6	2.2	11.5	108.3			3.2	3.2	51.5	85.7	626.3
1957	399.6	33.6	50.0	1.7	10.5	95.8			0.2	0.2	84.1	184.7	764.3
1958	469.4	33.0	52.8	2.4	9.7	97.8			0.2	0.2	98.4	150.1	815.9
1959	536.6	33.5	58.8	3.2	7.2	102.7			0.2	0.2	116.6	133.3	889.4
1960	577.3	33.5	60.6	3.6	8.3	105.9			0.3	0.3	112.6	133.0	929.1
1961	493.3	35.1	69.0	3.9	12.2	120.1			0.4	0.4	129.1	132.9	875.9
1962	609.8	36.5	77.4	4.4	12.1	130.5			0.5	0.5	190.5	142.4	1073.8
1963	712.9	43.2	83.8	7.8	4.7	139.5			0.2	0.2	307.1	144.0	1303.7
1964	764.1	34.1	81.7	8.6	5.2	129.7			0.1	0.1	284.5	149.3	1327.7
1965	754.2	35.4	73.8	8.4	3.0	120.6			0.1	0.1	250.9	158.8	1284.7
1966	684.6	39.1	66.0	8.7	0.9	114.8			0.4	0.4	277.5	160.7	1238.0
1967	789.3	38.9	74.5	8.1	1.5	123.0			1.0	1.0	318.1	181.3	1412.7
1968	931.8	40.9	78.5	9.9	1.2	130.5			0.0	0.0	341.7	200.4	1605.3

CTN BROAD DIVISIONS AND CATEGORIES

I. 1. INDUSTRIAL MACHINERY AND EQUIPMENT (INCLUDING SPARE PARTS)

II. FUELS, RAW MATERIALS (OTHER THAN FOR FOOD), OTHER MATERIALS

2. FUELS, MINERAL RAW MATERIALS, METALS
3. CHEMICALS, FERTILIZERS, RUBBER
4. BUILDING MATERIALS AND CONSTRUCTION PARTS
5. RAW MATERIALS OF VEGETABLE AND ANIMAL ORIGIN (NOT FOOD)

III. FOODSTUFFS AND RAW MATERIAL FOR FOODSTUFFS

6. LIVE ANIMALS (NOT FOR SLAUGHTER)
7. RAW MATERIAL FOR THE PRODUCTION OF FOODSTUFFS
8. FOODSTUFFS

IV. 9. INDUSTRIAL CONSUMER GOODS (OTHER THAN FOOD)

* CONVERTED FROM NATIONAL DEVISA UNITS THROUGH OFFICIAL EXCHANGE RATES. NOTE THE LIMITATIONS DISCUSSED IN THE EXPLANATORY TEXT.

TABLE III.CTN.M.U-H
USSR IMPORTS FROM HUNGARY, 1946-68
(MILLIONS OF CURRENT DOLLARS,* F.O.B.)

YEAR	BROAD DIV I 1	BROAD DIV II (2-5)					6	7	8	BROAD DIV III (6-8)	BROAD DIV IV 9	NOT SPECIFIED	TOTAL IMPORTS
		2	3	4	5	(2-5)							
1946	0.0	1.8				1.8			0.2	0.2	4.8	3.7	10.6
1947	0.6	3.7				3.7			0.2	0.2	3.0	9.8	17.2
1948	8.8	2.9				2.9		1.7	0.4	2.1	5.6	9.3	28.6
1949	23.7	3.4				3.4		4.6	1.2	5.8	13.0	21.1	66.9
1950	37.2	4.2				4.2		3.6	2.0	5.6	12.8	23.5	83.2
1951	35.7	5.0				5.0		2.6	2.0	4.5	25.6	43.4	114.1
1952	51.9	4.7				4.7		7.5	2.2	9.6	25.7	48.6	140.6
1953	86.7	5.0				5.0		5.2	5.2	10.4	26.8	43.5	172.3
1954	91.5	3.7				3.7		2.3	5.1	7.4	23.4	40.5	166.7
1955	89.0	15.5			2.0	17.5		3.5	12.9	16.4	20.4	3.2	146.4
1956	71.0	14.3		0.8	1.2	16.3		4.5	7.3	11.8	20.8	0.9	120.8
1957	77.2	4.8			3.5	8.3		0.2	6.8	7.0	11.2	3.1	106.8
1958	93.3	7.6		0.5	4.0	12.1		3.9	9.4	13.3	35.7	7.5	161.9
1959	116.1	5.9	0.9		4.5	11.3		3.5	9.6	13.1	54.7	11.4	206.6
1960	144.3	6.5	5.4		5.3	17.2		2.6	10.6	13.2	58.9	14.6	248.2
1961	179.0	6.5	7.4		4.7	18.6		2.0	21.1	23.1	88.3	17.8	326.8
1962	206.7	6.0	6.8		4.1	16.9		1.1	29.0	30.1	111.2	23.9	388.8
1963	230.2	5.3	8.4		4.4	18.1		0.8	34.0	34.8	111.5	28.5	423.1
1964	244.7	5.1	12.6		6.5	24.1		0.3	47.2	47.5	118.7	46.5	481.6
1965	254.6	7.9	8.4		6.1	22.4		2.8	50.3	53.1	132.4	52.8	515.3
1966	244.2	8.9	7.3		6.6	22.8		0.4	57.8	58.3	150.0	36.7	511.9
1967	263.7	16.1	8.8		6.8	31.8		0.4	79.7	80.1	179.7	41.7	597.1
1968	308.0	20.6	9.3		6.6	36.5		0.5	83.1	83.6	194.2	46.6	669.0

CTN BROAD DIVISIONS AND CATEGORIES

I.   1. INDUSTRIAL MACHINERY AND EQUIPMENT (INCLUDING SPARE PARTS)

II. FUELS, RAW MATERIALS (OTHER THAN FOR FOOD), OTHER MATERIALS

     2. FUELS, MINERAL RAW MATERIALS, METALS
     3. CHEMICALS, FERTILIZERS, RUBBER
     4. BUILDING MATERIALS AND CONSTRUCTION PARTS
     5. RAW MATERIALS OF VEGETABLE AND ANIMAL ORIGIN (NOT FOOD)

III. FOODSTUFFS AND RAW MATERIAL FOR FOODSTUFFS

     6. LIVE ANIMALS (NOT FOR SLAUGHTER)
     7. RAW MATERIAL FOR THE PRODUCTION OF FOODSTUFFS
     8. FOODSTUFFS

IV. 9. INDUSTRIAL CONSUMER GOODS (OTHER THAN FOOD)

* CONVERTED FROM NATIONAL DEVISA UNITS THROUGH OFFICIAL EXCHANGE
  RATES. NOTE THE LIMITATIONS DISCUSSED IN THE EXPLANATORY TEXT.

TABLE III-CTN.M.U-P
USSR IMPORTS FROM POLAND, 1946-68
(MILLIONS OF CURRENT DOLLARS,* F.O.B.)

YEAR	BROAD DIV I 1	2	3	4	5	BROAD DIV II (2-5)	6	7	8	BROAD DIV III (6-8)	BROAD DIV IV 9	NOT SPECIFIED	TOTAL IMPORTS
1946	—	83.9				83.9			2.4	2.4	6.9	15.2	108.4
1947	—	81.9				81.9			17.1	17.1	16.9	21.2	137.1
1948	—	93.0				93.0			17.1	17.1	38.5	25.0	173.7
1949	4.7	109.0				109.0			13.0	13.0	35.1	24.6	186.4
1950	36.8	95.0				95.0			21.7	21.7	29.9	26.5	210.0
1951	40.6	119.3				119.3			25.5	25.5	39.3	39.5	264.1
1952	60.4	160.9				160.9			29.3	29.3	46.6	53.7	350.9
1953	77.0	166.3				166.3			30.6	30.6	50.7	42.7	367.3
1954	73.3	155.4				155.4			22.6	22.6	39.4	47.4	338.0
1955	74.3	152.6	3.7	0.7	3.6	160.6			26.7	26.7	21.7	3.5	286.7
1956	72.5	155.0	6.0	3.4	3.0	167.5			6.7	6.7	32.8	3.8	283.3
1957	91.4	124.5	4.2	0.2	2.5	131.4			2.6	2.6	17.5	13.0	255.9
1958	86.4	104.6	4.7	1.9	2.2	113.4		3.1	14.2	17.3	20.7	27.4	265.1
1959	102.7	117.4	7.1	1.7	2.5	128.7			13.7	13.7	31.2	40.3	316.6
1960	121.0	128.7	6.3	1.2	3.2	139.4			15.6	15.6	65.5	45.2	386.7
1961	137.8	132.3	6.5	2.4	4.2	145.4		15.8	31.1	46.9	80.2	66.6	476.9
1962	194.4	130.9	9.3	2.7	4.9	147.8		8.1	32.7	40.8	103.0	78.2	564.2
1963	222.4	135.4	16.2	3.5	4.4	159.5		0.4	3.6	4.0	113.5	115.2	614.5
1964	262.4	138.3	25.3	1.2	6.0	170.7		0.8	18.7	19.6	116.8	148.4	717.9
1965	278.6	164.6	22.1	1.1	4.8	192.6		1.4	34.6	36.0	117.2	156.3	780.7
1966	259.2	141.0	21.9	1.0	4.8	168.8		1.1	9.9	11.0	154.9	139.3	733.2
1967	329.7	156.4	25.3	0.1	3.6	185.4		1.8	14.5	16.3	220.0	151.0	902.4
1968	393.1	155.2	34.3		3.4	192.8		1.4	12.4	13.8	242.9	189.0	1031.5

CTN BROAD DIVISIONS AND CATEGORIES

I. 1. INDUSTRIAL MACHINERY AND EQUIPMENT (INCLUDING SPARE PARTS)

II.   FUELS, RAW MATERIALS (OTHER THAN FOR FOOD), OTHER MATERIALS

    2. FUELS, MINERAL RAW MATERIALS, METALS
    3. CHEMICALS, FERTILIZERS, RUBBER
    4. BUILDING MATERIALS AND CONSTRUCTION PARTS
    5. RAW MATERIALS OF VEGETABLE AND ANIMAL ORIGIN (NOT FOOD)

III.   FOODSTUFFS AND RAW MATERIAL FOR FOODSTUFFS

    6. LIVE ANIMALS (NOT FOR SLAUGHTER)
    7. RAW MATERIAL FOR THE PRODUCTION OF FOODSTUFFS
    8. FOODSTUFFS

IV. 9. INDUSTRIAL CONSUMER GOODS (OTHER THAN FOOD)

* CONVERTED FROM NATIONAL DEVISA UNITS THROUGH OFFICIAL EXCHANGE

TABLE III.CTN.M.U-R
USSR IMPORTS FROM RUMANIA, 1946-68
(MILLIONS OF CURRENT DOLLARS,* F.O.B.)

YEAR	BROAD DIV I 1	2	3	4	5	BROAD DIV II (2-5)	6	7	8	BROAD DIV III (6-8)	BROAD DIV IV 9	NOT SPECIFIED	TOTAL IMPORTS
1946	-	7.1		0.8	1.9	9.8						12.7	22.4
1947	0.1	6.4		1.5	1.2	9.2		3.9		3.9		14.2	27.3
1948	0.0	19.4		2.5	3.1	25.0		43.7		43.7		21.9	91.6
1949	6.8	46.3		4.8	6.2	57.3		1.1		1.1	0.4	34.0	99.6
1950	8.3	58.3		4.8	9.2	72.4		6.1		6.1	0.4	52.0	139.2
1951	8.4	65.9		3.5	12.2	81.6		2.2		4.0	1.9	43.3	139.2
1952	10.6	88.9		6.9	15.5	111.4		10.5	1.8	12.8	4.6	56.6	196.0
1953	15.9	111.2		7.8	22.8	141.8		0.0	2.2	2.3	5.7	63.9	229.7
1954	19.1	95.0		4.6	19.9	119.5		4.8	2.2	7.0	4.7	44.4	194.7
1955	14.5	95.3	2.0	6.3	31.1	134.7		21.5	1.7	23.1	2.8	34.7	209.8
1956	14.8	94.2	2.5	7.8	35.4	139.9		6.1	7.9	14.0	7.0	59.6	235.3
1957	11.9	77.7	2.8	8.1	34.5	123.1		6.9	6.8	13.7	6.6	34.7	190.0
1958	10.0	103.3	3.8	11.0	32.8	150.9		21.8	7.1	28.9	13.2	30.5	233.6
1959	20.5	131.8	5.1	9.1	34.5	180.6		4.4	7.7	12.1	19.8	16.5	249.4
1960	23.7	135.2	4.9	9.6	39.9	189.5		11.9	14.7	26.5	26.9	13.4	280.0
1961	44.3	140.1	9.1	9.6	45.5	204.3		19.9	29.4	49.3	33.4	9.5	340.8
1962	58.6	141.3	11.3	10.2	42.7	205.5		5.1	26.4	31.5	38.3	14.9	348.8
1963	63.7	137.7	16.1	11.6	45.0	210.4		41.5	33.1	74.6	50.8	10.8	410.2
1964	78.7	144.4	23.7	5.8	45.9	219.8		7.1	36.1	43.2	63.5	16.0	421.1
1965	80.7	140.3	22.5	2.6	43.1	208.4		15.8	37.4	53.2	88.0	10.6	441.0
1966	56.5	116.2	20.0	3.5	42.1	181.7		27.9	39.5	67.4	95.6	4.2	405.4
1967	78.2	100.2	24.7	5.7	49.0	179.6		16.7	37.9	54.7	106.2	5.6	424.3
1968	104.7	91.7	24.5	4.9	46.6	167.7		9.3	33.3	42.6	136.7	4.6	456.4

CTN BROAD DIVISIONS AND CATEGORIES

I. 1. INDUSTRIAL MACHINERY AND EQUIPMENT (INCLUDING SPARE PARTS)

II. FUELS, RAW MATERIALS (OTHER THAN FOOD), OTHER MATERIALS

2. FUELS, MINERAL RAW MATERIALS, METALS
3. CHEMICALS, FERTILIZERS, RUBBER
4. BUILDING MATERIALS AND CONSTRUCTION PARTS
5. RAW MATERIALS OF VEGETABLE AND ANIMAL ORIGIN (NOT FOOD)

III. FOODSTUFFS AND RAW MATERIAL FOR FOODSTUFFS

6. LIVE ANIMALS (NOT FOR SLAUGHTER)
7. RAW MATERIAL FOR THE PRODUCTION OF FOODSTUFFS
8. FOODSTUFFS

IV. 9. INDUSTRIAL CONSUMER GOODS (OTHER THAN FOOD)

* CONVERTED FROM NATIONAL DEVISA UNITS THROUGH OFFICIAL EXCHANGE RATES. NOTE THE LIMITATIONS DISCUSSED IN THE EXPLANATORY TEXT.

TABLE III.CTN.M.U-Y
USSR IMPORTS FROM YUGOSLAVIA, 1946-68
(MILLIONS OF CURRENT DOLLARS,* F.O.B.)

YEAR	BROAD DIV I 1	2	3	4	5	BROAD DIV II (2-5)	6	7	8	BROAD DIV III (6-8)	BROAD DIV IV 9	NOT SPECIFIED	TOTAL IMPORTS
1946	—	3.6	0.1		4.6	8.3			0.1	0.1	0.0	16.3	24.8
1947	—	5.8	0.2		6.6	12.6			2.7	2.7	0.0	14.3	29.6
1948	—	5.5	0.8		15.2	21.5			1.7	1.7	0.0	23.1	46.3
1949	—	2.7	0.4		2.3	5.4			0.4	0.4		4.9	10.7
1950	—												—
1951	—												—
1952	—												—
1953	—												—
1954	—	0.2	0.0		0.2	0.3			0.5	0.5	0.0	0.3	1.1
1955	—	0.2	0.9	0.4	6.7	8.2		0.4	6.7	7.1	1.7	0.5	17.4
1956	0.9	16.1	2.2	1.8	7.9	28.1		2.8	8.0	10.8	3.8	6.1	49.7
1957	2.7	13.2	3.2	3.2	5.3	24.8		1.9	8.7	10.5	9.2	9.6	56.9
1958	4.3	20.7	2.8	1.4	2.6	27.4		4.1	7.6	11.7	6.7	0.8	50.9
1959	5.1	24.0	3.0	1.8	2.9	31.7		0.5	7.7	8.2	7.6	0.6	53.1
1960	7.7	25.0	3.2		3.0	31.2		2.0	2.3	4.3	6.9	3.0	53.1
1961	13.8	21.9	3.2		2.4	27.5		1.4	1.1	2.5	7.5	3.2	54.6
1962	10.3	20.0	3.0		3.2	26.2		0.5	0.0	1.5	7.1	1.1	46.1
1963	10.9	27.7	7.6		4.5	39.8		1.5	9.2	10.7	24.3	1.3	87.0
1964	13.0	33.9	10.0		12.6	56.4		2.3	13.4	15.7	32.9	2.8	120.9
1965	68.2	37.8	11.6		12.1	61.5		2.5	19.7	22.2	31.9	4.8	188.7
1966	77.0	33.9	12.7		11.2	57.7		1.2	9.8	11.0	41.4	5.7	192.8
1967	60.0	40.7	18.0		10.2	68.9			14.1	14.1	84.0	5.6	232.6
1968	64.1	40.4	11.7		11.6	63.7			8.5	8.5	77.7	3.1	217.1

CTN BROAD DIVISIONS AND CATEGORIES

I. 1. INDUSTRIAL MACHINERY AND EQUIPMENT (INCLUDING SPARE PARTS)

II. FUELS, RAW MATERIALS (OTHER THAN FOR FOOD), OTHER MATERIALS
  2. FUELS, MINERAL RAW MATERIALS, METALS
  3. CHEMICALS, FERTILIZERS, RUBBER
  4. BUILDING MATERIALS AND CONSTRUCTION PARTS
  5. RAW MATERIALS OF VEGETABLE AND ANIMAL ORIGIN (NOT FOOD)

III. FOODSTUFFS AND RAW MATERIAL FOR FOODSTUFFS
  6. LIVE ANIMALS (NOT FOR SLAUGHTER)
  7. RAW MATERIAL FOR THE PRODUCTION OF FOODSTUFFS
  8. FOODSTUFFS

IV. 9. INDUSTRIAL CONSUMER GOODS (OTHER THAN FOOD)

* CONVERTED FROM NATIONAL DEVISA UNITS THROUGH OFFICIAL EXCHANGE RATES. NOTE THE LIMITATIONS DISCUSSED IN THE EXPLANATORY TEXT.

TABLE III.CTN.M.U-CEMA
USSR IMPORTS FROM EUROPEAN CEMA (EXCLUDING ALBANIA), 1946-68
(MILLIONS OF CURRENT DOLLARS,* F.O.B.)

YEAR	BROAD DIV I 1	BROAD DIV II (2-5)	2	3	4	5	6	7	8	BROAD DIV III (6-8)	BROAD DIV IV 9	NOT SPECIFIED	TOTAL IMPORTS
1946	7.6	144.2	115.2		0.8	28.2		3.0	5.4	8.3	18.0	97.6	275.7
1947	9.8	151.8	114.4		1.5	35.9		4.4	27.6	31.9	25.7	61.4	280.7
1948	37.1	225.7	162.3	0.5	2.5	60.5		46.8	26.6	73.4	77.1	143.0	556.3
1949	93.1	266.0	219.5	2.1	4.8	39.6		12.5	23.2	35.7	95.3	269.2	759.4
1950	202.9	295.8	251.4	6.3	4.8	33.3		21.3	39.7	60.9	73.6	227.7	861.0
1951	309.3	393.6	338.4	11.7	3.5	40.0		11.8	51.8	63.6	101.1	304.8	1172.4
1952	429.0	510.6	438.4	13.0	6.9	52.3		29.4	56.5	85.8	112.0	323.5	1461.0
1953	646.6	567.1	496.3	10.2	7.8	52.8		15.1	66.4	81.5	114.0	280.5	1689.6
1954	795.4	513.5	441.3	13.8	4.6	53.7		14.2	57.8	71.9	102.1	288.9	1771.8
1955	733.6	601.1	454.0	62.8	10.0	74.3		32.4	80.1	112.5	76.3	133.8	1657.3
1956	655.9	628.5	462.8	66.5	16.2	82.9		21.6	66.4	88.0	214.8	219.6	1806.9
1957	713.9	552.1	388.0	62.6	12.6	89.0		17.9	66.2	84.0	248.7	301.9	1900.6
1958	861.6	591.8	422.4	69.7	20.0	79.7		41.0	95.7	136.7	333.6	267.9	2191.6
1959	1040.0	629.4	423.3	83.9	20.9	101.3		23.9	118.2	142.2	434.7	258.4	2504.6
1960	1208.6	650.7	444.1	91.0	17.9	97.7		30.7	151.0	181.7	511.0	242.9	2795.0
1961	1245.2	692.5	457.3	108.0	20.3	107.0		50.9	214.4	265.4	583.6	257.3	3044.1
1962	1623.9	711.7	459.7	123.9	22.6	105.5		26.9	216.0	242.9	718.2	293.6	3590.3
1963	1858.5	770.1	482.7	145.6	28.9	112.9		59.5	221.9	281.4	886.2	350.6	4146.8
1964	2024.9	832.5	496.2	176.0	23.0	137.4		26.8	269.2	296.1	869.1	427.8	4450.4
1965	2113.7	817.1	517.0	161.4	22.4	116.3		35.5	347.0	382.5	881.5	477.8	4672.6
1966	1926.2	737.3	440.1	156.3	23.8	117.1		41.5	332.8	374.3	994.1	430.2	4462.1
1967	2184.8	777.1	436.1	179.2	28.9	132.9		33.6	399.6	433.2	1203.0	494.4	5092.5
1968	2508.9	807.7	445.6	196.7	31.5	133.8		27.6	421.7	449.3	1332.5	545.2	5643.6

CTN BROAD DIVISIONS AND CATEGORIES

I. 1. INDUSTRIAL MACHINERY AND EQUIPMENT (INCLUDING SPARE PARTS)

II. FUELS, RAW MATERIALS (OTHER THAN FOR FOOD), OTHER MATERIALS
2. FUELS, MINERAL RAW MATERIALS, METALS
3. CHEMICALS, FERTILIZERS, RUBBER
4. BUILDING MATERIALS AND CONSTRUCTION PARTS
5. RAW MATERIALS OF VEGETABLE AND ANIMAL ORIGIN (NOT FOOD)

III. FOODSTUFFS AND RAW MATERIAL FOR FOODSTUFFS
6. LIVE ANIMALS (NOT FOR SLAUGHTER)
7. RAW MATERIAL FOR THE PRODUCTION OF FOODSTUFFS
8. FOODSTUFFS

IV. 9. INDUSTRIAL CONSUMER GOODS (OTHER THAN FOOD)

* CONVERTED FROM NATIONAL DEVISA UNITS THROUGH OFFICIAL EXCHANGE RATES. NOTE THE LIMITATIONS DISCUSSED IN THE EXPLANATORY TEXT.

TABLE III.CTN.M.C-U
CZECHOSLOVAKIA'S IMPORTS FROM USSR, 1958-68
(MILLIONS OF CURRENT DOLLARS,* F.O.B.)

YEAR	BROAD DIV I 1	2	3	4	5	BROAD DIV II (2-5)	6	7	8	BROAD DIV III (6-8)	BROAD DIV IV 9	NOT SPECIFIED	TOTAL IMPORTS
1958	42.7	154.9	16.1		62.2	233.1		93.9	18.1	112.0	12.7	51.2	451.8
1959	52.1	186.4	18.2		65.8	270.3		137.0	45.3	182.4	11.2	82.0	598.0
1960	46.6	156.1	20.5	0.5	67.7	244.8		129.4	34.9	164.3	13.8	161.0	630.5
1961	74.7	179.3	23.1	1.6	75.2	279.3		90.2	33.2	123.4	10.7	168.0	656.0
1962	92.1	206.5	26.5	2.4	62.5	297.9		114.7	47.1	161.9	20.0	209.6	781.5
1963	101.8	235.2	26.2	1.4	65.7	328.5		106.8	55.6	162.5	15.1	234.8	842.7
1964	121.6	264.9	22.6	1.0	85.4	374.0		78.0	26.4	104.5	8.1	304.8	912.9
1965	116.4	294.9	21.0	2.8	85.4	404.1		77.1	43.8	120.8	7.4	306.0	954.8
1966	116.2	246.8	19.7	5.0	83.3	354.8		88.0	56.8	144.7	9.1	289.8	914.7
1967	107.0	386.0	20.3	1.9	82.3	490.4		116.5	53.9	170.4	11.2	186.3	965.4
1968	91.0	310.3	21.6	1.7	91.1	424.7		117.6	40.6	158.2	14.1	348.2	1036.2

CTN BROAD DIVISIONS AND CATEGORIES

I. 1. INDUSTRIAL MACHINERY AND EQUIPMENT (INCLUDING SPARE PARTS)

II. FUELS, RAW MATERIALS (OTHER THAN FOR FOOD), OTHER MATERIALS

2. FUELS, MINERAL RAW MATERIALS, METALS
3. CHEMICALS, FERTILIZERS, RUBBER
4. BUILDING MATERIALS AND CONSTRUCTION PARTS
5. RAW MATERIALS OF VEGETABLE AND ANIMAL ORIGIN (NOT FOOD)

III. FOODSTUFFS AND RAW MATERIAL FOR FOODSTUFFS

6. LIVE ANIMALS (NOT FOR SLAUGHTER)
7. RAW MATERIAL FOR THE PRODUCTION OF FOODSTUFFS
8. FOODSTUFFS

IV. 9. INDUSTRIAL CONSUMER GOODS (OTHER THAN FOOD)

* CONVERTED FROM NATIONAL DEVISA UNITS THROUGH OFFICIAL EXCHANGE RATES. NOTE THE LIMITATIONS DISCUSSED IN THE EXPLANATORY TEXT.

TABLE III.CTN.M.C-B
CZECHOSLOVAKIA'S IMPORTS FROM BULGARIA, 1958-68
(MILLIONS OF CURRENT DOLLARS,* F.O.B.)

YEAR	BROAD DIV I 1	2	3	4	5	BROAD DIV II (2-5)	6	7	8	BROAD DIV III (6-8)	BROAD DIV IV 9	NOT SPECIFIED	TOTAL IMPORTS
1958	5.4	7.0	0.3	0.5	6.7	14.1		0.8	15.4	16.2	1.2	4.4	41.4
1959	11.3	6.9	0.6	0.8	8.7	16.3		0.8	12.3	13.2	0.5	3.0	44.3
1960	11.2	6.8	0.5	0.5	15.4	23.1		1.2	17.1	18.4	0.7	3.7	57.1
1961	17.5	5.2	1.1	0.8	12.7	19.8		1.1	23.2	24.3	1.4	2.7	65.7
1962	19.3	6.6	1.1	0.8	7.8	16.3		0.7	26.2	26.9	1.2	1.3	65.0
1963	18.6	7.2	1.5	1.1	11.5	21.2		1.1	23.4	24.5	0.4	4.6	69.3
1964	20.8	8.0	2.0	1.4	14.1	25.5		0.6	19.2	19.9	1.2	5.2	72.6
1965	31.8	7.4	0.0	1.5	17.0	26.8		0.4	20.3	20.7	3.3	6.5	89.2
1966	25.2	2.7	1.0	2.2	8.9	14.8		0.1	12.4	12.5	4.4	7.0	63.9
1967	25.3	9.7	2.1	0.8	17.2	29.7		0.0	16.6	16.6	2.2	4.9	78.8
1968	20.1	7.5	2.1	0.9	32.2	42.6		0.0	14.1	14.1	2.0	11.5	90.3

CTN BROAD DIVISIONS AND CATEGORIES

I. 1. INDUSTRIAL MACHINERY AND EQUIPMENT (INCLUDING SPARE PARTS)

II. FUELS, RAW MATERIALS (OTHER THAN FOR FOOD), OTHER MATERIALS

2. FUELS, MINERAL RAW MATERIALS, METALS
3. CHEMICALS, FERTILIZERS, RUBBER
4. BUILDING MATERIALS AND CONSTRUCTION PARTS
5. RAW MATERIALS OF VEGETABLE AND ANIMAL ORIGIN (NOT FOOD)

III. FOODSTUFFS AND RAW MATERIAL FOR FOODSTUFFS

6. LIVE ANIMALS (NOT FOR SLAUGHTER)
7. RAW MATERIAL FOR THE PRODUCTION OF FOODSTUFFS
8. FOODSTUFFS

IV. 9. INDUSTRIAL CONSUMER GOODS (OTHER THAN FOOD)

* CONVERTED FROM NATIONAL DEVISA UNITS THROUGH OFFICIAL EXCHANGE
  RATES. NOTE THE LIMITATIONS DISCUSSED IN THE EXPLANATORY TEXT.

TABLE III.CTN.M.C-G
CZECHOSLOVAKIA'S IMPORTS FROM EAST GERMANY, 1958-68
(MILLIONS OF CURRENT DOLLARS,* F.O.B.)

YEAR	BROAD DIV I 1	2	3	4	5	BROAD DIV II (2-5)	6	7	8	BROAD DIV III (6-8)	BROAD DIV IV 9	NOT SPECIFIED	TOTAL IMPORTS
1958	71.0	9.0	35.7	2.3	5.0	51.1		2.5	4.7	7.3	11.0	21.7	162.1
1959	82.5	14.7	37.3	2.5	7.1	61.7			0.3	0.3	11.6	18.9	175.0
1960	85.4	17.5	42.8	3.2	3.7	67.2			4.7	4.7	18.9	22.0	198.2
1961	92.1	20.0	51.0	3.0	4.1	78.3			3.1	3.1	31.5	25.1	230.0
1962	108.8	19.5	46.2	2.8	0.0	69.6			2.7	2.7	27.2	20.1	228.4
1963	112.1	18.5	45.4	2.5	1.9	68.2		2.5	3.6	6.2	26.2	19.9	232.7
1964	142.9	18.9	38.5	2.6	2.2	62.2			4.1	4.1	24.6	20.3	254.0
1965	169.8	16.8	44.9	3.6	1.5	66.8			2.8	2.8	31.3	17.2	287.9
1966	186.5	19.4	46.0	3.4	2.0	70.9			4.1	4.1	29.0	27.7	318.2
1967	169.6	18.4	49.0	4.6	1.3	73.3			4.6	4.6	38.3	34.3	320.2
1968	193.5	20.1	57.8	7.0	2.2	87.1			5.2	5.2	57.3	56.5	399.6

CTN BROAD DIVISIONS AND CATEGORIES

I. 1. INDUSTRIAL MACHINERY AND EQUIPMENT (INCLUDING SPARE PARTS)

II. FUELS, RAW MATERIALS (OTHER THAN FOR FOOD), OTHER MATERIALS

2. FUELS, MINERAL RAW MATERIALS, METALS
3. CHEMICALS, FERTILIZERS, RUBBER
4. BUILDING MATERIALS AND CONSTRUCTION PARTS
5. RAW MATERIALS OF VEGETABLE AND ANIMAL ORIGIN (NOT FOOD)

III. FOODSTUFFS AND RAW MATERIAL FOR FOODSTUFFS

6. LIVE ANIMALS (NOT FOR SLAUGHTER)
7. RAW MATERIAL FOR THE PRODUCTION OF FOODSTUFFS
8. FOODSTUFFS

IV. 9. INDUSTRIAL CONSUMER GOODS (OTHER THAN FOOD)

* CONVERTED FROM NATIONAL DEVISA UNITS THROUGH OFFICIAL EXCHANGE RATES. NOTE THE LIMITATIONS DISCUSSED IN THE EXPLANATORY TEXT.

TABLE III.CTN.M.C-H
CZECHOSLOVAKIA'S IMPORTS FROM HUNGARY, 1958-68
(MILLIONS OF CURRENT DOLLARS,* F.O.B.)

YEAR	BROAD DIV I 1	2	3	4	5	BROAD DIV II (2-5)	6	7	8	BROAD DIV III (6-8)	BROAD DIV IV 9	NOT SPECIFIED	TOTAL IMPORTS
1958	18.0	31.3	0.8	3.0	2.9	38.0		4.0	23.2	27.1	3.7	3.6	90.4
1959	17.2	27.1	1.0	2.2	2.9	33.2		4.3	24.2	28.5	3.8	4.4	87.0
1960	23.0	16.4	3.1	0.7	3.2	23.4		4.4	24.3	28.6	4.1	14.8	93.9
1961	45.2	32.7	2.8	1.5	4.0	40.9		5.0	25.6	30.6	11.9	7.1	135.8
1962	40.3	45.9	1.8	1.0	3.5	52.2		1.3	27.6	28.8	10.1	8.0	139.5
1963	32.7	44.0	2.4	0.8	4.3	51.4		0.0	32.1	33.1	10.1	3.7	131.1
1964	27.3	43.6	5.1	1.4	3.5	53.5		1.3	34.6	35.9	18.9	11.3	146.8
1965	32.6	40.6	7.2	3.8	3.1	54.7		3.7	35.7	39.3	28.6	16.2	171.4
1966	44.0	28.4	3.1	4.6	3.8	39.8		2.4	37.6	40.1	29.1	18.9	171.8
1967	42.5	20.4	1.8	2.1	2.5	26.7		0.9	41.2	42.1	21.7	17.8	150.8
1968	48.0	19.9	2.6	4.2	4.9	31.5		1.2	45.0	46.2	31.9	23.5	181.3

CTN BROAD DIVISIONS AND CATEGORIES

I. 1. INDUSTRIAL MACHINERY AND EQUIPMENT (INCLUDING SPARE PARTS)

II. FUELS, RAW MATERIALS (OTHER THAN FOR FOOD), OTHER MATERIALS

2. FUELS, MINERAL RAW MATERIALS, METALS
3. CHEMICALS, FERTILIZERS, RUBBER
4. BUILDING MATERIALS AND CONSTRUCTION PARTS
5. RAW MATERIALS OF VEGETABLE AND ANIMAL ORIGIN (NOT FOOD)

III. FOODSTUFFS AND RAW MATERIAL FOR FOODSTUFFS

6. LIVE ANIMALS (NOT FOR SLAUGHTER)
7. RAW MATERIAL FOR THE PRODUCTION OF FOODSTUFFS
8. FOODSTUFFS

IV. 9. INDUSTRIAL CONSUMER GOODS (OTHER THAN FOOD)

* CONVERTED FROM NATIONAL DEVISA UNITS THROUGH OFFICIAL EXCHANGE
RATES. NOTE THE LIMITATIONS DISCUSSED IN THE EXPLANATORY TEXT.

TABLE III.CTN.M.C-P
CZECHOSLOVAKIA'S IMPORTS FROM POLAND, 1958-68
(MILLIONS OF CURRENT DOLLARS,* F.O.B.)

YEAR	BROAD DIV I 1	2	3	4	5	BROAD DIV II (2-5)	6	7	8	BROAD DIV III (6-8)	BROAD DIV IV 9	NOT SPECIFIED	TOTAL IMPORTS
1958	11.8	41.8	1.5	2.0	0.5	45.7		4.7	2.0	6.7	0.3	7.0	71.5
1959	13.9	48.2	2.0	1.7	0.6	52.5		1.4	3.2	4.6	0.3	10.7	82.0
1960	27.6	58.1	2.5	1.1		61.7		0.8	3.5	4.3	2.1	14.8	110.6
1961	35.9	63.7	4.8	1.0		69.5		4.2	2.3	6.5	3.4	25.9	141.1
1962	46.3	62.3	5.9	2.6	0.8	71.6		0.9	3.7	4.6	3.4	19.2	145.0
1963	40.4	66.8	5.1	3.6	0.7	76.2		0.5	7.5	8.0	4.7	16.8	146.1
1964	52.5	79.9	5.2	3.0	0.5	88.5		1.3	17.9	19.2	5.8	27.4	193.3
1965	61.4	73.0	8.1	3.6	0.2	84.9		1.7	9.9	11.6	6.9	43.8	208.6
1966	57.5	57.6	5.3	1.9	2.1	66.9		0.8	9.9	10.7	4.9	39.8	179.7
1967	60.1	56.4	4.7	2.8	0.4	64.2		0.5	11.3	11.9	8.8	54.2	199.2
1968	75.5	65.6	5.2	4.4	0.2	75.5		0.8	15.6	16.5	18.5	62.0	247.9

CTN BROAD DIVISIONS AND CATEGORIES

I. 1. INDUSTRIAL MACHINERY AND EQUIPMENT (INCLUDING SPARE PARTS)

II. FUELS, RAW MATERIALS (OTHER THAN FOR FOOD), OTHER MATERIALS

2. FUELS, MINERAL RAW MATERIALS, METALS
3. CHEMICALS, FERTILIZERS, RUBBER
4. BUILDING MATERIALS AND CONSTRUCTION PARTS
5. RAW MATERIALS OF VEGETABLE AND ANIMAL ORIGIN (NOT FOOD)

III. FOODSTUFFS AND RAW MATERIAL FOR FOODSTUFFS

6. LIVE ANIMALS (NOT FOR SLAUGHTER)
7. RAW MATERIAL FOR THE PRODUCTION OF FOODSTUFFS
8. FOODSTUFFS

IV. 9. INDUSTRIAL CONSUMER GOODS (OTHER THAN FOOD)

* CONVERTED FROM NATIONAL DEVISA UNITS THROUGH OFFICIAL EXCHANGE RATES. NOTE THE LIMITATIONS DISCUSSED IN THE EXPLANATORY TEXT.

TABLE III.CTN.M.C-R
CZECHOSLOVAKIA'S IMPORTS FROM RUMANIA, 1958-68
(MILLIONS OF CURRENT DOLLARS,* F.O.B.)

YEAR	BROAD DIV I 1	2	3	4	5	BROAD DIV II (2-5)	6	7	8	BROAD DIV III (6-8)	BROAD DIV IV 9	NOT SPECIFIED	TOTAL IMPORTS
1958	1.7	5.3	0.8	1.5	1.7	9.3		0.9	9.1	10.0		1.3	22.4
1959	3.4	18.8	1.4	1.1	2.2	23.5		1.4	12.5	13.9		1.8	42.5
1960	10.1	16.0	1.4	1.7	1.8	20.9		8.9	17.5	26.4	0.0	5.9	64.3
1961	16.7	13.3	3.0	1.8	2.4	20.6		2.1	10.4	12.6	1.2	3.1	54.0
1962	15.7	9.0	4.0	2.8	3.4	19.2		5.9	14.7	20.6	1.2	3.5	60.1
1963	10.6	11.6	5.0	2.6	2.8	22.0		3.8	10.8	14.7	1.2	4.5	52.9
1964	17.3	10.6	8.5	2.5	4.3	25.8		9.5	16.0	25.5	1.7	4.2	74.6
1965	19.1	17.6	8.6	10.6	5.3	42.1		1.7	19.1	20.8	6.2	6.1	94.3
1966	27.1	18.3	3.8	11.0	4.1	37.2		4.0	14.3	18.4	2.4	7.2	92.2
1967	14.0	30.0	3.7	7.1	5.2	46.0		3.0	14.5	17.5	0.4	8.6	86.5
1968	13.0	30.6	6.4	11.1	6.9	55.0		4.1	16.8	20.9	1.4	19.0	109.3

CTN BROAD DIVISIONS AND CATEGORIES

I. 1. INDUSTRIAL MACHINERY AND EQUIPMENT (INCLUDING SPARE PARTS)

II. FUELS, RAW MATERIALS (OTHER THAN FOR FOOD), OTHER MATERIALS

2. FUELS, MINERAL RAW MATERIALS, METALS
3. CHEMICALS, FERTILIZERS, RUBBER
4. BUILDING MATERIALS AND CONSTRUCTION PARTS
5. RAW MATERIALS OF VEGETABLE AND ANIMAL ORIGIN (NOT FOOD)

III. FOODSTUFFS AND RAW MATERIAL FOR FOODSTUFFS

6. LIVE ANIMALS (NOT FOR SLAUGHTER)
7. RAW MATERIAL FOR THE PRODUCTION OF FOODSTUFFS
8. FOODSTUFFS

IV. 9. INDUSTRIAL CONSUMER GOODS (OTHER THAN FOOD)

* CONVERTED FROM NATIONAL DEVISA UNITS THROUGH OFFICIAL EXCHANGE RATES. NOTE THE LIMITATIONS DISCUSSED IN THE EXPLANATORY TEXT.

CZECHOSLOVAKIA'S IMPORTS FROM YUGOSLAVIA, 1958-66
TABLE III.CTN.M.C-Y
(MILLIONS OF CURRENT DOLLARS,* F.O.B.)

YEAR	BROAD DIV I 1	2	3	4	5	BROAD DIV II (2-5)	6	7	8	BROAD DIV III (6-8)	BROAD DIV IV 9	NOT SPECIFIED	TOTAL IMPORTS
1958		2.6	0.6		3.3	6.5		1.2	3.0	4.1		4.4	15.0
1959		2.6	0.9		3.0	6.5		0.9	2.3	3.2		1.0	10.7
1960	0.2	5.1	1.5	0.5	3.6	10.7		1.6	9.1	10.7	0.5	2.7	24.7
1961	0.2	5.6	1.1	0.3	1.5	8.5			6.5	6.5	0.3	1.3	16.8
1962	0.4	6.7	0.9		3.4	11.1		0.2	8.7	8.8	0.3	0.6	21.3
1963	0.6	5.6	0.5	0.3	6.0	12.3		0.2	8.4	8.6	0.9	0.3	22.6
1964	2.8	5.4	0.0	0.8	9.3	16.5		1.3	14.0	15.4	8.2	1.5	44.3
1965	18.0	9.0	1.2	1.6	8.0	19.8		1.4	12.7	14.0	14.0	5.9	71.8
1966	28.2	11.1	0.6	0.7	4.3	16.7		0.4	10.9	11.2	11.0	6.6	73.8

CTN BROAD DIVISIONS AND CATEGORIES

I. 1. INDUSTRIAL MACHINERY AND EQUIPMENT (INCLUDING SPARE PARTS)

II.   FUELS, RAW MATERIALS (OTHER THAN FOR FOOD), OTHER MATERIALS

2: FUELS, MINERAL RAW MATERIALS, METALS
3: CHEMICALS, FERTILIZERS, RUBBER
4: BUILDING MATERIALS AND CONSTRUCTION PARTS
5: RAW MATERIALS OF VEGETABLE AND ANIMAL ORIGIN (NOT FOOD)

III.   FOODSTUFFS AND RAW MATERIAL FOR FOODSTUFFS

6. LIVE ANIMALS (NOT FOR SLAUGHTER)
7. RAW MATERIAL FOR THE PRODUCTION OF FOODSTUFFS
8. FOODSTUFFS

IV. 9. INDUSTRIAL CONSUMER GOODS (OTHER THAN FOOD)

* CONVERTED FROM NATIONAL DEVISA UNITS THROUGH OFFICIAL EXCHANGE RATES. NOTE THE LIMITATIONS DISCUSSED IN THE EXPLANATORY TEXT.

TABLE III.CTN.M.C-CEMA
CZECHOSLOVAKIA'S IMPORTS FROM EUROPEAN CEMA (EXCLUDING ALBANIA), 1958-68
(MILLIONS OF CURRENT DOLLARS,* F.O.B.)

YEAR	BROAD DIV I 1	2	3	4	5	BROAD DIV II (2-5)	6	7	8	BROAD DIV III (6-8)	BROAD DIV IV 9	NOT SPECIFIED	TOTAL IMPORTS
1958	150.7	248.3	55.2	8.7	79.1	391.3		106.9	72.5	179.4	29.0	89.3	839.7
1959	180.4	302.1	60.5	7.5	87.3	457.4		145.0	97.8	242.8	27.4	120.7	1028.7
1960	203.8	271.0	70.8	7.6	91.8	441.2		144.6	102.0	246.7	40.6	222.2	1154.5
1961	282.0	314.3	85.5	9.7	98.5	508.4		102.6	97.9	200.4	60.1	231.9	1282.7
1962	322.6	349.9	85.5	12.5	78.9	526.7		123.5	122.0	245.5	63.0	261.6	1419.4
1963	316.3	383.3	85.5	11.9	86.8	567.6		115.7	133.1	248.8	57.8	284.4	1474.8
1964	382.5	425.8	82.0	11.8	109.9	629.5		90.8	118.2	209.0	60.2	373.1	1654.3
1965	431.2	450.3	90.9	25.9	112.4	679.4		84.5	131.6	216.1	83.7	395.8	1806.3
1966	456.4	373.3	78.9	28.0	104.2	584.4		95.4	135.1	230.5	78.8	390.5	1740.6
1967	418.5	520.9	81.5	19.2	108.8	730.4		121.0	142.1	263.2	82.7	306.0	1800.8
1968	441.1	454.0	95.8	29.2	137.4	716.4		123.7	137.4	261.1	125.2	520.8	2064.6

CTN BROAD DIVISIONS AND CATEGORIES

I. 1. INDUSTRIAL MACHINERY AND EQUIPMENT (INCLUDING SPARE PARTS)

II. FUELS, RAW MATERIALS (OTHER THAN FOR FOOD), OTHER MATERIALS

2. FUELS, MINERAL RAW MATERIALS, METALS
3. CHEMICALS, FERTILIZERS, RUBBER
4. BUILDING MATERIALS AND CONSTRUCTION PARTS
5. RAW MATERIALS OF VEGETABLE AND ANIMAL ORIGIN (NOT FOOD)

III. FOODSTUFFS AND RAW MATERIAL FOR FOODSTUFFS

6. LIVE ANIMALS (NOT FOR SLAUGHTER)
7. RAW MATERIAL FOR THE PRODUCTION OF FOODSTUFFS
8. FOODSTUFFS

IV. 9. INDUSTRIAL CONSUMER GOODS (OTHER THAN FOOD)

* CONVERTED FROM NATIONAL DEVISA UNITS THROUGH OFFICIAL EXCHANGE
RATES. NOTE THE LIMITATIONS DISCUSSED IN THE EXPLANATORY TEXT.

TABLE III.CTN.M-P-U
POLAND'S IMPORTS FROM USSR, 1958-68
(MILLIONS OF CURRENT DOLLARS,* F.O.B.)

YEAR	BROAD DIV I 1	2	3	4	5	BROAD DIV II (2-5)	6	7	8	BROAD DIV III (6-8)	BROAD DIV IV 9	NOT SPECIFIED	TOTAL IMPORTS
1958	37.8	145.6	9.2	0.1	41.2	196.0	0.1	22.3	2.2	24.5	16.0	59.6	334.0
1959	49.9	160.1	8.8	0.6	51.7	221.1	0.1	67.1	22.5	89.6	20.3	71.3	452.3
1960	56.8	179.3	10.8	0.8	64.5	255.3		59.5	12.1	71.6	17.7	63.9	465.3
1961	61.4	195.2	10.4	0.9	65.7	272.3		34.3	9.8	44.1	22.8	89.1	489.7
1962	92.5	221.4	10.5	0.2	60.7	292.8		54.5	6.5	61.0	24.1	107.4	577.8
1963	124.4	248.3	14.6	0.2	52.5	315.6		51.5	24.9	76.3	18.4	112.5	647.2
1964	87.1	267.7	13.1	0.9	72.5	354.1		10.2	9.6	19.8	21.7	159.7	642.4
1965	99.2	275.8	18.3	1.5	79.8	375.4		38.8	14.2	53.0	30.5	170.3	728.4
1966	136.2	297.7	21.6	4.9	86.2	410.5		34.8	15.1	49.8	21.9	173.2	791.7
1967	145.9	335.9	21.5	4.4	77.2	438.9	0.0	80.4	30.1	110.5	27.6	198.2	921.1
1968	154.4	392.0	26.3	5.9	90.6	514.8	0.0	62.5	31.0	93.5	26.0	221.9	1010.7

CTN BROAD DIVISIONS AND CATEGORIES

I. 1. INDUSTRIAL MACHINERY AND EQUIPMENT (INCLUDING SPARE PARTS)

II. FUELS, RAW MATERIALS (OTHER THAN FOR FOOD), OTHER MATERIALS

2. FUELS, MINERAL RAW MATERIALS, METALS
3. CHEMICALS, FERTILIZERS, RUBBER
4. BUILDING MATERIALS AND CONSTRUCTION PARTS
5. RAW MATERIALS OF VEGETABLE AND ANIMAL ORIGIN (NOT FOOD)

III. FOODSTUFFS AND RAW MATERIAL FOR FOODSTUFFS

6. LIVE ANIMALS (NOT FOR SLAUGHTER)
7. RAW MATERIAL FOR THE PRODUCTION OF FOODSTUFFS
8. FOODSTUFFS

IV. 9. INDUSTRIAL CONSUMER GOODS (OTHER THAN FOOD)

* CONVERTED FROM NATIONAL DEVISA UNITS THROUGH OFFICIAL EXCHANGE RATES. NOTE THE LIMITATIONS DISCUSSED IN THE EXPLANATORY TEXT.

TABLE III.CTN.M.P-B
POLAND'S IMPORTS FROM BULGARIA, 1958-68
(MILLIONS OF CURRENT DOLLARS,* F.O.B.)

YEAR	BROAD DIV I 1	2	3	4	5	BROAD DIV II (2-5)	6	7	8	BROAD DIV III (6-8)	BROAD DIV IV 9	NOT SPECIFIED	TOTAL IMPORTS
1958	0.3	4.4		0.0	6.5	10.9		0.2	5.4	5.6	0.7	1.2	18.7
1959	0.3	4.0	0.1		8.1	12.2		0.4	7.4	7.8	0.9	0.8	22.1
1960	0.3	3.8	0.0		8.1	11.9		0.3	6.7	7.0	0.5	0.4	20.2
1961	0.4	4.3		0.1	6.3	10.8		0.2	8.7	8.9	0.6	0.1	20.8
1962	3.3	3.0		0.3	4.7	8.0		0.2	17.9	18.1	1.2	0.7	31.2
1963	5.3	3.3	0.1	0.6	7.4	11.4		0.2	13.0	13.2	1.9	1.2	32.9
1964	4.8	4.4	0.1		7.7	12.1		0.1	10.3	10.4	1.8	2.7	31.9
1965	6.3	4.1	0.0		10.2	14.3		0.1	13.9	14.0	2.0	3.2	39.8
1966	10.1	1.7	0.1		10.9	12.7		0.1	12.6	12.7	3.3	5.0	43.8
1967	17.9	2.0	0.2		6.1	8.3		0.2	8.9	9.1	4.3	5.4	45.0
1968	19.0	2.0	0.8		0.4	3.2		0.8	11.3	12.1	5.9	7.1	47.3

CTN BROAD DIVISIONS AND CATEGORIES

I. 1. INDUSTRIAL MACHINERY AND EQUIPMENT (INCLUDING SPARE PARTS)

II. FUELS, RAW MATERIALS (OTHER THAN FOR FOOD), OTHER MATERIALS

2. FUELS, MINERAL RAW MATERIALS, METALS
3. CHEMICALS, FERTILIZERS, RUBBER
4. BUILDING MATERIALS AND CONSTRUCTION PARTS
5. RAW MATERIALS OF VEGETABLE AND ANIMAL ORIGIN (NOT FOOD)

III. FOODSTUFFS AND RAW MATERIAL FOR FOODSTUFFS

6. LIVE ANIMALS (NOT FOR SLAUGHTER)
7. RAW MATERIAL FOR THE PRODUCTION OF FOODSTUFFS
8. FOODSTUFFS

IV. 9. INDUSTRIAL CONSUMER GOODS (OTHER THAN FOOD)

* CONVERTED FROM NATIONAL DEVISA UNITS THROUGH OFFICIAL EXCHANGE RATES. NOTE THE LIMITATIONS DISCUSSED IN THE EXPLANATORY TEXT.

TABLE III.CTN.M.P-C
POLAND'S IMPORTS FROM CZECHOSLOVAKIA, 1958-68
(MILLIONS OF CURRENT DOLLARS.* F.O.B.)

YEAR	BROAD DIV I 1	2	3	4	5	BROAD DIV II (2-5)	6	7	8	BROAD DIV III (6-8)	BROAD DIV IV 9	NOT SPECIFIED	TOTAL IMPORTS
1958	47.6	15.4	2.0	0.4	3.8	21.7			0.2	0.2	14.7	10.3	94.5
1959	59.2	21.7	1.5	0.5	2.8	26.5			0.1	0.1	16.8	10.2	112.9
1960	67.8	35.0	2.2	0.8	3.5	41.6			0.3	0.3	12.5	4.9	127.1
1961	84.1	49.2	2.0	1.7	2.9	55.8			0.1	0.1	16.4	6.5	162.9
1962	96.8	55.5	3.0	2.4	3.8	64.7			0.2	0.2	22.6	14.3	198.6
1963	96.8	50.9	3.9	3.0	5.0	62.8		2.8	0.1	3.0	20.6	9.8	193.0
1964	89.3	47.2	3.0	2.2	5.4	57.8			0.1		12.6	33.5	193.1
1965	107.9	56.5	8.3	3.4	8.1	76.2			0.2	0.2	19.3	40.6	244.1
1966	114.3	37.4	6.7	1.1	9.0	54.2					18.4	46.2	233.1
1967	116.6	38.0	6.9	1.3	8.5	54.6			0.1	0.1	14.1	49.9	235.2
1968	107.9	40.5	9.3	1.0	8.6	59.5			2.1	2.1	11.5	47.7	228.6

CTN BROAD DIVISIONS AND CATEGORIES

I. 1. INDUSTRIAL MACHINERY AND EQUIPMENT (INCLUDING SPARE PARTS)

II. FUELS, RAW MATERIALS (OTHER THAN FOR FOOD), OTHER MATERIALS

   2. FUELS, MINERAL RAW MATERIALS, METALS
   3. CHEMICALS, FERTILIZERS, RUBBER
   4. BUILDING MATERIALS AND CONSTRUCTION PARTS
   5. RAW MATERIALS OF VEGETABLE AND ANIMAL ORIGIN (NOT FOOD)

III. FOODSTUFFS AND RAW MATERIAL FOR FOODSTUFFS

   6. LIVE ANIMALS (NOT FOR SLAUGHTER)
   7. RAW MATERIAL FOR THE PRODUCTION OF FOODSTUFFS
   8. FOODSTUFFS

IV. 9. INDUSTRIAL CONSUMER GOODS (OTHER THAN FOOD)

* CONVERTED FROM NATIONAL DEVISA UNITS THROUGH OFFICIAL EXCHANGE RATES. NOTE THE LIMITATIONS DISCUSSED IN THE EXPLANATORY TEXT.

TABLE III.CTN.M.P-G
POLAND'S IMPORTS FROM EAST GERMANY, 1958-68
(MILLIONS OF CURRENT DOLLARS,* F.O.B.)

YEAR	BROAD DIV I	2	3	4	5	BROAD DIV II (2-5)	6	7	8	BROAD DIV III (6-8)	BROAD DIV IV 9	NOT SPECIFIED	TOTAL IMPORTS
1958	52.5	27.4	32.0	2.2	3.4	60.0	0.0	0.0	6.9	6.9	26.4	9.6	155.5
1959	62.3	38.2	33.7	1.8	1.5	75.3	0.0	0.1	3.0	3.2	28.6	17.9	187.2
1960	79.7	23.8	38.8	1.6	3.0	67.2		0.1	5.0	5.0	25.0	9.5	186.4
1961	91.2	37.2	36.1	1.2	2.2	76.7		0.1	0.0	1.1	27.4	6.3	202.7
1962	110.3	31.6	42.5	1.9	3.1	79.1		0.0	1.4	1.4	39.5	4.6	234.9
1963	132.4	22.2	35.7	2.8	4.0	64.7		0.1	1.4	1.5	43.5	11.3	253.4
1964	101.1	29.7	37.2	2.4	4.7	74.1		0.1	3.8	3.8	31.6	25.2	235.8
1965	130.3	25.9	43.0	1.3	4.5	74.6		1.1	5.2	6.3	40.8	19.2	271.4
1966	138.4	26.9	40.2	0.3	4.0	71.4		0.4	1.0	1.5	38.7	30.3	280.3
1967	134.3	30.0	45.7	1.1	4.6	81.3		1.2	1.0	2.3	42.4	31.9	292.1
1968	115.0	39.8	45.7	1.5	4.7	91.7		1.3	2.5	3.8	48.0	37.7	296.2

CTN BROAD DIVISIONS AND CATEGORIES

I. 1. INDUSTRIAL MACHINERY AND EQUIPMENT (INCLUDING SPARE PARTS)

II. FUELS, RAW MATERIALS (OTHER THAN FOR FOOD), OTHER MATERIALS

2. FUELS, MINERAL RAW MATERIALS, METALS
3. CHEMICALS, FERTILIZERS, RUBBER
4. BUILDING MATERIALS AND CONSTRUCTION PARTS
5. RAW MATERIALS OF VEGETABLE AND ANIMAL ORIGIN (NOT FOOD)

III. FOODSTUFFS AND RAW MATERIAL FOR FOODSTUFFS

6. LIVE ANIMALS (NOT FOR SLAUGHTER)
7. RAW MATERIAL FOR THE PRODUCTION OF FOODSTUFFS
8. FOODSTUFFS

IV. 9. INDUSTRIAL CONSUMER GOODS (OTHER THAN FOOD)

* CONVERTED FROM NATIONAL DEVISA UNITS THROUGH OFFICIAL EXCHANGE RATES. NOTE THE LIMITATIONS DISCUSSED IN THE EXPLANATORY TEXT.

TABLE III.CTN.M.P-H
POLAND'S IMPORTS FROM HUNGARY, 1958-68
(MILLIONS OF CURRENT DOLLARS,* F.O.B.)

YEAR	BROAD DIV I 1	2	3	4	5	BROAD DIV II (2-5)	6	7	8	BROAD DIV III (6-8)	BROAD DIV IV 9	NOT SPECIFIED	TOTAL IMPORTS
1958	7.4	6.6	0.7	0.1	1.1	8.5	0.0	0.3	0.9	1.3	13.8	2.8	33.8
1959	7.6	9.1	0.6		1.9	11.7		1.1	3.0	4.2	11.4	1.8	36.6
1960	15.3	13.1	0.6	0.6	2.4	16.7		1.4	1.8	3.2	9.3	1.7	46.1
1961	21.7	17.5	0.3	0.4	2.4	20.5		0.1	2.3	2.3	13.6	0.8	59.0
1962	27.5	18.9	0.7	0.3	1.0	21.0		0.1	2.2	2.3	14.5	3.0	68.2
1963	32.1	16.3	0.6	0.9	1.3	19.1		0.0	4.0	4.0	12.9	7.7	75.9
1964	30.4	17.7	0.3	0.6	1.5	20.1	0.0	0.3	4.1	4.3	12.1	15.6	82.6
1965	33.4	22.1	2.6	0.0	1.9	27.5		0.1	6.6	6.6	21.4	16.8	105.7
1966	29.1	24.6	3.9	1.2	1.6	31.3		0.0	7.4	7.4	22.3	14.0	104.1
1967	28.9	23.2	2.4	0.3	2.0	28.0			6.1	6.1	20.3	20.7	104.0
1968	27.6	25.9	1.9	0.4	2.6	30.8	0.0	0.1	5.5	5.6	16.9	16.8	97.7

CTN BROAD DIVISIONS AND CATEGORIES

I. 1. INDUSTRIAL MACHINERY AND EQUIPMENT (INCLUDING SPARE PARTS)

II. FUELS, RAW MATERIALS (OTHER THAN FOR FOOD), OTHER MATERIALS

2. FUELS, MINERAL RAW MATERIALS, METALS
3. CHEMICALS, FERTILIZERS, RUBBER
4. BUILDING MATERIALS AND CONSTRUCTION PARTS
5. RAW MATERIALS OF VEGETABLE AND ANIMAL ORIGIN (NOT FOOD)

III. FOODSTUFFS AND RAW MATERIAL FOR FOODSTUFFS

6. LIVE ANIMALS (NOT FOR SLAUGHTER)
7. RAW MATERIAL FOR THE PRODUCTION OF FOODSTUFFS
8. FOODSTUFFS

IV. 9. INDUSTRIAL CONSUMER GOODS (OTHER THAN FOOD)

* CONVERTED FROM NATIONAL DEVISA UNITS THROUGH OFFICIAL EXCHANGE RATES. NOTE THE LIMITATIONS DISCUSSED IN THE EXPLANATORY TEXT.

TABLE III.CTN.M.P-R
POLAND'S IMPORTS FROM RUMANIA, 1958-68
(MILLIONS OF CURRENT DOLLARS,* F.O.B.)

YEAR	BROAD DIV I 1	2	3	4	5	BROAD DIV II (2-5)	6	7	8	BROAD DIV III (6-8)	BROAD DIV IV 9	NOT SPECIFIED	TOTAL IMPORTS
1958	0.3	7.3	0.3	1.7	1.2	10.6	0.0	0.1	1.1	1.2	0.1	0.2	12.3
1959	2.5	10.7	0.3	2.2	2.0	15.1	0.0	0.1	2.5	2.6	0.6	0.3	21.1
1960	3.1	9.6	0.4	1.2	1.8	13.0		0.6	2.0	2.6	0.4	1.4	20.5
1961	4.6	12.4	0.4	1.5	2.1	16.5			1.6	1.6	0.6	0.8	24.0
1962	14.8	14.6	0.3	0.7	1.4	17.0		1.2	4.8	6.0	1.4	1.0	40.2
1963	11.8	14.0	0.2	0.0	0.3	15.4		0.2	3.4	3.5	1.9	0.7	33.3
1964	5.2	16.4	0.7	0.4	0.7	18.2		0.2	3.2	3.4	1.2	1.5	29.5
1965	21.6	13.4	0.9	0.5	0.6	15.5		0.1	3.8	3.9	2.4	1.3	44.7
1966	16.6	15.4	0.8	0.6	0.5	17.3		0.3	3.1	3.4	1.6	2.1	41.0
1967	20.5	19.3	0.8	0.1	0.4	20.6		0.2	4.4	4.6	2.5	1.8	50.2
1968	24.9	21.1	0.3	0.4	0.5	22.4			6.4	6.4	2.4	1.4	57.5

CTN BROAD DIVISIONS AND CATEGORIES

I. 1. INDUSTRIAL MACHINERY AND EQUIPMENT (INCLUDING SPARE PARTS)

II. FUELS, RAW MATERIALS (OTHER THAN FOR FOOD), OTHER MATERIALS

2. FUELS, MINERAL RAW MATERIALS, METALS
3. CHEMICALS, FERTILIZERS, RUBBER
4. BUILDING MATERIALS AND CONSTRUCTION PARTS
5. RAW MATERIALS OF VEGETABLE AND ANIMAL ORIGIN (NOT FOOD)

III. FOODSTUFFS AND RAW MATERIAL FOR FOODSTUFFS

6. LIVE ANIMALS (NOT FOR SLAUGHTER)
7. RAW MATERIAL FOR THE PRODUCTION OF FOODSTUFFS
8. FOODSTUFFS

IV. 9. INDUSTRIAL CONSUMER GOODS (OTHER THAN FOOD)

* CONVERTED FROM NATIONAL DEVISA UNITS THROUGH OFFICIAL EXCHANGE
RATES. NOTE THE LIMITATIONS DISCUSSED IN THE EXPLANATORY TEXT.

TABLE III.CTN.M.P-Y
POLAND'S IMPORTS FROM YUGOSLAVIA, 1958-68
(MILLIONS OF CURRENT DOLLARS,* F.O.B.)

YEAR	BROAD DIV I 1	2	3	4	5	BROAD DIV II (2-5)	6	7	8	BROAD DIV III (6-8)	BROAD DIV IV 9	NOT SPECIFIED	TOTAL IMPORTS
1958	2.0	3.0	0.3	0.4	7.3	11.0		0.0	1.6	1.6	6.7	1.0	22.3
1959	1.6	5.0	0.2	0.3	10.5	16.1		0.1	1.9	1.9	4.6	0.8	25.0
1960	2.9	4.9	0.4	0.2	4.4	9.9		0.1	1.2	1.2	1.1	0.2	15.3
1961	14.7	7.1	1.6	0.3	9.6	18.5		0.2	1.9	2.0	3.4	0.5	39.0
1962	15.9	9.6	0.7	1.1	8.2	19.5		0.2	1.8	1.8	1.1	0.8	39.2
1963	9.7	8.1	0.6	0.1	12.3	21.1		0.2	1.8	1.9	2.2		34.8**
1964	7.1	10.0	1.8	1.3	12.2	25.3		0.4	2.3	2.7	3.2	2.2	40.5
1965	11.9	12.4	4.6	1.6	10.7	29.3		0.3	5.6	5.9	13.3	2.7	63.0
1966	16.4	9.0	4.8	1.6	5.4	20.8		0.2	1.7	1.9	10.6	6.9	56.6
1967	19.4	12.3	0.1	1.8	3.5	17.7		0.3	0.6	0.9	4.8	4.4	47.3
1968	10.0	11.0	0.3	2.0	3.5	16.7		0.9	4.1	5.0	5.4	2.9	40.0

CTN BROAD DIVISIONS AND CATEGORIES

I. 1. INDUSTRIAL MACHINERY AND EQUIPMENT (INCLUDING SPARE PARTS)

II. FUELS, RAW MATERIALS (OTHER THAN FOR FOOD), OTHER MATERIALS

2. FUELS, MINERAL RAW MATERIALS, METALS
3. CHEMICALS, FERTILIZERS, RUBBER
4. BUILDING MATERIALS AND CONSTRUCTION PARTS
5. RAW MATERIALS OF VEGETABLE AND ANIMAL ORIGIN (NOT FOOD)

III. FOODSTUFFS AND RAW MATERIAL FOR FOODSTUFFS

6. LIVE ANIMALS (NOT FOR SLAUGHTER)
7. RAW MATERIAL FOR THE PRODUCTION OF FOODSTUFFS
8. FOODSTUFFS

IV. 9. INDUSTRIAL CONSUMER GOODS (OTHER THAN FOOD)

* CONVERTED FROM NATIONAL DEVISA UNITS THROUGH OFFICIAL EXCHANGE RATES. NOTE THE LIMITATIONS DISCUSSED IN THE EXPLANATORY TEXT.

** SUM OF COMPONENTS GREATER THAN GIVEN TOTAL - ERROR IN ORIGINAL SOURCE.

TABLE III.CTN.M.P-CEMA
POLAND'S IMPORTS FROM EUROPEAN CEMA (EXCLUDING ALBANIA), 1958-68
(MILLIONS OF CURRENT DOLLARS,* F.O.B.)

YEAR	BROAD DIV I 1	2	3	4	5	BROAD DIV II (2-5)	6	7	8	BROAD DIV III (6-8)	BROAD DIV IV 9	NOT SPECIFIED	TOTAL IMPORTS
1958	146.0	201.7	44.2	4.5	57.2	307.7	0.1	22.8	16.8	39.7	71.7	83.7	648.8
1959	181.9	243.8	45.0	5.1	68.1	362.0	0.1	68.8	38.5	107.4	78.6	102.3	832.2
1960	223.0	264.6	52.8	4.9	83.3	405.7		61.8	27.9	89.7	65.4	81.7	865.6
1961	263.5	315.8	49.3	5.8	81.7	452.6		34.7	23.3	58.0	81.4	103.6	959.2
1962	345.2	345.1	57.0	5.8	74.7	482.6		56.0	32.9	88.9	103.3	130.9	1151.0
1963	402.7	355.0	55.1	8.6	70.4	489.1		54.8	46.7	101.5	99.3	143.0	1235.5
1964	317.9	383.2	54.4	6.5	92.4	536.5	0.0	10.9	30.9	41.8	81.0	238.1	1215.4
1965	398.7	397.7	73.0	7.6	105.0	583.5		40.1	43.9	84.1	116.4	251.4	1434.0
1966	444.7	403.7	73.2	8.2	112.2	597.4		35.6	39.2	74.8	106.3	270.8	1494.0
1967	464.0	448.3	77.4	7.1	98.8	631.7	0.0	82.0	50.6	132.7	111.3	307.9	1647.6
1968	448.9	521.3	84.3	9.4	107.4	722.4	0.0	64.6	58.9	123.5	110.7	332.4	1737.9

CTN BROAD DIVISIONS AND CATEGORIES

I. 1. INDUSTRIAL MACHINERY AND EQUIPMENT (INCLUDING SPARE PARTS)

III.   FOODSTUFFS AND RAW MATERIAL FOR FOODSTUFFS

II.   FUELS, RAW MATERIALS (OTHER THAN FOR FOOD), OTHER MATERIALS

6. LIVE ANIMALS (NOT FOR SLAUGHTER)
7. RAW MATERIAL FOR THE PRODUCTION OF FOODSTUFFS
8. FOODSTUFFS

2. FUELS, MINERAL RAW MATERIALS, METALS
3. CHEMICALS, FERTILIZERS, RUBBER
4. BUILDING MATERIALS AND CONSTRUCTION PARTS
5. RAW MATERIALS OF VEGETABLE AND ANIMAL ORIGIN (NOT FOOD)

IV. 9. INDUSTRIAL CONSUMER GOODS (OTHER THAN FOOD)

* CONVERTED FROM NATIONAL DEVISA UNITS THROUGH OFFICIAL EXCHANGE
RATES. NOTE THE LIMITATIONS DISCUSSED IN THE EXPLANATORY TEXT.

TABLE III-CTN-X-U-B
USSR EXPORTS TO BULGARIA, 1946-68
(MILLIONS OF CURRENT DOLLARS,* F.O.B.)

YEAR	BROAD DIV I 1	2	3	4	5	BROAD DIV II (2-5)	6	7	8	BROAD DIV III (6-8)	BROAD DIV IV 9	NOT SPECIFIED	TOTAL EXPORTS
1946	24.7	7.3	6.2		13.5	27.0		9.1		9.1	0.5	22.5	83.9
1947	5.7	5.3	4.0		12.4	21.7		1.8		1.8	0.5	32.8	62.4
1948	12.1	19.0	3.5		14.9	37.4		8.7		8.7	0.6	20.6	79.4
1949	15.5	21.3	4.6		15.1	41.1		14.0		14.0	0.8	22.6	94.0
1950	24.0	20.2	4.5		8.8	33.5		4.4		4.4	1.4	36.7	100.0
1951	35.1	18.9	4.7		15.5	39.2					1.2	40.4	115.9
1952	35.3	22.7	4.8		13.8	41.3					1.3	40.0	117.9
1953	36.0	24.6	4.6		16.2	45.4					1.2	27.0	109.6
1954	33.5	20.5	4.9		11.0	36.4					1.4	37.2	108.4
1955	40.4	29.4	4.9	0.5	10.4	45.2	0.3	4.3		4.6	2.4	34.9	127.4
1956	39.4	37.5	5.3	0.8	8.5	52.1	0.2	0.9		1.0	3.0	13.0	108.4
1957	35.4	49.0	11.1	0.8	18.1	79.0	0.1	14.4		14.5	26.4	17.1	172.4
1958	50.7	58.5	11.9	0.0	19.4	90.8	0.0	1.9	0.1	2.0	25.3	31.9	200.6
1959	88.4	65.6	16.4	1.5	27.1	110.6	0.1	11.7	0.2	12.0	31.5	47.4	289.9
1960	108.6	78.8	18.5	1.8	32.2	131.2	0.1	11.2	0.4	11.8	23.8	53.6	329.0
1961	124.2	91.1	15.3	2.2	32.9	141.5	0.1	0.7	1.3	1.8	24.3	64.4	356.2
1962	167.7	113.4	14.7	2.8	38.0	168.9	0.1	8.7	2.4	11.1	27.1	72.9	447.8
1963	207.5	137.4	18.5	2.7	34.4	193.1	0.2	12.4	9.9	22.5	27.0	45.3	495.4
1964	231.6	185.1	19.7	3.6	42.5	250.8	0.1	9.1	6.7	15.9	16.8	52.3	567.4
1965	249.7	201.8	20.3	3.9	51.5	277.5	0.1	7.5	0.8	8.4	16.3	36.5	588.4
1966	320.1	233.5	24.1	4.3	59.0	321.0	0.0	0.0	10.7	10.8	17.7	27.5	697.1
1967	362.9	244.7	28.1	6.2	51.6	330.6		0.0	22.3	22.3	21.4	25.5	762.8
1968	416.4	302.1	40.7	6.9	61.2	410.9		0.0	32.9	33.0	35.6	53.4	949.3

CTN BROAD DIVISIONS AND CATEGORIES

I. 1. INDUSTRIAL MACHINERY AND EQUIPMENT (INCLUDING SPARE PARTS)

II. FUELS, RAW MATERIALS (OTHER THAN FOR FOOD), OTHER MATERIALS

2. FUELS, MINERAL RAW MATERIALS, METALS
3. CHEMICALS, FERTILIZERS, RUBBER
4. BUILDING MATERIALS AND CONSTRUCTION PARTS
5. RAW MATERIALS OF VEGETABLE AND ANIMAL ORIGIN (NOT FOOD)

III. FOODSTUFFS AND RAW MATERIAL FOR FOODSTUFFS

6. LIVE ANIMALS (NOT FOR SLAUGHTER)
7. RAW MATERIAL FOR THE PRODUCTION OF FOODSTUFFS
8. FOODSTUFFS

IV. 9. INDUSTRIAL CONSUMER GOODS (OTHER THAN FOOD)

* CONVERTED FROM NATIONAL DEVISA UNITS THROUGH OFFICIAL EXCHANGE RATES. NOTE THE LIMITATIONS DISCUSSED IN THE EXPLANATORY TEXT.

TABLE III.CTN.X.U-C
USSR EXPORTS TO CZECHOSLOVAKIA, 1946-68
(MILLIONS OF CURRENT DOLLARS,* F.O.B.)

YEAR	BROAD DIV I 1	2	3	4	5	BROAD DIV II (2-5)	6	7	8	BROAD DIV III (6-8)	BROAD DIV IV 9	NOT SPECIFIED	TOTAL EXPORTS
1946	0.0	7.1	4.9		5.7	17.8		2.5		2.5	0.9	7.7	29.0
1947	0.1	10.5	5.6		5.6	21.6		13.6		13.6	0.6	8.3	44.3
1948	1.3	17.8	5.0		31.1	53.9		62.2	1.9	64.0	0.9	21.6	141.8
1949	6.4	31.1	9.1		30.3	70.5		41.9	41.5	83.4	0.7	45.0	206.0
1950	12.3	29.1	7.7		31.9	68.7		60.4	14.0	74.4	2.1	62.9	220.4
1951	26.7	39.5	9.8		43.4	92.7		99.6	19.4	119.0	3.2	48.5	290.1
1952	45.3	65.1	10.7		52.7	128.5		93.3	18.3	111.6	3.9	74.1	363.3
1953	41.8	61.6	10.9		56.1	128.6		87.7	21.3	109.1	2.5	66.8	348.8
1954	43.3	76.1	9.5		51.6	137.1		86.6	20.1	106.7	4.1	60.3	351.6
1955	36.9	94.7	13.3	0.2	57.5	165.6	0.1	88.9	15.2	104.1	5.9	43.3	355.9
1956	32.8	114.2	18.7	0.4	61.4	194.7	0.1	51.8	13.0	64.9	8.8	72.5	373.7
1957	46.8	172.2	16.9	0.4	65.0	254.5	0.0	134.1	20.8	154.9	18.2	77.0	551.3
1958	47.4	155.6	11.9	0.1	68.7	236.2	0.0	96.0	19.4	115.4	13.8	34.0	446.8
1959	58.9	183.1	18.5	0.2	66.5	268.3	0.0	141.8	44.6	186.5	11.7	77.6	603.0
1960	60.4	214.7	19.8	0.8	68.4	303.8	0.0	128.0	33.8	161.8	13.1	91.8	630.8
1961	82.8	249.5	22.7	1.3	77.2	350.6	0.1	89.1	32.7	121.9	11.3	86.0	652.7
1962	110.9	298.3	24.7	1.8	64.2	389.2	0.0	115.5	43.1	158.7	20.7	91.3	770.7
1963	129.1	343.8	25.6	2.5	67.1	439.0		117.1	55.5	172.6	15.9	92.5	849.0
1964	149.5	380.6	33.8	0.9	86.2	501.5	0.0	67.0	29.2	96.2	9.0	144.6	900.8
1965	131.1	410.0	29.9	1.7	87.9	529.5	0.0	77.4	40.6	117.9	9.7	137.6	925.9
1966	152.6	347.7	31.0	0.0	84.3	463.9		89.6	63.9	153.5	11.3	112.6	894.0
1967	140.8	404.4	32.6	3.8	83.3	524.2		110.8	67.7	178.4	13.8	110.1	967.4
1968	148.7	450.9	37.2	6.6	92.5	587.2		119.4	46.8	166.2	15.2	120.9	1038.1

CTN BROAD DIVISIONS AND CATEGORIES

I. 1. INDUSTRIAL MACHINERY AND EQUIPMENT (INCLUDING SPARE PARTS)

II.   FUELS, RAW MATERIALS (OTHER THAN FOR FOOD), OTHER MATERIALS

    2. FUELS, MINERAL RAW MATERIALS, METALS
    3. CHEMICALS, FERTILIZERS, RUBBER
    4. BUILDING MATERIALS AND CONSTRUCTION PARTS
    5. RAW MATERIALS OF VEGETABLE AND ANIMAL ORIGIN (NOT FOOD)

III.   FOODSTUFFS AND RAW MATERIAL FOR FOODSTUFFS

    6. LIVE ANIMALS (NOT FOR SLAUGHTER)
    7. RAW MATERIAL FOR THE PRODUCTION OF FOODSTUFFS
    8. FOODSTUFFS

IV. 9. INDUSTRIAL CONSUMER GOODS (OTHER THAN FOOD)

* CONVERTED FROM NATIONAL DEVISA UNITS THROUGH OFFICIAL EXCHANGE
  RATES. NOTE THE LIMITATIONS DISCUSSED IN THE EXPLANATORY TEXT.

TABLE III.CTN.X.U-G
USSR EXPORTS TO EAST GERMANY, 1946-68
(MILLIONS OF CURRENT DOLLARS,* F.O.B.)

YEAR	BROAD DIV I 1	2	3	4	5	BROAD DIV II (2-5)	6	7	8	BROAD DIV III (6-8)	BROAD DIV IV 9	NOT SPECIFIED	TOTAL EXPORTS
1946	-	0.7			23.1	23.7						17.3	41.0
1947	0.4	1.4	0.3		18.2	19.8						23.4	43.7
1948	1.3	25.9	0.4		9.9	36.2		19.0	6.6	25.6		28.4	91.4
1949	10.3	46.4	0.6		17.0	64.0		8.1	8.2	16.3		25.6	116.1
1950	8.8	41.5	0.0		35.3	77.7		33.3	40.8	74.0		25.1	185.8
1951	9.6	59.2	1.3		68.2	128.7		55.6	50.0	105.6		54.8	298.7
1952	9.9	68.3	1.7		84.5	154.6		73.3	53.7	126.9		141.5	432.9
1953	9.6	131.0	1.7		81.0	213.8		86.6	88.3	174.9		106.8	505.1
1954	6.8	156.8	3.0		86.0	245.8		82.9	59.2	142.1		88.0	482.7
1955	4.8	185.5	14.9	0.0	102.9	303.3		87.1	9.2	96.3	3.7	70.5	478.7
1956	8.9	228.2	20.5	0.2	110.1	358.9		65.4	62.7	128.1	3.0	72.4	571.3
1957	17.9	329.8	23.8	0.0	117.7	471.3		143.5	108.4	251.9	2.4	118.6	862.1
1958	27.2	365.0	23.6	0.0	118.9	507.5		127.3	49.6	177.0	2.6	85.4	799.8
1959	32.3	411.7	26.1	0.1	133.1	571.0		141.9	137.9	279.8	3.4	143.5	1030.1
1960	37.4	502.8	30.7	0.1	147.1	680.7		148.8	73.3	222.2	7.1	104.3	1051.7
1961	56.9	569.0	40.3	0.3	174.5	784.0		146.1	85.6	231.8	8.9	127.6	1209.1
1962	77.5	619.6	42.0	2.5	183.1	847.2		174.4	122.7	297.0	6.8	144.1	1372.7
1963	79.9	625.2	41.7	2.6	182.2	851.6		128.4	112.4	240.8	6.4	135.2	1313.9
1964	97.5	708.1	44.2	3.7	189.5	945.4		98.8	64.3	163.1	4.3	174.9	1385.2
1965	106.5	685.6	47.3	5.2	202.7	940.7		83.9	62.6	146.4	4.6	164.7	1363.0
1966	119.9	652.8	45.7	4.9	206.2	909.6		91.6	91.9	183.5	8.8	185.0	1406.8
1967	163.0	645.9	46.8	5.2	194.7	892.7		101.1	76.5	177.7	9.5	173.3	1416.2
1968	230.2	612.4	54.7	5.0	186.2	858.2		106.4	81.8	188.2	10.2	219.6	1506.4

CTN BROAD DIVISIONS AND CATEGORIES

I. 1. INDUSTRIAL MACHINERY AND EQUIPMENT (INCLUDING SPARE PARTS)

II. RAW MATERIALS (OTHER THAN FOR FOOD), OTHER MATERIALS

2. FUELS, MINERAL RAW MATERIALS, METALS
3. CHEMICALS, FERTILIZERS, RUBBER
4. BUILDING MATERIALS AND CONSTRUCTION PARTS
5. RAW MATERIALS OF VEGETABLE AND ANIMAL ORIGIN (NOT FOOD)

III. FOODSTUFFS AND RAW MATERIAL FOR FOODSTUFFS

6. LIVE ANIMALS (NOT FOR SLAUGHTER)
7. RAW MATERIAL FOR THE PRODUCTION OF FOODSTUFFS
8. FOODSTUFFS

IV. 9. INDUSTRIAL CONSUMER GOODS (OTHER THAN FOOD)

* CONVERTED FROM NATIONAL DEVISA UNITS THROUGH OFFICIAL EXCHANGE

TABLE III.CTN.X.U-H
USSR EXPORTS TO HUNGARY, 1946-68
(MILLIONS OF CURRENT DOLLARS,* F.O.B.)

YEAR	BROAD DIV I 1	2	3	4	5	BROAD DIV II (2-5)	6	7	8	BROAD DIV III (6-8)	BROAD DIV IV 9	NOT SPECIFIED	TOTAL EXPORTS
1946	-	2.2	0.5		4.9	7.6					0.1	2.5	10.2
1947	0.0	5.4	0.5		6.3	12.2					0.1	3.9	16.2
1948	0.9	10.3	0.4		8.2	18.8					0.2	14.5	34.4
1949	11.3	13.5	2.3		24.4	40.3					0.1	32.0	83.7
1950	13.2	17.6	2.1		27.7	47.5		2.2		2.2	0.2	63.7	126.9
1951	15.8	23.1	3.7		34.9	61.7		3.4		3.4	0.6	40.3	121.8
1952	22.1	31.2	4.3		39.6	75.1		0.3		0.3	0.7	52.0	150.3
1953	21.3	34.1	4.0		39.3	77.4		11.4		11.4	0.0	46.6	157.7
1954	17.5	43.0	4.2		48.4	95.6					0.0	38.8	153.0
1955	14.2	40.1	5.1		34.6	79.8	0.0	2.8	0.1	2.9	1.6	16.7	115.3
1956	15.0	46.7	5.4		40.1	92.3	0.0	0.2	0.1	0.4	2.9	16.4	126.9
1957	16.5	109.5	8.9		63.8	182.2	0.0	34.4	0.0	34.5	7.4	9.2	249.7
1958	20.7	88.0	8.8		57.4	154.1	0.0	11.6	0.3	11.9	6.1	7.8	200.6
1959	63.0	89.9	8.8		54.2	152.9	0.0	18.1	2.9	21.0	3.9	19.0	259.8
1960	70.7	103.9	10.5		66.5	181.0	0.0	14.7	3.7	18.4	5.8	35.6	311.4
1961	57.1	118.5	14.7		69.9	203.2	0.0	30.2	3.7	33.9	4.3	60.9	359.3
1962	66.5	133.8	19.2		80.9	233.9	0.0	19.9	5.6	25.5	4.3	80.9	411.1
1963	95.6	150.3	24.1		77.7	252.1	0.0	9.8	4.8	14.6	4.4	76.7	443.4
1964	125.0	179.3	27.6		84.4	291.3	0.0	1.7	4.5	6.2	6.4	63.7	492.7
1965	110.3	195.5	30.0		91.0	316.5	0.0	25.0	7.9	33.0	9.0	77.1	545.9
1966	121.5	195.5	34.5	1.9	99.8	331.6		0.0	11.3	12.3	8.9	30.4	504.6
1967	147.2	198.1	35.0	4.9	105.9	343.9		10.3	21.5	31.7	11.0	51.8	585.5
1968	138.5	247.5	38.9	6.6	125.9	418.8		22.0	17.8	39.8	13.6	64.7	675.4

CTN BROAD DIVISIONS AND CATEGORIES

I. 1. INDUSTRIAL MACHINERY AND EQUIPMENT (INCLUDING SPARE PARTS)

II. FUELS, RAW MATERIALS (OTHER THAN FOR FOOD), OTHER MATERIALS

2. FUELS, MINERAL RAW MATERIALS, METALS
3. CHEMICALS, FERTILIZERS, RUBBER
4. BUILDING MATERIALS AND CONSTRUCTION PARTS
5. RAW MATERIALS OF VEGETABLE AND ANIMAL ORIGIN (NOT FOOD)

III. FOODSTUFFS AND RAW MATERIAL FOR FOODSTUFFS

6. LIVE ANIMALS (NOT FOR SLAUGHTER)
7. RAW MATERIAL FOR THE PRODUCTION OF FOODSTUFFS
8. FOODSTUFFS

IV. 9. INDUSTRIAL CONSUMER GOODS (OTHER THAN FOOD)

* CONVERTED FROM NATIONAL DEVISA UNITS THROUGH OFFICIAL EXCHANGE RATES. NOTE THE LIMITATIONS DISCUSSED IN THE EXPLANATORY TEXT.

TABLE III.CTN.X.U-P
USSR EXPORTS TO POLAND, 1946-68
(MILLIONS OF CURRENT DOLLARS,* F.O.B.)

YEAR	BROAD DIV I	2	3	4	5	BROAD DIV II (2-5)	6	7	8	BROAD DIV III (6-8)	BROAD DIV IV 9	NOT SPECIFIED	TOTAL EXPORTS
1946	4.2	9.5	1.1		21.6	32.1		52.6		52.6	0.9	16.6	106.4
1947	1.7	10.2	0.8		27.6	38.6		34.3		34.3	0.6	29.2	104.4
1948	4.3	17.9	0.5		63.3	81.7		32.7		32.7	0.8	13.4	132.9
1949	21.9	23.7	0.0		46.4	71.1		6.1		6.1	2.8	34.9	136.9
1950	42.2	21.4	1.3		65.2	87.8		20.8		20.8	5.2	85.5	241.4
1951	63.6	29.9	2.0		81.0	112.8		25.8		25.8	4.9	103.5	310.7
1952	78.3	35.3	2.2		69.9	107.5		51.2		51.2	4.7	120.7	362.3
1953	105.5	41.4	1.8		65.4	108.6		10.5		10.5	6.1	98.2	328.9
1954	117.3	57.1	2.0		72.0	131.1		44.2		44.2	4.2	116.6	413.4
1955	134.5	74.0	10.1	2.0	62.3	148.3	0.1	31.3	3.3	34.7	5.7	108.6	431.8
1956	75.4	85.2	15.9	1.1	60.8	163.0	0.1	9.0	5.5	14.5	8.6	95.7	357.2
1957	60.0	137.7	10.9	0.6	57.9	207.0		96.6	6.4	103.0	7.3	53.6	430.9
1958	42.3	146.0	9.0	0.2	49.1	204.3		23.6	6.9	30.5	19.4	80.3	376.8
1959	52.6	166.7	9.5	0.6	49.4	226.3		65.6	24.4	90.0	19.7	97.8	486.4
1960	55.1	188.4	8.6	0.7	64.8	262.4		61.0	12.0	73.0	15.0	85.3	490.8
1961	64.2	204.3	9.7	1.1	64.2	279.2		42.2	10.1	52.3	24.0	110.9	530.7
1962	94.6	227.9	9.8	0.3	60.2	298.2		63.2	6.4	69.7	23.2	108.4	594.1
1963	127.5	258.6	11.8	0.2	51.3	322.0		57.7	24.3	82.0	18.0	113.1	662.5
1964	97.6	284.6	12.7	0.9	73.1	371.4		13.8	8.7	22.5	22.3	146.2	660.0
1965	108.9	284.8	17.2	2.1	73.7	377.8		38.3	18.1	56.4	24.2	159.4	726.7
1966	144.4	317.5	21.7	5.5	83.2	427.8		36.7	12.5	49.1	18.4	163.4	803.2
1967	169.4	356.5	23.0	6.3	74.9	460.7		80.0	24.5	104.5	23.4	154.3	912.2
1968	178.7	409.8	25.9	9.8	84.9	530.3		62.9	20.4	83.3	23.8	233.9	1050.1

CTN BROAD DIVISIONS AND CATEGORIES

I. 1. INDUSTRIAL MACHINERY AND EQUIPMENT (INCLUDING SPARE PARTS)

II. FUELS, RAW MATERIALS (OTHER THAN FOOD), OTHER MATERIALS

2. FUELS, MINERAL RAW MATERIALS, METALS
3. CHEMICALS, FERTILIZERS, RUBBER
4. BUILDING MATERIALS AND CONSTRUCTION PARTS
5. RAW MATERIALS OF VEGETABLE AND ANIMAL ORIGIN (NOT FOOD)

III. FOODSTUFFS AND RAW MATERIAL FOR FOODSTUFFS

6. LIVE ANIMALS (NOT FOR SLAUGHTER)
7. RAW MATERIAL FOR THE PRODUCTION OF FOODSTUFFS
8. FOODSTUFFS

IV. 9. INDUSTRIAL CONSUMER GOODS (OTHER THAN FOOD)

* CONVERTED FROM NATIONAL DEVISA UNITS THROUGH OFFICIAL EXCHANGE
RATES. NOTE THE LIMITATIONS DISCUSSED IN THE EXPLANATORY TEXT

TABLE III.CTN.X.U-R
USSR EXPORTS TO RUMANIA, 1946-68
(MILLIONS OF CURRENT DOLLARS,* F.O.B.)

YEAR	BROAD DIV I 1	2	3	4	5	BROAD DIV II (2-5)	6	7	8	BROAD DIV III (6-8)	BROAD DIV IV 9	NOT SPECIFIED	TOTAL EXPORTS
1946	2.5	2.4			4.9	7.3		17.1		17.1	0.2	3.2	30.3
1947	3.3	8.3			12.2	20.5		8.2		8.2	0.3	5.4	37.7
1948	11.3	7.5			17.0	24.5		4.2		4.2	1.1	7.1	48.2
1949	23.6	30.5			22.6	53.1		2.0		2.0	0.8	31.8	111.3
1950	39.7	30.4			24.6	54.9					0.9	18.3	113.9
1951	39.5	30.3			37.8	68.1		1.9		1.9	2.1	31.2	142.9
1952	68.2	35.1			35.7	70.8					2.1	84.9	226.0
1953	94.5	54.3			28.5	82.8					1.5	41.9	220.8
1954	59.8	59.0			27.5	86.5		4.9		4.9	2.2	59.2	212.7
1955	65.0	61.4	13.0	1.2	27.5	103.1	0.1	26.6	0.5	27.2	6.9	65.6	267.8
1956	37.3	75.8	10.7	2.2	29.4	118.1	0.0	4.0	0.4	4.5	8.7	43.4	212.0
1957	30.7	95.4	13.4	1.9	23.1	133.8	0.0	41.4	0.3	41.8	9.0	35.5	250.8
1958	33.8	116.9	13.7	1.1	26.9	158.6	0.0	16.5	0.4	17.0	8.4	33.5	251.3
1959	49.0	123.6	13.4	1.3	20.2	158.5	0.5	0.1	1.2	1.7	4.1	19.2	232.4
1960	57.3	130.9	13.9	1.4	24.6	170.8	1.1	8.4	0.9	10.4	9.6	12.5	260.7
1961	64.9	145.9	14.3	1.7	22.6	184.2	0.7	0.0	0.5	1.3	8.7	32.8	291.8
1962	89.5	188.8	11.0	1.7	22.4	224.0	0.4	0.0	0.6	1.0	10.5	49.8	374.8
1963	95.3	190.9	11.1	1.9	21.6	225.5	0.2	0.0	0.4	0.6	14.5	63.1	399.0
1964	85.7	227.0	10.2	2.4	23.2	262.8		33.6	1.0	34.6	11.2	98.9	493.1
1965	80.0	184.1	10.1	2.3	22.9	219.4	0.0	0.3	1.6	1.9	10.6	90.9	402.8
1966	101.3	186.0	16.0	2.6	23.5	228.1		0.0	1.1	1.1	13.7	42.0	386.3
1967	116.4	174.4	15.4	1.3	24.8	215.9			1.6	1.6	13.0	47.6	394.6
1968	117.6	177.9	14.7	1.6	24.9	219.1			4.0	4.0	10.3	65.6	416.7

CTN BROAD DIVISIONS AND CATEGORIES

I. 1. INDUSTRIAL MACHINERY AND EQUIPMENT (INCLUDING SPARE PARTS)

II. FUELS, RAW MATERIALS (OTHER THAN FOR FOOD), OTHER MATERIALS

2. FUELS, MINERAL RAW MATERIALS, METALS
3. CHEMICALS, FERTILIZERS, RUBBER
4. BUILDING MATERIALS AND CONSTRUCTION PARTS
5. RAW MATERIALS OF VEGETABLE AND ANIMAL ORIGIN (NOT FOOD)

III. FOODSTUFFS AND RAW MATERIAL FOR FOODSTUFFS

6. LIVE ANIMALS (NOT FOR SLAUGHTER)
7. RAW MATERIAL FOR THE PRODUCTION OF FOODSTUFFS
8. FOODSTUFFS

IV. 9. INDUSTRIAL CONSUMER GOODS (OTHER THAN FOOD)

* CONVERTED FROM NATIONAL DEVISA UNITS THROUGH OFFICIAL EXCHANGE RATES. NOTE THE LIMITATIONS DISCUSSED IN THE EXPLANATORY TEXT.

TABLE III.CTN.X.U-Y
USSR EXPORTS TO YUGOSLAVIA, 1946-68
(MILLIONS OF CURRENT DOLLARS,* F.O.B.)

YEAR	BROAD DIV I 1	2	3	4	5	BROAD DIV II (2-5)	6	7	8	BROAD DIV III (6-8)	BROAD DIV IV 9	NOT SPECIFIED	TOTAL EXPORTS
1946	2.6	3.5	0.2		1.5	5.1		1.3		1.3	0.8	8.7	18.4
1947	2.3	9.1	0.3		2.1	11.4					0.9	23.0	37.7
1948	2.9	6.4	0.0		1.0	8.4					1.3	21.9	34.4
1949	0.0	1.1	0.4			1.5					0.2	1.1	2.9
1950	–										0.0		–
1951	–										0.0		–
1952	–										0.0		–
1953	0.0										0.0		–
1954	–	0.9			0.1	0.9					0.0	1.0	2.0
1955	0.0	8.3	0.5		6.3	15.1		0.5	0.4	0.9	0.1	0.4	16.4
1956	2.9	23.2	0.9		6.7	30.7		34.5	0.4	34.9	0.3	0.2	69.1
1957	15.8	33.8	1.5		9.2	44.5		10.0		10.0	0.5	2.4	73.1
1958	11.4	24.3	4.4		3.5	32.1		6.0		6.0	0.9	0.7	51.1
1959	5.4	25.2	3.5		2.9	31.6		7.6		7.6	1.1	0.5	46.2
1960	14.9	29.0	4.7		0.6	34.3					1.4	4.5	55.1
1961	4.6	19.3	1.9		0.6	21.8					2.0	7.5	35.9
1962	11.7	31.7	4.8		0.0	37.4		1.4		1.4	2.5	19.3	72.3
1963	17.7	35.8	8.2		1.1	45.1		2.8	1.1	3.9	4.6	25.1	96.3
1964	29.8	50.8	6.9	0.2	1.1	59.1			0.5	0.5	5.7	39.8	134.9
1965	26.0	55.1	12.6	0.3	3.7	71.7		0.9	2.8	3.7	5.9	37.8	145.1
1966	34.0	60.6	19.1		6.0	85.8		0.0	28.0	29.0	7.3	57.8	213.9
1967	39.2	65.5	17.7		12.5	95.7		0.7	26.4	27.1	5.8	112.5	280.3
1968	50.4	77.6	17.7		19.4	114.7		4.4	23.1	27.5	4.8	91.7	289.1

CTN BROAD DIVISIONS AND CATEGORIES

I. 1. INDUSTRIAL MACHINERY AND EQUIPMENT (INCLUDING SPARE PARTS)

II. FUELS, RAW MATERIALS (OTHER THAN FOR FOOD), OTHER MATERIALS

2. FUELS, MINERAL RAW MATERIALS, METALS
3. CHEMICALS, FERTILIZERS, RUBBER
4. BUILDING MATERIALS AND CONSTRUCTION PARTS
5. RAW MATERIALS OF VEGETABLE AND ANIMAL ORIGIN (NOT FOOD)

III. FOODSTUFFS AND RAW MATERIAL FOR FOODSTUFFS

6. LIVE ANIMALS (NOT FOR SLAUGHTER)
7. RAW MATERIAL FOR THE PRODUCTION OF FOODSTUFFS
8. FOODSTUFFS

IV. 9. INDUSTRIAL CONSUMER GOODS (OTHER THAN FOOD)

* CONVERTED FROM NATIONAL DEVISA UNITS THROUGH OFFICIAL EXCHANGE RATES. NOTE THE LIMITATIONS DISCUSSED IN THE EXPLANATORY TEXT.

TABLE III.CTN.X.U-CEMA
USSR EXPORTS TO EUROPEAN CEMA (EXCLUDING ALBANIA), 1946-68
(MILLIONS OF CURRENT DOLLARS,* F.O.B.)

YEAR	BROAD DIV I 1	2	3	4	5	BROAD DIV II (2-5)	6	7	8	BROAD DIV III (6-8)	BROAD DIV IV 9	NOT SPECIFIED	TOTAL EXPORTS
1946	31.5	29.1	12.7		73.7	115.6		81.4		81.4	2.6	69.8	300.9
1947	11.3	41.1	11.1		82.2	134.4		57.9		57.9	2.1	103.0	308.8
1948	31.1	98.3	9.9		144.4	252.6		126.8	8.5	135.2	3.8	105.5	528.2
1949	88.9	166.5	17.6		155.9	340.0		72.2	49.7	121.9	5.2	192.0	748.0
1950	140.3	160.2	16.5		193.5	370.3		121.0	54.8	175.8	9.8	292.3	988.4
1951	190.3	200.8	21.5		280.8	503.1		186.3	69.4	255.7	12.1	318.8	1280.0
1952	259.1	257.7	23.9		296.2	577.7		218.0	72.0	290.0	12.7	513.3	1652.8
1953	308.7	347.0	23.1		286.5	656.7		196.2	109.6	305.8	12.3	387.3	1670.8
1954	278.2	412.5	23.6		296.5	732.5		218.5	79.3	297.9	12.9	400.2	1721.8
1955	295.9	485.1	61.2	3.9	295.2	845.4	0.5	241.1	28.1	269.7	26.2	339.7	1776.9
1956	208.7	587.5	76.5	4.7	310.2	979.0	0.3	131.3	81.8	213.5	35.0	313.4	1749.5
1957	207.3	893.7	85.0	3.7	345.6	1327.9	0.1	464.5	135.9	600.5	70.6	310.9	2517.2
1958	222.2	930.0	78.7	2.4	340.3	1351.5	0.1	276.8	76.8	353.7	75.6	272.8	2275.8
1959	344.3	1040.7	92.7	3.6	350.5	1487.5	0.6	379.2	211.3	591.1	74.3	404.5	2901.6
1960	389.5	1219.4	102.0	4.8	403.7	1729.9	1.3	372.1	124.1	497.5	74.4	383.1	3074.3
1961	450.0	1378.4	116.9	6.2	441.3	1942.8	0.9	308.0	134.0	442.9	81.6	482.4	3399.7
1962	606.6	1581.9	121.5	9.1	448.9	2161.4	0.5	381.8	180.8	563.1	92.6	547.4	3971.1
1963	734.9	1706.1	132.8	10.0	434.3	2283.3	0.4	325.4	207.3	533.1	86.2	525.9	4163.3
1964	786.9	1964.6	148.1	11.4	499.0	2623.1	0.1	224.0	114.5	338.6	70.0	680.6	4499.2
1965	786.6	1961.9	154.8	15.1	529.6	2661.4	0.1	232.4	131.5	364.0	74.4	666.1	4552.6
1966	959.9	1932.8	173.0	20.1	556.0	2682.0	0.0	218.9	191.4	410.3	78.8	561.0	4692.0
1967	1099.8	2023.9	180.9	27.8	535.2	2767.9		302.2	214.1	516.3	92.1	562.6	5038.7
1968	1230.1	2200.6	212.1	36.4	575.5	3024.6		310.8	203.8	514.5	108.7	758.1	5636.1

CTN BROAD DIVISIONS AND CATEGORIES

I. 1. INDUSTRIAL MACHINERY AND EQUIPMENT (INCLUDING SPARE PARTS)   III.   FOODSTUFFS AND RAW MATERIAL FOR FOODSTUFFS

II. FUELS, RAW MATERIALS (OTHER THAN FOR FOOD), OTHER MATERIALS
   6. LIVE ANIMALS (NOT FOR SLAUGHTER)
   7. RAW MATERIAL FOR THE PRODUCTION OF FOODSTUFFS
   8. FOODSTUFFS

2. FUELS, MINERAL RAW MATERIALS, METALS
3. CHEMICALS, FERTILIZERS, RUBBER
4. BUILDING MATERIALS AND CONSTRUCTION PARTS
5. RAW MATERIALS OF VEGETABLE AND ANIMAL ORIGIN (NOT FOOD)

IV. 9. INDUSTRIAL CONSUMER GOODS (OTHER THAN FOOD)

* CONVERTED FROM NATIONAL DEVISA UNITS THROUGH OFFICIAL EXCHANGE RATES. NOTE THE LIMITATIONS DISCUSSED IN THE EXPLANATORY TEXT.

TABLE III.CTN.X.C-U
CZECHOSLOVAKIA'S EXPORTS TO USSR, 1958-68
(MILLIONS OF CURRENT DOLLARS,* F.O.B.)

YEAR	BROAD DIV I 1	2	3	4	5	BROAD DIV II (2-5)	6	7	8	BROAD DIV III (6-8)	BROAD DIV IV 9	NOT SPECIFIED	TOTAL EXPORTS
1958	179.6	126.5	2.5			129.0		2.8	17.0	19.8	98.2	70.5	497.1
1959	201.2	116.9	6.0			122.9		5.2	20.7	25.9	148.3	89.1	587.4
1960	252.8	118.5	5.2	1.9		125.6		3.5	21.8	25.3	167.9	87.0	658.7
1961	322.8	122.3	8.1	1.9		132.2		4.8	23.8	28.6	169.4	60.5	713.4
1962	424.1	122.1	14.0	2.5		138.7		3.6	19.3	22.9	180.0	62.8	828.4
1963	502.8	133.5	18.6	2.5	3.2	157.8		4.4	21.9	26.3	204.7	64.8	956.5
1964	508.0	147.8	29.9	3.1	3.5	184.3		0.0	3.7	4.6	187.7	77.2	961.7
1965	565.3	73.9	31.9	4.5	6.7	117.0		3.0	4.4	7.3	170.7	162.6	1022.9
1966	480.7	118.2	35.5	5.6	5.2	164.5		2.6	6.6	9.2	173.9	92.1	920.5
1967	478.1	116.5	38.8	5.3	4.5	165.0			13.8	13.8	215.4	104.9	977.2
1968	490.2	126.0	44.1	5.8	4.5	180.4			7.5	7.5	227.7	102.2	1008.0

CTN BROAD DIVISIONS AND CATEGORIES

I. 1. INDUSTRIAL MACHINERY AND EQUIPMENT (INCLUDING SPARE PARTS)

II. FUELS, RAW MATERIALS (OTHER THAN FOR FOOD), OTHER MATERIALS

2. FUELS, MINERAL RAW MATERIALS, METALS
3. CHEMICALS, FERTILIZERS, RUBBER
4. BUILDING MATERIALS AND CONSTRUCTION PARTS
5. RAW MATERIALS OF VEGETABLE AND ANIMAL ORIGIN (NOT FOOD)

III. FOODSTUFFS AND RAW MATERIAL FOR FOODSTUFFS

6. LIVE ANIMALS (NOT FOR SLAUGHTER)
7. RAW MATERIAL FOR THE PRODUCTION OF FOODSTUFFS
8. FOODSTUFFS

IV. 9. INDUSTRIAL CONSUMER GOODS (OTHER THAN FOOD)

* CONVERTED FROM NATIONAL DEVISA UNITS THROUGH OFFICIAL EXCHANGE RATES. NOTE THE LIMITATIONS DISCUSSED IN THE EXPLANATORY TEXT.

TABLE III.CTN.X.C-B
CZECHOSLOVAKIA'S EXPORTS TO BULGARIA, 1958-68
(MILLIONS OF CURRENT DOLLARS,* F.O.B.)

YEAR	BROAD DIV I 1	2	3	4	5	BROAD DIV II (2-5)	6	7	8	BROAD DIV III (6-8)	BROAD DIV IV 9	NOT SPECIFIED	TOTAL EXPORTS
1958	12.5	8.0	1.6	0.6	2.9	13.0					4.0	6.6	36.3
1959	20.6	9.6	1.9	0.8	3.5	15.9					6.4	10.6	53.5
1960	23.5	14.7	1.8	1.2	5.1	22.8					4.7	10.5	61.5
1961	23.1	15.0	2.3	0.9	4.2	22.4					3.3	8.3	57.1
1962	28.8	15.6	2.7	0.9	3.4	22.6					5.5	7.8	64.7
1963	43.0	17.1	3.3	1.1	1.6	23.2					7.4	6.4	80.0
1964	29.6	17.8	2.9	1.4	1.9	24.0					5.1	4.4	63.1
1965	27.5	20.4	2.2	0.0	1.5	25.1					4.7	4.6	61.8
1966	48.8	13.7	2.8	1.6	1.1	19.2					4.2	9.4	81.5
1967	54.4	17.0	2.7	1.4	1.1	22.2					5.2	10.0	91.7
1968	48.7	12.9	2.2	1.5	1.1	17.7					6.3	9.2	82.0

CTN BROAD DIVISIONS AND CATEGORIES

I. 1. INDUSTRIAL MACHINERY AND EQUIPMENT (INCLUDING SPARE PARTS)

II. FUELS, RAW MATERIALS (OTHER THAN FOR FOOD), OTHER MATERIALS

2. FUELS, MINERAL RAW MATERIALS, METALS
3. CHEMICALS, FERTILIZERS, RUBBER
4. BUILDING MATERIALS AND CONSTRUCTION PARTS
5. RAW MATERIALS OF VEGETABLE AND ANIMAL ORIGIN (NOT FOOD)

III. FOODSTUFFS AND RAW MATERIAL FOR FOODSTUFFS

6. LIVE ANIMALS (NOT FOR SLAUGHTER)
7. RAW MATERIAL FOR THE PRODUCTION OF FOODSTUFFS
8. FOODSTUFFS

IV. 9. INDUSTRIAL CONSUMER GOODS (OTHER THAN FOOD)

* CONVERTED FROM NATIONAL DEVISA UNITS THROUGH OFFICIAL EXCHANGE
RATES. NOTE THE LIMITATIONS DISCUSSED IN THE EXPLANATORY TEXT.

TABLE III.CTN.X.C-G
CZECHOSLOVAKIA'S EXPORTS TO EAST GERMANY, 1958-68
(MILLIONS OF CURRENT DOLLARS,* F.O.B.)

YEAR	BROAD DIV I 1	2	3	4	5	BROAD DIV II (2-5)	6	7	8	BROAD DIV III (6-8)	BROAD DIV IV 9	NOT SPECIFIED	TOTAL EXPORTS
1958	40.2	45.6	3.2	0.5	6.2	55.5		5.4	3.6	9.0	29.6	23.2	157.5
1959	54.5	43.2	6.0	1.1	5.2	55.5		4.3	3.7	8.0	37.2	22.9	178.1
1960	57.8	50.6	8.7	1.5	3.1	63.9		3.8	3.7	7.5	42.7	23.7	195.6
1961	68.2	62.6	10.0	1.8	4.2	78.6		4.5	3.5	8.0	52.2	6.7	213.6
1962	79.4	61.7	11.9	2.3	4.0	79.9		4.7	2.8	7.5	47.9	15.1	229.9
1963	83.5	55.7	11.7	1.7	3.1	72.3	0.0	8.6	2.7	11.3	34.5	20.5	222.1
1964	91.9	78.6	9.2	3.3	4.5	95.6	0.0	6.0	3.8	10.7	37.8	29.9	266.0
1965	100.7	86.7	13.3	3.5	3.1	106.6	2.1	2.9	3.2	8.2	39.5	22.2	277.1
1966	103.8	80.0	12.6	3.2	4.4	100.2	0.0	3.5	3.8	7.3	43.5	42.6	297.4
1967	110.6	73.4	15.4	4.2	4.5	97.6	0.7	3.3	3.9	7.8	47.6	54.9	318.6
1968	119.7	65.7	14.9	4.3	6.7	91.6	0.7	3.3	2.9	6.9	45.2	64.6	328.1

CTN BROAD DIVISIONS AND CATEGORIES

I. 1. INDUSTRIAL MACHINERY AND EQUIPMENT (INCLUDING SPARE PARTS)

II. FUELS, RAW MATERIALS (OTHER THAN FOR FOOD), OTHER MATERIALS

2. FUELS, MINERAL RAW MATERIALS, METALS
3. CHEMICALS, FERTILIZERS, RUBBER
4. BUILDING MATERIALS AND CONSTRUCTION PARTS
5. RAW MATERIALS OF VEGETABLE AND ANIMAL ORIGIN (NOT FOOD)

III. FOODSTUFFS AND RAW MATERIAL FOR FOODSTUFFS

6. LIVE ANIMALS (NOT FOR SLAUGHTER)
7. RAW MATERIAL FOR THE PRODUCTION OF FOODSTUFFS
8. FOODSTUFFS

IV. 9. INDUSTRIAL CONSUMER GOODS (OTHER THAN FOOD)

* CONVERTED FROM NATIONAL DEVISA UNITS THROUGH OFFICIAL EXCHANGE
  RATES. NOTE THE LIMITATIONS DISCUSSED IN THE EXPLANATORY TEXT.

TABLE III.CTN.X.C-H
CZECHOSLOVAKIA'S EXPORTS TO HUNGARY, 1958-68
(MILLIONS OF CURRENT DOLLARS,* F.O.B.)

YEAR	BROAD DIV I 1	BROAD DIV II (2-5)	2	3	4	5	6	7	8	BROAD DIV III (6-8)	BROAD DIV IV 9	NOT SPECIFIED	TOTAL EXPORTS
1958	20.3	47.5	37.2	1.7	2.1	6.5		0.9	0.6	1.5	4.5	3.6	77.4
1959	26.7	44.7	33.6	2.3	3.3	5.4		0.5	0.4	0.9	7.5	6.4	86.1
1960	39.0	54.2	43.2	3.4	2.6	5.0		0.4	0.4	0.8	11.0	6.6	111.7
1961	26.9	65.4	53.2	2.8	2.8	6.6		0.3	0.5	0.8	6.7	4.4	104.2
1962	36.4	76.3	64.4	2.8	3.3	5.9		0.6	0.5	1.0	6.8	4.4	125.0
1963	45.1	84.8	69.9	3.9	3.8	7.2		0.4	1.2	1.7	13.4	7.7	152.7
1964	39.6	91.3	74.1	7.2	3.8	6.2		0.5	0.3	0.8	12.1	14.3	158.1
1965	38.1	71.9	55.3	6.4	3.7	6.5		0.5	0.2	0.7	11.4	10.1	132.2
1966	47.4	62.4	44.9	5.9	4.7	6.9		0.8	0.6	1.4	9.8	11.2	132.2
1967	60.1	61.3	41.3	7.9	5.1	6.9		0.9	2.2	3.1	14.1	13.9	152.4
1968	63.5	62.2	40.7	6.9	6.0	8.5		1.1	2.9	4.0	16.7	21.0	167.4

CTN BROAD DIVISIONS AND CATEGORIES

I. 1. INDUSTRIAL MACHINERY AND EQUIPMENT (INCLUDING SPARE PARTS)

II. FUELS, RAW MATERIALS (OTHER THAN FOR FOOD), OTHER MATERIALS

2. FUELS, MINERAL RAW MATERIALS, METALS
3. CHEMICALS, FERTILIZERS, RUBBER
4. BUILDING MATERIALS AND CONSTRUCTION PARTS
5. RAW MATERIALS OF VEGETABLE AND ANIMAL ORIGIN (NOT FOOD)

III. FOODSTUFFS AND RAW MATERIAL FOR FOODSTUFFS

6. LIVE ANIMALS (NOT FOR SLAUGHTER)
7. RAW MATERIAL FOR THE PRODUCTION OF FOODSTUFFS
8. FOODSTUFFS

IV. 9. INDUSTRIAL CONSUMER GOODS (OTHER THAN FOOD)

* CONVERTED FROM NATIONAL DEVISA UNITS THROUGH OFFICIAL EXCHANGE RATES. NOTE THE LIMITATIONS DISCUSSED IN THE EXPLANATORY TEXT.

TABLE III.CTN.X.C-P
CZECHOSLOVAKIA'S EXPORTS TO POLAND, 1958-68
(MILLIONS OF CURRENT DOLLARS,* F.O.B.)

YEAR	BROAD DIV I 1	2	3	4	5	BROAD DIV II (2-5)	6	7	8	BROAD DIV III (6-8)	BROAD DIV IV 9	NOT SPECIFIED	TOTAL EXPORTS
1958	47.9	15.0	2.1	2.0	3.6	22.6					14.6	9.7	94.9
1959	56.7	21.2	2.0	2.2	2.3	27.7					17.0	13.5	114.9
1960	66.2	34.3	2.1	2.5	2.1	41.1					12.3	8.8	128.3
1961	83.6	45.0	2.6	2.5	2.3	52.4					14.5	13.5	164.0
1962	102.4	54.3	2.8	2.6	3.2	62.9					21.0	14.8	201.0
1963	95.0	51.2	3.7	4.9	4.5	64.2					19.9	16.5	195.6
1964	92.8	47.5	3.8	3.7	4.8	59.8			0.0	0.0	14.7	25.5	192.8
1965	118.0	55.8	10.0	5.4	6.8	78.0			0.2	0.2	20.4	32.1	248.8
1966	128.1	37.9	7.6	3.5	8.5	57.5			0.0	0.0	17.7	33.2	236.5
1967	119.6	37.8	4.5	4.8	8.0	55.1					13.5	46.7	234.9
1968	116.4	40.6	6.4	4.7	7.5	59.2					11.7	44.5	231.7

CTN BROAD DIVISIONS AND CATEGORIES

I. 1. INDUSTRIAL MACHINERY AND EQUIPMENT (INCLUDING SPARE PARTS)

II. FUELS, RAW MATERIALS (OTHER THAN FOR FOOD), OTHER MATERIALS

2. FUELS, MINERAL RAW MATERIALS, METALS
3. CHEMICALS, FERTILIZERS, RUBBER
4. BUILDING MATERIALS AND CONSTRUCTION PARTS
5. RAW MATERIALS OF VEGETABLE AND ANIMAL ORIGIN (NOT FOOD)

III. FOODSTUFFS AND RAW MATERIAL FOR FOODSTUFFS

6. LIVE ANIMALS (NOT FOR SLAUGHTER)
7. RAW MATERIAL FOR THE PRODUCTION OF FOODSTUFFS
8. FOODSTUFFS

IV. 9. INDUSTRIAL CONSUMER GOODS (OTHER THAN FOOD)

* CONVERTED FROM NATIONAL DEVISA UNITS THROUGH OFFICIAL EXCHANGE RATES. NOTE THE LIMITATIONS DISCUSSED IN THE EXPLANATORY TEXT.

TABLE III.CTN.X.C-R
CZECHOSLOVAKIA'S EXPORTS TO RUMANIA, 1958-68
(MILLIONS OF CURRENT DOLLARS,* F.O.B.)

YEAR	BROAD DIV I 1	2	3	4	5	BROAD DIV II (2-5)	6	7	8	BROAD DIV III (6-8)	BROAD DIV IV 9	NOT SPECIFIED	TOTAL EXPORTS
1958	10.5	13.8	0.5	0.9	0.6	15.9		0.8	0.5	1.4	3.0	7.0	37.8
1959	21.6	25.9	0.7	1.3	0.5	28.4		1.5	0.3	1.8	2.1	6.6	60.6
1960	25.3	24.1	0.7	1.6	1.1	27.6		0.9		0.9	4.3	5.6	63.6
1961	38.9	21.7	0.8	1.9	0.8	25.4		0.2	0.2	0.4	7.6	3.5	75.7
1962	47.3	25.5	1.6	1.5	1.0	29.6		0.2	0.2	0.4	6.9	3.8	88.1
1963	54.6	27.9	1.3	1.7	0.4	31.3		0.7	2.0	2.7	8.7	3.4	100.7
1964	53.3	24.4	1.7	1.5	0.8	28.5		0.3	1.1	1.4	6.9	2.8	92.9
1965	36.7	21.3	0.0	1.3	0.6	24.1		0.1	0.8	0.9	4.2	2.9	68.9
1966	34.3	22.5	1.7	1.6	0.5	26.4		0.7	0.8	1.5	4.5	2.8	69.4
1967	37.8	28.4	2.7	4.0	0.0	35.2		0.7	0.8	1.5	7.4	7.6	89.5
1968	41.2	35.2	2.3	4.7	0.0	42.2		0.7	0.8	1.5	5.2	9.6	99.7

CTN BROAD DIVISIONS AND CATEGORIES

I. 1. INDUSTRIAL MACHINERY AND EQUIPMENT (INCLUDING SPARE PARTS)

II. FUELS, RAW MATERIALS (OTHER THAN FOR FOOD), OTHER MATERIALS

2. FUELS, MINERAL RAW MATERIALS, METALS
3. CHEMICALS, FERTILIZERS, RUBBER
4. BUILDING MATERIALS AND CONSTRUCTION PARTS
5. RAW MATERIALS OF VEGETABLE AND ANIMAL ORIGIN (NOT FOOD)

III. FOODSTUFFS AND RAW MATERIAL FOR FOODSTUFFS

6. LIVE ANIMALS (NOT FOR SLAUGHTER)
7. RAW MATERIAL FOR THE PRODUCTION OF FOODSTUFFS
8. FOODSTUFFS

IV. 9. INDUSTRIAL CONSUMER GOODS (OTHER THAN FOOD)

* CONVERTED FROM NATIONAL DEVISA UNITS THROUGH OFFICIAL EXCHANGE RATES. NOTE THE LIMITATIONS DISCUSSED IN THE EXPLANATORY TEXT.

TABLE III.CTN.X.C-Y
CZECHOSLOVAKIA'S EXPORTS TO YUGOSLAVIA, 1958-66
(MILLIONS OF CURRENT DOLLARS,* F.O.B.)

YEAR	BROAD DIV I 1	2	3	4	5	BROAD DIV II (2-5)	6	7	8	BROAD DIV III (6-8)	BROAD DIV IV 9	NOT SPECIFIED	TOTAL EXPORTS
1958	10.2	3.2	1.1	0.4	0.8	5.5		0.2	1.9	2.0	4.4	2.9	25.0
1959	7.3	4.9	1.7	0.4	0.9	7.9		0.2	0.7	0.9	4.1	1.8	21.9
1960	7.9	5.8	1.5	0.3	0.7	8.4		0.1	1.1	1.2	5.0	1.5	23.9
1961	5.7	4.3	0.8	0.3	0.4	5.8		0.5	0.7	1.2	4.4	0.9	18.1
1962	7.2	6.5	1.5	0.5	0.1	8.6		0.8	0.8	1.6	6.0	1.2	24.6
1963	17.8	13.8	1.9	1.2	0.7	17.5		1.3	0.0	1.3	8.7	1.5	46.8
1964	27.5	22.6	3.4	1.9	1.5	29.5		1.1		1.1	10.7	7.5	76.3
1965	21.2	25.8	4.1	2.0	2.1	34.0		1.8		1.8	9.8	2.4	69.2
1966	24.3	34.7	5.3	3.0	2.2	45.2		2.0		2.0	13.2	10.5	95.3

CTN BROAD DIVISIONS AND CATEGORIES

I. 1. INDUSTRIAL MACHINERY AND EQUIPMENT (INCLUDING SPARE PARTS)

II. FUELS, RAW MATERIALS (OTHER THAN FOR FOOD), OTHER MATERIALS

2. FUELS, MINERAL RAW MATERIALS, METALS
3. CHEMICALS, FERTILIZERS, RUBBER
4. BUILDING MATERIALS AND CONSTRUCTION PARTS
5. RAW MATERIALS OF VEGETABLE AND ANIMAL ORIGIN (NOT FOOD)

III. FOODSTUFFS AND RAW MATERIAL FOR FOODSTUFFS

6. LIVE ANIMALS (NOT FOR SLAUGHTER)
7. RAW MATERIAL FOR THE PRODUCTION OF FOODSTUFFS
8. FOODSTUFFS

IV. 9. INDUSTRIAL CONSUMER GOODS (OTHER THAN FOOD)

* CONVERTED FROM NATIONAL DEVISA UNITS THROUGH OFFICIAL EXCHANGE RATES. NOTE THE LIMITATIONS DISCUSSED IN THE EXPLANATORY TEXT.

TABLE III.CTN.X.C-CEMA
CZECHOSLOVAKIA'S EXPORTS TO EUROPEAN CEMA (EXCLUDING ALBANIA), 1958-68
(MILLIONS OF CURRENT DOLLARS,* F.O.B.)

YEAR	BROAD DIV I 1	2	3	4	5	BROAD DIV II (2-5)	6	7	8	BROAD DIV III (6-8)	BROAD DIV IV 9	NOT SPECIFIED	TOTAL EXPORTS
1958	311.1	246.1	11.6	6.1	19.8	283.6		9.9	21.7	31.6	154.0	120.6	900.9
1959	381.4	250.5	18.8	8.7	17.0	295.2		11.5	25.1	36.6	218.4	149.0	1080.5
1960	464.6	285.5	22.0	11.3	16.4	335.1		8.6	25.9	34.6	243.0	142.2	1219.4
1961	563.4	319.9	26.5	11.7	18.1	376.3		9.7	28.0	37.7	253.7	96.9	1328.0
1962	718.3	343.7	35.7	13.1	17.5	410.0		9.1	22.8	31.9	268.1	108.7	1537.1
1963	824.0	355.3	42.5	15.7	20.0	433.5	0.0	14.1	27.9	42.1	288.5	119.4	1707.5
1964	815.1	390.1	54.7	16.9	21.8	483.5	0.0	7.8	8.9	17.6	264.3	154.1	1734.6
1965	886.4	313.4	64.8	19.3	25.1	422.6	2.1	6.4	8.9	17.4	250.9	234.4	1811.7
1966	843.2	317.3	66.0	20.3	26.6	430.2	0.0	7.5	11.9	19.5	253.6	191.2	1737.6
1967	860.6	314.3	72.0	24.8	25.2	436.3	0.7	4.8	20.6	26.1	303.1	238.0	1864.2
1968	879.7	321.2	76.8	26.9	28.4	453.3	0.7	5.0	14.2	19.9	312.8	251.1	1916.8

CTN BROAD DIVISIONS AND CATEGORIES

I. 1. INDUSTRIAL MACHINERY AND EQUIPMENT (INCLUDING SPARE PARTS)

II. FUELS, RAW MATERIALS (OTHER THAN FOR FOOD), OTHER MATERIALS

2. FUELS, MINERAL RAW MATERIALS, METALS
3. CHEMICALS, FERTILIZERS, RUBBER
4. BUILDING MATERIALS AND CONSTRUCTION PARTS
5. RAW MATERIALS OF VEGETABLE AND ANIMAL ORIGIN (NOT FOOD)

III. FOODSTUFFS AND RAW MATERIAL FOR FOODSTUFFS

6. LIVE ANIMALS (NOT FOR SLAUGHTER)
7. RAW MATERIAL FOR THE PRODUCTION OF FOODSTUFFS
8. FOODSTUFFS

IV. 9. INDUSTRIAL CONSUMER GOODS (OTHER THAN FOOD)

* CONVERTED FROM NATIONAL DEVISA UNITS THROUGH OFFICIAL EXCHANGE
  RATES. NOTE THE LIMITATIONS DISCUSSED IN THE EXPLANATORY TEXT.

TABLE III.CTN.X.P-U
POLAND'S EXPORTS TO USSR, 1958-68
(MILLIONS OF CURRENT DOLLARS,* F.O.B.)

YEAR	BROAD DIV I 1	2	3	4	5	BROAD DIV II (2-5)	6	7	8	BROAD DIV III (6-8)	BROAD DIV IV 9	NOT SPECIFIED	TOTAL EXPORTS
1958	89.0	101.1	4.8	2.0	2.2	110.0	0.0		13.5	13.6	14.6	38.1	265.2
1959	102.5	116.7	5.8	1.6	2.8	126.9	0.1		14.1	14.1	33.3	36.2	313.0
1960	121.8	129.1	6.7	1.7	4.1	141.6	0.0	0.9	15.6	16.5	67.2	43.2	390.2
1961	125.2	127.9	6.4	2.4	4.1	140.9		16.2	35.3	51.5	91.4	76.0	485.0
1962	181.8	129.1	9.2	2.7	5.2	146.1		8.4	36.4	44.8	112.2	83.7	568.7
1963	222.6	131.7	15.9	3.6	4.6	155.8		0.6	8.9	9.6	121.3	108.1	617.5
1964	244.5	137.9	24.7	1.6	6.0	170.1		2.7	29.9	32.5	124.9	149.7	721.7
1965	263.1	163.3	23.2	1.1	4.8	192.4	0.1	2.8	28.6	31.5	128.1	166.4	781.4
1966	253.4	139.8	22.6	1.0	5.1	168.5	0.1	4.6	11.2	15.9	160.3	143.0	741.2
1967	319.2	157.4	25.7		5.4	188.5		3.8	14.5	18.2	221.4	154.4	901.8
1968	372.6	157.9	33.5		5.7	197.1		2.1	11.9	14.0	255.9	202.5	1042.1

CTN BROAD DIVISIONS AND CATEGORIES

I. 1. INDUSTRIAL MACHINERY AND EQUIPMENT (INCLUDING SPARE PARTS)

II. FUELS, RAW MATERIALS (OTHER THAN FOR FOOD), OTHER MATERIALS

2. FUELS, MINERAL RAW MATERIALS, METALS
3. CHEMICALS, FERTILIZERS, RUBBER
4. BUILDING MATERIALS AND CONSTRUCTION PARTS
5. RAW MATERIALS OF VEGETABLE AND ANIMAL ORIGIN (NOT FOOD)

III. FOODSTUFFS AND RAW MATERIAL FOR FOODSTUFFS

6. LIVE ANIMALS (NOT FOR SLAUGHTER)
7. RAW MATERIAL FOR THE PRODUCTION OF FOODSTUFFS
8. FOODSTUFFS

IV. 9. INDUSTRIAL CONSUMER GOODS (OTHER THAN FOOD)

* CONVERTED FROM NATIONAL DEVISA UNITS THROUGH OFFICIAL EXCHANGE RATES. NOTE THE LIMITATIONS DISCUSSED IN THE EXPLANATORY TEXT.

TABLE III.CTN.X.P-B
POLAND'S EXPORTS TO BULGARIA, 1958-68
(MILLIONS OF CURRENT DOLLARS,* F.O.B.)

YEAR	BROAD DIV I 1	2	3	4	5	BROAD DIV II (2-5)	6	7	8	BROAD DIV III (6-8)	BROAD DIV IV 9	NOT SPECIFIED	TOTAL EXPORTS
1958	2.0	8.1	0.3	0.1	0.1	8.5			0.0	0.0	0.4	6.2	17.1
1959	2.7	7.7	0.4	0.1	0.2	8.4	0.1		0.1	0.2	0.6	5.1	17.0
1960	7.1	8.6	1.4	0.2	0.3	10.5	0.1		0.1	0.1	1.8	8.2	27.6
1961	5.4	7.4	1.0	0.1	0.2	8.7	0.0		0.1	0.1	2.0	5.4	21.6
1962	8.4	7.2	1.5	0.0	0.3	9.1			0.3	0.3	2.3	4.3	24.3
1963	13.1	9.4	1.9	0.1	0.4	11.7			0.2	0.2	4.3	5.2	34.5
1964	14.2	8.7	1.8	0.2	0.3	10.9	0.0		0.0	0.1	4.5	5.5	35.2
1965	24.1	8.4	0.9	0.3	0.2	9.9			0.8	0.8	3.3	6.8	44.9
1966	27.0	5.7	0.9	0.5	0.1	7.2			0.4	0.4	3.6	6.5	44.5
1967	29.6	7.3	1.5	0.4	0.3	9.5			0.8	0.8	6.3	5.2	51.3
1968	34.0	7.9	2.3	0.3	0.8	11.3			1.5	1.5	10.1	6.6	63.4

CTN BROAD DIVISIONS AND CATEGORIES

I. 1. INDUSTRIAL MACHINERY AND EQUIPMENT (INCLUDING SPARE PARTS)

II. FUELS, RAW MATERIALS (OTHER THAN FOR FOOD), OTHER MATERIALS

2. FUELS, MINERAL RAW MATERIALS, METALS
3. CHEMICALS, FERTILIZERS, RUBBER
4. BUILDING MATERIALS AND CONSTRUCTION PARTS
5. RAW MATERIALS OF VEGETABLE AND ANIMAL ORIGIN (NOT FOOD)

III. FOODSTUFFS AND RAW MATERIAL FOR FOODSTUFFS

6. LIVE ANIMALS (NOT FOR SLAUGHTER)
7. RAW MATERIAL FOR THE PRODUCTION OF FOODSTUFFS
8. FOODSTUFFS

IV. 9. INDUSTRIAL CONSUMER GOODS (OTHER THAN FOOD)

* CONVERTED FROM NATIONAL DEVISA UNITS THROUGH OFFICIAL EXCHANGE RATES. NOTE THE LIMITATIONS DISCUSSED IN THE EXPLANATORY TEXT.

TABLE III.CTN.X.P-C
POLAND'S EXPORTS TO CZECHOSLOVAKIA, 1958-68
(MILLIONS OF CURRENT DOLLARS,* F.O.B.)

YEAR	BROAD DIV I 1	2	3	4	5	BROAD DIV II (2-5)	6	7	8	BROAD DIV III (6-8)	BROAD DIV IV 9	NOT SPECIFIED	TOTAL EXPORTS
1958	14.0	39.7	1.4	3.8	0.8	45.7		4.7	2.4	7.1	0.6	5.2	72.5
1959	17.1	44.6	2.3	1.9	1.2	50.0		1.6	3.6	5.2	0.9	7.6	80.6
1960	33.3	56.9	2.5	1.4	0.6	61.4	0.0	1.0	3.9	4.9	3.0	10.5	113.1
1961	42.3	68.8	4.9	1.8	0.5	76.1	0.1	4.5	2.9	7.4	4.8	16.2	146.8
1962	43.6	63.0	6.5	1.0	1.0	71.6	0.1	1.0	4.4	5.5	4.2	21.0	145.8
1963	43.7	63.3	4.8	3.0	1.5	72.4		0.8	7.8	8.7	5.1	14.9	144.7
1964	55.5	77.8	5.1	2.2	1.4	86.6		1.3	18.5	19.9	5.7	28.3	195.9
1965	62.8	75.4	7.1	3.5	1.2	87.2		2.5	9.8	12.2	6.1	40.1	208.4
1966	54.8	51.3	4.7	1.5	2.3	59.8		0.9	10.7	11.6	6.0	46.1	178.3
1967	69.4	54.2	4.0	3.7	2.5	64.4		0.8	12.9	13.7	9.8	45.4	202.7
1968	83.9	61.3	4.9	4.8	2.8	73.8		1.7	18.2	20.0	20.4	47.4	245.5

CTN BROAD DIVISIONS AND CATEGORIES

I. 1. INDUSTRIAL MACHINERY AND EQUIPMENT (INCLUDING SPARE PARTS)

II. FUELS, RAW MATERIALS (OTHER THAN FOR FOOD), OTHER MATERIALS
2. FUELS, MINERAL RAW MATERIALS, METALS
3. CHEMICALS, FERTILIZERS, RUBBER
4. BUILDING MATERIALS AND CONSTRUCTION PARTS
5. RAW MATERIALS OF VEGETABLE AND ANIMAL ORIGIN (NOT FOOD)

III. FOODSTUFFS AND RAW MATERIAL FOR FOODSTUFFS
6. LIVE ANIMALS (NOT FOR SLAUGHTER)
7. RAW MATERIAL FOR THE PRODUCTION OF FOODSTUFFS
8. FOODSTUFFS

IV. 9. INDUSTRIAL CONSUMER GOODS (OTHER THAN FOOD)

* CONVERTED FROM NATIONAL DEVISA UNITS THROUGH OFFICIAL EXCHANGE RATES. NOTE THE LIMITATIONS DISCUSSED IN THE EXPLANATORY TEXT.

TABLE III.CTN.X.P-G
POLAND'S EXPORTS TO EAST GERMANY, 1958-68
(MILLIONS OF CURRENT DOLLARS,* F.O.R.)

YEAR	BROAD DIV I 1	2	3	4	5	BROAD DIV II (2-5)	6	7	8	BROAD DIV III (6-8)	BROAD DIV IV 9	NOT SPECIFIED	TOTAL EXPORTS
1958	5.8	73.3	1.5		0.6	75.4		0.3	2.3	2.6	0.9	21.7	106.4
1959	17.4	82.4	0.9		0.6	83.9		0.3	3.7	4.0	0.8	30.8	136.9
1960	13.0	79.7	0.8	0.1	1.1	81.6		1.2	7.4	8.6	1.8	19.8	124.7
1961	7.8	74.0	1.1	0.1	0.9	76.1		1.1	8.1	9.1	2.5	14.2	109.7
1962	9.1	76.0	1.6	0.1	1.3	79.0	1.1	1.9	8.6	11.6	5.8	12.2	117.6
1963	11.7	73.6	1.7	0.2	2.9	78.4		0.9	7.7	8.6	7.4	14.3	120.5
1964	21.7	83.0	1.1	0.4	4.1	88.6		1.1	22.5	23.6	5.9	24.6	164.5
1965	29.5	79.2	1.2	0.4	3.9	84.7		1.7	6.9	8.6	6.1	24.1	153.1
1966	47.0	74.1	1.2	0.6	4.7	80.6		1.8	8.8	10.6	6.8	15.7	160.6
1967	47.3	77.8	2.3	0.6	3.8	84.6		4.6	14.2	18.7	9.3	15.7	175.7
1968	61.4	85.1	7.7	0.0	7.6	101.4		3.6	16.6	20.2	13.4	32.7	229.2

CTN BROAD DIVISIONS AND CATEGORIES

I. 1. INDUSTRIAL MACHINERY AND EQUIPMENT (INCLUDING SPARE PARTS)

II. FUELS, RAW MATERIALS (OTHER THAN FOR FOOD), OTHER MATERIALS

2. FUELS, MINERAL RAW MATERIALS, METALS
3. CHEMICALS, FERTILIZERS, RUBBER
4. BUILDING MATERIALS AND CONSTRUCTION PARTS
5. RAW MATERIALS OF VEGETABLE AND ANIMAL ORIGIN (NOT FOOD)

III. FOODSTUFFS AND RAW MATERIAL FOR FOODSTUFFS

6. LIVE ANIMALS (NOT FOR SLAUGHTER)
7. RAW MATERIAL FOR THE PRODUCTION OF FOODSTUFFS
8. FOODSTUFFS

IV. 9. INDUSTRIAL CONSUMER GOODS (OTHER THAN FOOD)

* CONVERTED FROM NATIONAL DEVISA UNITS THROUGH OFFICIAL EXCHANGE RATES. NOTE THE LIMITATIONS DISCUSSED IN THE EXPLANATORY TEXT.

TABLE III.CTN.X.P-H
POLAND'S EXPORTS TO HUNGARY, 1958-68
(MILLIONS OF CURRENT DOLLARS,* F.O.B.)

YEAR	BROAD DIV I 1	2	3	4	5	BROAD DIV II (2-5)	6	7	8	BROAD DIV III (6-8)	BROAD DIV IV 9	NOT SPECIFIED	TOTAL EXPORTS
1958	3.7	19.7	1.2	0.5	1.3	22.6	0.0	0.2	1.1	1.4	0.7	0.3	29.6
1959	7.3	21.1	4.1	0.6	1.7	27.4			0.2	0.2	1.2	0.9	37.1
1960	13.8	20.6	3.1	0.4	2.0	26.0			0.3	0.3	2.9	3.5	46.5
1961	15.1	24.6	1.3	0.4	1.2	27.5		1.1	2.6	3.7	3.0	5.8	55.1
1962	13.7	28.4	1.8	0.3	1.0	31.5		0.1	1.4	1.5	2.7	14.3	63.6
1963	28.8	29.6	1.8	0.3	2.5	34.1			0.4	0.4	3.3	12.4	79.0
1964	24.9	32.5	2.0	0.8	2.5	37.7		0.2	2.6	2.8	5.6	18.8	89.8
1965	25.0	34.0	3.0	1.1	2.5	40.6			1.4	1.6	6.3	12.4	85.9
1966	28.9	32.7	1.6	0.9	2.4	37.6		0.2	2.0	2.0	7.3	15.8	91.5
1967	38.8	28.4	2.5	2.0	3.3	36.3			6.2	6.2	10.1	22.1	113.4
1968	31.5	29.1	3.3	1.5	3.2	37.2			6.7	6.7	11.9	23.1	110.3

CTN BROAD DIVISIONS AND CATEGORIES

I. 1. INDUSTRIAL MACHINERY AND EQUIPMENT (INCLUDING SPARE PARTS)

II. FUELS, RAW MATERIALS (OTHER THAN FOR FOOD), OTHER MATERIALS

2. FUELS, MINERAL RAW MATERIALS, METALS
3. CHEMICALS, FERTILIZERS, RUBBER
4. BUILDING MATERIALS AND CONSTRUCTION PARTS
5. RAW MATERIALS OF VEGETABLE AND ANIMAL ORIGIN (NOT FOOD)

III. FOODSTUFFS AND RAW MATERIAL FOR FOODSTUFFS

6. LIVE ANIMALS (NOT FOR SLAUGHTER)
7. RAW MATERIAL FOR THE PRODUCTION OF FOODSTUFFS
8. FOODSTUFFS

IV. 9. INDUSTRIAL CONSUMER GOODS (OTHER THAN FOOD)

* CONVERTED FROM NATIONAL DEVISA UNITS THROUGH OFFICIAL EXCHANGE RATES. NOTE THE LIMITATIONS DISCUSSED IN THE EXPLANATORY TEXT.

TABLE III.CTN.X.P-R
POLAND'S EXPORTS TO RUMANIA, 1958-68
(MILLIONS OF CURRENT DOLLARS,* F.O.B.)

YEAR	BROAD DIV I 1	2	3	4	5	BROAD DIV II (2-5)	6	7	8	BROAD DIV III (6-8)	BROAD DIV IV 9	NOT SPECIFIED	TOTAL EXPORTS
1958	0.9	7.5	0.2		0.8	8.4		0.0	1.1	1.1	0.7	2.4	13.6
1959	5.0	8.9	0.2	0.1	0.7	9.9		0.1	1.5	1.5	0.4	0.9	17.6
1960	6.5	9.8	1.0	0.1	0.7	11.7	0.1	0.1	1.3	1.4	1.5	2.1	23.2
1961	10.7	9.8	2.3		1.6	13.7	0.1	0.1	1.7	1.9	4.9	1.3	32.5
1962	13.3	11.4	2.3	0.0	0.9	14.7	0.1	0.1	1.0	1.2	4.5	1.4	35.1
1963	18.3	11.3	1.9	0.1	0.7	13.9	0.1	0.2	2.0	2.3	4.6	2.2	41.2
1964	12.6	12.2	0.4	0.1	0.8	13.4		0.2	2.7	2.8	4.7	6.0	39.7
1965	12.2	11.7	0.8	0.0	1.2	13.8		0.6	3.0	3.5	3.0	3.3	35.8
1966	16.6	18.5	0.9	0.0	0.2	19.5		0.4	2.5	2.9	2.9	4.2	46.2
1967	19.2	17.3	0.8		0.2	18.3		0.1	1.9	2.0	3.4	3.7	46.5
1968	25.3	21.0	0.7	0.1	0.4	22.1			1.4	1.4	4.7	4.2	57.7

CTN BROAD DIVISIONS AND CATEGORIES

I. 1. INDUSTRIAL MACHINERY AND EQUIPMENT (INCLUDING SPARE PARTS)

II. FUELS, RAW MATERIALS (OTHER THAN FOR FOOD), OTHER MATERIALS

2. FUELS, MINERAL RAW MATERIALS, METALS
3. CHEMICALS, FERTILIZERS, RUBBER
4. BUILDING MATERIALS AND CONSTRUCTION PARTS
5. RAW MATERIALS OF VEGETABLE AND ANIMAL ORIGIN (NOT FOOD)

III. FOODSTUFFS AND RAW MATERIAL FOR FOODSTUFFS

6. LIVE ANIMALS (NOT FOR SLAUGHTER)
7. RAW MATERIAL FOR THE PRODUCTION OF FOODSTUFFS
8. FOODSTUFFS

IV. 9. INDUSTRIAL CONSUMER GOODS (OTHER THAN FOOD)

* CONVERTED FROM NATIONAL DEVISA UNITS THROUGH OFFICIAL EXCHANGE RATES. NOTE THE LIMITATIONS DISCUSSED IN THE EXPLANATORY TEXT.

TABLE III.CTN.X.P-Y
POLAND'S EXPORTS TO YUGOSLAVIA, 1958-68
(MILLIONS OF CURRENT DOLLARS,* F.O.B.)

YEAR	BROAD DIV I 1	2	3	4	5	BROAD DIV II (2-5)	6	7	8	BROAD DIV III (6-8)	BROAD DIV IV 9	NOT SPECIFIED	TOTAL EXPORTS
1958	12.3	9.5	3.2		0.6	13.2		2.6	4.3	6.9	1.3	0.4	34.0
1959	2.9	7.8	4.0	0.1	0.8	12.7		0.6	2.5	3.1	1.5	0.5	20.6
1960	7.9	12.0	4.5	0.1	0.8	17.4		1.6	4.5	6.1	4.9	0.5	36.7
1961	8.2	9.5	2.0	0.0	0.6	12.1		1.1	0.3	1.4	3.8	0.7	26.2
1962	7.3	10.1	3.7		0.5	14.2		4.9	2.3	7.2	2.5	0.3	31.5
1963	8.0	11.6	5.0	0.0	0.8	17.5		0.4	2.0	2.4	4.9	0.4	33.2
1964	16.9	19.8	4.1	0.2	0.3	24.5		0.4	1.2	1.6	5.9	6.9	55.7
1965	16.6	16.3	5.7	0.3	0.5	22.8		0.5	1.4	1.9	5.3	7.5	54.1
1966	28.0	12.2	4.3	0.4	0.8	17.6		0.3	2.6	2.8	6.7	19.9	75.0
1967	17.7	11.7	2.1	0.7	1.5	16.1		0.6	2.7	3.3	4.7	6.6	48.5
1968	15.6	11.6	2.0	0.3	2.6	16.5		0.6	5.4	6.0	6.0	7.8	51.9

CTN BROAD DIVISIONS AND CATEGORIES

I. 1. INDUSTRIAL MACHINERY AND EQUIPMENT (INCLUDING SPARE PARTS)

II. FUELS, RAW MATERIALS (OTHER THAN FOR FOOD), OTHER MATERIALS
2. FUELS, MINERAL RAW MATERIALS, METALS
3. CHEMICALS, FERTILIZERS, RUBBER
4. BUILDING MATERIALS AND CONSTRUCTION PARTS
5. RAW MATERIALS OF VEGETABLE AND ANIMAL ORIGIN (NOT FOOD)

III. FOODSTUFFS AND RAW MATERIAL FOR FOODSTUFFS
6. LIVE ANIMALS (NOT FOR SLAUGHTER)
7. RAW MATERIAL FOR THE PRODUCTION OF FOODSTUFFS
8. FOODSTUFFS

IV. 9. INDUSTRIAL CONSUMER GOODS (OTHER THAN FOOD)

* CONVERTED FROM NATIONAL DEVISA UNITS THROUGH OFFICIAL EXCHANGE RATES. NOTE THE LIMITATIONS DISCUSSED IN THE EXPLANATORY TEXT.

TABLE III.CTN.X.P-CEMA
POLAND'S EXPORTS TO EUROPEAN CEMA (EXCLUDING ALBANIA), 1958-68
(MILLIONS OF CURRENT DOLLARS,* F.O.B.)

YEAR	BROAD DIV I 1	2	3	4	5	BROAD DIV II (2-5)	6	7	8	BROAD DIV III (6-8)	BROAD DIV IV 9	NOT SPECIFIED	TOTAL EXPORTS
1958	115.4	249.3	9.3	6.3	5.7	270.7	0.1	5.2	20.5	25.7	17.9	73.8	503.4
1959	151.9	281.4	13.7	4.2	7.2	306.5	0.1	2.0	23.1	25.3	37.1	81.3	602.2
1960	195.4	304.6	15.4	3.7	8.9	332.7	0.1	3.2	28.6	31.9	78.1	87.2	725.2
1961	206.6	312.5	17.2	4.7	8.5	342.9	0.1	22.9	50.6	73.7	108.7	118.8	850.7
1962	269.8	315.2	22.9	4.0	9.8	351.9	1.2	11.4	52.2	64.9	131.6	136.8	955.1
1963	338.2	318.8	28.0	7.1	12.5	366.5	0.1	2.5	27.0	29.7	146.0	157.0	1037.4
1964	373.4	352.1	35.0	5.2	15.0	407.4	0.0	5.5	76.2	81.7	151.3	232.9	1246.8
1965	416.8	372.1	36.2	6.5	13.7	428.5	0.1	7.8	50.5	58.3	152.9	253.0	1309.6
1966	427.8	322.0	31.8	4.6	14.7	373.1	0.1	7.8	35.5	43.4	186.8	231.2	1262.4
1967	523.6	342.4	36.9	6.8	15.5	401.6		9.2	50.3	59.5	260.3	246.4	1491.5
1968	608.7	362.4	52.4	7.7	20.4	442.9		7.4	56.4	63.8	316.4	316.4	1748.2

CTN BROAD DIVISIONS AND CATEGORIES

I. 1. INDUSTRIAL MACHINERY AND EQUIPMENT (INCLUDING SPARE PARTS)

II. FUELS, RAW MATERIALS (OTHER THAN FOR FOOD), OTHER MATERIALS

2. FUELS, MINERAL RAW MATERIALS, METALS
3. CHEMICALS, FERTILIZERS, RUBBER
4. BUILDING MATERIALS AND CONSTRUCTION PARTS
5. RAW MATERIALS OF VEGETABLE AND ANIMAL ORIGIN (NOT FOOD)

III. FOODSTUFFS AND RAW MATERIAL FOR FOODSTUFFS

6. LIVE ANIMALS (NOT FOR SLAUGHTER)
7. RAW MATERIAL FOR THE PRODUCTION OF FOODSTUFFS
8. FOODSTUFFS

IV. 9. INDUSTRIAL CONSUMER GOODS (OTHER THAN FOOD)

* CONVERTED FROM NATIONAL DEVISA UNITS THROUGH OFFICIAL EXCHANGE RATES. NOTE THE LIMITATIONS DISCUSSED IN THE EXPLANATORY TEXT.

TABLE III.BEC-1.M.U-B
USSR IMPORTS FROM BULGARIA, 1946-68
(MILLIONS OF CURRENT DOLLARS,* F.O.B.)

YEAR	CLASS 1	111	112	121	122	CLASS 2	21	22	CLASS 3	31	32	CLASS 4+5	CLASS 6	CLASS 7	TOTAL IMPORTS
1946	4.9		.0	3.0	1.9	27.5	27.5						.0	19.3	51.7
1947	.5					37.1	37.1						.0	.5	38.2
1948	1.4		.2	1.4		62.2	62.2						.0	1.3	64.9
1949	7.0			6.8		41.6	41.6						.0	6.6	55.2
1950	14.1		2.6	11.5	.1	34.9	34.9					.7	.0	17.1	66.9
1951	13.4		4.6	7.0	1.8	46.8	46.8						.4	13.4	74.0
1952	21.2		6.9	11.4	2.9	66.2	66.2					1.9	1.1	18.6	109.0
1953	23.2		9.4	9.8	3.9	67.9	67.9					1.8	2.3	29.5	124.7
1954	22.2		9.5	7.1	5.6	77.3	77.3					3.6	2.3	31.3	136.7
1955	35.2	.0	11.0	7.3	16.9	63.4	59.3	4.1				5.6	15.6	1.6	121.4
1956	45.8	.2	14.4	9.2	22.0	65.1	58.7	6.4				6.2	27.2	.3	144.7
1957	45.5		14.6	8.2	22.7	66.9	57.9	9.1				11.4	71.1	3.2	198.1
1958	56.5	.0	20.7	8.5	27.3	61.8	51.5	10.3				15.5	68.5	.8	203.1
1959	76.8	.0	30.1	9.9	36.7	80.6	66.8	13.8				31.5	70.2	1.7	260.8
1960	100.9	.1	35.6	12.2	53.1	68.2	53.8	14.5				49.1	78.7	1.6	298.6
1961	117.3	.1	49.1	8.5	59.7	65.0	50.2	14.7				54.7	87.2	1.9	326.1
1962	116.9	.0	46.6	8.6	61.6	73.5	58.2	15.3				100.4	97.3	1.9	390.0
1963	141.8	.1	51.5	12.4	77.7	84.0	71.5	12.5				115.9	101.6	1.6	444.8
1964	179.8	.0	55.4	16.9	107.4	102.0	85.7	16.3				146.9	99.1	5.6	533.3
1965	223.6	.0	58.1	11.2	154.2	83.4	65.1	18.3				172.9	123.2	12.4	615.5
1966	228.1		52.0	9.3	166.8	86.8	68.3	18.5				190.6	143.5	5.0	654.1
1967	270.0		63.7	9.8	196.5	90.6	63.3	27.3				215.6	172.3	25.3	773.8
1968	296.0		61.5	9.9	224.6	105.9	68.2	37.7				253.7	204.0	31.7	891.3

* CONVERTED FROM NATIONAL DEVISA UNITS THROUGH
OFFICIAL EXCHANGE RATES. NOTE LIMITATIONS
DISCUSSED IN THE EXPLANATORY TEXT.

BEC CATEGORIES

1   FOOD AND BEVERAGES
    11   PRIMARY
         111   FOR INDUSTRY
         112   FOR HOUSEHOLD CONSUMPTION
    12   PROCESSED
         121   FOR INDUSTRY
         122   FOR HOUSEHOLD CONSUMPTION

2   INDUSTRIAL SUPPLIES (NON-FOOD)
    21   PRIMARY

3   FUELS AND LUBRICANTS
    31   PRIMARY
    32   PROCESSED

4   MACHINERY, EXC. TRANSPORT (W/PARTS)

5   TRANSPORT EQUIPMENT

6   CONSUMER GOODS, N.E.S.

TABLE III.BEC-2.M.U-B
USSR IMPORTS FROM BULGARIA, 1946-68
(MILLIONS OF CURRENT DOLLARS,* F.O.B.)

YEAR	AGGREGATION I. BASIC SNA CLASSES			AGGREGATION II. PRIMARY VS. PROCESSED				
	CAPITAL GOODS	INTERMEDIATE GOODS	CONSUMER GOODS	PRIMARY	PROCESSED	NOT SPECIFIED	TOTAL IMPORTS	RATIO SPECIFIED
1946	0.0	30.4	1.9	27.5	4.9	19.3	51.7	.6258
1947	0.0	37.7	.0	37.1	.5	.5	38.2	.9858
1948	0.0	63.6	.0	62.2	1.4	1.3	64.9	.9800
1949	0.0	48.4	.2	41.9	6.8	6.6	55.2	.8812
1950	.7	46.5	2.6	37.5	12.3	17.1	66.9	.7444
1951	0.0	53.8	6.8	51.4	9.2	13.4	74.0	.8190
1952	1.9	77.6	10.9	73.1	17.3	18.6	109.0	.8294
1953	1.8	77.7	15.6	77.3	17.9	29.5	124.7	.7637
1954	3.6	84.4	17.4	86.8	18.6	31.3	136.7	.7709
1955	5.6	70.7	43.5	70.3	49.5	1.6	121.4	.9865
1956	6.2	74.5	63.6	73.3	71.1	.3	144.7	.9980
1957	11.4	75.1	108.4	72.5	122.4	3.2	198.1	.9837
1958	15.5	70.3	116.5	72.1	130.2	.8	203.1	.9962
1959	31.5	90.5	137.1	97.0	162.1	1.7	260.8	.9935
1960	49.1	80.5	167.4	89.4	207.6	1.6	298.6	.9948
1961	54.7	73.5	196.0	99.4	224.9	1.9	326.1	.9942
1962	100.4	82.2	205.5	104.8	283.2	1.9	390.0	.9951
1963	115.9	96.5	230.9	123.1	320.1	1.6	444.8	.9965
1964	146.9	118.9	262.0	141.2	386.6	5.6	533.3	.9895
1965	172.9	94.7	335.5	123.2	479.9	12.4	615.5	.9798
1966	190.6	96.1	362.3	120.3	528.8	5.0	654.1	.9923
1967	215.6	100.4	432.4	127.0	621.5	25.3	773.8	.9673
1968	253.7	115.8	490.1	129.7	729.9	31.7	891.3	.9644

* CONVERTED FROM NATIONAL DEVISA-UNITS THROUGH
OFFICIAL EXCHANGE RATES. NOTE LIMITATIONS
DISCUSSED IN THE EXPLANATORY TEXT.

TABLE III.BEC-1.M.U-C
USSR IMPORTS FROM CZECHOSLOVAKIA, 1946-68
(MILLIONS OF CURRENT DOLLARS,* F.O.B.)

YEAR	CLASS 1	111	112	121	122	CLASS 2	21	22	CLASS 3	31	32	CLASS 4+5	CLASS 6	CLASS 7	TOTAL IMPORTS
1946	.8				.8	15.3	12.7	2.6				5.3	1.7	9.1	32.2
1947	10.3				10.3	17.8	13.9	3.9				8.7	.5	1.7	39.0
1948	9.1				9.1	41.0	31.4	9.5				24.9	18.1	42.9	135.9
1949	8.8				8.8	48.5	36.6	11.9				36.7	34.2	76.8	205.0
1950	13.3				13.3	78.1	63.2	14.9				59.1	21.8	29.2	201.6
1951	16.1				16.1	101.7	82.1	19.6				78.7	15.2	41.5	253.1
1952	13.0				13.0	127.0	103.3	23.7				107.1	16.2	36.1	299.3
1953	14.9				14.9	149.6	123.1	26.5				112.1	6.4	29.3	312.3
1954	12.8				12.8	117.4	95.4	22.0				145.9	7.0	35.1	318.1
1955	10.3				10.3	124.4	98.5	25.8				157.2	5.6	89.1	386.6
1956	6.5			1.0	5.5	131.4	96.1	35.3				113.8	75.5	69.3	396.4
1957	15.2			2.0	13.2	126.6	90.8	35.8				122.5	58.2	63.1	385.6
1958	20.5			2.8	17.7	155.9	110.7	45.2				187.0	97.1	51.7	512.1
1959	26.4			5.2	21.1	125.6	72.9	52.7				232.6	142.2	55.1	581.9
1960	25.2			3.4	21.8	130.5	75.6	54.8				293.2	168.3	35.2	652.4
1961	28.3			4.6	23.7	139.1	69.1	70.0				336.1	165.5	28.6	697.7
1962	23.1			3.8	19.2	137.6	61.4	76.2				454.0	177.9	32.2	824.8
1963	26.0			4.3	21.8	158.6	71.5	87.1				513.5	201.8	50.6	950.5
1964	6.0			1.7	4.3	186.3	75.6	110.7				528.1	186.4	62.0	968.9
1965	16.5	1.0		3.0	12.5	189.7	65.4	124.3				572.6	169.8	86.9	1035.4
1966	9.1			2.6	6.5	162.4	53.3	109.1				491.0	172.6	84.2	919.4
1967	11.1			4.5	6.6	166.8	52.6	114.2				508.3	206.7	89.4	982.2
1968	12.3			6.0	6.3	174.2	55.2	119.0				517.5	213.0	72.9	990.0

* CONVERTED FROM NATIONAL DEVISA UNITS THROUGH OFFICIAL EXCHANGE RATES. NOTE LIMITATIONS DISCUSSED IN THE EXPLANATORY TEXT.

BEC CATEGORIES

1 FOOD AND BEVERAGES
  11 PRIMARY
    111 FOR INDUSTRY
    112 FOR HOUSEHOLD CONSUMPTION
  12 PROCESSED
    121 FOR INDUSTRY
    122 FOR HOUSEHOLD CONSUMPTION

2 INDUSTRIAL SUPPLIES (NON-FOOD)
  21 PRIMARY

3 FUELS AND LUBRICANTS
  31 PRIMARY
  32 PROCESSED

4 MACHINERY, EXC. TRANSPORT (W/PARTS)

5 TRANSPORT EQUIPMENT

6 CONSUMER GOODS, N.E.S.

TABLE III.BEC-2.M.U-C
USSR IMPORTS FROM CZECHOSLOVAKIA, 1946-68
(MILLIONS OF CURRENT DOLLARS,* F.O.B.)

YEAR	AGGREGATION I. BASIC SNA CLASSES			AGGREGATION II. PRIMARY VS. PROCESSED		NOT SPECIFIED	TOTAL IMPORTS	RATIO SPECIFIED
	CAPITAL GOODS	INTERMEDIATE GOODS	CONSUMER GOODS	PRIMARY	PROCESSED			
1946	5.3	15.3	2.5	12.7	10.4	9.1	32.2	.7189
1947	8.7	17.8	10.8	13.9	23.4	1.7	39.0	.9566
1948	24.9	41.0	27.2	31.4	61.6	42.9	135.9	.6846
1949	36.7	48.5	43.0	36.6	91.6	76.8	205.0	.6255
1950	59.1	78.1	35.1	63.2	109.2	29.2	201.6	.8553
1951	78.7	101.7	31.2	82.1	129.5	41.5	253.1	.8361
1952	107.1	127.0	29.1	103.3	159.9	36.1	299.3	.8794
1953	112.1	149.6	21.3	123.1	159.9	29.3	312.3	.9062
1954	145.9	117.4	19.7	95.4	187.6	35.1	318.1	.8898
1955	157.2	124.4	15.9	98.5	198.9	89.1	386.6	.7694
1956	113.8	132.4	81.0	96.1	231.1	69.3	396.4	.8252
1957	122.5	128.6	71.4	90.8	231.7	63.1	385.6	.8364
1958	187.0	158.7	114.7	110.7	349.7	51.7	512.1	.8991
1959	232.6	130.9	163.3	72.9	453.9	55.1	581.9	.9053
1960	293.2	133.9	190.1	75.6	541.6	35.2	652.4	.9461
1961	336.1	143.7	189.2	69.1	600.0	28.6	697.7	.9590
1962	454.0	141.4	197.2	61.4	731.1	32.2	824.8	.9609
1963	513.5	162.9	223.6	71.5	828.5	50.6	950.5	.9468
1964	528.1	187.9	190.8	75.6	831.3	62.0	968.9	.9360
1965	572.6	193.7	182.3	66.5	882.1	86.9	1035.4	.9161
1966	491.0	165.0	179.1	53.3	781.9	84.2	919.4	.9084
1967	508.3	171.3	213.3	52.6	840.2	89.4	982.2	.9090
1968	517.5	180.3	219.3	55.2	861.8	72.9	990.0	.9263

* CONVERTED FROM NATIONAL DEVISA-UNITS THROUGH OFFICIAL EXCHANGE RATES. NOTE LIMITATIONS DISCUSSED IN THE EXPLANATORY TEXT.

TABLE III.BEC-1.M.U-G
USSR IMPORTS FROM EAST GERMANY, 1946-68
(MILLIONS OF CURRENT DOLLARS,* F.O.B.)

YEAR	CLASS 1	111	112	121	122	CLASS 2	21	22	CLASS 3	31	32	CLASS 4+5	CLASS 6	CLASS 7	TOTAL IMPORTS
1946						5.0		5.0	.9		.9	2.3	4.6	37.7	50.3
1947						1.7		1.7	.3		.3	.4	5.3	14.0	21.8
1948						.5	.5		1.2		1.2	2.5	15.0	42.7	61.8
1949						2.1	2.1		4.1		4.1	21.3	12.6	106.2	146.3
1950						6.3	6.3		4.9		4.9	60.7	8.6	79.5	160.1
1951						27.7	11.7	16.0	11.5		11.5	145.9	18.9	123.8	327.9
1952						26.5	13.0	13.5	13.9		13.9	197.0	17.9	109.9	365.2
1953						28.3	10.2	18.1	8.3		8.3	353.0	22.0	71.7	483.3
1954						30.7	13.8	17.0	9.5		9.5	461.9	25.3	90.2	617.7
1955	.9				.9	90.1	16.3	73.8	10.5		10.5	393.0	10.2	1.7	506.4
1956	3.2				3.2	99.0	14.3	84.7	9.3		9.3	377.6	51.5	85.7	626.3
1957	.2				.2	85.1	13.4	71.6	10.8		10.8	399.6	84.1	184.7	764.3
1958	.2				.2	86.2	14.7	71.6	11.6		11.6	469.4	98.4	150.1	815.9
1959	.2				.2	91.7	14.0	77.7	11.0		11.0	536.6	116.6	133.3	889.4
1960	.3				.3	94.2	13.9	80.3	11.7		11.7	577.3	112.6	133.0	929.1
1961	.4				.4	110.1	15.0	95.1	10.1		10.1	493.3	129.1	132.9	875.9
1962	.5				.5	119.2	13.1	106.0	11.4		11.4	609.8	190.5	142.0	1073.8
1963	.2				.2	128.7	16.0	112.8	10.8		10.8	712.9	307.1	144.0	1303.7
1964	.1				.1	120.6	8.6	111.9	9.1		9.1	764.1	284.5	149.3	1327.7
1965	.1				.1	111.3	6.5	104.8	9.3		9.3	754.2	250.9	158.8	1284.7
1966	.4				.4	106.3	3.7	102.5	8.5		8.5	684.6	277.5	160.7	1238.0
1967	1.0				1.0	113.8	4.8	109.1	9.2		9.2	789.3	318.1	181.3	1412.7
1968	1.0				1.0	120.3	4.1	116.2	10.2		10.2	931.8	341.7	200.4	1605.3

* CONVERTED FROM NATIONAL DEVISA UNITS THROUGH OFFICIAL EXCHANGE RATES. NOTE LIMITATIONS DISCUSSED IN THE EXPLANATORY TEXT.

BEC CATEGORIES

1   FOOD AND BEVERAGES
    11   PRIMARY
         111   FOR INDUSTRY
         112   FOR HOUSEHOLD CONSUMPTION
    12   PROCESSED
         121   FOR INDUSTRY
         122   FOR HOUSEHOLD CONSUMPTION

2   INDUSTRIAL SUPPLIES (NON-FOOD)
    21   PRIMARY

3   FUELS AND LUBRICANTS
    31   PRIMARY
    32   PROCESSED

4   MACHINERY, EXC. TRANSPORT (W/PARTS)

5   TRANSPORT EQUIPMENT

6   CONSUMER GOODS, N.E.S.

TABLE III.BEC-2.M.U-G
USSR IMPORTS FROM EAST GERMANY, 1946-68
(MILLIONS OF CURRENT DOLLARS,* F.O.B.)

YEAR	AGGREGATION I. BASIC SNA CLASSES			AGGREGATION II. PRIMARY VS. PROCESSED		NOT SPECIFIED	TOTAL IMPORTS	RATIO SPECIFIED
	CAPITAL GOODS	INTERMEDIATE GOODS	CONSUMER GOODS	PRIMARY	PROCESSED			
1946	2.3	5.8	4.6	0.0	12.7	37.7	50.3	.2518
1947	.4	2.1	5.3	0.0	7.8	14.0	21.8	.3573
1948	2.5	1.6	15.0	.5	18.6	42.7	61.8	.3092
1949	21.3	6.2	12.6	2.1	38.0	106.2	146.3	.2740
1950	60.7	11.2	8.6	6.3	74.3	79.5	160.1	.5033
1951	145.9	39.2	18.9	11.7	192.3	123.8	327.9	.6224
1952	197.0	40.4	17.9	13.0	242.3	109.9	365.2	.6990
1953	353.0	36.6	22.0	10.2	401.4	71.7	483.3	.8516
1954	461.9	40.2	25.3	13.8	513.7	90.2	617.7	.8539
1955	393.0	100.6	11.1	16.3	488.5	1.7	506.4	.9966
1956	377.6	108.3	54.7	14.3	526.3	85.7	626.3	.8631
1957	399.6	95.8	84.2	13.4	566.2	184.7	764.3	.7584
1958	469.4	97.8	98.5	14.7	651.1	150.1	815.9	.8160
1959	536.6	102.7	116.8	14.0	742.1	133.3	889.4	.8501
1960	577.3	105.9	112.9	13.9	782.3	133.0	929.1	.8569
1961	493.3	120.1	129.5	15.0	728.0	132.9	875.9	.8483
1962	609.8	130.5	191.0	13.1	918.2	142.4	1073.8	.8673
1963	712.9	139.5	307.3	16.0	1143.7	144.0	1303.7	.8896
1964	764.1	129.7	284.6	8.6	1169.7	149.3	1327.7	.8875
1965	754.2	120.6	251.0	6.5	1119.3	158.8	1284.7	.8764
1966	684.6	114.8	277.9	3.7	1073.5	160.7	1238.0	.8702
1967	789.3	123.0	319.1	4.8	1226.6	181.3	1412.7	.8717
1968	931.8	130.5	342.6	4.1	1400.8	200.4	1605.3	.8752

* CONVERTED FROM NATIONAL DEVISA-UNITS THROUGH OFFICIAL EXCHANGE RATES. NOTE LIMITATIONS DISCUSSED IN THE EXPLANATORY TEXT.

TABLE III.BEC-1.M.U-H
USSR IMPORTS FROM HUNGARY, 1946-68
(MILLIONS OF CURRENT DOLLARS,* F.O.B.)

YEAR	CLASS 1	111	112	121	122	CLASS 2	21	22	CLASS 3	31	32	CLASS 4+5	CLASS 6	CLASS 7	TOTAL IMPORTS
1946	.2		.2		.0				1.8		1.8	.0	4.8	3.7	10.6
1947	.2		.0		.1				3.7		3.7	.6	3.0	9.8	17.2
1948	2.1	1.7	.3		.1				2.9		2.9	8.8	5.6	9.3	28.6
1949	5.8	4.6	1.1		.0				3.4		3.4	23.7	13.0	21.1	66.9
1950	5.6	3.6	2.0		.0				4.2		4.2	37.2	12.8	23.5	83.2
1951	4.5	2.6	1.7		.3				5.0		5.0	35.7	25.6	43.4	114.1
1952	9.6	7.5	.7		1.5				4.7		4.7	51.9	25.7	48.6	140.6
1953	10.4	5.2	1.2		4.0				5.0		5.0	86.7	26.8	43.5	172.3
1954	7.4	2.3	2.0		3.1				3.7		3.7	91.5	23.4	40.5	166.7
1955	16.4	3.1	.8	.2	12.2	13.9	1.4	12.6	3.6	.2	3.4	89.0	20.4	3.2	146.4
1956	11.8	3.3	.2	1.2	7.2	13.3	.6	12.6	3.0	.3	2.7	71.0	20.8	.9	120.8
1957	7.0		.8	.2	5.9	5.7	2.9	2.8	2.6	.2	2.4	77.2	11.2	3.1	106.8
1958	13.3	3.0	4.1	.2	6.1	7.7	2.7	5.0	4.4	.6	3.7	93.3	35.7	7.5	161.9
1959	13.1	2.8	5.0	.0	5.3	8.1	2.7	5.4	3.2	.6	2.6	116.1	54.7	11.4	206.6
1960	13.2	2.6	3.3		7.3	13.9	3.3	10.6	3.3	.7	2.7	144.3	58.9	14.6	248.2
1961	23.1	1.8	8.5		12.8	15.4	2.1	13.3	3.2	.6	2.6	179.0	88.3	17.8	326.8
1962	30.1	.9	11.6		17.6	14.2	1.8	12.4	2.6		2.6	206.7	111.2	23.9	388.8
1963	34.8	.6	16.7		17.6	15.5	2.2	13.3	2.6		2.6	230.2	111.5	28.5	423.1
1964	47.5		23.9		23.6	21.5	3.2	18.2	2.7		2.7	244.7	118.7	46.5	481.6
1965	53.1	2.5	20.7		29.9	19.7	2.9	16.8	2.7		2.7	254.6	132.4	52.8	515.3
1966	58.3		32.3		26.0	20.2	4.4	15.7	2.6		2.6	244.2	150.0	36.7	511.9
1967	80.1		45.5		34.7	29.3	12.3	17.1	2.5		2.5	263.7	179.7	41.7	597.1
1968	83.6		45.3		38.3	34.5	17.2	17.3	2.0		2.0	308.0	194.2	46.6	669.0

* CONVERTED FROM NATIONAL DEVISA UNITS THROUGH OFFICIAL EXCHANGE RATES. NOTE LIMITATIONS DISCUSSED IN THE EXPLANATORY TEXT.

BEC CATEGORIES

1 FOOD AND BEVERAGES
  11 PRIMARY
    111 FOR INDUSTRY
    112 FOR HOUSEHOLD CONSUMPTION
  12 PROCESSED
    121 FOR INDUSTRY
    122 FOR HOUSEHOLD CONSUMPTION

2 INDUSTRIAL SUPPLIES (NON-FOOD)
  21 PRIMARY

3 FUELS AND LUBRICANTS
  31 PRIMARY
  32 PROCESSED

4 MACHINERY, EXC. TRANSPORT (W/PARTS)

5 TRANSPORT EQUIPMENT

6 CONSUMER GOODS, N.E.S.

TABLE III.BEC-2.M.U-H
USSR IMPORTS FROM HUNGARY, 1946-68
(MILLIONS OF CURRENT DOLLARS,* F.O.B.)

YEAR	AGGREGATION I. BASIC SNA CLASSES			AGGREGATION II. PRIMARY VS. PROCESSED		NOT SPECIFIED	TOTAL IMPORTS	RATIO SPECIFIED
	CAPITAL GOODS	INTERMEDIATE GOODS	CONSUMER GOODS	PRIMARY	PROCESSED			
1946	.0	1.8	5.1	.2	6.7	3.7	10.6	.6527
1947	.6	3.7	3.2	.0	7.4	9.8	17.2	.4327
1948	8.8	4.6	6.0	2.0	17.3	9.3	28.6	.6759
1949	23.7	8.0	14.2	5.7	40.1	21.1	66.9	.6852
1950	37.2	7.8	14.8	5.6	54.2	23.5	83.2	.7180
1951	35.7	7.6	27.5	4.2	66.5	43.4	114.1	.6200
1952	51.9	12.1	27.9	8.2	83.8	48.6	140.6	.6541
1953	86.7	10.2	32.0	6.4	122.5	43.5	172.3	.7479
1954	91.5	6.1	28.6	4.3	121.8	40.5	166.7	.7569
1955	89.0	20.9	33.4	5.6	137.6	3.2	146.4	.9781
1956	71.0	20.8	28.2	4.4	115.5	.9	120.8	.9926
1957	77.2	8.5	18.0	4.0	99.7	3.1	106.8	.9708
1958	93.3	15.2	45.9	10.4	144.1	7.5	161.9	.9539
1959	116.1	14.1	65.0	11.1	184.0	11.4	206.6	.9446
1960	144.3	19.8	69.6	9.9	223.7	14.6	248.2	.9411
1961	179.0	20.4	109.6	13.0	296.0	17.8	326.8	.9456
1962	206.7	17.8	140.4	14.4	350.5	23.9	388.8	.9385
1963	230.2	18.6	145.8	19.5	375.2	28.5	423.1	.9327
1964	244.7	24.1	166.2	27.1	408.0	46.5	481.6	.9035
1965	254.6	24.9	183.0	26.1	436.4	52.8	515.3	.8975
1966	244.2	22.8	208.3	36.7	438.5	36.7	511.9	.9283
1967	263.7	31.8	259.8	57.8	497.6	41.7	597.1	.9301
1968	308.0	36.5	277.9	62.5	559.9	46.6	669.0	.9303

* CONVERTED FROM NATIONAL DEVISA-UNITS THROUGH
OFFICIAL EXCHANGE RATES. NOTE LIMITATIONS
DISCUSSED IN THE EXPLANATORY TEXT.

TABLE III.BEC-1.M.U-P
USSR IMPORTS FROM POLAND, 1946-68
(MILLIONS OF CURRENT DOLLARS,* F.O.B.)

YEAR	CLASS 1	111	112	121	122	CLASS 2	21	22	CLASS 3	31	32	CLASS 4+5	CLASS 6	CLASS 7	TOTAL IMPORTS
1946	2.4				2.4	9.2		9.2	74.7	71.3	3.4		6.9	15.2	108.4
1947	17.1				17.1	4.2		4.2	77.7	75.1	2.6		16.9	21.2	137.1
1948	17.1				17.1	7.5		7.5	85.5	81.1	4.4		38.5	25.0	173.7
1949	13.0				13.0	11.0		11.0	98.0	93.2	4.8	4.7	35.1	24.6	186.4
1950	21.7				21.7	12.3		12.3	82.8	77.9	4.8	36.8	29.9	26.5	210.0
1951	25.5				25.5	22.2		22.2	97.2	92.8	4.3	40.6	39.3	39.5	264.1
1952	29.3				29.3	28.7		28.7	132.2	125.6	6.6	60.4	46.6	53.7	350.9
1953	30.6				30.6	33.8		33.8	132.5	125.1	7.4	77.0	50.7	42.7	367.3
1954	22.6				22.6	22.8		22.8	132.6	123.1	9.5	73.3	39.4	47.4	338.0
1955	26.7				26.7	39.3	6.0	33.3	121.3	112.5	8.8	74.3	21.7	3.5	286.7
1956	6.7		.0		6.7	50.5	7.6	42.9	117.0	102.3	14.6	72.5	32.8	3.8	283.3
1957	2.6	3.1	1.8		2.6	45.1	7.6	37.5	86.3	75.5	10.8	91.4	17.5	13.0	255.9
1958	17.3		.7		12.4	39.9	3.3	36.6	73.5	55.5	18.2	86.4	20.7	27.4	265.1
1959	13.7				12.9	46.3	3.0	43.3	82.4	65.5	16.8	102.7	31.2	40.3	316.6
1960	15.6		1.6		14.0	49.2	2.8	46.4	90.2	72.7	17.5	121.0	65.5	45.2	386.7
1961	46.9	15.8	2.1		29.0	54.8	3.8	51.0	90.6	73.4	17.2	137.8	80.2	66.6	476.9
1962	40.8	8.1	.2		32.5	55.9	4.0	51.9	91.9	75.8	16.1	194.4	103.0	78.2	564.2
1963	4.0		1.0	.4	2.6	65.9	2.4	63.5	93.6	76.5	17.1	222.4	113.5	115.2	614.5
1964	19.6		8.3	.8	10.4	77.5	4.6	72.9	93.2	75.7	17.5	262.4	116.8	148.4	717.9
1965	36.0		6.1	1.4	28.4	73.1	3.0	70.2	119.5	103.3	16.2	278.6	117.2	156.3	780.7
1966	11.0		5.1	1.1	4.7	42.1	3.6	38.5	126.6	111.9	14.7	259.2	154.9	139.3	733.2
1967	16.3		6.1	1.8	8.4	50.8	3.0	47.8	134.5	119.0	15.6	329.7	220.0	151.0	902.4
1968	13.8		3.4	1.4	9.0	70.8	3.4	67.5	122.0	107.0	15.0	393.1	242.9	189.0	1031.5

* CONVERTED FROM NATIONAL DEVISA UNITS THROUGH
OFFICIAL EXCHANGE RATES. NOTE LIMITATIONS
DISCUSSED IN THE EXPLANATORY TEXT.

BEC CATEGORIES

1 FOOD AND BEVERAGES
  11 PRIMARY
    111 FOR INDUSTRY
    112 FOR HOUSEHOLD CONSUMPTION
  12 PROCESSED
    121 FOR INDUSTRY
    122 FOR HOUSEHOLD CONSUMPTION

2 INDUSTRIAL SUPPLIES (NON-FOOD)

3 FUELS AND LUBRICANTS
  31 PRIMARY
  32 PROCESSED

4 MACHINERY, EXC. TRANSPORT (W/PARTS)

5 TRANSPORT EQUIPMENT

6 CONSUMER GOODS, N.E.S.

TABLE III.BEC-2.M.U-P
USSR IMPORTS FROM POLAND, 1946-68
(MILLIONS OF CURRENT DOLLARS,* F.O.B.)

YEAR	AGGREGATION I. BASIC SNA CLASSES			AGGREGATION II. PRIMARY VS. PROCESSED		NOT SPECIFIED	TOTAL IMPORTS	RATIO SPECIFIED
	CAPITAL GOODS	INTERMEDIATE GOODS	CONSUMER GOODS	PRIMARY	PROCESSED			
1946	0.0	83.9	9.3	71.3	21.9	15.2	108.4	.8597
1947	0.0	81.9	34.0	75.1	40.8	21.2	137.1	.8453
1948	0.0	93.0	55.6	81.1	67.5	25.0	173.7	.8558
1949	4.7	109.0	48.1	93.2	68.6	24.6	186.4	.8679
1950	36.8	95.0	51.7	77.9	105.6	26.5	210.0	.8740
1951	40.6	119.3	64.7	92.8	131.8	39.5	264.1	.8505
1952	60.4	160.9	75.9	125.6	171.6	53.7	350.9	.8470
1953	77.0	166.3	81.3	125.1	199.6	42.7	367.3	.8839
1954	73.3	155.4	61.9	123.1	167.5	47.4	338.0	.8599
1955	74.3	160.6	48.3	118.5	164.7	3.5	286.7	.9879
1956	72.5	167.5	39.5	110.0	169.6	3.8	283.3	.9867
1957	91.4	131.4	20.1	83.1	159.7	13.0	255.9	.9491
1958	86.4	116.5	34.8	63.5	174.2	27.4	265.1	.8965
1959	102.7	128.7	44.9	69.3	206.9	40.3	316.6	.8726
1960	121.0	139.4	81.1	77.1	264.4	45.2	386.7	.8831
1961	137.8	161.2	111.3	95.1	315.7	66.6	476.9	.8604
1962	194.4	155.9	135.7	88.1	397.9	78.2	564.2	.8613
1963	222.4	159.9	117.1	79.8	419.5	115.2	614.5	.8125
1964	262.4	171.5	135.5	88.6	480.8	148.4	717.9	.7932
1965	278.6	194.0	151.8	112.4	512.0	156.3	780.7	.7998
1966	259.2	169.9	164.8	120.7	473.2	139.3	733.2	.8100
1967	329.7	187.1	234.5	128.1	623.3	151.0	902.4	.8326
1968	393.1	194.2	255.2	113.7	728.8	189.0	1031.5	.8168

* CONVERTED FROM NATIONAL DEVISA-UNITS THROUGH OFFICIAL EXCHANGE RATES. NOTE LIMITATIONS DISCUSSED IN THE EXPLANATORY TEXT.

TABLE III.BEC-1.M.U-R
USSR IMPORTS FROM RUMANIA, 1946-68
(MILLIONS OF CURRENT DOLLARS,* F.O.B.)

YEAR	CLASS 1	111	112	121	122	CLASS 2	21	22	CLASS 3	31	32	CLASS 4+5	CLASS 6	CLASS 7	TOTAL IMPORTS
1946						2.7		2.7	7.1		7.1			12.7	22.4
1947	3.9	3.9				4.7		4.7	4.5		4.5			14.2	27.3
1948	43.7	43.7				9.3		9.3	15.7		15.7	1.0		21.9	91.6
1949	1.1	1.1				14.6		14.6	42.7		42.7	6.8	.4	34.0	99.6
1950	6.1	6.1				17.5		17.5	54.8		54.8	8.3	.4	52.0	139.2
1951	4.0	2.2			1.8	20.0		20.0	61.6		61.6	8.4	1.9	43.3	139.2
1952	12.8	10.5			2.2	24.2		24.2	87.3		87.3	10.6	4.6	56.6	196.0
1953	2.3	.0			2.3	32.3		32.3	109.5		109.5	15.9	5.7	63.9	229.7
1954	7.0	4.8			2.2	24.5		24.5	95.0		95.0	19.1	4.7	44.4	194.7
1955	23.1	20.3	1.0	1.1	.7	39.4	.7	38.7	95.3		95.3	14.5	2.8	34.7	209.8
1956	14.0	2.4	2.4	3.8	5.5	45.7	2.3	43.3	94.2		94.2	14.8	7.0	59.6	235.3
1957	13.7	1.7	3.6	4.8	3.6	45.4	1.4	43.9	77.7		77.7	11.9	6.6	34.7	190.0
1958	28.9	15.7	5.5	5.3	2.4	54.7	1.5	53.2	96.2		96.2	10.0	13.2	30.5	233.6
1959	12.1	.3	4.7	4.0	3.1	73.5	1.7	71.8	107.0		107.0	20.5	19.8	16.5	249.4
1960	26.5	7.5	6.4	4.3	8.3	86.6	4.0	82.6	102.9		102.9	23.7	26.9	13.4	280.0
1961	49.3	14.0	9.6	5.9	19.8	115.8	4.6	111.2	88.4		88.4	44.3	33.4	9.5	340.8
1962	31.5	9.4	9.4	4.4	8.3	128.8	1.2	127.6	76.7		76.7	58.6	38.3	14.9	348.8
1963	74.6	33.2	13.2	8.3	20.0	135.4	3.5	131.9	75.0		75.0	63.7	50.8	10.8	410.2
1964	43.2	.7	12.3	6.4	23.8	149.7	9.7	140.0	70.1		70.1	78.7	63.5	16.0	421.1
1965	53.2	10.6	11.1	5.2	26.3	150.4	11.0	139.4	58.0		58.0	80.7	88.0	10.6	441.0
1966	67.4	21.7	10.5	6.2	29.0	144.5	10.7	133.7	37.3		37.3	56.5	95.6	4.2	405.4
1967	54.7	11.2	10.3	5.6	27.7	149.8	14.1	135.6	29.8		29.8	78.2	106.2	5.6	424.3
1968	42.6	2.6	9.6	6.7	23.7	141.5	11.3	130.2	26.2		26.2	104.7	136.7	4.6	456.4

* CONVERTED FROM NATIONAL DEVISA UNITS THROUGH OFFICIAL EXCHANGE RATES. NOTE LIMITATIONS DISCUSSED IN THE EXPLANATORY TEXT.

BEC CATEGORIES

1   FOOD AND BEVERAGES
     11   PRIMARY
           111   FOR INDUSTRY
           112   FOR HOUSEHOLD CONSUMPTION
     12   PROCESSED
           121   FOR INDUSTRY
           122   FOR HOUSEHOLD CONSUMPTION

2   INDUSTRIAL SUPPLIES (NON-FOOD)
     21   PRIMARY

3   FUELS AND LUBRICANTS
     31   PRIMARY
     32   PROCESSED

4   MACHINERY, EXC. TRANSPORT (W/PARTS)

5   TRANSPORT EQUIPMENT

6   CONSUMER GOODS, N.E.S.

YEAR	AGGREGATION I. BASIC SNA CLASSES			AGGREGATION II. PRIMARY VS. PROCESSED		NOT SPECIFIED	TOTAL IMPORTS	RATIO SPECIFIED
	CAPITAL GOODS	INTERMEDIATE GOODS	CONSUMER GOODS	PRIMARY	PROCESSED			
1946	0.0	9.8	0.0	0.0	9.8	12.7	22.4	.4359
1947	.1	13.0	0.0	3.9	9.3	14.2	27.3	.4808
1948	1.0	68.7	0.0	43.7	25.9	21.9	91.6	.7606
1949	6.8	58.4	.4	1.1	64.5	34.0	99.6	.6586
1950	8.3	78.5	.4	6.1	81.1	52.0	139.2	.6265
1951	8.4	83.8	3.8	2.2	93.7	43.3	139.2	.6889
1952	10.6	121.9	6.8	10.5	128.9	56.6	196.0	.7111
1953	15.9	141.8	8.1	.0	165.7	63.9	229.7	.7216
1954	19.1	124.2	7.0	4.8	145.5	44.4	194.7	.7718
1955	14.5	156.1	4.5	22.0	153.1	34.7	209.8	.8347
1956	14.8	146.0	14.8	7.1	168.6	59.6	235.3	.7466
1957	11.9	129.6	13.8	6.8	148.5	34.7	190.0	.8172
1958	10.0	171.9	21.2	22.7	180.4	30.5	233.6	.8695
1959	20.5	184.8	27.6	6.8	226.2	16.5	249.4	.9339
1960	23.7	201.4	41.6	17.9	248.7	13.4	280.0	.9522
1961	44.3	224.2	62.8	28.2	303.0	9.5	340.8	.9720
1962	58.6	210.6	64.7	11.3	322.6	14.9	348.8	.9572
1963	63.7	251.9	83.9	49.8	349.7	10.8	410.2	.9738
1964	78.7	226.8	99.6	22.7	382.4	16.0	421.1	.9620
1965	80.7	224.2	125.4	32.7	397.6	10.6	441.0	.9759
1966	56.5	209.6	135.1	43.0	358.2	4.2	405.4	.9896
1967	78.2	196.3	144.1	35.6	383.1	5.6	424.3	.9868
1968	104.7	177.0	170.1	23.5	428.3	4.6	456.4	.9899

* CONVERTED FROM NATIONAL DEVISA-UNITS THROUGH OFFICIAL EXCHANGE RATES. NOTE LIMITATIONS DISCUSSED IN THE EXPLANATORY TEXT.

TABLE III.BEC-1.M.U-Y
USSR IMPORTS FROM YUGOSLAVIA, 1946-68
(MILLIONS OF CURRENT DOLLARS,* F.O.B.)

YEAR	CLASS 1	111	112	121	122	CLASS 2	21	22	CLASS 3	31	32	CLASS 4+5	CLASS 6	CLASS 7	TOTAL IMPORTS
1946	.1		.1			8.3	4.6	3.7					.0	16.3	24.8
1947	2.7		2.7			12.6	6.6	6.0					.0	14.3	29.6
1948	1.7		1.7			21.5	15.2	6.3					.0	23.1	46.3
1949	.4		.4			5.4	2.3	3.1						4.9	10.7
1954	.5				.5	.3	.2	.0					.0	.3	1.1
1955	7.1		2.0	.4	4.8	8.2	5.1	3.1					1.7	.5	17.4
1956	10.8	1.3	1.0	1.3	7.2	28.1	6.4	21.7				.9	3.8	6.1	49.7
1957	10.5	.6	.5	1.2	8.2	24.8	2.3	22.6				2.7	9.2	9.6	56.9
1958	11.7		3.2	.4	4.4	27.4	.3	27.1				4.3	6.7	.8	50.9
1959	8.2	3.7	1.5	.5	6.2	31.7	.4	31.3				5.1	7.6	.6	53.1
1960	4.3		2.3	2.0		31.2	.4	30.8				7.7	6.9	3.0	53.1
1961	2.5		1.1	1.4		27.5	.4	27.1				13.8	7.5	3.2	54.6
1962	1.5		1.0	.5		26.2	.5	25.7				10.3	7.1	1.1	46.1
1963	10.7		6.2	1.5	3.0	39.8	.6	39.2				10.9	24.3	1.3	87.0
1964	15.7		3.2	2.3	10.2	56.4	7.2	49.3				13.0	32.9	2.8	120.9
1965	22.2		1.5	2.5	18.2	61.5	7.4	54.2				68.2	31.9	4.8	188.7
1966	11.0		.2	1.2	9.5	57.7	7.8	49.9				77.0	41.4	5.7	192.8
1967	14.1		.8		13.2	68.9	7.3	61.5				60.0	84.0	5.6	232.6
1968	8.5		2.5		6.0	63.7	12.5	51.2				64.1	77.7	3.1	217.1

* CONVERTED FROM NATIONAL DEVISA UNITS THROUGH OFFICIAL EXCHANGE RATES. NOTE LIMITATIONS DISCUSSED IN THE EXPLANATORY TEXT.

BEC CATEGORIES

1 FOOD AND BEVERAGES
    11 PRIMARY
        111 FOR INDUSTRY
        112 FOR HOUSEHOLD CONSUMPTION
    12 PROCESSED
        121 FOR INDUSTRY
        122 FOR HOUSEHOLD CONSUMPTION

2 INDUSTRIAL SUPPLIES (NON-FOOD)
    21 PRIMARY
    22 PROCESSED

3 FUELS AND LUBRICANTS
    31 PRIMARY
    32 PROCESSED

4 MACHINERY, EXC. TRANSPORT (W/PARTS)

5 TRANSPORT EQUIPMENT

6 CONSUMER GOODS, N.E.S.

7 GOODS N.E.S. AND UNSPECIFIED

TABLE III.BEC-2.M.U-Y
USSR IMPORTS FROM YUGOSLAVIA, 1946-68
(MILLIONS OF CURRENT DOLLARS.* F.O.B.)

YEAR	AGGREGATION I. BASIC SNA CLASSES			AGGREGATION II. PRIMARY VS. PROCESSED		NOT SPECIFIED	TOTAL IMPORTS	RATIO SPECIFIED
	CAPITAL GOODS	INTERMEDIATE GOODS	CONSUMER GOODS	PRIMARY	PROCESSED			
1946	0.0	8.3	.1	4.7	3.7	16.3	24.8	.3405
1947	0.0	12.6	2.7	9.2	6.0	14.3	29.6	.5163
1948	0.0	21.5	1.7	16.9	6.3	23.1	46.3	.5006
1949	0.0	5.4	.4	2.7	3.1	4.9	10.7	.5451
1954	0.0	.3	.5	.2	.6	.3	1.1	.7350
1955	0.0	8.5	8.5	7.0	10.0	.5	17.4	.9741
1956	.9	30.7	12.0	8.7	34.9	6.1	49.7	.8772
1957	2.7	26.7	17.9	3.4	43.9	9.6	56.9	.8316
1958	4.3	31.5	14.2	7.1	42.9	.8	50.9	.9838
1959	5.1	32.1	15.3	1.9	50.6	.6	53.1	.9887
1960	7.7	33.2	9.1	2.7	47.4	3.0	53.1	.9427
1961	13.8	28.9	8.6	1.5	49.9	3.2	54.6	.9412
1962	10.3	26.7	8.1	1.4	43.6	1.1	46.1	.9772
1963	10.9	41.3	33.5	6.8	78.9	1.3	87.0	.9848
1964	13.0	58.8	46.3	10.4	107.7	2.8	120.9	.9770
1965	68.2	64.0	51.6	8.9	175.0	4.8	188.7	.9746
1966	77.0	59.0	51.1	8.1	179.0	5.7	192.8	.9706
1967	60.0	68.9	98.1	8.1	218.8	5.6	232.6	.9759
1968	64.1	63.7	86.2	15.1	198.9	3.1	217.1	.9857

* CONVERTED FROM NATIONAL DEVISA-UNITS THROUGH
OFFICIAL EXCHANGE RATES. NOTE LIMITATIONS
DISCUSSED IN THE EXPLANATORY TEXT.

TABLE III.BEC-1.M.U-CEMA

USSR IMPORTS FROM EUROPEAN CEMA (EXCLUDING ALBANIA), 1946-68

(MILLIONS OF CURRENT DOLLARS,* F.O.B.)

YEAR	CLASS 1	111	112	121	122	CLASS 2	21	22	CLASS 3	31	32	CLASS 4+5	CLASS 6	CLASS 7	TOTAL IMPORTS
1946	8.3		.2	3.0	5.2	59.6	40.2	19.4	84.5	71.3	13.2	7.6	18.0	97.6	275.7
1947	31.9	3.9	.0	.5	27.5	65.6	51.1	14.5	86.2	75.1	11.1	9.8	25.7	61.4	280.7
1948	73.4	45.1	.3	1.4	26.3	120.4	94.1	26.3	105.2	81.1	24.1	37.1	77.1	143.0	556.3
1949	35.7	5.7	1.4	6.8	21.8	117.9	80.4	37.5	148.1	93.2	54.9	93.1	95.3	269.2	759.4
1950	60.9	9.8	4.5	11.5	35.1	149.2	104.4	44.8	146.7	77.9	68.8	202.9	73.6	227.7	861.0
1951	63.6	4.8	6.2	7.0	45.5	218.3	140.7	77.7	175.3	92.8	82.5	309.3	101.1	304.8	1172.4
1952	85.8	18.0	7.6	11.4	48.9	272.5	182.5	90.0	238.1	125.6	112.6	429.0	112.0	323.5	1461.0
1953	81.5	5.2	10.6	9.8	55.8	311.8	201.2	110.7	255.2	125.1	130.1	646.6	114.0	280.5	1689.6
1954	71.9	7.1	11.5	7.1	46.2	272.6	186.4	86.2	240.9	123.1	117.7	795.4	102.1	288.9	1771.8
1955	112.5	23.5	12.8	8.6	67.6	370.5	182.1	188.3	230.7	112.8	117.9	733.6	76.3	133.8	1657.3
1956	88.0	5.9	16.9	15.1	50.1	409.9	179.6	225.3	223.5	102.6	120.9	655.9	214.8	219.6	1806.9
1957	84.0	1.7	19.1	15.2	48.1	374.8	174.1	200.7	177.3	75.7	101.6	713.9	248.7	301.9	1900.6
1958	136.7	21.8	32.0	16.8	66.1	406.2	184.3	221.9	185.6	55.9	129.7	861.6	333.6	267.9	2191.6
1959	142.2	3.1	40.6	19.2	79.3	425.8	161.1	264.7	203.6	66.1	137.5	1040.0	434.7	258.4	2504.6
1960	181.7	10.2	46.9	19.9	104.8	442.6	153.4	289.2	208.2	73.3	134.8	1208.6	511.0	242.9	2795.0
1961	265.4	31.0	69.3	19.0	145.5	500.2	144.8	355.4	192.3	74.0	118.4	1245.2	583.6	257.3	3044.1
1962	242.9	9.7	67.8	16.9	148.4	529.1	139.8	389.3	182.6	75.8	106.8	1623.9	718.2	293.6	3590.3
1963	281.4	33.8	82.4	25.4	139.8	588.1	166.9	421.1	182.0	76.5	105.5	1858.6	886.2	350.6	4146.8
1964	296.1	.7	100.0	25.8	169.6	657.5	187.4	470.1	175.1	75.7	99.4	2024.9	869.1	427.8	4450.4
1965	382.5	14.2	96.1	20.8	251.4	627.6	154.0	473.7	189.5	103.3	86.2	2113.7	881.5	477.8	4672.6
1966	374.3	21.7	99.9	19.2	233.4	562.2	144.1	418.1	175.0	111.9	63.1	1926.2	994.1	430.2	4462.1
1967	433.2	11.2	125.6	21.7	274.8	601.1	150.1	451.0	176.0	119.0	57.1	2184.8	1203.0	499.4	5092.5
1968	449.3	2.6	119.8	24.0	302.8	647.3	159.3	488.0	160.4	107.0	53.4	2508.9	1332.5	545.2	5643.6

* CONVERTED FROM NATIONAL DEVISA UNITS THROUGH OFFICIAL EXCHANGE RATES. NOTE LIMITATIONS DISCUSSED IN THE EXPLANATORY TEXT.

BEC CATEGORIES

1 FOOD AND BEVERAGES
  11 PRIMARY
    111 FOR INDUSTRY
    112 FOR HOUSEHOLD CONSUMPTION
  12 PROCESSED
    121 FOR INDUSTRY
    122 FOR HOUSEHOLD CONSUMPTION

2 INDUSTRIAL SUPPLIES (NON-FOOD)
  21 PRIMARY
  22 PROCESSED

3 FUELS AND LUBRICANTS
  31 PRIMARY
  32 PROCESSED

4 MACHINERY, EXC. TRANSPORT (W/PARTS)

5 TRANSPORT EQUIPMENT

6 CONSUMER GOODS, N.E.S.

7 GOODS N.E.S. AND UNSPECIFIED

TABLE III.BEC-2.M.U-CEMA
USSR IMPORTS FROM EUROPEAN CEMA (EXCLUDING ALBANIA), 1946-68
(MILLIONS OF CURRENT DOLLARS,* F.O.B.)

YEAR	AGGREGATION I. BASIC SNA CLASSES			AGGREGATION II. PRIMARY VS. PROCESSED		NOT SPECIFIED	TOTAL IMPORTS	RATIO SPECIFIED
	CAPITAL GOODS	INTERMEDIATE GOODS	CONSUMER GOODS	PRIMARY	PROCESSED			
1946	7.6	147.1	23.3	111.7	66.3	97.6	275.7	.6460
1947	9.8	156.2	53.2	130.0	89.2	61.4	280.7	.7812
1948	37.1	272.5	103.7	220.9	192.4	143.0	556.3	.7429
1949	93.1	278.6	118.5	180.7	309.5	269.2	759.4	.6455
1950	202.9	317.1	113.3	196.6	436.7	227.7	861.0	.7355
1951	309.3	405.4	152.9	244.5	623.1	304.8	1172.4	.7400
1952	429.0	539.9	168.5	333.7	803.8	323.5	1461.0	.7786
1953	646.6	582.1	180.4	342.0	1067.1	280.5	1689.6	.8340
1954	795.4	527.6	159.9	328.2	1154.7	288.9	1771.8	.8370
1955	733.6	633.2	156.7	331.1	1192.4	133.8	1657.3	.9192
1956	655.9	649.5	281.8	305.0	1282.2	219.6	1806.9	.8784
1957	713.9	569.0	315.9	270.6	1328.2	301.9	1900.6	.8412
1958	861.6	630.4	431.7	294.1	1629.6	267.9	2191.6	.8778
1959	1040.0	651.7	554.6	270.9	1975.3	258.4	2504.6	.8968
1960	1208.6	680.8	662.6	283.8	2268.3	242.9	2795.0	.9131
1961	1245.2	743.1	798.4	319.7	2467.1	257.3	3044.1	.9155
1962	1623.9	738.3	934.5	293.2	3003.5	293.6	3590.3	.9182
1963	1858.5	829.3	1108.5	359.6	3436.7	350.6	4146.8	.9155
1964	2024.9	859.1	1138.7	363.8	3658.8	427.8	4450.4	.9039
1965	2113.7	852.1	1229.0	367.5	3827.3	477.8	4672.6	.8977
1966	1926.2	778.2	1327.4	377.7	3654.1	430.2	4462.1	.9036
1967	2184.8	810.0	1603.3	405.8	4192.3	494.4	5092.5	.9029
1968	2508.9	834.3	1755.2	388.8	4709.6	545.2	5643.6	.9034

* CONVERTED FROM NATIONAL DEVISA-UNITS THROUGH OFFICIAL EXCHANGE RATES. NOTE LIMITATIONS DISCUSSED IN THE EXPLANATORY TEXT.

TABLE III.BEC-1.M.C-U
CZECHOSLOVAKIA'S IMPORTS FROM USSR, 1958-68
(MILLIONS OF CURRENT DOLLARS,* F.O.B.)

YEAR	CLASS 1	111	112	121	122	CLASS 2	21	22	CLASS 3	31	32	CLASS 4+5	CLASS 6	CLASS 7	TOTAL IMPORTS
1958	112.0	93.9	.6		17.5	182.3	167.9	14.4	50.8	50.8		42.7	12.7	51.2	451.8
1959	182.4	137.0	1.6		43.8	208.8	191.9	16.9	61.5	61.5		52.1	11.2	82.0	598.0
1960	164.3	129.4	1.9		33.0	228.4	205.7	22.7	16.4	16.4		46.6	13.8	161.0	630.5
1961	123.4	90.2	2.0		31.2	249.9	226.0	23.8	29.4	29.4		74.7	10.7	168.0	656.0
1962	161.9	114.7	5.8		41.3	254.9	226.4	28.5	43.0	42.6	.4	92.1	20.0	209.6	781.5
1963	162.5	105.6	2.9	1.3	52.7	282.8	256.0	26.8	45.6	44.0	1.7	101.8	15.1	234.8	842.7
1964	104.5	76.6	2.1	1.4	24.4	318.8	289.1	29.7	55.1	50.5	4.7	121.6	8.1	304.8	912.9
1965	120.8	75.6	8.7	1.5	35.1	361.3	331.3	30.0	42.3	40.8	1.9	116.4	7.4	306.0	954.8
1966	144.7	87.0	6.6	1.0	50.1	328.6	295.0	33.6	26.3	26.0	.3	116.2	9.1	289.8	914.7
1967	170.4	115.2	1.4	1.3	52.5	455.2	421.1	34.1	35.2	30.8	4.5	107.0	11.2	186.3	965.4
1968	158.2	116.4	1.4	1.2	39.2	382.4	342.9	39.5	42.4	32.3	10.0	91.0	14.1	348.2	1036.2

* CONVERTED FROM NATIONAL DEVISA UNITS THROUGH OFFICIAL EXCHANGE RATES. NOTE LIMITATIONS DISCUSSED IN THE EXPLANATORY TEXT.

BEC CATEGORIES

1 FOOD AND BEVERAGES
  11 PRIMARY
    111 FOR INDUSTRY
    112 FOR HOUSEHOLD CONSUMPTION
  12 PROCESSED
    121 FOR INDUSTRY
    122 FOR HOUSEHOLD CONSUMPTION

2 INDUSTRIAL SUPPLIES (NON-FOOD)
  21 PRIMARY
  22 PROCESSED

3 FUELS AND LUBRICANTS
  31 PRIMARY
  32 PROCESSED

4 MACHINERY, EXC. TRANSPORT (W/PARTS)

5 TRANSPORT EQUIPMENT

6 CONSUMER GOODS, N.E.S.

7 GOODS N.E.S. AND UNSPECIFIED

TABLE III.BEC-2.M.C-U
CZECHOSLOVAKIA'S IMPORTS FROM USSR, 1958-68
(MILLIONS OF CURRENT DOLLARS,* F.O.B.)

YEAR	AGGREGATION I. BASIC SNA CLASSES			AGGREGATION II. PRIMARY VS. PROCESSED		NOT SPECIFIED	TOTAL IMPORTS	RATIO SPECIFIED
	CAPITAL GOODS	INTERMEDIATE GOODS	CONSUMER GOODS	PRIMARY	PROCESSED			
1958	42.7	327.1	30.8	313.3	87.4	51.2	451.8	.8866
1959	52.1	407.4	56.5	392.0	124.0	82.0	598.0	.8629
1960	46.6	374.2	48.7	353.4	116.1	161.0	630.5	.7446
1961	74.7	369.5	43.9	347.6	140.4	168.0	656.0	.7440
1962	92.1	412.6	67.1	389.5	182.4	209.6	781.5	.7318
1963	101.8	435.3	70.8	408.5	199.4	234.8	842.7	.7214
1964	121.6	452.0	34.5	418.3	189.8	304.8	912.9	.6661
1965	116.4	481.2	51.2	456.4	192.4	306.0	954.8	.6795
1966	116.2	442.8	65.9	414.6	210.3	289.8	914.7	.6832
1967	107.0	607.0	65.1	568.5	210.5	186.3	965.4	.8070
1968	91.0	542.3	54.7	493.1	194.9	348.2	1036.2	.6639

* CONVERTED FROM NATIONAL DEVISA-UNITS THROUGH
OFFICIAL EXCHANGE RATES. NOTE LIMITATIONS
DISCUSSED IN THE EXPLANATORY TEXT.

TABLE III.BEC-1.M.C-B
CZECHOSLOVAKIA'S IMPORTS FROM BULGARIA, 1958-68
(MILLIONS OF CURRENT DOLLARS,* F.O.B.)

YEAR	CLASS 1	111	112	121	122	CLASS 2	21	22	CLASS 3	31	32	CLASS 4+5	CLASS 6	CLASS 7	TOTAL IMPORTS
1958	16.2	.3	4.4	.5	11.0	14.1	13.4	.6				5.4	1.2	4.4	41.4
1959	13.2	.2	4.7	.6	7.7	16.3	15.4	.8				11.3	.5	3.0	44.3
1960	18.4	.6	6.4	.7	10.8	23.1	22.1	1.0				11.2	.7	3.7	57.1
1961	24.3	.3	8.0	.7	15.2	19.8	17.9	1.9				17.5	1.4	2.7	65.7
1962	26.9	.4	9.9	.3	16.3	16.3	14.4	1.9				19.3	1.2	1.3	65.0
1963	24.5	.4	9.2	.7	14.2	21.2	18.8	2.4				18.6	.4	4.6	69.3
1964	19.9	.4	7.6	.3	11.6	25.5	22.5	3.0	.0		.0	20.8	1.2	5.2	72.6
1965	20.7	.3	8.2	.1	12.1	26.8	24.3	2.5				31.8	3.3	6.5	89.2
1966	12.5	.0	4.0	.0	8.4	14.8	11.6	3.2				25.2	4.4	7.0	63.9
1967	16.6		5.7	.0	10.9	29.7	25.6	4.2				25.3	2.2	4.9	78.8
1968	14.1	.4	4.7	.3	9.4	42.6	38.2	4.4				20.1	2.0	11.5	90.3

* CONVERTED FROM NATIONAL DEVISA UNITS THROUGH OFFICIAL EXCHANGE RATES. NOTE LIMITATIONS DISCUSSED IN THE EXPLANATORY TEXT.

BEC CATEGORIES

1 FOOD AND BEVERAGES
  11 PRIMARY
     111 FOR INDUSTRY
     112 FOR HOUSEHOLD CONSUMPTION
  12 PROCESSED
     121 FOR INDUSTRY
     122 FOR HOUSEHOLD CONSUMPTION

2 INDUSTRIAL SUPPLIES (NON-FOOD)
  21 PRIMARY
  22 PROCESSED

3 FUELS AND LUBRICANTS
  31 PRIMARY
  32 PROCESSED

4 MACHINERY, EXC. TRANSPORT (W/PARTS)

5 TRANSPORT EQUIPMENT

6 CONSUMER GOODS, N.E.S.

7 GOODS N.E.S. AND UNSPECIFIED

TABLE III.BEC-2.M.C-B
CZECHOSLOVAKIA'S IMPORTS FROM BULGARIA, 1958-68
(MILLIONS OF CURRENT DOLLARS,* F.O.B.)

YEAR	AGGREGATION I. BASIC SNA CLASSES			AGGREGATION II. PRIMARY VS. PROCESSED		NOT SPECIFIED	TOTAL IMPORTS	RATIO SPECIFIED
	CAPITAL GOODS	INTERMEDIATE GOODS	CONSUMER GOODS	PRIMARY	PROCESSED			
1958	5.4	14.9	16.6	18.2	18.8	4.4	41.4	.8934
1959	11.3	17.1	12.9	20.3	21.0	3.0	44.3	.9326
1960	11.2	24.4	17.8	29.0	24.4	3.7	57.1	.9354
1961	17.5	20.9	24.6	26.3	36.7	2.7	65.7	.9595
1962	19.3	17.0	27.4	24.7	39.1	1.3	65.0	.9806
1963	18.6	22.3	23.8	28.4	36.3	4.6	69.3	.9335
1964	20.8	26.2	20.4	30.5	36.9	5.2	72.6	.9280
1965	31.8	27.2	23.6	32.9	49.8	6.5	89.2	.9270
1966	25.2	14.9	16.8	15.7	41.2	7.0	63.9	.8901
1967	25.3	29.8	18.8	31.3	42.6	4.9	78.8	.9377
1968	20.1	42.6	16.1	42.9	35.9	11.5	90.3	.8726

* CONVERTED FROM NATIONAL DEVISA-UNITS THROUGH
OFFICIAL EXCHANGE RATES. NOTE LIMITATIONS
DISCUSSED IN THE EXPLANATORY TEXT.

TABLE III.BEC-1.M.C-G
CZECHOSLOVAKIA'S IMPORTS FROM EAST GERMANY, 1958-68
(MILLIONS OF CURRENT DOLLARS,* F.O.B.)

YEAR	CLASS 1	111	112	121	122	CLASS 2	21	22	CLASS 3	31	32	CLASS 4+5	CLASS 6	CLASS 7	TOTAL IMPORTS
1958	7.3	2.5			4.7	47.2	14.2	33.0	3.9	2.3	1.6	71.0	11.0	21.7	162.1
1959	.3				.3	54.4	20.4	34.0	7.3	4.5	2.7	82.5	11.6	18.9	175.0
1960	4.7				4.7	53.5	14.3	39.2	13.7	5.7	8.0	85.4	18.9	22.0	198.2
1961	3.1				3.1	61.9	14.5	47.5	16.3	4.1	12.2	92.1	31.5	25.1	230.0
1962	2.7		.3		2.4	56.1	16.1	40.0	13.5	5.2	8.3	108.8	27.2	20.1	228.4
1963	6.2	2.5	.9		2.8	56.0	17.7	38.3	12.2	5.6	6.6	112.1	26.2	19.9	232.7
1964	4.1		1.4		2.7	47.4	14.3	33.2	14.8	6.9	7.9	142.9	24.6	20.3	254.0
1965	2.8		.4		2.4	56.5	19.5	36.9	10.3	4.9	5.5	169.8	31.3	17.2	287.9
1966	4.1		1.6		2.6	57.8	20.5	37.3	13.1	6.2	6.9	186.5	29.0	27.7	318.2
1967	4.6		1.8		2.8	62.4	19.7	42.7	10.9	4.7	6.2	169.6	38.3	34.3	320.2
1968	5.2		2.3		3.0	71.2	19.7	51.5	15.9	5.6	10.3	193.5	57.3	56.5	399.6

* CONVERTED FROM NATIONAL DEVISA UNITS THROUGH
OFFICIAL EXCHANGE RATES. NOTE LIMITATIONS
DISCUSSED IN THE EXPLANATORY TEXT.

BEC CATEGORIES

1　FOOD AND BEVERAGES
　　11　PRIMARY
　　　　111　FOR INDUSTRY
　　　　112　FOR HOUSEHOLD CONSUMPTION
　　12　PROCESSED
　　　　121　FOR INDUSTRY
　　　　122　FOR HOUSEHOLD CONSUMPTION

2　INDUSTRIAL SUPPLIES (NON-FOOD)
　　21　PRIMARY
　　22　PROCESSED

3　FUELS AND LUBRICANTS
　　31　PRIMARY
　　32　PROCESSED

4　MACHINERY, EXC. TRANSPORT (W/PARTS)

5　TRANSPORT EQUIPMENT

6　CONSUMER GOODS, N.E.S.

7　GOODS N.E.S. AND UNSPECIFIED

TABLE III.BEC-2.M.C-G
CZECHOSLOVAKIA'S IMPORTS FROM EAST GERMANY, 1958-68
(MILLIONS OF CURRENT DOLLARS,* F.O.B.)

YEAR	AGGREGATION I. BASIC SNA CLASSES			AGGREGATION II. PRIMARY VS. PROCESSED		NOT SPECIFIED	TOTAL IMPORTS	RATIO SPECIFIED
	CAPITAL GOODS	INTERMEDIATE GOODS	CONSUMER GOODS	PRIMARY	PROCESSED			
1958	71.0	53.6	15.8	19.0	121.4	21.7	162.1	.8660
1959	82.5	61.7	11.9	24.9	131.2	18.9	175.0	.8918
1960	85.4	67.2	23.6	20.0	156.2	22.0	198.2	.8890
1961	92.1	78.3	34.6	18.6	186.3	25.1	230.0	.8907
1962	108.8	69.6	29.8	21.6	186.7	20.1	228.4	.9120
1963	112.1	70.8	29.9	26.7	186.1	19.9	232.7	.9146
1964	142.9	62.2	28.6	22.5	211.3	20.3	254.0	.9203
1965	169.8	66.8	34.1	24.8	245.9	17.2	287.9	.9403
1966	186.5	70.9	33.1	28.3	262.2	27.7	318.2	.9129
1967	169.6	73.3	43.0	26.2	259.6	34.3	320.2	.8929
1968	193.5	87.1	62.5	27.5	315.6	56.5	399.6	.8586

* CONVERTED FROM NATIONAL DEVISA-UNITS THROUGH OFFICIAL EXCHANGE RATES. NOTE LIMITATIONS DISCUSSED IN THE EXPLANATORY TEXT.

TABLE III.BEC-1.M.C-H
CZECHOSLOVAKIA'S IMPORTS FROM HUNGARY, 1958-68
(MILLIONS OF CURRENT DOLLARS,* F.O.B.)

YEAR	CLASS 1	111	112	121	122	CLASS 2	21	22	CLASS 3	31	32	CLASS 4+5	CLASS 6	CLASS 7	TOTAL IMPORTS
1958	27.1	4.0	4.5	.2	18.4	37.4	33.1	4.3	.7		.7	18.0	3.7	3.6	90.4
1959	28.5	4.3	5.4	.1	18.6	32.2	28.7	3.5	1.0		1.0	17.2	3.8	4.4	87.0
1960	28.6	4.0	4.9	.4	19.3	21.8	17.3	4.4	1.6		1.6	23.0	4.1	14.8	93.9
1961	30.6	4.5	5.8	.5	19.9	37.5	33.0	4.4	3.5	.7	2.7	45.2	11.9	7.1	135.8
1962	28.8	1.1	5.0	.2	22.6	50.3	47.4	2.9	1.9	.1	1.9	40.3	10.1	8.0	139.5
1963	33.1	.6	6.9	.3	25.2	48.7	44.2	4.5	2.8	.3	2.4	32.7	10.1	3.7	131.1
1964	35.9	1.1	6.8	.2	27.8	51.3	44.3	7.0	2.1	.2	2.0	27.3	18.9	11.3	146.8
1965	39.3	3.7	6.7	.0	29.0	52.5	40.7	11.7	2.2		2.2	32.6	28.6	16.2	171.4
1966	40.1	2.3	7.6	.1	30.0	36.7	28.6	8.1	3.1		3.1	44.0	29.1	18.9	171.8
1967	42.1	.9	8.3		32.9	24.9	20.9	3.9	1.9		1.9	42.5	21.7	17.8	150.8
1968	46.2	1.2	7.0		38.0	29.3	22.3	7.0	2.2		2.2	48.0	31.9	23.5	181.3

* CONVERTED FROM NATIONAL DEVISA UNITS THROUGH OFFICIAL EXCHANGE RATES. NOTE LIMITATIONS DISCUSSED IN THE EXPLANATORY TEXT.

BEC CATEGORIES

1 FOOD AND BEVERAGES
  11 PRIMARY
     111 FOR INDUSTRY
     112 FOR HOUSEHOLD CONSUMPTION
  12 PROCESSED
     121 FOR INDUSTRY
     122 FOR HOUSEHOLD CONSUMPTION

2 INDUSTRIAL SUPPLIES (NON-FOOD)
  21 PRIMARY
  22 PROCESSED

3 FUELS AND LUBRICANTS
  31 PRIMARY
  32 PROCESSED

4 MACHINERY, EXC. TRANSPORT (W/PARTS)

5 TRANSPORT EQUIPMENT

6 CONSUMER GOODS, N.E.S.

7 GOODS N.E.S. AND UNSPECIFIED

TABLE III.BEC-2.M.C-H
CZECHOSLOVAKIA'S IMPORTS FROM HUNGARY, 1958-68
(MILLIONS OF CURRENT DOLLARS,* F.O.B.)

YEAR	AGGREGATION I. BASIC SNA CLASSES			AGGREGATION II. PRIMARY VS. PROCESSED		NOT SPECIFIED	TOTAL IMPORTS	RATIO SPECIFIED
	CAPITAL GOODS	INTERMEDIATE GOODS	CONSUMER GOODS	PRIMARY	PROCESSED			
1958	18.0	42.2	26.7	41.6	45.2	3.6	90.4	.9607
1959	17.2	37.6	27.8	38.4	44.2	4.4	87.0	.9498
1960	23.0	27.8	28.4	26.3	52.8	14.8	93.9	.8424
1961	45.2	45.9	37.6	44.0	84.8	7.1	135.8	.9478
1962	40.3	53.5	37.7	53.5	77.9	8.0	139.5	.9428
1963	32.7	52.4	42.2	52.0	75.4	3.7	131.1	.9714
1964	27.3	54.8	53.5	52.3	83.2	11.3	146.8	.9234
1965	32.6	58.4	64.2	51.1	104.1	16.2	171.4	.9053
1966	44.0	42.2	66.7	38.5	114.4	18.9	171.8	.8900
1967	42.5	27.7	62.9	30.2	102.9	17.8	150.8	.8821
1968	43.0	32.7	77.0	30.5	127.2	23.5	181.3	.8702

* CONVERTED FROM NATIONAL DEVISA-UNITS THROUGH OFFICIAL EXCHANGE RATES. NOTE LIMITATIONS DISCUSSED IN THE EXPLANATORY TEXT.

TABLE III. BEC-1. M. C-P
CZECHOSLOVAKIA'S IMPORTS FROM POLAND, 1958-68
(MILLIONS OF CURRENT DOLLARS,* F.O.B.)

YEAR	CLASS 1	111	112	121	122	CLASS 2	21	22	CLASS 3	31	32	CLASS 4+5	CLASS 6	CLASS 7	TOTAL IMPORTS
1958	6.7	4.7	.7		1.4	18.9	15.3	3.7	26.8	26.8		11.8	.3	7.0	71.5
1959	4.6	1.4	1.1		2.0	30.9	26.8	4.0	21.7	21.7		13.9	.3	10.7	82.0
1960	4.3	.8	1.7		1.8	37.4	33.8	3.6	24.3	21.2	3.1	27.6	2.1	14.8	110.6
1961	6.5	4.2	1.0		1.3	43.5	37.8	5.8	25.9	21.5	4.5	35.9	3.4	25.9	141.1
1962	4.6	.9	.9	.2	2.8	51.5	43.0	5.8	20.1	17.6	2.5	46.3	3.4	19.2	145.0
1963	8.0	.3	2.2	1.3	5.3	54.7	46.0	8.7	21.5	19.3	2.2	40.4	4.7	16.8	146.1
1964	19.2		8.0		9.9	52.4	46.0	6.4	36.1	25.8	10.3	52.5	5.8	27.4	193.3
1965	11.6	.5	4.3	1.2	5.6	53.5	45.1	8.5	31.4	25.1	6.2	61.4	6.9	43.8	208.6
1966	10.7		4.9	.8	5.0	38.8	33.0	5.8	28.1	27.9	.2	57.5	4.9	39.8	179.7
1967	11.9		5.4	.5	5.9	37.4	31.1	6.3	26.8	26.6	.2	60.1	8.8	54.2	199.2
1968	16.5		7.6	.8	8.0	44.4	35.4	9.0	31.1	31.0	.1	75.5	18.5	62.0	247.9

* CONVERTED FROM NATIONAL DEVISA UNITS THROUGH OFFICIAL EXCHANGE RATES. NOTE LIMITATIONS DISCUSSED IN THE EXPLANATORY TEXT.

BEC CATEGORIES

1 FOOD AND BEVERAGES
  11 PRIMARY
    111 FOR INDUSTRY
    112 FOR HOUSEHOLD CONSUMPTION
  12 PROCESSED
    121 FOR INDUSTRY
    122 FOR HOUSEHOLD CONSUMPTION

2 INDUSTRIAL SUPPLIES (NON-FOOD)
  21 PRIMARY
  22 PROCESSED

3 FUELS AND LUBRICANTS
  31 PRIMARY
  32 PROCESSED

4 MACHINERY, EXC. TRANSPORT (W/PARTS)

5 TRANSPORT EQUIPMENT

6 CONSUMER GOODS, N.E.S.

7 GOODS N.E.S. AND UNSPECIFIED

TABLE III.BEC-2.M.C-P
CZECHOSLOVAKIA'S IMPORTS FROM POLAND, 1958-68
(MILLIONS OF CURRENT DOLLARS,* F.O.B.)

YEAR	AGGREGATION I. BASIC SNA CLASSES			AGGREGATION II. PRIMARY VS. PROCESSED		NOT SPECIFIED	TOTAL IMPORTS	RATIO SPECIFIED
	CAPITAL GOODS	INTERMEDIATE GOODS	CONSUMER GOODS	PRIMARY	PROCESSED			
1958	11.8	50.4	2.3	47.4	17.2	7.0	71.5	.9019
1959	13.9	54.0	3.4	51.0	20.3	10.7	82.0	.8699
1960	27.6	62.5	5.6	57.6	38.2	14.8	110.6	.8662
1961	35.9	73.7	5.7	64.4	50.8	25.9	141.1	.8163
1962	46.3	72.5	7.0	62.4	63.4	19.2	145.0	.8677
1963	40.4	76.7	12.2	67.8	61.6	16.8	146.1	.8849
1964	52.5	89.8	23.6	79.8	86.2	27.4	193.3	.8583
1965	61.4	86.6	16.8	75.0	89.8	43.8	208.6	.7902
1966	57.5	67.7	14.7	65.8	74.2	39.8	179.7	.7786
1967	60.1	64.7	20.2	63.1	81.9	54.2	199.2	.7280
1968	75.5	76.3	34.1	74.1	111.8	62.0	247.9	.7498

* CONVERTED FROM NATIONAL DEVISA-UNITS THROUGH
OFFICIAL EXCHANGE RATES. NOTE LIMITATIONS
DISCUSSED IN THE EXPLANATORY TEXT.

TABLE III.BEC-1.M.C-R
CZECHOSLOVAKIA'S IMPORTS FROM RUMANIA, 1958-68
(MILLIONS OF CURRENT DOLLARS,* F.O.B.)

YEAR	CLASS 1	111	112	121	122	CLASS 2	21	22	CLASS 3	31	32	CLASS 4+5	CLASS 6	CLASS 7	TOTAL IMPORTS
1958	10.0	.9	3.0		6.1	5.5	2.7	2.8	3.7	3.7		1.7		1.3	22.4
1959	13.9	1.4	3.9		8.6	19.1	15.8	3.3	4.3	4.3		3.4		1.8	42.5
1960	26.4	6.0	4.2	2.8	13.3	17.8	14.7	3.1	3.1	3.1		10.1	1.0	5.9	64.3
1961	12.6	.4	2.7	1.7	7.8	18.8	13.9	4.9	1.8	1.8		16.7	1.2	3.1	54.0
1962	20.6	4.4	2.7	1.5	12.0	16.8	9.0	7.7	2.4	2.4		15.7	1.2	3.5	60.1
1963	14.7	2.1	2.6	1.7	8.2	21.5	13.3	8.2	.5	.5		10.6	1.2	4.5	52.9
1964	25.5	7.4	2.3	2.2	13.7	22.6	10.8	11.8	3.2	2.3	.9	17.3	1.7	4.2	74.6
1965	20.8	.3	5.3	1.4	13.8	31.0	10.9	20.1	11.1	5.0	6.1	19.1	6.2	6.1	94.3
1966	18.4	2.4	3.7	1.7	10.6	22.1	6.6	15.6	15.0	1.6	13.4	27.1	2.4	7.2	92.2
1967	17.5	2.3	4.5	.7	10.0	20.4	7.8	12.7	25.6	2.0	23.6	14.0	.4	8.6	86.5
1968	20.9	2.9	4.5	1.2	12.3	28.8	8.2	20.6	26.1	2.4	23.7	13.0	1.4	19.0	109.3

* CONVERTED FROM NATIONAL DEVISA UNITS THROUGH OFFICIAL EXCHANGE RATES. NOTE LIMITATIONS DISCUSSED IN THE EXPLANATORY TEXT.

BEC CATEGORIES

1 FOOD AND BEVERAGES
  11 PRIMARY
    111 FOR INDUSTRY
    112 FOR HOUSEHOLD CONSUMPTION
  12 PROCESSED
    121 FOR INDUSTRY
    122 FOR HOUSEHOLD CONSUMPTION

2 INDUSTRIAL SUPPLIES (NON-FOOD)
  21 PRIMARY
  22 PROCESSED

3 FUELS AND LUBRICANTS
  31 PRIMARY
  32 PROCESSED

4 MACHINERY, EXC. TRANSPORT (W/PARTS)

5 TRANSPORT EQUIPMENT

6 CONSUMER GOODS, N.E.S.

7 GOODS N.E.S. AND UNSPECIFIED

TABLE III.BEC-2.M.C-R
CZECHOSLOVAKIA'S IMPORTS FROM RUMANIA, 1958-68
(MILLIONS OF CURRENT DOLLARS,* F.O.B.)

YEAR	AGGREGATION I. BASIC SNA CLASSES			AGGREGATION II. PRIMARY VS. PROCESSED		NOT SPECIFIED	TOTAL IMPORTS	RATIO SPECIFIED
	CAPITAL GOODS	INTERMEDIATE GOODS	CONSUMER GOODS	PRIMARY	PROCESSED			
1958	1.7	10.2	9.1	10.4	10.6	1.3	22.4	.9405
1959	3.4	24.9	12.5	25.5	15.3	1.8	42.5	.9584
1960	10.1	29.8	18.5	28.0	30.3	5.9	64.3	.9077
1961	16.7	22.7	11.6	18.7	32.3	3.1	54.0	.9431
1962	15.7	25.0	15.9	18.5	38.1	3.5	60.1	.9411
1963	10.6	25.8	12.0	18.5	29.8	4.5	52.9	.9141
1964	17.3	35.4	17.7	22.8	47.6	4.2	74.6	.9436
1965	19.1	43.8	25.3	21.4	66.8	6.1	94.3	.9356
1966	27.1	41.2	16.7	14.2	70.7	7.2	92.2	.9215
1967	14.0	49.0	14.9	16.6	61.4	8.6	86.5	.9011
1968	13.0	59.0	18.2	18.0	72.3	19.0	109.3	.8260

* CONVERTED FROM NATIONAL DEVISA-UNITS THROUGH
OFFICIAL EXCHANGE RATES. NOTE LIMITATIONS
DISCUSSED IN THE EXPLANATORY TEXT.

TABLE III.BEC-1.M.C-Y
CZECHOSLOVAKIA'S IMPORTS FROM YUGOSLAVIA, 1958-66
(MILLIONS OF CURRENT DOLLARS,* F.O.B.)

YEAR	CLASS 1	111	112	121	122	CLASS 2	21	22	CLASS 3	31	32	CLASS 4+5	CLASS 6	CLASS 7	TOTAL IMPORTS
1958	4.1	1.2	1.3		1.7	6.5	5.7	.8						4.4	15.0
1959	3.2	.9	.8		1.5	6.5	5.3	1.2						1.0	10.7
1960	10.7	1.6	1.1		8.0	10.7	7.8	2.9				.2	.5	2.7	24.7
1961	6.5		.4		6.1	8.5	6.4	2.1				.2	.3	1.3	16.8
1962	8.8		1.7	.2	7.0	11.1	9.8	1.2				.4	.3	.6	21.3
1963	8.6		2.1		6.6	12.3	10.6	1.7				.6	.9	.3	22.6
1964	15.4		2.6	1.3	11.4	16.5	13.6	2.9				2.8	8.2	1.5	44.3
1965	14.0		1.9	1.4	10.7	19.8	13.3	6.5				18.0	14.0	5.9	71.8
1966	11.2		1.6	.4	9.3	16.7	12.7	4.0				28.2	11.0	6.6	73.8

* CONVERTED FROM NATIONAL DEVISA UNITS THROUGH
OFFICIAL EXCHANGE RATES. NOTE LIMITATIONS
DISCUSSED IN THE EXPLANATORY TEXT.

BEC CATEGORIES

1 FOOD AND BEVERAGES
   11   PRIMARY
        111 FOR INDUSTRY
        112 FOR HOUSEHOLD CONSUMPTION
   12   PROCESSED
        121 FOR INDUSTRY
        122 FOR HOUSEHOLD CONSUMPTION

2 INDUSTRIAL SUPPLIES (NON-FOOD)
   21   PRIMARY
   22   PROCESSED

3 FUELS AND LUBRICANTS
   31   PRIMARY
   32   PROCESSED

4 MACHINERY, EXC. TRANSPORT (W/PARTS)

5 TRANSPORT EQUIPMENT

6 CONSUMER GOODS, N.E.S.

7 GOODS N.E.S. AND UNSPECIFIED

TABLE III.BEC-2.M.C-Y
CZECHOSLOVAKIA'S IMPORTS FROM YUGOSLAVIA, 1958-66
(MILLIONS OF CURRENT DOLLARS,* F.O.B.)

YEAR	AGGREGATION I. BASIC SNA CLASSES			AGGREGATION II. PRIMARY VS. PROCESSED		NOT SPECIFIED	TOTAL IMPORTS	RATIO SPECIFIED
	CAPITAL GOODS	INTERMEDIATE GOODS	CONSUMER GOODS	PRIMARY	PROCESSED			
1958	0.0	7.6	3.0	8.1	2.4	4.4	15.0	.7051
1959	0.0	7.4	2.3	7.0	2.6	1.0	10.7	.9057
1960	.2	12.2	9.6	10.5	11.6	2.7	24.7	.8923
1961	.2	8.5	6.8	6.8	8.8	1.3	16.8	.9244
1962	.4	11.2	9.0	11.5	9.2	.6	21.3	.9725
1963	.6	12.3	9.5	12.6	9.7	.3	22.6	.9873
1964	2.8	17.8	22.2	16.2	26.6	1.5	44.3	.9668
1965	18.0	21.1	26.7	15.2	50.6	5.9	71.8	.9174
1966	28.2	17.1	21.9	14.3	52.9	6.6	73.8	.9108

* CONVERTED FROM NATIONAL DEVISA-UNITS THROUGH
OFFICIAL EXCHANGE RATES. NOTE LIMITATIONS
DISCUSSED IN THE EXPLANATORY TEXT.

TABLE III.BEC-1.M.C-CEMA
CZECHOSLOVAKIA'S IMPORTS FROM EUROPEAN CEMA (EXCLUDING ALBANIA), 1958-68
(MILLIONS OF CURRENT DOLLARS,* F.O.B.)

YEAR	CLASS 1	111	112	121	122	CLASS 2	21	22	CLASS 3	31	32	CLASS 4+5	CLASS 6	CLASS 7	TOTAL IMPORTS
1958	179.4	106.4	13.2	.7	59.0	305.4	246.6	58.8	85.9	83.6	2.3	150.7	29.0	89.3	839.7
1959	242.8	144.4	16.7	.8	81.0	361.7	299.1	62.6	95.7	92.0	3.7	180.4	27.4	120.7	1028.7
1960	246.7	140.8	19.1	3.9	82.9	382.1	307.9	74.1	59.1	46.4	12.7	203.8	40.6	222.2	1154.5
1961	200.4	99.5	19.4	3.0	78.5	431.5	343.1	88.4	76.9	57.5	19.4	282.0	60.1	231.9	1282.7
1962	245.5	121.4	24.6	2.0	97.4	445.7	356.3	89.5	80.9	67.9	13.1	322.6	63.0	261.6	1419.4
1963	248.8	111.5	24.7	4.2	108.4	484.9	396.0	88.9	82.7	69.7	13.0	316.3	57.8	284.4	1474.8
1964	209.0	85.4	28.1	5.3	90.0	518.1	427.0	91.1	111.4	85.6	25.8	382.5	60.2	373.1	1654.3
1965	216.1	80.3	33.6	4.2	98.0	581.6	471.9	109.8	97.8	75.8	22.0	431.2	83.7	395.8	1806.3
1966	230.5	91.7	28.4	3.6	106.7	498.8	395.3	103.5	85.6	61.7	23.9	456.4	78.8	390.5	1740.6
1967	263.2	118.5	27.2	2.5	115.0	630.1	526.2	103.9	100.4	64.0	36.3	418.5	82.7	306.0	1800.8
1968	261.1	120.5	27.6	3.2	109.8	598.7	466.8	132.0	117.7	71.3	46.4	441.1	125.2	520.8	2064.6

* CONVERTED FROM NATIONAL DEVISA UNITS THROUGH
OFFICIAL EXCHANGE RATES. NOTE LIMITATIONS
DISCUSSED IN THE EXPLANATORY TEXT.

BEC CATEGORIES

1 FOOD AND BEVERAGES
    11 PRIMARY
        111 FOR INDUSTRY
        112 FOR HOUSEHOLD CONSUMPTION
    12 PROCESSED
        121 FOR INDUSTRY
        122 FOR HOUSEHOLD CONSUMPTION

2 INDUSTRIAL SUPPLIES (NON-FOOD)
    21 PRIMARY
    22 PROCESSED

3 FUELS AND LUBRICANTS
    31 PRIMARY
    32 PROCESSED

4 MACHINERY, EXC. TRANSPORT (W/PARTS)

5 TRANSPORT EQUIPMENT

6 CONSUMER GOODS, N.E.S.

7 GOODS N.E.S. AND UNSPECIFIED

TABLE III.BEC-2.M.C-CEMA

CZECHOSLOVAKIA'S IMPORTS FROM EUROPEAN CEMA (EXCLUDING ALBANIA), 1958-68

(MILLIONS OF CURRENT DOLLARS,* F.O.B.)

YEAR	AGGREGATION I. BASIC SNA CLASSES			AGGREGATION II. PRIMARY VS. PROCESSED		NOT SPECIFIED	TOTAL IMPORTS	RATIO SPECIFIED
	CAPITAL GOODS	INTERMEDIATE GOODS	CONSUMER GOODS	PRIMARY	PROCESSED			
1958	150.7	498.4	101.3	449.9	300.5	89.3	839.7	.8937
1959	180.4	602.6	125.0	552.1	355.8	120.7	1028.7	.8827
1960	203.8	585.8	142.6	514.3	418.0	222.2	1154.5	.8075
1961	282.0	610.9	158.0	519.6	531.3	231.9	1282.7	.8193
1962	322.6	650.2	185.0	570.2	587.6	261.6	1419.4	.8157
1963	316.3	683.3	190.9	601.9	588.6	284.4	1474.8	.8072
1964	382.5	720.3	178.4	626.1	655.0	373.1	1654.3	.7745
1965	431.2	764.0	215.3	661.6	748.9	395.8	1806.3	.7809
1966	456.4	679.7	213.9	577.1	773.0	390.5	1740.6	.7757
1967	418.5	851.5	224.8	735.8	759.0	306.0	1800.8	.8301
1968	441.1	840.1	262.5	686.2	857.6	520.8	2064.6	.7477

* CONVERTED FROM NATIONAL DEVISA-UNITS THROUGH OFFICIAL EXCHANGE RATES. NOTE LIMITATIONS DISCUSSED IN THE EXPLANATORY TEXT.

TABLE III.BEC-1.M.P-U
POLAND'S IMPORTS FROM USSR, 1958-68
(MILLIONS OF CURRENT DOLLARS,* F.O.B.)

YEAR	CLASS 1	111	112	121	122	CLASS 2	21	22	CLASS 3	31	32	CLASS 4+5	CLASS 6	CLASS 7	TOTAL IMPORTS
1958	24.5	22.2	1.0	.1	1.1	142.5	112.6	29.9	53.5	20.8	32.7	37.8	16.0	59.6	334.0
1959	89.6	67.0	3.9	1.2	17.5	157.7	127.6	30.1	63.4	24.8	38.6	49.9	20.3	71.3	452.3
1960	71.6	59.4	3.7	.5	8.0	182.0	150.9	31.1	73.3	26.4	46.9	56.8	17.7	63.9	465.3
1961	44.1	32.8	1.0	.3	10.1	188.8	159.6	29.2	83.5	28.3	55.1	61.4	22.8	89.1	489.7
1962	61.0	52.7	.9	.5	6.8	188.2	150.4	37.7	104.6	38.9	65.7	92.5	24.1	107.4	577.8
1963	76.3	50.0	1.9	.2	24.3	190.1	151.2	38.9	125.5	49.5	76.0	124.4	18.4	112.5	647.2
1964	19.8	7.3	2.1	.1	10.4	227.9	177.3	50.5	126.2	55.7	70.5	87.1	21.7	159.7	642.4
1965	53.0	35.9	2.5	.0	14.5	249.1	169.5	79.6	126.3	79.2	47.0	99.2	30.5	170.3	728.4
1966	49.8	34.8	1.8		13.3	292.5	177.1	115.4	117.9	72.8	45.1	136.2	21.9	173.2	791.7
1967	110.5	80.4	1.4		28.6	298.3	170.5	127.9	140.6	88.2	52.3	145.9	27.6	198.2	921.1
1968	93.5	62.5	2.0		29.0	349.0	188.2	160.7	165.8	118.9	46.9	154.4	26.0	221.9	1010.7

* CONVERTED FROM NATIONAL DEVISA UNITS THROUGH
OFFICIAL EXCHANGE RATES. NOTE LIMITATIONS
DISCUSSED IN THE EXPLANATORY TEXT.

BEC CATEGORIES

1 FOOD AND BEVERAGES
  11 PRIMARY
    111 FOR INDUSTRY
    112 FOR HOUSEHOLD CONSUMPTION
  12 PROCESSED
    121 FOR INDUSTRY
    122 FOR HOUSEHOLD CONSUMPTION

2 INDUSTRIAL SUPPLIES (NON-FOOD)
  21 PRIMARY
  22 PROCESSED

3 FUELS AND LUBRICANTS
  31 PRIMARY
  32 PROCESSED

4 MACHINERY, EXC. TRANSPORT (W/PARTS)

5 TRANSPORT EQUIPMENT

6 CONSUMER GOODS, N.E.S.

7 GOODS N.E.S. AND UNSPECIFIED

TABLE III.BEC-2.M.P-U
POLAND'S IMPORTS FROM USSR, 1958-68
(MILLIONS OF CURRENT DOLLARS,* F.O.B.)

YEAR	AGGREGATION I. BASIC SNA CLASSES			AGGREGATION II. PRIMARY VS. PROCESSED				
	CAPITAL GOODS	INTERMEDIATE GOODS	CONSUMER GOODS	PRIMARY	PROCESSED	NOT SPECIFIED	TOTAL IMPORTS	RATIO SPECIFIED
1958	37.8	218.3	18.1	156.7	117.6	59.6	334.0	.8215
1959	49.9	289.4	41.6	223.3	157.6	71.3	452.3	.8423
1960	56.8	315.2	29.4	240.4	161.0	63.9	465.3	.8628
1961	61.4	305.3	33.9	221.7	178.9	89.1	489.7	.8180
1962	92.5	346.1	31.9	243.1	227.4	107.4	577.8	.8141
1963	124.4	365.8	44.5	252.5	282.2	112.5	647.2	.8262
1964	87.1	361.4	34.2	242.4	240.4	159.7	642.4	.7515
1965	99.2	411.3	47.5	287.2	270.9	170.3	728.4	.7662
1966	136.2	445.3	37.0	286.5	332.0	173.2	791.7	.7812
1967	145.9	519.3	57.7	340.5	382.4	198.2	921.1	.7849
1968	154.4	577.3	57.1	371.6	417.1	221.9	1010.7	.7805

* CONVERTED FROM NATIONAL DEVISA-UNITS THROUGH
OFFICIAL EXCHANGE RATES. NOTE LIMITATIONS
DISCUSSED IN THE EXPLANATORY TEXT.

TABLE III.BEC-1.M.P-B
POLAND'S IMPORTS FROM BULGARIA, 1958-68
(MILLIONS OF CURRENT DOLLARS,* F.O.B.)

YEAR	CLASS 1	111	112	121	122	CLASS 2	21	22	CLASS 3	31	32	CLASS 4+5	CLASS 6	CLASS 7	TOTAL IMPORTS
1958	5.6	.1	3.8		1.8	10.5	9.8	.6	.4	.4		.3	.7	1.2	18.7
1959	7.8	.2	3.8	.1	3.7	12.2	10.7	1.5				.3	.9	.8	22.1
1960	7.0	.1	4.1	.0	2.7	11.9	10.2	1.7	.4	.4		.3	.5	.4	20.2
1961	8.8	.0	5.9	.1	2.8	10.4	8.5	1.8	.2	.2		.4	.6	.1	20.8
1962	18.1		10.7	.4	6.9	7.8	5.4	2.3	.1		.0	3.3	1.2	.7	31.2
1963	13.2	.1	7.0	.3	5.8	11.3	8.0	3.3	.1		.1	5.3	1.9	1.2	32.9
1964	10.4		4.3	.0	6.1	12.0	7.4	4.6	.1		.1	4.8	1.8	2.7	31.9
1965	14.0		9.2		4.8	14.1	10.0	4.1	.2		.2	6.3	2.0	3.2	39.8
1966	12.7		5.6	.1	7.0	12.6	10.7	1.9	.1		.1	10.1	3.3	5.0	43.8
1967	9.1		4.1	.1	4.9	8.1	6.1	2.0	.2		.2	17.9	4.3	5.4	45.0
1968	12.1	.6	5.2		6.2	3.1	.4	2.7	.1		.1	19.0	5.9	7.1	47.3

* CONVERTED FROM NATIONAL DEVISA UNITS THROUGH
OFFICIAL EXCHANGE RATES. NOTE LIMITATIONS
DISCUSSED IN THE EXPLANATORY TEXT.

BEC CATEGORIES

1   FOOD AND BEVERAGES
    11   PRIMARY
         111   FOR INDUSTRY
         112   FOR HOUSEHOLD CONSUMPTION
    12   PROCESSED
         121   FOR INDUSTRY
         122   FOR HOUSEHOLD CONSUMPTION

2   INDUSTRIAL SUPPLIES (NON-FOOD)
    21   PRIMARY
    22   PROCESSED

3   FUELS AND LUBRICANTS
    31   PRIMARY
    32   PROCESSED

4   MACHINERY, EXC. TRANSPORT (W/PARTS)

5   TRANSPORT EQUIPMENT

6   CONSUMER GOODS, N.E.S.

7   GOODS N.E.S. AND UNSPECIFIED

TABLE III.BEC-2.M.P-B
POLAND'S IMPORTS FROM BULGARIA, 1958-68
(MILLIONS OF CURRENT DOLLARS,* F.O.B.)

YEAR	AGGREGATION I. BASIC SNA CLASSES			AGGREGATION II. PRIMARY VS. PROCESSED		NOT SPECIFIED	TOTAL IMPORTS	RATIO SPECIFIED
	CAPITAL GOODS	INTERMEDIATE GOODS	CONSUMER GOODS	PRIMARY	PROCESSED			
1958	.3	11.0	6.3	14.1	3.4	1.2	18.7	.9372
1959	.3	12.5	8.5	14.7	6.7	.8	22.1	.9650
1960	.3	12.1	7.4	14.5	5.2	.4	20.2	.9789
1961	.4	10.9	9.4	14.8	5.9	.1	20.8	.9964
1962	3.3	8.4	18.9	16.3	14.2	.7	31.2	.9792
1963	5.3	11.7	14.7	15.1	16.6	1.2	32.9	.9650
1964	4.8	12.2	12.2	11.7	17.4	2.7	31.9	.9145
1965	6.3	14.3	16.0	19.2	17.3	3.2	39.8	.9189
1966	10.1	12.8	15.9	16.3	22.5	5.0	43.8	.8870
1967	17.9	8.4	13.3	10.1	29.4	5.4	45.0	.8799
1968	19.0	3.8	17.3	6.2	34.0	7.1	47.3	.8510

* CONVERTED FROM NATIONAL DEVISA-UNITS THROUGH
OFFICIAL EXCHANGE RATES. NOTE LIMITATIONS
DISCUSSED IN THE EXPLANATORY TEXT.

TABLE III.BEC-1.M.P-C
POLAND'S IMPORTS FROM CZECHOSLOVAKIA, 1958-68
(MILLIONS OF CURRENT DOLLARS,* F.O.B.)

YEAR	CLASS 1	111	112	121	122	CLASS 2	21	22	CLASS 3	31	32	CLASS 4+5	CLASS 6	CLASS 7	TOTAL IMPORTS
1958	.2				.2	21.2	3.7	17.5	.4		.4	47.6	14.7	10.3	94.5
1959	.1			.0	.1	26.1	3.9	22.1	.4		.4	59.2	16.8	10.2	112.9
1960	.3			.0	.3	36.9	4.2	32.7	4.6		4.6	67.8	12.5	4.9	127.1
1961	.1		.1			47.5	4.0	43.5	8.3		8.3	84.1	16.4	6.5	162.9
1962	.1		.1		.1	58.7	4.2	54.5	6.0		5.5	96.8	22.6	14.3	198.6
1963	3.0	2.8	.1			57.2	4.9	52.4	5.6	.5	5.0	96.8	20.6	9.8	193.0
1964						54.7	4.2	50.6	3.0	.5	3.0	89.3	12.6	33.5	193.1
1965	.2				.2	72.0	5.6	66.4	4.2		4.2	107.9	19.3	40.6	244.1
1966						49.0	4.6	44.4	5.2		5.2	114.3	18.4	46.2	233.1
1967	.1				.1	52.0	5.7	46.3	2.6		2.6	116.6	14.1	49.9	235.2
1968	2.1				2.1	56.0	5.7	50.3	3.5		3.5	107.9	11.5	47.7	228.6

* CONVERTED FROM NATIONAL DEVISA UNITS THROUGH OFFICIAL EXCHANGE RATES. NOTE LIMITATIONS DISCUSSED IN THE EXPLANATORY TEXT.

BEC CATEGORIES

1 FOOD AND BEVERAGES
  11 PRIMARY
    111 FOR INDUSTRY
    112 FOR HOUSEHOLD CONSUMPTION
  12 PROCESSED
    121 FOR INDUSTRY
    122 FOR HOUSEHOLD CONSUMPTION

2 INDUSTRIAL SUPPLIES (NON-FOOD)
  21 PRIMARY
  22 PROCESSED

3 FUELS AND LUBRICANTS
  31 PRIMARY
  32 PROCESSED

4 MACHINERY, EXC. TRANSPORT (W/PARTS)

5 TRANSPORT EQUIPMENT

6 CONSUMER GOODS, N.E.S.

7 GOODS N.E.S. AND UNSPECIFIED

TABLE III.BEC-2.M.P-C
POLAND'S IMPORTS FROM CZECHOSLOVAKIA, 1958-68
(MILLIONS OF CURRENT DOLLARS,* F.O.B.)

YEAR	AGGREGATION I. BASIC SNA CLASSES			AGGREGATION II. PRIMARY VS. PROCESSED		NOT SPECIFIED	TOTAL IMPORTS	RATIO SPECIFIED
	CAPITAL GOODS	INTERMEDIATE GOODS	CONSUMER GOODS	PRIMARY	PROCESSED			
1958	47.6	21.7	14.9	3.7	80.5	10.3	94.5	.8912
1959	59.2	26.5	16.9	3.9	98.7	10.2	112.9	.9094
1960	67.8	41.6	12.8	4.2	118.0	4.9	127.1	.9613
1961	84.1	55.8	16.4	4.1	152.3	6.5	162.9	.9601
1962	96.8	64.7	22.7	4.7	179.6	14.3	198.6	.9279
1963	96.8	65.7	20.8	8.4	174.8	9.8	193.0	.9495
1964	89.3	57.8	12.6	4.2	155.5	33.5	193.1	.8267
1965	107.9	76.2	19.4	5.6	198.0	40.6	244.1	.8339
1966	114.3	54.2	18.4	4.6	182.3	46.2	233.1	.8018
1967	116.6	54.6	14.2	5.7	179.6	49.9	235.2	.7880
1968	107.9	59.5	13.6	5.7	175.2	47.7	228.6	.7914

* CONVERTED FROM NATIONAL DEVISA-UNITS THROUGH OFFICIAL EXCHANGE RATES. NOTE LIMITATIONS DISCUSSED IN THE EXPLANATORY TEXT.

TABLE III-BEC-1-M-P-G

POLAND'S IMPORTS FROM EAST GERMANY, 1958-68

(MILLIONS OF CURRENT DOLLARS,* F.O.B.)

YEAR	CLASS 1	111	112	121	122	CLASS 2	21	22	CLASS 3	31	32	CLASS 4+5	CLASS 6	CLASS 7	TOTAL IMPORTS
1958	6.9	.0		.0	6.9	39.4	21.3	18.1	20.6	11.9	8.6	52.5	26.4	9.6	155.5
1959	3.1	.0	.3	.7	2.1	40.6	22.7	17.9	34.7	26.9	7.8	62.3	28.6	17.9	187.2
1960	5.0		.1	1.1	3.9	46.7	25.3	21.4	20.5	10.8	9.7	79.7	25.0	9.5	186.4
1961	1.1	.1	.1		1.0	47.8	22.6	25.1	28.9	13.2	15.7	91.2	27.4	6.3	202.7
1962	1.4		.4		1.0	57.8	29.4	28.4	21.2	11.9	9.3	110.3	39.5	4.6	234.9
1963	1.5			.6	.9	48.1	24.4	23.7	16.6	12.2	4.4	132.4	43.5	11.3	253.4
1964	3.8			.1	3.8	50.1	26.0	24.2	23.9	13.6	10.3	101.1	31.6	25.2	235.8
1965	6.3	1.0		.1	5.2	54.4	27.5	26.9	20.2	13.1	7.2	130.3	40.8	19.2	271.4
1966	1.4	.3		.1	1.0	54.9	28.9	26.0	16.5	10.3	6.2	138.4	38.7	30.3	280.3
1967	2.2	1.2	.2		.9	67.7	33.2	34.4	13.6	6.9	6.7	134.3	42.4	31.9	292.1
1968	3.8	1.3	.2		2.4	75.1	34.3	40.8	16.6	5.7	10.8	115.0	48.0	37.7	296.2

* CONVERTED FROM NATIONAL DEVISA UNITS THROUGH OFFICIAL EXCHANGE RATES. NOTE LIMITATIONS DISCUSSED IN THE EXPLANATORY TEXT.

BEC CATEGORIES

1 FOOD AND BEVERAGES
  11 PRIMARY
    111 FOR INDUSTRY
    112 FOR HOUSEHOLD CONSUMPTION
  12 PROCESSED
    121 FOR INDUSTRY
    122 FOR HOUSEHOLD CONSUMPTION

2 INDUSTRIAL SUPPLIES (NON-FOOD)
  21 PRIMARY
  22 PROCESSED

3 FUELS AND LUBRICANTS
  31 PRIMARY
  32 PROCESSED

4 MACHINERY, EXC. TRANSPORT (W/PARTS)

5 TRANSPORT EQUIPMENT

6 CONSUMER GOODS, N.E.S.

7 GOODS N.E.S. AND UNSPECIFIED

TABLE III.BEC-2.M.P-G
POLAND'S IMPORTS FROM EAST GERMANY, 1958-68
(MILLIONS OF CURRENT DOLLARS,* F.O.B.)

YEAR	AGGREGATION I. BASIC SNA CLASSES			AGGREGATION II. PRIMARY VS. PROCESSED		NOT SPECIFIED	TOTAL IMPORTS	RATIO SPECIFIED
	CAPITAL GOODS	INTERMEDIATE GOODS	CONSUMER GOODS	PRIMARY	PROCESSED			
1958	52.5	60.1	33.3	33.3	112.6	9.6	155.5	.9384
1959	62.3	76.1	31.0	49.9	119.4	17.9	187.2	.9044
1960	79.7	68.3	28.9	36.1	140.8	9.5	186.4	.9493
1961	91.2	76.7	28.4	35.9	160.5	6.3	202.7	.9688
1962	110.3	79.1	40.9	41.8	188.4	4.6	234.9	.9804
1963	132.4	65.3	44.4	36.6	205.5	11.3	253.4	.9556
1964	101.1	74.1	35.4	39.5	171.1	25.2	235.8	.8931
1965	130.3	75.7	46.1	41.6	210.5	19.2	271.4	.9292
1966	138.4	71.8	39.7	39.6	210.4	30.3	280.3	.8918
1967	134.3	82.5	43.4	41.5	218.7	31.9	292.1	.8908
1968	115.0	93.0	50.6	41.4	217.1	37.7	296.2	.8728

* CONVERTED FROM NATIONAL DEVISA-UNITS THROUGH
OFFICIAL EXCHANGE RATES. NOTE LIMITATIONS
DISCUSSED IN THE EXPLANATORY TEXT.

POLAND'S TABLE III.BEC-1.M.P-H
IMPORTS FROM HUNGARY, 1958-68
(MILLIONS OF CURRENT DOLLARS,* F.O.B.)

YEAR	CLASS 1	111	112	121	122	CLASS 2	21	22	CLASS 3	31	32	CLASS 4+5	CLASS 6	CLASS 7	TOTAL IMPORTS
1958	1.3	.3	.3		.6	7.1	4.3	2.8	1.4		1.4	7.4	13.8	2.9	33.8
1959	4.1	1.1	.3	.3	2.4	8.5	4.6	3.9	3.2		3.2	7.6	11.4	1.8	36.6
1960	3.1	1.3	.2	.2	1.4	12.2	7.9	4.3	4.4		4.4	15.3	9.3	1.7	46.1
1961	2.3	.1	1.6	.0	.7	15.8	8.9	6.9	4.8		4.8	21.7	13.6	.8	59.0
1962	2.3		1.3		.9	16.6	7.2	9.4	4.4		4.4	27.5	14.5	3.0	68.2
1963	4.0	.3	1.6		2.4	16.3	7.9	8.4	2.8		2.8	32.1	12.9	7.7	75.9
1964	4.3	.3	1.3		2.8	15.9	8.6	7.3	4.2		4.2	30.4	12.1	15.6	82.6
1965	6.6	.1	2.8		3.8	22.2	9.4	12.8	5.3		5.3	33.4	21.4	16.8	105.7
1966	7.4		2.3		5.1	26.5	9.8	16.8	4.7		4.7	29.1	22.3	14.0	104.1
1967	6.1		3.4		2.7	23.7	12.4	11.3	4.3		4.3	28.9	20.3	20.7	104.0
1968	5.6		1.5		4.0	25.7	15.1	10.7	5.0		5.0	27.6	16.9	16.8	97.7

* CONVERTED FROM NATIONAL DEVISA UNITS THROUGH
OFFICIAL EXCHANGE RATES. NOTE LIMITATIONS
DISCUSSED IN THE EXPLANATORY TEXT.

BEC CATEGORIES

1   FOOD AND BEVERAGES
    11   PRIMARY
       111   FOR INDUSTRY
       112   FOR HOUSEHOLD CONSUMPTION
    12   PROCESSED
       121   FOR INDUSTRY
       122   FOR HOUSEHOLD CONSUMPTION

2   INDUSTRIAL SUPPLIES (NON-FOOD)
    21   PRIMARY
    22   PROCESSED

3   FUELS AND LUBRICANTS
    31   PRIMARY
    32   PROCESSED

4   MACHINERY, EXC. TRANSPORT (W/PARTS)

5   TRANSPORT EQUIPMENT

6   CONSUMER GOODS, N.E.S.

7   GOODS N.F.S. AND UNSPECIFIED

TABLE III.BEC-2.M.P-H
POLAND'S IMPORTS FROM HUNGARY, 1958-68
(MILLIONS OF CURRENT DOLLARS,* F.O.B.)

YEAR	AGGREGATION I. BASIC SNA CLASSES			AGGREGATION II. PRIMARY VS. PROCESSED		NOT SPECIFIED	TOTAL IMPORTS	RATIO SPECIFIED
	CAPITAL GOODS	INTERMEDIATE GOODS	CONSUMER GOODS	PRIMARY	PROCESSED			
1958	7.4	8.8	14.8	5.0	26.0	2.9	33.8	.9158
1959	7.6	13.1	14.1	6.0	28.8	1.8	36.6	.9515
1960	15.3	18.2	10.9	9.4	35.0	1.7	46.1	.9636
1961	21.7	20.5	15.9	10.5	47.6	.8	59.0	.9864
1962	27.5	21.0	16.7	8.5	56.7	3.0	68.2	.9567
1963	32.1	19.1	16.9	9.5	58.7	7.7	75.9	.8988
1964	30.4	20.4	16.2	10.1	56.9	15.6	82.6	.8112
1965	33.4	27.6	28.0	12.2	76.7	16.8	105.7	.8413
1966	29.1	31.3	29.7	12.1	78.0	14.0	104.1	.8652
1967	28.9	28.0	26.4	15.8	67.5	20.7	104.0	.8008
1968	27.6	30.8	22.5	16.6	64.3	16.8	97.7	.8285

* CONVERTED FROM NATIONAL DEVISA-UNITS THROUGH OFFICIAL EXCHANGE RATES. NOTE LIMITATIONS DISCUSSED IN THE EXPLANATORY TEXT.

TABLE III. BEC-1.M.P-R,
POLAND'S IMPORTS FROM RUMANIA, 1958-68
(MILLIONS OF CURRENT DOLLARS,* F.O.B.)

YEAR	CLASS 1	111	112	121	122	CLASS 2	21	22	CLASS 3	31	32	CLASS 4+5	CLASS 6	CLASS 7	TOTAL IMPORTS
1958	1.2	.1	.3		.8	3.3	1.1	2.2	7.3		7.3	.3	.1	.2	12.3
1959	2.6	.1	.7	.5	1.2	5.5	1.4	4.1	9.6		9.6	2.5	.6	.3	21.1
1960	2.6	.6		.0	2.0	5.1	1.5	3.6	7.8		7.8	3.1	.4	1.4	20.5
1961	1.6		.4		1.1	4.4	1.7	2.7	12.1		12.1	4.6	.6	.8	24.0
1962	6.0		3.5	1.1	1.3	3.6	1.1	2.5	13.4		13.4	14.8	1.4	1.0	40.2
1963	3.5		2.0	.1	1.4	3.1	.3	2.8	12.3	.3	12.1	11.8	1.9	.7	33.3
1964	3.4		1.9		1.5	3.0	.4	2.6	15.2	1.1	14.1	5.2	1.2	1.5	29.5
1965	3.9		2.7		1.2	4.2	.6	3.6	11.3		11.3	21.6	2.4	1.3	44.7
1966	3.4	.2	2.1	.3	1.0	5.3	.4	4.9	12.0		12.0	16.6	1.6	2.1	41.0
1967	4.6		2.4		2.0	8.0	.4	7.6	12.6		12.6	20.5	2.5	1.8	50.2
1968	6.4		4.3		2.1	9.2	.2	9.0	13.2		13.2	24.9	2.4	1.4	57.5

* CONVERTED FROM NATIONAL DEVISA UNITS THROUGH
OFFICIAL EXCHANGE RATES. NOTE LIMITATIONS
DISCUSSED IN THE EXPLANATORY TEXT.

BEC CATEGORIES

1　FOOD AND BEVERAGES
　　11　PRIMARY
　　　　111　FOR INDUSTRY
　　　　112　FOR HOUSEHOLD CONSUMPTION
　　12　PROCESSED
　　　　121　FOR INDUSTRY
　　　　122　FOR HOUSEHOLD CONSUMPTION

2　INDUSTRIAL SUPPLIES (NON-FOOD)
　　21　PRIMARY
　　22　PROCESSED

3　FUELS AND LUBRICANTS
　　31　PRIMARY
　　32　PROCESSED

4　MACHINERY, EXC. TRANSPORT (W/PARTS)

5　TRANSPORT EQUIPMENT

6　CONSUMER GOODS, N.E.S.

7　GOODS N.E.S. AND UNSPECIFIED

TABLE III.BEC-2.M.P-R
POLAND'S IMPORTS FROM RUMANIA, 1958-68
(MILLIONS OF CURRENT DOLLARS,* F.O.B.)

YEAR	AGGREGATION I. BASIC SNA CLASSES			AGGREGATION II. PRIMARY VS. PROCESSED		NOT SPECIFIED	TOTAL IMPORTS	RATIO SPECIFIED
	CAPITAL GOODS	INTERMEDIATE GOODS	CONSUMER GOODS	PRIMARY	PROCESSED			
1958	.3	10.6	1.2	1.5	10.6	.2	12.3	.9858
1959	2.5	15.7	2.5	2.2	18.5	.3	21.1	.9858
1960	3.1	13.6	2.4	2.1	17.0	1.4	20.5	.9318
1961	4.6	16.5	2.2	2.1	21.1	.8	24.0	.9667
1962	14.8	18.2	6.2	4.6	34.5	1.0	40.2	.9751
1963	11.8	15.5	5.3	2.5	30.1	.7	33.3	.9805
1964	5.2	18.2	4.6	3.4	24.6	1.5	29.5	.9508
1965	21.6	15.5	6.3	3.3	40.1	1.3	44.7	.9720
1966	16.6	17.6	4.8	2.5	36.4	2.1	41.0	.9494
1967	20.5	20.8	6.9	3.1	45.2	1.8	50.2	.9636
1968	24.9	22.4	8.8	4.6	51.6	1.4	57.5	.9765

* CONVERTED FROM NATIONAL DEVISA-UNITS THROUGH
OFFICIAL EXCHANGE RATES. NOTE LIMITATIONS
DISCUSSED IN THE EXPLANATORY TEXT.

TABLE III.BEC-1.M.P-Y
POLAND'S IMPORTS FROM YUGOSLAVIA, 1958-68
(MILLIONS OF CURRENT DOLLARS,* F.O.B.)

YEAR	CLASS 1	111	112	121	122	CLASS 2	21	22	CLASS 3	31	32	CLASS 4+5	CLASS 6	CLASS 7	TOTAL IMPORTS
1958	1.6		.6		1.0	11.0	4.9	6.1				2.0	6.7	1.0	22.3
1959	1.9		.3	.0	1.6	16.1	6.5	9.5				1.6	4.6	.8	25.0
1960	1.2		.6	.1	.6	9.9	3.9	6.0				2.9	1.1	.2	15.3
1961	2.0		.4	.1	1.5	18.5	9.0	9.5				14.7	3.4	.5	39.0
1962	1.8		.2	.1	1.5	19.1	7.4	11.7				15.9	1.1	.8	39.2
1963	1.9		.3	.2	1.5	21.1	12.7	8.4	.4		.4	9.7	2.2		34.8**
1964	2.7		.6	.2	1.9	25.3	14.0	11.3				7.1	3.2	2.2	40.5
1965	5.9		1.1	.2	4.5	28.7	10.7	18.0	.6		.6	11.9	13.3	2.7	63.0
1966	1.9		.4	.2	1.3	20.8	9.6	11.2				16.4	10.6	6.9	56.6
1967	.9		.3	.3	.6	17.7	3.1	14.6				19.4	4.8	4.4	47.3
1968	5.0	.9	.5		3.6	16.7	3.4	13.3				10.0	5.4	2.9	40.0

* CONVERTED FROM NATIONAL DEVISA UNITS THROUGH
OFFICIAL EXCHANGE RATES. NOTE LIMITATIONS
DISCUSSED IN THE EXPLANATORY TEXT.

** SUM OF COMPONENTS GREATER THAN GIVEN
TOTAL - ERROR IN ORIGINAL SOURCE.

BEC CATEGORIES

1 FOOD AND BEVERAGES
  11 PRIMARY
    111 FOR INDUSTRY
    112 FOR HOUSEHOLD CONSUMPTION
  12 PROCESSED
    121 FOR INDUSTRY
    122 FOR HOUSEHOLD CONSUMPTION

2 INDUSTRIAL SUPPLIES (NON-FOOD)
  21 PRIMARY
  22 PROCESSED

3 FUELS AND LUBRICANTS
  31 PRIMARY
  32 PROCESSED

4 MACHINERY, EXC. TRANSPORT (W/PARTS)

5 TRANSPORT EQUIPMENT

6 CONSUMER GOODS, N.E.S.

7 GOODS N.E.S. AND UNSPECIFIED

TABLE III.BEC-2.M.P-Y
POLAND'S IMPORTS FROM YUGOSLAVIA, 1958-68
(MILLIONS OF CURRENT DOLLARS,* F.O.B.)

YEAR	AGGREGATION I. BASIC SNA CLASSES			AGGREGATION II. PRIMARY VS. PROCESSED		NOT SPECIFIED	TOTAL IMPORTS	RATIO SPECIFIED
	CAPITAL GOODS	INTERMEDIATE GOODS	CONSUMER GOODS	PRIMARY	PROCESSED			
1958	2.0	11.0	8.3	5.5	15.8	1.0	22.3	.9540
1959	1.6	16.1	6.5	6.8	17.4	.8	25.0	.9690
1960	2.9	9.9	2.3	4.5	10.6	.2	15.3	.9886
1961	14.7	18.6	5.3	9.4	29.1	.5	39.0	.9872
1962	15.9	19.7	2.8	7.6	30.7	.8	39.2	.9789
1963	9.7	21.2	4.1	13.0	22.0	-.2	34.8**	1.0050
1964	7.1	25.5	5.7	14.6	23.7	2.2	40.5	.9468
1965	11.9	29.5	18.9	11.9	48.5	2.7	63.0	.9580
1966	16.4	21.0	12.3	9.9	39.7	6.9	56.6	.8777
1967	19.4	18.1	5.4	3.1	39.8	4.4	47.3	.9064
1968	10.0	17.6	9.5	4.8	32.3	2.9	40.0	.9282

* CONVERTED FROM NATIONAL DEVISA-UNITS THROUGH OFFICIAL EXCHANGE RATES. NOTE LIMITATIONS DISCUSSED IN THE EXPLANATORY TEXT.

** SUM OF COMPONENTS GREATER THAN GIVEN TOTAL - ERROR IN ORIGINAL SOURCE.

Series III. BEC-1. M. P-CEMA

TABLE III.BEC-1.M.P-CEMA
POLAND'S IMPORTS FROM EUROPEAN CEMA (EXCLUDING ALBANIA), 1958-68
(MILLIONS OF CURRENT DOLLARS,* F.O.B.)

YEAR	CLASS 1	111	112	121	122	CLASS 2	21	22	CLASS 3	31	32	CLASS 4+5	CLASS 6	CLASS 7	TOTAL IMPORTS
1958	39.7	22.7	5.4	.1	11.4	224.1	152.9	71.2	83.6	33.2	50.4	146.0	71.7	83.7	648.8
1959	107.4	68.5	9.0	2.9	27.0	250.7	170.9	79.7	111.3	51.7	59.6	181.9	78.6	102.3	832.2
1960	89.7	61.4	8.1	1.9	18.3	295.0	200.2	94.8	110.7	37.2	73.5	223.0	65.4	81.7	865.6
1961	58.0	32.8	9.1	.4	15.7	314.6	205.3	109.3	138.0	41.9	96.1	263.5	81.4	103.6	959.2
1962	88.9	52.8	17.0	2.1	17.0	332.7	197.8	134.9	149.8	51.5	98.3	345.2	103.3	130.9	1151.0
1963	101.5	52.8	12.6	1.2	34.8	326.2	196.7	129.5	162.9	62.5	100.4	402.7	99.3	143.0	1235.5
1964	41.8	7.6	9.5	.1	24.6	363.7	223.9	139.8	162.7	70.4	102.4	317.9	81.0	238.1	1215.4
1965	84.1	37.0	17.2	.1	29.7	416.0	222.6	193.4	167.4	92.3	75.1	398.7	116.4	251.4	1434.0
1966	74.8	35.1	11.8	.4	27.4	440.9	231.5	209.4	156.4	83.1	73.3	444.7	106.3	270.8	1494.0
1967	132.7	81.8	11.5	.2	39.2	457.8	228.3	229.5	173.9	95.1	78.8	464.0	111.3	307.9	1647.6
1968	123.5	64.4	13.2	.0	45.9	518.1	243.9	274.2	204.2	124.6	79.6	448.9	110.7	332.4	1737.9

* CONVERTED FROM NATIONAL DEVISA UNITS THROUGH
OFFICIAL EXCHANGE RATES. NOTE LIMITATIONS
DISCUSSED IN THE EXPLANATORY TEXT.

BEC CATEGORIES

1   FOOD AND BEVERAGES
    11   PRIMARY
        111   FOR INDUSTRY
        112   FOR HOUSEHOLD CONSUMPTION
    12   PROCESSED
        121   FOR INDUSTRY
        122   FOR HOUSEHOLD CONSUMPTION

2   INDUSTRIAL SUPPLIES (NON-FOOD)
    21   PRIMARY
    22   PROCESSED

3   FUELS AND LUBRICANTS
    31   PRIMARY
    32   PROCESSED

4   MACHINERY, EXC. TRANSPORT (W/PARTS)

5   TRANSPORT EQUIPMENT

6   CONSUMER GOODS, N.E.S.

7   GOODS N.E.S. AND UNSPECIFIED

TABLE III.BEC-2.M.P-CEMA
POLAND'S IMPORTS FROM EUROPEAN CEMA (EXCLUDING ALBANIA), 1958-68
(MILLIONS OF CURRENT DOLLARS,* F.O.B.

YEAR	AGGREGATION I. BASIC SNA CLASSES			AGGREGATION II. PRIMARY VS. PROCESSED		NOT SPECIFIED	TOTAL IMPORTS	RATIO SPECIFIED
	CAPITAL GOODS	INTERMEDIATE GOODS	CONSUMER GOODS	PRIMARY	PROCESSED			
1958	146.0	330.5	88.6	214.3	350.8	83.7	648.8	.8710
1959	181.9	433.4	114.6	300.1	429.8	102.3	832.2	.8771
1960	223.0	469.0	91.8	306.8	477.0	81.7	865.6	.9056
1961	263.5	485.9	106.2	289.2	566.4	103.6	959.2	.8920
1962	345.2	537.5	137.3	319.2	700.8	130.9	1151.0	.8862
1963	402.7	543.2	146.7	324.6	768.0	143.0	1235.5	.8843
1964	317.9	544.2	115.1	311.4	665.9	238.1	1215.4	.8041
1965	398.7	620.6	163.3	369.1	813.5	251.4	1434.0	.8247
1966	444.7	632.9	145.5	361.6	861.6	270.8	1494.0	.8187
1967	464.0	713.7	162.0	416.8	922.9	307.9	1647.6	.8131
1968	448.9	786.8	169.9	446.2	959.4	332.4	1737.9	.8088

* CONVERTED FROM NATIONAL DEVISA-UNITS THROUGH
OFFICIAL EXCHANGE RATES. NOTE LIMITATIONS
DISCUSSED IN THE EXPLANATORY TEXT.

TABLE III.BEC-1.X.U-B
USSR EXPORTS TO BULGARIA, 1946-68
(MILLIONS OF CURRENT DOLLARS,* F.O.B.)

YEAR	CLASS 1	111	112	121	122	CLASS 2	21	22	CLASS 3	31	32	CLASS 4+5	CLASS 6	CLASS 7	TOTAL EXPORTS
1946	9.1	9.1				21.7	14.2	7.5	5.3		5.3	24.7	.5	22.5	83.9
1947	1.8	1.8				18.0	11.5	6.5	3.7		3.7	5.7	.5	32.8	62.4
1948	8.7	8.7				32.5	12.1	20.5	4.9		4.9	12.1	.6	20.6	79.4
1949	14.0	14.0				34.8	14.0	20.8	6.2		6.2	15.5	.8	22.6	94.0
1950	4.4	4.4				27.6	9.9	17.7	5.9		5.9	24.0	1.4	36.7	100.0
1951						31.6	15.8	15.8	7.6		7.6	35.1	1.2	40.4	115.9
1952						33.6	12.4	21.1	7.8		7.8	35.3	1.3	40.0	117.9
1953						36.9	15.8	21.0	8.6		8.6	36.0	1.2	27.0	109.6
1954						33.4	9.7	23.7	3.0		3.0	33.5	1.4	37.2	108.4
1955	4.6	4.6		.0		40.0	9.1	30.9	5.2		5.2	40.4	2.4	34.9	127.4
1956	1.0	.9		.1		45.2	8.5	36.6	6.8		6.8	39.4	3.0	13.0	108.4
1957	14.5	14.5		.0		64.1	18.4	45.6	15.0		15.0	35.4	26.4	17.1	172.4
1958	2.0	1.9	.1	.0		73.0	22.1	50.9	17.7		17.7	50.7	25.3	31.9	200.6
1959	12.0	11.8	.1	.0	.1	87.7	26.0	61.7	22.9		22.9	88.4	31.5	47.4	289.9
1960	11.8	11.3	.2	.0	.2	101.7	30.6	71.1	29.6	.1	29.4	108.6	23.8	53.6	329.0
1961	1.8	.4	.4	.0	.9	100.2	29.4	70.8	41.4	5.5	35.8	124.2	24.3	64.4	356.2
1962	11.1	8.8	.4	.0	1.9	117.5	33.5	84.0	51.4	9.9	41.5	167.7	27.1	72.9	447.8
1963	22.5	12.6	2.0	.0	7.9	125.8	34.4	91.4	67.3	23.7	43.6	207.5	27.0	45.3	495.4
1964	15.9	9.1	1.2	.0	5.5	158.1	44.9	113.2	97.7	57.6	35.1	231.6	16.8	52.3	567.4
1965	8.4	7.6	.6	.0	.2	174.0	56.0	118.1	103.5	71.1	32.4	249.7	16.3	36.5	588.4
1966	10.8	.0	1.1	.0	9.6	198.3	69.2	129.2	122.7	87.3	35.4	320.1	17.7	27.5	697.1
1967	22.3		1.2	.0	21.1	204.6	56.9	147.7	126.0	81.3	44.7	362.9	21.4	25.5	762.8
1968	33.0		1.6	.0	31.4	261.6	68.9	192.7	149.3	98.8	50.5	416.4	35.6	53.4	949.3

* CONVERTED FROM NATIONAL DEVISA UNITS THROUGH OFFICIAL EXCHANGE RATES. NOTE LIMITATIONS DISCUSSED IN THE EXPLANATORY TEXT.

BEC CATEGORIES

1 FOOD AND BEVERAGES
   11 PRIMARY
     111 FOR INDUSTRY
     112 FOR HOUSEHOLD CONSUMPTION
   12 PROCESSED
     121 FOR INDUSTRY
     122 FOR HOUSEHOLD CONSUMPTION

2 INDUSTRIAL SUPPLIES (NON-FOOD)

3 FUELS AND LUBRICANTS
   31 PRIMARY
   32 PROCESSED

4 MACHINERY, EXC. TRANSPORT (W/PARTS)

5 TRANSPORT EQUIPMENT

6 CONSUMER GOODS, N.E.S.

TABLE III.BEC-2.X.U-B
USSR EXPORTS TO BULGARIA, 1946-68
(MILLIONS OF CURRENT DOLLARS,* F.O.B.)

YEAR	AGGREGATION I. BASIC SNA CLASSES			AGGREGATION II. PRIMARY VS. PROCESSED		NOT SPECIFIED	TOTAL EXPORTS	RATIO SPECIFIED
	CAPITAL GOODS	INTERMEDIATE GOODS	CONSUMER GOODS	PRIMARY	PROCESSED			
1946	24.7	36.1	.5	23.2	38.1	22.5	83.9	.7314
1947	5.7	23.5	.5	13.3	16.4	32.8	62.4	.4750
1948	12.1	46.1	.6	20.8	38.1	20.6	79.4	.7411
1949	15.5	55.1	.8	28.1	43.3	22.6	94.0	.7595
1950	24.0	37.9	1.4	14.3	49.0	36.7	100.0	.6327
1951	35.1	39.2	1.2	15.8	59.6	40.4	115.9	.6510
1952	35.3	41.3	1.3	12.4	65.5	40.0	117.9	.6609
1953	36.0	45.4	1.2	15.8	66.7	27.0	109.6	.7536
1954	33.5	36.4	1.4	9.7	61.5	37.2	108.4	.6569
1955	40.4	49.8	2.4	13.7	78.8	34.9	127.4	.7262
1956	39.4	53.1	3.0	9.6	85.9	13.0	108.4	.8805
1957	35.4	93.6	26.4	32.9	122.5	17.1	172.4	.9011
1958	50.7	92.6	25.4	24.1	144.6	31.9	200.6	.8411
1959	88.4	122.4	31.7	37.9	204.6	47.4	289.9	.8365
1960	108.6	142.5	24.2	42.2	233.2	53.6	329.0	.8370
1961	124.2	142.0	25.7	35.8	256.1	64.4	356.2	.8193
1962	167.7	177.7	29.5	52.6	322.3	72.9	447.8	.8372
1963	207.5	205.7	36.9	72.7	377.4	45.3	495.4	.9085
1964	231.6	260.0	23.5	112.8	402.3	52.3	567.4	.9078
1965	249.7	285.1	17.0	135.2	416.7	36.5	588.4	.9379
1966	320.1	321.0	28.4	157.5	512.0	27.5	697.1	.9605
1967	362.9	330.6	43.7	139.4	597.9	25.5	762.8	.9665
1968	416.4	410.9	68.5	169.3	726.6	53.4	949.3	.9437

* CONVERTED FROM NATIONAL DEVISA-UNITS THROUGH OFFICIAL EXCHANGE RATES. NOTE LIMITATIONS DISCUSSED IN THE EXPLANATORY TEXT.

TABLE III.BEC-1.X.U-C
USSR EXPORTS TO CZECHOSLOVAKIA, 1946-68
(MILLIONS OF CURRENT DOLLARS,* F.O.B.)

YEAR	CLASS 1	111	112	121	122	CLASS 2	21	22	CLASS 3	31	32	CLASS 4+5	CLASS 6	CLASS 7	TOTAL EXPORTS
1946	2.5	2.5				15.9	15.1	.8	1.9	.0	1.9	.0	.9	7.7	29.0
1947	13.6	13.6				17.5	16.5	1.0	4.2	.1	4.1	.1	.6	8.3	44.3
1948	64.0	62.2				49.9	43.3	6.6	4.0	.1	3.9	1.3	.9	21.6	141.8
1949	83.4	41.9			41.5	65.2	49.2	16.0	5.3	1.7	3.7	6.4	.7	45.0	206.0
1950	74.4	60.4			14.0	64.0	51.3	12.7	4.7	1.7	3.0	12.3	2.1	62.9	220.4
1951	119.0	99.6			19.4	87.1	62.1	25.0	5.5	5.4	.1	26.7	3.2	48.5	290.1
1952	111.6	93.3			18.3	116.2	79.3	36.9	12.2	8.0	4.2	45.3	3.9	74.1	363.3
1953	109.1	87.7			21.3	119.3	80.5	38.7	9.3	6.8	2.5	41.8	2.5	66.8	348.8
1954	106.7	86.6			20.1	124.4	84.7	39.7	12.8	6.9	5.9	43.3	4.1	60.3	351.6
1955	104.1	88.7		1.2	14.3	149.9	95.2	54.7	15.7	10.2	5.5	36.9	5.9	43.3	355.9
1956	64.9	51.7		.8	12.4	174.8	104.0	70.8	19.9	16.5	3.3	32.8	8.8	72.5	373.7
1957	154.9	133.9		.2	20.8	203.6	116.4	87.2	50.9	46.9	4.0	46.8	18.2	77.0	551.3
1958	115.4	95.5	.7	.5	18.7	185.0	116.2	68.8	51.2	47.1	4.1	47.4	13.8	34.0	446.8
1959	186.5	139.3	1.0	2.5	43.7	204.5	134.3	70.2	63.8	58.9	4.9	58.9	11.7	77.6	603.0
1960	161.8	127.1	1.5	.9	32.2	221.8	139.8	82.0	82.0	70.7	11.3	60.4	13.1	91.8	630.8
1961	121.9	89.0	1.6	.3	31.1	243.6	150.6	93.0	107.0	92.8	14.2	82.8	11.3	86.0	652.7
1962	158.7	114.9	2.0	.6	41.2	251.1	147.7	103.4	138.0	124.8	13.3	110.9	20.7	91.3	770.7
1963	172.6	115.8	2.6	1.3	52.9	283.5	161.3	122.3	155.5	139.2	16.3	129.1	15.9	92.5	849.0
1964	96.2	65.6	2.1	1.4	27.1	324.9	191.4	133.5	176.6	156.2	20.4	149.5	9.0	144.6	900.8
1965	117.9	75.9	8.3	1.5	32.2	352.8	180.5	172.3	176.8	160.4	16.4	131.1	9.7	137.6	925.9
1966	153.5	88.6	6.8	1.0	57.1	310.8	167.6	143.2	153.2	136.1	17.1	152.6	11.3	112.6	894.0
1967	178.4	109.5	1.7	1.3	65.9	346.6	174.7	171.9	177.6	160.3	17.3	140.8	13.8	110.1	967.4
1968	166.2	118.2	1.4	1.2	45.5	393.8	191.6	202.2	193.4	176.6	16.8	148.7	15.2	120.8	1038.1

* CONVERTED FROM NATIONAL DEVISA UNITS THROUGH
  OFFICIAL EXCHANGE RATES. NOTE LIMITATIONS
  DISCUSSED IN THE EXPLANATORY TEXT.

BEC CATEGORIES

1 FOOD AND BEVERAGES
   11 PRIMARY
       111 FOR INDUSTRY
       112 FOR HOUSEHOLD CONSUMPTION
   12 PROCESSED
       121 FOR INDUSTRY
       122 FOR HOUSEHOLD CONSUMPTION

2 INDUSTRIAL SUPPLIES (NON-FOOD)
   21 PRIMARY
   22 PROCESSED

3 FUELS AND LUBRICANTS
   31 PRIMARY
   32 PROCESSED

4 MACHINERY, EXC. TRANSPORT (W/PARTS)

5 TRANSPORT EQUIPMENT

6 CONSUMER GOODS, N.E.S.

TABLE III.BEC-2.X.U-C
USSR EXPORTS TO CZECHOSLOVAKIA, 1946-68
(MILLIONS OF CURRENT DOLLARS,* F.O.B.)

YEAR	AGGREGATION I. BASIC SNA CLASSES			AGGREGATION II. PRIMARY VS. PROCESSED		NOT SPECIFIED	TOTAL EXPORTS	RATIO SPECIFIED
	CAPITAL GOODS	INTERMEDIATE GOODS	CONSUMER GOODS	PRIMARY	PROCESSED			
1946	.0	20.3	.9	17.7	3.6	7.7	29.0	.7331
1947	.1	35.3	.6	30.2	5.8	8.3	44.3	.8125
1948	1.3	116.1	2.8	105.6	14.5	21.6	141.8	.8476
1949	6.4	112.5	42.2	92.8	68.2	45.0	206.0	.7816
1950	12.3	129.2	16.0	113.4	44.2	62.9	220.4	.7147
1951	26.7	192.3	22.6	167.1	74.5	48.5	290.1	.8329
1952	45.3	221.8	22.2	180.6	108.6	74.1	363.3	.7960
1953	41.8	216.4	23.8	175.1	106.9	66.8	348.8	.8085
1954	43.3	223.7	24.2	178.2	113.1	60.3	351.6	.8285
1955	36.9	255.5	20.1	194.1	118.5	43.3	355.9	.8782
1956	32.8	247.2	21.2	172.2	128.9	72.5	373.7	.8059
1957	46.8	388.6	39.0	297.2	177.2	77.0	551.3	.8604
1958	47.4	332.2	33.2	259.5	153.3	34.0	446.8	.9240
1959	58.9	410.1	56.4	333.4	191.9	77.6	603.0	.8713
1960	60.4	431.8	46.9	339.2	199.8	91.8	630.8	.8545
1961	82.8	439.9	44.0	334.0	232.7	86.0	652.7	.8683
1962	110.9	504.7	63.8	389.3	290.0	91.3	770.7	.8815
1963	129.1	556.1	71.4	418.8	337.7	92.5	849.0	.8911
1964	149.5	568.5	38.2	415.2	341.0	144.6	900.8	.8395
1965	131.1	606.9	50.3	425.1	363.2	137.6	925.9	.8514
1966	152.6	553.5	75.2	399.1	382.2	112.6	894.0	.8740
1967	140.8	635.0	81.5	446.2	411.1	110.1	967.4	.8861
1968	148.7	706.5	62.0	487.7	429.5	120.8	1038.1	.8836

* CONVERTED FROM NATIONAL DEVISA-UNITS THROUGH OFFICIAL EXCHANGE RATES. NOTE LIMITATIONS DISCUSSED IN THE EXPLANATORY TEXT.

TABLE III.BEC-1.X.U-G
USSR EXPORTS TO EAST GERMANY, 1946-68
(MILLIONS OF CURRENT DOLLARS,* F.O.B.)

YEAR	CLASS 1	111	112	121	122	CLASS 2	21	22	CLASS 3	31	32	CLASS 4+5	CLASS 6	CLASS 7	TOTAL EXPORTS
1946						23.1	23.1							17.3	41.0
1947						18.9	18.4	.4	.7	.7		.4		23.4	43.7
1948	25.6	19.0			6.6	36.2	10.3	25.9	.9	.9		1.3		28.4	91.4
1949	16.3	8.1			8.2	61.8	18.1	43.8	2.1	.2	1.9	10.3		25.6	116.1
1950	74.0	33.3			40.8	69.6	36.8	32.7	8.2	3.5	4.7	8.8		25.1	185.8
1951	105.6	55.6			50.0	116.3	70.4	45.9	12.3	7.7	4.6	9.6		54.8	298.7
1952	126.9	73.3			53.7	142.0	92.5	49.5	12.5	7.3	5.2	9.9		141.5	432.9
1953	174.9	86.6			88.3	167.8	89.1	78.7	46.0	39.8	6.2	9.6		106.8	505.1
1954	142.1	82.9			59.2	187.6	99.0	88.6	58.2	46.9	11.3	6.8		88.0	482.7
1955	96.3	86.5	.1	1.7	8.1	242.4	125.4	117.1	60.9	48.0	12.9	4.8	3.7	70.5	478.7
1956	128.1	64.5		5.4	58.1	272.7	129.3	143.4	86.2	64.3	21.9	8.9	3.0	72.4	571.3
1957	251.9	141.6	3.8	5.5	100.9	338.4	131.6	206.8	132.9	103.1	29.8	17.9	2.4	118.6	862.1
1958	177.0	126.9	.0	2.8	47.2	383.0	127.6	255.4	124.5	98.7	25.7	27.2	2.6	85.4	799.8
1959	279.8	137.8	1.1	4.1	136.9	426.7	149.3	277.3	144.4	111.4	32.9	32.3	3.4	143.5	1030.1
1960	222.2	143.1	5.6	5.7	67.7	524.6	154.0	370.6	156.1	114.8	41.3	37.4	7.1	104.3	1051.7
1961	231.8	136.6	.7	10.0	84.5	602.2	190.2	411.9	181.8	127.1	54.7	56.9	8.9	127.6	1209.1
1962	297.0	169.6	.8	4.8	121.8	638.8	192.1	446.8	208.4	155.4	52.9	77.5	6.8	144.1	1372.7
1963	240.8	120.3	5.4	8.0	107.0	638.9	181.0	457.9	212.7	151.7	61.0	79.9	6.4	135.2	1313.9
1964	163.1	92.3	3.5	6.5	60.9	718.4	186.3	532.0	227.0	170.0	57.0	97.5	4.3	174.9	1385.2
1965	146.4	73.9	3.5	10.0	59.1	716.6	184.1	532.5	224.1	170.8	53.3	106.5	4.6	164.7	1363.0
1966	183.5	90.1	9.5	1.5	82.4	699.3	184.0	515.3	210.3	171.7	38.6	119.9	8.8	185.0	1406.8
1967	177.7	100.1	6.8	1.0	69.8	699.2	166.1	533.0	193.5	161.4	32.1	163.0	9.5	173.3	1416.2
1968	188.2	105.3	5.8	1.2	76.0	676.2	169.0	507.2	182.0	148.8	33.2	230.2	10.2	219.6	1506.4

* CONVERTED FROM NATIONAL DEVISA UNITS THROUGH OFFICIAL EXCHANGE RATES. NOTE LIMITATIONS DISCUSSED IN THE EXPLANATORY TEXT.

BEC CATEGORIES

1 FOOD AND BEVERAGES
  11 PRIMARY
    111 FOR INDUSTRY
    112 FOR HOUSEHOLD CONSUMPTION
  12 PROCESSED
    121 FOR INDUSTRY
    122 FOR HOUSEHOLD CONSUMPTION

2 INDUSTRIAL SUPPLIES (NON-FOOD)
  21 PRIMARY
  22 PROCESSED

3 FUELS AND LUBRICANTS
  31 PRIMARY
  32 PROCESSED

4 MACHINERY, EXC. TRANSPORT (W/PARTS)

5 TRANSPORT EQUIPMENT

6 CONSUMER GOODS, N.E.S.

7 GOODS N.E.S. AND UNSPECIFIED

TABLE III.BEC-2.X.U-G
USSR EXPORTS TO EAST GERMANY, 1946-68
(MILLIONS OF CURRENT DOLLARS,* F.O.B.)

YEAR	AGGREGATION I. BASIC SNA CLASSES			AGGREGATION II. PRIMARY VS. PROCESSED		NOT SPECIFIED	TOTAL EXPORTS	RATIO SPECIFIED
	CAPITAL GOODS	INTERMEDIATE GOODS	CONSUMER GOODS	PRIMARY	PROCESSED			
1946	0.0	23.7	0.0	23.7	0.0	17.3	41.0	.5792
1947	.4	19.8	0.0	19.4	.9	23.4	43.7	.4640
1948	1.3	55.2	6.6	29.3	33.8	28.4	91.4	.6900
1949	10.3	72.1	8.2	26.4	64.1	25.6	116.1	.7795
1950	8.8	111.0	40.8	73.6	87.1	25.1	185.8	.8646
1951	9.6	184.3	50.0	133.7	110.2	54.8	298.7	.8165
1952	9.9	227.8	53.7	173.1	118.2	141.5	432.9	.6730
1953	9.6	300.3	88.3	215.4	182.8	106.8	505.1	.7885
1954	6.8	328.6	59.2	228.7	165.9	88.0	482.7	.8176
1955	4.8	391.5	11.8	259.9	148.3	70.5	478.7	.8527
1956	8.9	428.8	61.2	258.2	240.7	72.4	571.3	.8732
1957	17.9	618.5	107.1	380.1	363.4	118.6	862.1	.8624
1958	27.2	637.2	49.9	353.3	361.0	85.4	799.8	.8932
1959	32.3	713.0	141.3	399.7	486.9	143.5	1030.1	.8607
1960	37.4	829.5	80.4	417.5	529.8	104.3	1051.7	.9008
1961	56.9	930.6	94.1	454.6	626.9	127.6	1209.1	.8945
1962	77.5	1021.6	129.4	517.9	710.6	144.1	1372.7	.8950
1963	79.9	980.0	118.8	458.5	720.2	135.2	1313.9	.8971
1964	97.5	1044.2	68.6	452.0	758.3	174.9	1385.2	.8737
1965	106.5	1024.6	67.2	432.2	766.1	164.7	1363.0	.8792
1966	119.9	1001.1	100.7	455.2	766.5	185.0	1406.8	.8685
1967	163.0	993.8	86.1	434.4	808.5	173.3	1416.2	.8776
1968	230.2	964.7	92.0	428.9	858.0	219.6	1506.4	.8542

* CONVERTED FROM NATIONAL DEVISA-UNITS THROUGH
OFFICIAL EXCHANGE RATES. NOTE LIMITATIONS
DISCUSSED IN THE EXPLANATORY TEXT.

TABLE III.BEC-1.X.U-H
USSR EXPORTS TO HUNGARY, 1946-68
(MILLIONS OF CURRENT DOLLARS,* F.O.B.)

YEAR	CLASS 1	111	112	121	122	CLASS 2	21	22	CLASS 3	31	32	CLASS 4+5	CLASS 6	CLASS 7	TOTAL EXPORTS
1946						5.9	5.1	.8	1.7		1.7		.1	2.5	10.2
1947						9.2	8.0	1.3	2.9		2.9	.0	.1	3.9	16.2
1948						12.3	10.4	1.9	6.5		6.5	.9	.2	14.5	34.4
1949						34.6	27.1	7.5	5.7		5.7	11.3	.1	32.0	83.7
1950	2.2	2.2				42.4	30.4	11.9	5.1		5.1	13.2	.2	63.7	126.9
1951	3.4	3.4				52.9	37.5	15.4	8.8	3.5	5.3	15.8	.6	40.3	121.8
1952	.3	.3				61.3	42.4	18.9	13.8	6.0	7.8	22.1	.7	52.0	150.3
1953	11.4	11.4				63.5	43.9	19.7	13.9	5.9	8.0	21.3	1.0	46.6	157.7
1954	.1	.1				82.0	52.4	29.6	13.6	5.5	8.2	17.5	1.0	38.8	153.0
1955	2.9	2.7		.2	.1	67.7	42.4	25.3	12.1	3.5	8.6	14.2	1.6	16.7	115.3
1956	.4	.1		.2	.1	74.0	41.9	32.0	18.3	8.6	9.7	15.0	2.9	16.4	126.9
1957	34.5	34.1		.4	.0	122.5	54.8	67.7	59.6	45.7	13.9	16.5	7.4	9.2	249.7
1958	11.9	11.4		.2	.3	110.2	61.8	48.4	43.9	25.3	18.6	20.7	6.1	7.8	200.6
1959	21.0	17.7		.4	2.9	107.5	61.0	46.4	45.4	28.1	17.3	63.0	3.9	19.0	259.8
1960	18.4	14.5		.2	3.7	127.5	76.2	51.3	53.5	34.3	19.2	70.7	5.8	35.6	311.4
1961	33.9	29.8		.3	3.7	146.5	78.3	68.2	56.6	36.8	19.8	57.1	4.3	60.9	359.3
1962	25.5	19.8		.2	5.6	172.7	90.0	82.7	61.2	38.1	23.1	66.5	4.3	80.9	411.1
1963	14.6	9.3	.2	.5	4.6	171.2	86.6	84.5	80.9	46.6	34.3	95.6	4.4	76.7	443.4
1964	6.2	1.3	.1	.4	4.4	196.6	101.3	95.3	94.7	56.5	38.2	125.0	6.4	63.7	492.7
1965	33.0	24.7	.1	.4	7.8	213.9	100.2	113.7	102.6	59.5	43.1	110.3	9.0	77.1	545.9
1966	12.3	.6	.0	.4	11.3	228.1	105.7	122.4	103.5	60.7	42.8	121.5	8.9	30.4	504.6
1967	31.7	9.9	.2	.4	21.3	246.0	106.1	139.9	97.9	52.9	45.0	147.2	11.0	51.8	585.5
1968	39.8	21.7	.3	.3	17.5	312.5	114.0	198.5	106.3	54.5	51.8	138.5	13.6	64.7	675.4

* CONVERTED FROM NATIONAL DEVISA UNITS THROUGH OFFICIAL EXCHANGE RATES. NOTE LIMITATIONS DISCUSSED IN THE EXPLANATORY TEXT.

BEC CATEGORIES

1 FOOD AND BEVERAGES
  11 PRIMARY
    111 FOR INDUSTRY
    112 FOR HOUSEHOLD CONSUMPTION
  12 PROCESSED
    121 FOR INDUSTRY
    122 FOR HOUSEHOLD CONSUMPTION

2 INDUSTRIAL SUPPLIES (NON-FOOD)
  21 PRIMARY

3 FUELS AND LUBRICANTS
  31 PRIMARY
  32 PROCESSED

4 MACHINERY, EXC. TRANSPORT (W/PARTS)

5 TRANSPORT EQUIPMENT

6 CONSUMER GOODS, N.E.S.

TABLE III.BEC-2.X.U-H
USSR EXPORTS TO HUNGARY, 1946-68
(MILLIONS OF CURRENT DOLLARS,* F.O.B.)

YEAR	AGGREGATION I. BASIC SNA CLASSES			AGGREGATION II. PRIMARY VS. PROCESSED		NOT SPECIFIED	TOTAL EXPORTS	RATIO SPECIFIED
	CAPITAL GOODS	INTERMEDIATE GOODS	CONSUMER GOODS	PRIMARY	PROCESSED			
1946	0.0	7.6	.1	5.1	2.6	2.5	10.2	.7520
1947	.0	12.2	.1	8.0	4.3	3.9	16.2	.7581
1948	.9	18.8	.2	10.4	9.5	14.5	34.4	.5795
1949	11.3	40.3	.1	27.1	24.6	32.0	83.7	.6171
1950	13.2	49.8	.2	32.7	30.5	63.7	126.9	.4977
1951	15.8	65.0	.6	44.3	37.1	40.3	121.8	.6688
1952	22.1	75.4	.7	48.7	49.6	52.0	150.3	.6538
1953	21.3	88.8	1.0	61.1	50.0	46.6	157.7	.7047
1954	17.5	95.6	1.0	57.9	56.2	38.8	153.0	.7461
1955	14.2	82.7	1.7	48.6	50.0	16.7	115.3	.8548
1956	15.0	92.5	3.0	50.6	59.9	16.4	126.9	.8706
1957	16.5	216.6	7.4	134.6	105.9	9.2	249.7	.9633
1958	20.7	165.7	6.4	98.5	94.2	7.8	200.6	.9611
1959	63.0	171.0	6.8	106.8	133.9	19.0	259.8	.9267
1960	70.7	195.7	9.5	125.0	150.9	35.6	311.4	.8858
1961	57.1	233.3	8.0	145.0	153.4	60.9	359.3	.8306
1962	66.5	253.9	9.9	147.9	182.3	80.9	411.1	.8033
1963	95.6	261.9	9.3	142.7	224.0	76.7	443.4	.8271
1964	125.0	293.0	10.9	159.3	269.7	63.7	492.7	.8707
1965	110.3	341.6	16.9	184.5	284.3	77.1	545.9	.8588
1966	121.5	332.6	20.2	167.0	307.2	30.4	504.6	.9398
1967	147.2	354.2	32.4	169.1	364.7	51.8	585.5	.9116
1968	138.5	440.8	31.4	190.5	420.2	64.7	675.4	.9042

* CONVERTED FROM NATIONAL DEVISA-UNITS THROUGH
OFFICIAL EXCHANGE RATES. NOTE LIMITATIONS
DISCUSSED IN THE EXPLANATORY TEXT.

TABLE III.BEC-1.X.U-P
USSR EXPORTS TO POLAND, 1946-68
(MILLIONS OF CURRENT DOLLARS,* F.O.B.)

YEAR	CLASS 1	111	112	121	122	CLASS 2	21	22	CLASS 3	31	32	CLASS 4+5	CLASS 6	CLASS 7	TOTAL EXPORTS
1946	52.6	52.6				26.0	25.7	.3	6.1	.7	5.5	4.2	.9	16.6	106.4
1947	34.3	34.3				32.6	32.4	.2	6.0	.6	5.4	1.7	.6	29.2	104.4
1948	32.7	32.7				73.5	73.0	.5	8.2	.8	7.4	4.3	.8	13.4	132.9
1949	6.1	6.1				63.1	61.5	1.6	8.0	.7	7.3	21.9	2.8	34.9	136.9
1950	20.8	20.8				82.0	78.2	3.7	5.8	1.4	4.5	42.2	5.2	85.5	241.4
1951	25.8	25.8				101.1	90.3	10.7	11.8	2.7	9.0	63.6	4.9	103.5	310.7
1952	51.2	51.2				96.2	86.8	9.4	11.3	4.8	6.5	78.3	4.7	120.7	362.3
1953	10.5	10.5				97.1	86.5	10.6	11.6	6.3	5.3	105.5	6.1	98.2	328.9
1954	44.2	44.2				114.8	104.1	10.7	16.3	7.5	8.9	117.3	4.2	116.6	413.4
1955	34.7	29.1	.1	.2	5.3	130.5	107.1	23.4	17.8	9.9	7.9	134.5	5.7	108.6	431.8
1956	14.5	7.7	.1	.1	6.6	139.7	131.9	25.8	23.3	11.3	12.0	75.4	8.6	95.7	357.2
1957	103.0	96.5	.2	.2	6.2	164.4	131.4	33.0	42.7	16.8	25.9	60.0	7.3	53.6	430.9
1958	30.5	23.4	1.4	.2	5.5	150.5	118.5	32.0	53.8	20.2	33.6	42.3	19.4	80.3	376.8
1959	90.0	65.4	3.7	1.4	19.6	159.6	126.9	32.7	66.6	28.3	38.4	52.6	19.7	97.8	486.4
1960	73.0	60.8	3.8	.5	7.9	183.1	151.7	31.4	79.4	32.1	47.3	55.1	15.0	85.3	490.8
1961	52.3	40.5	1.0	.3	10.5	188.5	156.5	31.9	90.8	33.5	57.3	64.2	24.0	110.9	530.7
1962	69.7	61.5	.6	.5	7.0	189.3	150.6	38.7	108.9	44.3	64.6	94.6	23.2	108.4	594.1
1963	82.0	55.0	1.4	.4	24.2	193.1	150.8	42.3	128.9	54.2	74.7	127.5	18.0	113.1	662.5
1964	22.5	10.3	1.7	.2	9.9	239.0	176.5	62.4	132.4	60.2	72.2	97.6	22.3	146.2	660.0
1965	56.4	35.1	1.7	.1	19.4	246.8	168.3	78.5	131.0	83.1	47.9	108.9	24.2	159.4	726.7
1966	49.1	36.6	.8	.1	11.6	301.9	173.9	128.1	125.8	77.5	48.4	144.4	18.4	163.4	803.2
1967	104.5	79.9	.7	.1	23.9	315.7	173.2	142.5	145.0	90.7	54.3	169.4	23.4	154.3	912.2
1968	83.3	62.9	.8		19.6	358.7	186.9	171.8	171.7	106.3	65.4	178.7	23.8	233.9	1050.1

* CONVERTED FROM NATIONAL DEVISA UNITS THROUGH
OFFICIAL EXCHANGE RATES. NOTE LIMITATIONS
DISCUSSED IN THE EXPLANATORY TEXT.

BEC CATEGORIES

1   FOOD AND BEVERAGES
    11   PRIMARY
         111   FOR INDUSTRY
         112   FOR HOUSEHOLD CONSUMPTION
    12   PROCESSED
         121   FOR INDUSTRY
         122   FOR HOUSEHOLD CONSUMPTION

2   INDUSTRIAL SUPPLIES (NON-FOOD)
    21   PRIMARY

3   FUELS AND LUBRICANTS
    31   PRIMARY
    32   PROCESSED

4   MACHINERY, EXC. TRANSPORT (W/PARTS)

5   TRANSPORT EQUIPMENT

6   CONSUMER GOODS, N.E.S.

TABLE III.BEC-2.X.U-P
USSR EXPORTS TO POLAND, 1946-68
(MILLIONS OF CURRENT DOLLARS,* F.O.B.)

YEAR	AGGREGATION I. BASIC SNA CLASSES			AGGREGATION II. PRIMARY VS. PROCESSED		NOT SPECIFIED	TOTAL EXPORTS	RATIO SPECIFIED
	CAPITAL GOODS	INTERMEDIATE GOODS	CONSUMER GOODS	PRIMARY	PROCESSED			
1946	4.2	84.7	.9	79.0	10.9	16.6	106.4	.8444
1947	1.7	72.9	.6	67.3	8.0	29.2	104.4	.7207
1948	4.3	114.4	.8	106.5	13.0	13.4	132.9	.8994
1949	21.9	77.2	2.8	68.4	33.6	34.9	136.9	.7448
1950	42.2	108.6	5.2	100.3	55.6	85.5	241.4	.6459
1951	63.6	138.7	4.9	118.9	88.2	103.5	310.7	.6667
1952	78.3	158.6	4.7	142.7	98.9	120.7	362.3	.6669
1953	105.5	119.1	6.1	103.3	127.4	98.2	328.9	.7014
1954	117.3	175.3	4.2	155.8	141.1	116.6	413.4	.7180
1955	134.5	177.5	11.1	146.2	177.0	108.6	431.8	.7484
1956	75.4	170.8	15.3	133.0	128.5	95.7	357.2	.7321
1957	60.0	303.7	13.6	244.8	132.6	53.6	430.9	.8757
1958	42.3	227.9	26.3	163.5	133.0	80.3	376.8	.7870
1959	52.6	293.1	42.9	224.3	164.4	97.8	486.4	.7989
1960	55.1	323.7	26.7	248.4	157.1	85.3	490.8	.8262
1961	64.2	320.1	35.5	231.5	188.3	110.9	530.7	.7911
1962	94.6	360.2	30.9	257.0	228.7	108.4	594.1	.8175
1963	127.5	378.3	43.6	262.3	287.1	113.1	662.5	.8294
1964	97.6	382.3	33.9	249.2	264.6	146.2	660.0	.7785
1965	108.9	413.1	45.3	288.2	279.0	159.4	726.7	.7806
1966	144.4	464.5	30.9	288.7	351.1	163.4	803.2	.7966
1967	169.4	540.7	47.9	344.4	413.5	154.3	912.2	.8309
1968	178.7	593.2	44.2	356.8	459.3	233.9	1050.1	.7772

* CONVERTED FROM NATIONAL DEVISA-UNITS THROUGH
OFFICIAL EXCHANGE RATES. NOTE LIMITATIONS
DISCUSSED IN THE EXPLANATORY TEXT.

TABLE III.BEC-1.X.U-R
USSR EXPORTS TO RUMANIA, 1946-68
(MILLIONS OF CURRENT DOLLARS,* F.O.B.)

YEAR	CLASS 1	111	112	121	122	CLASS 2	21	22	CLASS 3	31	32	CLASS 4+5	CLASS 6	CLASS 7	TOTAL EXPORTS
1946	17.1	17.1				7.3	5.6	1.7	.0		.0	2.5	.2	3.2	30.3
1947	8.2	8.2				20.5	13.2	7.3	.0		.0	3.3	.3	5.4	37.7
1948	4.2	4.2				24.5	17.3	7.2	.0		.0	11.3	1.1	7.1	48.2
1949	2.0	2.0				53.1	24.2	28.9	.0		.0	23.6	.8	31.8	111.3
1950	1.9	1.9				54.8	26.6	28.1	.1		.1	39.7	.9	18.3	113.9
1951						68.0	40.8	27.1	.1		.1	39.5	2.1	31.2	142.9
1952						70.5	39.7	30.8	.3		.3	68.2	2.1	84.9	226.0
1953						82.5	32.7	49.8	.3		.3	94.5	1.5	41.9	220.8
1954	4.9	4.9				85.8	32.8	53.0	.7		.7	59.8	2.2	59.2	212.7
1955	27.2	26.6		.1	.5	94.0	35.7	58.2	9.1		9.1	65.0	6.9	65.6	267.8
1956	4.5	4.0		.1	.4	108.9	36.9	72.0	9.3		9.3	37.3	8.7	43.4	212.0
1957	41.8	41.4		.1	.3	121.4	33.6	87.9	12.4		12.4	30.7	9.0	35.5	250.8
1958	17.0	16.5	.2	.1	.3	147.6	39.4	108.2	11.0	.1	10.9	33.8	8.4	33.5	251.3
1959	1.7	.5	.0	.1	1.1	146.9	34.6	112.3	11.6	.4	11.2	49.0	4.1	19.2	232.4
1960	10.4	9.4	.7	.1	.2	157.8	40.6	117.2	13.0	2.3	10.7	57.3	9.6	12.5	260.7
1961	1.3	.7	.3	.0	.2	175.3	41.4	133.9	8.9	2.5	6.4	64.9	8.7	32.8	291.8
1962	1.0	.4	.4	.0	.2	206.4	43.3	162.8	17.9	6.7	11.2	89.5	10.5	49.8	374.8
1963	.6	.2	.1	.0	.2	206.6	44.7	161.9	18.9	3.2	15.6	95.3	14.5	63.1	399.0
1964	34.6	33.6	1.0	.0	.2	243.9	47.5	196.4	18.8	3.4	15.4	85.7	11.2	98.9	493.1
1965	1.9	.3	1.2	.0	.3	202.4	47.8	154.7	16.9	3.9	13.1	80.0	10.6	90.9	402.8
1966	1.1		.5	.0	.6	210.1	57.7	152.4	18.0	5.0	13.1	101.3	13.7	42.0	386.3
1967	1.6		1.0		.6	198.2	59.1	139.1	17.7	5.5	12.2	116.4	13.0	47.6	394.6
1968	4.0		3.9		.2	197.9	61.6	136.3	21.2	5.1	16.1	117.6	10.3	65.6	416.7

* CONVERTED FROM NATIONAL DEVISA UNITS THROUGH OFFICIAL EXCHANGE RATES. NOTE LIMITATIONS DISCUSSED IN THE EXPLANATORY TEXT.

BEC CATEGORIES

1   FOOD AND BEVERAGES
  11   PRIMARY
    111   FOR INDUSTRY
    112   FOR HOUSEHOLD CONSUMPTION
  12   PROCESSED
    121   FOR INDUSTRY
    122   FOR HOUSEHOLD CONSUMPTION

2   INDUSTRIAL SUPPLIES (NON-FOOD)
  21   PRIMARY

3   FUELS AND LUBRICANTS
  31   PRIMARY
  32   PROCESSED

4   MACHINERY, EXC. TRANSPORT (W/PARTS)

5   TRANSPORT EQUIPMENT

6   CONSUMER GOODS, N.E.S.

TABLE III.BEC-2.X.U-R
USSR EXPORTS TO RUMANIA, 1946-68
(MILLIONS OF CURRENT DOLLARS,* F.O.B.)

YEAR	AGGREGATION I. BASIC SNA CLASSES			AGGREGATION II. PRIMARY VS. PROCESSED		NOT SPECIFIED	TOTAL EXPORTS	RATIO SPECIFIED
	CAPITAL GOODS	INTERMEDIATE GOODS	CONSUMER GOODS	PRIMARY	PROCESSED			
1946	2.5	24.5	.2	22.8	4.4	3.2	30.3	.8952
1947	3.3	28.7	.3	21.3	10.9	5.4	37.7	.8559
1948	11.3	28.7	1.1	21.5	19.7	7.1	48.2	.8533
1949	23.6	55.1	.8	26.2	53.3	31.8	111.3	.7142
1950	39.7	54.9	.9	26.6	68.9	18.3	113.9	.8390
1951	39.5	70.0	2.1	42.8	68.9	31.2	142.9	.7815
1952	68.2	70.8	2.1	39.7	101.4	84.9	226.0	.6244
1953	94.5	82.8	1.5	32.7	146.1	41.9	220.8	.8100
1954	59.8	91.4	2.2	37.7	115.8	59.2	212.7	.7215
1955	65.0	129.8	7.4	62.4	139.8	65.6	267.8	.7551
1956	37.3	122.2	9.1	40.9	127.7	43.4	212.0	.7955
1957	30.7	175.2	9.3	74.9	140.3	35.5	250.8	.8584
1958	33.8	175.1	8.8	56.1	161.7	33.5	251.3	.8667
1959	49.0	159.0	5.3	35.6	177.7	19.2	232.4	.9175
1960	57.3	180.3	10.5	53.0	195.1	12.5	260.7	.9519
1961	64.9	184.9	9.2	44.9	214.1	32.8	291.8	.8877
1962	89.5	224.4	11.1	50.8	274.2	49.8	374.8	.8672
1963	95.3	225.7	14.8	48.3	287.6	63.1	399.0	.8418
1964	85.7	296.3	12.2	85.5	308.8	98.9	493.1	.7995
1965	80.0	219.7	12.2	53.2	258.7	90.9	402.8	.7744
1966	101.3	228.1	14.8	63.1	281.2	42.0	386.3	.8912
1967	116.4	215.9	14.6	65.6	281.4	47.6	394.6	.8794
1968	117.6	219.1	14.3	70.6	280.5	65.6	416.7	.8425

* CONVERTED FROM NATIONAL DEVISA-UNITS THROUGH OFFICIAL EXCHANGE RATES. NOTE LIMITATIONS DISCUSSED IN THE EXPLANATORY TEXT.

TABLE III-BEC-1-X-U-Y
USSR EXPORTS TO YUGOSLAVIA, 1946-68
(MILLIONS OF CURRENT DOLLARS,* F.O.B.)

YEAR	CLASS 1	111	112	121	122	CLASS 2	21	22	CLASS 3	31	32	CLASS 4+5	CLASS 6	CLASS 7	TOTAL EXPORTS
1946	1.3	1.3				3.0	.2	2.8	2.1	.1	2.0	2.6	.8	8.7	18.4
1947						4.6	.3	4.4	6.8	.9	5.9	2.3	.9	23.0	37.7
1948						5.1	1.0	4.1	3.3	.8	2.5	2.9	1.3	21.9	34.4
1949						.6	.4	.2	.9	.2	.7	.0	.2	1.1	2.9
1954						.1		.1	.9	.7	.2		.0	1.0	2.0
1955	.9	.5			.4	7.5	6.2	1.3	7.6	6.7	1.0	.0	.1	.4	16.4
1956	34.9	34.5			.4	13.3	7.5	5.8	17.4	16.3	1.0	2.9	.3	.2	69.1
1957	10.0	10.0				18.9	11.5	7.4	25.6	24.6	1.0	15.8	.5	2.4	73.1
1958	6.0	6.0				14.4	6.0	8.4	17.7	17.2	.5	11.4	.9	.7	51.1
1959	7.6	7.6				13.9	5.0	8.8	17.7	16.8	1.0	5.4	1.1	.5	46.2
1960	1.4	1.4				14.4	3.0	11.4	19.9	15.3	4.5	14.9	1.4	4.5	55.1
1961	3.9	2.8			1.1	10.0	2.1	7.9	11.8	9.3	2.4	4.6	2.0	7.5	35.9
1962	.5				.5	19.4	5.4	14.0	18.0	13.2	4.8	11.7	2.5	19.3	72.3
1963						24.5	5.5	19.0	20.6	13.9	6.7	17.7	4.6	25.1	96.3
1964						36.7	3.6	33.1	22.4	15.2	7.2	29.8	5.7	39.8	134.9
1965	3.7	.9	.4		2.4	48.6	6.7	41.9	23.1	17.2	5.9	26.0	5.9	37.8	145.1
1966	29.0	1.0	.3		27.8	60.5	12.9	47.6	25.2	17.8	7.4	34.0	7.3	57.8	213.9
1967	27.1	.7	.2		26.2	66.1	19.8	46.3	29.7	18.0	11.7	39.2	5.8	112.5	280.3
1968	27.5	4.4	.1	.0	23.1	69.5	24.7	44.8	45.1	24.3	20.8	50.4	4.8	91.7	289.1

* CONVERTED FROM NATIONAL DEVISA UNITS THROUGH OFFICIAL EXCHANGE RATES. NOTE LIMITATIONS DISCUSSED IN THE EXPLANATORY TEXT.

BEC CATEGORIES

1 FOOD AND BEVERAGES
  11 PRIMARY
    111 FOR INDUSTRY
    112 FOR HOUSEHOLD CONSUMPTION
  12 PROCESSED
    121 FOR INDUSTRY
    122 FOR HOUSEHOLD CONSUMPTION

2 INDUSTRIAL SUPPLIES (NON-FOOD)
  21 PRIMARY
  22 PROCESSED

3 FUELS AND LUBRICANTS
  31 PRIMARY
  32 PROCESSED

4 MACHINERY, EXC. TRANSPORT (W/PARTS)

5 TRANSPORT EQUIPMENT

6 CONSUMER GOODS, N.E.S.

7 GOODS N.E.S. AND UNSPECIFIED

TABLE III.BEC-2.X.U-Y
USSR EXPORTS TO YUGOSLAVIA, 1946-68
(MILLIONS OF CURRENT DOLLARS,* F.O.B.)

YEAR	AGGREGATION I. BASIC SNA CLASSES			AGGREGATION II. PRIMARY VS. PROCESSED			TOTAL EXPORTS	RATIO SPECIFIED
	CAPITAL GOODS	INTERMEDIATE GOODS	CONSUMER GOODS	PRIMARY	PROCESSED	NOT SPECIFIED		
1946	2.6	6.4	.8	1.6	8.2	8.7	18.4	.5305
1947	2.3	11.4	.9	1.2	13.5	23.0	37.7	.3884
1948	2.9	8.4	1.3	1.7	10.8	21.9	34.4	.3634
1949	.0	1.5	.2	.6	1.2	1.1	2.9	.6196
1954	0.0	.9	.0	.7	.3	1.0	2.0	.4761
1955	.0	15.6	.5	13.3	2.7	.4	16.4	.9776
1956	2.9	65.2	.7	58.4	10.5	.2	69.1	.9964
1957	15.8	54.5	.5	46.0	24.7	2.4	73.1	.9676
1958	11.4	38.1	.9	29.3	21.2	.7	51.1	.9867
1959	5.4	39.2	1.1	29.5	16.3	.5	46.2	.9896
1960	14.9	34.3	1.4	18.4	32.2	4.5	55.1	.9179
1961	4.6	21.8	2.0	11.4	17.0	7.5	35.9	.7910
1962	11.7	38.8	2.5	20.0	33.1	19.3	72.3	.7334
1963	17.7	47.8	5.7	22.1	49.1	25.1	96.3	.7394
1964	29.8	59.1	6.2	18.8	76.3	39.8	134.9	.7049
1965	26.0	72.6	8.7	25.2	82.1	37.8	145.1	.7394
1966	34.0	86.7	35.3	31.9	124.2	57.8	213.9	.7297
1967	39.2	96.4	32.3	38.6	129.3	112.5	280.3	.5988
1968	50.4	119.1	27.9	53.5	143.8	91.7	289.1	.6827

* CONVERTED FROM NATIONAL DEVISA-UNITS THROUGH
OFFICIAL EXCHANGE RATES. NOTE LIMITATIONS
DISCUSSED IN THE EXPLANATORY TEXT.

TABLE III.BEC-1.X.U-CEMA
USSR EXPORTS TO EUROPEAN CEMA (EXCLUDING ALBANIA), 1946-68
(MILLIONS OF CURRENT DOLLARS,* F.O.B.)

YEAR	CLASS 1	111	112	121	122	CLASS 2	21	22	CLASS 3	31	32	CLASS 4+5	CLASS 6	CLASS 7	TOTAL EXPORTS
1946	81.4	81.4				99.9	88.7	11.1	15.7	1.3	14.4	31.5	2.6	69.8	300.9
1947	57.9	57.9				116.7	99.9	16.8	17.7	1.7	16.0	11.3	2.1	103.0	308.8
1948	135.2	126.8			8.5	229.0	166.3	62.6	23.6	1.0	22.7	31.1	3.8	105.5	528.2
1949	121.9	72.2			49.7	312.6	194.0	118.6	27.4	2.6	24.8	88.9	5.2	192.0	748.0
1950	175.8	121.0			54.8	340.3	233.3	107.0	29.9	6.5	23.4	140.3	9.8	292.3	988.4
1951	255.7	186.3			69.4	457.0	317.0	140.0	46.1	19.3	26.8	190.3	12.1	318.8	1280.0
1952	290.0	218.0			72.0	519.8	353.1	166.7	57.9	26.1	31.8	259.1	12.7	513.3	1652.8
1953	305.8	196.2			109.6	567.0	348.4	218.6	89.7	58.8	30.8	308.7	12.3	387.3	1670.8
1954	297.9	218.5			79.3	627.9	382.7	245.2	104.7	66.7	38.0	278.2	12.9	400.2	1721.8
1955	269.7	238.2	.1	3.2	28.2	724.5	414.9	309.6	120.8	71.6	49.2	295.9	26.2	339.7	1776.9
1956	213.5	128.9	.2	6.7	77.6	815.3	434.6	380.7	163.7	100.7	63.0	208.7	35.0	313.4	1749.5
1957	600.5	461.9	4.0	6.3	128.5	1014.4	486.2	528.2	313.5	212.4	101.0	207.3	70.6	310.9	2517.2
1958	353.7	275.6	2.3	3.8	72.0	1049.4	485.7	563.7	302.1	191.4	110.7	222.2	75.6	272.8	2275.8
1959	591.1	372.6	5.8	8.4	204.2	1132.8	532.2	600.7	354.6	227.1	127.5	344.3	74.3	404.5	2901.6
1960	497.5	366.3	11.8	7.3	112.0	1316.6	592.9	723.6	413.5	254.2	159.2	389.5	74.4	383.1	3074.3
1961	442.9	297.1	4.0	11.0	130.9	1456.2	646.4	809.8	486.6	298.3	188.2	450.0	81.6	482.4	3399.7
1962	563.1	375.0	4.2	6.2	177.6	1575.6	657.1	918.5	585.8	379.2	206.6	606.6	92.6	547.4	3971.1
1963	533.1	314.2	11.8	10.3	196.8	1619.2	658.9	960.3	664.1	418.5	245.6	734.9	86.2	525.9	4163.3
1964	338.6	212.7	9.6	8.5	107.8	1880.8	747.9	1132.9	742.2	503.8	238.5	786.9	70.0	680.6	4499.2
1965	364.0	217.4	15.4	12.1	119.1	1906.5	736.8	1169.7	754.9	548.7	206.1	786.6	74.4	666.1	4552.6
1966	410.3	215.9	18.7	3.0	172.6	1948.4	757.9	1190.5	733.5	538.2	195.4	959.9	78.8	561.0	4692.0
1967	516.3	299.3	11.6	2.8	202.5	2010.2	736.0	1274.2	757.7	552.1	205.6	1099.8	92.1	562.6	5038.7
1968	514.5	308.0	13.6	2.8	190.1	2200.7	792.1	1408.7	823.8	590.1	233.8	1230.1	108.7	758.1	5636.1

* CONVERTED FROM NATIONAL DEVISA UNITS THROUGH
OFFICIAL EXCHANGE RATES. NOTE LIMITATIONS
DISCUSSED IN THE EXPLANATORY TEXT.

BEC CATEGORIES

1   FOOD AND BEVERAGES
    11   PRIMARY
        111   FOR INDUSTRY
        112   FOR HOUSEHOLD CONSUMPTION
    12   PROCESSED
        121   FOR INDUSTRY
        122   FOR HOUSEHOLD CONSUMPTION

2   INDUSTRIAL SUPPLIES (NON-FOOD)
    21   PRIMARY

3   FUELS AND LUBRICANTS
    31   PRIMARY
    32   PROCESSED

4   MACHINERY, EXC. TRANSPORT (W/PARTS)

5   TRANSPORT EQUIPMENT

6   CONSUMER GOODS, N.E.S.

TABLE III.BEC-2.X.U-CEMA
USSR EXPORTS TO EUROPEAN CEMA (EXCLUDING ALBANIA), 1946-68
(MILLIONS OF CURRENT DOLLARS,* F.O.B.)

YEAR	AGGREGATION I. BASIC SNA CLASSES			AGGREGATION II. PRIMARY VS. PROCESSED		NOT SPECIFIED	TOTAL EXPORTS	RATIO SPECIFIED
	CAPITAL GOODS	INTERMEDIATE GOODS	CONSUMER GOODS	PRIMARY	PROCESSED			
1946	31.5	197.0	2.6	171.5	59.6	69.8	300.9	.7680
1947	11.3	192.3	2.1	159.5	46.3	103.0	308.8	.6663
1948	31.1	379.4	12.3	294.1	128.7	105.5	528.2	.8004
1949	88.9	412.2	54.9	268.8	287.2	192.0	748.0	.7433
1950	140.3	491.3	64.5	360.9	335.2	292.3	988.4	.7043
1951	190.3	689.4	81.4	522.7	438.5	318.8	1280.0	.7509
1952	259.1	795.7	84.7	597.3	542.2	513.3	1652.8	.6894
1953	308.7	852.9	121.9	603.5	680.0	387.3	1670.8	.7682
1954	278.2	951.1	92.3	667.9	653.6	400.2	1721.8	.7676
1955	295.9	1086.9	54.5	724.8	712.4	339.7	1776.9	.8088
1956	208.7	1114.6	112.8	664.4	771.7	313.4	1749.5	.8209
1957	207.3	1796.1	202.9	1164.5	1041.8	310.9	2517.2	.8765
1958	222.2	1630.8	149.9	955.0	1048.0	272.8	2275.8	.8801
1959	344.3	1868.5	284.3	1137.7	1359.4	404.5	2901.6	.8606
1960	389.5	2103.6	198.2	1225.3	1465.9	383.1	3074.3	.8754
1961	450.0	2250.9	216.4	1245.8	1671.5	482.4	3399.7	.8581
1962	606.6	2542.6	274.5	1415.6	2008.1	547.4	3971.1	.8622
1963	734.9	2607.7	294.8	1403.4	2234.1	525.9	4163.3	.8737
1964	786.9	2844.3	187.4	1474.0	2344.6	680.6	4499.2	.8487
1965	786.6	2891.0	208.9	1518.4	2368.1	666.1	4552.6	.8537
1966	959.9	2900.9	270.2	1530.7	2600.2	561.0	4692.0	.8804
1967	1099.8	3070.1	306.2	1599.1	2877.0	562.6	5038.7	.8883
1968	1230.1	3335.4	312.5	1703.8	3174.1	758.1	5636.1	.8655

* CONVERTED FROM NATIONAL DEVISA-UNITS THROUGH OFFICIAL EXCHANGE RATES. NOTE LIMITATIONS DISCUSSED IN THE EXPLANATORY TEXT.

TABLE III.BEC-1.X.C-U
CZECHOSLOVAKIA'S EXPORTS TO USSR, 1958-68
(MILLIONS OF CURRENT DOLLARS,* F.O.B.)

YEAR	CLASS 1	111	112	121	122	CLASS 2	21	22	CLASS 3	31	32	CLASS 4+5	CLASS 6	CLASS 7	TOTAL EXPORTS
1958	19.8			2.8	17.0	129.0	111.4	17.6				179.6	98.2	70.5	497.1
1959	25.9			5.2	20.7	122.9	102.9	20.0				201.2	148.3	89.1	587.4
1960	25.3			3.5	21.8	125.6	105.8	19.8				252.8	167.9	87.0	658.7
1961	28.6			4.8	23.8	132.2	103.7	28.5				322.8	169.4	60.5	713.4
1962	22.9			3.6	19.3	138.7	105.0	33.7				424.1	180.0	62.8	828.4
1963	26.3			4.4	21.9	157.8	116.1	41.7				502.8	204.7	64.8	956.5
1964	4.6			1.0	3.7	184.3	127.2	57.1				508.0	187.7	77.2	961.7
1965	7.3			3.0	4.4	117.0	56.4	60.6				565.3	170.7	162.6	1022.9
1966	9.2			2.6	6.6	164.5	105.4	59.1				480.7	173.9	92.1	920.5
1967	13.8				13.8	165.0	104.4	60.6				478.1	215.4	104.9	977.2
1968	7.5				7.5	180.4	116.6	63.8				490.2	227.7	102.2	1008.0

* CONVERTED FROM NATIONAL DEVISA UNITS THROUGH
OFFICIAL EXCHANGE RATES. NOTE LIMITATIONS
DISCUSSED IN THE EXPLANATORY TEXT.

BEC CATEGORIES

1   FOOD AND BEVERAGES
    11   PRIMARY
        111   FOR INDUSTRY
        112   FOR HOUSEHOLD CONSUMPTION
    12   PROCESSED
        121   FOR INDUSTRY
        122   FOR HOUSEHOLD CONSUMPTION

2   INDUSTRIAL SUPPLIES (NON-FOOD)
    21   PRIMARY
    22   PROCESSED

3   FUELS AND LUBRICANTS
    31   PRIMARY
    32   PROCESSED

4   MACHINERY, EXC. TRANSPORT (W/PARTS)

5   TRANSPORT EQUIPMENT

6   CONSUMER GOODS, N.E.S.

7   GOODS N.E.S. AND UNSPECIFIED

TABLE III.BEC-2.X.C-U
CZECHOSLOVAKIA'S EXPORTS TO USSR, 1958-68
(MILLIONS OF CURRENT DOLLARS,* F.O.B.)

| YEAR | AGGREGATION I. BASIC SNA CLASSES | | | AGGREGATION II. PRIMARY VS. PROCESSED | | NOT SPECIFIED | TOTAL EXPORTS | RATIO SPECIFIED |
	CAPITAL GOODS	INTERMEDIATE GOODS	CONSUMER GOODS	PRIMARY	PROCESSED			
1958	179.6	131.8	115.2	111.4	315.3	70.5	497.1	.8583
1959	201.2	128.1	168.9	102.9	395.4	89.1	587.4	.8483
1960	252.8	129.1	189.7	105.8	465.8	87.0	658.7	.8679
1961	322.8	137.0	193.2	103.7	549.2	60.5	713.4	.9152
1962	424.1	142.3	199.2	105.0	660.6	62.8	828.4	.9242
1963	502.8	162.2	226.6	116.1	775.5	64.8	956.5	.9322
1964	508.0	185.2	191.4	127.2	757.4	77.2	961.7	.9198
1965	565.3	119.9	175.0	56.4	803.8	162.6	1022.9	.8410
1966	480.7	167.1	180.6	105.4	723.0	92.1	920.5	.8999
1967	478.1	165.0	229.1	104.4	767.9	104.9	977.2	.8927
1968	490.2	180.4	235.2	116.6	789.2	102.2	1008.0	.8986

* CONVERTED FROM NATIONAL DEVISA-UNITS THROUGH
OFFICIAL EXCHANGE RATES. NOTE LIMITATIONS
DISCUSSED IN THE EXPLANATORY TEXT.

TABLE III.BEC-1.X.C-B
CZECHOSLOVAKIA'S EXPORTS TO BULGARIA, 1958-68
(MILLIONS OF CURRENT DOLLARS,* F.O.B.)

YEAR	CLASS 1	111	112	121	122	CLASS 2	21	22	CLASS 3	31	32	CLASS 4+5	CLASS 6	CLASS 7	TOTAL EXPORTS
1958						11.2	.8	10.4	1.8	.9	.9	12.5	4.0	6.6	36.3
1959						12.2	1.0	11.2	3.7	1.9	1.9	20.6	6.4	10.6	53.5
1960						17.5	1.9	15.6	5.3	2.7	2.7	23.5	4.7	10.5	61.5
1961						16.7	1.6	15.1	5.7	2.9	2.9	23.1	3.3	8.3	57.1
1962						17.2	1.1	16.2	5.4	2.7	2.7	28.8	5.5	7.8	64.7
1963						18.8	.6	18.2	4.4	1.8	2.6	43.0	7.4	6.4	80.0
1964						20.2	.6	19.6	3.8	1.9	1.9	29.6	5.1	4.4	63.1
1965						21.0	.5	20.5	4.1	2.1	2.1	27.5	4.7	4.6	61.8
1966						17.3	.7	16.6	1.9	.9	.9	48.8	4.2	9.4	81.5
1967						20.3	.5	19.8	1.9	1.0	1.0	54.4	5.2	10.0	91.7
1968						15.4	.2	15.3	2.3	1.1	1.1	48.7	6.3	9.2	82.0

* CONVERTED FROM NATIONAL DEVISA UNITS THROUGH OFFICIAL EXCHANGE RATES. NOTE LIMITATIONS DISCUSSED IN THE EXPLANATORY TEXT.

BEC CATEGORIES

1 FOOD AND BEVERAGES
  11 PRIMARY
    111 FOR INDUSTRY
    112 FOR HOUSEHOLD CONSUMPTION
  12 PROCESSED
    121 FOR INDUSTRY
    122 FOR HOUSEHOLD CONSUMPTION

2 INDUSTRIAL SUPPLIES (NON-FOOD)
  21 PRIMARY
  22 PROCESSED

3 FUELS AND LUBRICANTS
  31 PRIMARY
  32 PROCESSED

4 MACHINERY, EXC. TRANSPORT (W/PARTS)

5 TRANSPORT EQUIPMENT

6 CONSUMER GOODS, N.E.S.

7 GOODS N.E.S. AND UNSPECIFIED

TABLE III.BEC-2.X.C-B
CZECHOSLOVAKIA'S EXPORTS TO BULGARIA, 1958-68
(MILLIONS OF CURRENT DOLLARS,* F.O.B.)

YEAR	AGGREGATION I. BASIC SNA CLASSES			AGGREGATION II. PRIMARY VS. PROCESSED		NOT SPECIFIED	TOTAL EXPORTS	RATIO SPECIFIED
	CAPITAL GOODS	INTERMEDIATE GOODS	CONSUMER GOODS	PRIMARY	PROCESSED			
1958	12.5	13.0	4.0	1.7	27.9	6.6	36.3	.8169
1959	20.6	15.9	6.4	2.9	40.1	10.6	53.5	.8024
1960	23.5	22.8	4.7	4.6	46.4	10.5	61.5	.8287
1961	23.1	22.4	3.3	4.4	44.4	8.3	57.1	.8549
1962	28.8	22.6	5.5	3.7	53.2	7.8	64.7	.8799
1963	43.0	23.2	7.4	2.4	71.2	6.4	80.0	.9197
1964	29.6	24.0	5.1	2.5	56.1	4.4	63.1	.9300
1965	27.5	25.1	4.7	2.5	54.7	4.6	61.8	.9262
1966	48.8	19.2	4.2	1.6	70.6	9.4	81.5	.8852
1967	54.4	22.2	5.2	1.4	80.3	10.0	91.7	.8910
1968	48.7	17.7	6.3	1.3	71.4	9.2	82.0	.8874

* CONVERTED FROM NATIONAL DEVISA-UNITS THROUGH
OFFICIAL EXCHANGE RATES. NOTE LIMITATIONS
DISCUSSED IN THE EXPLANATORY TEXT.

TABLE III.BEC-1.X.C-G
CZECHOSLOVAKIA'S EXPORTS TO EAST GERMANY, 1958-68
(MILLIONS OF CURRENT DOLLARS,* F.O.B.)

YEAR	CLASS 1	111	112	121	122	CLASS 2	21	22	CLASS 3	31	32	CLASS 4+5	CLASS 6	CLASS 7	TOTAL EXPORTS
1958	9.0		.7	5.4	2.8	24.9	18.2	6.8	30.6	15.3	15.3	40.2	29.6	23.2	157.5
1959	8.0		.8	4.3	2.9	25.9	17.4	8.6	29.6	14.8	14.8	54.5	37.2	22.9	178.1
1960	7.5		.7	3.8	3.0	30.3	20.9	9.4	33.6	16.8	16.8	57.8	42.7	23.7	195.6
1961	8.0		.5	4.5	3.0	36.4	24.6	11.8	42.1	21.1	21.1	68.2	52.2	6.7	213.6
1962	7.5	.3	.7	4.4	2.2	41.0	26.3	14.7	38.9	19.4	19.4	79.4	47.9	15.1	229.9
1963	11.3	3.2	.9	5.4	1.9	32.0	19.2	12.8	40.3	20.1	20.1	83.5	34.5	20.5	222.1
1964	10.7	1.5	1.3	5.5	2.5	50.3	34.0	16.3	45.3	22.7	22.7	91.9	37.8	29.9	266.0
1965	8.2	2.3	.7	2.6	2.5	66.4	48.5	17.9	40.2	20.1	20.1	100.7	39.5	22.2	277.1
1966	7.3	.1	.8	3.4	2.9	65.0	47.6	17.4	35.2	17.6	17.6	103.8	43.5	42.6	297.4
1967	7.8	.7	.8	3.3	3.1	66.3	43.9	22.4	31.3	15.6	15.6	110.6	47.6	54.9	318.6
1968	6.9	.7	.7	3.3	2.3	60.6	37.9	22.6	31.1	15.5	15.5	119.7	45.2	64.6	328.1

* CONVERTED FROM NATIONAL DEVISA UNITS THROUGH OFFICIAL EXCHANGE RATES. NOTE LIMITATIONS DISCUSSED IN THE EXPLANATORY TEXT.

BEC CATEGORIES

1 FOOD AND BEVERAGES
  11 PRIMARY
    111 FOR INDUSTRY
    112 FOR HOUSEHOLD CONSUMPTION
  12 PROCESSED
    121 FOR INDUSTRY
    122 FOR HOUSEHOLD CONSUMPTION

2 INDUSTRIAL SUPPLIES (NON-FOOD)
  21 PRIMARY
  22 PROCESSED

3 FUELS AND LUBRICANTS
  31 PRIMARY
  32 PROCESSED

4 MACHINERY, EXC. TRANSPORT (W/PARTS)

5 TRANSPORT EQUIPMENT

6 CONSUMER GOODS, N.E.S.

7 GOODS N.E.S. AND UNSPECIFIED

TABLE III.BEC-2.X.C-G
CZECHOSLOVAKIA'S EXPORTS TO EAST GERMANY, 1958-68
(MILLIONS OF CURRENT DOLLARS,* F.O.B.)

YEAR	AGGREGATION I. BASIC SNA CLASSES			AGGREGATION II. PRIMARY VS. PROCESSED		NOT SPECIFIED	TOTAL EXPORTS	RATIO SPECIFIED
	CAPITAL GOODS	INTERMEDIATE GOODS	CONSUMER GOODS	PRIMARY	PROCESSED			
1958	40.2	60.9	33.1	34.2	100.1	23.2	157.5	.8527
1959	54.5	59.8	40.9	33.0	122.2	22.9	178.1	.8716
1960	57.8	67.7	46.4	38.4	133.5	23.7	195.6	.8790
1961	68.2	83.1	55.7	46.2	160.7	6.7	213.6	.9684
1962	79.4	84.6	50.8	46.7	168.1	15.1	229.9	.9342
1963	83.5	80.9	37.2	43.4	158.2	20.5	222.1	.9077
1964	91.9	102.6	41.6	59.4	176.7	29.9	266.0	.8875
1965	100.7	111.5	42.7	71.6	183.3	22.2	277.1	.9201
1966	103.8	103.7	47.3	66.2	188.7	42.6	297.4	.8569
1967	110.6	101.5	51.5	61.0	202.7	54.9	318.6	.8276
1968	119.7	95.6	48.2	54.8	208.7	64.6	328.1	.8031

* CONVERTED FROM NATIONAL DEVISA-UNITS THROUGH
OFFICIAL EXCHANGE RATES. NOTE LIMITATIONS
DISCUSSED IN THE EXPLANATORY TEXT.

TABLE III.BEC-1.X.C-H
CZECHOSLOVAKIA'S EXPORTS TO HUNGARY, 1958-68
(MILLIONS OF CURRENT DOLLARS,* F.O.B.)

YEAR	CLASS 1	111	112	121	122	CLASS 2	21	22	CLASS 3	31	32	CLASS 4+5	CLASS 6	CLASS 7	TOTAL EXPORTS
1958	1.5			.9	.6	28.3	6.5	21.8	19.1	9.6	9.5	20.3	4.5	3.6	77.4
1959	.9			.5	.4	28.5	4.8	23.7	16.1	7.6	8.5	26.7	7.5	6.4	86.1
1960	.8			.4	.4	30.9	5.6	25.3	23.4	11.5	11.9	39.0	11.0	6.6	111.7
1961	.8			.3	.5	42.2	6.1	36.1	23.2	11.3	11.9	26.9	6.7	4.4	104.2
1962	1.0			.6	.5	52.4	6.1	46.3	23.9	11.5	12.5	36.4	6.8	4.4	125.0
1963	1.7		.9	.4	.4	58.6	7.0	51.6	26.2	13.0	13.2	45.1	13.4	7.7	152.7
1964	.8			.5	.3	63.9	5.8	58.1	27.4	14.8	12.7	39.6	12.1	14.3	158.1
1965	.7			.5	.2	48.0	6.8	41.2	23.9	12.4	11.5	38.1	11.4	10.1	132.2
1966	1.4			.8	.6	40.3	7.2	33.2	22.1	11.8	10.3	47.4	9.8	11.2	132.2
1967	3.1	.9			2.2	39.0	6.4	32.6	22.2	10.6	11.6	60.1	14.1	13.9	152.4
1968	4.0	1.1			2.9	42.1	7.9	34.2	20.1	10.9	9.2	63.5	16.7	21.0	167.4

* CONVERTED FROM NATIONAL DEVISA UNITS THROUGH
OFFICIAL EXCHANGE RATES. NOTE LIMITATIONS
DISCUSSED IN THE EXPLANATORY TEXT.

BEC CATEGORIES

1 FOOD AND BEVERAGES
   11 PRIMARY
       111 FOR INDUSTRY
       112 FOR HOUSEHOLD CONSUMPTION
   12 PROCESSED
       121 FOR INDUSTRY
       122 FOR HOUSEHOLD CONSUMPTION

2 INDUSTRIAL SUPPLIES (NON-FOOD)
   21 PRIMARY
   22 PROCESSED

3 FUELS AND LUBRICANTS
   31 PRIMARY
   32 PROCESSED

4 MACHINERY, EXC. TRANSPORT (W/PARTS)

5 TRANSPORT EQUIPMENT

6 CONSUMER GOODS, N.E.S.

7 GOODS N.E.S. AND UNSPECIFIED

TABLE III.BEC-2.X.C-H
CZECHOSLOVAKIA'S EXPORTS TO HUNGARY, 1958-68
(MILLIONS OF CURRENT DOLLARS,* F.O.B.)

YEAR	AGGREGATION I. BASIC SNA CLASSES			AGGREGATION II. PRIMARY VS. PROCESSED		NOT SPECIFIED	TOTAL EXPORTS	RATIO SPECIFIED
	CAPITAL GOODS	INTERMEDIATE GOODS	CONSUMER GOODS	PRIMARY	PROCESSED			
1958	20.3	48.3	5.1	16.1	57.6	3.6	77.4	.9530
1959	26.7	45.1	7.9	12.4	67.3	6.4	86.1	.9260
1960	39.0	54.6	11.4	17.1	87.9	6.6	111.7	.9405
1961	26.9	65.6	7.2	17.4	82.4	4.4	104.2	.9580
1962	36.4	76.9	7.3	17.6	103.0	4.4	125.0	.9645
1963	45.1	85.2	14.6	20.9	124.1	7.7	152.7	.9496
1964	39.6	91.8	12.4	20.5	123.3	14.3	158.1	.9097
1965	38.1	72.4	11.6	19.2	102.9	10.1	132.2	.9236
1966	47.4	63.2	10.4	18.9	102.1	11.2	132.2	.9153
1967	60.1	62.2	16.2	18.0	120.5	13.9	152.4	.9091
1968	63.5	63.2	19.6	19.8	126.5	21.0	167.4	.8743

* CONVERTED FROM NATIONAL DEVISA-UNITS THROUGH
OFFICIAL EXCHANGE RATES. NOTE LIMITATIONS
DISCUSSED IN THE EXPLANATORY TEXT.

TABLE III.BEC-1.X.C-P
CZECHOSLOVAKIA'S EXPORTS TO POLAND, 1958-68
(MILLIONS OF CURRENT DOLLARS,* F.O.B.)

YEAR	CLASS 1	111	112	121	122	CLASS 2	21	22	CLASS 3	31	32	CLASS 4+5	CLASS 6	CLASS 7	TOTAL EXPORTS
1958						22.4	14.7	7.7	.2		.2	47.9	14.6	9.7	94.9
1959						27.5	20.9	6.5	.3		.3	56.7	17.0	13.5	114.9
1960						36.1	29.3	6.7	5.0		5.0	66.2	12.3	8.8	128.3
1961						44.2	36.8	7.4	8.2	.1	8.1	83.6	14.5	13.5	164.0
1962						57.4	48.8	8.6	5.5	.2	5.3	102.4	21.0	14.8	201.0
1963						58.2	45.2	13.0	6.0	.3	5.7	95.0	19.9	16.5	195.6
1964	.0				.0	56.6	44.9	11.6	3.2	.0	3.2	92.8	14.7	25.5	192.8
1965	.2				.2	73.8	56.3	17.5	4.2		4.2	118.0	20.4	32.1	248.8
1966	.0				.0	53.9	36.1	17.8	3.6		3.6	128.1	17.7	33.2	236.5
1967						52.4	35.1	17.3	2.7		2.7	119.6	13.5	46.7	234.9
1968						55.8	37.3	18.5	3.3		3.3	116.4	11.7	44.5	231.7

* CONVERTED FROM NATIONAL DEVISA UNITS THROUGH
OFFICIAL EXCHANGE RATES. NOTE LIMITATIONS
DISCUSSED IN THE EXPLANATORY TEXT.

BEC CATEGORIES

1 FOOD AND BEVERAGES
  11 PRIMARY
    111 FOR INDUSTRY
    112 FOR HOUSEHOLD CONSUMPTION
  12 PROCESSED
    121 FOR INDUSTRY
    122 FOR HOUSEHOLD CONSUMPTION

2 INDUSTRIAL SUPPLIES (NON-FOOD)
  21 PRIMARY
  22 PROCESSED

3 FUELS AND LUBRICANTS
  31 PRIMARY
  32 PROCESSED

4 MACHINERY, EXC. TRANSPORT (W/PARTS)

5 TRANSPORT EQUIPMENT

6 CONSUMER GOODS, N.E.S.

7 GOODS N.E.S. AND UNSPECIFIED

TABLE III.BEC-2.X.C-P
CZECHOSLOVAKIA'S EXPORTS TO POLAND, 1958-68
(MILLIONS OF CURRENT DOLLARS,* F.O.B.)

YEAR	AGGREGATION I. BASIC SNA CLASSES			AGGREGATION II. PRIMARY VS. PROCESSED		NOT SPECIFIED	TOTAL EXPORTS	RATIO SPECIFIED
	CAPITAL GOODS	INTERMEDIATE GOODS	CONSUMER GOODS	PRIMARY	PROCESSED			
1958	47.9	22.6	14.6	14.7	70.4	9.7	94.9	.8976
1959	56.7	27.7	17.0	20.9	80.5	13.5	114.9	.8828
1960	66.2	41.1	12.3	29.3	90.2	8.8	128.3	.9318
1961	83.6	52.4	14.5	36.9	113.6	13.5	164.0	.9175
1962	102.4	62.9	21.0	49.0	137.2	14.8	201.0	.9265
1963	95.0	64.2	19.9	45.5	133.5	16.5	195.6	.9155
1964	92.8	59.8	14.7	44.9	122.3	25.5	192.8	.8676
1965	118.0	78.0	20.7	56.3	160.4	32.1	248.8	.8710
1966	128.1	57.5	17.8	36.1	167.3	33.2	236.5	.8599
1967	119.6	55.1	13.5	35.1	153.1	46.7	234.9	.8012
1968	116.4	59.2	11.7	37.3	149.9	44.5	231.7	.8081

* CONVERTED FROM NATIONAL DEVISA-UNITS THROUGH OFFICIAL EXCHANGE RATES. NOTE LIMITATIONS DISCUSSED IN THE EXPLANATORY TEXT.

TABLE III.BEC-1.X.C-R
CZECHOSLOVAKIA'S EXPORTS TO RUMANIA, 1958-68
(MILLIONS OF CURRENT DOLLARS,* F.O.B.)

YEAR	CLASS 1	111	112	121	122	CLASS 2	21	22	CLASS 3	31	32	CLASS 4+5	CLASS 6	CLASS 7	TOTAL EXPORTS
1958	1.4			.8	.5	9.5	7.6	1.8	6.4	3.2	3.2	10.5	3.0	7.0	37.8
1959	1.8			1.5	.3	20.5	18.2	2.3	7.9	4.0	4.0	21.6	2.1	6.8	60.6
1960	.9			.9		17.7	14.4	3.3	9.8	4.9	4.9	25.3	4.3	5.6	63.6
1961	.4			.2	.2	15.3	11.7	3.6	10.0	5.0	5.0	38.9	7.6	3.5	75.7
1962	.4			.2	2.0	19.9	16.1	3.7	9.8	4.9	4.9	47.3	6.9	3.8	88.1
1963	2.7			.7	1.1	20.6	17.3	3.3	10.6	5.3	5.3	54.6	8.7	3.4	100.7
1964	1.4			.3		18.6	14.6	4.0	9.9	4.8	5.1	53.3	6.9	2.8	92.9
1965	1.0			.1	.8	14.4	11.6	2.8	9.8	4.5	5.3	36.7	4.2	2.9	68.9
1966	1.5			.7	.8	12.8	9.0	3.8	13.6	6.7	6.9	34.3	4.5	2.8	69.4
1967	1.5			.7	.8	20.3	13.5	6.8	14.8	7.4	7.4	37.8	7.4	7.6	89.5
1968	1.5			.7	.8	25.6	18.7	6.9	16.6	8.3	8.3	41.2	5.2	9.6	99.7

* CONVERTED FROM NATIONAL DEVISA UNITS THROUGH OFFICIAL EXCHANGE RATES. NOTE LIMITATIONS DISCUSSED IN THE EXPLANATORY TEXT.

BEC CATEGORIES

1 FOOD AND BEVERAGES
  11 PRIMARY
    111 FOR INDUSTRY
    112 FOR HOUSEHOLD CONSUMPTION
  12 PROCESSED
    121 FOR INDUSTRY
    122 FOR HOUSEHOLD CONSUMPTION

2 INDUSTRIAL SUPPLIES (NON-FOOD)
  21 PRIMARY
  22 PROCESSED

3 FUELS AND LUBRICANTS
  31 PRIMARY
  32 PROCESSED

4 MACHINERY, EXC. TRANSPORT (W/PARTS)

5 TRANSPORT EQUIPMENT

6 CONSUMER GOODS, N.E.S.

7 GOODS N.E.S. AND UNSPECIFIED

TABLE III.BEC-2.X.C-R
CZECHOSLOVAKIA'S EXPORTS TO RUMANIA, 1958-68
(MILLIONS OF CURRENT DOLLARS,* F.O.B.)

| YEAR | AGGREGATION I. BASIC SNA CLASSES | | | AGGREGATION II. PRIMARY VS. PROCESSED | | NOT SPECIFIED | TOTAL EXPORTS | RATIO SPECIFIED |
	CAPITAL GOODS	INTERMEDIATE GOODS	CONSUMER GOODS	PRIMARY	PROCESSED			
1958	10.5	16.7	3.5	10.8	20.0	7.0	37.8	.8156
1959	21.6	29.9	2.4	22.1	31.8	6.6	60.6	.8915
1960	25.3	28.4	4.3	19.3	38.7	5.6	63.6	.9126
1961	38.9	25.5	7.8	16.7	55.4	3.5	75.7	.9533
1962	47.3	29.8	7.1	21.0	63.2	3.8	88.1	.9566
1963	54.6	32.0	10.7	22.6	74.6	3.4	100.7	.9659
1964	53.3	28.8	8.0	19.4	70.7	2.8	92.9	.9694
1965	36.7	24.3	5.0	16.0	50.0	2.9	68.9	.9583
1966	34.3	27.0	5.3	15.7	50.9	2.8	69.4	.9592
1967	37.8	35.8	8.2	20.9	60.9	7.6	89.5	.9146
1968	41.2	42.9	6.1	27.0	63.2	9.6	99.7	.9040

* CONVERTED FROM NATIONAL DEVISA-UNITS THROUGH
OFFICIAL EXCHANGE RATES. NOTE LIMITATIONS
DISCUSSED IN THE EXPLANATORY TEXT.

TABLE III.BEC-1.X.C-Y
CZECHOSLOVAKIA'S EXPORTS TO YUGOSLAVIA, 1958-66
(MILLIONS OF CURRENT DOLLARS,* F.O.B.)

YEAR	CLASS 1	111	112	121	122	CLASS 2	21	22	CLASS 3	31	32	CLASS 4+5	CLASS 6	CLASS 7	TOTAL EXPORTS
1958	2.0			.2	1.9	5.3	.5	4.8	.2	.1	.1	10.2	4.4	2.9	25.0
1959	.9			.2	.7	7.3	.6	6.7	.6	.3	.3	7.3	4.1	1.8	21.9
1960	1.2			.1	1.1	7.4	.7	6.7	1.0	.4	.6	7.9	5.0	1.5	23.9
1961	1.2			.5	.7	4.6	.5	4.1	1.2	.5	.7	5.7	4.4	.9	18.1
1962	1.6			.8	.8	6.9	.6	6.3	1.7	.8	.9	7.2	6.0	1.2	24.6
1963	1.3			1.3	.0	15.3	.7	14.5	2.3	.7	1.5	17.8	8.7	1.5	46.8
1964	1.1			1.1		26.3	1.1	25.2	3.2	1.3	2.0	27.5	10.7	7.5	76.3
1965	1.8			1.8		32.4	1.7	30.7	1.6	.6	1.0	21.2	9.8	2.4	69.2
1966	2.0			2.0		42.9	.4	42.6	2.3	.9	1.4	24.3	13.2	10.5	95.3

* CONVERTED FROM NATIONAL DEVISA UNITS THROUGH OFFICIAL EXCHANGE RATES. NOTE LIMITATIONS DISCUSSED IN THE EXPLANATORY TEXT.

BEC CATEGORIES

1 FOOD AND BEVERAGES
  11 PRIMARY
    111 FOR INDUSTRY
    112 FOR HOUSEHOLD CONSUMPTION
  12 PROCESSED
    121 FOR INDUSTRY
    122 FOR HOUSEHOLD CONSUMPTION

2 INDUSTRIAL SUPPLIES (NON-FOOD)
  21 PRIMARY
  22 PROCESSED

3 FUELS AND LUBRICANTS
  31 PRIMARY
  32 PROCESSED

4 MACHINERY, EXC. TRANSPORT (W/PARTS)

5 TRANSPORT EQUIPMENT

6 CONSUMER GOODS, N.E.S.

7 GOODS N.E.S. AND UNSPECIFIED

TABLE III.BEC-2.X.C-Y
CZECHOSLOVAKIA'S EXPORTS TO YUGOSLAVIA, 1958-66
(MILLIONS OF CURRENT DOLLARS,* F.O.B.)

YEAR	AGGREGATION I. BASIC SNA CLASSES			AGGREGATION II. PRIMARY VS. PROCESSED		NOT SPECIFIED	TOTAL EXPORTS	RATIO SPECIFIED
	CAPITAL GOODS	INTERMEDIATE GOODS	CONSUMER GOODS	PRIMARY	PROCESSED			
1958	10.2	5.6	6.3	.6	21.5	2.9	25.0	.8823
1959	7.3	8.1	4.8	.9	19.3	1.8	21.9	.9170
1960	7.9	8.5	6.0	1.1	21.3	1.5	23.9	.9370
1961	5.7	6.4	5.1	1.1	16.1	.9	18.1	.9505
1962	7.2	9.4	6.8	1.4	21.9	1.2	24.6	.9509
1963	17.8	18.9	8.7	1.5	43.9	1.5	46.8	.9689
1964	27.5	30.6	10.7	2.3	66.5	7.5	76.3	.9023
1965	21.2	35.8	9.8	2.3	64.5	2.4	69.2	.9650
1966	24.3	47.2	13.2	1.2	83.6	10.5	95.3	.8897

* CONVERTED FROM NATIONAL DEVISA-UNITS THROUGH
OFFICIAL EXCHANGE RATES. NOTE LIMITATIONS
DISCUSSED IN THE EXPLANATORY TEXT.

TABLE III.BEC-1.X.C-CEMA
CZECHOSLOVAKIA'S EXPORTS TO EUROPEAN CEMA (EXCLUDING ALBANIA), 1958-68
(MILLIONS OF CURRENT DOLLARS,* F.O.B.)

YEAR	CLASS 1	111	112	121	122	CLASS 2	21	22	CLASS 3	31	32	CLASS 4+5	CLASS 6	CLASS 7	TOTAL EXPORTS
1958	31.6		.7	9.9	20.9	225.4	159.2	66.2	58.2	29.0	29.2	311.1	154.0	120.6	900.9
1959	36.6		.8	11.5	24.3	237.5	165.2	72.4	57.6	28.2	29.4	381.4	218.4	149.0	1080.5
1960	34.6		.7	8.6	25.2	258.1	178.0	80.1	77.0	35.9	41.2	464.6	243.0	142.2	1219.4
1961	37.7		.5	9.7	27.5	287.0	184.5	102.6	89.3	40.3	48.9	563.4	253.7	96.9	1328.0
1962	31.9		.7	8.8	22.1	326.6	203.4	123.2	83.5	38.7	44.8	718.3	268.7	108.7	1537.1
1963	42.1	3.2	1.7	10.9	26.2	346.0	205.4	140.6	87.5	40.6	46.9	824.0	288.5	119.4	1707.5
1964	17.6	1.5	1.3	7.2	7.6	393.8	227.0	166.8	89.7	44.2	45.5	815.1	264.3	154.1	1734.6
1965	17.4	2.3	.7	6.2	8.1	340.4	180.0	160.4	82.2	39.0	43.2	886.4	250.9	234.4	1811.7
1966	19.5	.1	.8	7.4	11.1	353.9	206.0	147.9	76.3	37.0	39.3	843.2	253.6	191.2	1737.6
1967	26.1	1.6	.8	3.9	19.8	363.3	203.9	159.5	73.0	34.7	38.3	860.6	303.1	238.0	1864.2
1968	19.9	1.7	.7	4.0	13.5	380.0	218.5	161.4	73.3	35.8	37.5	879.7	312.8	251.1	1916.8

* CONVERTED FROM NATIONAL DEVISA UNITS THROUGH
OFFICIAL EXCHANGE RATES. NOTE LIMITATIONS
DISCUSSED IN THE EXPLANATORY TEXT.

BEC CATEGORIES

1   FOOD AND BEVERAGES
    11   PRIMARY
         111   FOR INDUSTRY
         112   FOR HOUSEHOLD CONSUMPTION
    12   PROCESSED
         121   FOR INDUSTRY
         122   FOR HOUSEHOLD CONSUMPTION

2   INDUSTRIAL SUPPLIES (NON-FOOD)
    21   PRIMARY
    22   PROCESSED

3   FUELS AND LUBRICANTS
    31   PRIMARY
    32   PROCESSED

4   MACHINERY, EXC. TRANSPORT (W/PARTS)

5   TRANSPORT EQUIPMENT

6   CONSUMER GOODS, N.E.S.

7   GOODS N.E.S. AND UNSPECIFIED

TABLE III.BEC-2.X.C-CEMA
CZECHOSLOVAKIA'S EXPORTS TO EUROPEAN CEMA (EXCLUDING ALBANIA), 1958-68
(MILLIONS OF CURRENT DOLLARS,* F.O.B.)

YEAR	AGGREGATION I. BASIC SNA CLASSES			AGGREGATION II. PRIMARY VS. PROCESSED		NOT SPECIFIED	TOTAL EXPORTS	RATIO SPECIFIED
	CAPITAL GOODS	INTERMEDIATE GOODS	CONSUMER GOODS	PRIMARY	PROCESSED			
1958	311.1	293.5	175.7	189.0	591.3	120.6	900.9	.8661
1959	381.4	306.6	243.5	194.2	737.3	149.0	1080.5	.8621
1960	464.6	343.8	268.9	214.5	862.7	142.2	1219.4	.8834
1961	563.4	386.0	281.7	225.3	1005.7	96.9	1328.0	.9270
1962	718.3	419.1	290.9	243.0	1185.3	108.7	1537.1	.9293
1963	824.0	447.7	316.4	250.9	1337.1	119.4	1707.5	.9301
1964	815.1	492.2	273.2	274.0	1306.5	154.1	1734.6	.9111
1965	886.4	431.1	259.7	222.1	1355.2	234.4	1811.7	.8706
1966	843.2	437.7	265.6	244.0	1302.5	191.2	1737.6	.8900
1967	860.6	441.8	323.8	240.9	1385.3	238.0	1864.2	.8723
1968	879.7	459.0	327.0	256.8	1409.0	251.1	1916.8	.8690

* CONVERTED FROM NATIONAL DEVISA-UNITS THROUGH
OFFICIAL EXCHANGE RATES. NOTE LIMITATIONS
DISCUSSED IN THE EXPLANATORY TEXT.

TABLE III.BEC-1.X.P-U
POLAND'S EXPORTS TO USSR, 1958-68
(MILLIONS OF CURRENT DOLLARS,* F.O.B.)

YEAR	CLASS 1	111	112	121	122	CLASS 2	21	22	CLASS 3	31	32	CLASS 4+5	CLASS 6	CLASS 7	TOTAL EXPORTS
1958	13.5	.0	1.6		11.9	36.4	.4	36.1	73.5	55.3	18.2	89.0	14.6	38.1	265.2
1959	14.1	.1	.9		13.2	44.5	.8	43.7	82.4	65.5	16.9	102.5	33.3	36.2	313.0
1960	16.5		1.6	.9	14.0	51.0	1.5	49.5	90.5	73.0	17.5	121.8	67.2	43.2	390.2
1961	51.5	15.9	2.4	.3	32.9	50.0	2.0	48.0	90.8	73.5	17.3	125.2	91.4	76.0	485.0
1962	44.8	8.3	.1	.2	36.3	54.2	3.2	51.1	91.8	76.0	15.8	181.8	112.2	83.7	568.7
1963	9.5		2.9	.6	6.0	62.0	2.4	59.6	93.8	76.5	17.2	222.6	121.3	108.1	617.5
1964	32.5		12.2	2.7	17.6	75.6	4.1	71.5	94.5	76.5	18.0	244.5	124.9	149.7	721.7
1965	31.5	.1	7.5	2.8	21.1	74.9	3.1	71.8	117.5	101.1	16.4	263.1	128.1	166.4	781.4
1966	15.9	.1	4.9	4.6	6.3	43.0	3.7	39.3	125.5	109.4	16.0	253.4	160.3	143.0	741.2
1967	18.2		6.6	3.8	7.9	54.0	3.4	50.6	134.5	118.8	15.6	319.2	221.4	154.4	901.8
1968	14.0		4.0	2.1	8.0	75.0	3.9	71.1	122.1	106.9	15.2	372.6	255.9	202.5	1042.1

* CONVERTED FROM NATIONAL DEVISA UNITS THROUGH OFFICIAL EXCHANGE RATES. NOTE LIMITATIONS DISCUSSED IN THE EXPLANATORY TEXT.

BEC CATEGORIES

1 FOOD AND BEVERAGES
  11 PRIMARY
    111 FOR INDUSTRY
    112 FOR HOUSEHOLD CONSUMPTION
  12 PROCESSED
    121 FOR INDUSTRY
    122 FOR HOUSEHOLD CONSUMPTION

2 INDUSTRIAL SUPPLIES (NON-FOOD)
  21 PRIMARY
  22 PROCESSED

3 FUELS AND LUBRICANTS
  31 PRIMARY
  32 PROCESSED

4 MACHINERY, EXC. TRANSPORT (W/PARTS)

5 TRANSPORT EQUIPMENT

6 CONSUMER GOODS, N.E.S.

7 GOODS N.E.S. AND UNSPECIFIED

TABLE III.BEC-2.X.P-U
POLAND'S EXPORTS TO USSR, 1958-68
(MILLIONS OF CURRENT DOLLARS,* F.O.B.)

YEAR	AGGREGATION I. BASIC SNA CLASSES			AGGREGATION II. PRIMARY VS. PROCESSED		NOT SPECIFIED	TOTAL EXPORTS	RATIO SPECIFIED
	CAPITAL GOODS	INTERMEDIATE GOODS	CONSUMER GOODS	PRIMARY	PROCESSED			
1958	89.0	110.0	28.1	57.3	169.8	38.1	265.2	.8565
1959	102.5	126.9	47.4	67.2	209.6	36.2	313.0	.8845
1960	121.8	142.4	82.8	76.1	270.9	43.2	390.2	.8894
1961	125.2	157.0	126.8	93.8	315.2	76.0	485.0	.8433
1962	181.8	154.5	148.6	87.6	397.3	83.7	568.7	.8528
1963	222.6	156.4	130.3	81.8	427.5	108.1	617.5	.8249
1964	244.5	172.8	154.8	92.8	479.3	149.7	721.7	.7926
1965	263.1	195.3	156.6	111.7	503.2	166.4	781.4	.7871
1966	253.4	173.2	171.5	118.1	480.1	143.0	741.2	.8071
1967	319.2	192.3	235.9	128.8	618.5	154.4	901.8	.8288
1968	372.6	199.2	267.8	114.8	724.8	202.5	1042.1	.8057

* CONVERTED FROM NATIONAL DEVISA-UNITS THROUGH
OFFICIAL EXCHANGE RATES. NOTE LIMITATIONS
DISCUSSED IN THE EXPLANATORY TEXT.

TABLE III.BEC-1.X.P-B
POLAND'S EXPORTS TO BULGARIA, 1958-68
(MILLIONS OF CURRENT DOLLARS,* F.O.B.)

YEAR	CLASS 1	111	112	121	122	CLASS 2	21	22	CLASS 3	31	32	CLASS 4+5	CLASS 6	CLASS 7	TOTAL EXPORTS
1958	.0				.0	7.4	.0	7.4	1.1		1.1	2.0	.4	6.2	17.1
1959	.2	.1			.1	7.4	.1	7.4	1.0		1.0	2.7	.6	5.1	17.0
1960	.1	.1			.1	9.5	.6	8.9	1.0		1.0	7.1	1.8	8.2	27.6
1961	.1	.0			.1	8.0	.6	7.4	.7		.7	5.4	2.0	5.4	21.6
1962	.2				.2	8.1	.9	7.3	.9		.9	8.4	2.3	4.3	24.3
1963	.1	.0			.1	10.7	1.2	9.5	1.0		.9	13.1	4.3	5.2	34.5
1964	.1				.0	9.8	1.0	8.8	1.1	.1	1.1	14.2	4.5	5.6	35.2
1965	.8		.5		.3	8.8	.1	8.7	1.1	.0	1.1	24.1	3.3	6.8	44.9
1966	.4				.4	5.9		5.9	1.3		1.3	27.0	3.6	6.5	44.5
1967	.8				.8	8.1	.5	7.6	1.4		1.4	29.6	6.3	5.2	51.3
1968	1.5		.4		1.2	10.7	.3	10.4	.5		.5	34.0	10.1	6.6	63.4

* CONVERTED FROM NATIONAL DEVISA UNITS THROUGH OFFICIAL EXCHANGE RATES. NOTE LIMITATIONS DISCUSSED IN THE EXPLANATORY TEXT.

BEC CATEGORIES

1 FOOD AND BEVERAGES
  11 PRIMARY
    111 FOR INDUSTRY
    112 FOR HOUSEHOLD CONSUMPTION
  12 PROCESSED
    121 FOR INDUSTRY
    122 FOR HOUSEHOLD CONSUMPTION

2 INDUSTRIAL SUPPLIES (NON-FOOD)
  21 PRIMARY
  22 PROCESSED

3 FUELS AND LUBRICANTS
  31 PRIMARY
  32 PROCESSED

4 MACHINERY, EXC. TRANSPORT (W/PARTS)

5 TRANSPORT EQUIPMENT

6 CONSUMER GOODS, N.E.S.

7 GOODS N.E.S. AND UNSPECIFIED

TABLE III.BEC-2.X.P-B
POLAND'S EXPORTS TO BULGARIA, 1958-68
(MILLIONS OF CURRENT DOLLARS,* F.O.B.)

YEAR	AGGREGATION I. BASIC SNA CLASSES			AGGREGATION II. PRIMARY VS. PROCESSED		NOT SPECIFIED	TOTAL EXPORTS	RATIO SPECIFIED
	CAPITAL GOODS	INTERMEDIATE GOODS	CONSUMER GOODS	PRIMARY	PROCESSED			
1958	2.0	8.5	.4	.0	10.9	6.2	17.1	.6394
1959	2.7	8.5	.6	.1	11.7	5.1	17.0	.7000
1960	7.1	10.5	1.9	.7	18.8	8.2	27.6	.7041
1961	5.4	8.7	2.0	.6	15.6	5.4	21.6	.7523
1962	8.4	9.1	2.5	.9	19.1	4.3	24.3	.8218
1963	13.1	11.7	4.5	1.3	28.1	5.2	34.5	.8508
1964	14.2	11.0	4.5	1.0	28.7	5.6	35.2	.8426
1965	24.1	9.9	4.1	.6	37.5	6.8	44.9	.8481
1966	27.0	7.1	4.0	0.0	38.1	6.5	44.5	.8547
1967	29.6	9.5	7.0	.5	45.7	5.2	51.3	.8997
1968	34.0	11.3	11.6	.7	56.2	6.6	63.4	.8967

* CONVERTED FROM NATIONAL DEVISA-UNITS THROUGH
OFFICIAL EXCHANGE RATES. NOTE LIMITATIONS
DISCUSSED IN THE EXPLANATORY TEXT.

TABLE III.BEC-1.X.P-C
POLAND'S EXPORTS TO CZECHOSLOVAKIA, 1958-68
(MILLIONS OF CURRENT DOLLARS,* F.O.B.)

YEAR	CLASS 1	111	112	121	122	CLASS 2	21	22	CLASS 3	31	32	CLASS 4+5	CLASS 6	CLASS 7	TOTAL EXPORTS
1958	7.0	4.7	.2		2.1	19.3	.6	18.6	26.4	26.3	.0	14.0	.6	5.2	72.5
1959	5.1	1.4	1.1	.2	2.4	28.5	1.1	27.4	21.4	21.3	.1	17.1	.9	7.6	80.6
1960	4.9	.8	2.1	.2	1.8	37.0	1.1	35.9	24.3	21.0	3.3	33.3	3.0	10.5	113.1
1961	7.4	4.4	1.9	.1	1.0	45.8	4.9	40.9	30.2	21.4	8.8	42.3	4.8	16.2	146.8
1962	5.5	.9	1.6	.1	2.8	49.5	3.0	46.5	22.0	17.5	4.6	43.6	4.2	21.0	145.8
1963	8.7	.3	4.2	.5	3.6	52.4	2.6	49.8	20.0	19.7	.3	43.7	5.1	14.9	144.7
1964	19.8		15.7	1.3	2.8	48.9	3.8	45.1	37.7	25.5	12.2	55.5	5.7	28.3	195.9
1965	12.2	1.3	8.4	1.2	1.4	56.4	4.9	51.4	30.8	24.6	6.1	62.8	6.1	40.1	208.4
1966	11.6		9.7	.9	.9	31.6	2.2	29.4	28.1	27.8	.3	54.8	6.0	46.1	178.3
1967	13.7	.2	9.9	.5	3.1	36.1	1.7	34.4	28.3	25.8	2.5	69.4	9.8	45.4	202.7
1968	19.9	.4	13.8	1.0	4.8	40.1	1.3	38.8	33.7	30.6	3.1	83.9	20.4	47.4	245.5

* CONVERTED FROM NATIONAL DEVISA UNITS THROUGH OFFICIAL EXCHANGE RATES. NOTE LIMITATIONS DISCUSSED IN THE EXPLANATORY TEXT.

BEC CATEGORIES

1 FOOD AND BEVERAGES
 11 PRIMARY
   111 FOR INDUSTRY
   112 FOR HOUSEHOLD CONSUMPTION
 12 PROCESSED
   121 FOR INDUSTRY
   122 FOR HOUSEHOLD CONSUMPTION

2 INDUSTRIAL SUPPLIES (NON-FOOD)
 21 PRIMARY
 22 PROCESSED

3 FUELS AND LUBRICANTS
 31 PRIMARY
 32 PROCESSED

4 MACHINERY, EXC. TRANSPORT (W/PARTS)

5 TRANSPORT EQUIPMENT

6 CONSUMER GOODS, N.E.S.

7 GOODS N.E.S. AND UNSPECIFIED

TABLE III.BEC-2.X.P-C
POLAND'S EXPORTS TO CZECHOSLOVAKIA, 1958-68
(MILLIONS OF CURRENT DOLLARS,* F.O.B.)

YEAR	AGGREGATION I. BASIC SNA CLASSES			AGGREGATION II. PRIMARY VS. PROCESSED		NOT SPECIFIED	TOTAL EXPORTS	RATIO SPECIFIED
	CAPITAL GOODS	INTERMEDIATE GOODS	CONSUMER GOODS	PRIMARY	PROCESSED			
1958	14.0	50.3	3.0	31.9	35.4	5.2	72.5	.9286
1959	17.1	51.6	4.3	24.9	48.1	7.6	80.6	.9060
1960	33.3	62.4	6.9	25.1	77.5	10.5	113.1	.9073
1961	42.3	80.5	7.7	32.6	97.9	16.2	146.8	.8895
1962	43.6	72.6	8.6	23.0	101.8	21.0	145.8	.8563
1963	43.7	73.3	12.9	26.9	102.9	14.9	144.7	.8972
1964	55.5	87.9	24.2	45.0	122.5	28.3	195.9	.8556
1965	62.8	89.6	15.8	39.2	129.1	40.1	208.4	.8075
1966	54.8	60.7	16.7	39.8	92.4	46.1	178.3	.7416
1967	69.4	65.1	22.8	37.6	119.8	45.4	202.7	.7762
1968	83.9	75.2	39.0	46.0	152.1	47.4	245.5	.8068

* CONVERTED FROM NATIONAL DEVISA-UNITS THROUGH
OFFICIAL EXCHANGE RATES. NOTE LIMITATIONS
DISCUSSED IN THE EXPLANATORY TEXT.

TABLE III.BEC-1.X.P-G
POLAND'S EXPORTS TO EAST GERMANY, 1958-68
(MILLIONS OF CURRENT DOLLARS,* F.O.B.)

YEAR	CLASS 1	111	112	121	122	CLASS 2	21	22	CLASS 3	31	32	CLASS 4+5	CLASS 6	CLASS 7	TOTAL EXPORTS
1958	2.6		1.1	.3	1.1	7.0	.1	6.9	68.4	47.2	21.3	5.8	.9	21.7	106.4
1959	4.0		1.1	.3	2.6	8.9	.6	8.3	75.0	53.2	21.8	17.4	.8	30.8	136.9
1960	8.6	.7	1.7	.5	5.7	6.6	1.0	5.6	74.9	51.8	23.1	13.0	1.8	19.8	124.7
1961	9.1	.4	3.5	.6	4.6	7.4	.7	6.7	68.7	45.2	23.5	7.8	2.5	14.2	109.7
1962	11.6	2.5	3.9	.4	4.7	9.4	1.2	8.3	69.5	46.3	23.2	9.1	5.8	12.2	117.6
1963	8.6		5.2	.9	2.4	10.6	3.0	7.6	67.8	43.7	24.1	11.7	7.4	14.3	120.5
1964	23.6		20.6	1.1	1.9	12.1	4.5	7.6	76.5	51.9	24.6	21.7	5.9	24.6	164.5
1965	8.6		5.5	1.7	1.4	14.9	3.9	11.0	69.8	47.7	22.1	29.5	6.1	24.1	153.1
1966	10.5	3.1	5.4	1.8	3.4	16.1	3.6	12.5	64.5	44.5	20.0	47.0	6.8	15.7	160.6
1967	18.7	.8	9.3	1.4	4.9	23.2	3.6	19.6	61.4	41.6	19.8	47.3	9.3	15.7	175.7
1968	20.2		11.1	2.8	5.5	35.3	7.2	28.1	66.0	47.0	19.0	61.4	13.4	32.7	229.2

* CONVERTED FROM NATIONAL DEVISA UNITS THROUGH OFFICIAL EXCHANGE RATES. NOTE LIMITATIONS DISCUSSED IN THE EXPLANATORY TEXT.

BEC CATEGORIES

1 FOOD AND BEVERAGES
  11 PRIMARY
    111 FOR INDUSTRY
    112 FOR HOUSEHOLD CONSUMPTION
  12 PROCESSED
    121 FOR INDUSTRY
    122 FOR HOUSEHOLD CONSUMPTION

2 INDUSTRIAL SUPPLIES (NON-FOOD)
  21 PRIMARY
  22 PROCESSED

3 FUELS AND LUBRICANTS
  31 PRIMARY
  32 PROCESSED

4 MACHINERY, EXC. TRANSPORT (W/PARTS)

5 TRANSPORT EQUIPMENT

6 CONSUMER GOODS, N.E.S.

7 GOODS N.E.S. AND UNSPECIFIED

TABLE III.BEC-2.X.P-G
POLAND'S EXPORTS TO EAST GERMANY, 1958-68
(MILLIONS OF CURRENT DOLLARS,* F.O.B.)

YEAR	AGGREGATION I. BASIC SNA CLASSES			AGGREGATION II. PRIMARY VS. PROCESSED		NOT SPECIFIED	TOTAL EXPORTS	RATIO SPECIFIED
	CAPITAL GOODS	INTERMEDIATE GOODS	CONSUMER GOODS	PRIMARY	PROCESSED			
1958	5.8	75.7	3.2	48.4	36.3	21.7	106.4	.7962
1959	17.4	84.3	4.5	54.9	51.2	30.8	136.9	.7753
1960	13.0	82.7	9.1	55.1	49.7	19.8	124.7	.8412
1961	7.8	77.2	10.6	49.8	45.7	14.2	109.7	.8708
1962	9.1	81.9	14.4	54.0	51.4	12.2	117.6	.8963
1963	11.7	79.3	15.1	51.9	54.2	14.3	120.5	.8815
1964	21.7	89.8	28.4	77.1	62.8	24.6	164.5	.8505
1965	29.5	86.5	13.0	57.1	71.9	24.1	153.1	.8428
1966	47.0	82.3	15.5	53.4	91.4	15.7	160.6	.9021
1967	47.3	89.2	23.5	57.6	102.4	15.7	175.7	.9108
1968	61.4	105.0	30.0	66.0	130.4	32.7	229.2	.8572

* CONVERTED FROM NATIONAL DEVISA-UNITS THROUGH
OFFICIAL EXCHANGE RATES. NOTE LIMITATIONS
DISCUSSED IN THE EXPLANATORY TEXT.

TABLE III.BEC-1.X.P-H
POLAND'S EXPORTS TO HUNGARY, 1958-68
(MILLIONS OF CURRENT DOLLARS,* F.O.B.)

YEAR	CLASS 1	111	112	121	122	CLASS 2	21	22	CLASS 3	31	32	CLASS 4+5	CLASS 6	CLASS 7	TOTAL EXPORTS
1958	1.4	.2			1.1	4.5	.7	3.8	18.2	10.6	7.6	3.7	.7	.3	28.6
1959	.2		.1		.2	8.5	1.9	6.6	18.9	11.7	7.2	7.3	1.2	.9	37.1
1960	.3		.1		.3	8.6	2.4	6.2	17.4	9.9	7.5	13.8	2.9	3.5	46.5
1961	3.7	1.1	.3		2.2	9.1	.9	8.2	18.4	11.6	6.8	15.1	3.0	5.8	55.1
1962	1.5		.9	.1	.5	10.5	.8	9.7	21.0	13.8	7.3	13.7	2.7	14.3	63.6
1963	.4		.2		.2	13.3	2.1	11.3	20.8	13.7	7.1	28.8	3.3	12.4	79.0
1964	2.8		2.4	.2	.2	11.7	2.0	9.6	26.0	18.5	7.5	24.9	5.6	18.8	89.8
1965	1.6		1.3	.2	.2	14.4	2.4	12.0	26.2	18.7	7.4	25.0	6.3	12.4	85.9
1966	2.0		.8		1.2	15.6	2.6	12.9	22.0	15.1	6.9	28.9	7.3	15.8	91.5
1967	6.1		2.2		4.0	16.1	2.5	13.5	20.2	13.4	6.8	38.8	10.1	22.1	113.4
1968	6.7		1.9		4.8	15.1	2.6	12.5	22.1	15.1	7.0	31.5	11.9	23.1	110.3

* CONVERTED FROM NATIONAL DEVISA UNITS THROUGH OFFICIAL EXCHANGE RATES. NOTE LIMITATIONS DISCUSSED IN THE EXPLANATORY TEXT.

BEC CATEGORIES

1   FOOD AND BEVERAGES
    11   PRIMARY
         111   FOR INDUSTRY
         112   FOR HOUSEHOLD CONSUMPTION
    12   PROCESSED
         121   FOR INDUSTRY
         122   FOR HOUSEHOLD CONSUMPTION

2   INDUSTRIAL SUPPLIES (NON-FOOD)
    21   PRIMARY
    22   PROCESSED

3   FUELS AND LUBRICANTS
    31   PRIMARY
    32   PROCESSED

4   MACHINERY, EXC. TRANSPORT (W/PARTS)

5   TRANSPORT EQUIPMENT

6   CONSUMER GOODS, N.E.S.

7   GOODS N.E.S. AND UNSPECIFIED

TABLE III.BEC-2.X.P-H
POLAND'S EXPORTS TO HUNGARY, 1958-68
(MILLIONS OF CURRENT DOLLARS,* F.O.B.)

YEAR	AGGREGATION I. BASIC SNA CLASSES			AGGREGATION II. PRIMARY VS. PROCESSED		NOT SPECIFIED	TOTAL EXPORTS	RATIO SPECIFIED
	CAPITAL GOODS	INTERMEDIATE GOODS	CONSUMER GOODS	PRIMARY	PROCESSED			
1958	3.7	22.9	1.8	11.5	16.9	.3	28.6	.9913
1959	7.3	27.4	1.4	13.6	22.5	.9	37.1	.9757
1960	13.8	26.0	3.3	12.4	30.7	3.5	46.5	.9258
1961	15.1	28.6	5.6	13.9	35.4	5.8	55.1	.8951
1962	13.7	31.6	4.1	15.5	33.9	14.3	63.6	.7760
1963	28.8	34.1	3.7	15.9	50.7	12.4	79.0	.8431
1964	24.9	37.9	8.2	23.0	48.0	18.8	89.8	.7907
1965	25.0	40.8	7.7	22.4	51.2	12.4	85.9	.8563
1966	28.9	37.6	9.2	18.5	57.2	15.8	91.5	.8279
1967	38.8	36.3	16.3	18.1	73.2	22.1	113.4	.8055
1968	31.5	37.2	18.6	19.5	67.8	23.1	110.3	.7911

* CONVERTED FROM NATIONAL DEVISA-UNITS THROUGH
OFFICIAL EXCHANGE RATES. NOTE LIMITATIONS
DISCUSSED IN THE EXPLANATORY TEXT.

TABLE III.BEC-1.X.P-R
POLAND'S EXPORTS TO RUMANIA, 1958-68
(MILLIONS OF CURRENT DOLLARS,* F.O.B.)

YEAR	CLASS 1	111	112	121	122	CLASS 2	21	22	CLASS 3	31	32	CLASS 4+5	CLASS 6	CLASS 7	TOTAL EXPORTS
1958	1.1		.0	.0	1.1	5.8	.0	5.8	2.6		2.6	.9	.7	2.4	13.6
1959	1.5		.1	.1	1.3	6.7	.0	6.7	3.1		3.1	5.0	.4	.9	17.6
1960	1.4	.1	.3	.1	1.0	8.9	.8	8.0	2.8		2.8	6.5	1.5	2.1	23.2
1961	1.8	.1	.3	.1	1.4	10.6	1.9	8.7	3.1		3.1	10.7	4.9	1.3	32.5
1962	1.2	.1	.3	.1	1.0	11.4	1.8	9.6	3.3		3.3	13.3	4.5	1.4	35.1
1963	2.3	.1	.0	.2	2.0	10.1	1.5	8.6	3.8		3.8	18.3	4.6	2.2	41.2
1964	2.8			.2	2.7	9.1	.1	9.0	4.2	.1	4.2	12.6	4.7	6.0	39.7
1965	3.5		.2	.6	2.8	9.4	.6	8.8	4.3	1.1	3.3	12.2	3.0	3.3	35.8
1966	2.9		.1	.4	2.3	10.6	.2	10.5	8.9	.2	8.7	16.6	2.9	4.2	46.2
1967	1.9		.2	.1	1.6	14.9	.2	14.7	3.4	.0	3.4	19.2	3.4	3.7	46.5
1968	1.4		.5		.8	17.6	.4	17.1	4.6		4.6	25.3	4.7	4.2	57.7

* CONVERTED FROM NATIONAL DEVISA UNITS THROUGH OFFICIAL EXCHANGE RATES. NOTE LIMITATIONS DISCUSSED IN THE EXPLANATORY TEXT.

BEC CATEGORIES

1 FOOD AND BEVERAGES
  11 PRIMARY
    111 FOR INDUSTRY
    112 FOR HOUSEHOLD CONSUMPTION
  12 PROCESSED
    121 FOR INDUSTRY
    122 FOR HOUSEHOLD CONSUMPTION

2 INDUSTRIAL SUPPLIES (NON-FOOD)
  21 PRIMARY
  22 PROCESSED

3 FUELS AND LUBRICANTS
  31 PRIMARY
  32 PROCESSED

4 MACHINERY, EXC. TRANSPORT (W/PARTS)

5 TRANSPORT EQUIPMENT

6 CONSUMER GOODS, N.E.S.

7 GOODS N.E.S. AND UNSPECIFIED

TABLE III.BEC-2.X.P-R
POLAND'S EXPORTS TO RUMANIA, 1958-68
(MILLIONS OF CURRENT DOLLARS,* F.O.B.)

YEAR	AGGREGATION I. BASIC SNA CLASSES			AGGREGATION II. PRIMARY VS. PROCESSED		NOT SPECIFIED	TOTAL EXPORTS	RATIO SPECIFIED
	CAPITAL GOODS	INTERMEDIATE GOODS	CONSUMER GOODS	PRIMARY	PROCESSED			
1958	.9	8.4	1.8	.1	11.1	2.4	13.6	.8217
1959	5.0	9.9	1.9	.1	16.6	.9	17.6	.9518
1960	6.5	11.8	2.8	1.2	19.9	2.1	23.2	.9106
1961	10.7	13.8	6.7	2.2	29.0	1.3	32.5	.9615
1962	13.3	14.8	5.6	2.0	31.7	1.4	35.1	.9608
1963	18.3	14.2	6.5	1.6	37.4	2.2	41.2	.9472
1964	12.6	13.6	7.4	.2	33.4	6.0	39.7	.8480
1965	12.2	14.3	6.0	1.9	30.7	3.3	35.8	.9085
1966	16.6	20.0	5.4	.4	41.6	4.2	46.2	.9091
1967	19.2	18.4	5.3	.4	42.4	3.7	46.5	.9211
1968	25.3	22.1	6.0	.9	52.5	4.2	57.7	.9272

* CONVERTED FROM NATIONAL DEVISA-UNITS THROUGH
OFFICIAL EXCHANGE RATES. NOTE LIMITATIONS
DISCUSSED IN THE EXPLANATORY TEXT.

TABLE III.BEC-1.X.P-Y
POLAND'S EXPORTS TO YUGOSLAVIA, 1958-68
(MILLIONS OF CURRENT DOLLARS,* F.O.B.)

YEAR	CLASS 1	111	112	121	122	CLASS 2	21	22	CLASS 3	31	32	CLASS 4+5	CLASS 6	CLASS 7	TOTAL EXPORTS
1958	6.9	2.6			4.3	10.0	.1	9.9	3.1	2.2	.9	12.3	1.3	.4	34.0
1959	3.1	.6	.6		1.9	10.1	.2	9.9	2.6		2.6	2.9	1.5	.5	20.6
1960	6.1	1.6	.4		4.1	15.7	.5	15.2	1.6	.1	1.5	7.9	4.9	.5	36.7
1961	1.4	1.1	.3		1.0	9.5	.3	9.2	2.6	1.2	1.4	8.2	3.8	.7	26.2
1962	7.2	4.8	1.2	.1	1.1	12.5	2.0	10.5	1.7	.2	1.5	7.3	2.5	.3	31.5
1963	2.4	.4	1.9	.4	.2	15.6	2.6	13.0	1.8	.1	1.7	8.0	4.9	.4	33.2
1964	1.6		1.1		.0	16.5	.7	15.8	7.9	6.3	1.7	16.9	5.9	6.9	55.7
1965	1.9		1.3	.5	.1	14.3	.8	13.5	8.5	6.7	1.8	16.6	5.3	7.5	54.1
1966	2.8		2.6	.3		14.4	.6	13.8	3.3	1.9	1.4	28.0	6.7	19.9	75.0
1967	3.3		1.6	.6	1.0	14.4	.8	13.5	1.7	.6	1.1	17.7	4.7	6.6	48.5
1968	6.0		.2	.6	5.2	14.9	.9	14.0	1.6	.4	1.2	15.6	6.0	7.8	51.9

* CONVERTED FROM NATIONAL DEVISA UNITS THROUGH
OFFICIAL EXCHANGE RATES. NOTE LIMITATIONS
DISCUSSED IN THE EXPLANATORY TEXT.

BEC CATEGORIES

1   FOOD AND BEVERAGES
    11   PRIMARY
         111   FOR INDUSTRY
         112   FOR HOUSEHOLD CONSUMPTION
    12   PROCESSED
         121   FOR INDUSTRY
         122   FOR HOUSEHOLD CONSUMPTION

2   INDUSTRIAL SUPPLIES (NON-FOOD)
    21   PRIMARY
    22   PROCESSED

3   FUELS AND LUBRICANTS
    31   PRIMARY
    32   PROCESSED

4   MACHINERY, EXC. TRANSPORT (W/PARTS)

5   TRANSPORT EQUIPMENT

6   CONSUMER GOODS, N.E.S.

7   GOODS N.E.S. AND UNSPECIFIED

TABLE III.BEC-2.X.P-Y
POLAND'S EXPORTS TO YUGOSLAVIA, 1958-68
(MILLIONS OF CURRENT DOLLARS,* F.O.B.)

YEAR	AGGREGATION I. BASIC SNA CLASSES			AGGREGATION II. PRIMARY VS. PROCESSED		NOT SPECIFIED	TOTAL EXPORTS	RATIO SPECIFIED
	CAPITAL GOODS	INTERMEDIATE GOODS	CONSUMER GOODS	PRIMARY	PROCESSED			
1958	12.3	15.7	5.5	4.9	28.7	.4	34.0	.9875
1959	2.9	13.3	4.0	1.4	18.8	.5	20.6	.9782
1960	7.9	18.9	9.4	2.6	33.7	.5	36.7	.9871
1961	8.2	13.2	4.1	3.0	22.5	.7	26.2	.9724
1962	7.3	19.1	4.8	8.1	23.1	.3	31.5	.9913
1963	8.0	17.9	6.9	5.0	27.8	.4	33.2	.9880
1964	16.9	24.9	7.1	8.1	40.7	6.9	55.7	.8770
1965	16.6	23.3	6.6	8.8	37.8	7.5	54.1	.8614
1966	28.0	17.9	9.2	5.1	50.0	19.9	75.0	.7343
1967	17.7	16.7	7.4	3.1	38.8	6.6	48.5	.8638
1968	15.6	17.0	11.4	1.5	42.6	7.8	51.9	.8493

* CONVERTED FROM NATIONAL DEVISA-UNITS THROUGH
OFFICIAL EXCHANGE RATES. NOTE LIMITATIONS
DISCUSSED IN THE EXPLANATORY TEXT.

TABLE III.BEC-1.X.P-CEMA
POLAND'S EXPORTS TO EUROPEAN CEMA (EXCLUDING ALBANIA), 1958-68
(MILLIONS OF CURRENT DOLLARS,* F.O.B.)

YEAR	CLASS 1	111	112	121	122	CLASS 2	21	22	CLASS 3	31	32	CLASS 4+5	CLASS 6	CLASS 7	TOTAL EXPORTS
1958	25.7	4.9	3.0	.3	17.4	80.5	1.8	78.6	190.2	139.4	50.8	115.4	17.9	73.8	503.4
1959	25.3	1.6	3.2	.7	19.8	104.7	4.6	100.1	201.8	151.7	50.1	151.9	37.1	81.3	602.2
1960	31.9	1.6	5.7	1.7	22.9	121.7	7.5	114.1	211.0	155.7	55.2	195.4	78.1	87.2	725.2
1961	73.7	21.9	8.4	1.1	42.2	131.0	11.1	119.9	211.9	151.6	60.3	206.6	108.7	118.8	850.7
1962	64.9	11.8	6.7	.8	45.5	143.2	10.8	132.4	208.7	153.6	55.1	269.8	131.6	136.8	955.1
1963	29.7	.4	12.6	2.3	14.4	159.3	12.8	146.5	207.2	153.7	53.5	338.2	146.0	157.0	1037.4
1964	81.7	.0	51.0	5.5	25.1	167.2	15.6	151.7	240.2	172.4	67.7	373.4	151.3	232.9	1246.8
1965	58.3	1.3	23.3	6.5	27.1	178.8	15.0	163.8	249.7	193.2	56.5	416.8	152.9	253.0	1309.6
1966	43.4	.1	20.9	7.8	14.6	122.8	12.3	110.6	250.3	197.0	53.3	427.8	186.8	231.2	1262.4
1967	59.5	3.3	28.2	5.8	22.2	152.4	11.8	140.5	249.3	199.7	49.6	523.6	260.3	246.4	1491.5
1968	63.8	1.1	31.6	5.9	25.1	193.8	15.7	178.1	249.1	199.5	49.5	608.7	316.4	316.5	1748.2

* CONVERTED FROM NATIONAL DEVISA UNITS THROUGH
OFFICIAL EXCHANGE RATES. NOTE LIMITATIONS
DISCUSSED IN THE EXPLANATORY TEXT.

BEC CATEGORIES

1   FOOD AND BEVERAGES
    11   PRIMARY
         111   FOR INDUSTRY
         112   FOR HOUSEHOLD CONSUMPTION
    12   PROCESSED
         121   FOR INDUSTRY
         122   FOR HOUSEHOLD CONSUMPTION

2   INDUSTRIAL SUPPLIES (NON-FOOD)
    21   PRIMARY
    22   PROCESSED

3   FUELS AND LUBRICANTS
    31   PRIMARY
    32   PROCESSED

4   MACHINERY, EXC. TRANSPORT (W/PARTS)

5   TRANSPORT EQUIPMENT

6   CONSUMER GOODS, N.E.S.

7   GOODS N.E.S. AND UNSPECIFIED

TABLE III.BEC-2.X.P-CEMA
POLAND'S EXPORTS TO EUROPEAN CEMA (EXCLUDING ALBANIA), 1958-68
(MILLIONS OF CURRENT DOLLARS,* F.O.B.)

YEAR	AGGREGATION I. BASIC SNA CLASSES			AGGREGATION II. PRIMARY VS. PROCESSED		NOT SPECIFIED	TOTAL EXPORTS	RATIO SPECIFIED
	CAPITAL GOODS	INTERMEDIATE GOODS	CONSUMER GOODS	PRIMARY	PROCESSED			
1958	115.4	275.9	38.4	149.2	280.5	73.8	503.4	.8535
1959	151.9	308.7	60.2	161.0	359.8	81.3	602.2	.8650
1960	195.4	336.0	106.7	170.5	467.5	87.2	725.2	.8798
1961	206.6	365.9	159.3	193.0	538.9	118.8	850.7	.8604
1962	269.8	364.6	183.8	182.9	635.3	136.8	955.1	.8567
1963	338.2	369.2	173.0	179.5	700.9	157.0	1037.4	.8487
1964	373.4	413.0	227.5	239.1	774.8	232.9	1246.8	.8132
1965	416.8	436.4	203.4	232.9	823.7	253.0	1309.6	.8068
1966	427.8	381.0	222.4	230.3	800.8	231.2	1262.4	.8168
1967	523.6	410.8	310.7	243.0	1002.1	246.4	1491.5	.8348
1968	608.7	450.0	373.1	248.0	1183.8	316.5	1748.2	.8190

* CONVERTED FROM NATIONAL DEVISA-UNITS THROUGH
OFFICIAL EXCHANGE RATES. NOTE LIMITATIONS
DISCUSSED IN THE EXPLANATORY TEXT.

TABLE IV.SITC.M.U
WEST EUROPE'S IMPORTS FROM USSR, 1950-68
(MILLIONS OF CURRENT DOLLARS, C.I.F.)

YEAR	PRIMARY 0	1	2	3	4	TOTAL PRIMARY	MANUFACTURED 5	6	7	8	TOTAL MANUFACT.	9	TOTAL IMPORTS
1950	82.00	1.10	49.70	.90		133.70	.50	4.50	1.50		6.50	33.90	174.10
1951	157.90	1.20	89.20	9.20		257.50	1.00	17.70	1.50		20.20	35.00	312.70
1952	248.80		71.40	26.40	0.00	346.60	5.50	26.30	1.60	.10	33.50	3.10	383.20
1953	130.30		104.30	29.70	.30	264.60	7.20	23.40	3.60	.30	34.50	33.50	332.60
1954	99.90	.50	160.50	63.40	3.90	328.20	13.40	55.80	7.30	.30	76.80	8.20	413.20
1955	84.60	.70	233.10	83.50	.50	402.40	11.80	80.10	11.40	.20	103.50	15.50	521.40
1956	92.20	1.30	238.60	122.00	1.00	455.10	10.20	109.60	14.90	.10	134.80	5.90	595.80
1957	123.80	1.20	263.90	207.90	1.00	597.80	12.70	135.30	15.80	.60	164.40	7.30	769.50
1958	102.60	1.20	244.90	196.90	.70	546.30	16.80	127.00	12.70	1.50	158.00	2.70	707.00
1959	172.50	1.40	279.10	250.70	1.60	705.30	22.70	124.70	21.80	1.40	170.60	4.20	880.10
1960	154.40	2.30	351.70	303.70	5.30	817.40	26.40	127.40	21.00	.60	175.40	7.40	1000.20
1961	191.20	1.90	337.50	323.90	4.00	858.50	24.70	129.20	28.00	1.10	183.00	26.20	1067.70
1962	150.70	2.90	355.60	362.40	8.60	879.70	23.80	193.60	25.70	.70	243.80	15.20	1138.70
1963	171.50	2.30	385.60	430.80	8.50	998.70	22.10	194.80	26.30	1.40	244.60	17.30	1260.60
1964	54.68	2.50	439.52	467.98	16.77	981.45	24.42	204.13	46.38	3.75	278.68	17.45	1277.60
1965	89.26	2.97	519.74	464.18	28.66	1104.81	29.30	287.95	45.15	4.46	366.86	17.23	1488.90
1966	102.39	2.27	529.13	539.42	35.43	1208.64	33.61	323.15	51.11	5.38	413.25	17.17	1639.01
1967	118.28	2.89	515.50	633.14	49.56	1319.37	43.98	307.15	59.55	9.39	420.07	19.53	1758.99
1968	133.44	2.59	492.59	634.02	38.73	1301.37	54.87	354.39	65.97	8.24	483.47	17.65	1802.51

SITC CATEGORIES

0   FOOD AND LIVE ANIMALS
1   BEVERAGES AND TOBACCO
2   CRUDE MATERIALS, INEDIBLE, EXCEPT FUELS
3   MINERAL FUELS, LUBRICANTS AND RELATED MATERIALS
4   ANIMAL AND VEGETABLE OILS AND FATS
5   CHEMICALS
6   MANUFACTURED GOODS CLASSIFIED CHIEFLY BY MATERIAL
7   MACHINERY AND TRANSPORT EQUIPMENT
8   MISCELLANEOUS MANUFACTURED ARTICLES
9   COMMODITIES AND TRANSACTIONS NOT CLASSIFIED
     ACCORDING TO KIND PLUS NOT SPECIFIED

TABLE IV.SITC.M.B
WEST EUROPE'S IMPORTS FROM BULGARIA, 1950-68
(MILLIONS OF CURRENT DOLLARS, C.I.F.)

YEAR	0	1	2	3	4	TOTAL PRIMARY	5	6	7	8	TOTAL MANUFACT.	9	TOTAL IMPORTS
1950	2.30	.10	1.00				3.40						4.30	7.70
1951	1.60	.60	1.70				3.90						4.50	8.40
1952	10.80		1.90				12.70	.50	.50			1.00	1.70	15.40
1953	15.30		2.80				18.10	.80	2.90	.20		4.00	2.80	24.90
1954	17.00	1.40	1.60				20.00	1.70	2.80		.10	4.50	1.90	26.40
1955	6.40	5.40	1.50	.30			13.30	1.70	2.90	.20		4.80	2.20	20.30
1956	14.10	5.80	2.00	1.80			22.20	1.50	3.60	.20		5.30	2.30	29.80
1957	14.00	6.50	1.80	.70			24.10	1.40	4.40	.40		6.20	3.10	33.40
1958	23.60	6.30	3.20	.70			33.80	2.00	3.40	.40		5.80	1.10	40.70
1959	24.70	6.50	3.80	.40			35.40	1.40	5.00	.30	.10	6.80	1.10	43.30
1960	29.60	6.50	12.30	.30	1.40		50.10	2.30	6.10	.40	.20	9.00	2.20	61.30
1961	32.90	7.30	16.90	.90	2.30		60.30	1.90	4.50	.10	.30	6.80	6.50	73.60
1962	38.50	12.40	14.50	.90	1.40		67.70	2.00	8.10	.60	.30	11.00	6.50	85.20
1963	38.90	20.10	18.00	1.10	2.40		80.50	3.30	11.20	.90	.50	15.90	7.70	104.10
1964	40.50	18.88	13.79	.48	3.41		77.06	3.83	19.41	1.98	1.38	26.60	1.44	105.10
1965	65.28	18.82	17.00	.95	1.78		103.83	5.15	37.00	2.62	1.43	46.20	.84	150.87
1966	84.38	22.79	21.20	1.10	1.49		130.96	6.14	35.39	3.32	2.54	47.39	1.98	180.33
1967	82.46	18.41	26.82	1.29	3.96		132.94	7.26	29.02	4.40	3.15	43.83	3.23	180.00
1968	77.25	16.86	26.85	3.93	1.72		126.61	12.30	37.17	8.36	5.51	63.34	3.67	193.62

SITC CATEGORIES

0 FOOD AND LIVE ANIMALS
1 BEVERAGES AND TOBACCO
2 CRUDE MATERIALS, INEDIBLE, EXCEPT FUELS
3 MINERAL FUELS, LUBRICANTS AND RELATED MATERIALS
4 ANIMAL AND VEGETABLE OILS AND FATS
5 CHEMICALS
6 MANUFACTURED GOODS CLASSIFIED CHIEFLY BY MATERIAL
7 MACHINERY AND TRANSPORT EQUIPMENT
8 MISCELLANEOUS MANUFACTURED ARTICLES
9 COMMODITIES AND TRANSACTIONS NOT CLASSIFIED
   ACCORDING TO KIND PLUS NOT SPECIFIED

TABLE IV.SITC.M.C
WEST EUROPE'S IMPORTS FROM CZECHOSLOVAKIA, 1950-68
(MILLIONS OF CURRENT DOLLARS, C.I.F.)

YEAR	PRIMARY					TOTAL PRIMARY	MANUFACTURED				TOTAL MANUFACT.	9	TOTAL IMPORTS
	0	1	2	3	4		5	6	7	8			
1950	34.00		4.90	20.90		59.80		41.60	27.30	.30	69.20	81.30	210.30
1951	40.00		7.40	15.90		63.30		28.90	20.10	.60	49.60	61.70	174.60
1952	46.90		20.20	15.90	1.00	84.00	5.20	28.30	17.30	3.00	53.80	17.70	155.50
1953	28.80		19.20	11.60	.50	60.10	5.90	31.40	19.50	3.40	60.20	21.10	141.40
1954	21.20		20.70	10.90	.30	53.10	7.60	38.10	17.40	6.10	69.20	17.80	140.10
1955	24.70		25.90	14.60	.20	65.40	11.10	55.70	25.40	11.00	103.20	24.10	192.70
1956	28.10		30.40	21.60	.20	80.30	12.20	72.00	37.60	11.70	133.50	20.40	234.20
1957	31.60		38.80	20.70	.90	92.00	13.80	58.80	47.40	8.60	128.60	27.20	247.80
1958	37.80	.60	34.60	19.00	.10	92.00	14.40	57.50	33.50	13.80	119.20	8.40	219.70
1959	44.60	.50	34.90	20.70	.40	101.10	15.60	59.30	39.30	17.10	131.30	9.30	241.70
1960	31.70	.60	45.80	24.20	.60	102.90	21.50	64.70	47.90	14.00	148.10	14.80	265.80
1961	40.70	.90	49.20	25.80	.30	116.90	21.90	59.60	48.40	16.10	146.00	30.40	293.30
1962	44.50	.60	50.40	29.10	.30	125.50	17.80	59.00	54.40	17.80	149.00	23.20	297.70
1963	60.50	1.30	54.30	33.10	.20	149.40	16.00	57.70	49.60	18.10	141.40	29.00	319.80
1964	54.15	1.11	62.99	34.32	.31	152.88	23.67	82.35	55.34	27.69	189.05	10.14	352.06
1965	55.72	1.57	67.65	35.62	.52	161.08	26.16	102.01	62.35	29.37	219.89	12.32	393.29
1966	51.77	1.53	69.19	42.41	.82	165.72	28.04	107.97	64.58	34.36	234.95	16.72	417.39
1967	59.01	1.69	62.55	45.47	3.45	172.17	30.88	113.93	65.18	36.02	246.01	18.68	436.86
1968	71.09	1.87	68.27	50.98	2.75	194.96	33.34	124.18	76.33	40.24	274.09	15.24	484.28

SITC CATEGORIES

0   FOOD AND LIVE ANIMALS
1   BEVERAGES AND TOBACCO
2   CRUDE MATERIALS, INEDIBLE, EXCEPT FUELS
3   MINERAL FUELS, LUBRICANTS AND RELATED MATERIALS
4   ANIMAL AND VEGETABLE OILS AND FATS
5   CHEMICALS
6   MANUFACTURED GOODS CLASSIFIED CHIEFLY BY MATERIAL
7   MACHINERY AND TRANSPORT EQUIPMENT
8   MISCELLANEOUS MANUFACTURED ARTICLES
9   COMMODITIES AND TRANSACTIONS NOT CLASSIFIED
     ACCORDING TO KIND PLUS NOT SPECIFIED

TABLE IV.SITC.M.G
WEST EUROPE'S IMPORTS FROM EAST GERMANY,* 1951-68
(MILLIONS OF CURRENT DOLLARS, C.I.F.)

YEAR	PRIMARY					TOTAL PRIMARY	MANUFACTURED				TOTAL MANUFACT.	9	TOTAL IMPORTS
	0	1	2	3	4		5	6	7	8			
1951	3.10		.30	13.90	.20	17.50	19.20	3.10	9.90	2.80	35.00	28.30	80.80
1952	8.10		1.30	13.10	0.00	22.50	30.00	8.50	14.90	7.20	60.60	6.10	89.20
1953	2.10		.60	8.70	.30	11.70	27.90	13.10	17.40	7.80	66.20	6.40	84.30
1954	4.00			11.00	.30	15.30	33.80	15.20	27.10	10.40	86.50	11.20	113.00
1955	1.60		1.80	12.30	.30	14.20	38.40	18.20	31.70	12.00	100.30	15.30	129.80
1956	4.90		1.30	12.60		19.30	36.50	20.20	35.50	12.40	104.60	12.80	136.70
1957	1.60		1.30	11.80		14.70	37.80	20.20	35.40	13.50	106.90	15.70	137.30
1958	7.30		1.20	12.00	.10	20.60	38.50	24.50	33.90	11.40	108.30	9.60	138.50
1959	13.30		3.10	9.20	.40	26.00	42.30	25.10	33.20	11.80	112.40	10.00	148.40
1960	17.30		2.50	11.10	.70	31.60	45.50	32.80	31.30	13.00	122.60	12.30	166.50
1961	11.60		3.70	11.20	.60	27.10	41.80	27.80	32.80	13.50	115.90	25.30	168.30
1962	7.50		5.20	12.80	.20	25.70	41.60	31.20	32.10	14.40	119.30	21.00	166.00
1963	13.30		5.50	14.90	0.00	33.70	42.60	33.90	30.80	15.00	122.30	25.60	181.60
1964	17.65	.09	18.22	15.57	.59	52.12	51.22	49.76	45.20	20.69	166.87	10.93	229.92
1965	19.05	.04	24.65	16.43	.92	61.09	51.96	57.42	54.39	23.59	187.36	12.44	260.88
1966	33.24	.17	26.92	14.76	1.08	76.17	52.17	58.98	55.48	25.34	191.97	13.49	281.62
1967	39.41	.48	24.81	21.53	2.18	88.41	55.17	54.89	62.32	26.20	198.58	13.63	300.61
1968	28.67	.16	31.18	20.50	5.66	86.17	54.20	60.84	71.47	29.55	216.06	14.38	316.61

* EXCLUDING TRADE BETWEEN WEST GERMANY AND EAST GERMANY. SEE EXPLANATORY TEXT.

SITC CATEGORIES

0 FOOD AND LIVE ANIMALS
1 BEVERAGES AND TOBACCO
2 CRUDE MATERIALS, INEDIBLE, EXCEPT FUELS
3 MINERAL FUELS, LUBRICANTS AND RELATED MATERIALS
4 ANIMAL AND VEGETABLE OILS AND FATS
5 CHEMICALS
6 MANUFACTURED GOODS CLASSIFIED CHIEFLY BY MATERIAL
7 MACHINERY AND TRANSPORT EQUIPMENT
8 MISCELLANEOUS MANUFACTURED ARTICLES
9 COMMODITIES AND TRANSACTIONS NOT CLASSIFIED
    ACCORDING TO KIND PLUS NOT SPECIFIED

TABLE IV.SITC.M.H
WEST EUROPE'S IMPORTS FROM HUNGARY, 1950-68
(MILLIONS OF CURRENT DOLLARS, C.I.F.)

YEAR	PRIMARY					TOTAL PRIMARY	MANUFACTURED				TOTAL MANUFACT.	9	TOTAL IMPORTS
	0	1	2	3	4		5	6	7	8			
1950	44.80	.10	2.00	.30		47.20	.40	6.10	2.20		8.30	24.90	80.40
1951	30.50	.70	3.00	.90		35.10		6.90	3.10		10.40	23.40	68.90
1952	33.00		1.20	.10	3.60	37.90	2.10	6.70	2.60	2.90	14.30	9.10	61.30
1953	14.90		.90	.10	2.20	18.10	2.00	7.90	4.20	3.70	17.80	9.60	45.50
1954	32.50	.10	1.30	.50	3.60	38.00	2.00	7.80	4.10	3.20	17.10	8.30	63.40
1955	52.70	.30	1.40	3.00	4.00	61.40	3.00	13.00	4.70	4.10	24.80	14.80	101.00
1956	64.20	.60	7.00	2.60	2.50	76.90	4.20	15.40	5.10	4.30	29.00	10.10	116.00
1957	46.20	.40	8.20	3.90	3.00	61.70	4.60	9.20	4.30	3.40	21.50	9.20	92.40
1958	55.90	2.00	7.80	6.70	3.10	75.50	7.50	13.80	4.40	5.20	30.90	4.00	110.40
1959	67.60	2.60	9.80	7.60	4.50	92.10	8.10	16.90	5.60	5.50	36.10	5.10	133.30
1960	74.40	3.30	12.10	7.90	5.10	102.80	7.50	19.60	8.80	6.40	42.30	7.60	152.70
1961	68.60	2.40	12.10	9.30	2.60	95.00	6.20	15.80	5.40	6.80	34.20	20.20	149.40
1962	75.40	3.40	15.50	12.60	4.10	111.00	6.80	22.20	7.90	8.80	45.70	18.50	175.20
1963	112.10	3.00	18.50	14.10	6.20	153.90	8.20	30.80	7.80	11.90	58.70	23.20	235.80
1964	107.17	3.85	25.68	11.61	4.81	153.12	11.29	44.45	13.04	19.66	88.44	7.06	248.62
1965	130.66	3.93	26.51	9.20	4.62	174.92	9.59	53.53	11.72	20.28	95.12	7.94	277.99
1966	151.93	3.76	31.14	12.46	5.55	204.84	16.36	56.23	15.93	24.65	113.17	9.79	327.80
1967	154.06	3.61	31.94	17.37	7.40	214.38	16.85	54.66	17.22	25.89	114.62	12.21	341.20
1968	143.54	3.72	34.25	19.00	5.02	205.53	17.86	61.41	20.00	26.42	125.69	11.97	343.20

SITC CATEGORIES

0 FOOD AND LIVE ANIMALS
1 BEVERAGES AND TOBACCO
2 CRUDE MATERIALS, INEDIBLE, EXCEPT FUELS
3 MINERAL FUELS, LUBRICANTS AND RELATED MATERIALS
4 ANIMAL AND VEGETABLE OILS AND FATS
5 CHEMICALS
6 MANUFACTURED GOODS CLASSIFIED CHIEFLY BY MATERIAL
7 MACHINERY AND TRANSPORT EQUIPMENT
8 MISCELLANEOUS MANUFACTURED ARTICLES
9 COMMODITIES AND TRANSACTIONS NOT CLASSIFIED
   ACCORDING TO KIND PLUS NOT SPECIFIED

TABLE IV.SITC.M.P
WEST EUROPE'S IMPORTS FROM POLAND, 1950-68
(MILLIONS OF CURRENT DOLLARS, C.I.F.)

YEAR	PRIMARY 0	1	2	3	4	TOTAL PRIMARY	MANUFACTURED 5	6	7	8	TOTAL MANUFACT.	9	TOTAL IMPORTS
1950	67.60		8.90	130.50		207.00	.30	11.20	1.20	.10	12.80	28.10	247.90
1951	77.60		10.40	207.40		295.40	2.40	3.40	.20	.30	6.30	23.90	325.60
1952	77.90		14.30	150.50		242.70	5.20	4.10	.10		9.40	5.10	257.20
1953	87.90		15.50	114.60		218.00	4.20	6.90	.30	.10	11.50	5.40	234.90
1954	53.30		24.10	97.50		174.90	9.40	10.40	.80	.20	20.80	5.10	200.80
1955	55.30		28.30	135.50		219.10	11.90	19.00	2.40	.10	33.40	11.30	263.80
1956	75.00		37.70	164.10		276.80	9.80	22.30	3.90	.30	36.30	6.30	319.40
1957	76.50		30.50	135.60		242.60	12.20	22.40	4.70	.80	40.10	9.50	292.20
1958	114.80	.40	27.90	112.90		256.00	17.70	30.80	4.00	1.60	54.10	4.00	314.10
1959	144.10	.70	32.30	92.60		269.70	23.40	38.70	4.30	2.40	68.80	6.40	344.90
1960	156.60	.80	44.50	96.60		298.50	28.50	37.50	7.30	2.70	76.00	8.90	383.40
1961	179.70	.90	45.50	95.10		321.20	23.40	30.20	5.50	2.00	61.10	18.90	401.20
1962	182.20	1.60	59.60	101.20		344.60	22.80	44.20	8.30	3.00	78.30	20.80	443.70
1963	187.30	1.60	65.60	102.30		357.40	22.40	42.40	7.10	4.30	76.20	25.80	459.40
1964	206.67	1.48	83.84	113.68		405.67	28.49	62.21	10.96	10.59	112.25	7.54	525.45
1965	233.75	1.72	98.89	116.89	1.61	451.25	35.09	60.66	14.51	14.35	124.61	9.66	585.53
1966	244.54	2.75	106.25	109.48	5.62	466.63	43.64	73.81	20.14	16.33	153.92	11.56	630.11
1967	236.28	3.25	93.67	117.22	5.62	456.04	42.74	76.89	26.17	18.17	163.97	12.52	632.53
1968	221.30	4.03	115.12	139.96	6.62	487.03	40.92	73.87	34.23	23.04	172.06	12.26	671.36

SITC CATEGORIES

0 FOOD AND LIVE ANIMALS
1 BEVERAGES AND TOBACCO
2 CRUDE MATERIALS, INEDIBLE, EXCEPT FUELS
3 MINERAL FUELS, LUBRICANTS AND RELATED MATERIALS
4 ANIMAL AND VEGETABLE OILS AND FATS
5 CHEMICALS
6 MANUFACTURED GOODS CLASSIFIED CHIEFLY BY MATERIAL
7 MACHINERY AND TRANSPORT EQUIPMENT
8 MISCELLANEOUS MANUFACTURED ARTICLES
9 COMMODITIES AND TRANSACTIONS NOT CLASSIFIED
  ACCORDING TO KIND PLUS NOT SPECIFIED

TABLE IV.SITC.M.R
WEST EUROPE'S IMPORTS FROM RUMANIA, 1950-68
(MILLIONS OF CURRENT DOLLARS, C.I.F.)

YEAR	PRIMARY					TOTAL PRIMARY	MANUFACTURED				TOTAL MANUFACT.		TOTAL IMPORTS
	0	1	2	3	4		5	6	7	8		9	
1950	6.90		.50			7.40						5.60	13.00
1951	11.60		1.60			13.20						9.10	22.30
1952	10.90		2.10	11.80	0.00	24.80	.10	.10			.20	1.20	26.20
1953	15.70		2.30	28.30	.10	46.40		.20			.20	2.10	48.70
1954	13.20		13.70	39.50	1.20	67.60	.30	.80			1.10	2.00	70.70
1955	21.50		17.00	42.30	1.70	82.50	.30	4.60	.20		5.10	2.60	90.20
1956	33.50	.10	13.10	33.60	2.00	82.30	.90	2.90	.20		4.00	1.30	87.60
1957	13.00	.20	26.00	37.70	1.40	78.30	.90	1.90	.30		3.10	2.00	83.40
1958	21.00	2.10	26.40	32.40	1.20	83.10	1.10	5.90	.10		7.10	.90	91.10
1959	10.40	.30	25.70	32.60	1.70	70.70	1.30	5.50	2.00		8.80	.70	80.20
1960	36.70	.70	38.40	37.90	6.20	119.90	2.40	11.20	.40	.10	14.00	2.40	136.30
1961	53.60	.60	48.60	43.70	11.90	158.40	1.10	11.90	.10		13.20	6.90	178.50
1962	59.50	.80	47.80	46.80	7.60	162.50	1.70	12.00	.20	.60	14.50	7.70	184.70
1963	71.90	1.40	63.90	52.30	5.80	195.30	3.40	23.50	.50	.90	28.30	8.00	231.60
1964	79.09	.94	75.20	47.06	5.53	207.82	5.03	17.42	1.04	3.34	26.83	.91	235.56
1965	95.06	1.45	79.32	42.39	8.83	227.05	8.03	20.91	1.58	3.96	34.48	5.02	266.55
1966	92.79	2.01	88.22	52.69	7.06	242.77	14.20	43.16	3.31	6.78	67.45	2.98	313.20
1967	157.35	2.96	87.28	46.93	12.12	306.64	15.77	41.46	4.49	11.27	72.99	2.54	382.17
1968	115.84	2.50	82.65	64.20	13.49	278.68	17.07	54.75	18.15	18.64	108.61	4.53	391.82

SITC CATEGORIES

0   FOOD AND LIVE ANIMALS
1   BEVERAGES AND TOBACCO
2   CRUDE MATERIALS, INEDIBLE, EXCEPT FUELS
3   MINERAL FUELS, LUBRICANTS AND RELATED MATERIALS
4   ANIMAL AND VEGETABLE OILS AND FATS
5   CHEMICALS
6   MANUFACTURED GOODS CLASSIFIED CHIEFLY BY MATERIAL
7   MACHINERY AND TRANSPORT EQUIPMENT
8   MISCELLANEOUS MANUFACTURED ARTICLES
9   COMMODITIES AND TRANSACTIONS NOT CLASSIFIED
    ACCORDING TO KIND PLUS NOT SPECIFIED

TABLE IV.SITC.M.CEMA
WEST EUROPE'S IMPORTS FROM EUROPEAN CEMA (EXCLUDING ALBANIA)* 1950-68
(MILLIONS OF CURRENT DOLLARS, C.I.F.)

YEAR	PRIMARY					TOTAL PRIMARY	MANUFACTURED				TOTAL MANUFACT.	9	TOTAL IMPORTS
	0	1	2	3	4		5	6	7	8			
1950	237.6	1.3	67.0	152.6	0.0	458.5	.8	63.4	32.2	.4	96.8	178.1	733.4**
1951	322.3	2.5	113.6	247.3	.2	685.9	23.0	60.0	34.8	3.7	121.5	185.9	993.3
1952	436.4	0.0	112.4	217.8	4.6	771.2	48.6	74.5	36.5	13.2	172.8	44.0	988.0
1953	295.0	0.0	145.6	193.0	3.4	637.0	48.0	85.8	45.2	15.4	194.4	80.9	912.3
1954	241.1	2.0	221.9	222.8	9.3	697.1	68.2	130.9	56.7	20.2	276.0	54.5	1027.6
1955	246.8	6.4	307.2	291.2	6.7	858.3	78.2	193.5	76.0	27.4	375.1	85.8	1319.2
1956	312.0	7.8	330.6	356.8	5.7	1012.9	75.3	246.0	97.4	28.8	447.5	59.1	1519.5
1957	306.7	8.3	370.5	419.4	6.3	1111.2	83.4	252.2	108.3	26.9	470.8	74.0	1656.0
1958	363.0	12.6	346.0	380.6	5.2	1107.4	98.0	262.9	89.0	33.5	483.4	30.7	1621.5
1959	477.2	12.0	388.7	413.8	8.6	1300.3	114.8	275.2	106.5	38.3	534.8	36.8	1871.9
1960	500.7	14.2	507.3	481.7	19.3	1523.2	134.1	299.3	117.1	36.9	587.4	55.6	2166.2
1961	578.3	14.0	513.5	509.9	21.7	1637.4	121.0	279.0	120.3	39.9	560.2	134.4	2332.0
1962	557.8	21.7	548.6	566.4	22.2	1716.7	116.5	370.3	129.2	45.6	661.6	112.9	2491.2
1963	656.1	29.7	611.4	648.6	23.1	1968.9	118.0	394.3	123.0	52.1	687.4	136.6	2792.9
1964	559.9	28.8	719.2	690.7	31.4	2030.1	147.9	479.7	173.9	87.1	888.7	55.5	2974.3
1965	688.8	30.5	833.8	685.7	45.3	2284.0	165.3	619.5	192.3	97.4	1074.5	65.5	3424.0
1966	761.0	35.3	872.0	772.3	53.0	2493.7	194.2	698.7	213.9	115.4	1222.1	73.7	3789.5
1967	846.8	33.3	842.6	882.9	84.3	2689.9	212.6	678.0	239.3	130.1	1260.1	82.3	4032.4
1968	791.1	31.7	850.9	932.6	74.0	2680.3	230.6	766.6	294.5	151.6	1443.3	79.7	4203.4

* EXCLUDING TRADE BETWEEN WEST GERMANY AND
  EAST GERMANY.   SEE EXPLANATORY TEXT.

** TOTAL AND COMPONENTS EXCLUDE EAST GERMANY.

SITC CATEGORIES

0 FOOD AND LIVE ANIMALS
1 BEVERAGES AND TOBACCO
2 CRUDE MATERIALS, INEDIBLE, EXCEPT FUELS
3 MINERAL FUELS, LUBRICANTS AND RELATED MATERIALS
4 ANIMAL AND VEGETABLE OILS AND FATS
5 CHEMICALS
6 MANUFACTURED GOODS CLASSIFIED CHIEFLY BY MATERIAL
7 MACHINERY AND TRANSPORT EQUIPMENT
8 MISCELLANEOUS MANUFACTURED ARTICLES
9 COMMODITIES AND TRANSACTIONS NOT CLASSIFIED
   ACCORDING TO KIND PLUS NOT SPECIFIED

TABLE IV.SITC.X.U
WEST EUROPE'S EXPORTS TO USSR, 1950-68
(MILLIONS OF CURRENT DOLLARS, F.O.B.)

YEAR	PRIMARY					TOTAL PRIMARY	MANUFACTURED				TOTAL MANUFACT.	9	TOTAL EXPORTS
	0	1	2	3	4		5	6	7	8			
1950	3.10	.30	10.90		4.40	18.70	1.20	29.30	123.20		153.70	3.70	176.10
1951	9.00	2.30	31.00		7.50	49.80	1.10	37.60	133.60		172.30	6.00	228.10
1952	22.80	1.80	40.90		5.30	70.80	6.10	67.70	91.90	8.20	173.90	4.50	249.20
1953	57.30	3.30	36.20		8.20	105.00	5.70	78.30	106.60	8.70	199.30	2.40	306.70
1954	69.00	6.40	36.50		12.10	124.00	8.10	86.50	145.10	14.60	254.30	8.00	386.30
1955	47.70	1.30	32.30		12.40	93.70	3.90	87.80	184.10	2.70	278.50	6.90	379.10
1956	33.90	4.40	45.80		11.60	95.70	10.10	157.70	215.80	2.90	386.50	9.60	491.80
1957	66.30	5.40	47.70		11.90	131.30	14.90	190.30	208.40	10.30	423.90	15.20	570.40
1958	45.30	12.80	44.20		8.50	110.80	19.20	191.40	183.50	10.50	404.60	10.60	526.00
1959	31.20	6.00	37.90		9.70	84.80	23.10	215.60	246.70	12.30	497.70	17.50	600.00
1960	31.50	10.30	36.30		7.10	85.20	42.00	286.80	360.20	17.80	706.80	15.60	807.60
1961	22.80	8.20	56.90	.10	7.80	95.80	35.50	258.10	399.90	18.50	712.00	32.10	839.90
1962	46.00	6.10	57.50	.20	5.30	115.10	53.40	335.20	483.10	17.90	889.60	23.80	1028.50
1963	45.80	9.50	53.90	1.30	8.00	118.50	76.30	258.80	426.60	18.10	779.80	22.50	920.80
1964	90.23	8.36	64.76	.45	9.58	173.38	89.10	168.97	430.40	20.80	709.27	7.58	890.22
1965	87.98	12.70	81.65	.85	12.47	195.65	110.12	197.25	390.81	42.00	740.18	8.82	944.65
1966	76.99	14.10	61.39	.54	9.27	162.29	123.07	189.32	375.17	61.30	748.86	12.50	923.65
1967	73.73	15.65	81.66	1.14	4.71	176.89	154.84	297.64	517.16	120.97	1090.61	13.47	1280.98
1968	80.12	14.71	65.21	1.16	1.46	162.66	185.13	379.64	709.29	142.61	1416.67	11.68	1591.02

SITC CATEGORIES

0 FOOD AND LIVE ANIMALS
1 BEVERAGES AND TOBACCO
2 CRUDE MATERIALS, INEDIBLE, EXCEPT FUELS
3 MINERAL FUELS, LUBRICANTS AND RELATED MATERIALS
4 ANIMAL AND VEGETABLE OILS AND FATS
5 CHEMICALS
6 MANUFACTURED GOODS CLASSIFIED CHIEFLY BY MATERIAL
7 MACHINERY AND TRANSPORT EQUIPMENT
8 MISCELLANEOUS MANUFACTURED ARTICLES
9 COMMODITIES AND TRANSACTIONS NOT CLASSIFIED
   ACCORDING TO KIND PLUS NOT SPECIFIED

TABLE IV.SITC.X.B
WEST EUROPE'S EXPORTS TO BULGARIA, 1950-68
(MILLIONS OF CURRENT DOLLARS, F.O.B.)

YEAR	PRIMARY					TOTAL PRIMARY	MANUFACTURED				TOTAL MANUFACT.	9	TOTAL EXPORTS
	0	1	2	3	4		5	6	7	8			
1950	.30		.90		0.00	1.20	2.50	2.60	4.70		9.80	2.00	13.00
1951	.40		.60		0.00	1.00	1.10	.70	2.40		4.20	.90	6.10
1952	.30		1.70		.20	2.20	3.00	2.70	2.50	.20	8.40	1.00	11.60
1953	2.40		2.00		.80	5.20	4.00	8.80	4.30	.20	17.30	1.20	23.70
1954	1.80	.10	1.80		.10	3.80	2.90	5.30	4.70	.30	13.20	1.00	18.00
1955	1.20		2.40		.10	3.70	3.20	7.10	3.60	.40	14.30	2.70	20.70
1956	1.60		4.00		.50	6.10	5.90	11.00	2.70	.50	20.10	2.90	29.10
1957	1.90	.20	6.60		.30	9.00	5.40	16.80	4.30	.80	27.30	2.70	39.00
1958	2.00		7.10		.40	9.50	4.00	15.90	5.20	1.00	26.10	1.80	37.40
1959	4.90		11.70	.30	.40	17.30	17.80	39.00	19.60	1.70	78.10	4.50	99.90
1960	2.20		8.80		.50	11.50	6.30	35.40	20.80	1.20	63.70	1.40	76.60
1961	4.90		5.60		.60	11.10	9.10	33.90	8.90	.70	52.60	8.50	72.20
1962	8.10	.20	7.80		.50	16.60	10.30	33.40	13.40	.70	57.80	6.60	81.00
1963	12.90	.30	10.50		.50	24.20	12.00	27.00	28.10	1.10	68.20	8.50	100.90
1964	11.97	.07	14.61	.26	.64	27.55	18.35	49.95	47.75	1.80	117.85	1.25	146.65
1965	17.70	.51	16.45	.29	.92	35.87	22.95	72.65	64.70	3.06	163.36	2.02	201.25
1966	20.14	2.50	16.95	.66	1.14	41.39	33.29	100.27	139.31	5.01	277.88	2.66	321.93
1967	9.64	1.44	15.96	1.16	.73	28.93	37.48	96.17	130.81	5.13	269.59	3.57	302.10
1968	25.88	2.00	22.70	1.96	.41	52.95	39.93	84.48	88.53	4.06	217.00	3.74	273.69

SITC CATEGORIES

0 FOOD AND LIVE ANIMALS
1 BEVERAGES AND TOBACCO
2 CRUDE MATERIALS, INEDIBLE, EXCEPT FUELS
3 MINERAL FUELS, LUBRICANTS AND RELATED MATERIALS
4 ANIMAL AND VEGETABLE OILS AND FATS
5 CHEMICALS
6 MANUFACTURED GOODS CLASSIFIED CHIEFLY BY MATERIAL
7 MACHINERY AND TRANSPORT EQUIPMENT
8 MISCELLANEOUS MANUFACTURED ARTICLES
9 COMMODITIES AND TRANSACTIONS NOT CLASSIFIED
  ACCORDING TO KIND PLUS NOT SPECIFIED

TABLE IV.SITC.X.C
WEST EUROPE'S EXPORTS TO CZECHOSLOVAKIA, 1950-68
(MILLIONS OF CURRENT DOLLARS, F.O.B.)

YEAR	PRIMARY					TOTAL PRIMARY	MANUFACTURED				TOTAL MANUFACT.	9	TOTAL EXPORTS
	0	1	2	3	4		5	6	7	8			
1950	10.10	3.20	42.40		3.90	59.60	16.90	42.30	39.80		99.00	11.00	169.60
1951	17.90	1.90	45.30		2.60	67.70	20.30	34.50	42.50		97.30	15.00	180.00
1952	9.00	.30	22.90		2.30	34.50	11.80	26.90	27.40		68.50	6.50	109.50
1953	14.90	2.30	16.30		1.90	35.40	8.90	12.60	16.70	2.40	39.80	7.60	82.80
1954	38.50	2.90	20.00		3.90	65.30	12.40	14.90	7.40	1.60	37.00	8.20	110.50
1955	32.40	4.90	24.20		2.70	64.20	18.20	17.00	7.30	2.30	45.90	18.00	128.10
1956	22.70	10.00	23.70		4.90	61.30	20.30	45.50	19.70	3.40	89.00	16.20	166.50
1957	20.00	13.10	30.20		4.40	67.70	25.60	54.50	31.50	3.30	117.40	27.10	212.20
1958	16.30	10.00	34.80	.30	5.40	66.80	23.30	69.00	38.80	5.80	135.60	5.90	208.30
1959	20.20	10.90	34.80	.20	2.20	68.30	25.80	66.00	45.90	4.50	142.70	6.20	217.20
1960	22.20	8.70	33.90	1.30	1.70	67.80	33.00	103.20	44.90	4.20	185.50	7.10	260.40
1961	30.30	9.70	37.30	1.50	3.60	82.40	38.50	113.80	58.10	4.40	215.20	15.90	313.50
1962	23.50	9.40	33.80	.40	2.40	69.50	38.40	101.60	69.90	4.80	214.70	14.80	299.00
1963	23.60	8.20	38.80	.20	5.70	76.50	36.90	52.80	70.40	4.80	164.90	20.20	261.60
1964	34.61	4.13	39.52	1.12	5.04	84.42	53.35	62.84	81.09	5.10	206.17	2.92	293.50
1965	47.92	8.08	48.91	2.47	3.95	111.33	60.89	82.04	102.17	8.89	257.43	4.81	373.57
1966	61.75	8.92	51.92	1.36	3.33	127.28	72.89	103.69	150.55	12.33	343.21	5.68	476.17
1967	36.49	8.73	47.74	1.99	1.97	96.92	77.21	93.57	133.50	16.08	320.49	6.58	423.99
1968	40.04	8.72	49.09	2.40	3.26	103.51	88.76	104.93	176.69	16.21	393.37	7.85	504.74

SITC CATEGORIES

0 FOOD AND LIVE ANIMALS
1 BEVERAGES AND TOBACCO
2 CRUDE MATERIALS, INEDIBLE, EXCEPT FUELS
3 MINERAL FUELS, LUBRICANTS AND RELATED MATERIALS
4 ANIMAL AND VEGETABLE OILS AND FATS
5 CHEMICALS
6 MANUFACTURED GOODS CLASSIFIED CHIEFLY BY MATERIAL
7 MACHINERY AND TRANSPORT EQUIPMENT
8 MISCELLANEOUS MANUFACTURED ARTICLES
9 COMMODITIES AND TRANSACTIONS NOT CLASSIFIED
ACCORDING TO KIND PLUS NOT SPECIFIED

TABLE IV.SITC.X.G
WEST EUROPE'S EXPORTS TO EAST GERMANY,* 1951-68
(MILLIONS OF CURRENT DOLLARS, F.O.B.)

YEAR	\ PRIMARY \ 0	1	2	3	4	TOTAL PRIMARY	MANUFACTURED \ 5	6	7	8	TOTAL MANUFACT.	9	TOTAL EXPORTS
1951	33.60		8.20		.60	42.40	6.00	6.70	.50		13.20	9.20	64.80
1952	34.20	1.00	10.60		1.90	47.70	11.00	8.20	1.00	3.60	23.80	6.30	77.80
1953	40.90	2.60	10.30		1.60	55.40	12.00	11.60	2.30	3.10	29.00	8.30	92.70
1954	72.70	10.40	15.50		1.40	100.00	11.00	15.40	2.20	3.70	32.30	9.10	141.40
1955	50.30	9.50	22.60		2.60	85.00	8.80	17.00	2.50	3.80	32.10	11.20	128.30
1956	41.70	12.40	23.10		4.20	81.40	7.10	25.30	5.00	3.60	41.00	8.10	130.50
1957	36.20	18.50	21.80		4.20	80.70	7.70	26.50	5.40	4.00	43.60	11.60	135.90
1958	37.40	13.90	21.00	.10	2.90	75.30	8.50	35.90	13.20	2.80	60.40	3.00	138.70
1959	39.10	6.00	21.90	.10	1.40	68.50	10.00	41.10	11.70	3.10	65.90	3.30	137.70
1960	39.50	3.40	23.90	.40	2.50	69.70	12.80	65.10	17.50	2.10	97.50	6.10	173.30
1961	35.10	8.40	25.00	.40	2.10	71.00	12.30	66.70	20.60	2.30	101.90	9.60	182.50
1962	47.70	3.50	19.10	.30	2.90	73.50	10.40	37.30	35.00	1.50	84.20	9.50	167.20
1963	38.50	6.80	19.70	.40	1.20	66.60	9.80	40.10	43.30	1.80	95.00	13.00	174.60
1964	60.23	6.93	25.66	1.80	1.46	96.08	13.84	37.96	39.95	3.26	95.01	1.40	192.49
1965	99.76	9.32	27.85	1.08	2.06	140.07	13.32	63.19	54.55	4.35	135.41	1.91	277.38
1966	82.45	10.03	33.08	1.06	.79	127.41	14.47	84.26	102.49	4.60	205.82	1.74	334.98
1967	54.31	10.69	32.17	2.11	1.37	100.65	17.99	74.88	111.13	6.60	210.60	2.61	313.85
1968	38.08	7.71	33.48	.64	.99	80.90	25.88	68.61	86.87	6.89	188.25	1.51	270.66

SITC CATEGORIES

0   FOOD AND LIVE ANIMALS
1   BEVERAGES AND TOBACCO
2   CRUDE MATERIALS, INEDIBLE, EXCEPT FUELS
3   MINERAL FUELS, LUBRICANTS AND RELATED MATERIALS
4   ANIMAL AND VEGETABLE OILS AND FATS
5   CHEMICALS
6   MANUFACTURED GOODS CLASSIFIED CHIEFLY BY MATERIAL
7   MACHINERY AND TRANSPORT EQUIPMENT
8   MISCELLANEOUS MANUFACTURED ARTICLES
9   COMMODITIES AND TRANSACTIONS NOT CLASSIFIED
    ACCORDING TO KIND PLUS NOT SPECIFIED

*   EXCLUDING TRADE BETWEEN WEST GERMANY AND
    EAST GERMANY. SEE EXPLANATORY TEXT.

TABLE IV.SITC.X.H
WEST EUROPE'S EXPORTS TO HUNGARY, 1950-68
(MILLIONS OF CURRENT DOLLARS, F.O.B.)

YEAR	PRIMARY					TOTAL PRIMARY	MANUFACTURED				TOTAL MANUFACT.	9	TOTAL EXPORTS
	0	1	2	3	4		5	6	7	8			
1950	.80		17.80		.10	18.70	9.90	29.40	24.70		64.00	7.60	90.30
1951	1.00	.10	23.20		.10	24.40	6.60	17.20	16.50		40.30	9.60	74.30
1952	1.10	1.10	16.80		1.00	20.00	5.60	17.20	14.10	4.00	40.90	5.70	66.60
1953	3.40	1.60	19.50		1.10	25.60	5.50	13.50	10.70	2.90	32.60	9.60	67.80
1954	15.60	1.10	23.70		1.40	41.80	10.60	16.60	9.30	3.00	39.50	12.70	94.00
1955	39.70	2.30	35.40		4.80	82.20	10.90	30.20	8.00	3.10	52.20	16.80	151.20
1956	22.80	1.60	30.80		1.40	56.60	12.10	24.30	8.20	1.40	46.00	10.90	113.50
1957	23.30	2.30	26.30		1.90	53.80	17.50	24.80	14.20	2.60	59.10	9.30	122.20
1958	6.30	2.90	24.80		1.70	33.50	15.00	36.10	18.40	2.70	72.20	3.90	109.60
1959	6.10	3.40	25.80		1.40	38.00	20.70	47.10	29.10	4.30	101.20	6.10	145.30
1960	8.60	2.10	31.00		2.60	44.30	26.30	64.30	38.30	4.00	132.90	7.20	184.40
1961	10.60	4.30	24.90		1.90	41.70	24.90	60.90	34.60	3.00	123.40	19.90	185.00
1962	24.10	3.00	24.20		2.60	53.90	28.30	52.60	37.40	3.40	121.70	22.00	197.60
1963	36.50	1.20	31.60	.60	2.60	71.60	34.20	59.50	51.60	4.20	149.50	29.80	250.90
1964	21.56	4.54	37.44	1.23	2.58	67.35	45.22	72.43	68.05	7.18	192.88	3.02	263.25
1965	26.98	2.85	37.85	.78	3.03	71.49	42.47	76.84	65.51	8.36	193.18	3.35	268.02
1966	28.68	6.53	40.74	.55	1.94	78.44	53.13	77.95	82.68	11.38	225.14	4.65	308.22
1967	24.10	10.46	41.49	.66	2.25	78.96	61.15	86.16	109.98	14.20	271.49	5.34	355.79
1968	20.96	4.19	41.78	.73	1.63	69.29	72.24	101.23	87.40	13.64	274.51	5.32	349.11

SITC CATEGORIES

0   FOOD AND LIVE ANIMALS
1   BEVERAGES AND TOBACCO
2   CRUDE MATERIALS, INEDIBLE, EXCEPT FUELS
3   MINERAL FUELS, LUBRICANTS AND RELATED MATERIALS
4   ANIMAL AND VEGETABLE OILS AND FATS
5   CHEMICALS
6   MANUFACTURED GOODS CLASSIFIED CHIEFLY BY MATERIAL
7   MACHINERY AND TRANSPORT EQUIPMENT
8   MISCELLANEOUS MANUFACTURED ARTICLES
9   COMMODITIES AND TRANSACTIONS NOT CLASSIFIED
    ACCORDING TO KIND PLUS NOT SPECIFIED

TABLE IV.SITC.X.P
WEST EUROPE'S EXPORTS TO POLAND, 1950-68
(MILLIONS OF CURRENT DOLLARS, F.O.B.)

YEAR	PRIMARY					TOTAL PRIMARY	MANUFACTURED				TOTAL MANUFACT.	9	TOTAL EXPORTS
	0	1	2	3	4		5	6	7	8			
1950	6.30	3.40	31.30		2.80	43.80	12.90	26.30	67.60		106.80	13.90	164.50
1951	5.10	.10	56.20		1.80	63.10	19.70	25.10	89.30		134.10	10.30	207.50
1952	2.70	.10	44.20		2.00	49.00	14.90	21.90	67.60	4.70	109.10	13.80	171.90
1953	1.30	.30	35.80		.50	37.90	10.50	33.40	51.00	3.60	98.50	17.20	153.60
1954	13.10	3.60	43.40		2.30	62.40	14.50	29.30	38.10	5.80	87.70	14.70	164.80
1955	21.40	10.30	40.20		3.00	74.90	14.50	45.60	35.30	7.50	102.90	19.80	197.60
1956	34.80	7.00	38.60		2.70	83.10	17.20	81.30	47.30	6.70	152.50	19.80	255.40
1957	11.60	10.50	46.80		2.10	71.00	24.00	66.90	75.40	9.70	176.00	22.00	269.00
1958	4.60	8.60	43.20	.20	1.40	58.00	24.80	87.20	97.30	9.30	218.60	12.00	288.60
1959	12.20	7.50	36.00	.40	1.80	57.90	25.50	64.90	112.00	6.80	209.20	11.90	279.00
1960	7.80	5.40	45.70	2.50	2.40	63.80	32.40	73.30	97.10	5.90	208.70	13.90	286.40
1961	16.10	3.10	50.50	1.40	2.30	73.40	36.30	85.50	101.20	4.90	227.90	19.40	320.70
1962	18.90	4.30	42.70	1.70	1.20	68.80	41.00	79.10	123.70	6.20	250.00	19.20	338.00
1963	50.90	7.30	45.40	1.10	1.60	106.30	41.70	55.50	125.40	7.30	229.90	29.20	365.40
1964	53.61	9.81	56.11	2.14	4.44	126.11	49.31	71.27	98.29	8.01	226.88	7.83	360.82
1965	55.64	10.98	61.45	2.29	5.86	136.22	70.29	99.24	110.31	10.75	290.59	9.40	436.21
1966	70.97	9.99	55.31	2.92	5.31	144.50	86.70	122.68	146.19	14.78	370.35	10.37	525.24
1967	54.56	11.55	56.14	4.92	2.88	130.05	94.52	149.36	206.40	18.68	468.96	11.33	610.34
1968	67.07	4.39	48.34	5.57	4.61	129.98	102.92	156.81	226.42	21.10	507.25	11.77	649.01

SITC CATEGORIES

0   FOOD AND LIVE ANIMALS
1   BEVERAGES AND TOBACCO
2   CRUDE MATERIALS, INEDIBLE, EXCEPT FUELS
3   MINERAL FUELS, LUBRICANTS AND RELATED MATERIALS
4   ANIMAL AND VEGETABLE OILS AND FATS
5   CHEMICALS
6   MANUFACTURED GOODS CLASSIFIED CHIEFLY BY MATERIAL
7   MACHINERY AND TRANSPORT EQUIPMENT
8   MISCELLANEOUS MANUFACTURED ARTICLES
9   COMMODITIES AND TRANSACTIONS NOT CLASSIFIED
    ACCORDING TO KIND PLUS NOT SPECIFIED

TABLE IV.SITC.X.R
WEST EUROPE'S EXPORTS TO RUMANIA, 1950-68
(MILLIONS OF CURRENT DOLLARS, F.O.B.)

YEAR	\ PRIMARY \ 0	1	2	3	4	TOTAL PRIMARY	\ MANUFACTURED \ 5	6	7	8	TOTAL MANUFACT.	9	TOTAL EXPORTS
1950	.40		3.20			3.60	1.00	3.60	14.10		18.70	2.20	24.50
1951	.20		5.50			5.70	3.10	5.80	11.50		20.40	4.80	30.90
1952	.50		3.80		0.00	4.30	5.40	19.20	12.60		38.50	2.10	44.90
1953	2.10		5.50		0.00	7.60	2.10	27.10	15.50	1.30	45.50	2.70	55.80
1954	10.60		6.90		1.70	19.20	3.90	12.10	5.70	.80	22.50	2.40	44.10
1955	8.90		7.70		.20	16.80	7.50	19.80	4.20	.60	32.10	3.60	52.50
1956	6.00		7.10		.70	13.80	8.80	18.80	3.80	.60	32.00	6.00	51.80
1957	13.20	.20	9.90		2.70	25.80	10.30	18.00	7.80	.70	36.80	4.30	66.90
1958	3.50		12.10		3.60	19.40	7.30	26.30	10.90	.80	45.30	1.00	65.70
1959	2.70		11.30		1.70	15.70	8.40	19.80	18.30	.80	47.30	2.90	65.90
1960	4.80		14.40		.10	19.30	13.00	48.70	41.40	1.60	104.70	3.90	127.90
1961	4.40		16.60		.10	21.10	17.90	47.60	90.60	2.30	158.40	13.20	192.70
1962	6.00		13.20		.20	19.40	16.40	53.50	115.60	3.40	188.90	12.90	221.20
1963	7.20		14.80	2.90	.10	25.00	26.70	56.60	97.40	3.50	184.20	14.30	223.30
1964	10.33	.14	22.87	3.26	.74	37.34	30.74	77.55	106.77	4.06	219.12	2.18	258.64
1965	10.83	.24	27.60	2.92	.53	42.12	34.46	80.26	132.99	5.78	253.49	1.97	297.57
1966	12.43	.43	24.62	1.58	.71	39.77	40.26	99.62	166.30	6.10	312.28	2.56	354.62
1967	15.78	.52	23.62	1.36	.83	42.11	47.99	143.25	332.89	10.78	534.91	3.90	580.92
1968	13.91	1.61	31.37	3.65	1.71	52.25	48.33	147.44	314.35	11.22	521.34	4.66	578.27

SITC CATEGORIES

0   FOOD AND LIVE ANIMALS
1   BEVERAGES AND TOBACCO
2   CRUDE MATERIALS, INEDIBLE, EXCEPT FUELS
3   MINERAL FUELS, LUBRICANTS AND RELATED MATERIALS
4   ANIMAL AND VEGETABLE OILS AND FATS
5   CHEMICALS
6   MANUFACTURED GOODS CLASSIFIED CHIEFLY BY MATERIAL
7   MACHINERY AND TRANSPORT EQUIPMENT
8   MISCELLANEOUS MANUFACTURED ARTICLES
9   COMMODITIES AND TRANSACTIONS NOT CLASSIFIED
    ACCORDING TO KIND PLUS NOT SPECIFIED

TABLE IV.SITC.X.CEMA
WEST EUROPE'S EXPORTS TO EUROPEAN CEMA (EXCLUDING ALBANIA)* 1950-68
(MILLIONS OF CURRENT DOLLARS, F.O.B.)

YEAR	PRIMARY						MANUFACTURED						TOTAL EXPORTS
	0	1	2	3	4	TOTAL PRIMARY	5	6	7	8	TOTAL MANUFACT.	9	
1950	21.0	6.9	106.5	0.0	11.2	145.6	44.4	133.5	274.1	0.0	452.0	40.4	638.0**
1951	67.2	4.3	170.0	0.0	12.6	254.1	57.9	127.6	296.3	0.0	481.8	55.8	791.7
1952	70.6	4.3	140.9	0.0	12.7	228.5	57.8	163.8	217.1	24.4	463.1	39.9	731.5
1953	122.3	10.1	125.6	0.0	14.1	272.1	48.7	185.3	207.1	20.9	462.0	49.0	783.1
1954	221.3	24.5	147.8	0.0	22.9	416.5	63.4	180.1	212.5	30.5	486.5	56.1	959.1
1955	201.6	28.3	164.8	0.0	25.8	420.5	67.0	224.5	245.0	21.5	558.0	79.0	1057.5
1956	163.5	35.4	173.1	0.0	26.0	398.0	81.5	364.1	302.5	19.0	767.1	73.5	1238.6
1957	172.5	50.0	189.3	0.0	27.5	439.3	105.4	397.8	347.0	33.9	884.1	92.2	1415.6
1958	113.2	48.4	187.2	.6	23.9	373.3	102.1	461.8	367.3	31.6	962.8	38.2	1374.3
1959	116.6	33.8	180.5	1.0	18.6	350.5	131.3	494.3	483.3	33.2	1142.1	52.4	1545.0
1960	116.6	29.9	194.0	4.2	16.9	361.6	165.8	676.8	620.2	37.0	1499.8	55.2	1916.6
1961	124.2	33.7	216.8	3.4	18.4	396.5	174.5	666.5	713.9	36.5	1591.4	118.6	2106.5
1962	174.3	26.5	198.3	2.6	15.1	416.8	198.2	692.7	878.1	37.9	1806.9	108.8	2332.5
1963	215.4	33.3	214.5	6.5	19.0	488.7	237.6	550.0	842.8	41.1	1671.5	137.5	2297.7
1964	282.5	34.0	261.0	10.3	24.5	612.2	299.9	541.0	872.3	54.0	1767.2	26.2	2405.6
1965	346.8	44.7	301.8	10.7	28.8	732.7	354.5	671.5	921.0	86.6	2033.6	32.3	2798.7
1966	353.4	52.5	284.2	8.7	22.5	721.1	423.8	777.8	1162.7	119.2	2483.5	40.2	3244.8
1967	268.6	59.0	298.8	13.3	14.7	654.5	491.2	941.0	1541.9	192.6	3166.6	46.8	3868.0
1968	286.1	43.3	292.0	16.1	14.1	651.5	563.2	1043.1	1689.5	222.5	3518.4	46.5	4216.5

SITC CATEGORIES

0 FOOD AND LIVE ANIMALS
1 BEVERAGES AND TOBACCO
2 CRUDE MATERIALS, INEDIBLE, EXCEPT FUELS
3 MINERAL FUELS, LUBRICANTS AND RELATED MATERIALS
4 ANIMAL AND VEGETABLE OILS AND FATS
5 CHEMICALS
6 MANUFACTURED GOODS CLASSIFIED CHIEFLY BY MATERIAL
7 MACHINERY AND TRANSPORT EQUIPMENT
8 MISCELLANEOUS MANUFACTURED ARTICLES
9 COMMODITIES AND TRANSACTIONS NOT CLASSIFIED
  ACCORDING TO KIND PLUS NOT SPECIFIED

* EXCLUDING TRADE BETWEEN WEST GERMANY AND
  EAST GERMANY. SEE EXPLANATORY TEXT.

** TOTAL AND COMPONENTS EXCLUDE EAST GERMANY.

TABLE IV.BEC-1.M.U
WEST EUROPE'S IMPORTS FROM USSR, 1950-68
(MILLIONS OF CURRENT DOLLARS, C.I.F.)

YEAR	CLASS 1	111	112	121	122	CLASS 2	21	22	CLASS 3	31	32	CLASS 4+5	CLASS 6	CLASS 7	TOTAL IMPORTS
1950	77.30	72.30	5.00			60.50	32.50	28.00	.90	.90		1.50		33.90	174.10
1951	145.00	138.30	6.70			122.00	69.80	52.20	9.20	9.00	.20	1.50		35.00	312.70
1952	237.00	216.80	.20		20.00	115.00	58.80	56.20	26.40	16.40	10.00	1.60	.10	3.10	383.20
1953	119.10	100.30	.90	.30	17.60	146.40	76.90	69.50	29.70	13.60	16.10	3.60	.30	33.50	332.60
1954	90.20	67.60	1.20	3.90	17.50	243.80	118.60	125.20	63.40	23.70	39.70	7.30	.30	8.20	413.20
1955	71.30	48.50	.40	.50	21.90	339.50	148.30	191.20	83.50	36.50	47.00	11.40	.20	15.50	521.40
1956	82.00	56.60	.50	1.00	23.90	370.90	166.50	204.40	122.00	49.80	72.20	14.90	.10	5.90	595.80
1957	103.00	73.70		1.00	28.30	434.90	180.50	254.40	207.90	76.20	131.70	15.80	.60	7.30	769.50
1958	81.00	56.60	.20	.70	23.50	412.20	164.50	247.70	196.90	83.00	113.90	12.70	1.50	2.70	707.00
1959	130.90	107.40	.50	1.60	21.40	471.10	213.50	257.60	250.70	119.30	131.40	21.80	1.40	4.20	880.10
1960	117.20	85.40	.30	5.30	26.20	550.30	259.40	290.90	303.70	147.30	156.40	21.00	.60	7.40	1000.20
1961	156.80	131.10	.20	4.00	21.50	531.70	233.70	298.00	323.90	175.70	148.20	28.00	1.10	26.20	1067.70
1962	130.80	95.80	.90	8.60	25.50	603.70	233.20	370.70	362.40	193.40	169.00	25.70	.70	15.20	1138.70
1963	157.10	92.00	.70	8.50	55.90	627.70	239.20	388.50	430.80	248.20	182.60	26.30	1.40	17.30	1260.60
1964	68.65	11.49	.77	16.90	39.49	668.30	219.12	449.18	472.87	286.22	186.65	46.38	3.93	17.45	1277.60
1965	113.27	34.56	19.20	28.82	30.69	835.13	284.75	550.38	473.36	280.03	193.33	45.15	4.76	17.23	1488.90
1966	110.81	11.72	20.90	35.63	42.56	904.51	339.82	564.69	549.61	320.72	228.89	51.11	5.85	17.17	1639.01
1967	142.20	38.33	6.30	49.85	47.72	880.76	326.38	554.38	646.23	400.82	245.41	59.55	10.70	19.53	1758.99
1968	161.57	59.89	12.56	39.01	50.01	903.41	295.50	607.91	644.61	374.72	269.89	65.97	9.28	17.65	1802.51

BEC CATEGORIES AND LARGE ECONOMIC CLASSES

1 FOOD AND BEVERAGES
  11 PRIMARY
    111 FOR INDUSTRY
    112 FOR HOUSEHOLD CONSUMPTION
  12 PROCESSED
    121 FOR INDUSTRY
    122 FOR HOUSEHOLD CONSUMPTION

2 INDUSTRIAL SUPPLIES (NON-FOOD)
  21 PRIMARY
  22 PROCESSED

3 FUELS AND LUBRICANTS
  31 PRIMARY
  32 PROCESSED

4 MACHINERY, EXC. TRANSPORT (W/PARTS)

5 TRANSPORT EQUIPMENT

6 CONSUMER GOODS, N.E.S.

7 GOODS N.E.S. AND NOT SPECIFIED

TABLE IV.BEC-2.M.U
WEST EUROPE'S IMPORTS FROM USSR, 1950-68
(MILLIONS OF CURRENT DOLLARS, C.I.F.)

YEAR	AGGREGATION I. BASIC SNA CLASSES			AGGREGATION II. PRIMARY VS. PROCESSED		NOT SPECIFIED	TOTAL IMPORTS	RATIO SPECIFIED
	CAPITAL GOODS	INTERMEDIATE GOODS	CONSUMER GOODS	PRIMARY	PROCESSED			
1950	1.50	133.70	5.00	110.70	29.50	33.90	174.10	.805
1951	1.50	269.50	6.70	223.80	53.90	35.00	312.70	.888
1952	1.60	358.20	20.30	292.20	87.90	3.10	383.20	.992
1953	3.60	276.70	18.80	191.70	107.40	33.50	332.60	.899
1954	7.30	378.70	19.00	211.10	193.90	8.20	413.20	.980
1955	11.40	472.00	22.50	233.70	272.20	15.50	521.40	.970
1956	14.90	550.50	24.50	273.40	316.50	5.90	595.80	.990
1957	15.80	717.50	28.90	330.40	431.80	7.30	769.50	.991
1958	12.70	666.40	25.20	304.30	400.00	2.70	707.00	.996
1959	21.80	830.80	23.30	440.70	435.20	4.20	880.10	.995
1960	21.00	944.70	27.10	492.40	500.40	7.40	1000.20	.993
1961	28.00	990.70	22.80	540.70	500.80	26.20	1067.70	.975
1962	25.70	1070.70	27.10	523.30	600.20	15.20	1138.70	.987
1963	26.30	1159.00	58.00	580.10	663.20	17.30	1260.60	.986
1964	46.38	1169.56	44.19	517.60	742.53	17.45	1277.60	.986
1965	45.15	1371.87	54.65	618.54	853.13	17.23	1488.90	.988
1966	51.11	1501.47	69.31	693.16	928.73	17.17	1639.01	.990
1967	59.55	1615.17	64.72	771.83	967.61	19.53	1758.99	.989
1968	65.97	1646.92	71.95	742.67	1042.17	17.65	1802.51	.990

TABLE IV.BEC-1.M.B
WEST EUROPE'S IMPORTS FROM BULGARIA, 1950-68
(MILLIONS OF CURRENT DOLLARS, C.I.F.)

YEAR	CLASS 1	111	112	121	122	CLASS 2	21	22	CLASS 3	31	32	CLASS 4+5	CLASS 6	CLASS 7	TOTAL IMPORTS
1950	2.60	1.70	.90			.80	.10	.70						4.30	7.70
1951	2.50	1.50	1.00			1.40	.80	.60						4.50	8.40
1952	11.90	6.60	3.90		1.40	1.80	.30	1.50						1.70	15.40
1953	16.60	11.00	3.90		1.70	5.20	.70	4.50				.20	.10	2.80	24.90
1954	18.60	11.20	4.40		3.00	5.90	1.40	4.50						1.90	26.40
1955	7.60	2.30	3.90		1.40	10.30	5.70	4.60	.30		.30	.20		2.20	20.30
1956	14.40	5.00	6.80		2.60	12.60	7.50	5.10	1.80		1.80	.20		2.30	29.80
1957	14.20	3.40	7.40		3.40	13.90	8.10	5.80	.70		.70	.40		3.10	33.40
1958	24.80	6.40	8.30		10.10	13.70	7.50	6.20	.40	.20	.20	.40		1.10	40.70
1959	25.70	7.90	7.20		10.60	15.70	8.60	7.10		.20		.30	.10	1.10	43.30
1960	36.40	12.20	10.40	1.40	12.40	21.80	12.60	9.20	.30	.30		.40	.20	2.20	61.30
1961	44.80	16.20	12.40	2.30	13.90	21.00	14.00	7.00	.90	.90		.10	.30	6.50	73.60
1962	45.70	11.60	15.60	1.40	17.10	30.30	18.50	11.80	.90	.90		.60	1.20	6.50	85.20
1963	50.90	16.70	15.00	2.40	16.80	41.50	25.40	16.10	1.10	1.10		.90	2.00	7.70	104.10
1964	50.80	18.30	11.19	4.24	17.07	48.88	22.04	26.84	.48	.47	.01	1.98	1.52	1.44	105.10
1965	76.38	26.17	18.82	2.29	29.10	68.42	22.73	45.69	.95	.01	.94	2.62	1.66	.84	150.87
1966	98.55	46.64	15.15	2.33	34.43	72.60	27.60	45.00	1.10	.01	1.09	3.32	2.78	1.98	180.33
1967	104.45	49.54	18.10	4.91	31.90	62.97	23.69	39.28	1.29	.07	1.22	4.40	3.66	3.23	180.00
1968	95.22	38.20	18.70	2.67	35.65	76.00	21.53	54.47	3.93	3.78	.15	8.36	6.44	3.67	193.62

BEC CATEGORIES AND LARGE ECONOMIC CLASSES

1 FOOD AND BEVERAGES
  11 PRIMARY
     111 FOR INDUSTRY
     112 FOR HOUSEHOLD CONSUMPTION
  12 PROCESSED
     121 FOR INDUSTRY
     122 FOR HOUSEHOLD CONSUMPTION

2 INDUSTRIAL SUPPLIES (NON-FOOD)
  21 PRIMARY
  22 PROCESSED

3 FUELS AND LUBRICANTS
  31 PRIMARY
  32 PROCESSED

4 MACHINERY, EXC. TRANSPORT (W/PARTS)

5 TRANSPORT EQUIPMENT

6 CONSUMER GOODS, N.E.S.

7 GOODS N.E.S. AND NOT SPECIFIED

TABLE IV.BEC-2.M.B
WEST EUROPE'S IMPORTS FROM BULGARIA, 1950-68
(MILLIONS OF CURRENT DOLLARS, C.I.F.)

YEAR	AGGREGATION I. BASIC SNA CLASSES			AGGREGATION II. PRIMARY VS. PROCESSED		NOT SPECIFIED	TOTAL IMPORTS	RATIO SPECIFIED
	CAPITAL GOODS	INTERMEDIATE GOODS	CONSUMER GOODS	PRIMARY	PROCESSED			
1950	0.00	2.50	.90	2.70	.70	4.30	7.70	.442
1951	0.00	2.90	1.00	3.30	.60	4.50	8.40	.464
1952	0.00	8.40	5.30	10.80	2.90	1.70	15.40	.890
1953	.20	16.20	5.70	15.60	6.50	2.80	24.90	.888
1954	0.00	17.10	7.40	17.00	7.50	1.90	26.40	.928
1955	.20	12.60	5.30	11.90	6.20	2.20	20.30	.892
1956	.20	17.90	9.40	19.30	8.20	2.30	29.80	.923
1957	.40	19.10	10.80	18.90	11.40	3.10	33.40	.907
1958	.40	20.80	18.40	22.20	17.40	1.10	40.70	.973
1959	.30	24.00	17.90	23.90	18.30	1.10	43.30	.975
1960	.40	35.70	23.00	35.50	23.60	2.20	61.30	.964
1961	.10	40.40	26.60	43.50	23.60	6.50	73.60	.912
1962	.60	44.20	33.90	46.60	32.10	6.50	85.20	.924
1963	.90	61.70	33.80	58.20	38.20	7.70	104.10	.926
1964	1.98	71.90	29.78	52.00	51.66	1.44	105.10	.986
1965	2.62	97.83	49.58	67.73	82.30	.84	150.87	.994
1966	3.32	122.67	52.36	89.40	88.95	1.98	180.33	.989
1967	4.40	118.71	53.66	91.40	85.37	3.23	180.00	.982
1968	8.36	120.80	60.79	82.21	107.74	3.67	193.62	.981

TABLE IV.BEC-1.M.C
WEST EUROPE'S IMPORTS FROM CZECHOSLOVAKIA, 1950-68
(MILLIONS OF CURRENT DOLLARS, C.I.F.)

YEAR	CLASS 1	111	112	121	122	CLASS 2	21	22	CLASS 3	31	32	CLASS 4+5	CLASS 6	CLASS 7	TOTAL IMPORTS
1950	34.00	10.50		5.90	17.60	46.50	2.80	43.70	20.90	16.70	4.20	27.30	.30	81.30	210.30
1951	40.00	2.80	1.10	6.10	30.00	36.30	5.00	31.30	15.90	12.70	3.20	20.10	.60	61.70	174.60
1952	48.70	2.90	8.20	12.20	25.40	52.90	11.70	41.20	15.90	12.10	3.80	17.30	3.00	17.70	155.50
1953	29.80	1.20	5.10	7.70	15.80	56.00	11.20	44.80	11.60	9.00	2.60	19.50	3.40	21.10	141.40
1954	21.60	2.60	4.90	6.10	8.00	66.30	11.90	54.40	10.90	7.20	3.70	17.40	6.10	17.80	140.10
1955	25.00	4.60	4.20	9.20	7.00	92.60	16.30	76.30	14.60	10.60	4.00	25.40	11.00	24.10	192.70
1956	28.40	2.10	7.70	10.10	8.50	114.50	20.20	94.30	21.60	15.10	6.50	37.60	11.70	20.40	234.20
1957	33.30	5.60	11.00	8.80	7.90	110.60	25.20	85.40	20.70	14.30	6.40	47.40	8.60	27.20	247.80
1958	38.60	5.20	9.40	8.40	15.60	109.00	22.00	88.10	19.00	13.50	5.50	33.50	11.20	8.40	219.70
1959	45.90	7.50	10.60	8.00	19.60	112.90	22.00	90.90	20.70	14.80	5.90	39.30	13.60	9.30	241.70
1960	33.50	6.40	7.70	6.80	12.60	134.30	28.20	106.10	24.20	16.20	8.00	47.90	11.10	14.80	265.80
1961	41.70	4.10	7.80	7.30	22.50	133.10	30.80	102.30	25.80	15.70	10.10	48.40	13.90	30.40	293.30
1962	45.70	5.80	10.00	10.00	19.90	129.30	30.70	98.60	29.70	15.50	14.20	54.40	15.40	23.20	297.70
1963	61.50	5.20	12.20	7.70	36.50	130.50	33.20	97.30	33.10	15.40	17.70	49.60	16.00	29.00	319.80
1964	56.06	5.99	11.22	7.82	31.03	170.72	29.45	141.27	34.84	16.53	18.31	55.34	24.97	10.14	352.06
1965	58.42	6.14	14.63	9.23	28.42	197.04	33.99	163.05	36.39	16.20	20.19	62.35	26.77	12.32	393.29
1966	54.68	3.61	12.97	9.89	28.21	206.79	36.35	170.44	43.27	18.47	24.80	64.58	31.35	16.72	417.39
1967	64.68	7.11	13.36	12.47	31.74	208.49	32.16	176.33	46.74	17.65	29.09	65.18	33.09	18.68	436.86
1968	76.59	20.17	12.45	10.25	33.72	226.57	40.44	186.13	52.00	19.28	32.72	76.33	37.56	15.24	484.28

BEC CATEGORIES AND LARGE ECONOMIC CLASSES

1 FOOD AND BEVERAGES
  11 PRIMARY
     111 FOR INDUSTRY
     112 FOR HOUSEHOLD CONSUMPTION
  12 PROCESSED
     121 FOR INDUSTRY
     122 FOR HOUSEHOLD CONSUMPTION

2 INDUSTRIAL SUPPLIES (NON-FOOD)
  21 PRIMARY
  22 PROCESSED

3 FUELS AND LUBRICANTS
  31 PRIMARY
  32 PROCESSED

4 MACHINERY, EXC. TRANSPORT (W/PARTS)

5 TRANSPORT EQUIPMENT

6 CONSUMER GOODS, N.E.S.

7 GOODS N.E.S. AND NOT SPECIFIED

TABLE IV.BEC-2.M.C
WEST EUROPE'S IMPORTS FROM CZECHOSLOVAKIA, 1950-68
(MILLIONS OF CURRENT DOLLARS, C.I.F.)

YEAR	AGGREGATION I. BASIC SNA CLASSES			AGGREGATION II. PRIMARY VS. PROCESSED		NOT SPECIFIED	TOTAL IMPORTS	RATIO SPECIFIED
	CAPITAL GOODS	INTERMEDIATE GOODS	CONSUMER GOODS	PRIMARY	PROCESSED			
1950	27.30	83.80	17.90	30.00	99.00	81.30	210.30	.613
1951	20.10	61.10	31.70	21.60	91.30	61.70	174.60	.647
1952	17.30	83.90	36.60	34.90	102.90	17.70	155.50	.886
1953	19.50	76.50	24.30	26.50	93.80	21.10	141.40	.851
1954	17.40	85.90	19.00	26.60	95.70	17.80	140.10	.873
1955	25.40	121.00	22.20	35.70	132.90	24.10	192.70	.875
1956	37.60	148.30	27.90	45.10	168.70	20.40	234.20	.913
1957	47.40	145.70	27.50	56.10	164.50	27.20	247.80	.890
1958	33.50	141.60	36.20	49.00	162.30	8.40	219.70	.962
1959	39.30	149.30	43.80	54.90	177.50	9.30	241.70	.962
1960	47.90	171.70	31.40	58.50	192.50	14.80	265.80	.944
1961	48.40	170.30	44.20	58.40	204.50	30.40	293.30	.896
1962	54.40	176.80	45.30	62.00	212.50	23.20	297.70	.922
1963	49.60	176.50	64.70	66.00	224.80	29.00	319.80	.909
1964	55.34	219.37	67.22	63.19	278.74	10.14	352.06	.971
1965	62.35	248.80	69.82	70.96	310.01	12.32	393.29	.969
1966	64.58	263.56	72.53	71.40	329.27	16.72	417.39	.960
1967	65.18	274.81	78.19	70.28	347.90	18.68	436.86	.957
1968	76.33	308.99	83.73	92.34	376.71	15.24	484.28	.969

TABLE IV.BEC-1.M.G
WEST EUROPE'S IMPORTS FROM EAST GERMANY,* 1951-68
(MILLIONS OF CURRENT DOLLARS, C.I.F.)

YEAR	CLASS 1	111	112	121	122	CLASS 2	21	22	CLASS 3	31	32	CLASS 4+5	CLASS 6	CLASS 7	TOTAL IMPORTS
1951	3.30			1.80	1.50	22.60		22.60	13.90	13.90		9.90	2.80	28.30	80.80
1952	8.10	.10	.60	.30	7.10	39.80	1.30	38.50	13.10	12.50	.60	14.90	7.20	6.10	89.20
1953	2.40	.10	.30	.40	1.60	41.60	.60	41.00	8.70	7.60	1.10	17.40	7.80	6.40	84.30
1954	4.30		.30	1.40	2.60	45.00		49.00	11.00	8.20	2.80	27.10	10.40	11.20	113.00
1955	1.90		.30	.40	1.20	56.60		56.60	12.30	10.80	1.50	31.70	12.00	15.30	129.80
1956	4.90		.30	1.10	3.50	58.50	1.80	56.70	12.60	11.10	1.50	35.50	12.40	12.80	136.70
1957	1.60		.10		1.50	59.30	1.30	58.00	11.80	9.90	1.90	35.40	13.50	15.70	137.30
1958	7.40		.40	.10	6.90	64.20	1.20	63.00	12.00	9.80	2.20	33.90	11.40	9.60	138.50
1959	13.70	4.00	.50	1.20	8.00	70.50	3.10	67.40	9.20	7.20	2.00	33.20	11.80	10.00	148.40
1960	18.00	6.20	.70	5.00	6.10	80.80	2.50	78.30	11.10	8.90	2.20	31.30	13.00	12.30	166.50
1961	12.20	3.60		1.60	7.00	73.30	3.20	70.10	11.20	8.80	2.40	32.80	13.50	25.30	168.30
1962	7.70	3.90		.20	3.60	78.00	2.60	75.40	12.80	10.60	2.20	32.10	14.40	21.00	166.00
1963	13.30	1.70		2.30	9.30	82.00	2.40	79.60	14.90	12.10	2.80	30.80	15.00	25.60	181.60
1964	18.04	3.38	.09	1.12	13.45	116.87	12.89	105.98	15.57	11.93	3.64	45.20	21.31	10.93	229.92
1965	20.00	4.87	.12	5.57	9.44	133.15	18.65	114.50	16.43	9.80	6.63	54.39	24.48	12.44	260.88
1966	36.41	18.46	.21	1.58	16.16	135.17	20.39	114.78	14.76	8.81	5.95	55.48	26.32	13.49	281.62
1967	43.45	22.69	1.04	3.63	16.09	132.58	19.36	113.22	21.53	9.34	12.19	62.32	27.11	13.63	300.61
1968	40.36	22.93	.52	7.37	9.54	139.33	21.01	118.32	20.50	7.34	13.16	71.47	30.57	14.38	316.61

* EXCLUDING TRADE BETWEEN WEST GERMANY AND EAST GERMANY. SEE EXPLANATORY TEXT.

BEC CATEGORIES AND LARGE ECONOMIC CLASSES

1 FOOD AND BEVERAGES
  11 PRIMARY
    111 FOR INDUSTRY
    112 FOR HOUSEHOLD CONSUMPTION
  12 PROCESSED
    121 FOR INDUSTRY
    122 FOR HOUSEHOLD CONSUMPTION

2 INDUSTRIAL SUPPLIES (NON-FOOD)
  21 PRIMARY
  22 PROCESSED

3 FUELS AND LUBRICANTS
  31 PRIMARY
  32 PROCESSED

4 MACHINERY, EXC. TRANSPORT (W/PARTS)

5 TRANSPORT EQUIPMENT

6 CONSUMER GOODS, N.E.S.

7 GOODS N.E.S. AND NOT SPECIFIED

TABLE IV.BEC-2.M.G
WEST EUROPE'S IMPORTS FROM EAST GERMANY,* 1951-68
(MILLIONS OF CURRENT DOLLARS, C.I.F.)

YEAR	AGGREGATION I. BASIC SNA CLASSES			AGGREGATION II. PRIMARY VS. PROCESSED			TOTAL IMPORTS	RATIO SPECIFIED
	CAPITAL GOODS	INTERMEDIATE GOODS	CONSUMER GOODS	PRIMARY	PROCESSED	NOT SPECIFIED		
1951	9.90	38.30	4.30	13.90	38.60	28.30	80.80	.650
1952	14.90	53.30	14.90	14.50	68.60	6.10	89.20	.932
1953	17.40	50.80	9.70	8.60	69.30	6.40	84.30	.924
1954	27.10	61.40	13.30	8.50	93.30	11.20	113.00	.901
1955	31.70	69.30	13.50	11.10	103.40	15.30	129.80	.882
1956	35.50	72.20	16.20	13.20	110.70	12.80	136.70	.906
1957	35.40	71.10	15.10	11.30	110.30	15.70	137.30	.886
1958	33.90	76.30	18.70	11.40	117.50	9.60	138.50	.931
1959	33.20	84.90	20.30	14.80	123.60	10.00	148.40	.933
1960	31.30	103.10	19.80	18.30	135.90	12.30	166.50	.926
1961	32.80	89.70	20.50	15.60	127.40	25.30	168.30	.850
1962	32.10	94.90	18.00	17.10	127.90	21.00	166.00	.873
1963	30.80	100.90	24.30	16.20	139.80	25.60	181.60	.859
1964	45.20	138.94	34.85	28.29	190.70	10.93	229.92	.952
1965	54.39	160.02	34.04	33.44	215.01	12.44	260.88	.952
1966	55.48	169.97	42.69	47.87	220.27	13.49	281.62	.952
1967	62.32	180.43	44.24	52.43	234.56	13.63	300.61	.955
1968	71.47	190.13	40.63	51.80	250.43	14.38	316.61	.955

* EXCLUDING TRADE BETWEEN WEST GERMANY
  AND EAST GERMANY. SEE EXPLANATORY TEXT.

TABLE IV.BEC-1.M.H
WEST EUROPE'S IMPORTS FROM HUNGARY, 1950-68
(MILLIONS OF CURRENT DOLLARS, C.I.F.)

YEAR	CLASS 1	111	112	121	122	CLASS 2	21	22	CLASS 3	31	32	CLASS 4+5	CLASS 6	CLASS 7	TOTAL IMPORTS
1950	44.10	33.00	2.60	.90	7.60	8.90	2.80	6.10	.30	.30		2.20		24.90	80.40
1951	30.20	20.50	1.70	.60	7.40	11.30	4.00	7.30	.90	.90		3.10		23.40	68.90
1952	37.70	14.40	4.00	4.40	14.90	8.90	.10	8.80	.10		.10	2.60	2.90	9.10	61.30
1953	17.90	8.00	2.00	2.80	5.10	10.00	.10	9.90	.10		.10	4.20	3.70	9.60	45.50
1954	37.30	19.60	5.50	4.20	8.00	10.00	.20	9.80	.50		.50	4.10	3.20	8.30	63.40
1955	58.10	24.10	12.30	4.50	17.20	16.30	.30	16.00	3.00		2.70	4.70	4.10	14.80	101.00
1956	66.80	33.00	12.70	2.90	18.20	27.10	7.50	19.60	2.60		2.60	5.10	4.30	10.10	116.00
1957	50.00	16.70	13.00	3.20	17.10	21.60	7.80	13.80	3.90		3.90	4.30	3.40	9.20	92.40
1958	61.30	21.50	10.60	3.10	26.10	28.80	7.30	21.50	6.70		6.70	4.40	5.20	4.00	110.40
1959	75.20	25.50	11.60	4.50	33.60	34.30	8.80	25.50	7.60	.10	7.50	5.60	5.50	5.10	133.30
1960	82.70	28.00	10.30	5.10	39.30	39.30	11.90	27.40	7.90	.20	7.70	8.80	6.40	7.60	152.70
1961	73.60	22.00	13.50	2.60	35.50	34.10	11.00	23.10	9.30	.50	8.80	5.40	6.80	20.20	149.40
1962	82.80	25.50	14.20	4.10	39.00	44.60	12.90	31.70	12.60	1.80	10.80	7.90	8.80	18.50	175.20
1963	122.10	35.60	19.50	6.20	60.80	56.70	14.30	42.40	14.10	3.40	10.70	7.80	11.90	23.20	235.80
1964	116.15	38.10	20.66	4.88	52.51	77.36	19.80	57.56	11.73	2.48	9.25	13.04	23.28	7.06	248.62
1965	138.59	51.59	25.31	4.72	56.97	86.85	19.36	67.49	9.40	2.31	7.09	11.72	23.48	7.94	277.99
1966	161.86	63.74	25.93	5.68	66.51	97.90	18.88	79.02	13.25	3.31	9.94	15.93	29.07	9.79	327.80
1967	166.14	62.69	29.84	7.48	66.13	96.04	19.40	76.64	19.25	6.94	12.31	17.22	30.35	12.21	341.20
1968	153.57	61.31	23.67	5.13	63.46	105.05	20.24	84.81	22.13	9.06	13.07	20.00	30.47	11.97	343.20

BEC CATEGORIES AND LARGE ECONOMIC CLASSES

1 FOOD AND BEVERAGES
  11 PRIMARY
    111 FOR INDUSTRY
    112 FOR HOUSEHOLD CONSUMPTION
  12 PROCESSED
    121 FOR INDUSTRY
    122 FOR HOUSEHOLD CONSUMPTION

2 INDUSTRIAL SUPPLIES (NON-FOOD)
  21 PRIMARY
  22 PROCESSED

3 FUELS AND LUBRICANTS
  31 PRIMARY
  32 PROCESSED

4 MACHINERY, EXC. TRANSPORT (W/PARTS)

5 TRANSPORT EQUIPMENT

6 CONSUMER GOODS, N.E.S.

7 GOODS N.E.S. AND NOT SPECIFIED

TABLE IV.BEC-2.M.H
WEST EUROPE'S IMPORTS FROM HUNGARY, 1950-68
(MILLIONS OF CURRENT DOLLARS, C.I.F.)

YEAR	AGGREGATION I. BASIC SNA CLASSES			AGGREGATION II. PRIMARY VS. PROCESSED		NOT SPECIFIED	TOTAL IMPORTS	RATIO SPECIFIED
	CAPITAL GOODS	INTERMEDIATE GOODS	CONSUMER GOODS	PRIMARY	PROCESSED			
1950	2.20	43.10	10.20	38.70	16.80	24.90	80.40	.690
1951	3.10	33.30	9.10	27.10	18.40	23.40	68.90	.660
1952	2.60	27.80	21.80	18.50	33.70	9.10	61.30	.852
1953	4.20	20.90	10.80	10.10	25.80	9.60	45.50	.789
1954	4.10	34.30	16.70	25.30	29.80	8.30	63.40	.869
1955	4.70	47.90	33.60	37.00	49.20	14.80	101.00	.853
1956	5.10	65.60	35.20	53.20	52.70	10.10	116.00	.913
1957	4.30	45.40	33.50	37.50	45.70	9.20	92.40	.900
1958	4.40	60.10	41.90	39.40	67.00	4.00	110.40	.964
1959	5.60	71.90	50.70	46.00	82.20	5.10	133.30	.962
1960	8.80	80.30	56.00	50.40	94.70	7.60	152.70	.950
1961	5.40	68.00	55.80	47.00	82.20	20.20	149.40	.865
1962	7.90	86.80	62.00	54.40	102.30	18.50	175.20	.894
1963	7.80	112.60	92.20	72.80	139.80	23.20	235.80	.902
1964	13.04	132.07	96.45	81.04	160.52	7.06	248.62	.972
1965	11.72	152.56	105.76	98.57	171.47	7.94	277.99	.971
1966	15.93	180.57	121.51	111.86	206.15	9.79	327.80	.970
1967	17.22	185.46	126.32	118.87	210.13	12.21	341.20	.964
1968	20.00	193.62	117.60	114.28	216.94	11.97	343.20	.965

TABLE IV.BEC-1.M.P
WEST EUROPE'S IMPORTS FROM POLAND, 1950-68
(MILLIONS OF CURRENT DOLLARS, C.I.F.)

YEAR	CLASS 1	111	112	121	122	CLASS 2	21	22	CLASS 3	31	32	CLASS 4+5	CLASS 6	CLASS 7	TOTAL IMPORTS
1950	67.60	18.30	7.80	.40	41.10	20.40	.30	20.10	130.50	130.50		1.20	.10	28.10	247.90
1951	77.30	12.90	5.90	1.60	56.90	16.50	4.50	12.00	207.40	207.40		.20	.30	23.90	325.60
1952	77.70	11.30	10.30	2.70	53.40	23.80	1.30	22.50	150.50	150.00	.50	.10		5.10	257.20
1953	87.60	11.30	14.70	1.40	60.20	26.90	1.50	25.40	114.60	114.00	.60	.30	.10	5.40	234.90
1954	53.40	2.10	9.60	1.00	40.70	43.80	.10	43.70	97.50	96.70	.80	.80	.20	5.10	200.80
1955	55.60	1.20	13.60	.90	39.90	58.90	1.20	57.70	135.50	133.90	1.60	2.40	.10	11.30	263.80
1956	75.30	8.80	14.60	.80	51.10	69.50	9.00	60.50	164.10	161.90	2.20	3.90	.30	6.30	319.40
1957	76.90	5.80	14.40	.70	56.00	64.70	7.30	57.40	135.60	134.10	1.50	4.70	.80	9.50	292.20
1958	116.50	13.60	17.60	1.40	83.90	75.10	8.40	66.70	112.90	110.30	2.60	4.00	1.60	4.00	314.10
1959	143.90	16.20	25.10	1.40	101.20	95.30	13.50	81.80	92.60	87.90	4.70	4.30	2.40	6.40	344.90
1960	156.10	20.20	27.70	1.80	106.40	111.80	18.90	92.90	96.60	91.90	4.70	7.30	2.70	8.90	383.40
1961	179.50	22.70	34.90	1.70	120.20	100.20	16.20	84.00	95.10	89.60	5.50	5.50	2.00	18.90	401.20
1962	182.00	23.90	37.90	.80	119.40	128.40	24.50	103.90	101.20	92.00	9.20	8.30	3.00	20.80	443.70
1963	189.50	32.20	31.00	1.40	124.90	130.40	23.20	107.20	102.30	92.00	10.30	7.10	4.30	25.80	459.40
1964	206.54	34.08	23.30	1.31	147.85	174.57	34.78	139.79	114.04	104.41	9.63	10.96	11.81	7.54	525.45
1965	236.89	42.31	39.16	1.49	153.93	191.69	44.91	146.78	117.21	103.95	13.26	14.51	15.56	9.66	585.53
1966	248.52	48.59	34.02	2.99	162.92	221.75	55.54	166.21	110.13	103.64	6.49	20.17	18.01	11.56	630.11
1967	249.89	42.18	29.51	6.53	171.67	206.44	44.45	161.99	117.99	109.55	8.44	26.17	19.52	12.52	632.53
1968	237.77	47.17	23.27	7.50	159.83	221.43	63.06	158.37	140.96	126.45	14.51	34.23	24.70	12.26	671.36

BEC CATEGORIES AND LARGE ECONOMIC CLASSES

1 FOOD AND BEVERAGES
  11 PRIMARY
     111 FOR INDUSTRY
     112 FOR HOUSEHOLD CONSUMPTION
  12 PROCESSED
     121 FOR INDUSTRY
     122 FOR HOUSEHOLD CONSUMPTION

2 INDUSTRIAL SUPPLIES (NON-FOOD)
  21 PRIMARY
  22 PROCESSED

3 FUELS AND LUBRICANTS
  31 PRIMARY
  32 PROCESSED

4 MACHINERY, EXC. TRANSPORT (W/PARTS)

5 TRANSPORT EQUIPMENT

6 CONSUMER GOODS, N.E.S.

7 GOODS N.E.S. AND NOT SPECIFIED

TABLE IV.BEC-2.M.P
WEST EUROPE'S IMPORTS FROM POLAND, 1950-68
(MILLIONS OF CURRENT DOLLARS, C.I.F.)

| | AGGREGATION I. BASIC SNA CLASSES | | | AGGREGATION II. PRIMARY VS. PROCESSED | | | | |
YEAR	CAPITAL GOODS	INTERMEDIATE GOODS	CONSUMER GOODS	PRIMARY	PROCESSED	NOT SPECIFIED	TOTAL IMPORTS	RATIO SPECIFIED
1950	1.20	169.60	49.00	156.90	62.90	28.10	247.90	.887
1951	.20	238.40	63.10	230.70	71.00	23.90	325.60	.927
1952	.10	188.30	63.70	172.90	79.20	5.10	257.20	.980
1953	.30	154.20	75.00	141.50	88.00	5.40	234.90	.977
1954	.80	144.40	50.50	108.50	87.20	5.10	200.80	.975
1955	2.40	196.50	53.60	149.90	102.60	11.30	263.80	.957
1956	3.90	243.20	66.00	194.30	118.80	6.30	319.40	.980
1957	4.70	206.80	71.20	161.60	121.10	9.50	292.20	.967
1958	4.00	203.00	103.10	149.90	160.20	4.00	314.10	.987
1959	4.30	205.50	128.70	142.70	195.80	6.40	344.90	.981
1960	7.30	230.40	136.80	158.70	215.80	8.90	383.40	.977
1961	5.50	219.70	157.10	163.40	218.90	18.90	401.20	.953
1962	8.30	254.30	160.30	178.30	244.60	20.80	443.70	.953
1963	7.10	266.30	160.20	178.40	255.20	25.80	459.40	.944
1964	10.96	324.00	182.96	196.57	321.35	7.54	525.45	.986
1965	14.51	352.70	208.65	230.33	345.53	9.66	585.53	.984
1966	20.14	383.46	214.95	241.79	376.76	11.56	630.11	.982
1967	26.17	373.14	220.70	225.69	394.32	12.52	632.53	.980
1968	34.23	417.06	207.80	259.95	399.14	12.26	671.36	.982

TABLE IV.BEC-1.M.R
WEST EUROPE'S IMPORTS FROM RUMANIA, 1950-68
(MILLIONS OF CURRENT DOLLARS, C.I.F.)

YEAR	CLASS 1	111	112	121	122	CLASS 2	21	22	CLASS 3	31	32	CLASS 4+5	CLASS 6	CLASS 7	TOTAL IMPORTS
1950	5.90	4.00	1.00		.90	1.50	1.30	.20						5.60	13.00
1951	11.20	10.40	.40		.40	2.00	1.20	.80						9.10	22.30
1952	10.50	9.60	.80	.10	.10	2.70	.40	2.30	11.80		11.80			1.20	26.20
1953	14.30	13.60	.50		.10	4.00	1.50	2.50	28.30		28.30			2.10	48.70
1954	12.60	10.90	.10	1.20	.40	16.60	4.80	11.80	39.50		39.50			2.00	70.70
1955	19.50	16.60	.40	1.70	.80	25.60	7.50	18.10	42.30		42.30	.20		2.60	90.20
1956	33.70	26.30	3.40	2.00	2.00	18.80	6.50	12.30	33.60		33.60	.20		1.30	87.60
1957	13.00	5.60	4.60	1.40	1.40	30.40	10.10	20.30	37.70		37.70	.30		2.00	83.40
1958	22.70	13.40	4.60	1.20	3.50	35.00	10.00	25.00	32.40		32.40	.10		.90	91.10
1959	11.10	3.60	2.90	1.70	2.90	33.80	10.20	23.60	32.60		32.60	2.00		.70	80.20
1960	42.00	21.20	5.10	6.20	9.50	53.60	13.70	39.90	37.90		37.90	.40	.10	2.40	136.30
1961	64.70	41.70	4.80	11.90	6.30	63.00	15.00	48.00	43.70		43.70	.10		6.90	178.50
1962	64.90	42.50	7.40	7.60	7.40	64.50	16.90	47.60	46.80		46.80	.20	.60	7.70	184.70
1963	78.00	47.40	10.60	5.80	14.20	91.90	17.50	74.40	52.30		52.30	.50	.90	8.00	231.60
1964	85.23	49.93	8.15	6.11	21.04	95.86	18.91	76.95	49.14	2.17	46.97	1.04	3.38	.92	235.56
1965	105.66	48.41	14.46	9.57	33.22	105.00	16.76	88.24	45.25	3.42	41.83	1.58	4.04	5.02	266.55
1966	105.70	40.24	15.30	8.06	42.10	138.60	16.26	122.34	55.72	3.22	52.50	3.31	6.89	2.98	313.20
1967	180.27	85.88	19.33	13.27	61.79	132.95	17.64	115.31	50.47	3.83	46.64	4.49	11.45	2.55	382.17
1968	134.84	44.64	22.97	14.86	52.37	146.78	19.64	127.14	68.46	4.48	63.98	18.15	19.06	4.54	391.82

BEC CATEGORIES AND LARGE ECONOMIC CLASSES

1 FOOD AND BEVERAGES
  11 PRIMARY
    111 FOR INDUSTRY
    112 FOR HOUSEHOLD CONSUMPTION
  12 PROCESSED
    121 FOR INDUSTRY
    122 FOR HOUSEHOLD CONSUMPTION

2 INDUSTRIAL SUPPLIES (NON-FOOD)
  21 PRIMARY
  22 PROCESSED

3 FUELS AND LUBRICANTS
  31 PRIMARY
  32 PROCESSED

4 MACHINERY, EXC. TRANSPORT (W/PARTS)

5 TRANSPORT EQUIPMENT

6 CONSUMER GOODS, N.E.S.

7 GOODS N.E.S. AND NOT SPECIFIED

TABLE IV.BEC-2.M.R
WEST EUROPE'S IMPORTS FROM RUMANIA, 1950-68
(MILLIONS OF CURRENT DOLLARS, C.I.F.)

YEAR	AGGREGATION I. BASIC SNA CLASSES			AGGREGATION II. PRIMARY VS. PROCESSED		NOT SPECIFIED	TOTAL IMPORTS	RATIO SPECIFIED
	CAPITAL GOODS	INTERMEDIATE GOODS	CONSUMER GOODS	PRIMARY	PROCESSED			
1950	0.00	5.50	1.90	6.30	1.10	5.60	13.00	.569
1951	0.00	12.40	.80	12.00	1.20	9.10	22.30	.592
1952	0.00	24.10	.90	10.80	14.20	1.20	26.20	.954
1953	0.00	46.00	.60	15.60	31.00	2.10	48.70	.957
1954	0.00	68.20	.50	15.80	52.90	2.00	70.70	.972
1955	.20	86.20	1.20	24.50	63.10	2.60	90.20	.971
1956	.20	80.70	5.40	36.20	50.10	1.30	87.60	.985
1957	.30	75.10	6.00	20.30	61.10	2.00	83.40	.976
1958	.10	82.00	8.10	28.00	62.20	.90	91.10	.990
1959	2.00	71.70	5.80	16.70	62.80	.70	80.20	.991
1960	.40	118.90	14.60	40.00	93.90	2.40	136.30	.982
1961	.10	160.30	11.20	61.50	110.10	6.90	178.50	.961
1962	.20	161.40	15.40	66.80	110.20	7.70	184.70	.958
1963	.50	197.40	25.70	75.50	148.10	8.00	231.60	.965
1964	1.04	201.04	32.57	79.16	155.49	.92	235.56	.996
1965	1.58	208.23	51.72	83.05	178.48	5.02	266.55	.981
1966	3.31	242.62	64.29	75.02	235.20	2.98	313.20	.990
1967	4.49	282.57	92.57	126.68	252.95	2.55	382.17	.993
1968	18.15	274.74	94.40	91.73	295.56	4.54	391.82	.988

TABLE IV.BEC-1.M.CEMA
WEST EUROPE'S IMPORTS FROM EUROPEAN CEMA* (EXCLUDING ALBANIA), 1950-68
(MILLIONS OF CURRENT DOLLARS, C.I.F.)

YEAR	CLASS 1	111	112	121	122	CLASS 2	21	22	CLASS 3	31	32	CLASS 4+5	CLASS 6	CLASS 7	TOTAL IMPORTS
1950	231.50	139.80	17.30	7.20	67.20	138.60	39.80	98.80	152.60	148.40	4.20	32.20	.40	178.10	733.40**
1951	309.50	186.40	16.80	10.10	96.20	212.10	85.30	126.80	247.30	243.90	3.40	34.80	3.70	185.90	993.30
1952	431.60	261.70	28.00	19.60	122.30	244.90	73.90	171.00	217.80	191.00	26.80	36.50	13.20	44.00	988.00
1953	287.70	145.50	27.40	12.70	102.10	290.10	92.50	197.60	193.00	144.20	48.80	45.20	15.40	80.90	912.30
1954	238.00	114.30	26.00	17.80	80.20	435.40	137.00	298.40	222.80	135.80	87.00	56.70	20.20	54.50	1027.60
1955	239.00	97.30	35.10	17.20	89.40	599.80	179.30	420.50	291.20	192.10	99.10	76.00	27.40	85.80	1319.20
1956	305.50	131.80	46.00	17.90	109.80	671.90	219.00	452.90	356.80	237.90	118.90	97.40	28.80	59.10	1519.50
1957	292.00	110.80	50.50	15.40	115.60	735.40	240.30	495.10	419.40	234.50	184.90	108.30	26.90	74.00	1656.00
1958	352.30	116.70	51.10	14.90	169.60	738.40	219.80	518.20	380.60	216.60	164.00	89.00	30.90	30.70	1621.50
1959	446.40	172.10	58.40	18.60	197.30	833.60	279.70	553.90	413.80	229.50	184.30	106.50	34.80	36.80	1871.90
1960	485.90	179.60	62.20	31.60	212.50	991.90	347.20	644.70	481.70	264.80	216.90	117.10	34.00	55.60	2166.20
1961	573.30	241.40	73.60	31.40	226.90	956.40	323.90	632.50	509.90	291.20	218.70	120.30	37.70	134.40	2332.00
1962	559.50	209.00	86.00	32.70	231.90	1079.00	339.30	739.70	566.40	314.20	252.20	129.20	44.10	112.90	2491.20
1963	672.50	210.80	89.00	34.30	318.40	1160.70	355.20	805.50	643.60	372.20	276.40	123.00	51.50	136.60	2792.90
1964	601.47	161.27	75.38	42.38	322.44	1354.56	356.99	997.57	698.67	424.21	274.46	173.94	90.20	55.48	2974.31
1965	749.21	214.05	131.70	61.69	341.77	1617.28	441.15	1176.13	698.99	415.72	283.27	192.32	100.75	65.45	3424.01
1966	816.53	233.00	124.48	66.16	392.89	1777.32	514.84	1262.48	787.84	458.18	329.66	213.87	120.27	73.69	3789.46
1967	951.08	308.42	117.48	98.14	427.04	1720.23	483.08	1237.15	903.50	548.20	355.30	239.33	135.88	82.35	4032.36
1968	899.92	294.31	114.14	86.79	404.68	1818.57	481.42	1337.15	952.59	545.11	407.48	294.51	158.08	79.71	4203.40

* EXCLUDING TRADE BETWEEN WEST GERMANY
  AND EAST GERMANY. SEE EXPLANATORY TEXT.

** TOTAL AND COMPONENTS EXCLUDE EAST GERMANY.

BEC CATEGORIES AND LARGE ECONOMIC CLASSES

1 FOOD AND BEVERAGES
   11 PRIMARY
       111 FOR INDUSTRY
       112 FOR HOUSEHOLD CONSUMPTION
   12 PROCESSED
       121 FOR INDUSTRY
       122 FOR HOUSEHOLD CONSUMPTION

2 INDUSTRIAL SUPPLIES (NON-FOOD)
   21 PRIMARY
   22 PROCESSED

3 FUELS AND LUBRICANTS
   31 PRIMARY
   32 PROCESSED

4 MACHINERY, EXC. TRANSPORT (W/PARTS)

5 TRANSPORT EQUIPMENT

6 CONSUMER GOODS, N.E.S.

7 GOODS N.E.S. AND NOT SPECIFIED

TABLE IV.BEC-2.M.CEMA
WEST EUROPE'S IMPORTS FROM EUROPEAN CEMA* (EXCLUDING ALBANIA), 1950-68
(MILLIONS OF CURRENT DOLLARS, C.I.F.)

YEAR	AGGREGATION I. BASIC SNA CLASSES			AGGREGATION II. PRIMARY VS. PROCESSED		NOT SPECIFIED	TOTAL IMPORTS	RATIO SPECIFIED
	CAPITAL GOODS	INTERMEDIATE GOODS	CONSUMER GOODS	PRIMARY	PROCESSED			
1950	32.20	438.20	84.90	345.30	210.00	178.10	733.40**	.757
1951	34.80	655.90	116.70	532.40	275.00	185.90	993.30	.813
1952	36.50	744.00	163.50	554.60	389.40	44.00	988.00	.955
1953	45.20	641.30	144.90	409.60	421.80	80.90	912.30	.911
1954	56.70	790.00	126.40	412.80	560.30	54.50	1027.60	.947
1955	76.00	1005.50	151.90	503.80	729.60	85.80	1319.20	.935
1956	97.40	1178.40	184.60	634.70	825.70	59.10	1519.50	.961
1957	108.30	1280.70	193.00	636.10	945.90	74.00	1656.00	.955
1958	89.00	1250.20	251.60	604.20	986.60	30.70	1621.50	.981
1959	106.50	1438.10	290.50	739.70	1095.40	36.80	1871.90	.980
1960	117.10	1684.80	308.70	853.80	1256.80	55.60	2166.20	.974
1961	120.30	1739.10	338.20	930.10	1267.50	134.40	2332.00	.942
1962	129.20	1887.10	362.00	948.50	1429.80	112.90	2491.20	.955
1963	123.00	2074.40	458.90	1017.20	1609.10	136.60	2792.90	.951
1964	173.94	2256.88	488.02	1017.85	1900.99	55.48	2974.31	.981
1965	192.32	2592.01	574.22	1202.62	2155.93	65.45	3424.01	.981
1966	213.87	2864.32	637.64	1330.50	2385.33	73.69	3789.46	.981
1967	239.33	3030.29	680.40	1457.18	2492.84	82.35	4032.36	.980
1968	294.51	3152.26	676.90	1434.98	2688.69	79.71	4203.40	.981

* EXCLUDING TRADE BETWEEN WEST GERMANY AND EAST GERMANY. SEE EXPLANATORY TEXT.

** TOTAL AND COMPONENTS EXCLUDE EAST GERMANY.

TABLE IV.BEC-1.X.U
WEST EUROPE'S EXPORTS TO USSR, 1950-68
(MILLIONS OF CURRENT DOLLARS, F.O.B.)

YEAR	CLASS 1	111	112	121	122	CLASS 2	21	22	CLASS 3	31	32	CLASS 4+5	CLASS 6	CLASS 7	TOTAL EXPORTS
1950	7.50		2.10	5.40		41.70	2.20	39.50				123.20		3.70	176.10
1951	16.50		7.40	9.10		72.00	6.40	65.60				133.60		6.00	228.10
1952	28.10		10.30	7.10	10.70	116.00	1.80	114.20				91.90	8.70	4.50	249.20
1953	65.50		17.50	9.70	38.30	123.10	3.30	119.80				106.60	9.10	2.40	306.70
1954	81.10	2.10	24.40	14.40	40.20	137.00	10.40	126.60				145.10	15.10	8.00	386.30
1955	60.10		22.00	14.70	23.40	124.80	4.20	120.60				184.10	3.20	6.90	379.10
1956	45.50		27.20	14.80	3.50	217.00	4.80	212.20				215.80	3.90	9.60	491.80
1957	78.20	.30	27.30	15.30	35.60	257.00	5.70	251.30				208.40	11.60	15.20	570.40
1958	53.80	.30	27.30	17.00	9.20	266.20	18.70	247.50				183.50	11.90	10.60	526.00
1959	41.00	1.30	22.20	11.90	5.60	280.50	12.50	268.00				246.70	14.30	17.50	600.00
1960	38.80		22.40	11.20	5.20	373.80	19.60	354.20	.10		.10	360.20	19.20	15.60	807.60
1961	30.70		13.10	11.30	6.30	357.90	19.63	338.30	.20		.20	399.90	19.20	32.10	839.90
1962	51.50		18.00	9.20	24.30	450.60	20.40	430.20	1.30		1.30	483.10	19.30	23.80	1028.50
1963	53.90		23.00	24.20	6.70	396.60	23.10	373.50	.45		.45	426.60	19.90	22.50	920.80
1964	100.03	1.46	32.79	37.78	28.00	327.94	31.78	296.16				430.40	23.83	7.58	890.22
1965	100.88	6.88	32.04	26.32	35.64	397.37	40.36	357.01	.85		.85	390.81	45.92	8.82	944.65
1966	86.90	12.02	39.90	21.16	13.82	384.56	34.16	350.40	.54		.54	375.17	63.98	12.50	923.65
1967	79.34	2.89	44.70	21.92	9.83	545.58	39.40	506.18	1.14		1.14	517.16	124.28	13.47	1280.98
1968	83.48	11.12	46.07	15.84	10.45	638.76	34.02	604.74	1.16		1.16	709.29	146.64	11.68	1591.02

BEC CATEGORIES AND LARGE ECONOMIC CLASSES

1 FOOD AND BEVERAGES
  11 PRIMARY
    111 FOR INDUSTRY
    112 FOR HOUSEHOLD CONSUMPTION
  12 PROCESSED
    121 FOR INDUSTRY
    122 FOR HOUSEHOLD CONSUMPTION

2 INDUSTRIAL SUPPLIES (NON-FOOD)
  21 PRIMARY
  22 PROCESSED

3 FUELS AND LUBRICANTS
  31 PRIMARY
  32 PROCESSED

4 MACHINERY, EXC. TRANSPORT (W/PARTS)

5 TRANSPORT EQUIPMENT

6 CONSUMER GOODS, N.E.S.

7 GOODS N.E.S. AND NOT SPECIFIED

TABLE IV.BEC-2.X.U
WEST EUROPE'S EXPORTS TO USSR, 1950-68
(MILLIONS OF CURRENT DOLLARS, F.O.B.)

YEAR	AGGREGATION I. BASIC SNA CLASSES			AGGREGATION II. PRIMARY VS. PROCESSED		NOT SPECIFIED	TOTAL EXPORTS	RATIO SPECIFIED
	CAPITAL GOODS	INTERMEDIATE GOODS	CONSUMER GOODS	PRIMARY	PROCESSED			
1950	123.20	47.10	2.10	4.30	168.10	3.70	176.10	.979
1951	133.60	81.10	7.40	13.80	208.30	6.00	228.10	.974
1952	91.90	123.10	29.70	12.10	232.60	4.50	249.20	.982
1953	106.60	132.80	64.90	20.80	283.50	2.40	306.70	.992
1954	145.10	153.50	79.70	36.90	341.40	8.00	386.30	.979
1955	184.10	139.50	48.60	26.20	346.00	6.90	379.10	.982
1956	215.80	231.80	34.60	32.00	450.20	9.60	491.80	.980
1957	208.40	272.60	74.20	33.00	522.20	15.20	570.40	.973
1958	183.50	283.50	48.40	46.30	469.10	10.60	526.00	.980
1959	246.70	293.70	42.10	36.00	546.50	17.50	600.00	.971
1960	360.70	385.00	46.80	42.00	750.00	15.60	807.60	.981
1961	399.90	369.30	38.60	32.70	775.10	32.10	839.90	.962
1962	483.10	460.00	61.60	38.40	966.30	23.80	1028.50	.977
1963	425.60	422.10	49.60	46.10	852.20	22.50	920.80	.976
1964	430.40	367.63	84.62	66.03	816.62	7.58	890.22	.991
1965	390.81	431.42	113.60	79.28	856.55	8.82	944.65	.991
1966	375.17	418.28	117.70	86.08	825.07	12.50	923.65	.986
1967	517.16	571.53	178.81	86.99	1180.51	13.47	1280.98	.989
1968	709.29	666.88	203.16	91.21	1488.12	11.68	1591.02	.993

TABLE IV.BEC-1.X.B
WEST EUROPE'S EXPORTS TO BULGARIA, 1950-68
(MILLIONS OF CURRENT DOLLARS, F.O.B.)

YEAR	CLASS 1	111	112	121	122	CLASS 2	21	22	CLASS 3	31	32	CLASS 4+5	CLASS 6	CLASS 7	TOTAL EXPORTS
1950	.30		.30			6.00		6.00				4.70		2.00	13.00
1951	.40		.40			2.40	.10	2.30				2.40		.90	6.10
1952	.60	.10	.30	.20		7.00	.50	6.50				2.50	.50	1.00	11.60
1953	3.60	.40	2.40	.80		14.20	.90	13.30				4.30	.40	1.20	23.70
1954	2.20	.40	1.50	.10	.20	9.70	1.10	8.60				4.70	.40	1.00	18.00
1955	1.30		1.10	.10	.10	12.50	1.50	11.00				3.60	.60	2.70	20.70
1956	2.10	.10	1.40	.50	.10	20.50	1.50	19.00				2.70	.90	2.90	29.10
1957	2.20		1.90	.30		28.60	2.40	26.20				4.30	1.20	2.70	39.00
1958	2.40		2.00	.40		26.40	2.80	23.60				5.20	1.60	1.80	37.40
1959	5.30	3.60	.80	.70	.20	67.70	5.80	61.90	.30		.30	19.60	2.50	4.50	99.90
1960	2.70	.20	1.80	.50	.20	50.00	4.50	45.50				20.80	1.70	1.40	76.60
1961	5.50	1.80	1.00	2.30	.40	47.50	3.50	44.00				8.90	1.80	8.50	72.20
1962	8.60	3.60	1.70	3.30		50.80	4.50	46.30				13.40	1.60	6.60	81.00
1963	13.90	4.30	2.80	4.90	1.30	48.60	6.20	42.40				28.10	2.40	8.50	100.90
1964	10.96	3.43	3.43	2.36	1.74	83.00	9.40	73.60	.26		.26	47.75	3.43	1.25	146.65
1965	15.44	4.55	5.56	1.82	3.51	113.67	11.83	101.84	.29		.29	64.70	5.13	2.02	201.25
1966	20.49	11.08	7.52	1.14	.75	150.91	13.09	137.82	.66		.66	139.31	7.90	2.66	321.93
1967	9.83	1.67	5.49	.73	1.94	143.51	11.17	137.34	1.16		1.16	130.81	8.21	3.57	302.10
1968	26.20	15.15	5.68	.41	4.96	146.09	14.56	131.53	1.96		1.96	88.53	7.17	3.74	273.69

BEC CATEGORIES AND LARGE ECONOMIC CLASSES

1 FOOD AND BEVERAGES
   11 PRIMARY
      111 FOR INDUSTRY
      112 FOR HOUSEHOLD CONSUMPTION
   12 PROCESSED
      121 FOR INDUSTRY
      122 FOR HOUSEHOLD CONSUMPTION

2 INDUSTRIAL SUPPLIES (NON-FOOD)
   21 PRIMARY
   22 PROCESSED

3 FUELS AND LUBRICANTS
   31 PRIMARY
   32 PROCESSED

4 MACHINERY, EXC. TRANSPORT (W/PARTS)

5 TRANSPORT EQUIPMENT

6 CONSUMER GOODS, N.E.S.

7 GOODS N.E.S. AND NOT SPECIFIED

TABLE IV.BEC-2.X.B
WEST EUROPE'S EXPORTS TO BULGARIA, 1950-68
(MILLIONS OF CURRENT DOLLARS, F.O.B.)

YEAR	AGGREGATION I. BASIC SNA CLASSES			AGGREGATION II. PRIMARY VS. PROCESSED		NOT SPECIFIED	TOTAL EXPORTS	RATIO SPECIFIED
	CAPITAL GOODS	INTERMEDIATE GOODS	CONSUMER GOODS	PRIMARY	PROCESSED			
1950	4.70	6.00	.30	.30	10.70	2.00	13.00	.846
1951	2.40	2.40	.40	.50	4.70	.90	6.10	.852
1952	2.50	7.30	.80	.90	9.70	1.00	11.60	.914
1953	4.30	15.40	2.80	3.70	18.80	1.20	23.70	.949
1954	4.70	10.20	2.10	3.00	14.00	1.00	18.00	.944
1955	3.60	12.60	1.80	2.60	15.40	2.70	20.70	.870
1956	2.70	21.10	2.40	3.00	23.20	2.90	29.10	.900
1957	4.30	28.90	3.10	4.30	32.00	2.70	39.00	.931
1958	5.20	26.80	3.60	4.80	30.80	1.80	37.40	.952
1959	19.60	72.30	3.50	10.20	85.20	4.50	99.90	.955
1960	20.80	50.70	3.70	6.50	68.70	1.40	76.60	.982
1961	8.90	51.60	3.20	6.30	57.40	8.50	72.20	.882
1962	13.40	57.70	3.30	9.80	64.60	6.60	81.00	.919
1963	28.10	57.80	6.50	13.30	79.10	8.50	100.90	.916
1964	47.75	89.05	8.60	16.26	129.14	1.25	146.65	.991
1965	64.70	120.33	14.20	21.94	177.29	2.02	201.25	.990
1966	139.31	163.79	16.17	31.69	287.58	2.66	321.93	.992
1967	130.81	152.07	15.64	18.33	280.19	3.57	302.10	.988
1968	88.53	163.61	17.81	35.39	234.56	3.74	273.69	.986

TABLE IV.BEC-1.X.C
WEST EUROPE'S EXPORTS TO CZECHOSLOVAKIA, 1950-68
(MILLIONS OF CURRENT DOLLARS, F.O.B.)

YEAR	CLASS 1	111	112	121	122	CLASS 2	21	22	CLASS 3	31	32	CLASS 4+5	CLASS 6	CLASS 7	TOTAL EXPORTS
1950	14.00		8.90	3.90	1.20	104.80	40.30	64.50				39.80		11.00	169.60
1951	20.50		12.80	2.60	5.10	102.00	40.90	61.10				42.50		15.00	180.00
1952	11.60	.30	7.50	2.30	1.50	58.80	20.70	38.10				27.40	5.20	6.50	109.50
1953	18.40	1.60	10.40	1.90	4.50	37.40	15.70	21.70				16.70	2.70	7.60	82.80
1954	42.90	1.00	13.30	3.90	24.70	48.40	21.30	27.10				7.40	3.60	8.20	110.50
1955	36.00	1.10	17.00	2.70	15.20	61.70	25.60	36.10				7.30	5.10	18.00	128.10
1956	28.20	3.80	15.90	4.90	3.60	96.80	30.40	66.40				19.70	5.60	16.20	166.50
1957	26.00	2.30	13.40	4.40	5.90	118.80	37.20	81.60				31.50	8.80	27.10	212.20
1958	22.90	1.60	13.20	5.40	2.70	132.90	38.50	94.40			.30	38.80	7.50	5.90	208.30
1959	21.70	.60	11.50	2.20	7.40	136.80	44.00	92.80			.20	45.90	6.40	6.20	217.20
1960	23.00	.80	12.20	1.70	8.30	176.80	39.30	137.50	1.30	1.20	.10	44.90	7.30	7.10	260.40
1961	34.30	2.43	12.80	3.60	15.50	196.30	41.60	154.70	1.50	1.30	.20	58.10	7.40	15.90	313.50
1962	26.70	2.70	11.40	2.40	10.20	180.50	36.50	144.00	.40	.20	.20	69.90	6.70	14.80	299.00
1963	29.90	5.30	12.20	5.70	6.70	134.10	38.90	95.20	.20		.20	70.40	6.80	20.20	261.60
1964	38.07	11.82	14.11	5.04	7.10	159.78	36.47	123.31	1.12		1.12	81.09	10.53	2.92	293.50
1965	50.16	19.89	19.65	3.95	6.67	199.60	45.98	153.62	2.47	.01	2.46	102.17	14.36	4.81	373.57
1966	65.74	35.76	19.44	3.33	7.21	234.70	45.49	189.21	1.36		1.36	150.55	18.14	5.68	476.17
1967	35.09	6.45	21.36	1.97	5.31	228.87	48.89	179.98	1.99		1.99	133.50	17.96	6.58	423.99
1968	39.14	6.89	21.52	3.26	7.67	252.87	48.15	204.72	2.40		2.40	176.69	25.78	7.85	504.74

BEC CATEGORIES AND LARGE ECONOMIC CLASSES

1 FOOD AND BEVERAGES
   11 PRIMARY
       111 FOR INDUSTRY
       112 FOR HOUSEHOLD CONSUMPTION
   12 PROCESSED
       121 FOR INDUSTRY
       122 FOR HOUSEHOLD CONSUMPTION

2 INDUSTRIAL SUPPLIES (NON-FOOD)
   21 PRIMARY
   22 PROCESSED

3 FUELS AND LUBRICANTS
   31 PRIMARY
   32 PROCESSED

4 MACHINERY, EXC. TRANSPORT (W/PARTS)

5 TRANSPORT EQUIPMENT

6 CONSUMER GOODS, N.E.S.

7 GOODS N.F.S. AND NOT SPECIFIED

TABLE IV.BEC-2.X.C
WEST EUROPE'S EXPORTS TO CZECHOSLOVAKIA, 1950-68
(MILLIONS OF CURRENT DOLLARS, F.O.B.)

YEAR	AGGREGATION I. BASIC SNA CLASSES			AGGREGATION II. PRIMARY VS. PROCESSED		NOT SPECIFIED	TOTAL EXPORTS	RATIO SPECIFIED
	CAPITAL GOODS	INTERMEDIATE GOODS	CONSUMER GOODS	PRIMARY	PROCESSED			
1950	39.80	108.70	10.10	49.20	109.40	11.00	169.60	.935
1951	42.50	104.60	17.90	53.70	111.30	15.00	180.00	.917
1952	27.40	61.40	14.20	28.50	74.50	6.50	109.50	.941
1953	16.70	40.90	17.60	27.70	47.50	7.60	82.80	.908
1954	7.40	53.30	41.60	35.60	66.70	8.20	110.50	.926
1955	7.30	65.50	37.30	43.70	66.40	18.00	128.10	.859
1956	19.70	105.50	25.10	50.10	100.20	16.20	166.50	.903
1957	31.50	125.50	28.10	52.90	132.20	27.10	212.20	.872
1958	38.80	140.20	23.40	53.30	149.10	5.90	208.30	.972
1959	45.90	139.80	25.30	56.10	154.90	6.20	217.20	.971
1960	44.90	180.60	27.80	53.50	199.80	7.10	260.40	.973
1961	58.10	203.80	35.70	58.10	239.50	15.90	313.50	.949
1962	69.90	186.00	28.30	50.80	233.40	14.80	299.00	.951
1963	70.40	145.30	25.70	56.40	185.00	20.20	261.60	.923
1964	81.09	177.76	31.74	62.40	228.19	2.92	293.50	.990
1965	102.17	225.91	40.68	85.53	283.23	4.81	373.57	.987
1966	150.55	275.15	44.79	100.69	369.80	5.68	476.17	.988
1967	133.50	239.28	44.63	76.70	340.71	6.58	423.99	.984
1968	176.69	265.42	54.77	76.36	420.52	7.85	504.74	.984

WEST EUROPE'S EXPORTS TO EAST GERMANY,* 1951-68
TABLE IV.BEC-1.X.G
(MILLIONS OF CURRENT DOLLARS, F.O.B.)

YEAR	CLASS 1	111	112	121	122	CLASS 2	21	22	CLASS 3	31	32	CLASS 4+5	CLASS 6	CLASS 7	TOTAL EXPORTS
1951	34.20		20.30	4.00	9.90	20.90	6.00	14.90				.50		9.20	64.80
1952	36.10		17.60	3.20	15.30	29.60	9.00	20.60				1.00	4.80	6.30	77.80
1953	42.50		19.40	3.50	19.60	35.60	10.00	25.60				2.30	4.00	8.30	92.70
1954	74.10	3.40	22.90	3.90	43.90	51.70	21.40	30.30				2.20	4.30	9.10	141.40
1955	52.90	2.30	22.60	4.90	23.10	57.30	25.10	32.20				2.50	4.40	11.20	128.30
1956	45.90	2.10	23.90	6.80	13.10	67.70	26.80	40.90				5.00	3.80	8.10	130.50
1957	40.40	1.80	21.80	6.30	10.50	73.90	31.20	42.70				5.40	4.60	11.60	135.90
1958	40.10	2.30	23.70	5.20	8.90	78.40	27.50	50.90	.10		.10	13.20	3.90	3.00	138.70
1959	40.50	2.80	20.50	3.40	13.80	78.10	21.80	56.30	.10		.10	11.70	4.00	3.30	137.70
1960	41.10	1.40	19.80	4.00	15.90	105.30	21.60	83.70	.40		.40	17.50	2.90	6.10	173.30
1961	37.90	.50	14.80	3.20	19.40	111.30	25.30	86.00	.40		.40	20.60	2.70	9.60	182.50
1962	51.60	2.40	14.50	4.20	30.50	69.20	15.90	53.30	.30		.30	35.00	1.60	9.50	167.20
1963	40.00	3.00	15.40	3.00	18.60	75.90	19.20	56.70	.40	.10	.30	43.30	2.00	13.00	174.60
1964	60.79	17.05	15.19	3.36	25.19	85.09	25.16	59.93	1.80		1.80	39.95	3.46	1.40	192.49
1965	99.25	56.97	18.51	4.00	19.77	115.57	30.59	84.98	1.08		1.08	54.55	5.03	1.91	277.38
1966	80.60	41.28	23.06	3.52	12.74	144.09	36.29	107.80	1.06	.42	.64	102.49	4.99	1.74	334.98
1967	53.67	6.64	24.69	3.64	18.70	137.35	33.96	103.39	2.11	1.39	.72	111.13	6.99	2.61	313.85
1968	34.53	5.57	19.71	3.39	5.86	139.74	34.71	105.03	.64		.64	86.87	7.37	1.51	270.66

* EXCLUDING TRADE BETWEEN WEST GERMANY AND EAST GERMANY. SEE EXPLANATORY TEXT.

BEC CATEGORIES AND LARGE ECONOMIC CLASSES

1 FOOD AND BEVERAGES
　11 PRIMARY
　　111 FOR INDUSTRY
　　112 FOR HOUSEHOLD CONSUMPTION
　12 PROCESSED
　　121 FOR INDUSTRY
　　122 FOR HOUSEHOLD CONSUMPTION

2 INDUSTRIAL SUPPLIES (NON-FOOD)
　21 PRIMARY
　22 PROCESSED

3 FUELS AND LUBRICANTS
　31 PRIMARY
　32 PROCESSED

4 MACHINERY, EXC. TRANSPORT (W/PARTS)

5 TRANSPORT EQUIPMENT

6 CONSUMER GOODS, N.E.S.

7 GOODS N.E.S. AND NOT SPECIFIED

TABLE IV.BEC-2.X.G
WEST EUROPE'S EXPORTS TO EAST GERMANY,* 1951-68
(MILLIONS OF CURRENT DOLLARS, F.O.B.)

YEAR	AGGREGATION I. BASIC SNA CLASSES			AGGREGATION II. PRIMARY VS. PROCESSED		NOT SPECIFIED	TOTAL EXPORTS	RATIO SPECIFIED
	CAPITAL GOODS	INTERMEDIATE GOODS	CONSUMER GOODS	PRIMARY	PROCESSED			
1951	.50	24.90	30.20	26.30	29.30	9.20	64.80	.858
1952	1.00	32.80	37.70	26.60	44.90	6.30	77.80	.919
1953	2.30	39.10	43.00	29.40	55.00	8.30	92.70	.910
1954	2.20	59.00	71.10	47.70	84.60	9.10	141.40	.936
1955	2.50	64.50	50.10	50.00	67.10	11.20	128.30	.913
1956	5.00	76.60	40.80	52.80	69.60	8.10	130.50	.938
1957	5.40	82.00	36.90	54.80	69.50	11.60	135.90	.915
1958	13.20	86.00	36.50	53.50	82.20	3.00	138.70	.978
1959	11.70	84.40	38.30	45.10	89.30	3.30	137.70	.976
1960	17.50	111.10	38.60	42.80	124.40	6.10	173.30	.965
1961	20.60	115.40	36.90	40.60	132.30	9.60	182.50	.947
1962	35.00	76.10	46.60	32.80	124.90	9.50	167.20	.943
1963	43.30	82.30	36.00	37.70	123.90	13.00	174.60	.926
1964	39.95	107.30	43.84	57.40	133.69	1.40	192.49	.993
1965	54.55	177.62	43.31	106.07	169.41	1.91	277.38	.993
1966	102.49	189.95	40.79	101.05	232.18	1.74	334.98	.995
1967	111.13	149.74	50.38	66.68	244.57	2.61	313.85	.992
1968	86.87	149.34	32.94	59.99	209.16	1.51	270.66	.994

* EXCLUDING TRADE BETWEEN WEST GERMANY AND EAST GERMANY. SEE EXPLANATORY TEXT.

TABLE IV.BEC-1.X.H
WEST EUROPE'S EXPORTS TO HUNGARY, 1950-68
(MILLIONS OF CURRENT DOLLARS, F.O.B.)

YEAR	CLASS 1	111	112	121	122	CLASS 2	21	22	CLASS 3	31	32	CLASS 4+5	CLASS 6	CLASS 7	TOTAL EXPORTS
1950	.90		.60	.30		57.10	12.30	44.80				24.70		7.60	90.30
1951	1.10		.80	.30		47.10	15.90	31.20				16.50		9.60	74.30
1952	2.60	.50	.60	1.20	.30	39.80	11.40	28.40				14.10	4.40	5.70	66.60
1953	4.90	.40	1.50	1.40	1.60	39.40	15.10	24.30				10.70	3.20	9.60	67.80
1954	17.70	11.10	1.20	1.60	3.80	50.70	14.10	36.60				9.30	3.60	12.70	94.00
1955	44.70	30.30	2.80	5.50	6.10	77.70	17.60	60.10				8.00	4.00	16.80	151.20
1956	24.40	19.00	1.50	1.70	2.20	67.90	12.10	55.80				8.20	2.10	10.90	113.50
1957	25.20	10.70	2.90	2.60	9.00	69.90	12.70	57.20				14.20	3.60	9.30	122.20
1958	5.60		2.80	2.40	.40	77.70	16.30	61.40				18.40	4.00	3.90	109.60
1959	6.90	1.00	2.50	1.90	1.50	97.50	20.20	77.30				29.10	5.70	6.10	145.30
1960	10.30	1.40	3.20	3.30	2.40	123.30	21.70	101.60				38.30	5.30	7.20	184.40
1961	12.80	2.00	2.00	2.30	6.50	113.20	19.70	93.50				34.60	4.50	19.90	185.00
1962	25.80	8.00	4.40	3.60	9.80	106.70	19.40	87.30				37.40	5.70	22.00	197.60
1963	37.20	18.80	4.00	2.90	11.50	125.20	21.50	103.70	.60	.10	.50	51.60	6.50	29.80	250.90
1964	22.87	6.91	4.90	6.91	4.15	157.66	26.72	130.94	1.23	.01	1.22	68.05	10.42	3.07	263.25
1965	28.12	6.13	5.94	7.70	8.35	158.24	28.05	130.19	.78		.78	65.51	12.02	3.35	268.02
1966	29.79	5.33	10.71	7.96	5.74	176.13	34.98	141.15	.55		.55	82.68	14.43	4.65	308.22
1967	25.65	2.99	8.07	3.89	10.70	196.63	38.08	158.55	.66		.66	109.98	17.53	5.34	355.79
1968	18.68	1.14	7.29	2.77	7.48	219.06	34.48	184.58	.73		.73	87.40	17.93	5.32	349.11

BEC CATEGORIES AND LARGE ECONOMIC CLASSES

1 FOOD AND BEVERAGES
  11 PRIMARY
    111 FOR INDUSTRY
    112 FOR HOUSEHOLD CONSUMPTION
  12 PROCESSED
    121 FOR INDUSTRY
    122 FOR HOUSEHOLD CONSUMPTION

2 INDUSTRIAL SUPPLIES (NON-FOOD)
  21 PRIMARY
  22 PROCESSED

3 FUELS AND LUBRICANTS
  31 PRIMARY
  32 PROCESSED

4 MACHINERY, EXC. TRANSPORT (W/PARTS)

5 TRANSPORT EQUIPMENT

6 CONSUMER GOODS, N.E.S.

7 GOODS N.E.S. AND NOT SPECIFIED

TABLE IV.BEC-2.X.H
WEST EUROPE'S EXPORTS TO HUNGARY, 1950-68
(MILLIONS OF CURRENT DOLLARS, F.O.B.)

YEAR	AGGREGATION I. BASIC SNA CLASSES			AGGREGATION II. PRIMARY VS. PROCESSED		NOT SPECIFIED	TOTAL EXPORTS	RATIO SPECIFIED
	CAPITAL GOODS	INTERMEDIATE GOODS	CONSUMER GOODS	PRIMARY	PROCESSED			
1950	24.70	57.40	.60	12.90	69.80	7.60	90.30	.916
1951	16.50	47.40	.80	16.70	48.00	9.60	74.30	.871
1952	14.10	41.50	5.30	12.50	48.40	5.70	66.60	.914
1953	10.70	41.20	6.30	17.00	41.20	9.60	67.80	.858
1954	9.30	63.40	8.60	26.40	54.90	12.70	94.00	.865
1955	8.00	113.50	12.90	50.70	83.70	16.80	151.20	.889
1956	8.20	88.60	5.80	32.60	70.00	10.90	113.50	.904
1957	14.20	83.20	15.50	26.30	86.60	9.30	122.20	.924
1958	18.40	80.10	7.20	19.10	86.60	3.90	109.60	.964
1959	29.10	100.40	9.70	23.70	115.50	6.10	145.30	.958
1960	38.30	128.00	10.90	26.30	150.90	7.20	184.40	.961
1961	34.60	117.50	13.00	23.70	141.40	19.90	185.00	.892
1962	37.40	118.30	19.90	31.80	143.80	22.00	197.60	.889
1963	51.60	147.50	22.00	44.40	176.70	79.80	250.90	.881
1964	68.05	172.71	19.47	38.54	221.69	3.02	263.25	.989
1965	65.51	172.85	26.31	40.12	224.55	3.35	268.02	.988
1966	82.68	190.02	30.88	51.07	252.51	4.65	308.22	.985
1967	109.98	204.17	36.30	49.14	301.31	5.34	355.79	.985
1968	87.40	223.70	32.70	42.91	300.89	5.32	349.11	.985

TABLE IV.BEC-1.X.P
WEST EUROPE'S EXPORTS TO POLAND, 1950-68
(MILLIONS OF CURRENT DOLLARS, F.O.B.)

YEAR	CLASS 1	111	112	121	122	CLASS 2	21	22	CLASS 3	31	32	CLASS 4+5	CLASS 6	CLASS 7	TOTAL EXPORTS
1950	9.10	4.70	1.60	2.80		73.90	27.50	46.40				67.60		13.90	164.50
1951	6.90	3.90	1.20	1.80		101.00	31.50	69.50				89.30		10.30	207.50
1952	4.90	.50	1.70	2.00	.70	79.10	29.60	49.50				67.60	6.50	13.80	171.90
1953	2.10	1.00	.60	.50		78.80	25.70	53.10				51.00	4.50	17.20	153.60
1954	15.90	10.90	2.10	2.30	.60	89.40	33.70	55.70				38.10	6.70	14.70	164.80
1955	25.20	19.80	2.20	3.00	.20	108.30	37.30	71.00				35.30	9.00	19.80	197.60
1956	37.80	32.10	2.90	2.70	.10	141.60	33.00	108.60				47.30	8.90	19.80	255.40
1957	14.00	2.10	4.70	2.10	5.10	143.20	44.00	99.20				75.40	14.40	22.00	269.00
1958	6.20	.10	3.60	1.40	1.10	158.30	39.50	118.80	.20		.20	97.30	14.60	12.00	288.60
1959	13.50	.10	4.10	1.80	7.50	129.10	33.80	95.30	.40		.40	112.00	12.10	11.90	279.00
1960	9.40	.10	5.10	2.40	1.80	153.00	36.50	116.50	2.50	2.10	.40	97.10	10.50	13.90	286.40
1961	16.20	7.80	5.40	2.30	.70	173.70	37.60	136.10	1.40	.60	.80	101.20	8.80	19.40	320.70
1962	18.30	13.30	3.30	1.60	.50	163.40	32.70	130.70	1.70	.70	1.00	123.70	11.70	19.20	338.00
1963	49.80	40.70	5.10	1.60	2.40	148.00	35.50	112.50	1.10		1.10	125.40	11.90	29.20	365.40
1964	56.02	40.83	5.54	6.57	3.08	185.09	41.15	143.94	2.14		2.14	98.29	11.45	7.83	360.82
1965	58.75	39.09	9.51	8.84	1.31	238.72	51.80	186.92	2.29		2.29	110.31	16.74	9.40	436.21
1966	71.16	43.85	14.11	11.05	2.15	273.71	52.00	221.71	2.92		2.92	146.19	20.87	10.37	525.24
1967	51.66	30.02	13.35	2.88	5.41	312.28	58.22	254.06	4.92		4.92	206.40	23.75	11.33	610.34
1968	65.40	33.69	14.14	6.34	11.23	313.23	48.07	265.16	5.57	.03	5.54	226.42	26.61	11.77	649.01

BEC CATEGORIES AND LARGE ECONOMIC CLASSES

1 FOOD AND BEVERAGES
　11 PRIMARY
　　111 FOR INDUSTRY
　　112 FOR HOUSEHOLD CONSUMPTION
　12 PROCESSED
　　121 FOR INDUSTRY
　　122 FOR HOUSEHOLD CONSUMPTION

2 INDUSTRIAL SUPPLIES (NON-FOOD)
　21 PRIMARY
　22 PROCESSED

3 FUELS AND LUBRICANTS
　31 PRIMARY
　32 PROCESSED

4 MACHINERY, EXC. TRANSPORT (W/PARTS)

5 TRANSPORT EQUIPMENT

6 CONSUMER GOODS, N.E.S.

7 GOODS N.E.S. AND NOT SPECIFIED

TABLE IV.BEC-2.X.P
WEST EUROPE'S EXPORTS TO POLAND, 1950-68
(MILLIONS OF CURRENT DOLLARS, F.O.B.)

YEAR	AGGREGATION I. BASIC SNA CLASSES			AGGREGATION II. PRIMARY VS. PROCESSED		NOT SPECIFIED	TOTAL EXPORTS	RATIO SPECIFIED
	CAPITAL GOODS	INTERMEDIATE GOODS	CONSUMER GOODS	PRIMARY	PROCESSED			
1950	67.60	81.40	1.60	33.80	116.80	13.90	164.50	.916
1951	89.30	106.70	1.20	36.60	160.60	10.30	207.50	.950
1952	67.60	81.60	8.90	31.80	126.30	13.80	171.90	.920
1953	51.00	80.50	5.10	27.30	109.10	17.20	153.60	.888
1954	38.10	102.60	9.40	46.70	103.40	14.70	164.80	.911
1955	35.30	131.10	11.40	59.30	118.50	19.80	197.60	.900
1956	47.30	176.40	11.90	68.00	167.60	19.80	255.40	.922
1957	75.40	147.40	24.20	50.80	196.20	22.00	269.00	.918
1958	97.30	160.00	19.30	43.20	233.40	12.00	288.60	.958
1959	112.00	131.40	23.70	38.00	229.10	11.90	279.00	.957
1960	97.10	158.00	17.40	43.80	228.70	13.90	286.40	.951
1961	101.20	185.20	14.90	51.40	249.90	19.40	320.70	.940
1962	123.70	179.60	15.50	50.00	268.80	19.20	338.00	.943
1963	135.40	191.40	19.40	81.30	254.90	29.20	365.40	.920
1964	98.29	234.63	20.07	87.52	265.47	7.83	360.82	.978
1965	110.31	288.94	27.56	100.40	326.41	9.40	436.21	.978
1966	146.19	331.53	37.13	109.96	404.89	10.37	525.24	.980
1967	206.40	350.10	42.51	101.59	497.42	11.33	610.34	.981
1968	226.42	358.83	51.98	95.93	541.30	11.77	649.01	.982

TABLE IV.BEC-1.X.R.
WEST EUROPE'S EXPORTS TO RUMANIA, 1950-68
(MILLIONS OF CURRENT DOLLARS, F.O.B.)

YEAR	CLASS 1	111	112	121	122	CLASS 2	21	22	CLASS 3	31	32	CLASS 4+5	CLASS 6	CLASS 7	TOTAL EXPORTS
1950	.40		.30		.10	7.80	1.10	6.70				14.10		2.20	24.50
1951	.20		.20			14.40	2.10	12.30				11.50		4.80	30.90
1952	.50	.30	.20		.30	27.40	2.20	25.20				12.60	2.30	2.10	44.90
1953	2.40	5.30	1.00		1.10	33.80	2.00	31.80				15.50	1.40	2.70	55.80
1954	12.50		1.30	2.20	3.70	21.80	2.10	19.70				5.70	1.70	2.40	44.10
1955	9.20	3.70	1.80	1.10	2.60	33.10	2.90	30.20				4.20	2.40	3.60	52.50
1956	6.80	.80	2.00	.70	3.30	32.30	3.30	29.00				3.80	2.90	6.00	51.80
1957	16.20	.30	2.00	2.70	11.20	35.80	5.60	30.20				7.80	2.80	4.30	66.90
1958	7.10		1.10	3.60	2.40	44.30	6.40	37.90				10.90	2.40	1.00	65.50
1959	4.40	.50	1.00	1.70	1.20	38.00	5.10	32.90				18.30	2.30	2.90	65.90
1960	4.90	.70	1.80	.10	2.30	75.00	7.90	67.10				41.40	2.70	3.90	127.90
1961	4.50		2.10	.10	2.30	81.10	10.70	70.40				90.60	3.30	13.20	192.70
1962	6.20	.20	2.80	1.30	1.90	81.50	4.80	76.70				115.60	5.00	12.90	221.20
1963	7.10	.20	4.20	.40	2.30	96.30	3.80	92.50	2.90	2.50	.40	97.40	5.50	14.30	223.50
1964	8.90	.13	4.22	.75	3.80	132.09	10.75	121.34	3.26	2.73	.53	106.77	5.44	2.18	258.64
1965	9.43	1.37	4.20	.61	3.25	142.05	15.25	126.80	2.92	2.47	.45	132.99	8.22	1.97	297.57
1966	10.45	.70	5.23	.78	3.74	165.07	18.36	146.71	1.58	.99	.59	166.30	8.65	2.56	354.62
1967	10.87	1.28	4.54	1.04	4.01	218.13	22.95	195.18	1.36	.96	.40	332.89	13.77	3.90	580.92
1968	9.84	1.12	3.00	2.03	3.69	231.91	28.74	203.17	3.65	3.14	.51	314.35	13.84	4.66	578.27

BEC CATEGORIES AND LARGE ECONOMIC CLASSES

1 FOOD AND BEVERAGES
  11 PRIMARY
    111 FOR INDUSTRY
    112 FOR HOUSEHOLD CONSUMPTION
  12 PROCESSED
    121 FOR INDUSTRY
    122 FOR HOUSEHOLD CONSUMPTION

2 INDUSTRIAL SUPPLIES (NON-FOOD)
  21 PRIMARY
  22 PROCESSED

3 FUELS AND LUBRICANTS
  31 PRIMARY
  32 PROCESSED

4 MACHINERY, EXC. TRANSPORT (W/PARTS)

5 TRANSPORT EQUIPMENT

6 CONSUMER GOODS, N.E.S.

7 GOODS N.E.S. AND NOT SPECIFIED

TABLE IV.BEC-2.X.R
WEST EUROPE'S EXPORTS TO RUMANIA, 1950-68
(MILLIONS OF CURRENT DOLLARS, F.O.B.)

YEAR	AGGREGATION I. BASIC SNA CLASSES			AGGREGATION II. PRIMARY VS. PROCESSED		NOT SPECIFIED	TOTAL EXPORTS	RATIO SPECIFIED
	CAPITAL GOODS	INTERMEDIATE GOODS	CONSUMER GOODS	PRIMARY	PROCESSED			
1950	14.10	7.80	.40	1.40	20.90	2.20	24.50	.910
1951	11.50	14.40	.20	2.30	23.80	4.80	30.90	.845
1952	12.60	27.40	2.80	2.40	40.40	2.10	44.90	.953
1953	15.50	34.10	3.50	3.30	49.80	2.70	55.80	.952
1954	5.70	29.30	6.70	8.70	33.00	2.40	44.10	.946
1955	4.20	37.90	6.80	8.40	40.50	3.60	52.50	.931
1956	3.80	33.80	8.20	6.10	39.70	6.00	51.80	.884
1957	7.80	38.80	16.00	7.90	54.70	4.30	66.90	.936
1958	10.90	47.90	5.90	7.50	57.20	1.00	65.70	.985
1959	18.30	40.20	4.50	6.60	56.40	2.90	65.90	.956
1960	41.40	75.80	6.80	10.40	113.60	3.90	127.90	.970
1961	90.60	81.20	7.70	12.80	166.70	13.20	192.70	.931
1962	115.60	83.00	9.70	7.80	200.50	12.90	221.20	.942
1963	97.40	99.80	12.00	10.70	198.50	14.30	223.50	.936
1964	106.77	136.23	13.46	17.83	238.63	2.18	258.64	.992
1965	132.99	146.95	15.67	23.29	272.32	1.97	297.57	.993
1966	166.30	168.13	17.62	25.28	326.77	2.56	354.62	.993
1967	332.89	221.81	22.32	29.73	547.29	3.90	580.92	.993
1968	314.35	238.71	20.53	36.00	537.59	4.66	578.27	.992

TABLE IV.BEC-1.X.CEMA
WEST EUROPE'S EXPORTS TO EUROPEAN CEMA* (EXCLUDING ALBANIA), 1950-68
(MILLIONS OF CURRENT DOLLARS, C.I.F.)

YEAR	CLASS 1	111	112	121	122	CLASS 2	21	22	CLASS 3	31	32	CLASS 4+5	CLASS 6	CLASS 7	TOTAL EXPORTS
1950	32.20	4.70	13.80	12.40	1.30	291.30	83.40	207.90				274.10		40.40	638.00**
1951	79.80	3.90	43.10	17.80	15.00	359.80	102.90	256.90				296.30		55.80	791.70
1952	84.40	1.40	38.20	16.00	28.80	357.70	75.20	282.50				217.10	32.40	39.90	731.50
1953	139.40	3.70	52.80	17.80	28.80	362.30	72.70	289.60				207.10	25.30	49.00	783.10
1954	246.40	34.20	66.70	28.40	117.10	408.70	104.10	304.60				212.50	35.40	56.10	959.10
1955	229.40	57.20	69.50	32.00	70.70	475.40	114.20	361.20				245.00	28.70	79.00	1057.50
1956	190.70	57.90	74.80	32.10	25.90	643.80	111.90	531.90				302.50	28.10	73.50	1238.60
1957	202.20	17.50	73.70	33.40	77.30	727.20	138.80	588.40				347.00	47.00	92.20	1415.60
1958	138.10	4.30	73.70	35.40	24.70	784.20	149.70	634.50	.60		.60	367.30	45.90	38.20	1374.30
1959	133.30	9.90	62.60	23.60	37.20	827.70	143.20	684.50	1.00		1.00	483.30	47.30	52.40	1545.00
1960	130.20	4.60	66.30	23.20	36.10	1057.20	151.10	906.10	4.20	3.30	.90	620.20	49.60	55.20	1916.60
1961	141.90	14.50	51.20	25.10	51.10	1081.00	158.00	923.00	3.40	1.90	1.50	713.90	47.70	118.60	2106.50
1962	188.70	30.20	56.10	25.20	77.20	1102.70	134.20	968.50	2.60	.90	1.70	878.10	51.60	108.80	2332.50
1963	231.20	72.30	66.70	42.70	49.50	1024.70	148.20	876.50	6.50	2.70	3.80	842.80	55.00	137.50	2297.70
1964	297.64	81.63	80.18	62.77	73.06	1130.65	181.43	949.22	10.26	2.74	7.52	872.30	68.56	26.18	2405.57
1965	362.03	134.88	95.41	53.24	78.50	1365.22	223.86	1141.36	10.68	2.48	8.20	921.04	107.42	32.28	2798.65
1966	365.13	150.07	119.97	48.94	46.15	1529.17	234.37	1294.80	8.67	1.41	7.26	1162.69	138.96	40.16	3244.81
1967	266.11	51.94	122.20	36.07	55.90	1787.35	252.67	1534.68	13.34	2.35	10.99	1541.87	212.49	46.80	3867.97
1968	277.27	74.68	117.21	34.04	51.34	1941.66	242.73	1698.93	16.11	3.17	12.94	1689.55	245.34	46.53	4216.50

* EXCLUDING TRADE BETWEEN WEST GERMANY AND EAST GERMANY. SEE EXPLANATORY TEXT.

** TOTAL AND COMPONENTS EXCLUDE EAST GERMANY.

BEC CATEGORIES AND LARGE ECONOMIC CLASSES

1 FOOD AND BEVERAGES
  11 PRIMARY
     111 FOR INDUSTRY
     112 FOR HOUSEHOLD CONSUMPTION
  12 PROCESSED
     121 FOR INDUSTRY
     122 FOR HOUSEHOLD CONSUMPTION

2 INDUSTRIAL SUPPLIES (NON-FOOD)
  21 PRIMARY
  22 PROCESSED

3 FUELS AND LUBRICANTS
  31 PRIMARY
  32 PROCESSED

4 MACHINERY, EXC. TRANSPORT (W/PARTS)

5 TRANSPORT EQUIPMENT

6 CONSUMER GOODS, N.E.S.

7 GOODS N.E.S. AND NOT SPECIFIED

TABLE IV.BEC-2.X.CEMA
WEST EUROPE'S EXPORTS TO EUROPEAN CEMA* (EXCLUDING ALBANIA), 1950-68
(MILLIONS OF CURRENT DOLLARS, C.I.F.)

YEAR	AGGREGATION I. BASIC SNA CLASSES			AGGREGATION II. PRIMARY VS. PROCESSED		NOT SPECIFIED	TOTAL EXPORTS	RATIO SPECIFIED
	CAPITAL GOODS	INTERMEDIATE GOODS	CONSUMER GOODS	PRIMARY	PROCESSED			
1950	274.10	308.40	15.10	101.90	495.70	40.40	638.00**	.937
1951	296.30	381.50	58.10	149.90	586.00	55.80	791.70	.930
1952	217.10	375.10	99.40	114.80	576.80	39.90	731.50	.945
1953	207.10	383.80	143.20	129.20	604.90	49.00	783.10	.937
1954	212.50	471.30	219.20	205.00	698.00	56.10	959.10	.942
1955	245.00	564.60	168.90	240.90	737.60	79.00	1057.50	.925
1956	302.50	733.80	128.80	244.60	920.50	73.50	1238.60	.941
1957	347.00	778.40	198.00	230.00	1093.40	92.20	1415.60	.935
1958	367.30	624.50	144.30	227.70	1108.40	38.20	1374.30	.972
1959	493.30	862.20	147.10	215.70	1276.90	52.40	1545.00	.966
1960	620.20	1089.20	152.00	225.30	1636.10	55.20	1916.60	.971
1961	713.90	1124.00	150.40	225.60	1762.30	118.60	2106.50	.944
1962	878.10	1160.70	184.90	221.40	2002.30	108.80	2332.50	.953
1963	842.80	1146.20	171.20	289.90	1870.30	137.50	2297.70	.940
1964	872.30	1285.31	221.80	345.98	2033.43	26.18	2405.57	.989
1965	921.04	1564.02	281.33	456.63	2309.76	32.28	2798.65	.988
1966	1162.69	1736.85	305.08	505.82	2698.80	40.16	3244.81	.988
1967	1541.87	1888.70	390.59	429.16	3392.00	46.80	3867.97	.988
1968	1689.55	2066.49	413.89	437.79	3732.14	46.53	4216.50	.989

* EXCLUDING TRADE BETWEEN WEST GERMANY AND EAST GERMANY. SEE EXPLANATORY TEXT.

** TOTAL AND COMPONENTS EXCLUDE EAST GERMANY.

TABLE V.CTN.MX.H-1
HUNGARY'S TRADE WITH CPES, 1946-69
(MILLIONS OF CURRENT DOLLARS,* IMPORTS C.I.F., EXPORTS F.O.B.)

YEAR	IMPORTS I	II	III	IV	TOTAL	EXPORTS I	II	III	IV	TOTAL
1946					21.9					25.0
1947					48.6					40.2
1948					87.8					87.4
1949	15.4	108.7	3.8	5.2	133.1	41.0	34.2	41.6	28.8	145.5
1950	28.6	134.4	6.8	9.0	178.8	68.5	40.5	64.7	43.0	216.8
1951	56.0	175.9	22.6	5.0	259.6	82.7	49.4	74.9	64.7	271.7
1952	77.1	231.4	17.5	5.2	331.3	106.5	66.3	91.0	60.5	324.3
1953	73.7	240.4	35.5	6.0	355.6	165.1	78.6	83.4	67.5	394.5
1954	62.3	258.8	23.5	15.8	360.4	159.7	82.0	86.5	57.4	385.6
1955	52.4	215.1	20.5	14.4	302.4	161.8	86.9	102.0	53.4	404.1
1956	48.4	216.9	16.4	16.7	298.5	134.4	68.8	66.5	37.4	307.1
1957					497.2					330.2
1958	83.3	312.4	34.6	20.4	450.6	228.0	102.8	79.4	81.4	491.6
1959	167.2	323.1	49.7	30.0	570.0	248.3	104.6	84.5	103.3	540.6
1960	225.8	369.5	50.8	41.4	687.5**	307.8	123.8	87.4	104.6	623.6**
1961	219.2	389.8	56.2	39.4	704.6**	353.9	144.2	102.0	156.2	756.3**
1962	291.7	436.0	50.5	42.5	820.7	365.3	157.4	108.9	179.0	810.7
1963	328.7	472.5	42.5	56.6	900.4	383.6	167.6	125.3	172.7	849.3
1964	357.0	553.2	26.3	59.6	996.2	430.4	202.0	146.8	183.6	962.8
1965	346.4	555.3	54.8	62.0	1018.5	456.7	207.3	167.9	226.2	1058.0
1966	349.4	563.4	35.9	63.3	1016.0	459.4	212.6	165.8	252.3	1089.2
1967	442.3	546.5	87.6	106.9	1183.3	497.5	188.9	190.8	289.9	1167.1
1968	372.2	657.0	88.1	117.1	1235.0	552.9	204.2	207.3	321.5	1285.9
1969	390.9	696.2	100.5	118.5	1306.2	591.9	233.8	241.2	351.1	1417.9

CTN BROAD DIVISIONS

I.   INDUSTRIAL MACHINERY AND EQUIPMENT (INCLUDING SPARE PARTS)
II. FUELS, RAW MATERIALS (OTHER THAN FOOD) AND OTHER MATERIALS
III. FOODSTUFFS AND RAW MATERIALS FOR THE PRODUCTION OF FOODSTUFFS
IV. INDUSTRIAL CONSUMER GOODS (OTHER THAN FOOD)

* CONVERTED FROM NATIONAL DEVISA UNITS THROUGH OFFICIAL EXCHANGE RATES. NOTE LIMITATIONS DISCUSSED IN THE EXPLANATORY TEXT.

** EXCLUDES TRADE WITH CUBA

	IMPORTS	EXPORTS
1960	0.0	1.1
1961	8.1	10.9

TABLE V.CTN.MX.H-2
HUNGARY'S TRADE WITH NON-CPE'S, 1946-69
(MILLIONS OF CURRENT DOLLARS,* IMPORTS C.I.F., EXPORTS F.O.B.)

YEAR	IMPORTS					EXPORTS				
	I	II	III	IV	TOTAL	I	II	III	IV	TOTAL
1946				2.5	9.6					10.6
1947					75.2					48.6
1948					80.5					77.3
1949	34.7	111.3	6.5		155.1	7.7	28.2	79.7	19.4	135.1
1950	36.9	93.3	4.5	2.3	137.0	5.4	20.1	64.2	22.1	111.8
1951	26.5	99.2	6.3	2.4	134.5	8.5	27.0	61.5	27.1	124.1
1952	22.1	95.1	8.4	2.5	128.3	7.9	23.4	54.9	27.7	113.9
1953	17.3	89.8	22.4	2.3	131.9	11.0	20.8	39.4	32.5	103.8
1954	13.9	103.4	50.9	3.2	171.4	11.2	23.7	63.8	35.0	133.7
1955	10.6	159.3	77.3	4.6	251.9	16.7	56.4	80.7	43.3	197.1
1956	10.2	123.6	45.9	3.1	182.8	14.4	44.3	83.7	37.5	180.0
1957	N.A.	N.A.	N.A.	N.A.	185.4	N.A.	N.A.	N.A.	N.A.	157.8
1958	22.9	129.9	19.1	8.5	180.5	16.9	57.6	76.5	41.1	192.1
1959	34.9	159.9	21.7	6.6	223.1	17.6	79.6	90.6	41.4	229.2
1960	45.5	205.3	29.8	7.9	289.5**	24.7	82.1	92.7	51.1	250.5**
1961	42.7	216.5	51.9	10.0	321.2**	29.1	86.3	101.6	55.9	272.9**
1962	53.4	203.3	60.3	11.3	328.4	32.0	88.1	108.0	60.8	288.9
1963	65.9	241.9	85.9	11.7	405.4	27.1	106.2	153.7	69.8	356.8
1964	80.4	298.9	101.9	17.5	499.8	27.5	135.0	138.5	88.3	389.3
1965	80.8	311.1	91.8	18.5	502.2	37.5	153.0	165.7	95.6	451.8
1966	97.1	338.3	92.5	22.0	549.9	39.7	179.4	179.1	106.3	504.5
1967	131.8	317.0	117.3	26.3	592.3	31.8	188.6	202.4	111.6	534.5
1968	95.6	346.1	106.1	20.2	568.0	30.8	185.2	172.8	114.8	503.6
1969	112.4	369.2	112.0	28.4	622.0	44.3	265.8	236.9	119.2	666.2

* CONVERTED FROM NATIONAL DEVISA UNITS THROUGH OFFICIAL EXCHANGE RATES. NOTE LIMITATIONS DISCUSSED IN THE EXPLANATORY TEXT.

** INCLUDES TRADE WITH CUBA

	IMPORTS	EXPORTS
1960	0.0	1.1
1961	8.1	10.9

CTN BROAD DIVISIONS

I.   INDUSTRIAL MACHINERY AND EQUIPMENT (INCLUDING SPARE PARTS)
II. FUELS, RAW MATERIALS (OTHER THAN FOOD) AND OTHER MATERIALS
III. FOODSTUFFS AND RAW MATERIALS FOR THE PRODUCTION OF FOODSTUFFS
IV. INDUSTRIAL CONSUMER GOODS (OTHER THAN FOOD)

TABLE V.CTN.MX.P-1
POLAND'S TRADE WITH CPE'S, 1946-69
(MILLIONS OF CURRENT DOLLARS,* F.O.B.)

YEAR	IMPORTS					EXPORTS				
	I	II	III	IV	TOTAL	I	II	III	IV	TOTAL
1946					114.1					75.7
1947					110.6					109.1
1948					245.4					234.9
1949					269.4					280.7
1950	140.1	209.9	41.5	16.9	408.3	48.9	219.6	50.2	42.2	360.8
1951	206.9	255.9	45.5	26.8	535.2	50.8	281.3	46.7	55.5	434.3
1952	235.1	239.6	83.6	24.4	582.6	78.6	319.7	47.5	59.5	505.3
1953	258.8	236.1	43.8	17.3	555.9	101.9	337.2	67.2	62.6	568.8
1954	252.1	279.0	85.9	24.2	641.3	95.5	391.4	58.8	55.9	601.7
1955	249.2	272.0	54.2	29.5	605.0	114.2	374.0	53.0	37.2	578.3
1956	289.1	291.1	46.1	51.0	677.4	133.2	379.6	19.6	47.7	580.2
1957	230.5	363.3	132.3	52.0	778.0	177.0	362.0	14.9	24.1	578.0
1958	219.7	356.7	54.8	83.1	714.3	240.0	315.5	37.8	27.1	620.4
1959	269.1	420.3	146.9	86.7	923.0	261.5	349.4	34.6	36.4	682.0
1960	294.9	449.7	134.2	70.7	949.5	322.1	372.9	47.0	88.2	830.2
1961	376.1	495.7	93.4	88.9	1054.2	368.8	368.2	88.5	113.7	939.1
1962	484.0	536.2	113.8	112.3	1246.2	436.6	380.5	78.9	138.2	1034.3
1963	544.6	543.9	125.2	112.2	1326.0	522.1	404.4	38.7	157.9	1123.1
1964	533.2	606.2	67.0	99.7	1306.2	627.9	458.6	90.9	173.2	1350.6
1965	643.0	653.8	108.4	142.2	1547.5	684.6	469.8	82.3	171.9	1408.7
1966	695.0	668.3	105.3	135.3	1603.8	708.4	424.0	57.1	210.6	1400.2
1967	757.7	697.1	154.7	127.4	1736.9	806.8	452.9	70.6	280.9	1611.2
1968	760.0	791.6	155.9	130.5	1838.0	945.9	511.4	79.8	341.5	1878.5
1969	884.5	886.4	194.4	148.2	2113.5	1087.3	542.2	61.2	373.3	2063.9

CTN BROAD DIVISIONS

I.   INDUSTRIAL MACHINERY AND EQUIPMENT (INCLUDING SPARE PARTS)
II.   FUELS, RAW MATERIALS (OTHER THAN FOOD) AND OTHER MATERIALS
III. FOODSTUFFS AND RAW MATERIALS FOR THE PRODUCTION OF FOODSTUFFS
IV.   INDUSTRIAL CONSUMER GOODS (OTHER THAN FOOD)

* CONVERTED FROM NATIONAL DEVISA UNITS THROUGH
OFFICIAL EXCHANGE RATES. NOTE LIMITATIONS
DISCUSSED IN THE EXPLANATORY TEXT.

TABLE V.CTN.MX.P-2
POLAND'S TRADE WITH NON-CPE'S, 1946-69
(MILLIONS OF CURRENT DOLLARS,* F.O.B.)

IMPORTS

YEAR	I	II	III	IV	TOTAL
1946					31.7
1947					209.6
1948					271.0
1949					363.0
1950	76.4	144.9	33.3	5.3	259.9
1951	106.1	232.9	36.8	13.2	389.0
1952	80.7	177.2	18.5	3.9	280.4
1953	62.6	144.4	8.1	3.3	218.4
1954	41.4	177.7	36.3	6.8	262.2
1955	38.9	210.0	67.1	10.9	326.9
1956	50.3	205.7	77.9	10.6	344.5
1957	66.9	301.4	85.7	19.5	473.5
1958	107.9	305.2	79.9	19.5	512.5
1959	121.1	268.8	93.7	13.0	496.6
1960	110.3	320.0	104.9	10.2	545.5
1961	115.1	342.2	164.1	11.1	632.5
1962	142.5	346.6	137.2	12.9	639.2
1963	129.9	337.1	173.6	12.4	653.0
1964	101.2	402.7	249.7	12.4	766.1
1965	123.7	453.1	200.7	15.3	792.8
1966	179.7	509.5	182.6	18.4	890.2
1967	220.1	531.7	134.5	21.6	907.9
1968	264.4	553.7	165.5	31.5	1015.1
1969	298.1	623.2	139.3	35.5	1096.2

EXPORTS

YEAR	I	II	III	IV	TOTAL
1946					50.8
1947					137.2
1948					296.4
1949					338.1
1950	.4	135.4	102.5	35.2	273.4
1951	.6	235.1	79.7	11.9	327.3
1952	.6	162.3	96.7	10.4	270.1
1953	.2	143.2	101.9	16.8	262.1
1954	.9	143.5	97.4	25.2	267.1
1955	5.9	218.1	88.0	29.2	341.3
1956	20.7	248.2	95.4	40.2	404.6
1957	18.0	232.7	108.2	38.1	397.0
1958	44.3	223.0	140.7	30.9	439.0
1959	40.0	211.4	174.0	37.7	463.2
1960	49.3	208.1	192.4	45.4	495.3
1961	52.8	218.9	233.7	59.1	564.5
1962	57.4	262.0	237.3	55.2	611.8
1963	63.7	267.8	245.4	70.1	647.0
1964	73.0	286.2	300.7	85.9	745.8
1965	82.7	312.5	321.8	102.2	819.2
1966	93.8	354.6	319.5	104.1	872.0
1967	104.5	381.0	321.7	108.1	915.3
1968	110.6	433.9	322.0	112.9	979.3
1969	142.4	494.7	319.6	120.8	1077.6

* CONVERTED FROM NATIONAL DEVISA UNITS THROUGH
OFFICIAL EXCHANGE RATES. NOTE LIMITATIONS
DISCUSSED IN THE EXPLANTORY TEXT.

CTN BROAD DIVISIONS

I. INDUSTRIAL MACHINERY AND EQUIPMENT (INCLUDING SPARE PARTS)
II. FUELS, RAW MATERIALS (OTHER THAN FOOD) AND OTHER MATERIALS
III. FOODSTUFFS AND RAW MATERIALS FOR THE PRODUCTION OF FOODSTUFFS
IV. INDUSTRIAL CONSUMER GOODS (OTHER THAN FOOD)

PART THREE

Notes and Documentation

Key to the Citations

Each source cited in the documentation in Part Three and in the appendices in Part Four is identified by a code consisting of one or more capital letters plus a number, which identify the full reference listed in the Bibliography at the end of the book. The letters indicate the source according to three classifications: Western government publications, international organizations, or country of publication.

GP = Government publications of Western countries

UN = United Nations

$CEMA$ = Council for Mutual Economic Assistance

U = U.S.S.R.

B = Bulgaria

C = Czechoslovakia

G = East Germany

H = Hungary

P = Poland

R = Rumania

Y = Yugoslavia

A = Albania

W = All Western countries

A. Constructing the Record

Origin-Destination of Total Trade (Series I)

Standardization

Series I records the origin of total imports and destination of total exports for each of the nine East European countries (including Albania), for East Europe by country (excluding Albania), and for the rest of the world by geographical groupings, as detailed below.

Trade by East European Partner. Most countries provide data on trade with individual nations. These statistics were obtained directly in most cases from a reporting country's official publications. If, in order to obtain a "Total CPEs" subtotal it was necessary to estimate trade with one, or at most, a few East European countries, then (but only then) trade-partner statistics were utilized. The use of such mirror statistics is always identified by the same footnote code, as shown in the legend to each table. Trade with Albania as a trade partner is not shown separately but is included with "OCPEs." This procedure was dictated in part by having to limit the number of columns per page and in part by the fact that trade with Albania tends to be negligible (because of its small size and — in more recent years — because its main trade links are with Mainland China rather than with East Europe). However, Albania's trade with East European countries for selected years is shown as obtained from Albanian sources. (Mirror statistics for Albania cannot be gained from the tables here provided.)

Trade with "Other Centrally Planned Economies." This grouping was obtained either directly as the sum of values for these individual countries, or indirectly as a residual, by subtracting the sum of trade with individual East European countries (except Albania) from officially reported trade with "Total CPEs." As a general procedure, both calculations were made in order to obtain a statistical check. A footnote code indicates when trade with OCPEs could be obtained only as a residual.

Trade with "Total Centrally Planned Economies." This subtotal was obtained in most cases by summing trade with individual East European countries and the OCPEs aggregate. If a component was not separately available, the subtotal was taken to be the officially published value given for this sum. Such "given" rather than "summed" subtotals are identified by a footnote code. Whenever possible, officially given and summed subtotals were compared as a statistical check. Cuba has been included with "Total CPEs" consistently since 1960.

278

Trade with "More Developed Countries." This group comprises what is also known as "developed countries," or Economic Class I, according to the U.N. definition, with Yugoslavia excluded. Table 5 compares U.N. and East European classifications of countries into MDC and LDC groups.

Trade values for the MDC group were obtained by the following procedures: (1) the sum of region or country components, (2) a directly given subtotal in a country's official statistics, (3) a residual, by subtracting trade with LDCs from trade with "Total Non-CPEs," or (4) as an interpolated estimate, provided that full information was available for a preceding and subsequent year and, further, that only the division of "Total Non-CPEs" trade between MDCs and LDCs had to be estimated. If obtained as shown in (3) or (4), a footnote code identifies the method.

Trade with "Less Developed Countries." This group consists of what is also known as "developing countries," or Economic Class II, according to the U.N. definition (see Table 5). Trade values were obtained according to one of the four methods just noted for MDCs.

Trade with "Total Non-Centrally Planned Economies." The subtotal is either (1) the sum of trade with MDCs and LDCs, (2) a subtotal reported in official publications, or (3) a "residual," derived by subtracting trade with "Total CPEs" from total trade. The latter two cases are identified by appropriate footnote codes.

Total Trade. In every case this statistic was independently given, obtained in most cases from the official publications of a reporting country and in a few instances from secondary sources.

Special Problems

Careful attention has been given in each table to internal statistical consistency. Many of the special problems encountered were in fact due to data revisions and other inconsistencies among sources. In general, the most recently published values have been utilized. Important discrepancies among sources and other special problems have been documented in notes to individual tables. Three problems are discussed next for illustration:

Hungarian Transport Charges. Between 1952 and 1956 Hungary reported trade according to "actual parity," a concept that corresponds neither to f.o.b. nor c.i.f. in its treatment of transport and related costs. Subsequently, revised figures were published for these years according to "border parity" (exports f.o.b., imports c.i.f.) for total trade and trade by two groups of trade partners, achieving consistency with other years. Trade by countries according to border parity were not, however, given. The revised and unrevised figures (total and by combined groups) were used to calculate a set of adjustment coefficients which were applied to the unrevised data by countries for 1952-1956, thereby achieving at least numerical consistency between country components and revised totals (see documentation to Tables I.M.H and I.X.H below).

Table 5

Classification of Countries into MDC and LDC Groups
by the United Nations and by East European Countries*

Classified by	More Developed Countries (MDCs)	Less Developed Countries (LDCs)
United Nations[1]	North America, West Europe (including Turkey and Yugoslavia), South Africa, Japan, and Oceania.	All other countries except CEMA, Albania, and the Asian CPEs. Cuba *is* included with LDCs.
U.S.S.R.[2]	Same as U.N. except for the exclusion of Turkey and Yugoslavia.	Same as U.N. except for the inclusion of Turkey and the exclusion of Cuba since 1960.
Bulgaria	Not known; appears to be the same as the U.S.S.R.	Not known; appears to be the same as the U.S.S.R.
Czechoslovakia[3]	Same as U.N. except for the exclusion of New Zealand and Yugoslavia.	Same as U.N. except for the inclusion of New Zealand and the exclusion of Cuba since 1960.
East Germany[4]	Same as U.N. except for the exclusion of Yugoslavia and South Africa.	Same as U.N. except for the inclusion of South Africa and the exclusion of Cuba since 1960.
Hungary[5]	"Total Capitalist" (i.e., all economies not centrally planned) less trade with LDCs. Same as U.N. except for the inclusion of Israel and the exclusion of Yugoslavia.	Sum of (a) Asia except Asian CPEs, Japan, and Israel; (b) Africa except South Africa; (c) the Americas except North America and Cuba since 1960. Same as U.N. except for the exclusion of Israel and Cuba since 1960.
Poland[6]	Same as U.N. except for the exclusion of Yugoslavia	Same as U.N. except for the exclusion of Cuba since 1960.
Rumania[7]	Sum of trade with individual West European countries,[8] Israel, Japan, Canada, the U.S., and Australia. Same as U.N. except for the inclusion of Israel and the exclusion of New Zealand and Yugoslavia.	Total trade less trade with "Total CPEs" and MDCs. Same as U.N. except for the inclusion of New Zealand and the exclusion of Israel and Cuba since 1960.
Yugoslavia[7]	Sum of Europe (given) less European CPEs, Japan, Canada, the U.S., and Oceania. Same as U.N. except for the exclusion of South Africa.	Sum of Asia less Asian CPEs plus Japan, Africa, Central America (excluding Cuba since 1960), and South America. Same as U.N. except for the exclusion of Cuba since 1960.
Albania[7]	Sum of trade with individual MDCs.[9] Probably understates somewhat trade with MDCs as compared to the U.N. definition.	Sum of trade with individual LDCs plus unspecified residual. Probably overstates somewhat trade with LDCs as compared to the U.N. definition.

*The classification shown here for East European countries refers to the appropriate columns of tables in Series I.

[1] See, for example, *UN-1*, pp. 2-8.

[2] *U-3*, September 1968, p. 48.

[3] *C-3*, 1969, p. 408.

[4] *G-2*, p. 97.

[5] Calculated on the basis of subtotal for "Total Capitalist," trade by continents and selected country totals.

[6] *P-2*. 1967 (translation), p. 8.

[7] Calculated by the author. See documentation to the statistical tables.

[8] Austria, Belgium, Denmark, England, Finland, France, Greece, Iceland, Italy, Netherlands, Norway, Portugal, Spain, West Germany.

[9] Austria, Belgium, Denmark, England, France, Italy, Netherlands, Sweden, West Germany.

East Germany's "Special" vs. "General Trade." Until 1966 East Germany's trade statistics were on a "special trade" basis, excluding re-exports; those published since 1966 are defined as "general trade," including re-exports. (See Part Four, pp. 349-53 for a more detailed discussion.) Statistics on total trade, trade by groups of countries and with the U.S.S.R. have been officially revised back to 1949 to correspond to the new definition, but the remaining country series were revised back only as far as 1960. To achieve at least numerical consistency in the revised series for 1949-59, the unrevised trade partner data were adjusted by assigning discrepancies (relatively small) to trade with OCPEs, as explained in the notes to the East German tables.

Statistical Revisions. A number of East European countries, e.g., Bulgaria, Hungary, Poland, and Rumania, have published revised trade series in the late 1950s without disclosing the nature of the revisions. Whenever possible, only revised figures consistent over time have been included. In cases where the revised figures of a series were published for scattered earlier years only, the unrevised figures have been included for intervening years, with footnote codes identifying unrevised entries.

Commodity Composition of Total Trade and Trade by
East European Trade Partner (Series II and III)

Series II presents the commodity composition of total trade by individual East European country according to the CTN, BEC, or SITC classification systems. Series III shows the commodity composition of trade by East European trade partner according to the CTN and BEC classification systems.

Standardization According to CTN

Criteria for Inclusion in the *Data Bank*. Although most East European countries publish information on commodity composition of both total trade and trade by major partners, details vary greatly. The number of commodity groups specified may number from four to several hundred, and in many cases the sum of the itemized components is less than the independently given total. Even though only the nine one-digit CTN *categories* plus the four *broad division* subtotals are shown here, more detailed commodity breakdown was processed for the *Data Bank* as useful information and also because such detail is required for conversion to SITC or BEC.

The commodity composition of total trade and intraregional bilateral trade was processed to three CTN digits provided that (1) the CTN code was either given or could be assigned; and (2) spotchecks indicated that for most years at least 80 percent of total trade would be specified according to assigned or assignable one-, two-, or three-digit CTN codes. (The 80 percent cut-off point was arbitrary.) For the U.S.S.R. and Poland, five-and seven-digit CTN details were aggregated into two- or three-digit subtotals if these figures were not published directly. No permanent record has been kept of details beyond three-digit CTN. The decision not to disaggregate below a three-digit CTN level was suggested by the availability of data in general as well as the relatively small expected payoff from additional detail wanting in completeness. Furthermore, a preliminary comparison of CTN with the SITC and BEC systems revealed that a reasonably good transformation could be made from three-digit CTN to the two Western nomenclatures if the purpose was to obtain one-digit SITC *categories* or BEC aggregates (by "broad-end-use" and "SNA classes").

Special Aggregation Problems and Procedures. In processing the data according to CTN, the unusual disclosure practices of certain CEMA countries raise problems requiring special procedures. One would expect, for instance, that the higher the level of aggregation, the more complete would be the coverage of published totals. This is the case for most CEMA countries but not for the U.S.S.R. or for the Polish series on trade by partner. The U.S.S.R. does not publish an exhaustive breakdown by one-digit CTN commodity categories in its basic statistical sources. The only one-digit subtotal given is for *Category* 1 (Machinery and Equipment), while very few two-digit subtotals are published. Conversely, three-, five-, and seven-digit CTN details are quite numerous (though not exhaustive) and five- or seven-digit CTN breakdowns may be shown without the corresponding three-digit CTN subtotals. In many instances, therefore, the two- or three-digit subtotals needed for present purposes had to be reconstructed by collecting lower-digit components.

A similar problem was faced in processing the commodity composition of Polish trade by partner. Since the data are shown mainly in five-digit CTN detail, three-, two-, and one-digit entries had to be reconstructed from their five-digit components by successive aggregations.

Thus, each statistical entry which has a CTN code is one of three types:

(1) Original entries, for which (it is logical to assume) the value given in primary sources exhausts trade at the indicated level;

(2) Reconstructed entries, obtained when higher-digit CTN components have been summed prior to the entry's inclusion in the computerized records. These entries may not exhaust values at the indicated level. For example, CTN 308 is obtained by summing CTN 30805 and 30818, the only components that are given. Reconstructed CTN 308 would be the correct subtotal only if the nomenclature contained no more than the two components shown or, in case there were additional code components, if their trade values were zero. Since neither the complete nomenclature code nor the list of all zero-trade items are available, whether *reconstructed* items are exhaustive or not cannot be determined.

(3) Collected entries, representing computer aggregation of already processed *original* or *reconstructed* CTN components. *Collected*

and *reconstructed* entries are thus conceptually similar in that each may be less than exhaustive, the difference being in the level of aggregation at which omissions may have occurred.

Each type of entry is identified by a special footnote code in the *Data Bank* but these special codes are not shown in the *Compendium*. For some countries, all nine CTN *categories* shown here represent *collected* entries and their sum does not exhaust total trade; for other countries the *categories* represent *original* entries whose sum equals the total, independently given. Since individual tables in most cases consist of only *collected* or only *original categories*, the special codes have been omitted. As a general rule, if the nine CTN *categories* exhaust total trade so that there is no column showing "unspecified," then each *category* represents a value taken directly from official publications. If, however, the sum of *categories* is less than the total so that there is an "unspecified" column, then each *category* represents a *collected* entry, obtained through computer aggregation of *original, reconstructed*, and *collected* components.

Verification of Statistical Accuracy. Considerable attention has been given to accuracy and internal consistency. All keypunched entries have been verified and auditing programs routinely utilized. But in the cases of countries providing less than exhaustive coverage, it was impossible to check fully for inaccuracies. For example, misprints and internal inconsistencies in official publications which could be detected under an exhaustive breakdown of total trade might well remain undetected otherwise.

Inconsistent Classification to CTN. A further problem stemmed from reclassification by a CEMA country of a commodity from one CTN *category* or *broad division* to another (to be distinguished from a general revision of the CTN code, discussed in Appendix A below). Thus, Hungary, like other CEMA countries officially adopting the CEMA code in 1962, originally included spare parts in *Category* 1 (Machinery and Equipment). Starting in 1967, however, Hungary alone (as far as is known) classified Spare Parts with *Broad Division* II (Fuels, Raw Materials, Other Materials). Since Spare Parts in this case represent approximately 20 percent of machinery exports and about 30 percent of machinery imports, failure to allow for variable classification would affect the comparability of some series substantially. Spare parts have therefore been retained with machinery trade for all years.

For other CEMA countries important reclassification problems have not been noted. As far as one can tell, the commodity classification by CTN *categories* published by CEMA countries during the 1960s is quite similar. (Small discrepancies in classification within *categories* have been noted. See, for example, the notes to Appendix Table A-1.) However, for statistics published during the 1950s, when the use of CTN was reportedly voluntary, non-uniformity of classifying commodities had been noted as a problem by the United Nations (*UN-3*, 1957, Chapter VI, p. 34) and (more extensively) by a more recent study *(W-17)*. During the 1960s several CEMA countries have published revised statistics for earlier years, apparently to make them more comparable with recent series. Since it is the revised series which have generally been included here, it is possible that the non-uniformity of classification noted earlier is no longer a serious problem. A firm conclusion, however, would require a more extensive examination of this problem than was found possible within the limitations of this project.

Standardization According to SITC and BEC

Standard International Trade Classification. SITC values for three countries' total trade are presented here at the one-digit *category* level, while the *Data Bank* includes SITC details for the same three countries to two digits. For Yugoslavia and Hungary the statistics are as originally reported; for the U.S.S.R. the data have been derived by conversion from CTN (see Appendix B for details). For other East European countries, and for trade by partner, there is not enough information to attempt such conversion.

Yugoslavia has provided one- and two-digit SITC details on total trade since the early 1950s, and is the only East European country which has consistently done so. Even finer SITC disaggregation is possible for Yugoslavia's trade with partners, including those in East Europe, reported in the official Yugoslav publications only by five-digit SITC codes. Because of the volume of data that would have had to be processed to obtain one-digit subtotals on trade composition by partner (several hundred commodities annually in exports and imports by partner), only three years, 1960, 1964, and 1968, have been so processed. The resulting series have not been included in the *Compendium* but are available in the *Data Bank*.

For Hungary, one-digit SITC has been available from secondary sources since 1960. During the mid-1960s that country switched from reporting total trade in two-digit CTN to two-digit SITC.

Czechoslovakia started in 1965 to publish total trade according to one-, two-, and three-digit SITC but the series were considered too short (1965-67) to be presented here. The information is available in the *Data Bank* and in recent issues of *UN-8*.

Other East European countries do not report commodity composition by SITC.

Broad Economic Categories. All tables showing the commodity composition by BEC have been derived through conversions from originally reported CTN or SITC data. The transformation process is discussed in Appendix B.

For total trade (Series II), BEC series are presented for three countries. For the U.S.S.R. and Bulgaria, these figures have been derived by conversion from CTN data; for Yugoslavia, from SITC data. For other East European countries, insufficient CTN or SITC detail is available to render conversion to BEC.

For trade by East European partner (Series III), BEC series are presented for three countries, the U.S.S.R., Czechoslovakia, and Poland. Each series has been derived by conversion from CTN data.

The reconciliation of CTN and BEC nomenclatures is based on one-, two-, or three-digit CTN (see Appendix Table B-4). However, in some cases when it was prescribed to convert from three-digit CTN, the required detail was not available. Thus, the more aggregated two-digit CTN had to be allocated among its three-digit components, according to one of the following methods:

(1) Information from trade-partner sources was utilized. For example, in Czechoslovakia's imports from the U.S.S.R., CTN 20 (Solid Fuels) is not specified in further detail. Since U.S.S.R. data show that nearly all of reported trade in this CTN *group* was in CTN 200 (Hard Coal), Czechoslovak exports to the U.S.S.R. were assigned to CTN 200.

(2) In some cases the usual importance of one CTN *subgroup* (or subgroup span) is such that it is probable that all or a substantial part of reported trade is covered by a particular *subgroup* (or subgroup span). To illustrate, if no three-digit detail was given, all of trade reported for CTN 23 (Fuel Gas, Electric Power, and Steam) was assigned to CTN 231 (Electric Power), unless there was information showing that other subgroups were also traded, in which case the procedure discussed below was followed.

(3) If no other basis could be found, an estimated, usually equiproportionate (such as "50-50"), allocation was made between two or more *subgroups* (or spans) corresponding to different BEC *categories*. For example, of CTN 34 (Fertilizers, Insecticides, and Pesticides), CTN 340 and 341 correspond to BEC 21, while CTN 342 and 343 correspond to BEC 22. Accordingly, CTN 34 was allocated "50-50" between CTN 340-341 and 342-343.

Three-digit CTN entries obtained through any of these allocation procedures are identified in the *Data Bank* by a special footnote code. Notes to individual tables list the individual allocations (which are the same from year to year) and show also, annually, the percent of total "specified trade" so allocated. Since these percentages are usually small, these special procedures are not believed to introduce a significant bias in the BEC series.

Commodity Composition of Trade with West Europe
(Series IV)

Underlying statistics have been obtained from West European sources, as compiled by the United Nations and reported in appendices to the annual *Economic Bulletin for Europe*. These are the only series in Part Two deriving from non-East European sources. The number of countries included by the U.N. in the West Europe total had increased from 13 in 1950 to 18 by 1964, as shown in Table 6; Yugoslavia has been consistently excluded here from the West Europe total (since U.N. publications include Yugoslavia with West Europe only in certain years).

West Germany's trade with East Germany is not included in the West Europe total because West Germany considers it domestic trade (previously called "Interzonenhandel," currently "Innerdeutscherhandel")

Table 6

Coverage by Country of West Europe
as a Group in Trade with East Europe, 1950-1968

	Since 1950	Since 1952	Since 1958	Since 1964
EEC				
	Belgium	Greece	Ireland[d]	Spain
	France	Iceland	Portugal	
	Luxembourg			
	Italy			
	Netherlands			
	West Germany[a]			
EFTA				
	Austria			
	Denmark[b]			
	Finland			
	Norway[b]			
	Sweden[b]			
	Switzerland			
	United Kingdom[c]			

a. Excludes trade with East Germany.
b. General trade.
c. General imports and special exports.
d. Excluded from the West Europe total during 1962-63;
all other years, general imports and special exports.

even though East Germany reports it as international trade (Aussen-handel). U.N., West German, and East German estimates of this trade differ somewhat, as is shown in Table 7.

West European countries report *special trade* (see Appendix D for definition), except as noted in Table 6. Transaction values are imports c.i.f., and exports f.o.b., border of the reporting country.

To improve the internal consistency of the statistics, selected adjustments were made in the original U.N. data, as explained and illustrated in Appendix B, pp. 333-36.

Tables showing the commodity composition of trade between East European countries and West Europe have been derived by conversion from original SITC series.

B. Documentation

Statistical Series I

Tables I.M.U and I.X.U

Note. For Soviet statistical definitions, including the system of trade, coverage, the treatment of transport and related costs, and the identification of trade partner, see Appendix D.

Table 7

Trade between West Germany* and East Germany, 1950-1969
(Millions of Dollars)

Year	West German Imports			West German Exports		
	Var. 1 (c.i.f.) (1)	Var. 2 (2)	GDR exp. (f.o.b.) (3)	Var. 1 (f.o.b.) (4)	Var. 2 (5)	GDR imp. (f.o.b.) (6)
1950	99.6	n.a.	79.3	92.6	n.a.	60.8
1951	44.3	n.a.	35.2	42.3	n.a.	43.6
1952	30.4	n.a.	33.1	39.3	n.a.	45.9
1953	67.6	69.5	69.7	60.5	57.1	62.7
1954	104.7	101.2	104.9	99.4	93.8	103.8
1955	138.8	135.1	136.4	131.7	120.0	131.1
1956	155.5	152.9	154.0	166.4	139.9	146.2
1957	194.5	197.4	204.6	201.3	181.8	183.9
1958	204.2	205.4	211.3	190.6	192.4	190.1
1959	212.3	218.4	229.7	256.8	233.4	228.6
1960	267.4	235.3	241.2**	228.5	220.6	213.7**
1961	233.9	225.2	219.5	216.6	203.4	203.9
1962	228.6	220.7	210.7	213.2	210.0	195.9
1963	255.6	251.2	242.9	214.9	208.5	197.2
1964	256.8	270.8	265.0	287.7	267.3	208.9
1965	315.7	303.4	293.9	297.8	276.5	263.4
1966	336.4	318.6	306.5	406.3	381.8	349.6
1967	316.0	n.a.	297.3	370.7	n.a.	306.7
1968	360.4	n.a.	335.6	359.0	n.a.	292.1
1969	399.2	n.a.	365.4	560.8	n.a.	465.0

*Includes trade of West Berlin.
**Revised series (see documentation to Statistical Tables I.M.G and I.X.G).
Source: Columns (1) and (4), 1950-53: *UN-8*, 1955 (converted to dollars at the rate of DM 1 = $.238); 1954-57: *UN-8*, 1958; 1958-61: *UN-8*, 1962; 1962-65: *UN-8*, 1966; 1966-68: *UN-8*, 1968; 1969: *UN-2*, Vol. 22, no. 1, Appendix Table A. Columns (2) and (5), K. Pritzel, "Der Interzonen Handel — Entwicklung, Wirtschaftliche Bedeutung, Politische Aspekte," *Aus Politik und Zeit Geschichte: Beilage zur Wochen Zeitung das Parlament*, Bd. 48:67 (November 29, 1967), p. 9, as quoted in *W-4*, p. 166. (Figures were originally shown in "accounting units," which are, for all practical purposes, the same as Deutsche Marks, converted to dollars at the rate of DM 1 = $.238 until the end of 1960 and DM 1 = $.25 since 1961.) Columns (3) and (6), 1950-55: *G-1*, 1955 (rubles converted to dollars at the rate of R 1 = $.25); 1956-59: *W-10*, pp. 65, 70 (series is consistent with East German series available to 1955 except in 1950, for which *W-10* shows much higher trade: $100.6 and $96.8 in West German imports and exports, respectively; rubles converted to dollars at R 1 = $.25); 1960-69: *G-1*, 1970 (valuta-marks converted to dollars at the rate of VM 1 = $.238 until 1961 and VM 1 = $.25 between 1961 and 1969).

Sources. Bulgaria, Czechoslovakia, East Germany, Hungary, Poland, Rumania, Yugoslavia, MDCs, LDCs, and Total, 1946-1966: *U-2*; 1967-1968: *U-1*, 1968; 1969: *U-1*, 1969.

Other CPEs, 1946-1969: balancing item, i.e., total trade with "socialist countries" (as reported in *U-2*, and various issues of *U-1*) less trade with East European countries except Albania. (Note: In some issues of *U-1* published in the mid-1960s, Cuba has been included among "socialist countries" for the period before 1960. In these cases appropriate adjustments have been made so that here Cuba is included with "socialist countries" only since 1960).

Tables I.M.B and I.X.B

Note. For Bulgarian statistical definitions, including the system of trade, coverage, the treatment of transport and related costs, and the identification of trade partner, see Appendix D.

Bulgarian foreign trade statistics were revised around 1958. Revised figures were published for 1950 and since 1955; the unrevised series are available for 1952-56. Thus, for 1955-56, revised and unrevised series can be compared in an attempt to throw some light on the nature of the revision.

Table 8

Bulgaria's Total Trade, Revised and Unrevised, 1955-1956
(Millions of New Levas)

Year	Imports			Exports		
	Revised (1)	Unrevised (2)	Ratio: (1):(2) (3)	Revised (4)	Unrevised (5)	Ratio: (4):(5) (6)
1955	292.4	227.7	1.28	276.4	268.2	1.03
1956	293.8	290.4	1.01	353.4	396.7	0.89

Source: Revised series, *B-1*, 1963, p. 306; unrevised series, *B-1*, 1956, p. 82 (old levas converted to new levas).

For 1955, Bulgaria's revised imports (total as well as imports from every CEMA country) are larger than the unrevised figures. Revised exports for 1955 also tend to be larger but by a smaller margin (except for exports to East Germany, where the revised figures are slightly smaller). The direction of the 1956 revision is less consistent; revised imports tend to be larger but often only by a small margin; while revised exports (total and to every CEMA country) are smaller than the unrevised figures.

The only official comment available on the revision states:

> The data on exports and imports for 1955 and 1956 differ from comparable data in previous publications due to adjustments made because of the clarification of certain indices and changes in the number of types of goods listed. For example, data on goods exchanged does not include figures for costs and quantities of goods given or received free of charge. Costs and quantities of goods exported and imported for processing and certain other purposes have also been adjusted. [*B-6*, p. 3.]

The exclusion of foreign aid from the revised series would be expected to reduce revised figures below those shown by the unrevised series. Similarly, adjustment of "improvement and repair trade" (i.e., goods "for processing") would also be expected to lower revised figures (provided that the revision followed the recommendations of CEMA's Standing Commission for Statistics to include "value added" only). Instead, we find that revised 1955 imports are substantially larger than unrevised figures, suggesting that major revision, at least for 1955, took place for reasons in addition to those officially reported. (For an informative Western hypothesis concerning the nature of similar revisions in Rumania, see Note to Table I.M.R and I.X.R.)

Sources. U.S.S.R., Czechoslovakia, East Germany, Hungary, Poland, Rumania, Yugoslavia, 1950: *B-4*, 1950-1967; 1952-54: *B-1*, 1956; 1955, 1957, 1960-62: *B-1*, 1963; 1956, 1963: *B-1*, 1965; 1958-59: *B-1*, 1961; 1964-67: *B-2*, 1968; 1968: *B-2*, 1969; 1969: *B-2*, 1970.

MDCs, LDCs, 1950: *B-4*, 1956-1967; 1952-54: interpolated by assuming that the rate of change of proportion relative to "Total Non-CPEs" between 1950 and 1955 was constant; 1955, 1960, 1962-65: *B-4*, 1950-1965; 1956: *B-2*, 1969; 1957-59: interpolated by assuming that the rate of change of proportion relative to "Total Non-CPEs" between 1956 and 1960 was constant; 1961: interpolated as above; 1966-69: *B-3*, 1970.

Total Non-CPEs, 1952-54: balancing item, i.e., total trade less total CPEs (as summed); 1957-59: *B-4*, 1955-1961; 1961: *B-4*, 1955-1961 (adjusted to exclude Cuba).

Total, 1950: *B-4*, 1950-1967; 1952-54: *B-1*, 1956; 1955-61: *B-4*, 1955-1961; 1962-65: *B-4*, 1950-1965; 1966-68: *B-2*, 1969; 1969: *B-2*, 1970.

Tables I.M.C and I.X.C

Note. For Czechoslovak statistical definitions, including the system of trade, coverage, the treatment of transport and related costs, and the identification of trade partner, see Appendix D.

Sources. U.S.S.R., Bulgaria, Hungary, Poland, Rumania, 1946: *C-1*, p. 149; U.S.S.R., 1952: *W-13*, p. 212 (based on official sources); U.S.S.R., Bulgaria, East Germany, Hungary, Poland, Rumania, Yugoslavia 1948, 1953, 1958-59: *C-2*, 1964; 1950: *C-2*, 1967; 1954-57: *C-3*, 1958; 1960-67: *C-3*, 1968; 1968: *C-3*, 1969; 1969: *C-4*, June 1970.

Other CPEs (sum of components), 1950: *C-2*, 1967; 1953-57: *C-3*, 1958; 1958-59: *C-2*, 1964; 1960-67: *C-3*, 1968; 1968: *C-3*, 1969; 1969: *C-4*, June 1970.

Total CPEs, 1948: *C-2*, 1964; 1951-52: *W-13*, p. 212. (Exports of $604.0 million to "socialist countries" in 1952 is a misprint. The entry should read $629.0 million. The correction was obtained through correspondence with the author.) 1969: *C-4*, June 1970.

MDCs, LDCs, 1948, 1953, 1956-59: *C-2*, 1962; 1950, 1955: *C-2*, 1967; 1951-52, 1954: interpolated by assuming that rate of change of proportion relative to "Total Non-CPEs" is constant. 1960-67: *C-3*, 1968; 1968: *C-3*, 1969; 1969: *C-4*, June 1970.

Total Non-CPEs, 1951-52: *W-13*, p. 212; 1969: *C-4*, June 1970.

Total, 1946-52: *C-1*, 1953-57: *C-3*, 1958; 1959: *C-3*, 1961; 1965-67: *C-3*, 1968; 1968: *C-3*, 1969; 1969: *C-4*, June 1970.

Tables I.M.G and I.X.G

Note. For East German statistical definitions, including the system of trade, coverage, the treatment of transport and related costs, and the identification of trade partner, see Appendix D.

Sources. U.S.S.R., 1946-48: *W-10*, pp. 63-68. (Kohler's series have been calculated from secondary East German sources that presumably relied on official series which were subsequently revised. There is a large discrepancy between Kohler's figures and the subsequently revised official figures for 1949 — the earliest year for which the two sets of statistics can be compared. According to the official revised figures, imports from the U.S.S.R. in 1949 were approximately 47 percent higher, and exports to the U.S.S.R. about 21 percent lower, than those reported by Kohler. Discrepancies, but of a smaller magnitude, exist also for 1950-52. The official revised figures for 1949 and thereafter are used here, but for 1946-48, Kohler's reconstructed figures are still the best available. The reader should note, however, that pre- and post-1949 figures very likely are not comparable.) 1949-69: *G-1*, 1970.

Bulgaria, Czechoslovakia, Hungary, Poland, Rumania, Yugoslavia, 1946-52: *W-10*, pp. 62-64, 67-69 (see note for trade with U.S.S.R.); 1953-54: *G-1*, 1955; 1955-58: *G-1*, 1958; 1959: *G-1*, 1960-61; 1960-67: *G-1*, 1968; 1968-69: *G-1*, 1970.

Other CPEs, 1946-48: *W-10*, pp. 62-69 (sum of components); 1949-59: balancing item, i.e., total trade with "socialist countries" (*G-1*, 1970) less trade with East European countries except Albania; 1960-69: *G-1*, 1970. (Note: In 1949, sum of components of "Total CPEs" exceeds the given total because different sources were used. In imports, the revised figure for the U.S.S.R. is much higher than that reported by Kohler. This suggests that at least some of the revision may represent a reassignment of imports from East Central European countries to the U.S.S.R. In exports, however, the revised figure for the U.S.S.R. is smaller than that reported by Kohler, yet the sum of exports to all East European countries still exceeds officially reported total exports to all "socialist countries," although only by a small amount.)

There are two methods of calculating trade with "Other CPEs": adding the country components ("summed OCPEs"), and subtracting from the officially reported trade with "Total CPEs" the sum of trade with all East European countries except Albania ("residual OCPEs"). These alternative calculations can be made only since 1953, the first year for which trade by countries has been disclosed. Since 1960, the two methods yield identical results. Between 1953-59, however, "residual OCPEs" is consistently larger than "summed OCPEs," and for the following reason: Trade with the U.S.S.R. and trade with "Total CPEs" are revised series defined as *general trade* while trade with individual East Central European countries until 1960 represents more narrowly defined *special trade* (see Appendix D for definition of terms and further discussion). Thus, when trade with OCPEs is calculated as a "residual," the figure includes actual transactions plus the difference between "general" and "special" coverages in trade with East Central European countries. So, "residual OCPEs" is upward biased because it includes an amount assignable to East Central European countries on account of the revision of statistics; while "summed OCPEs" is downward biased relative to the post-1960 series because it represents *special* rather than *general trade*. The difference between the two series is relatively small, as is shown by the tabulation below in Table 9.

Table 9

East Germany's Trade with Other
Centrally Planned Economies, 1953-1959
(Millions of Current Dollars)

Year	Imports from OCPEs			Exports to OCPEs		
	"Residual"	"Summed"	"Residual" less "Summed"	"Residual"	"Summed"	"Residual" less "Summed"
1953	54.0	54.0	---	70.6	70.5	.1
1954	71.1	68.2	2.9	113.4	111.9	1.5
1955	93.3	88.0	5.3	116.6	112.9	3.7
1956	92.4	89.9	2.5	116.3	112.6	3.7
1957	105.2	97.8	7.4	141.7	122.6	19.1
1958	124.2	115.4	8.8	172.7	152.4	20.3
1959	138.9	129.2	9.7	148.8	134.5	14.3

The reader may note that the discrepancy between the two OCPEs series corresponds to the estimated re-export trade with "Total CPEs" less that with the U.S.S.R., as is shown in Table D-1 in Appendix D.

MDCs, 1946-48: *W-10*, pp. 65, 70 (sum of columns 20, 21, and 22); 1949-69: *G-1*, 1970.

LDCs, 1946-48: *W-10*, pp. 65, 69 (column 19); 1949-69: *G-1*, 1970.

Total, 1946-48: *W-10*, pp. 61, 66; 1949-69: *G-1*, 1970. The reader may note that United Nations sources (*UN-8*, 1968, p. 290, as well as other issues of the same publication) incorrectly report total exports in 1954 as 7,103.5 million valuta-marks. The correct figure is either 5,376.4 or 5,401.7 million valuta-marks, showing *special* or *general trade*, respectively.

Tables I.M.H and I.X.H

Note. For Hungarian statistical definitions, including the system of trade, coverage, the treatment of transport and related costs, and the identification of trade partner, see Appendix D.

Sources. U.S.S.R., Czechoslovakia, 1946-48: *W-15*, p. 41.

Bulgaria, Poland, Rumania, Yugoslavia, 1946-47: sum of trade with these four countries calculated by applying percentage given in *W-5*, p. 59 to total trade (*H-1*, 1967, p. 219); trade with individual countries is then estimated by assuming that the percentage share of each in the four-country subtotal is the same as in 1948.

    Bulgaria, Poland, Rumania, 1948: The sum of trade with these three countries was calculated by applying the percentage given in *W-5*, p. 59, to total trade (*H-1*, 1967, p. 219); trade with individual countries is then estimated by assuming that the percentage share of each in the three-country subtotal is the same as in 1949.

    U.S.S.R., Bulgaria, Czechoslovakia, East Germany, Poland, Rumania, Yugoslavia, 1949-54: *H-1*, 1949-1955; 1955-57: *H-1*, 1957; 1958-61: *H-1*, 1961; 1962-63: *H-1*, 1963; 1964-65: *H-1*, 1965; 1966-68: *H-1*, 1968; 1969: *H-1*, 1969.

    Other CPEs (sum of country components except as noted), 1949-51: *H-1*, 1949-1955; 1952-56: *H-1*, 1949-1955 and *H-1*, 1957. Statistics reported in the latter two sources were adjusted as follows: Merchandise trade during 1952-56 was valued differently from other years by the inclusion (in exports) or exclusion (in imports) of certain transport charges (see discussion on p. 279 above). Revised figures, presenting a consistent series for all years, are available only for total trade and for two subtotals, "Total CPEs" and "Total Non-CPEs" (*H-1*, 1967). To be able to include these revised figures here, the unrevised country components need to be adjusted. Since the adjustment is related to "extra" transport costs (paid over f.o.b. Hungarian border in exports and received toward c.i.f. Hungarian border in imports), the small adjustment amounts are not distributed proportionately to trade but are assigned to trade with OCPEs and LDCs, the two groups of countries that are located the farthest from Hungary's borders. The revised and unrevised series, together with the corresponding adjustments, are shown in Table 10.

Table 10

Hungary: Revised and Unrevised Series
and Corresponding Adjustments, 1952-1956
(Millions of Current Dollars)

Year	Total Trade		Total CPEs		Total Non-CPEs		Other CPEs		LDCs	
	Rev.	Unrev.	Rev.	Unrev.	Rev.	Unrev.	Adj.	Unrev.	Adj.	Unrev.
					Imports					
1952	459.5	443.6	331.2	321.1	128.2	122.5	38.9	28.8	16.0	10.3
1953	487.4	471.1	355.5	345.0	131.9	126.1	45.0	34.4	14.3	8.5
1954	531.6	512.7	360.3	348.7	171.3	163.9	39.7	28.1	23.2	15.8
1955	554.2	534.4	302.4	293.4	251.8	241.0	39.5	30.6	39.2	28.4
1956	481.2	466.2	298.4	291.8	182.8	174.4	36.6	29.9	24.8	16.4
					Exports					
1952	438.1	442.7	324.3	324.9	113.8	117.8	26.6	27.3	21.1	25.1
1953	498.2	502.9	394.4	395.6	103.8	107.3	34.2	35.5	22.3	25.8
1954	519.2	525.0	385.5	386.6	133.7	138.4	35.7	36.8	29.8	34.5
1955	601.0	608.9	404.0	404.9	197.0	204.0	43.5	44.4	44.7	51.7
1956	486.9	494.8	307.0	307.3	179.9	187.5	37.8	38.1	35.6	43.2

Other CPEs (continued), 1957: *H-1*, 1957; 1958-61: *H-1*, 1961; 1962-63: *H-1*, 1963; 1964-65: *H-1*, 1965; 1966-68: *H-1*, 1968; 1969: *H-1*, 1969. Note. Trade with Mainland China since 1962 is estimated as a residual, "Total Socialist" trade less trade with individual "socialist" countries, all of which are shown except Mainland China.

MDCs, calculated as a residual, "Total Capitalist" trade less trade with LDCs. "Total Capitalist" trade, 1949: *H-1*, 1949-1955; 1950-67: *H-1*, 1967 (1960-61 totals adjusted by excluding trade with Cuba); 1968-69: *H-1*, 1969.

LDCs, calculated as the sum of trade with Asia, Africa, and the Americas, less CPE and MDC countries. 1949-51: *H-1*, 1949-1955; 1952-56: *H-1*, 1949-1955 and *H-1*, 1957 (note special adjustment described under OCPEs, above); 1957: *H-1*, 1958; 1958-61: *H-1*, 1961; 1962-63: *H-1*, 1963; 1964-65: *H-1*, 1965; 1966-68: *H-1*, 1968; 1969: *H-1*, 1969.

Total, 1946-51, 1957-67: *H-1*, 1967; 1952-56 unrevised: *H-1*, 1949-1955 and *H-1*, 1956; revised: *H-1*, 1967; 1968-69: *H-1*, 1969.

Tables I.M.P and I.X.P

Note. For Polish statistical definitions, including the system of trade, coverage, the treatment of transport and related costs, and the identification of trade-partner country, see Appendix D.

Sources. U.S.S.R., Bulgaria, Czechoslovakia, East Germany, Hungary, Rumania, 1946-49, 1951-54: *P-5*, June 1957 as quoted in *W-9;* 1950, 1955-65: *P-2*, 1965; 1966-68: *P-2*, 1968; 1969: *P-4*, 1970.

Yugoslavia, 1946-47: *P-6*, 1948; 1948 imports (balancing item): "Total CPEs" (*P-2*, 1965) less imports from individual CPEs. (Unusually large trade figures in 1948 are approximately matched by Yugoslav "mirror" statistics. *W-9*, reporting no imports, is apparently incorrect.) 1948 exports, 1949, 1951-54: *P-5*, June 1957, as quoted in *W-9*. (For 1954, *W-9* reports $4.7 million in imports. However, the sum of trade with "Total CPEs" by countries exceeds subsequently reported trade with "Total CPEs" by exactly this amount. It is assumed, therefore, that trade with Yugoslavia was not resumed until 1955.) 1950, 1955-65: *P-2*, 1965; 1966-68: *P-2*, 1968; 1969: *P-4*, 1970.

Other CPEs (sum of country components), 1946-49, 1951-54: *P-5*, June 1957, as quoted in *W-9;* 1950, 1955-65: *P-2*, 1965; 1966-68: *P-2*, 1968; 1969: *P-4*, 1970.

MDCs, LDCs, 1946-49: extrapolated by distributing trade with "Total Non-CPEs" (*P-2*, various issues) to MDCs and LDCs in the same proportion as in 1950; 1950, 1955-68: *P-2*, 1968; 1951-54: interpolated by distributing trade with "Total Non-CPEs" to MDCs and LDCs by assuming that their proportions change at a constant rate between 1950 and 1955; 1969: *P-4*, 1970.

Total, 1946-68: *P-2*, 1968; 1969: *P-4*, 1970.

Tables I.M.R and I.X.R

Note. For Rumanian statistical definitions, including the system of trade, coverage, the treatment of transport and related costs, and the identification of trade-partner country, see Appendix D.

1960 is the first postwar year in which the Central Statistical Office of Rumania published foreign trade data in its official statistical yearbooks, showing total imports and exports since 1958, index numbers linking these data to 1950 and 1955, trade by countries since 1958, and the volume of imports and exports by major commodities since 1958. In the more recent yearbooks, imports and exports by the nine CTN *categories* are also shown for 1950, 1955, and since 1959.

Scattered data for the earlier period from Rumanian and trade-partner sources have been collected and analyzed by J. M. Montias (*W-14*, pp. 136-47). He observed that data published prior to 1959 refer to statistical series that do not accord with those released more recently, except for the 1950 data. For 1951-54, only the old series are available; for 1955-57 both old and revised series are available but they diverge. Montias analyzed the nature of the revision (i.e., the discrepancy between the two series) by commodity groups and by countries. By comparing Rumanian and trade-partner statistics he found:

(1) Trade turnover with Rumania recorded in the official statistics of Hungary, Poland, Bulgaria, and East Germany nearly coincide with the value given in Rumanian statistics corresponding to the old series for the years 1955 to 1957 and to the revised series for subsequent years. (Note, however, one exception which Montias does not discuss: Polish-Rumanian trade in 1957 shows a 54 percent divergence between the figures released by the two countries. See *W-14*, Table 3.4, p. 143.) Since the coincidence of figures between Rumanian and trade-partner sources goes back to at least 1955, Montias tentatively concludes that the revision did not affect the Rumanian basis for valuation in trade with these countries.

(2) From an analysis of the old and revised commodity structure in 1955, Montias found that the revision affected mainly machinery imports and raw material exports and that the discrepancy was confined almost exclusively to trade with the U.S.S.R. and with Czechoslovakia. In 1955, 1956, and 1957 there were large discrepancies between Soviet and Czechoslovak statistics of trade turnover with Rumania and Rumanian statistics of trade with these two countries. These discrepancies dwindled to insignificant amounts from 1958 on, with the exception of Czechoslovak-Rumanian trade in 1959, when an appreciable gap opened up again for no apparent reason. Montias conjectures that these discrepancies (thus, by implication, the revisions) may be explained by Rumanian compensation for machinery and equipment invested by the U.S.S.R. in "joint-stock companies" between 1945 and 1956 after these companies were turned over to Rumania between 1954 and 1956, so that Soviet investments were recorded retroactively by Rumania as imports from the U.S.S.R. to accord with U.S.S.R. treatment of these investments as exports. Also by conjecture, those Soviet investments that originated in other countries, such as Czechoslovakia, were recorded in the revised statistics as imports from these countries, Montias argues.

In the *Compendium*, whenever available, revised series are shown; unrevised data are included for all other years, with appropriate footnote codes. (Total exports and imports for 1956-57, consistent with the revised series, have been obtained by us from a Hungarian source.)

Sources. U.S.S.R., Bulgaria, Czechoslovakia, East Germany, Hungary, Poland, Yugoslavia, Other CPEs (sum of country components), 1958-59: *R-1*, 1960; 1960-68: *R-1*, 1969; 1969: *R-1*, 1970.

Total CPEs, Total Non-CPEs, 1948-57: *W-7* (based on official Rumanian, official U.S.S.R., and U.S. Department of Commerce Sources). For Total CPEs, alternative estimates for 1950 and 1955 can be made by subtracting trade with MDCs and LDCs (in *W-9*, p. 72) from total trade (official, revised), while for Total Non-CPEs, the sum of MDCs and LDCs is an alternative estimate. Both sets of figures are shown in Table 11.

Table 11

Rumania: Alternative Estimates of Trade
with Total CPEs and Total Non-CPEs,* 1950, 1955
(Millions of Current Dollars)

Year	Trade with Total CPEs				Trade with Total Non-CPEs			
	Imports		Exports		Imports		Exports	
	W-7	*W-9*	*W-7*	*W-9*	*W-7*	*W-9*	*W-7*	*W-9*
1950	200.0	190.1	180.0	189.5	43.4	53.3	32.4	22.9
1955	344.0	377.8	303.0	344.5	117.9	84.1	118.7	77.2

*Sources of estimates are given in the column headings.

As comparisons of estimates in Table 11 indicate, the unrevised series obtained from official, secondary, or trade-partner sources can be used with reservations only.

MDCs (sum of trade with component countries), 1958-59: *R-1*, 1960; 1960-68: *R-1*, 1969; 1969: *R-1*, 1970. (Trade with MDCs for two earlier years are shown in *W-9*, p. 72, in millions of current dollars, as follows: Imports, 1950: 40.2; 1955: 62.4; exports, 1950: 11.7; 1955: 50.6.)

LDCs, 1958-69: calculated as residual by subtracting from total trade the sum of trade with CPEs and MDCs. (Trade with LDCs for two earlier years are shown in *W-9*, p. 72, in millions of current dollars, as follows: Imports, 1950: 13.2; 1955: 21.7; exports, 1950: 11.3; 1955: 26.6.)

Total, 1946-47: *W-14*, p. 137; 1948-49, 1951-54: *W-7*; 1950, 1955, 1960-68: *R-1*, 1969; 1956-57: *H-3*, p. 231; 1958-59: *R-1*, 1960; 1969: *R-1*, 1970. (The entries for 1950 and 1955-69 represent comparable, officially revised, figures.)

TABLES I.M.Y and I.X.Y

Note. For Yugoslav statistical definitions, including the system of trade, coverage, the treatment of transport and related costs, and the identification of trade-partner country, see Appendix D.

Sources. U.S.S.R., Bulgaria, Czechoslovakia, East Germany, Hungary, Poland, Total 1946-54: Y-3; 1955-57: Y-2, 1958; 1958-60: Y-2, 1961; 1961-63: Y-2, 1964; 1964-66: Y-2, 1967; 1967-69: Y-2, 1970.

Other CPEs (sum of components), 1946-54: Y-3 ("Other Asia" entry is used as the estimate because most of the important Asian countries, except the Asian CPEs, were specified. To the extent that "Other Asia" includes non-CPEs, the estimate is upward biased. No trade figure was found for Albania; since there was probably some trade with this country during 1946-49, the OCPEs estimate for these years is downward biased. Maximum trade with Albania is trade with "Other Europe," i.e., the unspecified residual, which in millions of current dollars, was as follows: Imports, 1946: 0.0; 1947: 0.4; 1948: 0.0; 1949: 0.1; exports, 1946: 0.5; 1947: 0.7; 1948: 2.3; 1949: 3.1).

Other CPEs (continued), 1955-57 (sum of Albania, Mainland China, and "Other Asia"): Y-2, 1958; 1958-59 (sum of Albania, Mainland China, and "Other Asia" in imports; sum of Albania, Mainland China, Vietnam, and "Other Asia" in exports): Y-2, 1961; 1960 (same components as in 1958-59, plus Cuba): Y-2, 1961; 1961-63 (sum of Albania, Mainland China, "Other Asia" plus Cuba in imports; sum of Albania, "Other Asia," plus Cuba in exports): Y-2, 1964; 1964-66 (same components as in 1961-63): Y-2, 1967; 1967-69 (same components as in 1961-63): Y-2, 1970.

MDCs (sum of Europe less European CPEs, plus Japan, Canada, the United States, and Oceania), 1946-54: Y-3; 1955-57: Y-2, 1958; 1958-60: Y-2, 1961; 1961-63: Y-2, 1964; 1964-66: Y-2, 1967; 1967-69: Y-2, 1970.

LDCs (sum of Asia less Asian CPEs and Japan; Africa; Central America less Cuba since 1960; and South America), 1946-54: Y-3; 1955-57: Y-2, 1958; 1958-60: Y-2, 1961; 1961-63: Y-2, 1964; 1964-66: Y-2, 1967; 1967-69: Y-2, 1970.

Tables I.M.A and I.X.A

Note. For Albanian statistical definitions, including the system of trade, coverage, the treatment of transport and related costs, and the identification of trade-partner country, see Appendix D.

Sources. U.S.S.R., Bulgaria, Czechoslovakia, East Germany, Hungary, Poland, Rumania, Yugoslavia, other CPEs (sum of country components), MDCs (sum of country components), LDCs (sum of reported country components plus "Other"), 1950, 1955, 1960-64: A-1, 1965; 1951-54, 1956-58: UN-3, 1960, p. VI-13.

Total, 1946-64: A-1, 1965; 1965-67: P-9, p. 113.

Tables I.M.CEMA and I.X.CEMA

Summation of Tables I.M.U through I.M.R and Tables I.X.U through I.X.R, respectively.

Statistical Series II

Tables II.CTN.M.U and II.CTN.X.U

Note. Every CTN *category*, except *Category* 1, represents a summation of multi-digit CTN entries in the *Data Bank*, which have been obtained, together with *Category* 1 (always given) from Soviet sources as follows: 1946-66: *U-2*, and various issues of *U-1* up to and including *U-1*, 1967; 1967-69: *U-1*, 1967 through *U-1*, 1969. Each yearbook contains statistics for more than one year. Although the basic body of information for a given year, including the figure for total trade, is the same in all volumes, additional details not shown in one yearbook can often be found in subsequent editions. To obtain as complete information as possible, all volumes with overlapping information were consulted for each year.

Two troublesome features of Soviet foreign trade statistics may be noted: the problem of aggregation and the problem of incomplete coverage.

Official sources do not present systematic information by CTN *categories* or *broad divisions*, thus, even though there is a wealth of detail reported, it does not provide summary information without additional processing, involving laborious aggregation. The task of deriving CTN *category* and *broad division* aggregates was undertaken (see Section A above for a discussion of special aggregation problems and procedures).

A more serious difficulty is incomplete coverage, i.e., the sums of aggregated CTN *categories* or *broad divisions* do not add to total trade. The proportion of trade specified annually between 1946 and 1969 ranges from 89 to 98 percent in imports (average: 94 percent) and from 73 to 93 percent in exports (average: 84 percent); there is no significant trend in these proportions over time. However, by consulting various official statistical publications it is possible to derive, for selected years, unspecified residuals which are smaller than those shown in Tables II.CTN.M.U and II.CTN.X.U. Full details and calculations can be found in Appendix E.

Tables II.CTN.M.B and II.CTN.X.B

1950, 1955, 1960, 1965-68: *B-1*, 1969; 1956-59, 1961: *B-4*, 1955-1961; 1962-64: *B-4*, 1950-1965; 1969: *B-2*, 1970.

Tables II.CTN.M.C and II.CTN.X.C

1948, 1953, 1958-60: *C-2*, 1964 (1960 data were revised; see *C-3*, 1961, for unrevised figures); 1949-52, 1954: *C-3*, 1957; 1955-57: *C-3*, 1961; 1961-67: *C-3*, 1968; 1968: *C-3*, 1969; 1969: *C-4*, June 1970.

Tables II.CTN.M.G and II.CTN.X.G

1950, 1955, 1960-65: CTN *broad division* percentage composition reported in *H-3*, p. 234, which is applied to total trade shown in *E-1*,

1968; 1967: CTN *broad division* export percentage composition reported in *H-12*, p. 319, applied to total trade in *E-1*, 1968; 1969 (including 1960 and 1965 percentage composition for CTN *Category* 2), *CEMA-2*, pp. 356, 358.

Tables II.CTN.M.H and II.CTN.X.H

1949-54: *H-1*, 1949-1955 (see Note 1 below); 1955-57: *H-1*, 1957 (see Note 1 below); 1958-59: *H-1*, 1961; 1960-65: *H-1*, 1965 (see Note 2 below); 1966: *H-1*, 1966; 1967: *H-1*, 1967 (see Note 3 below); 1968: *H-1*, 1968 (see Note 3 below); 1969: *H-1*, 1969 (see Note 3 below).

Note 1. Exports and imports between 1952-56 were originally reported at so-called contract parity, for all other years at border parity, i.e., imports c.i.f., exports f.o.b. (The difference between contract and border parities is transport costs incurred in foreign exchange; in exports transport costs are subtracted from contract parity, in imports they are added to arrive at border parity.) In 1957 (*H-1*, 1957) the commodity composition (i.e., the share of CTN *categories* in the total) but not total trade, was revised for 1955-56 without explanation. This revision apparently reclassified items formerly in *Broad Division* IV into *Broad Division* I, and also affected slightly subtotals of the other two *broad divisions*. Subsequently, total trade and trade by "socialist" and "capitalist" groups of countries (but not by commodity groups) was revised for 1952-56 to correspond to the "border parity" concept. In order to present consistent series not only for total trade (officially revised) but also by CTN *categories*, the latter (unrevised) series were adjusted as follows: Ratios of revised to unrevised values were calculated annually for imports and exports by socialist and capitalist country groups. These ratios were applied as adjustment coefficients to the unrevised commodity series according to CTN *broad divisions*. The average adjustment coefficients for 1952-56 are:

	Socialist	Capitalist
Imports	+3.0%	+5.0%
Exports	-0.2%	-3.5%

Total trade by CTN *broad divisions* was obtained as the sum of the corresponding socialist and capitalist series. The more detailed CTN commodity *categories*, available only since 1955 and only for total trade, were adjusted by applying the ratios of revised to unrevised values calculated for corresponding CTN *broad divisions*.

Note 2. Total imports in *Category* 2 in 1962 have been revised downward, those of *Category* 3 revised upward, in more recent issues of *H-1*. Table II.CTN.M.H shows revised figures.

Note 3. The commodity composition of CTN *broad divisions* had been revised as of 1967. The most significant change was the reclassification of spare parts from CTN *Broad Division* I to II. Additional small changes, apparently reclassifying commodities from CTN *Broad*

Divisions I and II into III and IV, have also been made. (Compare unrevised 1967 structure shown in *UN-8*, 1967, p. 367, with revised series in *H-1*, 1967, pp. 223-24.) Since spare parts represent more than 30 percent of Hungary's machinery imports and over 20 percent of machinery exports, this reclassification would affect greatly the consistency of the important machinery series. Therefore, official statistics were adjusted here by reclassifying spare parts from CTN *Broad Division* II to I.

Tables II.CTN.M.P and II.CTN.X.P

1946-55: *P-2*, 1967; 1956-65: *P-2*, 1965; 1966-68: *P-2*, 1968; 1969: *P-4*, 1970.

Tables II.CTN.M.R and II.CTN.X.R

1950, 1955, 1960-66: *R-1*, 1967; 1959: *R-1*, 1964; 1967-68: *R-1*, 1969; 1969: *R-1*, 1970.

Tables II.CTN.M.A and II.CTN.X.A

1950, 1955, 1960-64: *A-1*, 1965.

Table II.CTN.M.CEMA

1950, 1955, 1959-69: Sum of Tables II.CTN.M.U, II.CTN.M.B, II.CTN.M.C, II.CTN.M.H, II.CTN.M.P, and II.CTN.M.R.

Table II.CTN.X.CEMA

1950, 1955, 1959-69: Sum of Tables II.CTN.X.U, II.CTN.X.B, II.CTN.X.C, II.CTN.X.H, II.CTN.X.P, and II.CTN.X.R.

Tables II.SITC.M.U and II.SITC.X.U

SITC conversion from multi-digit CTN data as recorded in the *Data Bank*. Sources of original data are shown in documentation to Tables II.CTN.M.U and II.CTN.X.U. The CTN/SITC conversion key shown in Table B-6 was applied. The percent of "specified trade" converted by each of the three keys is shown in Table 12.

Tables II.SITC.M.H and II.SITC.X.H

1960-63: Percentages reported in *H-7*, p. 315, were applied to total trade shown in *H-1*, 1967; 1964: *UN-3*, 1966, p. 351; 1965-68: *H-1*, 1968; 1969: *H-1*, 1969.

Tables II.SITC.M.Y and II.SITC.X.Y

1952-53: *Y-2*, 1953; 1953-54: *Y-2*, 1954; 1955-57: *Y-2*, 1957; 1958-60: *Y-2*, 1960; 1961-63: *Y-2*, 1963; 1964-66: *Y-2*, 1966; 1967-69: *Y-2*, 1969.

Table 12

Percent of "Specified Trade" Converted from CTN
to SITC by Each of the Three Conversion Keys. 1946-1969

Year	Imports (II.SITC.M.U)			Exports (II.SITC.X.U)		
	Primary Key	Secondary Key	Tertiary Key	Primary Key	Secondary Key	Tertiary Key
1946	95.92%	1.20%	2.88%	85.91%	12.83%	1.26%
1947	96.52	1.69	1.79	91.30	7.96	.74
1948	97.33	1.44	1.23	93.97	5.09	.94
1949	96.08	1.98	1.94	94.56	3.69	1.75
1950	96.19	1.45	2.36	94.31	3.77	1.92
1951	96.25	1.35	2.40	96.07	2.35	1.58
1952	96.79	1.14	2.07	95.64	1.79	2.57
1953	95.36	1.28	3.36	97.12	1.46	1.42
1954	96.04	1.33	2.63	97.93	1.28	.79
1955	97.75	.58	1.67	97.94	1.53	.53
1956	98.62	.25	1.13	98.03	1.49	.48
1957	98.29	.21	1.50	98.45	1.02	.53
1958	98.27	.17	1.56	98.49	1.07	.44
1959	98.26	.26	1.48	98.62	1.05	.33
1960	98.18	.22	1.60	98.27	1.20	.53
1961	97.51	.25	2.24	98.48	1.14	.38
1962	96.97	.23	2.80	98.32	1.20	.48
1963	96.48	.25	3.27	98.16	1.32	.52
1964	95.75	.28	3.97	98.44	1.04	.52
1965	95.45	.28	4.27	98.34	1.00	.66
1966	95.76	.31	3.93	98.25	1.09	.66
1967	96.92	.38	2.70	98.45	.91	.64
1968	96.73	.32	2.95	98.47	.78	.75
1969	93.72	.30	5.98	98.37	.72	.91
Unweighted Average	96.71	.71	2.57	96.75	2.37	.89

Tables II.BEC.M.U and II.BEC.X.U

BEC conversion from multi-digit CTN data as recorded in the
Data Bank. Sources of original data were shown in documentation to
Tables II.CTN.M.U and II.CTN.X.U. The CTN/BEC conversion key
shown in Appendix Table B-4 was applied to CTN data with the following special adjustments:

CTN 51, Fur and Pelts, was not disaggregated in the original
source. Based on the composition of this commodity *group* in trade
between the U.S.S.R. and West European countries as a group in recent
years, 80 percent of imports and 20 percent of exports were allocated
to BEC 22, the remaining percentages to BEC 21.

In exports only, CTN 83, Vegetables, Fruits, Berries and Related
Products, was not available in further detail. This CTN *group* was allocated equally to BEC 112 and 122.

The proportions of imports and exports transformed to BEC
through special conversions are shown in Table 13.

Table 13

Percent of U.S.S.R. Total Trade Converted
to BEC by Special Allocation, 1946-1969

Year	Imports (II.BEC.M.U)	Exports (II.BEC.X.U)	Year	Imports (II.BEC.M.U)	Exports (II.BEC.X.U)
1946	--	11.2%	1958	.1%	.9%
1947	--	6.4	1959	.1	.8
1948	--	4.1	1960	--	1.0
1949	--	2.7	1961	--	.8
1950	--	2.3	1962	--	.8
1951	--	1.7	1963	--	1.1
1952	--	1.2	1964	--	.9
1953	--	.9	1965	--	.9
1954	--	.9	1966	--	.9
1955	.1	1.1	1967	.1	.7
1956	.1	1.1	1968	.1	.6
1957	.1	.9	1969	--	.6

Tables II.BEC.M.B and II.BEC.X.B

BEC conversion from multi-digit CTN data as recorded in the *Data Bank*. Sources of original data are shown in documentation to Tables II.CTN.M.B and II.CTN.X.B. In addition, multi-digit CTN data required for the conversion have been obtained from *B-1*, 1961, 1963, 1965, 1968, 1969; *B-6*, 1955-57; *B-7*, 1958-1959; and *B-8*, pp. 35, 36, and 43. Inadequate CTN detail was available for 1950 and 1969 to permit meaningful conversion to BEC. The CTN/BEC conversion key shown in Appendix Table B-4 was applied.

For some years between 1955 and 1968, the CTN detail required for BEC conversion was not available for particular commodities. In most cases, however, the required details could be accurately estimated by indirect methods, such as: (1) if all but one CTN *group* within a CTN *category* was given, the unspecified residual in the given *category* total was estimated to represent the missing CTN *group*; (2) the identical procedure was used to estimate missing *subgroups* within *groups*; (3) in a few cases and for selected years only, the division of a *group* into component *subgroups* was estimated on the basis of trade in the *subgroup* shown in physical units. Estimated entries obtained through any of these methods are identified by a special footnote code in the *Data Bank*. Since each year these estimates represent less than 10 percent of total trade, and since the estimates are believed to be accurate, no significant bias is expected to result for the BEC series.

In addition to the above special procedures, the following CTN groups were converted to BEC by special allocation:

Imports		Exports	
CTN	BEC	CTN	BEC
53	21	35	22
56	{ 21 (50%) / 22 (50%)	51	{ 21 (50%) / 22 (50%)

	Imports		Exports
CTN	BEC	CTN	BEC
72	$\begin{cases} 111\ (50\%) \\ 121\ (50\%) \end{cases}$	53	$\begin{cases} 21\ (50\%) \\ 22\ (50\%) \end{cases}$
80	122	56	22
81	112		
83	$\begin{cases} 112\ (50\%) \\ 122\ (50\%) \end{cases}$		

The proportions of imports and exports transformed to BEC through special conversions are shown in Table 14.

Table 14

Percent of Bulgaria's Total Trade
Converted to BEC by Special Allocation, 1955-1968

Year	Imports (II.BEC.M.B)	Exports (II.BEC.X.B)	Year	Imports (II.BEC.M.B)	Exports (II.BEC.X.B)
1955	1.0%	4.2%	1962	1.7%	2.1%
1956	1.2	2.0	1963	2.2	2.1
1957	1.3	2.5	1964	2.5	1.7
1958	1.8	2.7	1965	2.9	1.8
1959	2.3	2.6	1966	2.2	1.9
1960	1.8	2.3	1967	2.5	2.2
1961	1.3	2.2	1968	3.0	2.1

Tables II.BEC.M.Y and II.BEC.X.Y

BEC conversion from two-digit SITC data as recorded in the *Data Bank*. Sources of original data are shown in documentation to Tables II.SITC.M.Y and II.SITC.X.Y. The SITC/BEC conversion key shown in Appendix Table B-5 was applied.

Statistical Series III

Tables III.CTN.M.U (B through Y) and III.CTN.X.U (B through Y)

In each table, every CTN *category* except *Category* 1 (always given) represents a summation of multi-digit CTN entries in the *Data Bank*, whose original sources are the same as those shown in documentation to Tables II.CTN.M.U and II.CTN.X.U. The first two paragraphs of the Note to the above tables are also applicable here.

Tables III.CTN.M.U-CEMA and III.CTN.X.U-CEMA

Summation of Tables III.CTN.M.U (B through R) and Tables III.CTN.X.U (B through R), respectively.

Tables III.CTN.M.C (U through Y) and III.CTN.X.C (U through Y)

In each Table, every CTN *category* represents a summation of multi-digit CTN entries in the *Data Bank,* whose original sources are: 1958-59: *C-6;* 1960-65: *C-2,* 1962, 1963, 1964, 1965, 1966; 1966: *C-2,* 1967 and *C-3,* 1967; 1967: *C-3,* 1967, 1968; 1968: *C-3,* 1968. The original sources show trade by partner according to commodity groups, without CTN numbers. On the basis of commodity designations, a two- or three-digit CTN number was assigned to each entry. (Since the sequence of commodity groups in the original sources always follows the CTN numerical sequence, this facilitated somewhat the assignment of CTN codes.) However, the proportion of trade specified is always less than 100 percent, i.e., there remains for each country in each year an undistributed residual. It is believed that in most cases the unspecified items represent unlisted CTN commodity *groups* or *subgroups,* but the possibility remains that reported trade in specified CTN *groups* and *subgroups* is less than exhaustive.

It may be noted that statistical series frequently overlap, i.e., the structure of trade for a given year may be reported in several issues of *C-2* and *C-3.* Additional commodity detail was obtained by consulting all relevant volumes.

Tables III.CTN.M.C-CEMA and III.CTN.X.C-CEMA

Summation of Tables III.CTN.M.C (U through R) and Tables III.CTN.X.C (U through R), respectively.

Tables III.CTN.M.P (U through Y) and III.CTN.X.P. (U through Y)

In each table, every CTN *category* represents a summation of three-digit CTN entries in the *Data Bank.* Entries in the *Data Bank* are based on three-, five-, and seven-digit entries (with CTN code numbers given) whose original sources are: 1958: *P-7,* 1958; 1959: *P-7,* 1959; 1960: *P-7,* 1960; 1961: *P-7,* 1961; 1962: *P-7,* 1962; 1963: *P-7,* 1963; 1964-65: *P-2,* 1965; 1966-67: *P-2,* 1967; 1968: *P-2,* 1968.

The proportion of trade specified is somewhat less than 100 percent, i.e., there remains for each country in each year an undistributed residual.

Tables III.CTN.M.P-CEMA and III.CTN.X.P-CEMA

Summation of Tables III.CTN.M.P (U through R) and Tables III.CTN.X.P (U through R), respectively.

Tables III.BEC.M.U (B through Y) and III.BEC.X.U (B through Y)

BEC conversion from multi-digit CTN data as recorded in the *Data Bank.* Sources of original data are shown in documentation to Tables II.CTN.M.U (B through Y) and II.CTN.X.U (B through Y). The CTN/BEC conversion key shown in Appendix Table B-4 was applied to CTN data.

In exports to Bulgaria, Czechoslovakia, and East Germany, an occasional special allocation was necessary. These allocations, as well as the proportions of exports to the respective countries transformed to BEC through special conversions, are shown in Table 15.

Table 15

U.S.S.R. Exports to Bulgaria, Czechoslovakia,
and East Germany: Percent of Total Exports
Converted to BEC by Special Allocation, 1946-1968

Year	Bulgaria[1] (III.BEC.X.U-B)	Czechoslovakia[2] (III.BEC.X.U-C)	East Germany[3] (III.BEC.X.U-G)
1946	3.8%		
1947	2.1		
1948	2.0		
1949	2.0		
1950	2.0		
1951	1.7		
1952	.6		
1953	.6		
1954	.6		
1955		.7	.2
1956		.5	.1
1957		.2	.1
1958		.2	.1
1959		.1	.1
1960		.1	.1
1961		.1	.1
1962		.1	.1
1963		.1	.1
1964		.1	.1
1965		.1	.1
1966		.1	.1
1967		.1	.1
1968		.1	.1

1. CTN 34 to BEC 21.
2. CTN 52 to BEC 21 (80%) and BEC 22 (20%).
3. CTN 34 to BEC 21; CTN 52 to BEC 21 (80%) and BEC 22 (20%).

Tables III.BEC.M.U-CEMA and III.BEC.X.U-CEMA

Summation of Tables III.BEC.M.U (B through R) and Tables III.BEC.X.U (B through R), respectively.

Tables III.BEC.M.C (U through Y) and III.BEC.X.C (U through Y)

BEC conversion from multi-digit CTN data as recorded in the *Data Bank*. Sources of original data are shown in documentation to Tables III.CTN.M.C (U through Y) and III.CTN.X.C (U through Y). The

CTN/BEC conversion key shown in Appendix Table B-4 was applied to CTN data, except for special allocations which, together with the proportions of trade so converted, are shown in Tables 16 and 17 for imports and exports, respectively.

Tables III.BEC.M.C-CEMA and III.BEC.X.C-CEMA

Summation of Tables III.BEC.M.C (U through R) and Tables III.BEC.X.C (U through R), respectively.

Tables III.BEC.M.P (U through Y) and III.BEC.X.P (U through Y)

BEC conversion from three-digit CTN data as recorded in the *Data Bank*. Sources of original data are shown in documentation to Tables III.CTN.M.P (U through Y) and III.CTN.X.P (U through Y). The CTN/BEC conversion key shown in Appendix Table B-4 was applied.

Tables III.BEC.M.P-CEMA and III.BEC.X.P-CEMA

Summation of Tables III.BEC.M.P (U through R) and Tables III.BEC.X.P (U through R), respectively.

Statistical Series IV

Tables IV.SITC.M (U through R) and IV.SITC.X (U through R)

In each table, every SITC *category* represents a summation of multi-digit SITC entries in the *Data Bank,* whose original sources are annual issues *UN-2.* See Part Three, Section A, above, for a discussion of data and adjustments.

Tables IV.SITC.M.CEMA and IV.SITC.X.CEMA

Summation of Tables IV.BEC.M (U through R) and IV.BEC.X (U through R), respectively.

Tables IV.BEC.M (U through R and IV.BEC.X (U through R)

BEC conversion from multi-digit SITC data as recorded in the *Data Bank,* applying the conversion key shown in Appendix Table B-5. Sources of original data are shown in documentation to Tables IV.SITC. (U through R) and IV.SITC. (U through R).

Tables IV.BEC.M.CEMA and IV.BEC.X.CEMA

Summation of Tables IV.BEC.M (U through R) and IV.BEC.X (U through R), respectively.

Table 16

Czechoslovakia's Imports from East European Countries:
Percent of Total Imports Converted to BEC by Special Allocation, 1958-1968

Year	U.S.S.R.[1] III.BEC.M.C-U	Bulgaria[2] III.BEC.M.C-B	East Germany[3] III.BEC.M.C-G	Hungary[4] III.BEC.M.C-H	Poland[5] III.BEC.M.C-P	Rumania[6] III.BEC.M.C-R	Yugoslavia[7] III.BEC.M.C-Y
1958	15.1	17.5	13.4	10.1	39.2	28.4	18.3
1959	12.6	20.2	15.1	11.6	29.1	19.3	16.5
1960	12.3	22.2	15.7	10.4	21.8	11.2	8.7
1961	14.8	22.8	12.4	8.7	16.6	9.2	4.8
1962	13.1	29.1	12.6	6.6	13.4	9.0	15.7
1963	12.1	25.8	13.8	11.4	16.2	9.9	16.7
1964	14.0	20.0	12.6	9.8	21.6	6.3	12.1
1965	13.2	17.6	11.9	7.6	16.2	11.2	4.9
1966	11.5	12.6	12.3	8.7	20.9	8.1	5.0
1967	10.0	14.5	10.6	10.6	18.8	10.5	--
1968	9.9	10.2	10.4	7.8	18.7	8.2	--

1. CTN 20 to BEC 31; CTN 51 to BEC 21; CTN 52 to BEC 21; CTN 81 to BEC 112 (50%) and 122 (50%); CTN 82 to BEC 122; CTN 83 to BEC 112.

2. CTN 34 to BEC 21 (50%) and 22 (50%); CTN 51 to BEC 21; CTN 83 to BEC 112 (50%) and 122 (50%).

3. CTN 20 to BEC 31 (50%) and 32 (50%); CTN 34 to BEC 21 (50%) and 22 (50%); CTN 51 to BEC 21 (50%) and 22 (50%); CTN 81 to BEC 112.

4. CTN 20 to BEC 31 (50%) and 32 (50%); CTN 34 to BEC 21 (50%) and 122 (50%); CTN 51 to BEC 21 (50%) and 22 (50%); CTN 83 to BEC 112 (50%) and 122 (50%); CTN 81 to BEC 112; CTN 83 to BEC 112 (20%) and 22 (80%).

5. CTN 20 to BEC 31; CTN 52 to BEC 21 (50%) and 22 (50%); CTN 81 to BEC 112; CTN 83 to BEC 112 (50%) and 122 (50%).

6. CTN 51 to BEC 21; CTN 83 to BEC 112 (50%) and 122 (50%).

7. CTN 51 to BEC 21; CTN 52 to BEC 21 (50%) and 22 (50%); CTN 81 to BEC 112; CTN 83 to BEC 112 (50%) and 122 (50%).

Table 17

Czechoslovakia's Exports to East European Countries:
Percent of Total Exports Converted to BEC by Special Allocation, 1958-1968

Year	U.S.S.R. III.BEC.X.C-U	Bulgaria[1] III.BEC.X.C-B	East Germany[2] III.BEC.X.C-G	Hungary[3] III.BEC.X.C-H	Poland[4] III.BEC.X.C-P	Rumania[5] III.BEC.X.C-R	Yugoslavia[6] III.BEC.X.C-Y
1958	--	8.9	22.3	18.9	2.9	18.4	1.9
1959	--	10.2	19.7	13.6	1.3	13.6	3.4
1960	--	14.8	20.4	16.5	1.2	16.5	4.3
1961	--	15.5	22.5	16.7	1.5	13.8	6.4
1962	--	11.6	19.5	13.9	2.2	11.9	6.9
1963	--	6.0	20.8	13.3	3.6	10.6	3.2
1964	--	8.1	17.8	14.0	1.7	10.5	3.8
1965	--	8.2	16.0	14.5	2.0	13.1	3.4
1966	--	4.0	13.2	13.3	2.5	19.4	2.5
1967	--	3.1	11.4	10.5	2.6	16.6	--
1968	--	3.2	11.2	9.8	2.6	16.6	--

1. CTN 20 to BEC 31 (50%) and 32 (50%); CTN 34 to BEC 21 (50%) and 22 (50%); CTN 51 to BEC 21 (50%) and 22 (50%); CTN 53 to BEC 21.

2. CTN 20 to BEC 31 (50%) and 32 (50%); CTN 231 to BEC 31 (50%) and 32 (50%); CTN 34 to BEC 21 (50%) and 22 (50%); CTN 51 to BEC 21 (50%) and 22 (50%); CTN 83 to BEC 112 (50%) and 122 (50%).

3. CTN 20 to BEC 31 (67%) and 32 (33%); CTN 34 to BEC 21 (50%) and 22 (50%); CTN 51 to BEC 21 (50%) and 22 (50%).

4. CTN 20 to BEC 31 (10%) and 32 (90%); CTN 51 to BEC 22.

5. CTN 20 to BEC 31 (50%) and 32 (50%); CTN 51 to BEC 21 (50%) and 22 (50%).

6. CTN 20 to BEC 31 (50%) and 32 (50%); CTN 51 to BEC 21 (50%) and 22 (50%).

Statistical Series V

Tables V.CTN.MX.H (1 and 2)

1949-55: *H-1* (see Note 1 to Tables II.CTN.M.H and II.CTN.X.H);
1956, CPEs: *H-2*, January 1957; 1956, Non-CPEs: calculated by ap-
plying percentages given in *H-8*, February-March 1967, p. 203, to "Total
Non-CPEs" (see documentation to Tables I.M.H and I.X.H); 1958, CPEs:
Total trade by CTN *broad divisions* (see Tables II.CTN.M.H and
II.CTN.X.H), less trade with "Non-CPEs"; 1958: Non-CPEs: calculated
by applying percentages given in *H-8*, February-March 1967 to "Total
Non-CPEs"; 1959-68: annual issues of *H-1* (see Note 3 to Tables
II.CTN.M.H and II.CTN.X.H); 1969: *H-2*, March 1970.

Note. The commodity composition of CTN *broad divisions* had
been revised as of 1967, the most significant change being the reclassification of spare parts from *Broad Division* I to II (see Note 3 to
Tables II.CTN.M.H and II.CTN.X.H). For consistency, the official statistics were adjusted here by reclassifying spare parts from CTN
Broad Division II to I. Trade in spare parts for 1968 and 1969 are
shown in *H-1*, 1968 and *H-1*, 1969, respectively; for 1967 it was assumed that the ratio of spare parts to machinery was the same as in
1968.

Tables V.CTN.MX.P (1 and 2)

1946-68: *P-2*, 1968; 1969: *P-2*, 1969.

PART FOUR
Appendices
ON SUBJECTS OF SPECIAL INTEREST

APPENDIX A

Three Commodity Trade Classifications

CEMA Trade Nomenclature (CTN)

History

A brief history of CTN, the "Uniform CEMA Foreign Trade Commodity Nomenclature," can be pieced together from various East European sources. In March 1959 a group of foreign trade statistical experts from CEMA countries recommended adoption of a uniform nomenclature as of 1960 (*U-3*,* 1968, p. 48), and the CEMA Secretariat prepared a draft CTN based on this recommendation. Apparently after some delay, the draft was examined by another CEMA expert committee in September 1960 and was superseded by a revised and expanded CTN (*H-8*, June 1964, p. 652 fn.). This last was formally adopted by CEMA members as of 1962 (*U-3*, January 1971, p. 49).

The 1962 CTN is a slightly modified version of the U.S.S.R.'s "Uniform Commodity Nomenclature of Foreign Trade," first published in 1954 (*U-4*, as quoted in *U-1*, 1960, p. 6). There are indications that the U.S.S.R. nomenclature was introduced about 1950.** Even before the modified U.S.S.R. code was officially adopted, it had been used by some CEMA countries as the "CEMA code." For example, Bulgarian foreign trade yearbooks published during the late 1950s show that the commodity classification is based on "1953 CEMA" nomenclature. (*B-1*, 1956, p. 156, and *B-7*, p. 13.) The 1956 Hungarian yearbook also indicates that commodity breakdowns are based on a "classification employed by countries participating in CEMA." (*H-1*, 1956.)

Both the original U.S.S.R. nomenclature of 1954 and the subsequent 1962 CTN have undergone revisions. These have affected neither the

---

*See Key to the Citations, p. 277 above.
**The January 1971 issue of an English language Soviet journal states: "For more than 20 years now, the Soviet Union has had a Uniform Foreign Trade Commodity Nomenclature, which has been widely used not only at home but also abroad, in other socialist countries." (*U-3*, p. 48.)

basic principles of classification nor the number and definition of one-digit *categories* and *broad divisions,* until the most recent revision in 1971, as noted below. Hence, revisions should not affect the comparability over time of series included in this *Compendium.* Revisions have added new multidigit commodity designations, reclassified others, and clarified definitions. A partial reconciliation list* for the original 1954 U.S.S.R. nomenclature, the 1962 CTN code (since 1962 the U.S.S.R. nomenclature and the CEMA Trade Nomenclature have become officially identical), and the 1967 revised second edition of the CTN, shown in a U.S. document (*W-3,* vol. I, pp. 166-215), indicated that the revisions at two- and three-digit levels were minor. A discussion of differences between the 1954 U.S.S.R. nomenclature and the 1962 CTN, including examples and the reason for the revision, can be found in *W-6,* pp. 277-78.

All CEMA countries record the commodity composition of trade in CTN even though not every set of CTN statistics is published. The CTN is also used in trade agreements involving CEMA countries.

Classification System

The CTN is a seven-digit code (compared to the six-digit U.S.S.R. code of 1954), with each commodity designation preceded by a code number. The first digit of the code indicates *categories,* also called sections (of which there are 9); the second digit, commodity *groups* (58); the third, commodity *subgroups* (309); the fourth and fifth, commodity *positions;* and the sixth and seventh, commodity *subpositions* (over 4000 *positions* and *subpositions,* combined) (*U-3,* September 1968, p. 48). Judging from the date of publication of the source cited, the numbers in parentheses refer to the 1967 second edition.

In constructing the CTN, it was intended that the classification allow division of commodities according to (1) investment vs. consumption goods, (2) fixed vs. variable capital, (3) industrial vs. agricultural commodities, and (4) degree of processing. Within commodity *categories,* two-digit *groups* usually indicate either the designation of industrial equipment (*category* 1 except 16), that of consumer goods (9), or nature of material (2 to 8). The third digit usually identifies the degree of processing from raw materials through intermediate products (however, in *Categories* 1 and 9, *subgroups* detail the type of machinery and equipment and type of industrial consumer good, respectively). A discussion of how well the CTN classification system fulfills its objectives can be found in *W-6,* pp. 274-77. The nine one-digit *categories* and four CTN *broad divisions* (in which data are shown in the statistical tables included here) are identified in Table 1 of the Introduction. Codes and designations to three digits (maximum detail in which data are shown in the *Data Bank* and used in conversion to BEC and SITC) are shown in Table A-1.

---

*The reconciliation list is partial because only those codes appear on the list for which trade was reported in U.S.S.R. yearbooks.

Table A-1

CEMA Trade Nomenclature (CTN), Three Digits
(Effective 1962-1970)

Cate-gory	Group	Sub-group	Designation
			I. Industrial Machinery and Equipment (including spare parts)
1			Machinery and Equipment
	10		Metalworking equipment
		100	Metal-cutting machine tools and spare parts
		101	Presses and spare parts
		102	Hammers and spare parts
		103	Other forge and press equipment
	11		Power and electric equipment
		110	Power equipment
		111	Electrical engineering equipment
		112	Electrode products
	12		Mining, metallurgical, and crude-oil industrial equipment
		120	Mining equipment
		121	Crushing, grinding, and concentrating equipment
		122	Coking equipment
		123	Blast furnace equipment
		124	Steel smelting equipment
		125	Rolling mill equipment
		126	Wire drawing equipment
		127	Foundry equipment
		128	Oil-drilling equipment
		129	Equipment for petroleum refineries
	13		Hoisting and conveying equipment
		130	Cranes and spare parts
		131	Charging and setting machines and spare parts
		132	Winches
		133	Hoisting machines and spare parts
		134	Power trucks and equipment
		135	Other hoisting and conveying equipment
	14		Equipment for food and light industries
		140	Equipment for the food industry
		141	Equipment for the soap industry
		142	Industrial refrigeration equipment
		143	Equipment for the tobacco industry
		144	Equipment for light industry
	15		Equipment for chemical, lumber, paper, and construction industries and other industrial equipment
		150	Equipment for the chemical industry
		151	Equipment for the lumber and paper industry
		152	Woodworking machines and spare parts
		153	Equipment for the building-materials industry
		154	Excavators and road-building equipment
		155	Pump and compressor equipment
		156	Public service and fire-fighting equipment
		157	Equipment for the printing industry
		158	Telecommunications equipment
		159	Equipment for other branches of industry

Table A-1 (cont'd)

Category	Group	Subgroup	Designation
	16		Equipment and parts for complete industrial plants
		161	Mining, metallurgical, and power plants
		162	Metalworking plants
		163	Chemical plants
		164	Complete equipment or machine units for chemical plants
		165	Plants for building-materials and lumber industries
		166	Textile, leather, and rubber industrial plants
		167	Plants for food and consumer-goods industries
		168	Plants and equipment for scientific, cultural, and welfare institutions
		169	Plants and equipment for underground construction
	17		Instruments, laboratory-medical equipment, bearings, tools, and abrasives
		170	Instruments
		171	Laboratory equipment
		172	Medical equipment and instruments
		173	Bearings (including balls and rollers)
		174	Tools
		175	Industrial diamonds and rubies
		176	Hard alloys
		177	Abrasives
		178	Process-control instruments, laboratory equipment
		179	Instruments for measuring mechanical magnitudes
	18		Tractors and agricultural machinery
		180	Tractors and spare parts
		181	Agricultural machinery
		182	Agricultural implements
	19		Means of transport
		190	Railroad rolling stock
		191	Motor transport and garage equipment
		192	Ships, marine, marine-hoisting, and diving equipment
		193	Means of air travel
		194	Other transport equipment
			II. Fuels, Raw Materials (other than for Food), Other Materials
2			Fuels, Mineral Raw Materials, Metals
	20		Solid fuels
		200	Hard coal
		201	Coke
		202	Brown coal
		203	Charcoal
		204	Other solid fuels
	21		Crude oil
		210	Crude oil
	22		Petroleum products and synthetic liquid fuel
		220	Gasoline
		221	Aviation fuel
		222	Ligroin
		223	Kerosene
		224	Diesel fuel
		225	Mazut

Table A-1 (cont'd)

Category	Group	Subgroup	Designation
		226	Lubricating oils
		227	Lubricating greases
		228	Oil additives
		229	Other petroleum products
	23		Fuel gas, electric power, and steam
		230	Combustible gas
		231	Electric power
		232	Steam
		233	Water
	24		Metallic ores and concentrates
		240	Ores of ferrous metals
		241	Ores of nonferrous metals
		242	Concentrates of nonferrous metals
		243	Other metallic ores
	25		Nonmetallic minerals, clays, earths
		250	Nonmetallic minerals
		251	Clays
		252	Nonmetallic ores
		253	Nonmetallic minerals, other
	26		Ferrous metals
		260	Pig iron and ingots
		261	Ferroalloys
		262	Scrap and wastes of ferrous metals
		263	Steel in ingots
		264	Rolled ferrous metals
		265	Products of rolled steel (ordinary and high-quality)
		266	Pipes
		267	Containers
		268	Metal products (hardware)
		269	Switching equipment, metal barrels, and other metal products
	27		Nonferrous metals
		270	Nonferrous metals and alloys
		271	Scrap and wastes of nonferrous metals
		272	Rolled nonferrous metals
		273	Products of nonferrous metals
	28		Precious metals and products
		280	Precious metals
		281	Precious metal products
	29		Cable and wire, including bare and insulated cables and wires
		290	Cable
		291	Wire
		292	Copper and aluminum rails and coils
3			Chemicals, Fertilizers, Rubber
	30		Chemical products
		300	Organic and inorganic acids
		301	Soda products and other alkalis
		302	Salts of organic and inorganic acids
		303	Coal and tar chemicals
		304	Plastics and materials for production of plastics
		305	Alcohols and aldehydes

Table A-1 (cont'd)

Cate-gory	Group	Sub-group	Designation
		306	Products of wood-chemical industry
		307	Intermediate products of aniline dye industry
		308	Inorganic oxides, etc.
		309	Other chemical products
	31		Dyes, paints, varnishes, and tanning materials
		310	Coal-tar dyes and natural indigo
		311	Paint and varnish materials
		312	Tanning and dyeing materials of vegetable origin
		313	Tanning extracts (natural and synthetic)
	32		Explosives and pyrotechnic products
		320	Explosives
		321	Pyrotechnic products
	33		Film and photographic materials
		330	Raw materials for film (celluloid)
		331	Movie and photographic film
		332	Photographic plates and paper, and photographic equipment
	34		Fertilizers, insecticides, and pesticides
		340	Phosphorous fertilizers, including phosphates and apatite concentrates
		341	Potassium fertilizers
		342	Nitrogen fertilizers
		343	Insecticides and pesticides
	35		Crude rubber, rubber, and rubber-asbestos products
		350	Crude rubber (natural and synthetic)
		351	Motor vehicle tires, inner tubes, and flaps
		352	Conveyor and drive belts
		353	Rubber sleeves and hoses
		354	Rubber mats and rubberized cloths
		355	Rubber-asbestos products
		356	Other insulation and technical-rubber products
	36		Isotopes and amorphous chemicals
		360	Radioactive isotopes
		361	Amorphous chemicals
4			Building Materials and Construction Parts
	40		Building materials
		400	Cement and related materials
		401	Sheet glass
		402	Roofing materials
		403	Wall covering and decorating materials
		404	Refractory materials
		405	Insulation materials
		406	Other building materials
		407	Products of basalt
	41		Prefabricated structures and parts
		410	Prefabricated buildings
		411	Prefabricated barracks
		412	Wooden construction materials (elements)
		413	Various other structures and parts
	42		Metal warehouses, metal structures, and tubings
		420	Metal warehouses
		421	Metal structures and tubings

Table A-1 (cont'd)

Cate-gory	Group	Sub-group	Designation
5			Raw Materials of Vegetable and Animal Origin (not food)
	50		Timber, pulp, and paper
		500	Round timber
		501	Lumber
		502	Veneer
		503	Wood articles for production purposes
		504	Cork bark, cork chips, and cork products
		505	Wood pulp and cellulose
		506	Paper
		507	Cardboard
		508	Paper and cardboard products for production purposes
		509	Reeds
	51		Textile raw materials and semifinished products
		510	Plant fibers
		511	Wool
		512	Natural silk
		513	Raw spinning materials, synthetic
		514	Semi-manufactured products from textile raw materials
		515	Other spinning raw materials and materials
	52		Fur and pelts
		520	Raw fur and pelts
		521	Natural prepared fur (undyed)
		522	Prepared, dyed fur
		523	Sample products of fur and pelts
	53		Unprepared leather and hides
		530	Hides and skins
		531	Finished leather (tanned hides)
	54		Tobacco (raw material)
		540	Tobacco leaves
		541	Wastes of tobacco industry
	55		Seed grain and planting materials
		550	Seed grains of cereals, groats, and legumes
		551	Seed grains of oil-bearing crops
		552	Seed grains of exotic and industrial plants
		553	Seed grains of vegetables
		554	Seed grains of fodder plants
		555	Other seed grains and planting materials
	56		Essential oils, exotic resins, and medicinal-pharmaceutical raw materials
		560	Essential oils and natural aromatics
		561	Synthetic aromatic products
		562	Exotic resins
		563	Medicinal-pharmaceutical raw materials
	57		Industrial fats and oils
		570	Industrial fats of animal origin
		571	Fish fats, industrial
		572	Industrial oils of vegetable origin
		573	Other industrial oils and waxes
	58		Feedstuff, regular (hay) and concentrated
		580	Oilcake and oilcake meal
		581	Mill waste products
		582	Hay-fodder

Table A-1 (cont'd)

Category	Group	Subgroup	Designation
		583	Fodder yeasts, albumen
		584	Other fodder and feedstuffs
	59		Other raw materials and materials
		590	Bristles, animal hair, and other raw materials of animal origin
		591	Artificial leather, intestines, and other artificial raw materials
		592	Ropes, fishing nets, industrial fabrics, and other materials
		593	Other raw materials and materials, n.e.s.

III. Foodstuffs and Raw Materials for Foodstuffs

Category	Group	Subgroup	Designation
6			<u>Live Animals (not for slaughter)</u>
	60		Live animals
		600	Draft animals
		601	Breeding stock
		602	Sheep and goats
		603	Other live animals
		604	Live birds and bird eggs
		605	Live roe and live fish
		606	Sperm of breeding stock
7			<u>Raw Materials for the Production of Foodstuffs</u>
	70		Cereals (including groats)
		700	Cereals (excluding groats)
		701	Groat cereals
	71		Live animals for slaughter
		710	Live animals (to be slaughtered for meat)
	72		Oil seeds and fruits, and other foodstuff raw materials
		720	Oil seeds and fruits for industrial purposes
		721	Coffee, cocoa, and tea
		722	Spices
		723	Products of the starch and hydrolysis industries
		724	Sea mammals (oils and meat) and fish fats
		725	Margarine products
		726	Other foodstuff raw materials
8			<u>Foodstuffs</u>
	80		Meat, dairy products, animal fats, and eggs
		800	Meat and meat products
		801	Fats for consumption, animal origin (including butter)
		802	Milk and dairy products (excluding butter)
		803	Eggs and egg products
	81		Fish and fish preparations
		810	Fresh and frozen fish
		811	Salted fish
		812	Smoked fish
		813	Canned fish
		814	Prepared fish, other
		815	Canned crustacea (crab, lobster, etc.)
		816	Caviar
		817	Dried spinal cord of fish (sturgeon)

Table A-1 (cont'd)

Cate-gory	Group	Sub-group	Designation
		818	Deepwater products
		819	Other products of the fishing industry
	82		Flour milling products, legumes
		820	Flour milling products
		821	Legumes
	83		Vegetables, fruits, berries, and related products
		830	Vegetables
		831	Melons
		832	Fresh fruits, berries, and related products
		833	Dried fruits, berries, and related products
		834	Canned fruits and berries
		835	Nuts, almonds, etc.
		836	Frozen fruits, berries, vegetables, etc.
	84		Sugar, vegetable oils, beverages, other foodstuffs, and related consumer goods
		840	Sugar and confectionery products
		841	Vegetable food oils
		842	Other food fats
		843	Processed fruits, berries, etc.
		844	Beverages, alcoholic and nonalcoholic
		845	Vitamins
		846	Tobacco products
		847	Other foodstuffs and related consumer goods

IV. Industrial Consumer Goods (other than Food)

Cate-gory	Group	Sub-group	Designation
9			Industrial Consumer Goods
	90		Cotton, wool and other fabrics (excluding industrial)
		900	Cotton fabrics
		901	Woolen fabrics
		902	Silk fabrics
		903	Linen fabrics
		904	Carpeting
		905	Other products of the weaving industry
		906	Other fabrics
		907	Fabrics from staple fiber
	91		Clothing and linen
		910	Topcoats and outer garments (except leather and fur)
		911	Leather clothing
		912	Fur clothing
		913	Linen garments (excluding knits)
		914	Knit linen garments
		915	Table linen, bedding, and toweling
		916	Hosiery
		917	Headgear
		918	Other clothing and linen
	92		Haberdashery goods
		920	Textile haberdashery
		921	Tulle and tulle goods
		922	Metal haberdashery
		923	Leather haberdashery
		924	Other haberdashery (fancy) goods

Table A-1 (cont'd)

Category	Group	Subgroup	Designation
	93		Leather, rubber, and other footwear
		930	Leather footwear
		931	Rubber footwear
		932	Textile and combination footwear
		933	Other footwear
	94		Household dishes and dining implements
		940	Metal dishes
		941	China and earthenware
		942	Glass dishes
		943	Metal silverware
		944	Other dishes
	95		Furniture
		950	Furniture
	96		Medicines and hygienic, pharmaceutical, and cosmetic products
		960	Narcotics
		961	Bacteriological compounds
		962	Other medicines
		963	Medicinal materials and related rubber articles
		964	Sanitation and hygienic articles
		965	Soaps, perfumes, and cosmetics
		966	Medicinal implements (containers)
	97		Household and cultural articles
		970	Household appliances
		971	Electrotechnical goods
		972	Other household articles
		973	Paper products
		974	Printed matter
		975	Musical instruments and accessories
		976	Sport and hunting equipment
		977	Handicraft, art supplies, and toys
		978	Motion pictures
		979	Other household and cultural articles
	98		Industrial consumer goods, n.e.s.
		980	Drawing and office supplies
		981	Jewelry, precious stones, and amber
		982	Other articles
		983	Samples of consumer articles

Source: Translated by the author (with notes in parentheses added to elucidate meaning) from *H-8*, June 1964, pp. 652-59, except for codes 13, 130-34 (which appear to be inadvertent omissions) which were obtained from U.S.S.R. sources as shown in *U-4*, 1962, p.388; CTN 233, obtained from Polish sources, shown in *P-2*, 1968, p.253; and CTN 178,179, and 907 (which appear to have been added after 1962), from U.S.S.R. sources as shown in *W-3*, vol. I, pp. 19-60.

CTN *Category* 6, shown in the original as a separate *broad division*, was included in *Broad Division* III, as is the more recent practice in CEMA countries.

Subgroup designated as 593 above is shown in *U-4*, 1962, p. 394, as 599. Poland makes use of CTN 160 as a separate *subgroup*, Equipment and Machinery for Mining, instead of grouping these commodities with CTN 161.

The CTN codes and designations shown in Table A-1 are largely based on a listing of the 1962 CTN found in a 1964 Hungarian journal. This source listed all 58 CTN *groups* but only 297 *subgroups,* i.e., 12 fewer than allegedly contained in the 1967 CTN (see above). Some of the missing *subgroups* represent obvious omissions, such as *subgroups* 130 through 134, but the discrepancy may also be due in part to *subgroups* added in the 1967 second edition. The CTN shown in Table A-1 was supplemented with additional *subgroups* shown in Soviet and Polish publications, bringing the number of *subgroups* to 306. Thus, three of the 309 *subgroups* are not shown because they cannot be identified.

Revised and Enlarged 1971 Edition

The 1971 revision does not affect the consistency of the statistical series presented here, which extend only to 1969, but in updating the series beyond 1970, the revision would have to be taken into account.

This new edition was prepared by CEMA experts during 1968 and 1969, was officially adopted at the December 1969 (14th) meeting of the CEMA Standing Commission for Statistics, and was introduced as of January 1971 (*U-3,* January 1971, p. 49). The publication which lists the revised nomenclature to its full seven digits covers more than 600 printed pages and appears to be a full listing (see CEMA-1). The possibility that some codes are not shown cannot of course be excluded. Explicit statements in the CEMA literature as well as the comparison of the 1971 CTN with the earlier versions down to the three-digit level disclose that this revision was more substantial than the ones in 1962 and 1967. A number of two-digit *groups* and three-digit *subgroups* have been added or deleted, while the content of still others has been changed. In terms of numbers, *groups* have been reduced from 58 to 57, *subgroups* increased from 309 to 317, and *positions* plus *subpositions* decreased from the previously reported "over 4,000" to 3,945 (*CEMA-1,* p. 4).

It is useful to distinguish two types of revisions in the CTN: a reclassification of commodities from one CTN *category* to another, which should be taken into account when updating the *Compendium* and *Data Bank* beyond 1970; and reclassifications, additions, or deletions *within* CTN *categories,* which also need to be taken into account when updating the *Data Bank* beyond 1970.

A comparison of the 1971 CTN with the earlier version shown in Table A-1 reveals three reclassifications across *categories:*

(1) The transfer of CTN 29 (Cable Products) to CTN 113 (Cable and Wire), i.e., a reclassification of a commodity *group* from a semi-finished metal product in *Category* 2 to a *subgroup* belonging to the power and electric equipment *group* in *Category* 1. It is interesting to note that a Soviet source states as an explanation that the U.N.'s SITC "also places cable products in the 'Machinery and Equipment' section." (*U-3,* January 1971, p. 49.)

(2) CTN 54 (Tobacco Raw Materials) has been moved to CTN 726.

Thus, raw tobacco is now considered a material for the food industry, a change which improves the internal consistency of CTN because tobacco products have always been included among foodstuffs in *Category* 8.

(3) CTN 845 (Vitamins) has been reclassified as CTN 967, i.e., moved from foodstuffs (*Category* 8) to industrial consumer goods (*Category* 9), a change which appears to be justified to improve the internal consistency of classification.

Changes involving reclassifications *within* CTN *categories* are much more numerous: codes have been added, deleted, transferred (i.e., a commodity *group* or *subgroup* designated by one code number in earlier CTN was given a new code number) or redesignated (i.e., the same code number assigned a new commodity designation). The most frequent type of change, the "miscellaneous" or "not elsewhere specified" *subgroup*, has been consistently given the last three-digit numerical position, i.e., the code always ending with 9. Thus, CTN 135 (Other Hoisting and Conveying Equipment) has been changed to CTN 139; CTN 194 (Other Transport Equipment), to 199; CTN 243 (Other Nonmetallic Minerals), to 249; and so on. About two dozen transfers or code additions of this kind can be noted.

A further apparently systematic change has been the moving of spare parts, previously generally included with the appropriate machinery *subgroup*, to the "not elsewhere specified" *subgroup*. This change in classification has been deduced from the new three-digit listing by noting that *subgroup* designations no longer include the phrase, "and spare parts." But whether the reallocation of spare parts has been consistent, and if so, always into the last *subgroup*, is not known for certain.

A careful study of the revisions indicates that their primary purpose was to make the CTN internally more consistent without changing any of the basic principles of classification. For example, *Group* 16 (Equipment and Parts for Complete Industrial Plants) was transferred to other *groups* in *Category* 1 in order to classify all machinery according to type. In the old CTN, *Group* 16 included all types of machinery and equipment if destined for assembling into complete plants. This practice clashed with the general principle of classifying machinery by type and also caused a significant portion of machinery shipments to be effectively lost from detailed commodity statistics.

Instead of listing the complete CTN-1971 to three digits, let us reconstruct the revisions by comparing codes and designations shown in Table A-1 with those published in CTN-1971 (official source: *CEMA-1*, pp. 623-34). The revisions are grouped into three categories: new codes, transferred codes, and old codes with new designations. These changes are shown in Tables A-2, A-3, and A-4, respectively.

An important innovation of the CTN-1971 is the inclusion of a 70-item Appendix, "Production Operations Not Included in Sections 1-9 of the Uniform CEMA Foreign Trade Commodity Nomenclature," which lists invisible commercial transactions. These entries have "O" codes (which can thus be considered a tenth CTN *category*), and are divided

Table A-2

Revisions in the 1971 CTN: New Codes

CTN Code	Commodity Designation
104	Precision metal-finishing equipment
105	Shop equipment for metallurgical processes
113	Cables and wires
145	Equipment for the sewing industry
146	Equipment for leather, footwear, and fur industries
195	Small autos, motorcycles, and mini-bikes
209	Other solid fuels
339	Other film and photographic materials
345	Mixed fertilizers
346	Natural (organic) fertilizers
414	Metal accessories in construction
415	Plastic accessories in construction
416	Ceramic and other construction parts
419	Other construction materials and parts
709	Other cultivated cereals
711	Fowl for slaughter
719	Other livestock for slaughter
822	Bakery products
837	Marinated fruits
838	Mushrooms
85	Beverages and tobacco products
850	Beverages, alcoholic and nonalcoholic
851	Tobacco products
967	Vitamins
984	Antiques

into nine two-digit groups (01 to 09), each comprised of several five-digit items (*CEMA-1*, pp. 601-15). The two-digit *group* classifications are:

01 = Patents, licenses, know-how
02 = Projects and exploratory activities
03 = Mounting and building activities
04 = Overall technical management and control
05 = Repairing
06 = Leasing and concessions
07 = Alterations and finishing
08 = Exchange of specialists (technical recruitment)
09 = Other services of productive character

A Soviet source states:

The need to classify such operations arises because the [CTN] is used not only for operational and statistical records but also for accounting and foreign exchange transactions records, where these transactions are relevant. [*U-3*, January 1971, p. 49.]

Table A-3

Revisions in the 1971 CTN: Transferred Codes

Old CTN[a]	New CTN[b]	Old CTN[a]	New CTN[b]
124	123**	54	726**
125	123**	540	726**
126	123**	541	726**
135	139	555	559
141	149	584	589
144*	149	593	599
168	164 **	603	609
194	199		
		726*	729
203	209	843	(831 through 836)***
204*	209	844	850
243	249	845	967
253	259	846	851
29	113	847	849
290	113		
291	113	906	909
292	113	918	919
		924*	929
343	348	933	939
356	359	944	949
406	409	982	989
515	(513 or 514)***	983	989

a. Old CTN codes have been deleted except those with an *, which have been given new designations, as shown in Table A-4.

b. The new CTN codes have been added except those identified with **, whose designation has been changed (as shown in Table A-4) or those with ***, whose designation has remained essentially unchanged.

Standard International Trade Classification (SITC)

History

The first edition of the United Nations Standard International Trade Classification (the "original SITC") was prepared by the organization's Secretariat in 1950. By 1960, governments of countries accounting for approximately 80 percent of world trade were compiling their commodity composition according to the SITC system, as had the major international agencies reporting trade. To facilitate regrouping data from the Brussels Tariff Nomenclature, still widely used in West Europe by customs authorities to record commodities crossing frontiers, the SITC was revised by the UN in 1960 ("SITC, Revised").

Classification System and Limitations

The 1960 edition essentially preserved the original SITC structure down to the three-digit level. The 1,312 five-digit items in the revised code are summarized into 625 *subgroups*, these into 177 *groups*, then 56 *divisions*, which are consolidated into 10 *sections* (or *categories*).

Table A-4

Revisions in the 1971 CTN: Changes in Commodity Designations[a]

CTN Code	Commodity Designation
123	Metallurgical equipment
127	Equipment for the petroleum refining industry
128	Equipment for geological exploration and extraction
129	Other metallurgical and petroleum equipment
144	Equipment for the textile industry
16	Engineering plants, structures, and public utilities
161	Industrial plants and buildings
162	Plants for lumber and other rural industries
163	Houses and complexes
165	Communications equipment (except for ships)
166	Hydrotechnical plants and equipment
167	Pipelines
169	Other buildings, plants, and structures for general public use
204	Coke and semicoke of lignite
269	Other ferrous metal products
710	Cattle for slaughter
726	Tobacco raw materials
836	Frozen fruits and berries
84	Sugar, vegetable oils, and other foodstuffs
901	Wool and synthetic fabrics
902	Silk and synthetic fabrics
903	Linen and synthetic fabrics
911	Leather and synthetic clothing

a. The exclusion of spare parts from machinery *subgroup* designations is not shown.

To facilitate aggregation, the first digit determines *section*, the second *division*, the third *group*, the fourth *subgroup*, the fifth *item*, the sixth and seventh (of interest only to particular groups of countries or international organizations) *article* or *subitem*. Codes and designations to two digits are shown in Table A-5; codes and designations to five digits can be found in *UN-7*.

Since SITC was developed from a customs nomenclature, SITC groupings may be according to nature of material, final use, or degree of processing. Accordingly, aggregates obtained by summing SITC codes have certain limitations for economic analysis.* For example, gasoline and various other processed petroleum products (SITC 332) are classified with primary products (SITC 0-4), while unrefined nonferrous metals (SITC 68), and lime and cement (SITC 661) are included with manufactured goods (SITC 5-8). These and similar problems have prompted the U.N. Statistical Commission to design a new "Broad Economic Categories" nomenclature.

*The Statistical Commission of the United Nations observes: "The SITC, Revised . . . as it stands is not entirely suitable for analysis by end-use. . . ." (*UN-4*, p. vii.)

Table A-5

Standard International Trade Classification, Revised (SITC), Two Digits

Section (Category)	Division	Designation
0		Food and Live Animals
	00	Live animals
	01	Meat and meat preparations
	02	Dairy products and eggs
	03	Fish and fish preparations
	04	Cereals and cereal preparations
	05	Fruit and vegetables
	06	Sugar, sugar preparations, and honey
	07	Coffee, tea, cocoa, spices, and manufactures thereof
	08	Feeding stuff for animals (not including unmilled cereals)
	09	Miscellaneous food preparations
1		Beverages and Tobacco
	11	Beverages
	12	Tobacco and tobacco manufactures
2		Crude Materials, Inedible, Except Fuels
	21	Hides, skins, and fur skins, undressed
	22	Oil seeds, oil nuts, and oil kernels
	23	Crude rubber (including synthetic and reclaimed)
	24	Wood, lumber, and cork
	25	Pulp and waste paper
	26	Textile fibres (not manufactured into yarn, thread, or fabrics) and their waste
	27	Crude fertilizers and crude minerals (excluding coal, petroleum, and precious stones)
	28	Metalliferous ores and metal scrap
	29	Crude animal and vegetable materials, n.e.s.
3		Mineral Fuels, Lubricants and Related Materials
	32	Coal, coke, and briquettes
	33	Petroleum and petroleum products
	34	Gas, natural and manufactured
	35	Electric energy
4		Animal and Vegetable Oils and Fats
	41	Animal oils and fats
	42	Fixed vegetable oils and fats
	43	Animal and vegetable oils and fats, processed, and waxes of animal or vegetable origin
5		Chemicals
	51	Chemical elements and compounds
	52	Mineral tar and crude chemicals from coal, petroleum, and natural gas
	53	Dyeing, tanning, and coloring materials
	54	Medicinal and pharmaceutical products
	55	Essential oils and perfume materials; toilet, polishing, and cleansing preparations
	56	Fertilizers, manufactured

Table A-5 (cont'd)

Section (Category)	Division	Designation
	57	Explosives and pyrotechnic products
	58	Plastic materials, regenerated cellulose, and artificial resins
	59	Chemical materials and products, n.e.s.
6		Manufactured Goods Classified Chiefly by Material
	61	Leather, leather manufactures, n.e.s., and dressed fur skins
	62	Rubber manufactures n.e.s.
	63	Wood and cork manufactures (excluding furniture)
	64	Paper, paperboard, and manufactures thereof
	65	Textile yarn, fabrics, made-up articles, and related products
	66	Nonmetallic mineral manufactures n.e.s.
	67	Iron and steel
	68	Nonferrous metals
	69	Manufactures of metal n.e.s.
7		Machinery and Transport Equipment
	71	Machinery, other than electric
	72	Electrical machinery, apparatus, and appliances
	73	Transport equipment
8		Miscellaneous Manufactured Articles
	81	Sanitary, plumbing, heating, and lighting fixtures and fittings
	82	Furniture
	83	Travel goods, handbags, and similar articles
	84	Clothing
	85	Footwear
	86	Professional, scientific, and controlling instruments; photographic and optical goods, watches, and clocks
	89	Miscellaneous manufactured articles n.e.s.
9		Commodities and Transactions Not Classified According to Kind
	91	Postal packages
	92	Special transactions
	93	Unclassified goods
	94	Animals n.e.s. (including zoo animals)
	95	Firearms and ammunition
	96	Coins (other than gold and legal tender)

Source: *UN-7*, pp. 3-4, 45; except *division* 92, added by Yugoslavia (*Y-2*, various issues).

Broad Economic Categories (BEC)

Classification System

A new and improved system, BEC is comprised of only 19 *basic categories* within 7 *large economic classes*, as shown in Table 3 of the Introduction. *Large economic classes* are one-digit entries 1 through 7; *basic categories* are one-, two-, or three-digit entries not further divided. Each BEC *category* is defined in terms of one- to five-digit codes of the SITC, as shown in *UN-4*.

The 19 *basic categories* ("elements") of BEC can be combined not only into the 7 *large economic classes* but also according to two additional and independent aggregation procedures: *broad end use* ("primary products" and "processed goods") and *basic SNA classes* ("capital goods," "intermediate goods," and "consumption goods").

The BEC system classified commodities as "primary" if (1) they are characteristically the products of primary sectors, i.e., farming, forestry, fishing, hunting, and the extractive industries; (2) transformation or processing of primary products accounts for only a small amount of value added; and (3) they are waste and scrap materials. Any commodity not defined as "primary" is classified as "processed." To illustrate, ginned cotton is classified as a primary commodity since almost all of its total value derives from agriculture. In contrast, canned and prepared foods, which receive much of their value in food processing, are counted as "processed" (*UN-6*, p. 34).

As far as matching BEC elements and SNA *basic classes* is concerned, it is recognized that a fully accurate alignment is not possible. The main problem is that SNA classifies commodities according to end use but a given good entering into international trade may often be put to alternative end uses. Accordingly, commodities are generally allocated in the BEC according to their customary end use. (*UN-4*, p. vii.)

The aggregation of BEC basic categories according to *broad end use* and SNA *basic classes* is shown in Table A-6.

Table A-6

BEC Aggregates by Broad End Use and Basic SNA Classes

A. Broad End Use	(2) Intermediate Goods
(1) Primary Products	111
11	121
21	2
31	31
	322
(2) Processed Goods	42
12	53
22	
32	(3) Consumer Goods
4	112
5	122
6	522
(3) Unspecified	6
7	(4) Unspecified
	7
B. Basic SNA Classes	
(1) Capital Goods	(5) To be Allocated by the User
41	321
521	51

Source: *UN-4.*

APPENDIX B

Reconciliation of Classifications

CTN to BEC

CTN and BEC Classifications Compared

The transformation of CTN to BEC is facilitated by the relatively small number of BEC *categories* as well as by similarities in the principles of classification in the two nomenclatures. The 7 *large economic classes* of the BEC correspond rather closely to combinations of CTN *categories* and *groups*, so any CEMA country's trade specified in two-digit CTN can be regrouped into the 7 *large economic classes* of the BEC, as is shown in Table B-1.

Table B-1

Correspondence of BEC Large Economic Classes
with CTN Commodity Categories and Groups

BEC Large Economic Classes	CTN Code
1 Food and Beverages	7-8
2 Industrial Supplies (non-Food)	2-5 (except 20-23)
3 Fuels and Lubricants	20-23
4 Machinery, Other Capital Equipment (except Transport), and Accessories	1 (except 19)
5 Transport Equipment	19
6 Consumer Goods Not Elsewhere Specified	9
7 Goods Not Elsewhere Specified	6

A highly accurate transformation of CTN to BEC can be made also from only one-digit CTN *categories* or the even more aggregated CTN *broad divisions*, if BEC's 7 *large economic classes* are combined into 4 *"larger" economic classes*. Since the commodity composition of CEMA countries' trade is available most readily according to *broad divisions*, it is of interest to examine how accurately these divisions can be aligned with BEC's 4 *"larger" economic classes*. A comparison of the most aggregate groupings of commodities in the two nomenclatures is shown in Table B-2.

The approximate correspondence of BEC *large economic classes* and CTN *broad divisions* and the required adjustments are discussed next.

$$(1) \quad BEC \ 1 + 7 \cong CTN \ III$$

327

Table B-2

A Comparison of BEC Large Economic Classes and CTN Broad Divisions

BEC Large Economic Classes	CTN Broad Divisions
1 Food and Beverages	I Industrial Machinery and Equipment (including Spare Parts)
2 Industrial Supplies (non-Food)	
3 Fuels and Lubricants	
4 Machinery, Other Capital Equipment (except Transport), and Accessories	II Fuels, Raw Materials (other than Food), Other Materials
	III Foodstuffs and Raw Materials for Foodstuffs
5 Transport Equipment	
6 Consumer Goods Not Elsewhere Specified	IV Industrial Consumer Goods (other than Food)
7 Goods Not Elsewhere Specified	

An item-by-item examination of the two nomenclatures revealed five commodities of some importance classified differently in the two systems: Unmilled Corn, Unmilled Oats, Live Animals Not for Slaughter, Tobacco Manufactures, and Vitamins are all included in CTN III but not in BEC 1. The BEC classifies Unmilled Corn and Oats with Industrial Supplies (BEC 2); Live Animals Not for Slaughter with goods Not Elsewhere Specified (BEC 7), and Tobacco Manufactures and Vitamins with Consumer Goods (BEC 6). Since as far as CEMA countries are concerned the only commodity of any importance included in their published trade statistics among those listed under BEC 7 is Live Animals Not for Slaughter, BEC 1 and 7 can be combined and aligned with CTN III except for the four commodities listed.

$$(2) \text{BEC } 2 + 3 \cong \text{CTN II}$$

$$(3) \text{BEC } 4 + 5 \cong \text{CTN I}$$

The main reason for showing Fuels and Lubricants (BEC 3) separately from Industrial Supplies (BEC 2) and Transport Equipment (BEC 5) separately from Machinery and Equipment (BEC 4) is that fuels and means of transport can be used for both industrial and household consumption. Thus, the complete BEC (see Table 3 in the Introduction) presents a further breakdown of fuels (which includes Motor Spirits) and means of transport (which includes Passenger Motor Vehicles) to permit the allocation of these categories between industrial and household uses as desired. (In fact, such an allocation is necessary when aggregating according to SNA *basic classes*.) However, according to CTN, all fuels are included with industrial supplies and all means of transport with industrial machinery and equipment. Thus, by combining BEC *large economic classes* 2 plus 3 and 4 plus 5 into *"larger"* economic classes, no inaccuracy whatever is introduced as far as alignment with CTN *Broad Divisions* II and I, respectively, is concerned.

To be sure, to the extent that not all CEMA exports and imports of transport equipment and fuels are destined for industrial use, the descriptive accuracy of CTN *Broad Divisions* I and II is impaired. One may add, however, that since the production and consumption of privately owned motor vehicles in East Europe was (and still is) limited, the assumption that transport equipment and fuels are destined for industry is much less inaccurate than a similar assumption would be for most Western countries.

(4) BEC 6 ≅ CTN IV

These two aggregates can be aligned quite accurately except for Tobacco Manufactures and Vitamins, which are included in BEC 6 and excluded from CTN IV.

Summarizing the above, we find the correspondence between BEC *"larger" economic classes* and CTN *broad divisions* as follows:

(1) BEC 1 + 7 ≅ CTN III less Unmilled Corn, Unmilled Oats,
        Tobacco Manufactures, and Vitamins

(2) BEC 2 + 3 ≅ CTN II plus Unmilled Corn and Unmilled Oats

(3) BEC 4 + 5 ≅ CTN I

(4) BEC 6   ≅ CTN IV plus Tobacco Manufactures and Vitamins

An Original Conversion Key

To convert CTN data to BEC aggregates by *broad end use* or SNA *basic classes* was much more difficult than regrouping by *large economic classes* because a satisfactory transformation involves disaggregation of trade flows in CTN and reaggregation on the basis of the BEC system. To facilitate conversion of East Europe's not fully detailed CTN data to BEC, the original 19 *basic categories* of BEC were combined here into 11, as shown in Table B-3.

The abridgement involved three changes in the original BEC classification, as follows:

(1) BEC categories 41, 42, 51, 522, and 523 were combined to new BEC 4, Machinery, Transport Equipment, Accessories, and Parts. For most CEMA countries total trade in machinery is available but further details, particularly on spare parts and accessories, tend to be sketchy. Since in the original BEC all five *categories* here combined were summed as Processed (see Table A-6), no significant information is lost when these categories are combined for greater comparability with CTN. However, in so doing, Spare Parts and Accessories (BEC 42 and 53), which would have been included in Intermediate Goods according to SNA *basic classes* (see Table A-6) are now included in Capital Goods, which is therefore biased upward. Similarly, all of BEC 51 (to be allocated by the user) is now included in Capital Goods, although a certain portion of trade in Passenger Motor Vehicles would need to be allocated to Consumer Goods.

Table B-3

Combined Broad Economic Categories (BEC) and Corresponding CTN Headings

Combined BEC Categories	Corresponding CTN Headings
1 Food and Beverages	
11 Primary	
111 For industry	6, 70, 71, 720, 721
112 For household consumption	722, 803, 810-12, 830-33
12 Processed	
121 For industry	723, 724, 726, 820
122 For household consumption	725, 800-802, 813-19, 821, 834-36, 84
2 Industrial Supplies (non-Food)	
21 Primary	24, 25, 340, 341, 350*, 500, 510-12, 520, 530, 54-56, 58, 590
22 Processed	26-29, 30-33, 342, 343, 351-56, 36, 4, 501-509, 513-15, 521-23, 531, 57, 591-93
3 Fuels and Lubricants	
31 Primary	200, 202, 204, 21, 230
32 Processed	201, 203, 22, 231, 232
4 Machinery, Transport Equipment, Accessories, and Parts (includes BEC 5)	1
6 Consumer Goods Not Elsewhere Specified	9
7 Goods Not Specified	Grand total less trade specified in CTN

*Special allocation between BEC 21 and 22 is required for Natural and Synthetic Raw Rubber, respectively.

(2) BEC 32, Processed Fuels and Lubricants, is not broken down into 321 (Motor Spirit) and 322 (Other Processed Fuels) because this CTN detail is generally not available. Once again, this elision does not affect the Primary and Processed subtotals. In the SNA subtotals all of BEC 32 is classified as Intermediate rather than Consumption goods, following the reasoning set forth on p. 328 above.

(3) The final such combination, to new BEC 6, Consumer Goods, of Durable (61), Semidurable (62), and Nondurable (63) articles, raises no problems of aggregation by degree of processing or SNA *classes*.

Next, a CTN/BEC conversion key was prepared, which made use of that most highly aggregated CTN code which could be assigned accurately to a BEC *combined category*. The key, classified by BEC headings, is shown in Table B-3; cross-classified in CTN sequence, in Table B-4.

Table B-4

Conversion of CEMA Trade Nomenclature (CTN)
to Combined Broad Economic Categories (BEC)

CTN	BEC	CTN	BEC
1	4	511	21
		512	21
200	31	513	22
201	32	514	22
202	31	515	22
203	32		
204	31	520	21
		521	22
21	31	522	22
22	32	523	22
230	31	530	21
231	32	531	22
232	32		
		54	21
24	21	55	21
25	21		
26	22	560	22
27	22	561	22
28	22	562	21
29	22	563	21
30	22	57	22
31	22	58	21
32	22		
33	22	590	21
		591	22
340	21	592	22
341	21	593	22
342	22		
343	22	60	111
		70	111
350	21	71	111
351	22		
352	22	720	111
353	22	721	111
354	22	722	112
355	22	723	121
356	22	724	121
		725	122
36	22	726	121
		800	122
4	22	801	122
500	21	802	122
501	22	803	112
502	22		
503	22	810	112
504	22	811	112
505	22	812	112.
506	22	813	122
507	22	814	122
508	22	815	122
509	22	816	122
510	21	817	122

Table B-4 (cont'd)

CTN	BEC	CTN	BEC
818	122	833	112
819	122	834	122
820	121	835	122
821	122	836	122
830	112	84	122
831	112	9	6
832	112		7*

*Total trade less trade specified in CTN.

The following simplifying conventions were found to be useful or necessary:

(1) Food and Beverages, Primary, for Industry (BEC 111) now includes Live Animals Not for Slaughter (CTN 6) to avoid retaining a separate BEC category just for this small item, and, also, to be able to allocate all of CTN *Broad Division* III to BEC *Large Economic Class* 1, as was discussed above. BEC 111 also includes (instead of BEC 21, as in the original) the feed cereals oats and corn (CTN 70004 and 70005) because CTN to three digits does not show them separately from wheat, rye, and barley (CTN 70001, -2, and -3, respectively). Since both BEC 111 and 21 are Primary as well as Intermediate goods, this raises no problem of aggregation by degree of processing or SNA classes.

(2) Food and Beverages, Processed, for Industry (BEC 121) omits unrefined sugar (CTN 80002) and some additional smaller items because they are not specified at three-digit CTN. They are included in BEC 122, which thus may be slightly upward biased. This will affect aggregation only by SNA classes, in favor of Consumer and at the expense of Intermediate goods.

(3) Industrial Supplies, Primary (BEC 21) is downward biased because it excludes oats and corn (see (1) above) as well as waste and scrap materials (except those of metals), the latter causing the Primary subtotal to be understated.

Special Problems and Evaluation

A special problem encountered during the CTN/BEC conversion was that for certain CEMA countries or years some CTN entries were not available in sufficient detail to use the conversion key without further adjustment. In these few cases, special allocations were made, and are documented in notes to the appropriate tables.

No attempt has been made as yet to quantify the bias introduced by combining original BEC categories and by simplifying assumptions. However, one may conclude that whenever CTN data were available in detail required by the conversion key, the resulting BEC series provide a reasonably reliable empirical foundation for analysis and international comparisons. It is believed that the classification of spare parts with Capital instead of Intermediate goods may result in the most significant bias.

SITC to BEC

The original BEC *categories* were designed by the U.N. to facilitate conversion from SITC data; in fact, BEC *categories* are defined in terms of SITC headings. This SITC/BEC conversion key has been prepared and published *(UN-4)*, and it individually assigns more than 600 two- to five-digit SITC headings to appropriate BEC *categories* (SITC contains a total of 1,312 five-digit items).

The trade of individual East European countries with West Europe as a group (Series IV) is the longest and most important SITC series in this collection which was to be converted to BEC. After preliminary processing of the data (including assigning the SITC code when not given), it was revealed that usually no more than two- or three-digit SITC details would be available, so the U.N.'s SITC/BEC key, requiring up to five-digit SITC detail, could not be applied. However, an item-by-item examination of the U.N. key revealed that in most cases two- or three-digit SITC can be matched accurately to one of the 11 *combined* (rather than the original 19) *basic categories* of BEC. Such an "abbreviated" key was constructed and is shown in Table B-5.

The new SITC/BEC key in turn was used as a guide to process East-West trade data, by computer, as summarized next.

In the U.N. publications on East-West trade, the number of component commodity groups has varied by subperiods, increasing from about 20 in 1950 to nearly 200 by 1964. Since 1964 the data have been published with three-digit SITC codes; before 1964 only commodity or commodity group designations were given, to which two- or three-digit SITC codes (or code spans) could be assigned. Even though only one-digit SITC *category* subtotals are shown in the *Compendium*, greater commodity detail was included in the *Data Bank*. The number of commodity series processed was determined, subject to data availability, by two objectives: to obtain a consistent series by SITC one-digit *categories* and two-digit *divisions*, and to convert SITC data to BEC. The decision to disregard SITC detail beyond two digits except when needed for more accurate transformation to BEC was made because SITC data even to two digits are voluminous, and also because the more aggregated the commodity groups the better the chances that data in comparable classification for earlier subperiods could be found. Approximately 50 export and import series were processed for each CEMA country.

The following example illustrates how the two criteria were jointly considered. Textile Fibers (SITC 26) is shown in U.N. publications for most years by commodities (wool, cotton, jute, etc.), each a three-digit component of SITC 26. Thus, only SITC 26 would need to be included to attain the first objective. However, conversion to BEC requires that

Table B-5

Conversion of Standard International Trade Classification (SITC)
to Combined Broad Economic Categories (BEC)[1]

SITC	BEC	SITC	BEC
00	111	242	21
01	122	243	22
022-024	122	244	21
025	112	25	22
031	112	261-265	21
032	122	266	22
041-045	111	267	21
046-048	121	27-29	21
051	112		
052	121	321.4[5]	31
053	122	321.8[6]	32
054	112	331	31
055	122	332	32
06	122[2]	34	31
071	111	35	32
072	111		
073	122	4	121
074	112		
075	112	51-53	22
08	21	54	6
09[3]	122	55-59	22
		6	22
11	122		
12	21[4]	7	4
21	21	81	22
22	111	82-89	6
23	21		
241	31	9	7

1. This key has been constructed primarily for application to trade between individual East European countries and West Europe as a group.

2. Trade assumed to consist of refined sugar and sugar products only. For U.S.S.R. trade with West Europe this assumption is valid on the basis of U.S.S.R. trade statistics.

3. East-West trade statistics usually include components of SITC 09 with 07 and other divisions in section "O."

4. Trade assumed to consist of unmanufactured tobacco.

5. Includes unprocessed lignite, peat, etc.

6. Includes coal, lignite, and peat briquettes.

SITC *group* 266 (Synthetic Fibers) be placed in one BEC *category*, while all other SITC *groups* (natural textile fibers and textile waste materials) tally with another *category* of BEC. Thus, SITC 26 would be too highly aggregated, but including all subgroups of SITC 26 would be unnecessarily detailed. Accordingly, two commodity groups were included: Natural Textile Fibers and Textile Wastes (SITC 261-65, 267) and Synthetic Fibers (SITC 266).

To construct East-West trade series that conform with the two objectives of consistency of SITC as well as BEC series over time, it was necessary to adjust the original U.N. data by making special allocations among SITC *categories* as well as SITC *groups*.

Allocations among SITC *Categories*. If in a subperiod a commodity group was found to correspond to an SITC code span which contained different SITC first digits, trade was allocated to two or more commodity designations by a special procedure. To illustrate, trade in Oil Seeds (SITC 22) and Animal and Vegetable Oils and Fats (SITC 4) were each reported for 1952-57 and again since 1964, but given only as a combined commodity group for 1958-63. Since the two groups have different SITC first digits, the value was distributed between the components by interpolation, on the basis of proportions calculated for subsequent and (if available) preceding years. Entries so obtained are identified by a special footnote code in the *Data Bank*.

The value of commodities so allocated is considerably less than 10 percent for each East European country for most years. Between 1952 and 1963 there were in fact only four commodity groups of importance for which special allocations were made: Oil Seeds, Fats, and Oils; Fur skins and Products (if Undressed, SITC 21; if Tanned and Dressed, SITC 61; if made into clothing, SITC 84); Fertilizers (if Crude, SITC 27; if Manufactured, SITC 56); and Textiles (Yarn and Fabrics, SITC 65; Clothing, SITC 84). Since 1964 adequate commodity detail has been published so that no special allocation was necessary; for 1950-52 additional allocations were made because the statistics then published were highly aggregated.

The accuracy of SITC one-digit *categories* shown in the *Compendium* would be affected adversely by these special allocations only if the composition of trade with respect to the allocated commodity groups was atypical for the years requiring adjustments.

Allocation among SITC *Groups*. For certain commodity groups, the SITC detail required for conversion was unavailable for some years. For example, within SITC 02, Dairy Products and Eggs, subgroups 022-024 (various dairy products) converts to one BEC category while SITC 025 (Eggs) converts to another. For 1957-63 only the combined commodity group was shown, so a special allocation by a method similar to that detailed above was made for each East European country's exports and imports. The additional allocations were also mostly for food items (which are all in SITC *category* "O") so these do not affect the accuracy of SITC *categories*.

For a few commodities, accurate BEC conversion required greater than three-digit SITC detail, which was not available in U.N. publications. The most important was SITC 321, Coal, Coke, and Briquettes (a principal Polish and U.S.S.R. export to West Europe) because BEC classifies coal as Primary, and coke and briquettes as Processed, industrial supplies. For Poland, all SITC 321 exports were classified as Coal (SITC 321.4), based on information obtained from the Polish Commercial Consulate that during the entire postwar period, Poland exported to West Europe almost exclusively coal. For the U.S.S.R., the

ratio of coal to coke-briquette exports to the main West European imports combined was calculated for each year from U.S.S.R. sources and
the ratios applied to SITC data obtained from West European sources.
A few further special allocations were made on a similar basis but the
relative importance of the additional commodity groups involved was
very small.

CTN to SITC

The United Nations' Conversion Key

In 1965, a subcommittee of the United Nations Statistical Commission prepared a preliminary key bridging SITC and CTN nomenclatures
(UN-5). It consists largely of a reconciliation of six- and seven-digit
SITC *items* with five-digit CTN *positions*. The key is cross-classified
in order of SITC and CTN headings. No conversion is shown for less
than five-digit entries in either nomenclature. Apparently the U.N.
itself has been unable to make use of the key, because of inadequate
knowledge of the details of CEMA foreign trade. The only official
statement that can be found with regard to the SITC/CTN conversion
project states:

> In considering the key, the Commission bore in mind the difficulties of rec-
> onciling the CMEA classification, which postulated the knowledge available in
> countries whose economies were centrally planned, of the end use of many of the
> articles classified, with the SITC. As the use of the key would undoubtedly reveal
> areas in which it could be improved, the Commission recommended that the Sta-
> tistical Office of the United Nations should co-operate with the secretariat of the
> CMEA in preparing a revised version. [*UN-6*, p. 32.]

That some CEMA countries and possibly the CEMA Secretariat
make use of the U.N. key is suggested by the fact that two CEMA countries, Hungary and Czechoslovakia, submitted to the U.N. the SITC
commodity composition of their trade not long after the key became
available. Another key, linking CTN, SITC, and the Brussels Tariff
Nomenclature (BTN), has reportedly been published in the U.S.S.R.
(*U-5*, as shown in *W-6*, p. 277, fn. 10). In the West, however, such conversions have not been made because in most cases only too highly
aggregated CTN statistics have been available.

New Conversion Key for U.S.S.R. Total Trade

To obtain adequate correspondence of CTN and SITC, a minimum
of three-digit CTN data would seem needed, a disclosure requirement
generally not met at the present time.

For U.S.S.R. total trade alone, which is the longest and most detailed (though still incomplete) published CTN series, a transformation
to SITC has been carried out by sequential application of a three-part
conversion key, shown in Table B-6.

Table B-6

Conversion of CEMA Trade Nomenclature (CTN)
to Standard International Trade Classification (SITC)

CTN	SITC	CTN	SITC
		Primary Key (First Iteration)	
10	71	290	72
110	71	291	72
111	72	292	68
112	72	30	51
12	71	31	53
13	71	32	57
14	71	33	86
150	71	340	27
151	71	341	27
152	71	342	28
153	71	343	59
154	71	350	23
155	71	351	62
156	81	352	62
157	71	353	62
158	72	354	62
159	71	355	62
16	71	356	62
170	86	360	51
171	86	361	59
172	86		
173	71	40	66
174	69	41	63
175	66	42	69
176	69	500	24
177	51	501	24
18	71	502	63
19	73	503	63
		504	63
20	32	505	25
21	33	506	64
22	33	507	64
230	34	508	64
231	35	509	29
232	34	510	26
24	28	511	26
25	27	512	26
260	67	513	26
261	67	514	65
262	67	515	65
263	67	520	21
264	67	521	61
265	67	522	61
266	67	523	61
267	69	530	21
268	69	531	61
269	69	54	12
27	68	550	04
28	68		

Table B-6 (cont'd)

CTN	SITC	CTN	SITC
551	22	81	03
552	29	82	04
553	29	83	05
554	29	840	06
555	29	841	42
560	55	842	09
561	51	843	05
562	29	844	11
563	29	845	54
570	41	846	12
571	41	847	09
572	42		
573	43	90	65
58	08	91	84
590	29	92	84
591	62	93	85
592	65	940	69
593	29	941	66
		942	66
60	00	943	69
		944	89
70	04	95	82
71	00	96	54
720	22	970	72
721	07	971	72
722	07	972	69
723	59	973	64
724	41	974	89
725	09	975	89
726	09	976	89
800	01	977	89
801	41	978	86
802	02	979	71
803	02	98	89

Secondary Key (Second Iteration)

CTN	SITC	CTN	SITC
11	72	52	21
15	71	53	21
17	86	55	29
23	35	56	29
26	67	57	41
29	72	59	29
34	27	72	07
35	23	80	01
36	51	84	06
50	24	94	69
51	26	97	72

Tertiary Key (Third Iteration)

CTN	SITC	CTN	SITC
1	7	6	0
2	2 and 3*	7	0
3	5	8	0 and 1*
4	6	9	6 and 8*
5	2 and 4*		

*Allocation proportions must be determined separately for imports and exports, uniquely for each country.

The new CTN/SITC conversion key was especially designed for CTN data which details all or a substantial part of trade at no less than two- or three-digit level codes, such as are published by the U.S.S.R. for total trade. A *primary key* was devised to convert two- or three-digit CTN codes into two-digit SITC codes, generally using three-digit CTN except when a two-digit level was sufficient; this would have been the only key needed if all reported trade were specified at the appropriate level. When this was not the case, a less accurate *secondary key* was employed to transform all remaining two-digit CTN codes (those not included in the *primary key* because conversion from three-digit CTN was needed but not available). Finally, when only one-digit CTN was available, a *tertiary key* was formed from one-digit CTN into one-digit SITC.

It is important to note that, in contradistinction to the CTN/SITC key prepared by the U.N. and other keys reconciling two nomenclatures, the purpose here is to obtain accurate SITC aggregates *(categories or divisions)* rather than a fully detailed CTN-SITC matching of homogeneous articles. Hence, the maximum SITC detail used in the conversion is two digits.

The *primary key* was prepared by matching commodity descriptions in the two systems. In some cases, exact correspondence between the two codes was not possible since CTN classifies commodities largely according to origin and end use, and SITC classifies them partly by stage of fabrication, partly by industrial origin, and partly by the nature of material. In some cases even three-digit CTN data permit only approximate transformation to two-digit SITC. Since the purpose here is to obtain broad SITC aggregates, differences between the codes was serious only when a given CTN item had to be allocated among two or more SITC *categories*. To illustrate, Fertilizers (classified by end use) belong to CTN *subgroups* 340 to 342 (Phosphorous, Potassium, and Nitrogen Fertilizers, respectively), which in the SITC system (classified by stage of fabrication) could be Crude (SITC 271) or Manufactured (SITC 561). Having determined from U.S.S.R. sources that the bulk of fertilizer exports are Crude, the conversion key allocates CTN *subgroups* 340, 341, and 342 to SITC 26, 27, and 28, respectively.*

The *secondary key* was designed on the basis of the *primary key*. To illustrate (see Table B-6), within CTN group 15 the *primary key* specifies eight *subgroups* to be converted to SITC 71 and two *subgroups* to other SITC divisions. If the *subgroups* of CTN 15 were not at all (or not fully) specified, all of CTN 15 (or its unspecified component) was converted by the *secondary key* into SITC 71. The tertiary key was devised by a procedure similar to that used for the *secondary key*.

---

*U.S.S.R. statistics specify most (but not all) five-digit components of CTN 340, 341, and 342. From the U.N.'s detailed CTN/SITC key it could be determined that most of the exports specified are Crude. In U.S.S.R. imports, the maximum CTN detail is two digits (CTN *group* 34).

As a general rule, the larger the proportion converted by the *primary key* the greater the accuracy of the SITC series. Notes to tables give the proportions.

The conversion involved the following iterative steps:

(1) All CTN entries that could be converted directly by the *primary key* were converted into two-digit SITC codes. For example (see Table B-6), CTN 10, 111, and 12 were converted to SITC 71, 72, and 71, respectively. Note that CTN 110 and 112 were skipped because (assuming that these commodities were traded) published statistics in *group* 11 do not specify trade in the full three digits. Whether there was in fact trade in CTN 110 or 112 could be determined by subtracting CTN 111 from CTN 11 (see step 3).

(2) Two-digit SITC entries obtained by *primary key* conversions were numerically ordered and summed so that the proportions of total trade converted by the *primary key* could be calculated.

(3) Converted CTN entries were subtracted from each of their respective higher-level subtotals and from the grand total in order to obtain so-called remainders. The purpose of this subtraction was to document in greatest possible detail all information which had not yet been converted, in preparation for subsequent iterations. To continue with the above example, CTN 111 was subtracted from CTN 11 while CTN 10, 11, and 12, etc., were subtracted from *Category* 1, from *Broad Division* I, and all of them from the grand total.

(4) The *secondary key* was applied to all the remaining two-digit CTN entries (i.e., two-digit codes where it would have been preferable to convert three-digit components but where these were not available). In the example above, the original data contained an entry for CTN group 11. If there had been no information at a *subgroup* level, the entire *group* 11 would have had to be converted by the *secondary key*. But one three-digit component of 11 (i.e., 111) was given, which, as the first step, was already converted by the *primary key*. If this *subgroup* (or the sum of *subgroups*, if applicable) exhausted *group* 11 — a question that is decided when it (or their sum) is subtracted from *group* 11 — this ends the matter. If the sum of *subgroups* is less than the given *group*, there will be a remainder under CTN 11, to be converted to SITC during the second iteration by the *secondary key*.

(5) Two-digit SITC entries obtained by *secondary key* conversion were numerically ordered and summed so that the proportion of total trade converted by the *secondary key* could be calculated.

(6) CTN entries converted by the *secondary key* were subtracted from their respective subtotals and from the grand total in order to obtain remainders for the third iteration. Thus, to continue with the example, CTN 11 (itself a remainder after CTN 111 was subtracted) and the other two-digit components of CTN 1 converted by the *secondary key* were subtracted from *Category* 1, *Broad Division* I, and from the grand total.

(7) The *tertiary key* converted remaining one-digit *categories* (remainders or original data not specified in greater detail) into SITC

one-digit *categories*. Since in the U.S.S.R. only the Machinery and Equipment (CTN 1) subtotal was originally given, there was a need to apply the *tertiary key* only to this *Category* (where the unspecified residual in both imports and exports fluctuated between 5 and 15 percent during 1946-1969).

(8) One digit SITC entries obtained by the *tertiary key* conversion were numerically ordered and summed.

(9) Converted CTN entries were subtracted from the grand total.

(10) All SITC data were merged. Proportions of trade converted by the three keys were combined and tabulated with the "final remainder," which could not be converted. This final remainder was checked against the "unspecified" column in Tables II. CTN. M.U and II. CTN. X.U; final remainders and unspecified had to be numerically identical.

APPENDIX C

Socialist Trade Prices and the Valuation Problem

Concept of Transaction Value

National statistics on external trade are compiled by most countries according to *transaction values*. For imports, these values are based on prices at which goods are purchased by the importer, plus transportation and insurance costs to the frontier of the importing country (c.i.f. valuation). For exports, they are based on the prices of sale by the exporter, including costs of transportation and insurance to the frontier of the exporting country (f.o.b. valuation). Since price is a market phenomenon, the concept of *transaction value* presumes that price is substantially the outcome of the interaction between international supply and demand, even though it is recognized that the recorded value of a commodity may differ on regional markets (*UN-6*, p. 39).

To compare foreign trade statistics of countries, commodities traded should have a similar base of valuation. Thus, regardless of how the goods traded may be valued or how much they sell for on the domestic market of the exporter or importer, for international comparisons they should be valued approximately at (actual or hypothetical) "world market" prices. This is the only interpretation one can give to the U.N.'s concept of comparable *transaction values*, even though "world market price" is not an unambiguous concept.

A country whose currency is free from exchange controls or major restrictions can be assumed to trade approximately at world market prices, in response to automatic market pressures. Such a country's *transaction values* serve to compare its external trade with both domestic transactions and corresponding external transactions by the rest of the world. In contrast, centrally planned economies, which rely on strict exchange controls and other institutional barriers between foreign and domestic markets, have no automatic mechanism maintaining foreign trade prices at or near world market levels. Thus, these countries' trade statistics may not be comparable with either the domestic transactions of the country itself or with the external transactions of the rest of the world, as can be deduced from certain institutional features of CPEs, to which we turn next.

Transaction Values in "National Devisa Units"

What are "National Devisa Units"? Domestic prices in East European countries are generally arbitrary or at least strongly manipulated

342

by central authorities. Official exchange rates are set on the basis of a stated gold content* that is essentially fictitious because currencies are not backed by gold and cannot be exchanged for convertible Western currencies, and also because the stated gold content frequently yields official exchange rates that overvalue East European currencies (according to purchasing power comparisons with Western currencies), often by two- to three-hundred percent or more. To distinguish external trade transactions which have been converted into national currencies at official exchange rates from purely domestic money transactions, the prefix "devisa" is attached to these values by CPEs. Thus, external trade transactions are reported in "national devisa units" (NDUs), that is, in "devisa-rubles" by the U.S.S.R., in "devisa zlotys" by Poland, and so on. The prefix "devisa" is assigned explicitly to trade statistics by East Germany, Hungary, and Poland, whose published foreign trade transactions are in devisa-marks, devisa-forints, and devisa-zlotys, respectively; in other East European countries the "devisa" prefix is implicit and reference to it is seen occasionally in their literature.

Significance of "National Devisa Unit" Values. To elucidate the meaning of values expressed in NDUs, it is necessary to know the prices used in foreign trade transactions. East European countries state that they trade with both other CPEs and Western countries approximately at world market prices. Let us accept this as if it were a fact, for the moment, and trace the recording of transactions accordingly.

In trade with Western countries, prices are nearly always quoted in dollars. The resulting dollar transaction values are converted to NDUs by the official $/NDU rate. In trade with other CPEs, prices are nearly always expressed in devisa-rubles (also called "accounting" or "transferable" rubles), which, given the above price assumption, are simply dollar (or other convertible-currency) world prices, converted into rubles at the official exchange rate of .9 rubles to the dollar. Each East European country (except of course the U.S.S.R.) converts its transactions stated in devisa-rubles to NDUs at the official ruble/NDU exchange rate. It follows that values recorded in NDUs can be reconverted to dollars at the official $/NDU rates because East European countries' exchange rates with the dollar and other Western currencies are consistent with the rate of .9 rubles to the dollar. Thus, East Europe's external trade statistics in NDUs can be converted into dollars at the official exchange rates so that the resulting values would compare with the external trade statistics of the rest of the world if, and only if, transaction prices were comparable to those on world markets.

*Except the East German valuta-mark, which has been defined in terms of the U.S. dollar (4.2 valuta-marks/$). Since the devaluation of the dollar in December 1971, CEMA countries have maintained the nominal gold contents of their currencies but revalued them approximately 8 percent higher in relation to the dollar.

Foreign Trade Prices of East European Countries

Evidence suggests that the assumption that East European countries trade at current world market prices is not correct for trade among CPEs or (fully) for trade between CPEs and non-CPEs.

Prices in Trade With CPEs. CEMA agreements specify that prices are to be based on average world market prices of some previous period as a point of departure. They are then adjusted to take into account various "considerations" stated in such general terms that wide latitude remains for negotiators to set prices. The result, called "adjusted historical world market prices," usually remain fixed for many years, depending on commodity and trade partner. Considering, further, that trade among CPEs is based substantially on long-term trade agreements specifying quantities of commodities to be exported and imported, and that exports and imports continue to be balanced bilaterally, *transaction values* in CPEs cannot be said to correspond to current world prices, nor to have been determined largely by regional market forces. The Statistical Office of the U.N. states the problem as follows:

> The trade of a centrally planned economy with another centrally planned economy may be carried out on a basis not comparable to that governing its trade with a country whose economy is not centrally planned. . . . [I]n the absence of data on the unit values of specific commodities entering the trade of the centrally planned economies with one another, it is difficult to assess the possible effects on the trade statistics of this kind of incomparability. [*UN-8*, 1966, p. 9.]

Recent statistical evidence, comparing unit values or actual foreign trade prices in intra-East European trade with unit values or price quotations of similar commodities on the world market, suggests that the former are substantially higher than the latter. One such estimate, made by this author on the basis of a CEMA statistical study (summarized in *H-13*, March 1967, pp. 283-300), would place the average markup in the mid-1960s close to 20 percent. The markup appears to have been somewhat higher for manufactures than for primary products, somewhat larger during the early 1960s than during more recent years, and greater in some bilateral relationships than in others *(W-11)*. Even though precise estimates of foreign trade price levels cannot be made at the present time, the conclusion that prices are generally higher in trade among CPEs than on the world market appears substantially correct. These findings, and their significance for interpreting East European statistics, have been confirmed by the following statement in a 1970 U.N. publication:

> Intra-east European trade is conducted in almost complete isolation from the rest of the world market, and investigations — whether conducted in eastern or western Europe — indicate that price levels ruling in that trade sector are significantly above those in east-west and intra-west trade. This suggests that trade data . . . for east European countries have an upward bias, but by how much cannot be ascertained. [*UN-2*, vol. 21, no. 1, p. 48.]

Prices in Trade with Non-CPEs. In East-West trade, prices in general could be expected to correspond to current world prices. Yet, studies comparing transaction prices in trade between CPEs and non-CPEs with world prices have shown that East European countries offer large discounts in their exports to the West — discounts that appear to be substantially greater than those which could be justified by lower quality. These may be due, *inter alia,* to Western discrimination in the form of higher tariffs and other obstacles to trade, CEMA countries exporting on the basis of plan directives rather than market considerations, and the need to dispose of unwanted surpluses acquired from other CPEs or other inconvertible currency areas as a result of bilateral agreements. A rough estimate by this author of such discounts would be about 20 percent. Discounts appear to be larger in manufactures than in primary products, and there is some evidence that they have been increasing over time *(W-11).*

Less evidence is available on prices in East Europe's imports from the West; what there is indicates that import prices are probably close to world prices, perhaps somewhat higher.

Conclusions

Given that prices at which CPEs trade on Eastern and Western markets apparently diverge from world market prices in opposite directions and by substantial margins (depending on trade partner, commodity, and year), official statistics in NDUs or their unadjusted dollar equivalents are not exact and can be misleading. For example, the trade dependence of an East European country on CEMA (or on the combined CPE group) appears to be higher on the basis of official statistics than it would be if calculated at comparable transaction (i.e., world market) prices. It follows, therefore, that the reorientation of trade from one trading area to another may indicate shifts of resources in real terms different than that which would be calculated on the basis of unadjusted NDU or dollar values. Furthermore, since relative prices of machinery and equipment — the fastest growing CTN *broad division* in intra-CEMA trade — appear to be high on the CEMA market as compared to price ratios on the world market, the rate of growth of intra-CEMA trade calculated from official statistics may be upward biased.

The inevitable conclusion is, therefore, that intraregional and international comparisons should take into account differences in *transaction prices* which are not reflected in official statistics as expressed in NDUs or their dollar equivalents obtained through official exchange rate conversions. If one could measure the deviation of an East European country's foreign trade prices from world market prices according to trade partners, commodities, and years, trade flows could be revealed. But since information on foreign trade prices (unit values) is too fragmentary to permit such an adjustment for every East European country, the value series in current NDUs have been recorded in the *Data Bank* without adjustments.* For presentation here, the NDU

*For an experimental adjustment of Hungary's foreign trade statistics at "Adjusted Dollar Prices," see *W-11.*

series have been converted to U.S. dollars at the official exchange rates shown in Table C-1.

Table C-1

Official Exchange Rates of East European Countries, 1946-1969

Country	Currency (as shown in official publications	Years Recorded in *Data Bank*	Exchange Rate Used for Conversion (NDU/$)
U.S.S.R.	Ruble	1946-69	.90[a]
Bulgaria	Leva	1950-69	1.17[b]
Czechoslovakia	Koruna	1946-69	7.20[c]
East Germany	Valuta-mark	1946-69	4.20[d]
Hungary	Devisa-forint	1946-69	11.74
Poland	Devisa-zloty	1946-69	4.00
Rumania	Lei	1946-69	6.00[e]
Yugoslavia	Dinar	1965-69	12.50[f]
		1946-64	300.00[g]
Albania	Lek	1950-67	50.00[h]

Note. For all countries except Yugoslavia, external trade statistics have been recorded in the *Data Bank,* for all years shown, in NDUs consistent with official currency values in effect in 1969. The official exchange rates of several East European countries were revised at times during the 1946-69 period. Series originally reported in "old" NDUs have been either revised subsequently by the countries themselves in "new" NDUs, or the "old" NDUs have been converted into "new" NDUs by the author before recording the series in the *Data Bank.* For Yugoslavia, statistics up to 1964 were recorded in the *Data Bank* at the former rate of 300 dinars per U.S. dollar.

a. New *ruble* introduced on January 1, 1961. (Prior to 1961, .25 old *rubles* per dollar.) Pre-1961 series have been revised in official publications to correspond with the new *ruble* rate.

b. New *leva* introduced on January 1, 1962. (Prior to 1962, 7.56 old *levas* per dollar.) Some pre-1962 series have been reported in recent publications in new *levas*, other pre-1962 series have been converted into new *levas* by the author before *Data Bank* processing (1 old leva = 0.171954 new *levas*).

c. New *koruna* introduced in 1948. (Prior to 1948, 50 old *korunas* per dollar.)

d. Prior to 1960, East German official publications reported trade in old *rubles*. These series have been converted into *valuta-marks* by the author (1 old ruble = 1.05 valuta marks).

e. Data for 1946-49, 1951-54, and 1956-57 obtained from secondary sources reporting either in *lei* or in dollars, with exchange rates consistent with the *lei* per dollar rate shown in the Table.

f. New *dinar* introduced on January 1, 1966. The new rate as of January 23, 1971 is 15 *dinars* per dollar.

g. 1946-51 exchange rate was 50 dinars per dollar, but pre-1952 series have been obtained from official publications already using the exchange rate in effect between 1952 and 1965.

h. New *lek* introduced on August 15, 1965; 10 old *leks* = 1 new *lek*.

APPENDIX D

Some Main Problems of Statistical Comparability

Introduction

Strict international comparability of foreign trade statistics continues to be handicapped by numerous differences in definitions and conventions used by individual countries. Statistical standardization has long been promoted by various international organizations such as the U.N. and CEMA, but national statistical practices often fail to conform to proposed international standards because of divergent historical developments and the political, economic, and administrative requirements of national policies.

To improve comparability of international trade statistics, in 1970 the U.N. Statistical Office compiled the explicit and implicit recommendations of the U.N.'s Statistical Commission on the methodology of reporting foreign trade statistics *(UN-6)*. Standardization within the CEMA framework is being promoted by the organization's Standing Commission for Statistics, which is concerned with broader issues, and by the Statistical Department of the CEMA Secretariat, which elaborates specific recommendations. (*U-3*, September 1968, p. 46.)

The purpose of this section is to summarize statistical concepts and definitions known to be used by individual East European countries in reporting trade statistics, and to compare their practices, as well as recommendations of the CEMA Standing Commission for Statistics, with the most recent recommendations of the U.N. Statistical Commission. Such comparison is useful in allowing for the limitations of the national series presented here for making intraregional and international comparisons.

Four comparative aspects are examined: (1) general and special systems of trade statistics, (2) coverage of merchandise trade, (3) treatment of transport and related expenses (f.o.b. and c.i.f.), and (4) identification of partner country. Two additional aspects, commodity classification systems and valuation, have already been discussed in Appendices A and C, respectively. In each subsection, a general discussion of concepts and the recommendations of the U.N. Statistical Commission will be followed by a summary description of statistical practices among East European countries.

General and Special Reporting Systems

Concepts and United Nations Recommendations

Systems of recording trade differ chiefly in their treatment of re-exported goods. *Special imports* are those directly for domestic consumption or use, including transformation and repair. *Special exports* comprise national exports — wholly or partly produced or manufactured in a country — plus those which, having originally been included in special imports, are re-exported without the intended transformation, i.e., exports of "nationalized" goods. (The above definition needs to be expanded where a distinction is to be made between national and customs frontiers. If so, *special imports* would also include imports into customs-bonded manufacturing plants plus imports withdrawn, inward from customs-bonded warehouses and free-trade zones; while *special exports* would include exports from customs-bonded manufacturing plants. *UN-6*, pp. 15-25.)

General imports are the combined total of imports for directly domestic consumption plus imports for re-exports. *General exports* are the combined total of national exports plus re-exports.

The meaning of re-exports is not unambiguous and is of considerable significance. CEMA recommends that all re-exports be included:

> Imports comprise foreign goods intended for home consumption or processing and also goods for re-export. The latter imply foreign goods imported and then exported without processing and also goods purchased abroad and then exported direct to a third country. [*U-3*, September 1968, p. 46.]

According to the U.N., a cargo must cross the national (or customs) frontier of a country to be included in the statistics. Thus, if a good is purchased by country *A* from country *B* for resale and is routed through country *C* (without crossing the frontier of *A*), "it is customary, expedient and correct to exclude these goods from recorded external trade [of both *A* and *C*]." (*UN-6*, p. 25.)*

According to the U.N., countries using the *general trade* system may also report separately the part of imports destined for domestic use. This is called "retained imports" and is usually calculated by subtracting re-exports (including "nationalized" goods) from *general imports*. Retained imports are likely to be smaller than *special imports* since the latter include goods purchased originally for domestic use but sebsequently re-exported. A recent U.N. source in fact refers to three systems of recording trade: *special, general*, and *semi-special*, the latter defined as *general trade* less all re-exports (*UN-1*, p. 16).

---

*For country *C* the transaction is *transit trade*, to be excluded from *general trade* by explicit recommendation (*UN-6*, pp. 24-25). For country *A*, the recommendation to exclude the transaction is implicit: "In the general trade system, the ... record is made when goods move across the national boundary...." (Ibid., p. 23.) And elsewhere, "in the case of imports, [the recording country] is the country from which the goods were first shipped to the reporting country." (Ibid., p. 61.)

The U.N. recommends that countries should, if practicable, report *general trade:*

> In order to maximize the usefulness of international trade statistics, the coverage of the statistics should be sufficiently wide to take account of all merchandise entering or leaving a country from or to another country with the exception of goods simply being transported through the territory. [*UN-6*, p. 3.]

CEMA's Standing Commission for Statistics also recommends that member countries record *general trade* (*U-3*, September 1968, p. 46), but the discrepancy noted above in defining re-exports makes the two recommendations unlike in detail.

East European Procedures

Data in this *Compendium* are believed to be consistent with the *general trade* concept as defined by CEMA, with the following known or possible exceptions, by country:

East Germany: The system of recording total trade and trade with the U.S.S.R., total CPEs, MDCs, and LDCs, 1946-48, is unknown, but is probably *special trade;* trade with individual East European countries other than the U.S.S.R., 1946-52, is unknown, but is probably *special trade.*

Rumania: For 1948-49 and 1951-54, the system of recording trade is unknown.

Yugoslavia: Not a CEMA member, Yugoslavia has consistently reported *special trade.*

Estimated Re-Export Trade of East Germany and Hungary

Re-export trade is of considerable interest to foreign trade specialists because, among other reasons, international comparisons of trade relative to national income are more meaningful if based on *special trade,* with re-exports excluded. Of special interest for East Europe, degrees of actual bilateralism can best be estimated by making allowance for financing imports with re-exports, a practice to which East European countries have been known to resort.* Primarily for these reasons, Haberler has suggested that the re-export trade of CPEs "should be made the object of systematic-factual-statistical studies."**

CEMA countries do not, as a general rule, publish re-export figures. But for two CEMA members, East Germany and Hungary, an attempt can be made to estimate re-export trade indirectly.

---

*Wiles distinguishes *natural re-exports* ("a big *entrepôt* like London buys and sells raw materials and semifabricates") and *financing re-exports* ("*A* wants convertible currency more than anything *B* can sell for [*A*'s] domestic use.... So *A* buys one of *B*'s principle exports...and resells it. Thus *A/B* trade is both bilateral and reciprocal; yet *A* acquires the convertible currency she wants.") (*W-18*, p. 261, with illustrative cases.) One may add that re-exports can arise also from the need to dispose of unwanted commodities acquired as a result of bilateral agreements with inconvertible-currency countries.

**"Theoretical Reflections on the Trade of Socialist Economies," in *W-2*, p. 45.

East German Re-Exports. The country's foreign trade statistics by geopolitical regions until 1966 (and by countries until 1960) have corresponded approximately to *special trade;* more recently, published statistics refer to *general trade* (CEMA definition). In 1970, revised statistical series of trade by regions were published retroactively to 1949, corresponding to *general trade.* By assuming, as a first approximation, that the revision was due simply to a change in the definition, differences between the two series (available for 1950-66 by regions and for 1953-60 in trade with the U.S.S.R.) would permit estimating re-export trade, which is shown in Table D-1 on the following page. However, when the resulting estimates are compared with those obtained for Hungary (see last paragraph of this page), we find that, in addition to switching from the *special trade* to the *general trade* system, some unexplained statistical revision may also have occurred.

Special imports (Wareneinfuhr) consist of commodities for domestic use, the standard definition. However, both *special imports* and *special exports* exclude value added by "improvement and repair trade" *(Lohnveredlungen)* as well as provisions for ships and aircraft, while *general trade* includes both of these items. Thus, estimated re-exports also include trade in these categories and could also reflect revisions for reasons not explained.

The estimated dollar value of re-export trade, its total, distribution by regions, and relative importance are shown in Table D-1.

Hungarian Re-Exports. Published foreign trade series cover *general trade,* but from secondary Hungarian sources it is possible to construct a *special trade* series for 1951-68. For an eleven-year subperiod, it is also possible to show actual foreign exchange costs of transporting Hungarian imports up to the Hungarian border and Hungarian exports to a "contract" point (outside Hungary's boundaries). Since Hungary is the only CEMA country reporting imports on a c.i.f. basis, transport and related costs need to be subtracted to make Hungarian statistics comparable with those of other CEMA countries. The respective series are presented in Table D-2.

Re-Export Estimates Compared. Comparison of the calculated relative shares of re-export trade, Column (2) of Table D-1 and Column (6) of Table D-2, would indicate that re-exports are more important for Hungary than for East Germany. Considering that East Germany's calculated re-export trade would even appear to be upward biased due to the inclusion of additional commercial items, its re-export figures are surprisingly low. While it cannot be excluded that observed differences between the estimated re-export trade of the two countries reflect actual differences, the gap strongly suggests the possibility that East Germany's calculated re-exports are incomplete because the estimates derived here are affected by unexplained adjustment in the revised series. This possibility is suggested also by the fact that while in Hungary's total trade the value of imports for re-export and re-exports parallel closely, the same series in East Germany's total trade diverge, estimated imports for re-export being substantially larger each year since 1958.

Table D-1

East German Imports for Re-Export, and Re-Exports,
by Region or Country of Provenance or Destination, 1950-1966
(Millions of Current Dollars)

Year	Total $ (1)	Total Percent[a] (2)	Total CPEs $ (3)	Total CPEs Percent[a] (4)	U.S.S.R. $ (5)	U.S.S.R. Percent[a] (6)	MDCs $ (7)	MDCs Percent[a] (8)	LDCs $ (9)	LDCs Percent[a] (10)
				Imports for Re-export[b]						
1950	-		-		-		-		-	
1951	-		-		-		-		-	
1952	-		-		-		-		-	
1953	-		-		-		-		-	
1954	3.8	0.4	2.9	0.4	-		.9	0.3	-	
1955	6.3	0.5	5.3	0.6	-		1.0	0.3	-	
1956	3.5	0.3	2.5	0.3	-		1.0	0.3	-	
1957	18.8	1.2	7.5	0.6	-		10.6	2.6	.7	1.2
1958	23.2	1.4	14.8	1.2	6.0	0.9	7.9	1.9	.5	0.6
1959	24.8	1.2	14.6	1.0	4.9	0.5	9.9	2.3	.3	0.4
1960	24.7	1.1	12.1	0.8	4.6	0.5	12.3	2.5	.3	0.3
1961	32.8	1.5	16.2	1.0	n.a.		15.6	3.5	1.0	1.0
1962	32.5	1.4	22.3	1.2	n.a.		10.1	3.7	.2	0.3
1963	32.8	1.4	20.6	1.2	n.a.		12.1	2.9	.1	0.1
1964	26.1	1.0	14.2	0.8	n.a.		11.4	2.1	.5	0.4
1965	55.2	2.0	23.0	1.1	n.a.		28.9	4.7	3.3	2.8
1966	67.6	2.2	28.3	1.2	n.a.		37.4	5.0	1.9	1.5
				Re-exports[c]						
1950	-		-		-		-		-	
1951	-		-		-		-		-	
1952	-		-		-		-		-	
1953	-		-		-		-		-	
1954	6.0	0.5	1.5	0.2			4.5	1.7	-	
1955	16.5	1.3	10.6	1.1	6.9	1.3	5.9	1.9	-	
1956	7.5	0.5	3.7	0.4	-		3.8	1.2	-	
1957	23.1	1.3	19.1	1.4	-		3.2	0.8	.8	1.1
1958	25.0	1.3	20.3	1.4	-		2.9	0.8	1.8	2.3
1959	20.0	0.9	14.3	0.9	-		4.6	1.1	1.1	1.5
1960	16.7	0.8	11.8	0.7	1.0	0.3	4.1	0.9	.8	0.9
1961	18.3	0.8	13.9	0.8	n.a.		4.1	0.9	.3	0.3
1962	15.4	0.7	12.9	0.7	n.a.		1.5	0.4	1.0	1.1
1963	18.9	0.7	16.5	0.8	n.a.		2.0	0.4	.4	0.4
1964	14.4	0.5	11.5	0.5	n.a.		2.8	0.5	.1	0.1
1965	38.2	1.3	15.6	0.7	n.a.		20.5	3.3	2.1	1.5
1966	25.4	0.8	14.1	0.6	n.a.		7.8	1.2	3.5	2.1

a. Percent of corresponding "general imports" or "general exports."
b. "General imports" less "special imports."
c. "General exports" less "special exports."

Source: *G-1*, various issues. Data shown in valuta-marks converted to dollars at the official exchange rate.

Table D-2

Hungarian Special Trade, General Trade, Imports
for Re-Export, and Re-Exports, 1951-1968
(Millions of Current Dollars)

Year	Special Imports[a]			Imports for Re-Export (4)	General Imports[a] (5)	Imports for Re-Export as % of General Imports (6)
	At Contract Prices[b] (1)	Transport Costs[c] (+) (2)	At Hungarian Border (c.i.f.) (3)			
1951	n.a.	n.a.	367.6	26.5	394.1	6.7%
1952	409.0	15.9	424.9	34.7	459.6	7.6
1953	435.8	16.3	452.1	35.5	487.5	7.3
1954	457.9	18.9	476.8	54.9	531.7	10.3
1955	461.8	19.8	481.7	72.7	554.4	13.1
1956	416.7	15.0	431.7	49.6	481.3	10.3
1957	n.a.	n.a.	654.4	28.2	682.6	4.1
1958	565.2	18.1	583.3	47.8	631.1	7.6
1959	710.2	20.4	730.6	62.5	793.1	7.9
1960	889.2	22.5	911.7	64.3	976.0	6.6
1961	935.5	24.1	959.6	66.2	1025.8	6.5
1962	1067.7	27.2	1094.9	54.0	1148.9	4.7
1963	n.a.	n.a.	1242.1	63.7	1305.8	4.9
1964	n.a.	n.a.	1406.3	88.6	1494.9	5.9
1965	n.a.	n.a.	1412.8	107.9	1520.7	7.1
1966	n.a.	n.a.	1459.1	106.8	1565.8	6.8
1967	n.a.	n.a.	1654.8	120.8	1775.7	6.8
1968	n.a.	n.a.	1696.4	106.6	1803.0	5.9

Year	Special Exports[a]			Re-Exports (4)	General Exports[a] (5)	Re-Exports as % of General Exports (6)
	At Contract Prices[b] (1)	Transport Costs[c] (-) (2)	At Hungarian Border (f.o.b.) (3)			
1951	n.a.	n.a.	365.5	30.3	395.8	7.7
1952	405.8	4.7	401.1	37.1	438.2	8.5
1953	462.6	4.7	458.1	40.2	498.3	8.1
1954	462.6	5.8	456.8	62.5	519.3	12.0
1955	537.0	7.9	529.1	72.0	601.1	12.0
1956	445.5	7.9	437.6	49.4	487.0	10.1
1957	n.a.	n.a.	459.5	28.6	488.1	5.9
1958	645.0	9.9	635.1	48.6	683.7	7.1
1959	720.6	12.2	708.4	61.4	769.8	8.0
1960	820.4	12.0	808.4	65.7	824.1	7.5
1961	974.4	13.0	961.4	67.8	1029.2	6.6
1962	1062.9	16.9	1046.0	53.5	1099.5	4.9
1963	n.a.	n.a.	1143.0	63.0	1206.0	5.2
1964	n.a.	n.a.	1262.9	89.2	1352.1	6.6
1965	n.a.	n.a.	1403.3	106.5	1509.8	7.1
1966	n.a.	n.a.	1491.3	102.4	1593.7	6.4
1967	n.a.	n.a.	1581.7	119.8	1701.5	7.0
1968	n.a.	n.a.	1678.5	111.1	1789.6	6.2

Table D-2 (cont'd)

a. *Special trade* and *general trade* concepts correspond to U.N. definitions, except for the definition of re-exports, which follows CEMA practice (*H-11*, 1963, p. 411).

b. The difference between "contract" and "border" parities are transportation costs incurred in foreign exchange; in imports transport costs are added to arrive at "imports c.i.f. Hungarian border" and in exports transport costs are subtracted to obtain "exports f.o.b. Hungarian border."

c. Includes only transport costs incurred in foreign exchange. See footnote above.

Sources: Columns (1) and (2): *H-1*, 1956, p. 183; *H-1*, 1957, p. 219; *H-8*, December 1964, p. 1239. Column (3): *H-4*, various issues as quoted in *H-9*, p. 84, and *H-10*, no. 105, p. 204, or derived by summing columns (1) and (2). Column (4): calculated as the difference between columns (5) and (3). Column (5): *H-1*, 1967, p. 219; *H-1*, 1968, pp. 258-59.

Coverage of Merchandise Trade

United Nations Recommendations

The coverage of categories singled out by U.N. recommendations relate to goods to be included in statistics on merchandise trade, excluded from the statistics, and separately recorded. Where such recommendations are contrary to the general practice of most Western countries, this fact is noted here. (Recommendations are given in *UN-6*, pp. 3-15; reporting practices of most Western countries are shown in *UN-8*, 1968, pp. 7-8.)

To be included:

(1) Transactions in ships and aircraft. (U.N. concern with the recording of these items focuses on changes in country of registration unaccompanied by actual movements of the vehicle from one country to another, i.e., shifts in flag of convenience.) Present practice of most Western countries is to include new ships and aircraft but to exclude transfer of ownership of second-hand ships and aircraft.

(2) Trade on government account, including civilian and military foreign aid shipments (whether or not under loan or grant); war reparations; and military goods (except if consigned to own armed forces abroad).

(3) Trade on the account of foreign concessions.

(4) Trade in gas, electricity, and water.

(5) Parcel post: No recommendation is made as to coverage, except that important commodities of light weight but high value, such as diamonds and gems, should be recorded in full.

(6) Silver ore and concentrates, bullion, unissued coin, scrap, and partly worked manufactures of silver.

To be excluded:

(7) Monetary gold.

(8) Securities, bank notes, and coins in circulation.

(9) Goods consigned by a government to its armed forces and diplomatic representatives abroad.

(10) Temporary trade, such as tourists' effects; animals for racing

and breeding; goods for exhibition only; returnable samples and con-
tainers; goods shipped for temporary storage; vehicles carrying goods
or passengers between countries.

(11) Transit trade.

To be separately recorded:

(12) Nonmonetary gold.

(13) Bunkers, stores, etc., supplied to foreign vehicles or acquired
abroad.

(14) Fish and salvage sold abroad off national vessels or purchased
in national ports from foreign vessels.

(15) Repairs to ships and aircraft (value added only).

(16) Improvement and repair trade: The general practice of Western countries is to include inward and outward movement of such trade
at full value and as regular merchandise trade. Goods moving abroad
for improvement or repair are described as "passive," and those cor-
respondingly received from other countries as "active." Returned
goods are most frequently recorded by the country engaged in active
repair trade as re-exports.

(17) Goods on lease (e.g., computer facilities, films). Present
practice is to include such transactions at full value as regular merchandise trade.

East European Procedures

Comprehensive information on the coverage of merchandise trade
is difficult to obtain for most East European countries, particularly for
1946-55. Some do not disclose any information and others report se-
lective information only. Notes to trade statistics may not indicate
whether the stated coverage is also applicable to earlier years. Revised series may be published without explaining fully the nature of the
revision. Since the statistical practices of most East European countries differed from one another considerably during the 1940s and
1950s, information available for one country may not shed light fully on
the statistical coverage of others. Since the early 1960s a move toward
more uniform statistical coverage within CEMA countries can be dis-
cerned, but differences continue as noted.

Table D-3 summarizes available information on the coverage of
merchandise trade by East European countries; national practices and
CEMA recommendations are compared with U.N. recommendations.
Additional details and the documentation can be found in the notes to
the Table.

The following main findings emerge:

(1) Trade in new ships, aircraft, etc., is included in the data for all
East European countries. How used ships, aircraft, etc., are treated
statistically is not known, but trade in them is believed to be small to
insignificant.

(2) The CEMA recommendation on government trade is to exclude
foreign aid, i.e., "goods exported as free assistance or as gifts," from
merchandise trade (*U-3,* September 1968, p. 47). But for CPEs

Table D-3

Coverage of East Europe's Foreign Trade Statistics
Compared with U.N. 1970 Recommendations

Coverage of Merchandise Trade: United Nations Recommendations	CEMA Recommendation[1]	U.S.S.R.	Bulgaria[9]	Czechoslovakia[11]	East Germany[13]	Hungary	Poland	Rumania[23]	Yugoslavia	Albania
To Be Included										
1. Ships, etc.	✓[2]	Consistent with CEMA recommendations	Consistent with CEMA recommendations, except as noted	✓	✓	✓	✓	Unknown (probably consistent with CEMA recommendations)	✓	Unknown
2. Government trade	excl.[3]			n.a.	excl.[3]	incl.[16]	excl.[19]		incl.[24]	
3. Concessions	n.a.			n.a.	n.a.	n.a.	n.a.		n.a.	
4. Gas, electricity, water	✓[4]			✓	✓	✓	✓		✓	
5. Parcel post	incl.[5]			n.a.	incl.[14]	incl.[17]	incl.[20]		incl.[25]	
6. Silver ore	✓[6]			✓	✓	✓	✓		✓	
To Be Excluded										
7. Monetary gold	✓			✓	✓	✓	✓		✓	
8. Securities, coins in circulation	✓			✓	✓	✓	✓		✓	
9. To own armed forces and diplomats	✓			✓	✓	✓[16]	✓		n.a.	
10. Temporary trade	✓			✓	✓	✓	✓		✓	
11. Transit trade	✓			✓	✓	✓	✓		✓	
To Be Shown Separately										
12. Nonmonetary gold	n.a.			n.a.	n.a.	n.a.	n.a.		n.a.	
13. Bunkers, etc.	incl.			n.a.	incl.	incl.	incl.[21]		incl.[26]	
14. Fish, etc., from vessels	n.a.			n.a.	n.a.	n.a.	n.a.		n.a.	
15. Ship, etc., repairs (value added)	incl.			n.a.	incl.	incl.	incl.		n.a.	
16. Improvement and repair trade	incl.[7]			incl.[12]	incl.[15]	incl.[18]	incl.[22]		excl.[27]	
17. Goods on lease	excl.[8]			n.a.	excl.[8]	excl.[8]	n.a.		n.a.	

✓ = Agrees with U.N. recommendation   incl. = Included in merchandise trade
n.a. = Not available   excl. = Excluded from merchandise trade

1. Made by the CEMA Standing Commission for Statistics (*U-3*, September 1968, pp. 46-48), and probably during the early 1960s.
2. Included in CTN (commodity *subgroup* 192).
3. Foreign aid is excluded, while trade in military goods is probably excluded.
4. Included in CTN (commodity *group* 23).
5. Private parcel post excluded.
6. Included in CTN (commodity *group* 24).
7. If a contractor's raw material is processed and the finished product is re-exported to the country supplying the raw material, then both parties take into account processing costs only. Value of raw materials and finished goods moving across boundaries is recorded separately but is not included in commodity trade. (*U-3*, September 1968, p. 47.) Apparently, only value added is included in merchandise trade.
8. Movie films for rent are excluded, while films purchased and sold, including license payments, are included.
9. For 1951-54, see General Note to Tables I.M.B and I.X.B in Part Three.
10. Foreign aid is excluded since 1955 (*B-6*, p. 3, and *B-2*, 1968, p. 169). The United Nations document stating that foreign aid has been included since 1953 appears to be erroneous. (*UN-8*, 1968, p. 121, and previous issues.)
11. For 1946-52 coverage is not known.

Table D-3 (cont'd)

12. Value added (*C-3*, 1969, p. 408).

13. For 1946-48 coverage is not known; it is probably *special trade*, which is known to exclude re-exports, value added by improvement and repair trade, and provisions for ships and aircraft. (*G-1*, 1967, p. 383.) The years 1949-59 are also exceptions, but only for trade with individual East European countries other than U.S.S.R. For 1949-52, probably *special trade;* for 1953-59, *special trade.*

14. Private ("gift") parcel post is excluded from both *general* and *special trade.* (*G-1*, 1967, p. 383.) Earlier source states that all postal packages were excluded from *special trade.* (*W-10*, p. 59.)

15. Apparently includes value added only.

16. Includes "government aids granted in form of goods, as far as such aids are based on international treaties" (*H-11*, 1963, p. 411). United Nations sources state that such aid is included in imports only. (*UN-8*, 1968, p. 368.) Also includes deliveries under war reparations (*H-11*, 1963, p. 411), but only since 1953 (*UN-8*, 1968, p. 368). Prior to 1958, goods destined for Hungarian diplomatic agencies stationed in Hungary are included. (*UN-8*, 1968, p. 368.)

17. Excludes parcel post since 1953. (*UN-8*, 1968, p. 368.)

18. Included in merchandise trade until 1958 at the full value of goods. Since 1959 only value added has been included, calculated (if applicable) as "the value of the raw material charged as fee for job-work." (*H-11*, 1963, p. 411.) U.N. sources state that inclusion at value added commenced in 1958 (*UN-8*, 1968, p. 368), a possible error.

19. Excludes "goods exported or imported free of charge" (*P-8*, 1967, p. 7). Also excludes "war reparations, purchases of surplus army property, purchase and sale of other military material." (*UN-8*, 1968, p. 677.)

20. Excludes "private postal matters" (*P-8*, 1967, p. 7); U.N. sources state that "beginning 1954, parcel post" is excluded (*UN-8*, 1968, p. 677).

21. Included in merchandise trade (*P-8*, 1967, p. 7); according to U.N. sources, since 1954 only (*UN-8*, 1968, p. 677).

22. Value added (*P-8*, 1967, p. 7).

23. For 1948-49 and 1951-54, coverage is not known. See General Note to Tables I.M.R and I.X.R in Part Three.

24. Includes imports "deriving from the Tripartite [U.S., French, U.K.] Economic Aid; since 1957 imports on account of long-term credit on the agricultural surpluses of the USA, as well as import on account of reparations and restitutions, of subsequent claims and grants from various international organizations." (*Y-2*, 1960, p. 8.) According to U.N. sources, the above items have been included only since 1951 (*UN-8*, 1968, p. 926). Also includes "imports of foreign army surplus property." (Ibid.)

25. Includes parcel post (*Y-2*, 1966, p. 9); "Prior to 1954, parcel post of non-commercial character" was excluded (*UN-8*, 1968, p. 926).

26. Included since 1958 (ibid).

27. Excluded from merchandise trade since 1960; shown separately. "Active improvement trade was included in the data on regular exports and imports" (*Y-2*, 1966, p. 9) "at full value" (*Y-2*, 1960, p. 8). Excluded prior to 1951 (*UN-8*, 1968, p. 926).

especially, it is difficult to separate strictly commercial from strictly governmental transactions. For instance, goods may be shipped on credit without obtaining full commercial reciprocity, a possible form of foreign aid.

Hungary is apparently an exception to the CEMA foreign-aid rule, since it includes (though possibly in imports only) "government aid granted in the form of goods . . . [if] based on international treaties" (*H-11*, 1963, p. 411). Until about 1955 Bulgaria reportedly also included foreign aid in its merchandise trade. Yugoslavia (not a CEMA member) has included goods received (supplied?) as aid since 1951.

Aid received by CEMA countries after the war from UNRRA was apparently excluded from merchandise trade, as stated explicitly by the U.N. for Czechoslovakia, Hungary, and Poland (*UN-8*, 1968). Reparations deliveries are also believed to have been excluded, except in the case of Hungary, which reports that reparations have been included in merchandise trade since 1953 (*H-11*, 1963, p. 411). As for the purchase or sale of military hardware, there is reason to believe that they are included in the trade statistics because CEMA recommends that "all goods and material values exported and imported on a commercial basis are the object of foreign trade registration" (*U-3*, September 1968, p. 46). To be sure, military items are not listed in the published CEMA Trade Nomenclature, nor are they shown in national publications. But since detailed commodity breakdowns, when published, are not exhaustive, the possibility that military items are included in reported trade totals cannot be excluded.

(3) CEMA recommendations (believed to have been made during the early 1960s) are more or less being followed by member countries, although statistical practices are still far from uniform. Except for government trade, as noted above, transactions that CEMA suggests should be included or excluded from merchandise trade correspond quite closely to the 1970 U.N. recommendations. The major difference between U.N. and CEMA standards concerns transactions that the U.N. suggests should be reported separately (e.g., improvement and repair trade; bunkers, stores, etc., supplied to foreign vehicles; and repairs to ships and aircraft) but that CEMA recommends should be included with merchandise trade. However, CEMA's Standing Commission for Statistics recently recommended that, as of 1971, certain invisible commercial transactions — including repairs as well as leasing, items which according to the U.N. should be reported separately — are to be shown separately also by CEMA countries, in a new appendix to the CTN (see Appendix A above for further details).

In sum, it appears that the trend is toward greater statistical standardization, not only in the West and in CEMA but also between CEMA and non-CEMA countries. Important differences do remain; moreover, statistical coverage during earlier years may not always correspond to the known coverage of the same country for more recent years.

Transport and Related Expenses

The U.N. recommends that valuation be c.i.f. imports and f.o.b. exports, border of reporting country. C.i.f. valuation is preferred over f.o.b. in imports because the former often or typically represents the total foreign exchange cost of imports. A further advantage of using different systems of valuation for imports and exports is that the difference between them provides an independent estimate of distribution costs (*UN-6*, pp. 46-47).

All East European countries except Hungary and Yugoslavia report both imports and exports f.o.b. border of supplying country. Hungary and Yugoslavia record imports c.i.f. and exports f.o.b. (Hungary's estimated foreign exchange cost of transporting imports to the Hungarian border can be found in Table D-2 above.) An advantage of having both imports and exports f.o.b. border of the supplying country is that it is possible to estimate imports of a country from the export data of its trade partner.

Identification of Partner Country

United Nations Recommendations

Differences among countries as to identifying trade partners is believed to be the most important cause of incomparability of mirror statistics. (*UN-6*, p. 58.) Therefore, the U.N. recommends recording trade on the basis of country of *consignment*, which is defined for imports as the country from which goods are directly received and for exports as the country to which goods are directly sent. (*UN-6*, p. 63.) This system offers the greatest possibility of attaining accuracy and comparability of trade flows reported independently by trading partners.* It is recognized that mirror statistics could still remain inconsistent, *inter alia*, because (1) goods are exported to countries compiling statistics solely according to the *special trade* system; (2) the coverage of re-exports differs; (3) goods are dispatched in transit through a second country to optional destinations; and (4) cargo shipped to one country is diverted on the high seas to another destination.

The U.N. appreciates that some countries might find it desirable to record statistics on alternative bases. For imports, this could be according to country of *production* (last country in which goods received appreciable physical transformation) or country of *purchase* (residence of seller); for exports, according to country of *consumption* (last known destination) or country of *sale* (residence of buyer). If the exact method used by the country reporting trade statistics is not known, for imports, the term country of *provenance*, for exports, the term country of *destination* is used (*UN-8*, 1968, p. 8).

Present practices of Western countries vary considerably with respect to the use of these definitions.

East European Procedures

Different sources frequently give conflicting definitions of trade partner as used by individual countries. The problem seems to be, at least in part, that the definition of trade partner given in East European documents, when translated literally, may not correspond in intended meaning to the U.N. terminology. The following information is available by country:

U.S.S.R. Trade partners are defined as countries of *production* and *consumption*. This is apparently the correct U.N. interpretation of U.S.S.R. methodology (*UN-8*, various issues). Literal translation (by the U.S.S.R.) reads "origin-destination" or "origin-designation" (*U-3*, September 1968, p. 47, and *U-2*, January 1971, p. 49), but the intended meaning is clarified by the statement:

*Identical definitions but a slightly different terminology are employed by another U.N. publication, where, for imports, the country of *first consignment* is defined as the country from which goods were first directed to the importing country, and for exports the country of *last consignment* is the last known destination to which goods are sent (*UN-8*, 1966, p. 8).

In most countries, a country of exports is defined as a country of destination, ... of imports ... as a country of origin. This definition is used by the USSR and some [!] other CEMA countries.... Along with this most widespread definition ... there is also the registration ... according to countries having a trade agreement or countries where the importer (exporter) lives or countries from or to which goods are delivered. [*U-3*, September 1968, p. 47.]

Bulgaria. Country of import is "the country from which the commodities are bought," and country of export is "the country to which the commodities are sold" (*B-2*, 1968, p. 169, and other issues of the same publication). This appears to correspond to the U.N. definition of countries of *purchase* and *sale*. (See also *UN-8*, 1967, p. 128, and other issues for a similar interpretation.)

Czechoslovakia. Statistics are recorded by countries of *purchase* and *sale*. Explanatory notes in the yearbooks state that the criterion is the residence of the contracting party (*C-3*, 1969, p. 408; also previous issues). The U.N., however, defines Czechoslovakia's trade partners as "countries of consignment" (*UN-8*, 1967, p. 230, and other issues), an apparent error.

East Germany. Trade partners are defined as countries of *purchase* and *sale* (*G-2*, pp. 93-94). The U.N. indicates *provenance* and *destination* (*UN-8*, 1967, p. 304, and other issues) because in the East German statistical yearbooks (*G-1*) no definition can be found.

Hungary. Based on official statements, trade partners are defined as countries of *purchase* and *sale:* "A partner country is the country where the party concluding a civil law contract with the Hungarian party (first buyer and last purchaser) is domiciled" (*H-11*, 1963, p. 411). The U.N. identifies Hungary's trade partners as "countries of *production* and *last consignment*" (*UN-8*, 1968, p. 374, and other issues), an apparent error; since 1971 by countries of *production* and *consumption* (*H-2*, 1972, no. 2-3, p. 51).

Poland. Partners are defined as countries of *purchase* and *sale*.

Rumania. Trade partners are given as countries of *purchase* and *sale* (*UN-8*, 1968, p. 700).

Yugoslavia. Imports are by country of *production*, exports by country of *consumption:*

The country in which the commodities have been manufactured in the condition as imported has been considered as country of origin. Basic raw materials ... have been shown by the producing countries even if the commodities have been shipped from the warehouses of some other country.... The country in which the commodities are consumed or have to undergo further processing is considered as the country of destination. [*Y-2*, 1969, p. 9, and other issues of the same publication.]

Albania. Definition of trade partner is not known, so *provenance* and *destination* are the terms used in international publications (*UN-8*, 1968, p. 45).

To summarize, all European CEMA countries except the U.S.S.R. apparently record statistics according to country of *purchase* or *sale*, while the U.S.S.R. keeps books according to country of *production* and *consumption*, a practice which is followed by Yugoslavia also.

APPENDIX E

The Case of the Unspecified U.S.S.R. Residuals

The available distributions of U.S.S.R. trade by known partner countries or by commodity categories leaves unspecified a significant proportion of the total. The problem of these unspecified residuals needs to be taken into consideration in any economic analysis of the geographic or commodity composition of U.S.S.R. trade, since the residuals are not randomly distributed.

Exports to Less Developed Countries

U.S.S.R. foreign trade yearbooks *(U-1)* report trade by both individual countries and groups of countries, the latter classified as "socialist" ("Total CPEs" in our terminology), "industrial capitalist" (MDCs), and "developing" (LDCs) countries. The composition of the LDC group follows the standard U.N. description for Economic Group II, except for the inclusion of Turkey and the exclusion of Cuba *(U-3,* September 1968, p. 48). Each year the sum of reported trade with these three groups adds precisely to the independently given total of exports or imports; moreover, the sum of reported trade with individual CPE and MDC countries adds to the independently given group totals. The one exception is in the case of U.S.S.R. exports by country to LDCs, for which the sum of individual national exports is substantially less each year than the independently given total exports to the group as a whole. (There is no corresponding discrepancy in imports.) In 1970 this unspecified residual amounted to $792 million, or close to two-fifths of total reported U.S.S.R. exports to LDCs and nearly 7 percent of global exports.

Calculated unspecified residuals are shown in Table E-1 for 1946-70. It is only since 1955, however, that the residuals can be meaningfully derived because only since then has trade with practically all countries been reported in the foreign trade yearbooks.*

Commodity Composition of Total Trade

U.S.S.R. tabulations of commodity composition for total trade (Tables II.CTN.M.U and II.CTN.X.U) and trade by country (Tables

---

*For each year, trade with individual countries is reported in several issues of *U-1*, among which there may be slight differences in the list of countries included. All issues of *U-1* were consulted to obtain maximum country coverage.

Table E-1

U.S.S.R. Trade with Less Developed Countries:
Comparison of LDC Group Total with Sum of Trade Reported by Component Countries, 1946-1970
(Millions of Dollars)

Year	Country Sums						Total of Sums		Given LDC Total		Percent*		Unspecified Value**	Exports % of Total Trade
	Asia		Africa		Latin America									
	Export	Import	Export	Import	Export	Import	Export	Import	Export	Import	Export	Import		
1946	39.2	27.3	1.7	2.1	1.9	18.8	42.8	48.2	43.0	58.9	99.5	81.9		
1947	14.7	34.8	3.7	2.9	1.7	17.2	20.0	54.9	21.6	62.7	92.6	87.6		
1948	25.1	94.6	46.2	65.1	.8	10.8	72.1	170.4	73.6	181.6	98.0	93.9		
1949	62.0	62.7	3.9	46.3	.7	4.3	66.6	113.3	71.1	121.6	93.6	93.2		
1950	9.4	52.8	21.6	37.0	0	1.7	31.0	91.4	32.3	92.7	95.9	98.7		
1951	46.4	66.4	24.7	20.2	0	7.4	71.1	94.1	73.3	95.3	97.0	98.7		
1952	43.0	57.8	30.0	44.0	0	5.1	73.0	106.9	74.6	113.9	97.9	93.9		
1953	35.4	44.9	13.1	22.7	.7	9.9	49.2	77.4	50.1	80.0	98.2	96.8		
1954	33.7	46.4	10.8	31.0	47.4	43.2	91.9	120.7	97.9	156.2	93.9	77.2		
1955	60.2	84.9	13.6	31.8	24.3	78.0	98.1	194.7	142.0	195.8	69.1	99.4	43.9	1.3
1956	98.2	170.2	42.2	61.7	22.1	43.2	162.6	275.1	267.8	276.6	60.7	99.5	105.2	2.9
1957	165.7	178.1	87.8	144.1	5.0	88.6	258.4	410.8	362.9	414.0	71.2	99.2	104.4	2.4
1958	241.9	269.6	92.6	121.4	23.3	57.6	357.8	448.6	460.6	450.6	77.7	99.6	102.8	2.4
1959	187.6	265.4	97.6	169.6	27.6	49.6	312.7	484.6	430.8	488.0	72.6	99.3	118.1	2.2
1960	175.3	294.0	99.8	201.6	31.9	35.7	307.0	531.2	337.4	534.6	91.0	99.4	30.4	0.5
1961	265.2	361.1	178.8	148.3	29.6	50.8	473.6	560.2	583.9	563.5	81.1	99.4	110.3	1.8
1962	334.1	374.1	164.8	133.7	38.4	74.0	537.3	581.8	988.3	584.3	54.4	99.6	451.0	6.4
1963	453.8	362.8	222.0	219.1	30.7	75.7	706.4	657.6	911.9	648.7	77.5	101.4	205.4	2.8
1964	469.2	379.4	246.8	182.8	29.0	64.1	745.0	626.3	964.4	626.4	77.2	100.0	219.4	2.9
1965	476.6	457.7	329.0	248.4	49.2	108.1	854.8	814.2	1122.7	815.7	76.1	99.8	267.9	3.3
1966	500.4	485.8	306.2	222.4	37.6	160.0	844.2	868.2	1211.8	870.5	69.7	99.7	367.6	4.2
1967	502.0	459.1	395.8	242.6	19.7	71.9	917.4	773.6	1341.1	775.9	68.4	99.7	423.7	4.8
1968	549.6	470.8	330.8	293.3	22.6	82.4	902.9	846.5	1403.4	860.0	64.3	98.4	500.6	5.2
1969	674.6	581.7	416.4	400.3	25.1	104.3	1116.1	1086.3	1689.0	1102.3	66.1	98.5	572.9	5.4
1970	659.6	642.3	579.7	536.4	8.7	78.0	1247.9	1256.8	2039.9	1272.9	61.2	98.7	792.0	6.8

*Total of Sums as percent of Given LDC Total.

**Given LDC Total less Total of Sums.

Source: 1946-54: U-2, 1955-70: U-2 and U-1, various issues. Devisa-rubles were converted here to dollars at the official ruble/dollar exchange rate.

Table E-2

U.S.S.R. Imports by CTN Categories: Comparison of Percentage
Composition Given (G) and Summed (S), 1946, 1950, 1955, 1958-1969

Year	CTN 1		CTN 2		CTN 3		CTN 4		CTN 5		CTN 7-8*		CTN 9		Total Imports		
	G	S	G	S	G	S	G	S	G	S	G	S	G	S	G	S	G or S
	(1)	(2)	(3)	(4)	(5)	(6)	(7)	(8)	(9)	(10)	(11)	(12)	(13)	(14)	(15)	(16)	(17)
1946	28.5	28.5	21.7	21.6	1.9	1.4		1.4	10.5	18.5	15.7	13.4	7.2	4.3	85.5	89.1	94.9
1947		17.8		21.4		2.9		1.1		18.5		22.7		5.0		89.4	
1948		9.0		19.0		5.6		1.2		28.0		19.7		9.1		91.6	
1949		14.4		22.8		4.6		1.7		20.1		15.5		10.4		89.5	
1950	21.5	21.5	26.8	25.5	6.9	5.8		1.4	11.5	15.4	17.5	16.8	7.4	6.6	91.6	93.0	96.9
1951		20.8		25.2		12.0		0.9		11.7		16.0		7.5		94.1	
1952		21.6		26.7		8.6		1.1		14.5		16.6		6.9		96.0	
1953		27.5		28.0		3.6		1.0		12.9		16.7		6.6		96.3	
1954		30.6		22.9		2.9		0.6		13.6		19.3		6.3		96.2	
1955	30.2	30.2	24.8	24.6	3.4	3.4		0.6	8.4	12.6	20.2	20.1	4.8	4.8	91.8	96.3	96.6
1956		24.8		27.4		5.8		0.9		13.0		16.2		9.4		97.5	
1957		23.9		26.1		5.2		1.0		15.8		14.3		11.4		97.7	
1958	24.5	24.5	23.0	23.1	6.4	6.4		1.1	9.5	13.7	14.8	14.5	14.5	14.2	92.7	97.7	98.1
1959	26.6	26.6	21.2	21.3	6.0	6.0		0.9	8.3	12.4	12.8	12.6	18.2	18.0	93.1	97.8	98.1
1960	29.8	29.8	21.0	20.9	6.0	6.0		0.8	8.4	11.5	12.1	12.0	17.2	17.1	94.5	98.1	98.4
1961	29.8	29.8	19.1	18.6	7.1	7.1		0.9	7.3	10.2	14.1	14.0	17.3	17.1	94.7	97.7	98.5
1962	34.8	34.8	17.7	17.7	6.6	6.6		0.9	6.2	9.1	11.5	11.5	17.8	17.6	94.6	98.2	98.4
1963	34.9	34.9	14.8	14.9	6.2	6.2		0.8	6.5	9.7	12.8	12.8	18.3	18.3	93.5	97.6	97.5
1964	34.4	34.4	12.0	12.2	5.5	5.5		0.5	5.5	9.2	20.1	19.8	15.4	15.3	92.9	96.9	97.2
1965	33.4	33.4	12.3	12.4	6.2	6.2		0.6	6.3	9.8	20.2	20.1	14.2	14.2	92.6	96.7	96.8
1966	32.4	32.4	11.1	11.2	6.4	6.4		0.6	6.7	10.4	19.6	19.5	16.4	16.3	92.6	96.8	96.9
1967	34.2	34.2	11.0	7.6**	6.1	6.1		0.7	6.2	9.8	15.8	15.7	19.6	19.5	92.9	93.6	97.2
1968	36.9	36.9	11.2	7.9**	6.0	5.9		0.8	6.0	8.5	13.6	13.6	19.9	19.6	93.6	93.2	96.9
1969	37.5	37.5	12.0	8.6**	6.2	6.0		0.7	6.4	8.8	12.9	12.8	19.0	18.6	94.0	93.0	97.1

*Trade in CTN *Category* 6 is insignificant.

**Total trade in CTN 24, Metallic Ores and Concentrates, is no longer reported. Only one component, CTN 24216, Alumina, is given.

Source: G columns, 1946, 1950, 1955, 1960, 1966: *U-1*, 1968; 1969: *U-1*, 1969. S columns, 1946-69: based on Statistical Table II.CTN.M.U.

$U-2$: 1958, 1963-64: *U-1*, 1964; 1959, 1961-66: *U-1*, 1959-1963, *U-1*, 1965, and *U-1*, 1966; 1967-68: *U-1*, 1968; 1969: *U-1*, 1969.

Table E-3

U.S.S.R. Exports by CTN Categories: Comparison of Percentage
Composition Given (G) and Summed (S), 1946, 1950, 1955, 1958-1969

Year	CTN 1 G (1)	CTN 1 S (2)	CTN 2 G (3)	CTN 2 S (4)	CTN 3 G (5)	CTN 3 S (6)	CTN 4 G (7)	CTN 4 S (8)	CTN 5 G (9)	CTN 5 S (10)	CTN 7-8* G (11)	CTN 7-8* S (12)	CTN 9 G (13)	CTN 9 S (14)	Total Exports G (15)	Total Exports S (16)	Total Exports G or S (17)
1946	5.8	5.8	15.1	12.3	5.0	4.8		0.1	30.5	36.0	29.8	28.3	7.4	5.1	93.6	92.4	99.2
1947		2.9		16.9		8.0		0.5		31.6		16.7		7.7		84.3	
1948		4.5		16.6		5.7		0.4		23.4		36.1		6.0		92.7	
1949		9.2		20.7		6.5		0.3		21.3		22.6		5.0		85.6	
1950	11.8	11.8	15.8	15.3	4.3	4.2		0.2	16.6	18.6	20.6	19.5	4.9	3.7	74.0	73.3	76.2
1951		14.9		17.5		3.7		0.2		20.4		21.2		3.7		81.6	
1952		16.2		18.1		2.9		0.2		16.3		21.6		2.4		77.7	
1953		17.8		21.8		2.7		0.3		16.3		17.9		2.4		79.2	
1954		16.5		26.6		3.1		0.5		18.0		14.6		2.5		81.8	
1955	17.5	17.5	27.8	26.3	3.1	3.0		0.5	16.3	17.5	12.0	12.0	3.0	3.0	79.7	79.8	81.4
1956		17.3		31.3		3.3		0.4		15.8		10.9		2.8		81.8	
1957		14.9		34.3		3.1		0.2		14.1		18.1		3.2		87.9	
1958	18.5	18.5	37.3	36.4	3.6	3.4		0.2	13.2	14.5	12.3	12.3	3.6	3.6	88.5	88.9	90.0
1959	21.5	21.6	33.8	32.9	3.2	2.9		0.2	11.2	12.7	15.1	15.0	2.9	2.8	87.7	88.1	89.4
1960	20.5	20.5	37.2	36.3	3.5	3.3		0.3	12.7	14.2	13.1	13.0	2.9	2.8	89.9	90.4	91.7
1961	16.1	16.1	38.8	37.8	3.9	3.7		0.3	12.8	14.2	13.7	13.6	2.9	2.9	88.2	88.6	89.9
1962	16.6	16.6	36.5	35.4	3.2	3.1		0.3	11.6	12.7	13.3	13.2	2.6	2.6	83.8	83.5	85.2
1963	19.7	19.7	37.4	36.4	3.4	3.3		0.3	11.3	12.2	12.9	12.9	2.6	2.6	87.3	87.4	88.7
1964	21.0	21.0	40.0	39.0	3.3	3.1		0.4	12.4	12.9	7.7	7.7	2.4	2.4	86.8	86.5	87.7
1965	20.0	20.0	39.6	37.9	3.6	3.4		0.5	13.1	13.7	8.4	8.3	2.4	2.3	87.1	86.1	88.2
1966	20.8	20.8	37.6	35.7	3.8	3.7		0.5	13.0	14.0	9.2	9.1	2.4	2.3	86.8	86.1	88.3
1967	21.1	21.1	35.9	34.1	4.0	3.9		0.5	11.8	12.8	11.8	11.7	2.6	2.5	87.2	86.6	88.7
1968	21.6	21.6	34.6**	33.8	4.1	3.9		0.6	11.4	12.3	10.3	10.2	2.7	2.4	84.7	84.8	86.2
1969	22.5	22.5	35.1**	34.5	3.9	3.8		0.6	10.2	10.6	10.7	10.4	2.6	2.3	85.0	84.7	86.0

*Trade in CTN *Category* 6 is insignificant.

**CTN 25, Nonmetallic Minerals, Clays, and Earth, are not included. In 1966 and 1967, this commodity group represented 1.1 percent of U.S.S.R. exports.

Source: G columns: same as in Table E-2; S columns: Statistical Table II.CTN.X.U.

III.CTN.M.U-B through CEMA and III.CTN.X.U-B through CEMA) reveal that in each year a certain proportion of trade (usually larger for
exports than for imports) is not specified according to any CTN *category*. Commodity composition cannot be accurately analyzed without
knowledge of which CTN *categories* are fully specified or which are incomplete, or without information on the composition of the unspecified
residual.

Recent issues of the U.S.S.R. foreign trade yearbook *(U-1)* indicate, for selected years, commodity structure — in the sense of aggregated commodity groupings — as a percent of total imports or exports.
The sum of the percentages each year is less than 100. Although no
CTN numbers are given with the commodity groupings, approximate
(one- and two-digit) CTN numbers can be assigned. To obtain additional information on the unspecified residual, the percentages given in
the yearbooks (here coded G for "given") and those obtained from the

Table E-4

U.S.S.R. Trade: Comparison of Alternative Estimates of Percentage Composition
by CTN Categories, 1946, 1950, 1955, 1958-1969

CTN Category	G and S Percentages Compared	Explanation
1	G = S	This is the only *category* total which is shown regularly in value terms. Thus, percentage totals are identical, except for rounding errors.
2	G > S	G may not be exhaustive in imports where it represents the sum of two components, Fuel and Electric Power (CTN 20-23) and Ores, Concentrates, Metals, and Products (CTN 24, 26-29). A separate additional entry, Nonmetallic Minerals, (CTN 25) is shown in exports only (except for 1968-69). S is incomplete because certain commodity groups in which the U.S.S.R. is known to trade are not listed.
3	G > S	G appears to be exhaustive on the basis of content description. S is, therefore, incomplete.
4	G < S	G is not reported. S may not be complete.
5	G < S	G is definitely incomplete because only two components, Timber, Pulp, and Paper Articles (CTN 50) and Textile Raw Materials and Semimanufactures (CTN 51) are given. S may be incomplete.
6,7,8	G > S	G appears to be exhaustive on the basis of content description. S is, therefore, incomplete.
9	G > S	G appears to be exhaustive on the basis of content description. S is, therefore, incomplete.

Data Bank after summation of two- and three-digit entries (here coded S for "summed") have been compared by CTN *categories* in Tables E-2 and E-3 for imports and exports, respectively.

The independent pairs of percentages obtained in this manner reveal a consistent pattern for 1946, 1950, 1955, and 1958-69, one that is much the same in imports and exports. For some *categories* the percentages from the two sources are always identical (except for rounding); for others, the percentages from one source are either always larger or always smaller. Differences between the G and S percentages can be explained satisfactorily in each case by examining the underlying commodity coverage in the two sources, as summarized in Table E-4.

From Table E-4 it appears that accepting for each CTN *category* the larger of the two percentages, G or S, permits reduction of the un-specified component, compared to taking either the G or the S percent-ages alone. For imports between 1958 and 1969, the average propor-tion of trade specified by CTN *categories* can be increased in this way to 97.6 percent (compared to 93.5 and 96.4 percent on the basis of G or S estimates alone); in exports, the average rises to 88.3 percent (com-pared with 86.9 and 86.8 percent). The new figures are shown in col-umn 17 of Tables E-2 and E-3, respectively.

Two recent publications from East Europe enable us to go a step further. They provide an exhaustive percentage breakdown of commod-ity composition for each CEMA country, including the U.S.S.R., for se-lected years according to five new aggregative commodity groupings. These groupings are identified by descriptive titles only, but it appears that they correspond to certain combinations of CTN *categories,* as shown in Table E-5. The five new groupings may indicate that CEMA or some CEMA countries have introduced alternative or revised defi-nitions of CTN *broad divisions.*

Table E-5

CTN Classification: Titles of "Alternative" Broad Divisions
and Corresponding One-Digit CTN Categories

CTN		
"Alternative" Broad Division	Category	Designation
I	1	Industrial Machinery and Equipment
II	2	Fuels, Mineral Raw Materials, Metals
III	3,4,6+ Unspecified	Chemical Products, Fertilizer, Rubber, Building Materials, and Other Products
IV	5,7,8	Agricultural Products and Foodstuffs, Including Agricultural Raw Materials
V	9	Industrial Consumer Goods

Source: *CEMA-2*, pp. 356-59, 446-47; *P-9*, p. 114.

Table E-6

U.S.S.R. Trade by CTN Categories: Comparison of Percentage Composition Shown in Various Sources

Year	"Alternative" Broad Divisions and Corresponding CTN Categories										Unspecified Col. (5) Less Col. (6) (11)
	I = 1		II = 2		III = 3 + 4 + 6 + Unspecified		IV = 5 + 7 + 8		V = 9		
	CEMA (1)	G or S (2)	CEMA (3)	G or S (4)	CEMA (5)	G or S (6)	CEMA (7)	G or S (8)	CEMA (9)	G or S (10)	
Imports											
1950	21.5	21.5	26.9	26.8	9.8	8.3	34.4	32.9	7.4	7.4	1.5
1955	30.2	30.2	24.9	24.8	7.1	4.0	33.0	32.8	4.8	4.8	3.1
1960	29.8	29.8	21.2	21.0	8.1	6.8	23.7	23.6	17.2	17.2	1.3
1965	33.4	33.4	12.5	12.4	9.7	6.8	30.2	30.0	14.2	14.2	2.9
1967	34.2	34.2	11.1	11.0	9.4	6.8	25.7	25.6	19.6	19.6	2.6
1969	37.5	37.5	12.2	12.0	9.3	6.9	22.0	21.7	19.0	19.0	2.4
Exports											
1950	11.8	11.8	15.7	15.8	28.1	4.5	39.5	39.2	4.9	4.9	23.6
1955	17.5	17.5	27.8	27.8	22.2	3.6	29.5	29.5	3.0	3.0	18.6
1960	20.5	20.5	37.2	37.2	12.1	3.8	27.3	27.3	2.9	2.9	8.3
1965	20.0	20.0	39.6	39.6	15.9	4.1	22.1	22.1	2.4	2.4	11.8
1967	21.1	21.1	35.9	35.9	15.8	4.5	24.6	24.6	2.6	2.6	11.3
1969	22.5	22.5	36.9	35.1*	16.4	4.5	21.6	21.3	2.6	2.6	11.9

*Discrepancy with percent shown in column (3) is explained by omission of CTN 25, as shown in footnote to Table E-3.
Source: CEMA columns, 1950, 1955, 1960, 1965, and 1969: CEMA-2, pp. 357, 359; 1967: P-9, p. 114.

Table E-6 compares the larger of either the given G or summed S percentages (from Tables E-2 and E-3) with the newly published "CEMA" percentages. Comparisons in Table E-6 confirm the previous findings of Tables E-2 and E-3 and provide additional information summarized in Table E-7.

A reconstructed distribution of U.S.S.R. imports and exports by CTN *categories* is shown for 1950, 1955, 1960, 1965, 1967, and 1969 in Table E-8. There still remains a significant component unspecified, which amounts to about $250 million (2.4 percent) of imports and $1.4 billion (11.9 percent) of exports in 1969. The fact that the proportions are considerably larger in exports than in imports suggests that all or a substantial part of the unspecified residual is comprised of commercially traded strategic items.

Table E-7

U.S.S.R. Trade: Comparison of Alternative Estimates of Percentage Composition by CTN Categories, 1950, 1955, 1960, 1965, 1967, 1969

CTN Category	Percentages Compared	Explanation
1	CEMA = G = S	Percentages shown are identical in all sources.
2	CEMA ≥ G	In imports, higher CEMA percentages are very likely accounted for by the inclusion of CTN 25 (see Table E-4). In exports, percentages are identical except in 1969; in that year CTN 25 was excluded, as shown in Table E-3. CEMA appears to be exhaustive on the basis of content description.
3+4+6 + unspecified	CEMA > G or S	CTN 3 appears to be exhaustive in G. Even though CTN 4 may be incomplete in S, it is usually of very small importance in the total trade of every CEMA country. Thus, whatever unspecified component there may be, it is likely to be small. CTN 6 is insignificant. It appears reasonable to conclude, therefore, that the observed difference between CEMA and G or S represents all, or practically all, the unspecified residual in U.S.S.R. imports or exports.
5+7+8	CEMA > G or S	Since the sum of CTN 7 and 8 appears to be exhaustive in G (CTN 6 being insignificant), the small remaining discrepancy appears to be the result of incomplete specification of CTN 5 in both G and S. Accordingly, the difference should be added to CTN 5 obtained from S.
9	CEMA = G	Both sources are identical and appear to be exhaustive on the basis of content description.

Table E-8

U.S.S.R.: Imports and Exports by CTN Categories
Plus Unspecified Trade, 1950, 1955, 1960, 1965, 1967, 1969
(as Percent of Total)

Year	CTN Categories							Unspecified	
	1	2	3	4	5	6-8	9	Percent	Millions of Dollars
					Imports				
1950	21.5	26.9	6.9	1.4	16.9	17.5	7.4	1.5	21.8
1955	30.2	24.9	3.4	0.6	12.8	20.2	4.8	3.1	94.9
1960	29.8	21.2	6.0	0.8	11.6	12.1	17.2	1.3	73.2
1965	33.4	12.5	6.2	0.6	10.0	20.2	14.2	2.9	233.7
1967	34.2	11.1	6.1	0.7	9.9	15.8	19.6	2.6	222.0
1969	37.5	12.2	6.2	0.7	9.1	12.9	19.0	2.4	247.8
					Exports				
1950	11.8	15.7	4.3	0.2	18.9	20.6	4.9	23.6	423.5
1955	17.5	27.8	3.1	0.5	17.5	12.0	3.0	18.6	637.3
1960	20.5	37.2	3.5	0.3	14.2	13.1	2.9	8.3	461.8
1965	20.0	39.6	3.6	0.5	13.7	8.4	2.4	11.8	964.6
1967	21.1	35.9	4.0	0.5	12.8	11.8	2.6	11.3	1090.7
1969	22.5	36.9	3.9	0.6	10.9	10.7	2.6	11.9	1387.4

Source: Imports, CTN 1, 3, 4, 6-8, and 9: Table E-2; CTN 2: Table E-6; CTN 5: Table E-2, col. (10) plus (col. 7 less col. 8 of Table E-6). Exports, CTN 1, 3, 4, 6-8, and 9: Table E-3; CTN 2: Table E-6; CTN 5: Table E-3, col (10) plus (col. 7 less col. 8 of Table E-6).

APPENDIX F

Trade with United States, Canada, Japan, and Australia

The statistics below supplement Series IV in Part Two on trade between individual East European countries and West Europe as a group. This essentially rounds out the MDC group, which, besides West Europe, includes the United States, Canada, Japan, Australia, New Zealand, and the Union of South Africa. East Europe's trade with the last two countries has been insignificant.

The present separate appendix has been prepared because in general commodity composition by SITC *categories* has been available for more recent years for these four countries than for West Europe (since 1961 for the United States and Canada; since 1964 for Japan; in the case of Australia only total trade can be shown).

Trade with the MDC group as reported by individual East European countries in Statistical Series I and "mirror" statistics compiled from trade-partner sources (i.e., the sum of trade with East European countries reported by West Europe, the United States, Canada, and Japan) will not be in exact agreement. There are differences in the systems of reporting trade ("general" vs. "special" systems), in the treatment of transportation and related charges (c.i.f. vs. f.o.b.), in identification of trade-partner countries (origin of imports and destination of exports), and in the dates at which trade is recorded as goods move from origin to destination.

Table F-1

United States Trade with U.S.S.R.: Total, 1946-1969, by SITC Categories, 1961-1969
(Millions of Current Dollars)

Year	Primary						Manufactured						Total Trade
	0	1	2	3	4	Total	5	6	7	8	9	Total	
Imports (f.o.b.)													
1946-50*													68.4
1951-55*													16.8
1956-60*													21.9
1961	.2	0	10.7	-	-	11.0	6.2	5.0	-	.4	.2	11.8	22.8
1962	.2	0	11.0	-	-	11.2	.6	4.0	0	.4	.2	5.1	16.4
1963	.2	0	13.2	-	-	13.4	.3	7.0	-	.4	.1	7.9	21.2
1964	.2	0	13.1	-	-	13.4	.2	7.1	0	.7	.1	8.2	21.5
1965	.6	0	13.9	0	0	14.5	.4	26.4	0	.6	.2	28.2	42.7
1966	.7	.1	16.4	0	0	17.1	1.4	30.3	.1	.5	.2	32.2	49.6
1967	.8	.1	14.4	0	2.0	17.3	1.1	21.8	.2	.6	.2	23.8	41.2
1968	.3	.1	15.5	0	0	15.9	1.0	39.7	.1	1.1	.2	42.2	58.1
1969	.5	.1	14.5	1.2	0	16.3	1.3	32.1	.1	1.6	.1	35.2	51.5
Exports (f.o.b.)													
1946-50*													108.6
1951-55*													.1
1956-60*													11.3
1961	0	-	6.0	0	15.1	21.2	2.8	4.3	16.8	.5	-	24.4	45.6
1962	.1	0	9.7	-	4.0	13.9	.8	.7	3.9	.8	0	6.1	20.1
1963	1.1	-	7.3	2.0	2.1	12.4	8.1	.7	1.1	.4	.1	10.5	22.9
1964	117.8	-	6.3	.3	8.3	132.7	8.1	.2	4.9	.4	0	13.6	146.4
1965	0	0	15.9	0	16.7	32.7	5.7	.3	5.1	.3	.2	11.7	44.3
1966	.1	0	23.2	-	7.6	30.9	4.9	1.2	4.1	.3	.2	10.7	41.7
1967	0	.2	32.1	.2	-	32.5	13.1	1.7	11.4	1.2	.2	27.6	60.2
1968	0	.9	18.0	0	-	18.9	20.6	.7	15.0	1.9	.2	38.4	57.4
1969	0	1.2	22.1	.3	-	23.6	27.5	7.7	41.6	4.1	.3	81.2	104.8

*Annual average.

Source: 1946-60: *GP-4*, pp. 21-22, 32-33; 1961-69: *W-20*, annual issues.

Note: General trade; country of production (imports) and consumption (exports). Figures may not add to total because of rounding.

Table F-2

United States Trade with Bulgaria: Total, 1946-1969, by SITC Categories, 1961-1969
(Millions of Current Dollars)

Year	Primary						Manufactured						Total Trade
	0	1	2	3	4	Total	5	6	7	8	9	Total	
Imports (f.o.b.)													
1946-50*													3.4
1951-55*													.4
1956-60*													.7
1961	.7	0	.1	–	–	.9	.2	.1	–	0	–	.3	1.2
1962	.6	0	.1	–	–	.7	.3	.1	–	0	0	.4	1.2
1963	.5	–	.2	–	–	.7	.2	.1	0	0	–	.3	1.1
1964	.6	–	.1	–	–	.7	.3	.1	0	.1	0	.5	1.1
1965	1.1	–	.1	–	–	1.2	.3	.2	0	.1	–	.5	1.7
1966	1.5	–	.3	–	–	1.8	.4	.2	0	0	0	.6	2.5
1967	1.9	–	.1	–	0	2.0	.4	.2	0	.1	0	.7	2.8
1968	2.7	0	.1	–	–	2.9	.6	.2	–	.1	0	.9	3.7
1969	.6	0	.1	–	–	.8	.3	.2	.1	.1	0	.8	1.6
Exports (f.o.b.)													
1946-50*													1.5
1951-55*													0
1956-60*													.2
1961	0	–	–	–	–	0	0	0	0	0	–	0	0
1962	0	–	0	–	–	0	0	–	–	0	–	0	0
1963	.1	–	–	–	–	.1	–	0	0	0	0	0	.1
1964	1.6	–	2.6	–	.2	4.4	.2	0	.2	0	–	.4	4.8
1965	2.3	–	0	–	.2	2.5	.5	0	.5	.1	–	1.1	3.6
1966	1.6	0	.1	0	–	1.7	.9	0	1.0	.1	–	1.9	3.6
1967	2.9	0	0	0	–	2.9	.8	0	.4	0	0	1.2	4.2
1968	2.4	0	.1	–	–	2.6	.5	0	.9	0	0	1.5	4.0
1969	2.3	–	0	0	–	2.4	.6	.1	1.5	.1	0	2.3	4.6

*Annual average.

Source: 1946-60: GP-4, pp. 21-22, 32-33; 1961-69: W-20, annual issues.
Note: General trade; country of production (imports) and consumption (exports). Figures may not add to total because of rounding.

Table F-3

United States Trade with Czechoslovakia: Total, 1946-1969, by SITC Categories, 1961-1969
(Millions of Current Dollars)

Imports (f.o.b.)

Year	Primary 0	1	2	3	4	Total	Manufactured 5	6	7	8	9	Total	Total Trade
1946-50*													22.4
1951-55*													6.6
1956-60*													9.1
1961	1.0	0	.7	0	-	1.7	.2	2.3	1.5	3.4	0	7.5	9.2
1962	.8	0	.6	0	-	1.4	.4	2.7	1.6	3.8	.1	8.5	9.9
1963	.8	.1	.6	0	-	1.5	.2	2.7	1.8	3.6	.1	8.4	9.9
1964	.8	.1	.5	0	0	1.3	.2	4.4	2.7	4.0	.2	11.5	12.8
1965	1.3	.1	.7	0	-	2.1	.3	4.5	4.0	5.7	.3	14.7	16.7
1966	1.4	.1	.9	0	0	2.4	.6	7.2	10.4	6.8	.3	25.3	27.7
1967	1.9	.1	.8	0	-	2.8	.8	5.0	9.6	7.9	.3	23.4	26.2
1968	2.0	.1	.4	-	0	2.6	.8	6.2	6.3	7.4	.4	21.2	23.8
1969	1.8	.1	.6	0	-	2.5	.6	6.5	5.3	8.9	.2	21.6	24.1

Exports (f.o.b.)

Year	Primary 0	1	2	3	4	Total	Manufactured 5	6	7	8	9	Total	Total Trade
1946-50*													41.9
1951-55*													.9
1956-60*													2.3
1961	.4	.4	3.2	.4	.7	5.1	.8	.8	.3	.1	0	2.1	7.2
1962	1.6	-	3.4	.1	.2	5.3	1.1	.4	.2	.1	0	1.7	7.0
1963	2.8	-	3.6	.7	.2	7.3	1.6	.3	.6	.1	0	2.5	9.8
1964	6.7	0	2.1	-	.7	9.5	.7	.6	.4	.3	0	1.7	11.3
1965	18.3	.3	6.4	0	-	25.0	.8	.6	.9	.4	0	2.6	27.6
1966	26.6	.1	6.8	0	.3	33.8	.5	.8	1.8	.5	0	3.5	37.2
1967	5.4	0	5.0	0	-	10.4	.9	1.0	6.1	1.3	.1	8.6	19.0
1968	4.7	.2	4.1	0	-	9.0	.9	.9	1.9	.8	0	5.0	14.1
1969	.3	.2	5.3	.5	0	6.4	.8	1.4	4.9	.8	0	7.9	14.3

*Annual average.

Source: 1946-60: GP-4, pp. 21-22, 32-33; 1961-69: W-20, annual issues.

Note: General trade; country of production (imports) and consumption (exports). Figures may not add to total because of rounding.

Table F-4

United States Trade with East Germany: Total, 1946-1969, by SITC Categories, 1961-1969
(Millions of Current Dollars)

Year	Primary						Manufactured						Total Trade
	0	1	2	3	4	Total	5	6	7	8	9	Total	
Imports (f.o.b.)													
1946-50*													n.a.
1951-55*													n.a.
1956-60*													4.7
1961	0	-	.2	.2	-	.4	.1	.4	.7	1.0	0	2.1	2.5
1962	.1	-	.6	.2	-	.9	.2	.3	.7	.8	.1	2.1	3.0
1963	0	-	1.0	.2	-	1.2	.3	.3	.7	.7	.1	2.0	3.2
1964	.2	-	2.1	.3	-	2.6	.2	2.3	.7	.8	.1	4.1	6.7
1965	.1	0	.9	.4	-	1.4	.2	3.3	.8	.8	.1	5.1	6.5
1966	.1	0	.9	.4	-	1.4	.3	4.1	1.6	.7	.1	6.8	8.2
1967	.1	0	.5	.4	0	1.0	.3	2.0	1.3	.9	.1	4.6	5.6
1968	.1	0	.5	.5	0	1.1	.3	.8	1.2	2.2	.2	4.8	5.9
1969	0	0	1.1	.4	0	1.5	.9	1.6	2.3	1.6	.2	6.5	8.0
Exports (f.o.b.)													
1946-50*													n.a.
1951-55*													n.a.
1956-60*													1.2
1961	.9	-	0	-	1.7	2.6	.1	.1	0	0	-	.2	2.8
1962	.4	1.1	.2	-	-	1.7	0	0	0	0	-	0	1.7
1963	4.6	.8	.7	.3	0	6.4	0	0	0	0	-	0	6.4
1964	13.5	1.1	1.4	2.9	-	18.9	.7	0	.2	.1	-	1.0	19.9
1965	8.5	1.4	1.0	1.3	-	12.2	.2	.2	0	.0	-	.4	12.6
1966	17.1	2.8	1.2	1.6	-	22.7	0	.2	1.9	.1	-	2.2	24.9
1967	18.4	2.7	1.6	.9	-	23.6	.1	.3	2.1	.3	-	2.8	26.3
1968	22.3	1.4	.8	1.2	-	25.7	.1	.7	2.4	.4	0	3.5	29.2
1969	22.2	1.3	5.2	1.1	-	29.8	.2	.3	1.8	.3	0	2.6	32.4

*Annual average.

Source: 1956-60: *GP-4*, pp. 21-22, 32-33; 1961-69: *W-20*, annual issues.

Note: General trade; country of production (imports) and consumption (exports). Figures may not add to total because of rounding.

Table F-5

United States Trade with Hungary: Total, 1946-1969, by SITC Categories, 1961-1969
(Millions of Current Dollars)

Year	Primary 0	1	2	3	4	Total	Manufactured 5	6	7	8	9	Total	Total Trade
						Imports (f.o.b.)							
1946-50*													1.4
1951-55*													2.2
1956-60*													1.4
1961	.5	.1	.2	—	—	.8	.1	.3	.2	.7	.1	1.2	2.0
1962	.2	.1	.1	—	—	.4	.1	.3	.1	.7	.1	1.3	1.7
1963	.1	.1	0	—	—	.2	.1	.2	.2	.7	.1	1.3	1.5
1964	.2	.1	.1	—	—	.3	0	.3	.2	.7	.1	1.3	1.7
1965	.1	.1	.2	—	—	.4	.1	.4	.3	.9	.1	1.7	2.1
1966	.2	.2	.2	—	—	.6	.2	.5	.5	1.2	.1	2.5	3.5
1967	.4	.2	.2	—	—	.8	.1	.8	.8	1.4	.1	3.2	3.9
1968	.2	.2	.1	—	—	.6	.1	1.2	.4	1.5	.1	3.3	3.8
1969	.4	.3	.1	—	—	.8	.2	1.1	.5	1.4	.1	3.3	4.1
						Exports (f.o.b.)							
1946-50*													7.2
1951-55*													.8
1956-60*													2.4
1961	0	—	.2	—	.3	.5	.4	.2	0	.1	0	.8	1.3
1962	0	—	.1	—	—	.1	.4	0	.2	.1	0	.7	.8
1963	15.1	—	1.3	.2	—	16.7	.2	0	.2	.1	0	.6	17.3
1964	7.7	—	5.1	—	.1	12.8	.4	.1	.2	.1	0	.8	13.6
1965	2.8	—	4.7	—	.5	8.0	.8	.1	.3	.1	0	1.3	9.3
1966	4.9	—	2.6	—	.2	7.7	.9	.3	.6	.4	0	2.2	10.0
1967	3.9	0	.6	—	—	4.5	.5	.6	1.5	.4	0	3.0	7.5
1968	8.0	0	.7	0	—	8.6	.6	.5	.9	.3	0	2.4	11.0
1969	3.6	—	.3	0	—	3.9	.9	.7	1.0	.6	0	3.2	7.1

*Annual average.

Source: 1946-60: *GP-4*, pp. 21-22, 32-33; 1961-69: *W-20*, annual issues.

Note: General trade; country of production (imports) and consumption (exports). Figures may not add to total because of rounding.

Table F-6

United States Trade with Poland: Total, 1946-1969, by SITC Categories, 1961-1969
(Millions of Current Dollars)

Year	Primary						Manufactured						Total Trade
	0	1	2	3	4	Total	5	6	7	8	9	Total	
Imports (f.o.b.)													
1946-50*													3.5
1951-55*													16.6
1956-60*													31.4
1961	26.9	.1	4.2	-	-	31.1	4.2	3.3	.8	1.8	.1	10.1	41.2
1962	26.3	.1	6.0	-	-	32.4	3.5	5.8	1.2	2.7	.1	13.1	45.6
1963	24.9	.1	5.5	.1	-	30.6	1.8	6.6	.4	3.0	.3	12.1	42.7
1964	27.9	.1	6.7	.2	-	35.0	1.6	13.4	.3	3.9	.1	19.2	54.2
1965	35.2	.1	5.6	.2	0	41.2	2.5	17.0	.5	4.5	.2	24.7	65.9
1966	42.9	.2	6.9	.2	0	50.2	6.1	20.0	1.1	5.2	.2	32.6	82.9
1967	48.1	.2	4.3	.2	0	52.8	5.2	25.6	1.7	5.4	.2	38.1	91.0
1968	46.0	.3	6.1	.2	0	52.7	5.5	32.1	.9	5.3	.3	44.2	96.9
1969	51.4	.3	5.8	.1	-	57.6	3.9	29.1	1.1	5.8	.3	40.2	97.8
Exports (f.o.b.)													
1946-50*													75.8
1951-55*													1.3
1956-60*													80.0
1961	36.1	.7	23.0	0	6.9	66.6	1.7	1.0	3.0	.5	1.9	8.1	74.7
1962	48.6	.3	24.5	-	11.6	85.0	1.5	1.0	3.0	.5	3.4	9.4	94.4
1963	73.7	3.2	17.5	0	5.4	99.8	.9	1.1	2.2	.5	4.1	8.9	108.7
1964	77.8	3.1	26.3	.1	20.7	128.0	1.9	1.5	1.2	.9	4.4	9.9	137.9
1965	8.0	.6	8.5	0	11.2	28.3	1.3	1.4	1.9	1.3	1.1	6.9	35.2
1966	25.2	.5	15.6	.1	5.4	46.7	1.2	.8	2.4	1.3	.5	6.2	52.9
1967	29.3	1.0	15.5	0	4.1	50.0	4.3	1.2	3.2	1.3	.7	10.7	60.8
1968	40.7	1.2	26.8	0	4.2	72.9	1.7	1.7	4.1	1.3	.4	9.3	82.2
1969	19.4	1.3	16.3	0	1.4	38.5	3.9	2.7	4.9	1.3	.9	13.8	52.6

*Annual average.

Source: 1946-60: *GP-4*, pp. 21-22, 32-33; 1961-69: *W-20*, annual issues.

Note: General trade; country of production (imports) and consumption (exports). Figures may not add to total because of rounding.

Table F-7

United States Trade with Rumania: Total, 1946-1969, by SITC Categories, 1961-1969
(Millions of Current Dollars)

Year	Primary						Manufactured						Total Trade
	0	1	2	3	4	Total	5	6	7	8	9	Total	
						Imports (f.o.b.)							
1946-50*													.4
1951-55*													.4
1956-60*													.8
1961	1.2	-	0	-	-	1.2	0	0	-	.1	-	.2	1.3
1962	.2	-	.1	-	-	.3	-	.2	-	.1	-	.3	.6
1963	.2	-	.1	-	-	.3	-	.2	-	.2	0	.4	.8
1964	.2	0	.1	-	-	.2	0	.4	-	.5	0	1.0	1.2
1965	.3	-	.2	-	-	.5	-	.5	-	.8	0	1.3	1.8
1966	.6	-	.5	-	-	1.1	.5	1.5	0	1.4	0	3.4	4.7
1967	1.0	0	.8	.5	-	2.3	0	.8	0	2.8	.3	3.9	6.2
1968	.9	0	.6	.8	-	2.3	0	.7	.1	2.6	.1	3.5	5.8
1969	.8	0	.3	2.7	-	3.8	.2	.8	0	3.0	.2	4.2	8.0
						Exports (f.o.b.)							
1946-50*													6.0
1951-55*													.1
1956-60*													1.1
1961	.2	-	0	-	-	.3	.3	.4	.4	.1	-	1.2	1.4
1962	0	-	.2	-	-	.2	.2	0	.3	0	-	.5	.8
1963	.1	-	0	.4	.4	.5	.2	0	.4	.1	-	.7	1.2
1964	.2	-	2.3	1.2	.1	4.1	.5	0	.4	.1	-	1.0	5.1
1965	.6	-	2.0	1.2	0	4.0	.2	.2	1.8	.1	-	2.3	6.3
1966	.2	-	8.4	.9	0	9.5	1.8	2.0	12.8	1.0	-	17.6	27.2
1967	.3	0	3.6	.1	0	4.0	3.0	3.3	5.9	.4	0	12.6	16.7
1968	.5	0	2.6	1.0	-	4.0	1.2	2.6	7.8	2.5	0	14.1	18.2
1969	1.1	0	5.0	4.1	-	10.2	1.1	10.6	9.8	.6	0	22.1	32.3

*Annual average.

Source: 1946-60: GP-4, pp. 21-22, 32-33; 1961-69: W-20, annual issues.

Note: General trade; country of production (imports) and consumption (exports). Figures may not add to total because of rounding.

Table F-8

United States Trade with Yugoslavia: Total, 1946-1969, by SITC Categories, 1961-1969
(Millions of Current Dollars)

Year	Primary						Manufactured						Total Trade
	0	1	2	3	4	Total	5	6	7	8	9	Total	
Imports (f.o.b.)													
1946-50*													9.1
1951-55*													28.7
1956-60*													34.6
1961	3.9	4.3	1.7	0	.4	10.3	.4	19.7	.3	8.1	.6	29.1	39.4
1962	5.6	4.7	3.5	0	.3	14.1	1.1	20.5	.7	11.3	.7	34.3	48.4
1963	7.0	5.7	4.1	0	0	16.8	1.1	20.1	.8	9.2	.6	31.8	48.6
1964	7.0	7.2	4.2	0	0	18.4	1.3	19.5	1.3	9.1	.8	32.0	50.4
1965	9.4	9.3	4.1	-	0	22.8	1.1	21.5	3.8	11.4	.6	38.4	61.2
1966	8.1	13.1	4.1	.5	-	25.3	1.8	26.6	7.1	13.5	.1	49.1	74.2
1967	12.6	13.6	3.3	0	-	30.0	2.4	27.9	9.8	15.9	.8	56.8	86.8
1968	11.8	11.0	5.0	0	0	27.8	2.2	41.0	10.9	20.0	.7	74.9	102.7
1969	12.9	12.4	4.4	0	0	29.7	2.8	31.1	15.1	22.7	.5	72.2	102.1
Exports (f.o.b.)													
1946-50*													45.9
1951-55*													108.9
1956-60*													115.2
1961	54.7	.4	26.3	5.7	12.1	99.2	3.6	14.8	33.0	1.1	2.2	54.7	153.9
1962	59.5	1.1	22.2	5.4	9.4	97.6	3.7	16.3	31.9	2.4	2.2	56.5	154.1
1963	96.0	.9	18.8	5.7	8.0	129.4	3.3	2.8	22.6	1.3	5.0	35.0	164.4
1964	59.5	.6	26.3	5.9	11.8	104.1	2.8	7.0	23.9	2.0	5.0	40.7	144.8
1965	72.2	1.0	29.0	7.9	13.3	123.4	2.8	4.3	15.3	2.5	.7	25.6	149.0
1966	87.7	1.4	33.8	7.4	4.9	135.2	2.9	2.7	28.3	3.4	.6	37.9	173.2
1967	36.6	1.8	9.7	6.3	11.0	65.4	3.9	1.9	22.0	2.6	.4	30.8	96.0
1968	11.6	2.7	15.7	5.6	0	35.6	6.5	6.7	35.8	2.6	.2	51.8	87.4
1969	12.9	3.2	15.5	2.3	0	33.9	10.2	8.0	28.2	2.6	.3	49.3	83.2

*Annual average.

Source: 1946-60: *GP-4*, pp. 21-22; 1961-69: *W-20*, annual issues.

Note: General trade; country of production (imports) and consumption (exports). Figures may not add to total because of rounding.

Table F-9

United States Trade with European CEMA: Total, 1946-1969, by SITC Categories, 1961-1969
(Millions of Current Dollars)

Year	Primary						Manufactured						Total Trade
	0	1	2	3	4	Total	5	6	7	8	9	Total	
Imports (f.o.b.)													
1946-50*													99.5**
1951-55*													43.0**
1956-60*													70.0
1961	30.5	.2	16.1	.2	—	47.1	11.0	11.4	3.2	7.4	.4	33.2	80.2
1962	28.3	.2	18.5	.2	—	47.3	5.1	13.4	3.6	8.5	.8	30.8	78.4
1963	26.7	.3	20.6	.3	—	47.9	2.9	17.1	3.1	8.6	.5	32.4	80.4
1964	30.1	.3	22.6	.5	0	53.5	2.5	28.0	3.9	10.7	.6	45.8	99.2
1965	38.6	.3	21.6	.6	0	61.3	3.8	52.2	5.6	13.4	.9	76.2	137.4
1966	47.4	.5	26.1	.6	0	74.6	9.5	63.8	13.6	15.8	.9	103.4	178.6
1967	54.2	.6	21.1	1.1	2.0	79.0	7.7	56.2	13.5	19.1	1.2	97.7	176.7
1968	52.2	.7	23.3	1.5	0	78.1	8.3	80.9	9.1	20.2	1.3	120.1	198.0
1969	55.5	.8	22.5	4.4	0	83.3	7.4	71.4	9.4	22.4	1.1	111.8	195.1
Exports (f.o.b.)													
1946-50*													241.0**
1951-55*													3.2**
1956-60*													98.5
1961	37.6	1.1	32.4	.4	24.7	96.3	6.1	6.8	20.5	1.3	1.9	36.8	133.0
1962	50.7	1.4	38.1	.1	15.8	106.2	4.0	2.1	7.6	1.5	3.4	18.4	125.0
1963	97.5	4.0	30.4	3.6	7.7	143.2	11.0	2.1	4.5	1.2	4.2	23.2	166.4
1964	225.3	4.2	46.1	4.5	30.4	310.4	12.5	2.4	7.5	1.7	4.4	28.4	339.0
1965	40.5	2.3	38.5	2.5	28.7	112.7	9.5	2.6	10.7	2.2	1.3	26.3	138.9
1966	75.7	3.4	57.9	2.5	13.5	153.0	10.2	5.3	24.6	3.6	.7	44.4	197.4
1967	60.2	3.9	58.4	1.3	4.1	127.9	22.7	8.1	30.6	4.1	1.0	66.5	194.7
1968	78.6	3.7	53.1	2.2	4.2	141.9	25.6	7.1	33.0	7.7	.6	74.2	216.1
1969	48.9	4.0	54.2	6.0	1.4	114.8	35.0	23.5	65.5	7.8	1.2	133.1	248.1

*Annual average.

**Excludes trade with East Germany.

Source: Tables F-1 through F-7.

Note: General trade; country of production (imports) and consumption (exports). Figures may not add to total because of rounding.

Table F-10

Canada's Trade with U.S.S.R.: Total, 1946-1969, by SITC Categories, 1961-1969
(Millions of Current U.S. Dollars)

Year	Primary						Manufactured						Total Trade
	0	1	2	3	4	Total	5	6	7	8	9	Total	
Imports (f.o.b.)													
1946-50*													.3
1951-55*													1.0
1956-60*													2.3
1961	0	-	1.4	-	-	1.4	.6	.7	0	0	0	1.3	2.7
1962	0	0	.7	-	-	.7	.5	.4	-	0	0	.9	1.7
1963	0	-	1.0	-	-	1.0	.4	.7	-	0	0	1.1	2.1
1964	0	-	1.1	-	-	1.1	.5	.9	0	.1	0	1.5	2.6
1965	0	0	5.9	-	-	5.9	.6	2.4	.1	.1	0	3.2	9.1
1966	0	0	7.2	-	-	7.2	.1	2.7	.4	.3	0	3.5	10.8
1967	.1	.3	13.7	-	-	14.1	.2	4.1	.8	2.1	0	7.2	21.3
1968	0	.1	11.2	.1	.8	12.2	.2	4.1	1.7	1.9	0	7.8	20.0
1969	.1	.1	5.0	-	-	5.2	.5	4.7	.1	.8	.1	6.2	11.4
Exports (f.o.b.)													
1946-50*													4.4
1951-55*													1.5
1956-60*													15.4
1961	12.9	-	1.6	-	-	14.5	.1	9.1	.3	0	0	9.4	24.0
1962	.1	-	1.3	-	-	1.4	0	.2	1.5	0	0	1.7	3.1
1963	137.2	-	1.8	-	-	139.0	.1	0	.1	0	0	.2	139.2
1964	289.1	1.0	1.6	-	-	291.7	.1	.1	1.2	0	0	1.5	293.2
1965	175.0	-	1.3	-	-	176.3	.1	-	6.4	.1	.1	6.6	182.9
1966	292.9	-	3.2	-	-	296.1	.2	-	.2	.1	.1	.6	296.6
1967	110.8	-	7.4	-	-	118.2	.2	.4	.2	.1	.1	1.0	119.2
1968	77.4	.1	3.2	-	-	80.7	.5	.6	.7	.2	.1	2.1	82.8
1969	2.8	-	3.2	-	-	5.9	.2	.1	2.7	0	.2	3.2	9.1

*Annual average.

Source: 1946-60: GP-2, 1954, 1957-58, and 1962-63 (Canadian $ converted to U.S. $ at the average conversion coefficient shown for each year in UN-8, 1966, p. 138); 1961-69: W-20, annual issues.

Note: Special trade; country of consignment (imports and exports). Figures may not add to total because of rounding.

Table F-11

Canada's Trade with Bulgaria: Total, 1946-1969, by SITC Categories, 1961-1969
(Millions of Current U.S. Dollars)

Imports (f.o.b.)

Year	Primary						Manufactured						Total Trade
	0	1	2	3	4	Total	5	6	7	8	9	Total	
1946-50*	0	–	–	–	–	0	–	–	–	–	–		0
1951-55*	0	–	0	–	–	0	–	–	–	–	–		0
1956-60*	0	–	–	–	–	0	–	0	–	0	–	0	0
1961	0	–	0	–	–	0	0	0	0	0	0	0	0
1962	0	–	–	–	–	0	0	.1	0	.1	0	.1	.1
1963	0	–	0	–	–	0	0	.1	.1	.1	0	.2	.1
1964	.3	–	–	–	–	.3	0	.1	0	.1	0	.3	.5
1965	.4	–	0	–	–	.4	0	.2	.1	.1	0	.3	.7
1966	.8	0	0	–	–	.8	0	.3	.1	.2	0	.6	1.2
1967	.8	0	0	–	0	.9	0	.2	.1	.4	0	.7	1.5
1968	.5	0	0	–	–	.5	0	.3	.2	.2	0	.7	1.2
1969	.5	0	0	–	0	.5	.1	.2	0	.4	0	.7	1.2

Exports (f.o.b.)

Year	Primary						Manufactured						Total Trade
	0	1	2	3	4	Total	5	6	7	8	9	Total	
1946-50*	–	–	–	–	–	–	–	.3	–	–	–	.3	.3
1951-55*	0	–	0	–	–	0	–	.4	–	–	–	.4	.4
1956-60*	17.8	–	–	–	–	17.8	0	–	0	–	0	0	0
1961	6.8	–	–	–	–	6.8	0	–	0	–	0	0	.3
1962	7.2	–	–	–	–	7.2	–	–	0	–	0	0	.4
1963	0	–	–	–	–	0	0	–	–	0	–	0	0
1964	–	–	–	–	–	17.8	0	–	0	0	–	–	17.8
1965	0	–	–	–	–	6.8	0	–	0	0	–	0	6.8
1966	–	–	–	–	–	7.2	–	–	0	0	–	0	7.0
1967	0	–	0	–	–	0	0	–	0	0	–	0	0
1968	–	–	0	–	–	0	0	–	0	0	–	.1	.1
1969	0	–	0	–	–	0	.1	–	0	0	–	.1	.1

*Annual average.

Source: 1946-60: *GP-2*, 1954, 1957-58, and 1962-63 (Canadian $ converted to U.S. $ at the average conversion coefficient shown for each year in *UN-8*, 1966, p. 138); 1961-69: *W-20*, annual issues.

Note: Special trade; country of consignment (imports and exports). Figures may not add to total because of rounding.

Table F-12

Canada's Trade with Czechoslovakia: Total, 1946-1969, by SITC Categories, 1961-1969
(Millions of Current U.S. Dollars)

Imports (f.o.b.)

Year	Primary					Manufactured						Total Trade
		2	3	4	Total	5	6	7	8	9	Total	
1946-50*												4.2
1951-55*												3.1
1956-60*												5.9
1961	.1	0	-	-	.1	.2	4.1	1.5	2.4	0	8.1	8.3
1962	.1	0	-	-	.1	.1	3.9	1.5	2.8	0	8.3	8.4
1963	.1	0	-	-	.1	.2	4.3	1.1	2.8	0	8.4	8.5
1964	.1	0	-	-	.1	.2	5.7	1.4	4.4	.2	11.8	11.9
1965	.1	0	-	-	.1	.1	7.3	2.0	5.0	.2	14.6	14.8
1966	.1	0	-	-	.1	.2	10.6	2.0	6.7	.4	19.8	20.1
1967	.2	.1	-	-	.3	.1	15.2	2.8	7.5	.4	26.1	26.4
1968	.1	.1	-	-	.2	.2	14.4	2.6	7.6	.3	25.1	25.3
1969	.2	.1	-	-	.2	.3	16.7	3.4	6.9	.3	27.6	27.8

Exports (f.o.b.)

Year	Primary					Manufactured						Total Trade
		2	3	4	Total	5	6	7	8	9	Total	
1946-50*												7.9
1951-55*												.5
1956-60*												8.0
1961	11.1	2.8	-	-	13.9	.1	6.4	.1	0	0	6.6	20.5
1962	0	2.0	-	-	2.0	0	1.1	.2	0	0	1.3	3.4
1963	9.7	1.2	-	-	10.9	.2	1.0	.2	0	0	1.4	12.3
1964	47.2	1.5	-	.5	49.2	.1	.7	.3	0	0	1.1	50.3
1965	28.0	2.8	-	-	30.7	0	1.2	.2	0	0	1.5	32.2
1966	0	4.3	-	-	4.3	0	.1	.4	0	-	.5	4.9
1967	6.8	2.8	-	-	9.6	0	.2	.3	.2	0	.7	10.4
1968	7.3	2.6	-	-	9.8	0	.1	.4	.1	0	.5	10.4
1969	0	2.7	-	-	2.7	.1	.1	.7	.1	0	.9	3.6

*Annual average.

Source: 1946-60: GP-2, 1954, 1957-58, and 1962-63 (Canadian $ converted to U.S. $ at the average conversion coefficient shown for each year in UN-8, 1966, p. 138); 1961-69: W-20, annual issues.

Note: Special trade; country of consignment (imports and exports). Figures may not add to total because of rounding.

Table F-13

Canada's Trade with East Germany: Total, 1946–1969, by SITC Categories, 1961–1969
(Millions of Current U.S. Dollars)

Year	Primary 0	1	2	3	4	Total	Manufactured 5	6	7	8	9	Total	Total Trade
Imports (f.o.b.)													
1946-50*													n.a.
1951-55**													.7
1956-60*													.9
1961	0	–	0	–	0	0	0	.4	.1	.4	0	.9	1.0
1962	0	–	0	–	0	0	0	.4	.1	.3	0	.8	.8
1963	0	–	.1	–	–	.1	0	.5	.1	.4	0	1.1	1.1
1964	0	–	0	–	–	0	0	.5	.2	.6	.1	1.3	1.4
1965	–	–	0	0	–	0	0	.5	.1	.8	0	1.4	1.5
1966	.1	–	0	0	–	.1	0	.7	.4	.7	.1	1.9	2.0
1967	.1	–	0	0	–	.1	0	1.0	1.0	.9	0	2.9	3.1
1968	0	–	.2	0	–	.2	0	.8	.8	.9	.1	2.5	2.7
1969	.1	–	.2	0	–	.3	0	.9	1.1	.9	0	3.0	3.2
Exports (f.o.b.)													
1946-50*													n.a.
1951-55**													.6
1956-60*													.5
1961	1.4	–	0	–	–	1.4	–	.1	0	0	–	.1	1.6
1962	–	–	1.3	–	–	1.3	–	0	–	–	–	0	1.3
1963	–	–	1.2	–	–	1.2	0	0	–	0	–	0	1.2
1964	10.8	–	0	–	–	10.9	0	–	–	0	–	0	10.9
1965	14.1	–	–	–	–	14.1	–	0	–	0	–	0	14.1
1966	10.6	–	.7	–	–	11.3	–	0	0	0	–	0	11.4
1967	5.0	–	.1	–	–	5.1	–	–	0	0	–	–	5.1
1968	–	–	1.0	–	–	1.1	–	–	0	0	–	0	1.1
1969	0	–	1.7	–	–	1.7	–	–	.1	0	–	.1	1.8

*Annual average.
**1952-55 average.

Source: 1946-60: GP-2, 1954, 1957-58, and 1962-63 (Canadian $ converted to U.S. $ at the average conversion coefficient shown for each year in UN-8, 1966, p. 138); 1961-69: W-20, annual issues.

Note: Special trade; country of consignment (imports and exports). Figures may not add to total because of rounding.

Table F-14

Canada's Trade with Hungary: Total, 1946-1969, by SITC Categories, 1961-1969
(Millions of Current U.S. Dollars)

Imports (f.o.b.)

Year	Primary						Manufactured						Total Trade
	0	1	2	3	4	Total	5	6	7	8	9	Total	
1946-50*													.1
1951-55*													.2
1956-60*													.3
1961	0	0	0	-	-	.1	0	.2	-	.1	0	.3	.4
1962	0	0	-	-	-	.1	0	.2	-	.1	0	.3	.4
1963	0	0	0	-	-	.1	0	.3	0	.1	0	.4	.5
1964	.1	0	0	-	-	.1	0	.3	.1	.2	0	.6	.7
1965	.1	.1	0	-	-	.3	0	.5	.1	.5	0	1.2	1.4
1966	.2	.1	0	-	-	.3	.1	1.4	.2	1.0	.1	2.7	3.1
1967	.5	.1	0	-	-	.6	.1	2.7	.2	2.3	.1	5.4	6.1
1968	.5	.1	0	-	-	.7	.1	2.7	.3	3.4	.1	6.7	7.3
1969	.5	.2	.1	-	-	.8	.2	2.8	.5	4.0	.1	7.7	8.5

Exports (f.o.b.)

Year	Primary						Manufactured						Total Trade
	0	1	2	3	4	Total	5	6	7	8	9	Total	
1946-50*													.6
1951-55*													.1
1956-60*													1.0
1961	0	-	.5	-	-	.5	0	0	0	0	0	.1	.6
1962	0	-	.3	-	-	.3	-	-	0	0	0	0	.3
1963	0	-	.3	-	-	.3	-	0	0	0	0	0	.4
1964	1.0	-	.7	-	-	1.8	-	-	0	0	0	0	1.8
1965	4.9	-	2.8	-	-	7.7	0	0	0	0	0	.1	7.7
1966	0	-	3.0	-	-	3.0	0	.1	0	0	-	.1	3.2
1967	0	-	3.1	-	-	3.1	.1	0	.1	0	0	.1	3.3
1968	6.6	-	4.7	-	-	11.2	.1	.1	.1	0	0	.2	11.5
1969	.4	-	2.0	-	-	2.4	.1	.2	0	0	0	.4	2.8

*Annual average.

Source: 1946-60: GP-2, 1954, 1957-58, and 1962-63 (Canadian $ converted to U.S. $ at the average conversion coefficient shown for each year in UN-8, 1966, p. 138); 1961-69: W-20, annual issues.

Note: Special trade; country of consignment (imports and exports). Figures may not add to total because of rounding.

Table F-15

Canada's Trade with Poland: Total, 1946–1969, by SITC Categories, 1961–1969
(Millions of Current U.S. Dollars)

Year	Primary						Manufactured						Total Trade
	0	1	2	3	4	Total	5	6	7	8	9	Total	
Imports (f.o.b.)													
1946–50*													.1
1951–55*													.6
1956–60*													1.6
1961	.6	.1	.4	–	–	1.1	.2	1.1	.3	.5	0	2.1	3.1
1962	1.1	0	.2	–	–	1.3	.2	1.5	.5	.9	.1	3.2	4.5
1963	1.2	0	.2	–	–	1.4	.3	2.9	.4	1.3	0	4.9	6.3
1964	1.4	0	0	–	–	1.5	.4	4.7	.4	1.6	.1	7.2	8.6
1965	1.9	.1	.3	–	0	2.3	.3	5.7	.6	2.0	.1	8.7	10.9
1966	1.6	.1	.2	–	–	1.9	.2	7.6	.6	2.2	.2	10.8	12.7
1967	1.3	.1	.6	–	–	2.0	.3	7.9	1.0	2.5	.2	11.9	13.9
1968	1.3	.1	.3	–	–	1.7	.3	6.9	.4	2.9	.1	10.6	12.3
1969	1.0	.1	.5	–	–	1.6	.4	6.0	.7	2.7	.1	9.9	11.5
Exports (f.o.b.)													
1946–50*													9.2
1951–55*													1.0
1956–60*													13.9
1961	34.2	0	2.8	–	–	37.1	–	3.5	0	0	0	3.6	40.7
1962	26.7	0	5.5	–	–	32.2	0	2.8	0	0	0	2.9	35.0
1963	17.0	0	5.1	–	–	22.1	.1	2.2	.8	0	0	3.0	25.2
1964	51.3	0	5.8	–	–	57.1	0	.7	.2	0	0	1.0	58.1
1965	20.2	–	8.8	–	–	29.0	0	.1	0	0	0	.2	29.2
1966	26.3	–	8.2	–	–	34.5	0	.1	.1	0	0	.2	34.7
1967	19.4	0	4.2	–	–	23.6	.1	.1	.1	0	0	.2	24.0
1968	12.9	0	4.1	–	–	17.0	.1	.1	.1	.1	0	.4	17.4
1969	2.1	0	3.6	–	–	5.8	0	.2	.2	.1	0	.4	6.2

*Annual average.

Source: 1946–60: *GP-2*, 1954, 1957–58, and 1962–63 (Canadian $ converted to U.S. $ at the average conversion coefficient shown for each year in *UN-8*, 1966, p. 138); 1961–69: *W-20*, annual issues.

Note: Special trade; country of consignment (imports and exports). Figures may not add to total because of rounding.

Table F-16

Canada's Trade with Rumania: Total, 1946-1969, by SITC Categories, 1961-1969
(Millions of Current U.S. Dollars)

Imports (f.o.b.)

Year	Primary 0	1	2	3	4	Total	Manufactured 5	6	7	8	9	Total	Total Trade
1946-50*						0							0
1951-55*						0							0
1956-60*						0							0
1961	.2	-	0	-	-	.2	-	-	-	0	-	0	.3
1962	0	-	-	-	-	0	-	-	-	0	0	0	.1
1963	0	-	0	-	-	0	-	0	-	.1	0	.1	.1
1964	.1	-	-	-	-	0	-	.1	-	0	0	0	.1
1965	.2	-	-	-	-	.2	-	.1	-	.1	0	.1	.2
1966	.2	-	-	-	-	.6	-	.1	-	.2	0	.3	.5
1967	.1	-	-	-	.4	.7	-	.4	0	.2	0	.3	.9
1968	.1	-	-	-	.7		-	1.4	0	.6	0	1.0	1.7
1969	.3	0	0	1.1	1.6	3.0	-		0	2.2	0	3.5	6.6

Exports (f.o.b.)

Year	Primary 0	1	2	3	4	Total	Manufactured 5	6	7	8	9	Total	Total Trade
1946-50*	.3												.2
1951-55*													.1
1956-60*													.9
1961	.3	-	.5	-	-	.7	0	.2	.2	0	-	.3	1.1
1962	0	-	.1	-	-	.1	0	.3	0	0	-	.4	.5
1963	.1	-	.1	-	-	.2	-	.9	.1	0	0	1.0	1.2
1964	.2	-	.1	-	-	.3	0	.2	0	0	0	.2	.5
1965	-	-	.4	-	-	.4	.2	-	-	-	0	.2	.6
1966	0	-	.6	-	-	.6	0	0	0	0	-	0	.6
1967	0	-	.3	-	-	.3	-	-	0	0	-	0	.3
1968	-	-	.5	-	-	.5	0	0	.5	0	0	.6	1.1
1969	.2	-	.6	-	-	.8	-	0	.3	0	0	.4	1.1

*Annual average.

Source: 1946-60: *GP-2*, 1954, 1957-58, and 1962-63 (Canadian \$ converted to U.S. \$ at the average conversion coefficient shown for each year in *UN-8*, 1966, p. 138); 1961-69: *W-20*, annual issues.

Note: Special trade; country of consignment (imports and exports). Figures may not add to total because of rounding.

Table F-17

Canada's Trade with Yugoslavia: Total, 1946-1969, by SITC Categories, 1961-1969
(Millions of Current U.S. Dollars)

Year	Primary 0	1	2	3	4	5	Total	Manufactured 6	7	8	9	Total	Total Trade
Imports (f.o.b.)													
1946-50*	.1	0											0
1951-55*	0	0											.2
1956-60*	.1	0											.6
1961	.2	0	.3	0	0	.2	.4	.5	.1	.6	0	1.4	1.8
1962	.2	0	.2	0	0	.1	.2	.6	0	.8	0	1.5	1.7
1963	.1	0	.2	0	0	.1	.3	.5	.1	.8	.1	1.5	1.8
1964	.1	0	.5	0	0	.1	.7	.7	.1	.7	.1	1.7	2.4
1965	.2	0	.4	–	–	.2	.6	1.0	.1	.8	.1	2.2	2.8
1966	.1	.1	.5	–	–	.1	.7	.9	.1	.7	.1	1.9	2.4
1967	.1	.1	.3	0	0	0	.5	1.4	.4	1.1	.1	3.0	3.5
1968	.3	.1	.5	0	0	.5	.9	1.6	.3	1.1	.1	3.6	4.5
1969	.6	.1	.9	0	0	.2	1.6	1.8	.3	1.3	.1	3.7	5.3
Exports (f.o.b.)													
1946-50*	0	0											4.4
1951-55*	0	0											7.1
1956-60*		0											1.3
1961	0	0	1.2	0	0	0	1.2	0	1.0	0	.1	1.1	2.3
1962	0	0	.7	0	0	0	.7	.1	.2	0	.1	.4	1.1
1963	13.9	0	2.1	0	0	0	16.0	.2	.1	0	.1	.4	16.4
1964	.1	0	4.4	0	0	0	4.5	.3	.2	0	0	.5	5.0
1965	.1	0	7.3	0	–	.1	7.4	.1	.5	0	.1	.8	8.2
1966	.1	0	2.7	–	–	0	2.8	.1	.7	0	.1	.9	3.8
1967	0	0	2.1	–	–	0	2.1	.7	.4	0	.1	1.2	3.4
1968	.1	0	0	3.8	0	0	3.9	1.8	.5	0	.1	2.4	6.3
1969	0	0	4.5	0	0	0	4.5	2.0	1.0	.1	.1	3.2	7.7

*Annual average.

Source: 1946-60: *GP-2*, 1954, 1957-58, and 1962-63 (Canadian $ converted to U.S. $ at the average conversion coefficient shown for each year in *UN-8*, 1966, p. 138); 1961-69: *W-20*, annual issues.

Note: Special trade; country of consignment (imports and exports). Figures may not add to total because of rounding.

Table F-18

Canada's Trade with European CEMA: Total, 1946-1969, by SITC Categories, 1961-1969
(Millions of Current U.S. Dollars)

Year	Primary						Manufactured						Total Trade
	0	1	2	3	4	Total	5	6	7	8	9	Total	
Imports (f.o.b.)													
1946-50*													4.7
1951-55*													5.6
1956-60*													11.0
1961	.9	.1	1.8	-	0	2.9	1.0	6.5	1.9	3.4	0	12.7	15.8
1962	1.2	0	.9	-	0	2.2	.8	6.4	2.1	4.1	.1	13.5	15.9
1963	1.3	0	.3	-	-	2.7	.9	8.7	1.6	4.7	0	16.0	18.7
1964	1.6	0	1.1	-	-	2.8	1.1	12.0	2.1	6.9	.4	22.5	25.4
1965	2.5	.1	6.2	-	-	8.9	1.1	16.6	2.9	8.6	.3	29.4	38.4
1966	2.5	.2	7.5	0	0	10.2	.4	23.2	3.7	11.2	.8	39.3	49.9
1967	3.2	.6	14.3	0	.4	18.5	.8	31.2	5.8	15.6	.7	54.1	72.9
1968	2.8	.4	11.7	.1	1.5	16.6	.7	29.6	5.9	17.5	.6	54.3	70.8
1969	2.6	.4	5.9	1.2	1.6	11.6	1.3	32.7	5.8	17.9	.6	58.6	70.2
Exports (f.o.b.)													
1946-50*													22.4
1951-55*													3.8
1956-60*													39.9
1961	59.9	0	8.2	-	-	68.1	.2	19.6	.6	0	0	20.4	88.8
1962	26.8	0	10.5	-	-	37.3	0	4.8	1.7	0	0	6.7	44.0
1963	163.9	0	9.7	-	-	173.7	.4	4.1	1.2	0	0	5.6	179.5
1964	417.4	1.5	9.7	-	-	428.8	.2	1.7	1.7	0	0	3.8	432.6
1965	249.0	-	16.1	-	-	265.0	.3	1.3	6.6	.1	.1	8.6	273.5
1966	337.0	-	20.0	-	-	357.0	.2	.7	.7	.1	.1	1.4	358.4
1967	142.0	0	17.9	-	-	159.9	.2	.7	.7	.3	.1	2.3	162.3
1968	104.3	.1	16.1	-	-	120.3	.7	.9	1.7	.5	.1	3.9	124.4
1969	5.3	0	13.8	-	-	19.3	.5	.6	4.0	.2	.2	5.5	24.7

*Annual average.

Source: Tables F-10 through F-16.

Note: Special trade; country of consignment (imports and exports). Figures may not add to total because of rounding.

Table F-19

Japan's Trade with U.S.S.R.: Total, 1950-1969, by SITC Categories, 1964-1969

(Millions of Current Dollars)

Year	Primary						Manufactured						Total Trade
	0	1	2	3	4	Total	5	6	7	8	9	Total	
Imports (c.i.f.)													
1950-55*													1.0
1956-60*													32.4
1961													145.4
1962													147.3
1963													161.9
1964	2.8	0	68.7	74.6	0	146.2	7.8	69.7	2.5	.5	.1	80.6	226.7
1965	4.8	0	81.4	78.3	0	164.7	8.8	64.0	2.2	.4	0	75.5	240.2
1966	6.4	0	116.7	90.5	.2	213.8	8.9	75.1	1.9	.4	.1	86.4	300.4
1967	8.0	0	204.3	96.4	.5	309.2	12.0	129.3	2.8	.6	.1	144.8	453.9
1968	6.5	0	259.9	82.0	.5	348.9	10.9	100.0	2.9	.6	.2	114.6	463.5
1969	8.3	0	263.9	67.4	.3	339.9	9.6	107.0	3.6	1.1	.4	121.7	461.6
Exports (f.o.b.)													
1950-55*													.5
1956-60*													20.3
1961													65.4
1962													149.4
1963													158.1
1964	.3	0	8.7	0	0	9.0	11.5	38.6	115.5	6.2	1.0	172.8	181.8
1965	.4	0	13.0	0	0	13.4	23.6	58.9	59.9	10.0	2.6	154.9	168.4
1966	.5	0	12.3	0	0	12.8	24.1	63.4	88.2	25.3	.3	201.3	214.0
1967	.3	.1	6.2	0	0	6.6	21.3	37.0	48.9	43.4	.5	151.1	157.7
1968	.6	0	4.6	0	.1	5.3	20.7	60.1	46.4	45.2	1.1	173.5	178.8
1969	.6	0	6.9	2.9	0	10.4	36.7	101.0	69.7	46.6	3.7	257.7	268.1

*Annual average.

Source: 1950-59: *GP-3*, 1962, p. 255; 1960-63: *GP-3*, 1970, p. 290; 1964-69: *W-20*, annual issues.

Note: General trade; country of production (imports) and last consignment (exports). Figures may not add to total because of rounding.

Table F-20

Japan's Trade with Bulgaria: Total, 1960, 1964-1969, by SITC Categories, 1964-1969
(Millions of Current Dollars)

Year	Primary						Manufactured						Total Trade
	0	1	2	3	4	Total	5	6	7	8	9	Total	
Imports (c.i.f.)													
1960													2.1
1961													n.a.
1962													n.a.
1963													n.a.
1964	1.1	0	.1	0	0	1.2	0	4.4	.1	0	0	4.5	5.7
1965	.9	.1	.1	0	0	1.1	0	4.8	.1	0	0	4.9	6.0
1966	1.3	.4	.8	0	0	2.5	.1	10.8	.1	.1	0	11.1	13.6
1967	1.2	.8	4.1	0	0	6.1	.2	8.4	.2	0	0	8.8	15.1
1968	2.1	1.2	1.9	0	0	5.2	.2	.8	.4	0	0	1.4	6.6
1969	3.0	1.7	2.3	0	0	7.0	.2	1.3	.3	0	0	1.8	8.8
Exports (f.o.b.)													
1960													1.2
1961													n.a.
1962													n.a.
1963													n.a.
1964	.2	0	.5	0	0	.7	.4	1.0	5.3	.2	0	6.9	7.6
1965	.2	0	.8	0	0	1.0	.2	3.0	6.6	.1	0	9.9	10.9
1966	0	-	1.3	-	-	1.3	.9	9.2	12.8	.3	0	23.2	24.6
1967	-	0	1.5	-	-	1.5	.4	3.4	19.0	.2	-	23.0	24.5
1968	0	0	.6	0	0	.6	.5	5.5	8.0	.4	0	14.4	15.0
1969	0	0	.4	0	0	.4	.5	5.5	8.0	.4	0	14.4	14.8

Source: 1960: *B-1*, 1970; 1964-1969: *W-20*, annual issues.
Note: General trade; country of production (imports) and last consignment (exports). Figures may not add to total because of rounding.

Table F-21

Japan's Trade with Czechoslovakia: Total, 1958-1969, by SITC Categories, 1964-1969
(Millions of Current Dollars)

Imports (c.i.f.)

Year	Primary						Manufactured						Total Trade
	0	1	2	3	4	Total	5	6	7	8	9	Total	
1958													1.7
1959													1.8
1960													3.2
1961													4.2
1962													2.9
1963													4.3
1964	3.0	0	.6	0	0	3.6	0	1.4	.8	.2	0	2.4	6.0
1965	2.3	0	2.9	0	0	5.2	0	.7	.8	.2	0	1.7	6.9
1966	2.5	0	2.8	0	0	5.3	.1	.6	.7	.3	0	1.7	6.9
1967	2.4	0	2.0	2.1	0	6.5	.2	9.2	1.5	.4	0	11.3	18.0
1968	3.5	0	.5	1.3	0	5.3	.6	4.3	4.0	.5	0	9.4	14.7
1969	2.6	0	0	0	0	2.6	.6	1.5	5.8	.3	0	8.2	10.8

Exports (f.o.b.)

Year	Primary						Manufactured						Total Trade
	0	1	2	3	4	Total	5	6	7	8	9	Total	
1958													.1
1959													4.3
1960													1.3
1961													3.8
1962													5.0
1963													7.2
1964	.7	0	0	0	0	.7	.2	0	1.4	.5	0	2.1	2.8
1965	.6	0	0	0	0	.6	.9	.2	6.5	.5	0	8.1	8.7
1966	.4	-	.2	-	-	.4	.7	.3	2.5	.3	0	3.8	4.3
1967	.3	-	0	0	0	.5	.9	1.8	3.0	.2	0	5.9	6.3
1968	.1	0	.1	0	0	.2	.3	.2	1.8	.8	0	3.1	3.3
1969	0	0	.3	0	0	.3	.9	1.5	9.9	1.8	0	14.1	14.4

Source: 1958-63: C-2, 1964, pp. 104-105; 1964-69: W-20, annual issues.
Note: General trade; country of production (imports) and last consignment (exports). Figures may not add to total because of rounding.

Table F-22

Japan's Trade with East Germany: Total, 1951-1969, by SITC Categories, 1964-1969
(Millions of Current Dollars)

Year	Primary						Manufactured						Total Trade
	0	1	2	3	4	Total	5	6	7	8	9	Total	
Imports (c.i.f.)													
1951-55*													3.8
1956-60*													2.7
1961													9.5
1962													4.7
1963													3.2
1964	.7	0	0	0	0	.7	.5	.5	1.0	.6	0	2.6	3.3
1965	0	0	.1	0	0	.1	0	.1	.6	.4	0	1.1	1.2
1966	0	0	.1	0	0	.1	0	2.1	.8	.4	0	3.3	3.6
1967	.3	0	.1	0	0	.4	.2	13.0	1.2	.5	0	14.9	15.3
1968	.6	0	.2	0	0	.8	0	25.8	3.1	1.0	0	29.9	30.7
1969	.6	0	.1	.1	0	.8	.2	22.5	6.0	1.5	0	30.2	31.0
Exports (f.o.b.)													
1951-55*													1.1
1956-60*													2.3
1961													1.6
1962													.4
1963													.6
1964	0	0	0	0	0	0	0	0	0	0	0	0	.1
1965	0	0	.1	0	0	.1	0	.2	.8	0	0	1.0	1.1
1966	-	-	0	0	-	0	0	0	2.4	.1	0	2.5	2.5
1967	-	-	.1	-	-	.1	0	.6	2.2	.1	.1	2.9	3.1
1968	0	0	.6	0	0	.6	.4	.3	1.3	.1	.1	2.2	2.8
1969	.5	.5	1.8	0	0	2.3	1.3	.5	1.5	.3	0	3.6	5.9

*Annual average.

Source: 1951-59: *GP-3*, 1962, p. 255; 1960-63: *GP-3*, 1970, p. 290; 1964-69: *W-20*, annual issues.

Note: General trade; country of production (imports) and last consignment (exports). Figures may not add to total because of rounding.

Table F-23

Japan's Trade with Hungary: Total, 1958-1969, by SITC Categories, 1964-1969
(Millions of Current Dollars)

Imports (c.i.f.)

Year	Primary						Manufactured						Total Trade
	0	1	2	3	4	Total	5	6	7	8	9	Total	
1958													0
1959													0
1960													0
1961													.7
1962													1.1
1963													1.0
1964	.1	0	0	0	0	.1	.2	0	.2	.2	0	.6	.7
1965	.1	0	0	0	0	.1	.2	0	.1	0	0	.3	.4
1966	.2	0	.1	0	0	.2	.4	.1	0	.1	0	.5	.7
1967	.5	0	0	0	0	.6	.5	.2	0	.1	0	.7	1.4
1968	1.2	0	0	0	0	1.2	.9	.2	0	.1	0	1.2	2.4
1969	2.5	0	0	0	0	2.5	1.3	.2	0	1.0	0	2.5	5.0

Exports (f.o.b.)

Year	Primary						Manufactured						Total Trade
	0	1	2	3	4	Total	5	6	7	8	9	Total	
1958													0
1959													.1
1960													.2
1961													1.4
1962													2.8
1963													4.1
1964	0	0	2.7	0	0	2.7	.4	.6	.4	0	0	1.4	4.1
1965	0	0	1.0	0	0	1.0	.3	.4	.6	0	0	1.3	2.3
1966	-	-	1.0	-	-	1.0	.4	.9	.5	0	0	1.8	2.8
1967	-	-	1.4	-	-	1.4	.5	1.1	.5	.1	-	2.2	3.6
1968	0	0	1.0	0	0	1.0	.9	1.2	.4	.1	0	2.7	3.7
1969	0	0	.8	0	0	.8	1.6	1.8	.7	.3	0	4.4	5.2

Source: 1958-63: *H-1*, annual issues; 1964-69: *W-20*, annual issues.

Note: General trade; country of production (imports) and last consignment (exports). Figures may not add to total because of rounding.

Table F-24

Japan's Trade with Poland: Total, 1951-1969, by SITC Categories, 1964-1969
(Millions of Current Dollars)

Year	Primary						Manufactured						Total Trade
	0	1	2	3	4	Total	5	6	7	8	9	Total	
Imports (c.i.f.)													
1951-55*													.1
1956-60*													.4
1961													1.8
1962													1.5
1963													1.3
1964	1.6	0	.2	0	0	1.8	0	0	.2	0	0	.2	2.0
1965	1.1	0	.7	0	0	1.8	0	.1	.1	0	0	.2	2.0
1966	.9	0	1.2	1.6	0	3.7	.3	.1	0	0	0	.4	4.1
1967	1.3	0	1.3	11.2	0	13.8	1.8	10.5	.1	0	0	12.4	26.3
1968	2.0	0	1.4	15.6	0	19.0	.8	19.5	.1	.1	0	20.5	39.5
1969	1.3	0	4.0	18.1	0	23.4	.3	19.3	.3	.3	.1	20.3	43.7
Exports (f.o.b.)													
1951-55*													.5
1956-60*													1.0
1961													1.7
1962													2.7
1963													1.2
1964	0	0	.1	0	0	.1	.3	.7	1.3	.1	0	2.4	2.5
1965	0	0	.9	0	0	.9	1.5	2.0	.9	.1	0	4.5	5.4
1966	-	-	.1	-	0	.1	1.6	.3	.7	.1	.2	2.9	3.0
1967	-	-	.7	-	-	.7	1.6	.8	2.0	.8	0	5.2	5.9
1968	0	0	2.6	0	0	2.6	.5	2.0	1.6	.3	0	4.4	7.0
1969	0	0	4.2	0	0	4.2	1.7	6.4	1.1	.7	0	9.9	14.1

*Annual average.

Source: 1946-1959: *GP-3*, 1962, p. 255; 1960-63: *GP-3*, 1970, p. 290; 1964-1969: *W-20*, annual issues.

Note: General trade; country of production (imports) and last consignment (exports). Figures may not add to total because of rounding.

Table F-25

Japan's Trade with Rumania: Total, 1960-1969, by SITC Categories, 1964-1969
(Millions of Current Dollars)

Year	Primary						Manufactured						Total Trade
	0	1	2	3	4	Total	5	6	7	8	9	Total	
	Imports (c.i.f.)												
1960													.3
1961													5.2
1962													3.5
1963													7.7
1964	3.0	0	.9	7.5	0	11.4	0	.4	0	.1	0	.5	11.9
1965	3.4	0	1.2	14.2	0	18.8	0	.2	.2	0	0	.2	19.0
1966	.8	0	.6	16.5	0	17.9	0	1.7	.1	0	0	1.9	19.8
1967	6.6	0	1.0	14.3	0	21.9	.7	9.2	.2	0	0	10.0	32.0
1968	.6	0	.5	7.9	0	9.0	.6	5.4	.2	0	0	6.2	15.2
1969	.8	0	4.8	2.4	0	8.0	.1	5.9	.2	0	0	6.2	14.2
	Exports (f.o.b.)												
1960													.1
1961													1.8
1962													6.4
1963													8.1
1964	.1	0	1.9	0	0	2.0	.3	9.1	7.7	.1	0	17.2	19.2
1965	.1	0	1.7	0	0	1.8	.3	6.0	7.0	.1	0	13.4	15.2
1966	-	-	2.5	0	-	2.5	.4	5.7	13.2	.2	0	19.5	22.0
1967	.2	-	.8	0	-	1.0	.4	2.7	22.6	.7	0	26.4	27.3
1968	0	0	.7	0	0	.7	1.6	7.7	11.2	.6	0	21.2	21.9
1969	0	0	1.5	0	0	1.5	1.3	10.9	7.7	.9	0	20.9	22.4

Source: 1960-63: *GP-3*, 1970, p. 291; 1964-69: *W-20*, annual issues.

Note: General trade; country of production (imports) and last consignment (exports). Figures may not add to total because of rounding.

Table F-26

Japan's Trade with Yugoslavia: Total, 1951-1969, by SITC Categories, 1964-1969
(Millions of Current Dollars)

Year	Primary						Manufactured						Total Trade
	0	1	2	3	4	Total	5	6	7	8	9	Total	
Imports (c.i.f.)													
1951-55*													0
1956-60*													.3
1961													1.3
1962													.5
1963													.5
1964	.3	.1	.4	0	0	.8	0	.1	0	0	0	.1	.9
1965	.1	.3	.1	0	0	.5	0	0	.1	0	0	.1	.6
1966	0	.5	.4	0	0	.9	0	.6	0	0	0	.6	1.6
1967	0	.6	.7	0	0	1.3	.8	8.4	.4	.4	.1	10.0	11.4
1968	.1	.9	1.1	0	0	2.1	1.4	1.1	.1	0	.1	2.7	4.8
1969	.2	.6	1.0	0	0	1.8	1.9	.2	0	.3	.1	2.5	4.4
Exports (f.o.b.)													
1951-55*													2.4
1956-60*													2.9
1961													5.8
1962													15.3
1963													7.8
1964	4.4	0	.2	0	0	4.6	.3	1.7	3.0	.2	0	5.2	9.8
1965	2.2	0	.5	0	0	2.7	1.9	7.4	18.6	.6	.1	28.6	31.3
1966	.2	-	.3	0	-	.5	.6	5.9	31.8	.6	0	38.9	39.5
1967	.3	-	.3	-	-	.6	.5	6.3	20.1	1.5	0	28.4	29.2
1968	.3	0	.7	0	0	1.0	.7	4.8	22.4	1.6	0	29.5	30.5
1969	.8	0	1.0	0	0	1.8	2.7	11.6	4.4	1.6	0	20.3	22.1

*Annual average.

Source: 1951-60: Y-2, annual issues; 1964-69: W-20, annual issues.

Note: General trade; country of production (imports) and last consignment (exports). Figures may not add to total because of rounding.

Table F-27

Japan's Trade with European CEMA: Total, 1961-1969, by SITC Categories, 1964-1969
(Millions of Current Dollars)

Year	Primary						Manufactured						Total Trade
	0	1	2	3	4	Total	5	6	7	8	9	Total	
Imports (c.i.f.)													
1961													166.8*
1962													161.0*
1963													179.4*
1964	12.3	0	70.5	82.1	0	164.9	8.5	76.4	4.8	1.6	.1	91.4	256.3
1965	12.6	.1	86.4	92.5	0	191.6	9.0	69.4	3.9	1.0	0	83.8	275.4
1966	12.1	.4	122.2	108.6	.2	243.5	9.8	90.4	3.7	1.3	.1	105.3	349.1
1967	20.3	.8	212.9	124.0	.5	358.5	15.6	179.7	5.9	1.6	.1	202.9	562.0
1968	16.5	1.2	164.4	106.8	.5	389.4	14.0	156.0	10.7	2.3	.2	183.2	572.6
1969	19.1	1.7	275.1	87.9	.3	384.1	12.3	157.7	16.2	4.2	.5	190.9	575.0
Exports (f.o.b.)													
1961													75.7*
1962													166.7*
1963													179.3*
1964	1.3	0	13.9	0	0	15.2	13.1	50.0	131.6	7.1	1.0	202.8	218.0
1965	1.3	0	17.5	0	0	18.8	26.8	70.7	82.3	10.8	2.6	193.2	212.0
1966	.9	0	17.2	0	0	18.1	28.1	79.8	120.3	26.3	.5	255.0	273.2
1967	.8	.1	10.9	0	.1	11.8	25.1	47.4	98.2	45.5	.5	216.7	228.4
1968	.7	0	10.2	0	0	11.0	24.9	77.0	70.7	47.5	1.2	221.3	232.3
1969	.6	.5	15.9	2.9	0	19.9	44.0	127.6	98.6	51.0	3.7	324.9	344.8

*Excludes trade with Bulgaria.

Source: Tables F-19 through F-25.
Note: General trade; country of production (imports) and last consignment (exports). Figures may not add to total because of rounding.

Table F-28

Australia's Trade with Individual East European Countries and European CEMA, 1949/50-1969/70

(Millions of Current U.S. Dollars)

Year*	U.S.S.R.	Bulgaria	Czechoslovakia	East Germany	Hungary	Poland	Rumania	Yugoslavia	European CEMA**
Imports (f.o.b.)									
1949/50-1954/55	1.7	-	8.3	.7	1.2	.6	.3	.4	12.8
1955/56-1959/60	1.1	-	5.6	1.6	.8	.5	0	.1	9.6
1960/61	1.9	-	6.9	2.2	1.2	.9	0	.1	13.1
1961/62	1.9	.1	5.8	1.8	1.1	.9	0	.3	11.6
1962/63	1.2	.3	6.1	2.2	1.2	1.2	0	.4	12.2
1963/64	2.0	.6	7.1	2.4	1.2	1.7	0	1.4	15.0
1964/65	2.4	.7	7.2	11.4	1.6	2.8	0	.6	26.1
1965/66	1.8	.9	7.3	5.4	1.6	2.1	.1	.8	19.2
1966/67	1.9	.7	7.2	3.6	1.4	2.1	.2	.4	17.1
1967/68	2.3	.7	7.6	3.4	1.8	2.6	.6	.7	19.0
1968/69	2.2	.6	9.1	3.7	2.9	3.7	.4	1.9	22.6
1969/70	3.9	.7	8.4	5.0	2.2	3.3	1.0	1.0	24.5
Exports (f.o.b.)									
1949/50-1954/55	17.6	.2	7.3	.1	.4	16.3	.6	3.2	44.7
1955/56-1959/60	5.7	.7	14.9	1.5	.3	25.3	1.0	5.8	49.4
1960/61	18.2	.8	13.9	1.2	.8	17.7	.9	9.4	53.5
1961/62	26.1	.8	10.9	.9	.4	21.1	0	6.8	60.2
1962/63	32.4	.3	10.4	.8	1.2	13.8	0	13.2	58.9
1963/64	126.8	.2	18.0	1.0	3.3	17.2	0	19.6	166.5
1964/65	84.9	.9	13.7	4.4	.9	16.0	.1	13.3	120.9
1965/66	53.2	.1	10.0	1.8	1.2	18.8	.1	16.8	85.2
1966/67	22.6	.2	11.3	2.4	2.6	20.8	.4	20.9	60.3
1967/68	30.4	.1	8.9	1.2	6.9	21.8	1.3	17.9	70.6
1968/69	44.8	.1	9.2	1.4	3.0	25.3	.2	16.6	84.0
1969/70	57.1	.3	9.7	1.9	1.9	22.3	4.7	19.0	97.9

*July - June.

**Excludes Yugoslavia.

Source: *GP-1*, annual issues. Original data shown in Australian pounds or dollars (introduced in February 1966 with a value of 0.5 Australian pounds) converted to U.S. dollars (Australian $ = 1.12 U.S. $).

Note: General trade; country of production (imports) and consumption (exports). Figures may not add to total because of rounding.

APPENDIX G

Available East European Foreign Trade Series
in Constant Prices, 1938-1970

Country	Years	Total Trade	By CTN Broad Divisions	By CTN Categories	By CPEs and Non-CPEs	Other (as specified)
U.S.S.R.	1938	X				
	1946-70	X				
	1960,63-70				X	X[a]
Bulgaria	1939,50,55-69	X				
	1939,50,55, 60,62-69		X	X		
Czechoslovakia	1948-69	X				
	1948-61				X	
East Germany	1950-69	X				
	1960-69				X	
Hungary	1949-70	X	X		X	X[b]
Poland	1947-70	X				
	1950,55,57-70		X			
Rumania	None					
Yugoslavia	1948-70	X				
	1950-70					X[c]
Albania	None					

Note: The series shown have been calculated on the basis of published or derived indices of physical volume or indices of price, based on East European country sources. The statistical series are presented in *W-12*.

a. CEMA plus (OCPEs and Yugoslavia).
b. Four CTN *broad divisions* for CPEs plus non-CPEs.
c. By SITC *categories* 0 through 8.

APPENDIX H

IDRC Soviet and East European Foreign Trade Data Bank, 1946-1969

The *IDRC Soviet and East European Foreign Trade Data Bank* consists of a computer system and accompanying programs which permit us to handle the data presented in Part Two and Appendix F above. In most cases it contains considerably more commodity detail than could be included in this volume.

The *Data Bank* also goes substantially beyond the *Compendium* in providing convenient, speedy, and versatile access to approximately a half million data entries. A major feature of the system for most purposes is its capability of retrieving information for immediate use without further programming, as described below. The system has been further designed so that updating and extensions can be done by routine procedures.

The *Data Bank* differs from a simple data base. Much more than a mere listing of numbers, it contains and identifies on request all titles, nomenclature definitions, and guides to coding, automatically providing the user a full set of word descriptions to match any data set that may be requested.

The computer programs and subroutines available with the *data tape,* a highly compact binary file, fall into four broad categories: Access Package, Auxiliary Routines, Special Programs, and Interactive Modes. A generalized diagram of the system, whose main components are described below, is shown in Figure 1.

1. The *data tape* is structured according to a tree hierarchy, as shown in Figure 2. In each year for which data are included, total imports and exports have been disaggregated by trade partners, by one of three commodity classification systems, or through a cross-classification involving both trade partners and commodity designations. Successively more detailed breakdowns are arranged on the *data tape* in branch-like fashion. Internally aggregated subtotals are always shown within each branch. Thus, even if values in an original source have been reported only at the *subgroup* (three-digit) and *category* (one-digit) levels, synthetic *group* (two-digit) values are obtained automatically. Briefly, the data tree is designed to be as complete as possible.

The user can identify special situations in the *Data Bank* via footnote-type codes attached to each entry. For instance, footnote code 8 signals that the value is an internally aggregated "synthetic" number, hence may not exhaust trade at the indicated level. Some twenty

Figure 1

Data Bank System Arrangement

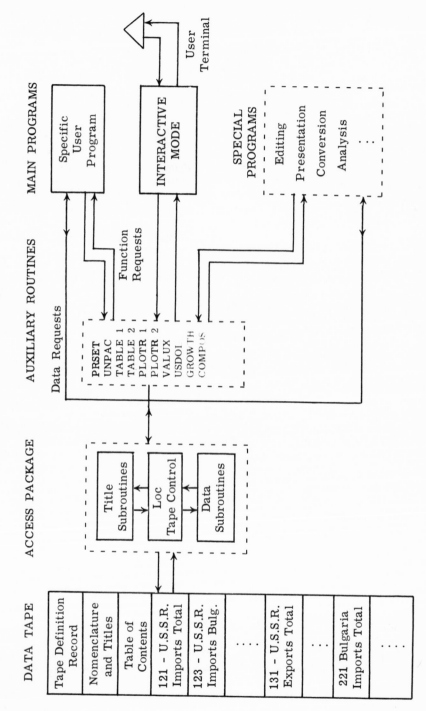

Figure 2

Data Structure

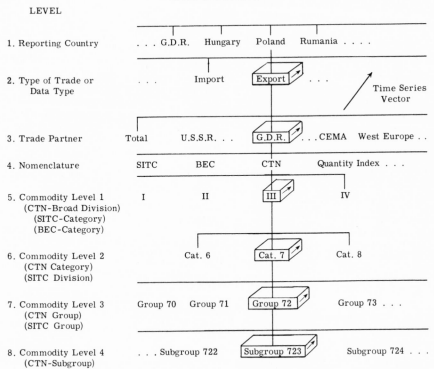

LEVEL

1. Reporting Country   . . . G.D.R.   Hungary   Poland   Rumania . . . .

2. Type of Trade or   Import   Export   . . .   Time Series
   Data Type   Vector

3. Trade Partner   Total   U.S.S.R. . .   G.D.R.   . . .CEMA   West Europe . .

4. Nomenclature   SITC   BEC   CTN   Quantity Index . . .

5. Commodity Level 1   I   II   III   IV
   (CTN-Broad Division)
   (SITC-Category)
   (BEC-Category)

6. Commodity Level 2   Cat. 6   Cat. 7   Cat. 8
   (CTN Category)
   (SITC Division)

7. Commodity Level 3   Group 70   Group 71   Group 72   Group 73 . . .
   (CTN Group)
   (SITC Group)

8. Commodity Level 4   . . . Subgroup 722   Subgroup 723   Subgroup 724 . . .
   (CTN-Subgroup)

different footnote codes appear in the *Data Bank,* an especially significant auxiliary identification since often the data provided by East European countries have gaps or special characteristics that may differ among classification systems, countries, and periods. For example, in one period the U.S.S.R. may show trade in CTN 24, Metallic Ores and Concentrates, and CTN 26, Ferrous Metals, plus some three- and five-digit components of CTN 27, Nonferrous Metals; in a subsequent period it may publish only a combined figure for CTN 24-27.

The *data tape* features a bootstrap mechanism: Any request for data automatically initializes a retrieval procedure, which includes inputs into core, a table of contents, written titles, and a set of internal instructions concerning options such as the currency units in which data could be provided.

2. The Access Package consists of a series of short subroutines which serve in "black box" fashion to connect user and data in a way which permits almost effortless random access to materials of interest. The user need only specify nomenclature, desired degree of detail, a code number for country or countries, whether import or export figures are involved, and trade partner. The data so requested are then

loaded from the *data tape* into core storage, where they become available for viewing, together with relevant country names, commodity titles, footnotes, and other explanatory information. If a data set being requested is not in a *Data Bank*, this information too is immediately communicated.

3. The Auxiliary Subroutines consist of special processing programs available upon request for performing operations on data, once these have been supplied. Examples are presentations of data in tabular form (programs TABLE 1 or TABLE 2 in Figure 1), conversion from national devisa units to U.S. dollars (program USDOL), or standard time series analysis on any specified set of factors (program GROWTH). Generally, the Auxiliary Subroutines programs perform single functions on the full *Data Bank* or subsets and then return for the next command.

4. The Special Programs component consists of an expandable set of algorithms for such specific tasks as editing, presentation of data in special tables, or conversions between classification systems. It also includes analysis procedures, such as methods for calculating mirror ratios from trade-partner sources. These algorithms generally utilize the Access Package and building blocks from the *Auxiliary Subroutines*.

5. The most versatile service in the software is the Interactive Mode program. It permits the user to select individual items or vectors from the *Data Bank* in isolation from the remainder of the system, and then to print, compare, and manipulate them via teletype or typewriter terminal.

In general, therefore, the researcher could expect to have at his disposal the entire *Data Bank* file, the capabilities of Special Programs and Auxiliary Subroutines, and, together with these, a number of manipulating algorithms applicable to interactive analysis.

The data storage system and subroutines have been designed to accommodate future expansion of the *Data Bank* through updating or inclusion of additional data, such as trade by partner countries, or further commodity detail for years through 1969. It also appears possible to catalogue efficiently entirely new types of data, such as industrial production and input-output transactions, for purposes of being analyzed in conjunction with foreign trade proper.

Copies of the *Data Bank* or portions thereof can be made available to individual scholars and institutions at reasonable charges. For further information, write to:

DATA BANK
International Development Research Center
Indiana University
1005 East Tenth Street
Bloomington, Indiana 47401

BIBLIOGRAPHY

Government Publications of Western Countries

GP-1   Australia, Bureau of Census and Statistics. *Oversea Trade Bulletin*. Canberra. Annual.

GP-2   Canada, Dominion Bureau of Statistics. *Canada Yearbook*. Ottawa. Annual.

GP-3   Japan, Bureau of Statistics. *Japan Statistical Yearbook*. Tokyo. Annual.

GP-4   United States, Bureau of the Census. *Foreign Commerce and Navigation of the United States, 1946-1963*. Washington, D.C.: 1965.

United Nations Publications

UN-1   Conference on Trade and Development. *Handbook of International Trade and Development Statistics, 1969*. New York, 1969.

UN-2   Economic Commission for Europe. *Economic Bulletin for Europe*. Annual.

UN-3   _____. *Economic Survey of Europe*. Annual.

UN-4   Economic and Social Council, Statistical Commission. "Classification by Broad Economic Categories." *Statistical Papers*, Series M, no. 53. New York, 1971.

UN-5   _____. "Predvaritel'nyĭ klíŭch mezhdu 'SITC' i 'ETNVT' po poríàdku zagolovkov klassifikatsionnoĭ skhemy 'SITC.' Preliminary Key between the SITC and ETNVT in the Order of the SITC Headings." (Dual language.) Parts 1 and 2. E/CN.3/314. 1965 (?).

UN-6   Statistical Office. "International Trade Statistics Concepts and Definitions." *Statistical Papers*, Series M, no. 52. New York, 1970.

UN-7   _____. "Standard International Trade Classification, Revised." *Statistical Papers*, Series M, no. 34. New York, 1961.

UN-8   _____. *Yearbook of International Trade Statistics*. Annual.

Council for Mutual Economic Assistance Publications

CEMA-1   *Edinaíà tovarnaíà nomenklatura vneshneĭ torgovli stran-chlenov soveta ekonomicheskoĭ vzaimopomoshchi* [Uniform Merchandise Nomenclature of Foreign Trade of the Member Nations of the Council for Mutual Economic Assistance], 3rd edition, enlarged and corrected. Moscow, 1970.

404 Soviet and East European Foreign Trade (1946-1969)

CEMA-2 Statisticheskiĭ ezhegodnik stran-chlenov soveta ekonomi-cheskoĭ vzaimopomoshchi, 1970 [Statistical Yearbook of the Member Nations of the Council for Mutual Economic Assistance, 1970]. Moscow, 1970.

U.S.S.R.

U-1 Vneshniaia torgovlia SSSR [Foreign Trade of the USSR]. Moscow: Ministerstvo Vneshneĭ Torgovli SSSR, Planovoekonomicheskoe upravlenie (Ministry of Foreign Trade of the U.S.S.R., Planning Economic Office). Annual.

U-2 Vneshniaia torgovlia SSSR; staticheskiĭ sbornik, 1918-1966 [Foreign Trade of the U.S.S.R.; statistical volume, 1918-1966]. Moscow: Ministerstvo Vneshneĭ Torgovli SSSR, Planovoekonomicheskoe upravlenie, 1967.

U-3 Foreign Trade [English version of *Vneshniaia Torgovlia SSSR*]. Moscow: Ministerstvo Vneishneĭ Torgovli SSSR. Monthly.

U-4 Edinaia tovarnaia nomenklatura vneshneĭ torgovli [Uniform Commodity Nomenclature of Foreign Trade]. Moscow: Vneshtorgizdat (Foreign Trade Publishing House), 1954, 1962.

U-5 Ministerstvo vneshneĭ torgovli, Nauchno-issledovatel'skoĭ institut (Ministry of Foreign Trade, Scientific Research Institute). *Alfavitnyĭ ukazatel' k edinoĭ tovarnoĭ nomenklature vneshneĭ torgovli stran SEV, Standartnoĭ mezhdunarodnoĭ torgovloĭ klassifikatsii OON i Briussel'skoĭ tamozhennoĭ nomenklature* [Alphabetical Index to the Unified Commodity Nomenclature of Foreign Trade of the CEMA Countries, the Standard International Trade Classification of the U.N. and the Brussels Tariff Nomenclature]. Moscow: no publisher, no date. Reported in Y. Romanov. "Vneshniaia torgovlia statistika v stranakh SEV" [Foreign Trade Statistics in the CEMA Countries]. *Vneshniaia Torgovlia*, July 1969.

Bulgaria

B-1 Staticheskii godishnik na Narodna Republika Bŭlgariia [Statistical Yearbook of the People's Republic of Bulgaria]. Sofia: Tsentralno Statichesko Upravlenie (Central Statistical Office). Annual.

B-2 Staticheskii ezhegodnik Narodna Respubliki Bolgarii. Statistical Yearbook of the People's Republic of Bulgaria. (Dual language.) Sofia: Tsentralno Statichesko Upravlenie. Annual.

B-3 Staticheski spravochnik. Durzhavno Upravlenie za Informatsii (Office of Information). Annual.

B-4 Vŭnshnata tŭrgoviia na NR Bulgariia, Staticheski danni [Foreign Trade of the People's Republic of Bulgaria, Statistical Collection]. (Also published under slightly different names like *Staticheski obzor.*) Sofia: Ministerstvo na vŭnshnata tŭrgoviia (Ministry of Foreign Trade). Annual.

B-5   *Staticheski Izvestiiă* [Statistical Bulletin]. Sofia: Tsentralno Statichesko Upravlenie. Monthly.

B-6   *Bulgarian Foreign Trade, 1955-1957.* Translation of the Bulgarian language *Staticheski Sbornik, 1955-1957.* Washington, D.C.: Joint Publications Research Service, no. 8033 (3 April 1961).

B-7   *Statistics on the Foreign Trade of the People's Republic of Bulgaria, 1958-1959.* Translation of the Bulgarian language *Staticheski Sbornik, 1958-1959.* Washington, D.C.: Joint Publications Research Service, no. 6884 (7 March 1961).

B-8   Nikolaenko, Zh. I., and Pitertsev, N. A. "People's Republic of Bulgaria." Translation from *Razvitie vneshneĭ torgovli sotsialisticheskikh stran Evropy za gody vlasti* [Development of the Foreign Trade of the Socialist Countries of Europe during the Years of the People's Authority]. *Bulletin of Foreign Commercial Information,* Supplement 22, Scientific Research Projection Institute. Moscow: U.S.S.R. Ministry of Foreign Trade, December 1965. Washington, D.C.: Joint Publications Research Service.

Czechoslovakia

C-1   *Dvacet let rozvoje československé socialistické republiky* [Twenty Years of Development of the Czechoslovak Socialist Republic]. Prague: Ústřední komise lidové kontroly a statistiky (People's Central Commission of Control and Statistics), 1965.

C-2   *Facts on Czechoslovak Foreign Trade.* Prague: Českovlovenská Obchodní Komora (Czechoslovak Chamber of Commerce). Annual.

C-3   *Statistická ročenka československé socialistické republiky* [Statistical Yearbook of the Czechoslovak Socialist Republic]. Prague: Státní Úřad Statistiky (State Statistical Office). Annual.

C-4   *Czechoslovak Foreign Trade.* (Title varies: *Foreign Trade*). Prague: Československá Obchodní Komora. Monthly.

C-5   Kamagancevová, Ludmila, ed. *Roční Ukazatelé Vývoje Ekonomiky Evropských Socialistických Zemí* [Annual Index of the Economic Development of the European Socialist Countries]. Prague: Výzkumný Ústav pro Zahraniční Obchod (Research Institute for Foreign Trade), 1968.

C-6   *Statistické zprávy* (Supplement 1959): *Zahraniční Obchod ČSSR.* Prague: Státní Úřad Statistiky, 1960.

East Germany

G-1   *Statistisches Jahrbuch der Deutschen Demokratischen Republik* [Statistical Yearbook of the German Democratic Republic]. Berlin: Staatliche Zentralverwaltung für Statistik. Annual.

G-2   *Definitionen für Planung, Rechnungsführung und Statistik,* Teil 4 [Definitions for Planning, Accounting and Statistics, Part 4]. Berlin: Staatliche Zentralverwaltung für Statistik, 1969.

406   Soviet and East European Foreign Trade (1946-1969)

Hungary

H-1 *Statisztikai évkönyv* [Statistical Yearbook]. Budapest: Központi Statisztikai Hivatal (Central Statistical Office), 1949-1955; annual issues thereafter.

H-2 *Statisztikai havi közlemények* [Monthly Statistical Bulletin]. Budapest: Központi Statisztikai Hivatal. Monthly.

H-3 Holka, Gyula, and Pócs, Ervin. *A szocialista országok gazdasági fejlődése* [The Economic Development of Socialist Countries]. Budapest: K. and J. Könyvkiadó, 1968.

H-4 *Külkereskedelmi statisztikai évkönyv* [Foreign Trade Statistical Yearbook]. Budapest: Központi Statisztikai Hivatal. Annual.

H-5 *Külkereskedelem* [Foreign Trade]. Budapest: A Magyar Kereskedelmi Kamara és a Konjunktura- és Piackutató Intézet (Hungarian Foreign Trade Chamber of Commerce and the Institute of Business Cycles- and Market-Research). Monthly.

H-6 *Statistical Pocket Book of Hungary.* Budapest: Központi Statisztikai Hivatal. Annual.

H-7 Vajda, Imre. *The Role of Foreign Trade in a Socialist Economy.* Budapest: Corvina Press, 1965.

H-8 *Statisztikai szemle* [Statistical Review]. Budapest: Központi Statisztikai Hivatal. Monthly.

H-9 Benedecki, J., ed. *Gazdaságstatisztika* [Economic Statistics]. Budapest: Tankönyvkiadó, 1970.

H-10 *Statisztikai idöszaki közlemények* [Occasional Statistical Reports]. Budapest: Központi Statisztikai Hivatal. Irregular.

H-11 *Statistical Yearbook.* Budapest: Central Statistical Office. Annual.

H-12 Kiss, Tibor. *Nemzetközi munkamegosztás es magyarország gazdasági növekedése* [International Division of Labor and Hungary's Economic Growth]. Budapest: Kossuth, 1969.

H-13 *Közgazdasági szemle* [Economic Review]. Budapest: Hungarian Academy of Sciences, Economic Committee. Monthly.

Poland

P-1 *Rocznik statystyczny* [Statistical Yearbook]. Warsaw: Glówny Urząd Statystyczny (Central Statistical Office). Annual.

P-2 *Statystyka handlu zagranicznego* [Statistics of Foreign Trade]. Warsaw: Glówny Urząd Statystyczny. Annual.

P-3 *Statystyka handlu zagranicznego — przywoz i wywoz towarow wedlug krajow* [Statistics of Foreign Trade — Imports and Exports according to Countries]. (Since 1961 title changed to *Import i eksport towarow wedlug krajow.*) Warsaw: Glówny Urząd Statystyczny. Annual.

P-4 *Maly rocznik statystyczny* [Concise Statistical Yearbook]. Warsaw: Glówny Urząd Statystyczny. Annual.

P-5 *Handel zagraniczny* [Foreign Trade]. Warsaw: Polska Izba Handlu Zagranicznego (Polish Chamber of Foreign Trade). Monthly.

P-6   *Statistical Yearbook of Poland.* 1948.
P-7   *Statystyka handlu zagranicznego — obroty handlowe Polski z poszczegolnymi krajami* [Statistics of Foreign Trade — Poland's Trade Turnovers with Individual Countries]. Warsaw: Główny Urząd Statystyczny. Annual.
P-8   *Yearbook of Foreign Trade Statistics: Translation.* Warsaw: Główny Urząd Statystyczny. Annual.
P-9   *Rozwoj gospodarczy krajow RWPG 1950-1968* [Economic Development of CEMA Countries 1950-1968]. Warsaw: Główny Urząd Statystyczny, 1969.

Rumania

R-1   *Anuarul statistic al R.P.R.* [Statistical Yearbook of the R.P.R.]. Bucharest: Directia Centrala de Statistica (Central Directorate of Statistics). Annual.
R-2   *Revista de statistica* [Review of Statistics]. Bucharest: Directia Centrala de Statistica. Monthly.

Yugoslavia

Y-1   *Statisticki godisnjak Jugoslavije* [Statistical Yearbook of Yugoslavia]. Belgrade: Savezni Zavod za Statistiku. (Federal Institute for Statistics). Annual.
Y-2   *Statistika spoljne trgovine SFR Jugoslavije. Statistics of Foreign Trade of the SFR Yugoslavia.* (Dual language.) Belgrade: Savezni Zavod za Statistiku. Annual.
Y-3   *Jugoslavija 1945-1964 — Statisticki Pregled* [Yugoslavia 1945-1964 — Statistical Review]. Belgrade: Savezni Zavod za Statistiku, 1965.

Albania

A-1   *Vjetare statistikor i R.P.Sh.* [Statistical Yearbook of the R.P.Sh.]. Tirana: Drejtoria e Statistiskes (Directorate of Statistics). Annual.

Western Articles and Books

W-1   Allen, Robert L. "A Note on Soviet Foreign Trade Statistics." *Soviet Studies,* X (April 1959).
W-2   Brown, Alan A., and Neuberger, Egon, eds. *International Trade and Central Planning: An Analysis of Economic Interactions.* Berkeley and Los Angeles: University of California Press, 1968.
W-3   Central Intelligence Agency. *USSR Foreign Trade, 1964-68,* vols. I-V. 1970.
W-4   Dean, Robert William. "The Politics of West German Trade with the Soviet Bloc, 1954-1968." Unpublished Ph.D. dissertation, University of Denver, 1970.

W-5   Dewar, Margaret. *Soviet Trade with Eastern Europe, 1945-1949*. London: Royal Institute of International Affairs, 1951.

W-6   Hewett, Edward A. "Foreign Trade Prices in the Council for Mutual Economic Assistance." Unpublished Ph.D. dissertation, University of Michigan, 1971.

W-7   International Monetary Fund. "Rumania: Background Information on the Economy." Mimeographed. November 30, 1951.

W-8   Kaser, Michael. *Comecon: Integration Problems of the Planned Economies*, second edition. London: Oxford University Press, 1967.

W-9   Kiesewetter, Bruno. *Der Ostblock*. Berlin: Safari-Verlag, 1960.

W-10 Köhler, Heinz. *Economic Integration in the Soviet Bloc: with an East German Case Study*. New York: Praeger, 1965. For derivation of East Germany's foreign trade data, see Supplement obtainable from the author upon request.

W-11 Marer, Paul. "Postwar Pricing and Price Patterns in Socialist Foreign Trade (1946-1970)." Indiana University International Development Research Center (IDRC) *Occasional Paper* no. 2 (1972).

W-12 _____. "Soviet and East European Foreign Trade (1950-1969): Statistical Series and Analysis at Constant Prices." *IDRC Working Paper* (1972).

W-13 Michal, Jan M. "Czechoslovakia's Foreign Trade." *Slavic Review*, XXVII (June 1968).

W-14 Montias, John Michael. *Economic Development in Communist Rumania*. Cambridge: MIT Press, 1967.

W-15 Spulber, Nicholas. "The Economic Relations between the USSR and the East European Countries after World War II." Unpublished Ph.D. dissertation, New School of Social Research, 1952.

W-16 U.S. Congress, Joint Economic Committee. *Economic Developments in Countries of Eastern Europe: A Compendium of Papers*. Washington, D.C.: Government Printing Office, 1970.

W-17 Van Brabant, Jozef M. "From 'Dolya i Naprimer' to External Flows by Commodity-Groups for the European Members of the Council for Mutual Economic Assistance." M.A. thesis submitted to Yale University, July 1967.

W-18 Wiles, P.J.D. *Communist International Economics*. New York: Praeger, 1969.

W-19 Wilczynski, Jozef. *The Economics and Politics of East-West Trade*. New York: Praeger, 1969.

W-20 Organisation for Economic Co-operation and Development. *Commodity Trade, Series C*. Paris. Annual since 1961.